The
First Amendment
in the
Balance

JOSEPH F. SCHUSTER, PH.D.

Eastern Washington University

WITHDRAWN

9/93

Austin & Winfield, Publishers
SAN FRANCISCO

Library of Congress Cataloging-in-Publication Data

Schuster, Joseph F.
 The first amendment in the balance / Joseph F. Schuster.
 458p.   cm.
 Includes bibliographical references and index.
 ISBN 1-880921-01-4 (pbk.) : $39.95. -- ISBN 1-880921-09-X Z(cloth) : $74.95
 1. United States--Constitutional law--Amendments--1st. 2. Freedom of speech
United States. 3. Freedom of the press--United States. 4. Freedom of religion--United
States. I. Title.
KF4770.S38   1992
342.73'03--dc20
[347.3023]

                                                          92-29492
                                                            CIP

Editorial Inquiries:

Austin & Winfield, Publishers
534 Pacific Avenue
San Francisco, CA 94133
Fax: (415) 434-3441

Order Fulfillment:

Austin & Winfield, Publishers
P.O. Box 2529
San Francisco, CA 94126
Fax: (415) 434-3441

This book is for

AMANDA

whose Love and Faith made it possible

TABLE OF CONTENTS

Preface i

Introduction 1

Part I: The Communications Clauses

Ch.	1	The Communications Clauses Considered	7
	2	National Defense and Security	25
	3	Public Order and Tranquility	51
	4	Necessary Activity in Controlled Environments	75
	5	Assuring the Fair Administration of Justice	97
	6	Protection of the Electoral Process	123
	7	The Advancement of Patriotism	157
	8	The Advancement of Equality	181
	9	Toward A Decent Society	199
	10	Protection from Libel and Invasion of Privacy	223
	11	Protection from Assaultive and Unwanted Stimuli	247
	12	Protection of Economic and Property Rights	267

Part II: The Religion Clauses

Ch.	13	Separatism, Secularism, and Accommodation	289
	14	The Rights and Duties of Citizens	297
	15	The State's Police Power	315
	16	The General Welfare	339
	17	Governmental Aid to Religious Schools	367
	18	Governmental Sponsorship of Religious Activity	397

Epilogue: The First Amendment in the Balance 435

Bibliographical Note 439

Table of Cases 443

Index 449

PREFACE

The writing of this book resulted from both opportunity and necessity. Opportunity derived from the fact that, at EWU, the study of "Civil Rights and Liberties" is divided between three courses, one of which is "The First Amendment." Necessity arose from the lack, over time, of a single satisfactory text for such a course. One could, of course, use part of a standard casebook. But that required students to spend considerable sums of their often hard earned money. One could piece together a course out of a number of smaller books. That was also expensive, and often resulted in a course which lacked any focus. Or one could make use of a number of excellent commentaries. That exposed the student, very desirably, to a number of viewpoints. But most such studies were a bit advanced for undergraduates, and contained few if any cases.

In the course of trying first one and then another of these solutions, I came to feel that almost all of the available materials lacked appropriate organization. Typically, and especially in the casebooks, students confronted cases employing different doctrinal approaches before having been introduced to the doctrines. And cases were often, and necessarily, bracketed with others utilizing quite different doctrines.

I thus began to construct my own course, using cases which I edited, assigning supplementary library readings, and imposing my own organization. That organization, which appears in final form in this book, developed from another factor which provided the eventual rationale for both it and the book. For it seems to me that the materials available for teaching the First Amendment too often assume that First Amendment values must necessarily outweigh all others. That perception, though understandable given the importance of those values, misrepresents the position of legislatures and, most importantly, courts, including the Supreme Court. Thus this text encourages consideration of competing values, and of the divergence of views which regularly occurs on First Amendment matters.

My own thinking on the "firstness" of the First has been shaped by confrontation with a number of different perspectives. Those which have been most influential are cited regularly in text and footnote, and are discussed in the Bibliographical Note. To the authors of these materials, and others unmentioned, I

i

owe an enormous debt. Each has stimulated me to think about and constantly reevaluate my own thinking on the Amendment. My greatest intellectual debt, however, is to those who have been my teachers over the years, from Sister Constance, who taught me to read and write, to R. Wallace Brewster and Ruth C. Silva, *emeriti* of the Pennsylvania State University, who introduced me to constitutional analysis.

Defects in this book are, of course, mine alone, but I could not have written it without the assistance of many at EWU. The Faculty Development Fund, the Northwest Institute for Advanced Study, and the Department of Government provided substantial funding and a partial release from teaching duties. Professor Janet Vinzant gave a timely and encouraging critique, and Allen Simon, Jr., researched the basics of "political correctness." Sonia Combs efficiently processed the case material, and her husband Carl, of the Computer Center, worked tirelessly and skillfully at improving the formatting. Both gave freely of their time and skills, in a manner far exceeding any contractual obligation. And Doreen Timm, secretary and "nerve center" of the Government Department, took on extra work as cheerfully and competently as she has performed more "routine" tasks over the years.

Above all else, however, the completion of this book is due to the talents and energy of Shannon Waechter, the remarkable young lady who has been my research assistant for the past two years. Ms. Waechter did much of the editing on the text, and was responsible for final preparation and editing of case materials. Without her, no deadline would have been met. Just as importantly, she lent to my prose a grace and facility it did not otherwise possess, advised me on numerous "judgment calls" that had to be made, and committed herself to the work as wholly and energetically as if it were her own. In a very real sense, it is, and I am most grateful for all that she has done. And I thank Kimberly and Lacey for sharing their mother's time with me.

On a personal level, I am thankful to have had as parents Fred and Jennie Schuster; to be brother to their children, and to have Dan, Ro, Jenny, and Alyssa, as son and family. And most of all I am grateful for the love, support, and companionship of the gentle and beautiful lady to whom this book is dedicated.

Spokane, WA
1 May, 1992

INTRODUCTION
THE FIRST AMENDMENT "PROBLEM"

"Congress shall make no law respecting an establishment of religion, or prohibiting the free exercise thereof; or abridging the freedom of speech, or of the press, or the right of the people peaceably to assemble, and to petition the Government for a redress of grievances."

The forty-five words quoted above comprise, of course, the First Amendment to the United States Constitution. Along with the commerce, due process, and equal protection clauses, the First Amendment is one of the most litigated sections of that constitution. That the First should have provoked so much controversy is remarkable. There was, with the exception of several cases having to do with certain beliefs and practices of the Mormon religion in the U. S. territories, almost no litigation concerning the Amendment and its meaning for the first century and a quarter of its existence. And the Amendment appears, on its face, to be virtually self-defining. Like the 22nd's proviso that "<u>no person</u> shall be elected to the office of the President more than twice," the First speaks in terms of absolute negation, stating that "Congress shall make <u>no law</u> . . . ."

The Fourth Amendment, by contrast, forbids not all searches and seizures but only those which are "unreasonable." The terms of the operative provisions of the 14th Amendment are even less precise. And, of course, the values inherent in the First Amendment, as much as any in the Constitution, seem central to the maintenance of a democratic society, as well as to the individualistic character of the particular democracy which is the United States.

But the extent to which Americans agree as to the desirable scope which should be given to the First Amendment is itself very much a matter of controversy.

And neither its words, their history, nor their implications necessarily lead to the conclusion that they are to be interpreted in absolute fashion. While it is true that the Amendment refers to "no law," it is also true that it refers (as to the units of government to be affected by its strictures) only to Congress. If the words are to be interpreted literally there is no reason for preferring "no law" over "Congress," and it would seem that, in so far as the First Amendment is concerned, the legislatures of the states are free to place whatever limitations they wish on the right of the people to worship or to communicate through speech and press.

The received answer is, of course, that the Fourteenth Amendment's "due process" clause has applied the First, along with most of the rest of the first ten amendments, to the states, and thus that the Amendment limits the states just as it does the national government. But there is still the fact that the Amendment, even as "incorporated," would seem to apply only to legislatures, or perhaps to all state entities but only to the national legislature. How then can one conclude, as did the Supreme Court long ago, that the First Amendment limits not only Congress and the states but also the national executive and even the national judiciary? Finally, there is the fact that the phrase "no law" does not refer, in the case of the communications clauses, simply to the abridging of "speech," but rather to the abridging of the "freedom of speech," a category which may have been intended by the Framers to be somewhat less broad. The answers to these questions cannot be determined solely on the basis of the words of the Amendment.

The truth of this assertion becomes even more obvious when one considers the difficulties attendant on attempting to interpret the Amendment in an absolute fashion. There is, for example, the fact that the first two of its provisions, collectively making up the "religion" clauses, can at least on some accounts be seen to contradict each other. Suppose, for example, that one must decide whether a group of youths wishing to pray together may do so on public school property. The decision must be made not only with reference to the "establishment" clause, which might be taken to forbid such activity, but also the "free exercise" clause, which arguably requires it's allowance. A literal reading of either of the two clauses would not seem particularly helpful in resolving the controversy.[1]

There is also the fact that some of the provisions of the Amendment may seem, at least in some circumstances, to contradict other and equally binding Constitutional provisions. Most obviously, though by no means exclusively, such a possible contradiction exists with respect to the guarantee of the freedom of the press, and the Sixth Amendment's requirement that "in all criminal prosecutions" the accused shall enjoy trial "by an impartial jury." Both provisions are couched in absolute terms, and yet in some circumstances the grant of absolute protection to one may interfere with the realization of the other.

Finally, there is the fact that an "absolutely absolute" interpretation of the First Amendment would lead to conclusions that reasonable people simply will not countenance. In its very first decision on a free speech problem, one written by the illustrious Oliver Wendell Holmes, the Court recognized that not even the most stringent theory of free speech would protect one who shouted "fire in a crowded theatre."[2] We may be equally confident that the Court would not, and should not, have protected a newspaper which, having obtained on June 1, 1944, the detailed plans for the June 6 Allied invasion of Europe, proposed to published them.

The necessity for the existence of such exceptions to the limitations of the communications clauses is all but universally recognized, and the same ought to be true with respect to the religion clauses. Pushed to the extreme, for example, the establishment clause might be held to require that government deny to churches elementary services like police and fire protection, services which undoubtedly contribute to church attendance. Just as obviously, the free exercise clause cannot be held to protect a religious group acting on the basis of a belief in the necessity of human sacrifice, even if it is able to recruit someone willing to serve in that role.

The meaning of the First Amendment, like the meaning of most other provisions of the Constitution, presents, then, a "problem," or more accurately a series of problems. How the Supreme Court has addressed these problems is the subject of this book. As the title indicates,[3] the book takes the position that the Court's answers to questions of First Amendment interpretation can best be understood by considering the provisions of the Amendment in the light of the values with which its application has allegedly been in conflict. This position assumes that those who seek to limit activity arguably protected by the First do not generally attempt to enforce such limitations without reason. Rather, they do so because they believe that such limitation is necessary or desirable in pursuit of certain societal goals. Furthermore the Court, in determining whether the acting agency has transgressed the Amendment, must and does weigh the importance of the goal sought by government against the degree of infringement on First

Amendment activity. In a word, both acting and reacting entities (typically legislature and Court) engage in *balancing*. How the balance should be struck in particular cases is a matter to be explored later. This book asserts only that: 1) the Court must and does engage in balancing; and 2) the best way to understand the body of doctrine which has grown up about the proper interpretation of the First Amendment is to look at the formulation and application of that doctrine as it has been used to solve real problems arising in the context of felt governmental need.

Thus the book is divided as follows: Part I, comprising approximately two-thirds of the book, is organized into two sections. In the first, we consider the conflict between free communication and the achievement of certain necessary and fundamental functions which any democratic government must perform, including the protection of national security, the maintenance of domestic order and tranquility, the assurance of the integrity of the political process, the fair administration of justice, and the ability of governmental agencies to perform their functions without undue hindrance. In the second, free communication is seen as conflicting with certain governmental goals that, while not absolutely necessary, may be seen as of importance for the promotion of a healthy society, particularly a healthy democratic society. Included are such goals as the promotion of patriotism, of equality, and of what many see as a decent society. In addition, we here consider the possible conflict between free communication and certain values of importance principally to individuals, but incapable of realization without governmental action. Included are such matters as the protection of economic rights, of the freedom from libel and invasion of privacy, and of freedom from unwanted stimuli.

In Part II we deal with problems arising under the religion clauses. In some of these conflicts there arise the same kinds of conflicts as those involved with the communications clauses. In others, however, it is the clash of values represented by the establishment and the free exercise clauses themselves that is at issue.

Most of the chapters which follow then, deal with a specific "problem" area, one which has necessitated a balancing of interests. In each chapter, an introductory essay seeks to clarify the goals to be weighed, to set forth the development of the topic in general, and to point out the particular doctrines and approaches which have been utilized by the Court in the resolution of the issues presented. Each essay is followed by three (in one case four) edited cases. The use of a relatively small number of cases allows for the inclusion of longer excerpts from the opinions, and for the generous use of concurring and dissenting opinions. Both are of particular value when dealing with First Amendment issues which, perhaps more than those in any other area of constitutional law involve questions as much of philosophy as of law, posing problems about the kind of society we wish to have. The cases selected are either classic or comparatively recent, and are ones which seem useful to illustrate such controversy, as well as to delineate the nature of the particular conflict involved, and the Court's response to it.

Parts I and II each begin with a chapter which provides an overview of the special problems involved with, respectively, the communications clauses and the religion clauses. These problems are set in political context, and the particular doctrines and approaches developed by the Court for the analysis of each are presented. In addition, the introductory chapters begin with a discussion of the values thought to be enhanced by religious and communicative freedom, values which provide the necessary justification for the First Amendment, and the necessary counterweights to be placed "in the balance" as we explore the meaning of that Amendment.

---

[1] The Supreme Court has had exactly this issue before it on two occasions. In the first case, Widmar v. Vincent (1981), involving a state university, the Court held that allowance of the religious group was required by the "free speech" provision of the First Amendment, and that the allowance of equal access to such groups would not violate the establishment clause. In the second, Board of Education of Westside Community Schools v. Mergens (1990), it upheld a Congressional statute mandating equal access for religious groups in high schools against an Establishment clause challenge.

[2] Schenck v. United States (1919)

[3] The title of this book, *The First Amendment in the Balance*, was first used in a article, critical of balancing, by Laurent B. Frantz which appeared in 71 *Yale Law Journal* 1424 (1962).

1
THE COMMUNICATIONS CLAUSES CONSIDERED

The framers of the First Amendment placed first those clauses dealing with religion, but it is conventional to begin by discussing the clauses relating to communication, including the rights of speech, press, assembly, and petition. Following that convention, we will first consider the particular values said to be enhanced by freedom of communication, and then the doctrines formulated by the Supreme Court to protect those values.

We could, of course, ignore the matter of First Amendment values and rest our case for its defense solely on the grounds that the Amendment is part of the Constitution. This would imply that what the Constitution requires must be implemented; certainly a defensible legal position. But, at least from the "balancing" perspective that this text adopts, such a viewpoint would be inadequate. For only if we understand the values to be derived from protecting freedom of communication, can we be in a position to understand the extraordinary lengths to which the Court has gone to protect such communication. And only then are we in a position to formulate our own views as to the proper balance to be struck between free communication and other governmental goals.

That there are important values to be served by free communication would seem to be self-evident. Not only did the framers of the First Amendment think so, but the very first provisions of the Bill of Rights to be "incorporated" into the meaning of the 14th Amendment's due process clause were the communications clauses.[1] And in the agenda outlined by Chief Justice Harlan Stone for a post-New Deal Court, free communication plays a prominent part.[2] Finally, freedom of communication is so central to our democratic system that it would have to be protected even if not specifically provided for by the Constitution.

But why do we especially value freedom of communication? What does it do for society, for government, or for the individual, which entitles it to special protection? Why must there be, as Frederick Schauer says, a "thumb on the scale"[3] when we balance the demands of the communications clauses against other governmental interests?

The ways of conceptualizing the values to be promoted by the communications clauses are as numerous as those who have considered the matter, but they generally fall into three categories. First, and central to any account of free communications values, has been what is called by Alexander Meiklejohn "political freedom,"[4] the right to give and receive information on political matters, a right obviously necessary for the very survival of democracy. Second, most observers have expanded this right to "political speech" to include communication in the pursuit of truth in any field.[5] Finally, some recent commentators have held that free communication is necessary not only in pursuit of these goals, but also as a way of promoting "self-expression" or "self-realization."[6]

In the landmark case of New York Times v. Sullivan (1964), a case which in the context of a suit for libel presented the issue of the freedom to criticize government officials, the Court observed that ". . . we consider this case against the background of a profound national commitment to the principle that debate on *public issues* should be uninhibited." And the juxtaposition of the provisions relating to speech and press with those protecting the right of assembly and petition does seem to imply that the framers were particularly concerned with political speech. The Meiklejohn position reflects this concern, resting as it does on the assumptions that all relevant information must be made available to the electorate as a prerequisite for their ballot decisions, and that free speech is a necessary consequence of the idea that the people are sovereign and government is their servant. For the sovereign people must be free to communicate their wishes to their servant, and for the servant to control such communication by the master would be anomalous, and dangerous in the extreme.

Limiting the protection of free communication to that relating to political speech might, as Meiklejohn hoped, have the advantage of providing the widest possible protection for such speech. But such a limitation would have severe disadvantages. First, the distinction between speech which is "political" and that which is not would sometimes be difficult to draw. Second, any definition of "political" speech which was drawn with any precision would seem to exclude from First Amendment protection material that many would wish to protect.

The United States Supreme Court has never accepted the Meiklejohn distinction. But the Court has, in a series of libel cases, drawn distinctions between "public" and "private" figures, and between "public" and "private" speech, which are reminiscent of that formulation.[7] And in Times, it indicated that the protection of "political" speech is at the "core" of the First Amendment. A balancing approach to freedom of communication would be free then, to weight the balance more heavily in favor of communication when clearly political speech is involved.

A somewhat broader view would hold that free communication is valuable generally as an aid to truth. One version of this theory holds that free communication is necessary, because only through exposure to all ideas can we sift out those that are true. A second holds that if all information is available, that which is accepted in the "marketplace of ideas" can be taken as true. Perhaps the best expression of this version is that provided by Justice Holmes in his famous dissent in Abrams v. United States (1919):

> But when men have realized that time has upset many fighting faiths, they may come to believe . . . that the ultimate good desired is better reached by free trade in ideas—that the best truth is the power of the thought to get itself accepted in the competition of the market, and that truth is the only ground upon which their wishes can be safely carried out. . . . That, at any rate, is the theory of our Constitution.

And, in Gitlow v. New York, Holmes expressed his willingness to accept the consequences of the "marketplace" idea:

> If in the long run the beliefs expressed in proletarian dictatorship are destined to be accepted by the dominant forces of the community, the only meaning of free speech is that they should be given their chance and have their way.

That, as Justice Douglas once remarked, "we have never been faithful" to Holmes' ideal,[8] will become obvious in the chapters to come; and the balancing approach adopted here implicitly denies that we should. For, as Frederick Schauer states, the concept that the "marketplace" will always yield "truth" is simply too contrary to observed experience to entertain.[9] And any theory of the First

Amendment (other than an absolutist one), will lead us to reject some consequences of speech, and thus *some* speech in *some* circumstances.

The first version of the argument from truth requires a belief that there is such a thing as objective truth, and that such truth is knowable by humans. Many would challenge the first premise, and most the second, at least if truth is taken to mean absolute, non-contingent truth. It also requires a belief, as does the "marketplace" idea, that people are both capable of deciding, and will do so rationally. But that too seems partially contradicted by experience.

The argument from truth may better be formulated as a negative. It may be argued that, since we can never be sure of what is true, we should be extremely cautious in suppressing anything, since unknowingly we may suppress the truth. Thus formulated, the argument from truth becomes an argument from error, one which may be combined with Meiklejohn's argument from political necessity into what Schauer terms the argument from "governmental incompetence." Government, it is asserted, is, like the citizen, generally unable to distinguish truth from falsehood. Moreover, government has its own particular interests in determining some things to be true and others to be false. Because of this, it should be *particularly disqualified* from making such determinations.

In Cohen v. California (1971), the Court first flirted with the idea that the value of the communications clauses is the aid that they give to "self-expression" or "self-realization." While communication seen as an aid to democracy or to the search for truth is valued for its benefit to the recipient or to society as a whole, the focus on "self-expression" emphasizes its utility for the communicator. Such a formulation would, of course, give protection to the widest range of human activity. Indeed, since almost any action can be seen as "expressive," there would seem to be virtually no limits on the kind of activity it would protect. Franklyn Haiman argues that the touchstone of whether an "expressive act" is, or is not protected by the First Amendment, should be whether and to what extent it does "harm."[10] But this has the effect of collapsing the meaning of the communications clauses into John Stuart Mill's famous dictum that "the only reason" for which society may interfere with a person's freedom of action is to prevent "harm to others." And what constitutes "harm" and "to others" is itself sufficiently debatable that we may hesitate to read into First Amendment jurisprudence the murky boundaries of Mill's formulation. As Meiklejohn knew, the wider we cast the net of First Amendment coverage, the more likely it is that the effectiveness of the coverage will be lessened. For purposes of the book then, we will assume that the values to be protected by the First Amendment does not include "self-expression," except and unless the Court itself has stressed this value.

We will, therefore, proceed on the assumption that the values to be protected by the communications clauses are those having to do with the necessity of communication for democratic government and with the search for truth generally. On any but an absolutist accounting, there must be times when the value of specific communicative activity is so marginal to either of these goals that it must bow to other needs. So the formulation of First Amendment doctrine and its application to specific cases always involves, at least potentially, two questions. Should this activity generally come under First Amendment protection, and should it be so protected in the specific circumstances of the instant case?[11]

One way to answer these questions is to distinguish "speech," which must in all but the most extreme cases be protected, from "action," which is not so protected. Justice Hugo Black, the Court's most fervent defender of First Amendment absolutism, saw this distinction as the key to that defense. But Black's position involved seeing, when necessary, "action" when most of us would have seen "speech." A more sophisticated version of this theory is that offered by Thomas Emerson, who made it the key to analysis in his *The System of Freedom of Expression*.[12]

For Emerson all behavior, verbal and non-verbal, which can be counted as "expression" is protected by the First Amendment. Further, the unprotected realm of "action" may include verbal as well as non-verbal "acts." Where, as will frequently be the case, expression and action are intermingled, whether or not the First Amendment comes into play depends upon which is predominant. If one is primary and the other is secondary, the conduct will or will not come under the First Amendment umbrella on this basis.

Recognizing the difficulty of making this determination with precision, Emerson tells us that the answer must be found in a "common sense reaction" aided by the consideration of two other factors: whether the conduct at issue is intended as communicative and capable of being understand as such; and whether the actions involved (divorced from their expressive aspects) are normally the subject of governmental control. On the basis of these criteria, he characterizes political assassination, physical interference with the movement of troop trains, and the pouring of blood on Selective Service files as "conduct." By contrast, burning a draft card to protest the nation's engagement in a war is "expression."

Emerson's first criterion turns out to be no criterion at all for, as we have noted, *any* conduct may be intended and understood as communicative. It is, then, his second criterion that really provides the basis for distinction. But the utility of that distinction is doubtful, as evidenced by United States v. O'Brien (1968) . For a draft card is the property of the government, and its preservation is, from the perspective of the government, essential to its utility. Why then, could O'Brien, having burned his draft card, not have been convicted under a general federal statute prohibiting the destruction of government property, every bit as easily as for pouring blood on government records?

There is little doubt that it is the second criterion which is, for Emerson, the really critical one. All of the examples that he gives, pouring blood on records equally with burning draft cards, may be seen as "communicative" in nature. It may be in some circumstances possible to make a reasonable determination of whether expressive "acts" are likely to be received as communicative in nature, but even this kind of distinction will not be easy to draw. Additionally, the matter of the intent of the "communicator" is virtually useless. It is not that the matter of intent is so difficult for the law to determine. We use intention in a great variety of legal circumstances and manage to muddle along rather well. But in First Amendment jurisprudence, "muddling along" is not enough. Given the importance of the First Amendment, it is virtually certain that we will accept as determinative the individual's own assertion of intention to communicate. Franklyn Haiman's observation that little is gained by distinguishing between "speech" and "action"" on such a basis seems then, to be correct.[13]

Haiman's own theory as to what is "speech" has the virtue of avoiding the artificiality of the "speech-action" distinction, but at the cost of blurring the line between *what* is protected and *when* First Amendment protection should be extended. For Haiman the First Amendment may protect all "expression" which he defines as all human behavior, at least potentially. This is so because all human behavior communicates. At the same time, the Amendment does not license all conduct.

The necessary distinction between that which is, and that which is not protected can be drawn by first recognizing three kinds of human behavior. The first is conduct that is "entirely symbolic" having as its function only the creation of ideas and feelings in others. These should be treated no differently than words. Second, there is conduct in which people engage primarily for its own sake, to satisfy some need, and without regard to its effect on others. To this the First Amendment has no application. The third and most problematic category, is conduct which is ordinarily non-symbolic, but which may be endowed by its actor or those who perceive it as symbolic. This includes, in some circumstances, virtually all included in the second group. For this we need a basis for distinguishing between that which is protected and that which is unprotected by the First Amendment. Such a basis for distinction Haiman finds in the degree of harm attached to the conduct.[14]

Haiman's theory, like that of Emerson, is vulnerable on a number of counts. His three categories do not really function very well to delineate how wide should be the protection afforded for various kinds of conduct. The line that he draws for example, between the "symbolism" involved when a stripper gyrates within inches of a spectator and her touching of that spectator is so thin as to be nonexistent, and depends not on the two being in different categories of conduct, but on the perception that the first act is purely symbolic while the second is not. In addition, Haiman's theory depends for much of its validity on seeing psychic harm as insignificant compared to physical harm, a proposition which, in view of modern psychology, is very much to be doubted.[15]

Finally, given its necessary reliance on degrees of "harm" to determine what is to be protected, Haiman's theory is virtually indistinguishable from Mill's "harm" principle. Thus, not only is it vulnerable to the difficulties associated with that theory, but like the "free expression" position with which it is closely associated, it leaves no basis for preferring "free communication" over liberty in general, or indeed, over a variety of other human desires.[16]

Frederick Schauer's discussion of the "speech umbrella" begins by noting that there are many forms of conduct not considered as speech in everyday conversation, but which are within the concept of "free speech." Thus freedom of speech must include all linguistic communication, certain signs and symbols which are the equivalent of language, commonly recognized symbols for which there is no exact linguistic analogue (e.g. Bronx Cheers), and pictures or pictorial representations. But, says Schauer, there are additionally many things which are in the ordinary sense considered "speech" which have nothing to do with speech; these include perjury, hiring another to commit a crime, and entering into a contract. Thus the issue of freedom of communications involves questions both of the "width" , and "porosity" of the "speech umbrella." Having said this, Schauer's analysis follows, in general, the process of inclusion and exclusion which has been followed by the Supreme Court.[17]

The Court's chief contribution to the issue of the width of the "speech umbrella" is to be found in the case of Chaplinsky v. New Hampshire (1942). In that case the Court held that libel, obscenity and (as in the instant case) "fighting words" could not be considered to come under the rubric of free speech. Rather, the Court tied that which is to be protected to the maintenance of other social interests, in particular to the "exposition of ideas." Another attempt to distinguish the protected from the unprotected, the initial holding that commercial speech was unprotected, proceeded on essentially the same grounds. And even the Court's most recent back-tracking on this issue has stemmed from the recognition that such speech may be of value to the search for truth.[18] Beyond this, the Court has generally held that "content-based" and "viewpoint-based" restrictions on communications are impermissible.

Most of the Court's effort to give meaning to the First Amendment has considered not the "width" of the umbrella, but rather the degree of its "porousness", i.e. the circumstances under which it is or is not permissible to regulate communication. Chief among the formulations intended to deal with this matter have been the doctrines of "no prior restraint," "clear and present danger," and "preferred position."

The doctrine of "no prior restraint" holds that government may not, except in the most extreme circumstances, suppress material which has not yet been published. The distinction in terms of effect on free communication is, therefore, the distinction between subsequent punishment for having made an utterance, and prevention of the utterance before the fact. The former may, under certain circumstances, be justified. The latter almost never is.[19]

The extraordinary deference accorded by the Court to this doctrine is partially due to historic factors, particularly the fact that prior restraint was once a favorite device of the English monarchy and that such eloquent spokesmen as John Milton inveighed against it. It is also due to the fact that true prior restraint involves censorship, i.e. some kind of determination by a government official that some material is not permissible to communicate, and presents in stark form the issue of governmental self-interest and consequent incompetence.

Prior restraint, the Court has held, is particularly dangerous to freedom of communication on a number of grounds. The standards involved are likely to be vague, and thus capable of being applied to materials not meant to be suppressed by those establishing the standards. Those who function as censors must justify their positions, and may thus be overly zealous in performing their duties. Most importantly, true prior restraint does not allow materials to be made public even once, making impossible an adequate and independent judgment of their true worth.

But, of course, prior restraint may be no worse than a system of subsequent punishment. For under the latter, the cautious person may prefer not to publish for fear of going over the permissible line, and might feel less at risk if able to submit his materials to the censor. Thus the fear of subsequent punishment may also operate to prevent materials from ever seeing the light of day.

Nevertheless, the very real problems and fears associated with censorship, as well as tradition, inertia, and the effect of precedent in American law, make likely the continued survival of the doctrine of "no prior restraint." But a full appreciation of the doctrine will note that it cannot be defended as an absolute. Indeed, our example of a situation where no reasonable person could argue for absolutism, the suppression of publication of the plans for the D-Day invasion, would be a classic case of prior restraint.[20]

The earliest and most famous of the doctrines attempting to deal with the "porousness" of the umbrella is the "clear and present danger" test, first enunciated by Justice Oliver Wendell Holmes in Schenck v. United States. Schenck was the very first free communications case ever decided by the Supreme Court. In his opinion for the Court, Justice Holmes delivered his famous dictum against First Amendment absolutism, that one who yelled "fire in a crowded theatre" would not be immune from prosecution, and continued:

> The question in every case is whether the words used are used in such circumstances as to create a clear and present danger of a substantive evil that government has a right to present. It is a question of proximity and degree.

Holmes' formulation contained only the seeds of stringent protection for First Amendment values. Its development was accomplished in two later cases, in neither of which was it adopted by a majority of the Court. In his own Abrams dissent, Holmes indicated that, for him, a danger sufficient to justify the suppression of speech would not only have to be probable, but must be present in the sense of "imminency," i.e. so close to happening that its occurrence could not be countered by the exercise of countervailing speech. And, in his concurrence in Whitney v. California (1927), Justice Brandeis, with Holmes in agreement, added that the "evil" apprehended must be not only one that government can lawfully prevent, but that it must be a relatively serious one.

It is in this modified form that the clear and present danger doctrine has survived. It may be restated as follows: The question in every case is whether there is a high probability of the imminent occurrence of a serious evil which government can legitimately prevent. So formulated the test would seem to be of doubtful utility as an across the board device for determining whether restrictions on First Amendment activity are justified. For one thing, there are many evils which government may prevent but which are not so serious that, under clear and present danger, they could be reached by devices impinging on the First Amendment. For another, the element of "immediacy" presents problems. In Schenck the "evil" that government was attempting to suppress was resistance to the draft, and it could be determined with relative ease whether Schenck's leaflets had indeed contributed significantly to such resistance. But what about those circumstances where the danger apprehended is one that is long-term and one which, by its nature, cannot be effectively dealt with only when immediate? Such a set of circumstances was arguably present in Dennis v. United States (1951). In a concurrence in which he recognized the difficulty just mentioned, Justice Robert Jackson argued that "clear and present danger" had no real application to such a case, and should be preserved as a "rule of reason" for the kind of case for which it had been designed.

Until recently the "clear and present danger" test, for all its reputation as a liberty-protecting device, has had a rather checkered career. The Court majority in the 1950s "Communist" cases felt it necessary to substantially alter its formulation in order to apply it. Nevertheless, it continues to be heavily employed in most varieties of "free communications" cases. Indeed, it is the impossibility of showing such a "clear and present danger" in the area of obscenity that is at the heart of at least one line of argument against the prohibition of such material. And the Court itself has reaffirmed the validity of the doctrine as applied to threats to public order:[21] ". . . the constitutional guarantees of free speech and free press do not permit a state to forbid or proscribe advocacy of the use of force or law violation except where such advocacy is directed to inciting or producing imminent lawless action and is likely to incite or produce such action."

Also of major importance, among the guidelines developed by the Court for use in solving "free communication" problems, is the doctrine of "preferred position." More an attitude than a test, since its principal function is to point out the direction in which one should face when dealing with such matters, "preferred position" does not specify how far in that direction one necessarily should go. As a matter of logic, at least, the idea of "preferred position" differs little from Schauer's argument that we should "put a thumb on the scales" in favor of communication.[22]

The problem with the preferred position doctrine arises when one confronts the question of just how "preferred" the allegedly protected activity is to be. Walter Berns criticizes the court's application of the doctrine by noting that, by his reckoning, it *always* results in protection for the "communicative" activity in question. For Berns, a test with only one result is not really a test, and results in an absolutism which cannot be defended. Further, says Berns, the preferred position doctrine could not always be followed even by its most ardent admirers, who upheld the conviction of a woman who allowed her Jehovah's Witness ward to distribute religious literature on the streets at night, in contravention of a state child labor statute. Here, says Berns, to have applied the doctrine would necessarily have resulted in striking down the conviction; it was, therefore, abandoned by its Court admirers, silently and without discussion. If Berns is right, "preferred position" in such a case is just a disguise for *ad hoc* balancing.[23]

Martin Shapiro on the other hand, defends preferred position. The First Amendment, he says, is not absolute, but to ignore preferred positions is to act as if the Amendment does not exist. In this respect his "preferred position" argument is similar to Schauer's "thumb on the scales," and indicates merely that the Amendment is to be given preference, unspecified as to degree, over other governmental concerns. This version of the doctrine is a far cry from the "absolutist" view characterized by Walter Berns.

Shapiro's second argument in favor of preferred position is more revealing of the results which he would like application of the doctrine to yield. For Shapiro not only admonishes the Court to remember that the First Amendment exists and that it was deliberately given special prominence by the Framers, but to remember that it is to be used in a particular way as well. The Court should be especially active in the area of First Amendment freedoms, not only for the sake of the values of that Amendment, but in order to protect the political process, and to aid those not likely to be served by the normal operation of that process. This argument marries "preferred position" doctrine with that of the second and third paragraphs of Carolene Product's footnote four. Thus "preferred position" is not only a device to protect First Amendment interests in general, but to assist other interests which are not "otherwise sufficiently represented." Such a "marriage" seems valid only if those who seek to limit speech always wish to restrict the "political processes" or that their purpose is always opposed to the interest of "discrete and insular minorities." But, it can be argued, limits on speech may be protective both of the political process and of minorities.[24]

In addition and more importantly for our purposes, such a theory does not reflect what the Court has recently been doing. In what sense can it be said that the media, one of the combatants in the conflicts over "free press-fair trial" and protection of reputational and privacy interests, is "insufficiently represented" in the political process? And what "insufficiently represented interests" were protected by the Court when it struck down, in Buckley v. Valeo, carefully tailored restrictions on campaign spending?

For Shapiro, the answer to "how preferred" First Amendment interests can be found in a revitalization of the clear and present danger test. But whatever its validity in some contexts, "clear and present danger," even undergirded by preferred position, seems of little help in solving others.[25] Such matters, along with most First Amendment problems, have been and indeed must be dealt with by the balancing of interests.

There are two quite different meanings to "balancing,"[26] one much more acceptable to contemporary scholarship. "Definitional balancing" weighs First Amendment values as opposed to others *before the fact* of the particular case. It thus involves the construction of abstract principles (or rules of thumb) as to how certain conflicts between First Amendment values and other interests are to be decided. These principles are then available for application to particular cases.

Thus, for example, the Court in New York Times v. Sullivan determined that, where First Amendment values conflicted with the right of public officials to be free from libelous falsehood, the Amendment must take precedence unless the statements in question were published with *actual malice*. This principle may then be used to determine the outcome of all future cases involving public officials. It may also be useful in determining the degree of protection to be given to First Amendment rights in the context of libel as the person harmed becomes less and less "public."

Similarly, "definitional balancing," although of a slightly different order, exists in the Court's posture on obscenity. That which is obscene, the Court has held, is not protected by the First Amendment. But in order to protect things entitled to such protection, the definition of what is obscene is couched in quite narrow terms. This approach in effect attempts to balance beforehand the right of the society to maintain its "decency" with the First Amendment interests involved. In the same vein, the "clear and present danger test" can be seen as a type of "definitional balancing." For under it certain societal interests can be served, despite the First Amendment, but only if the danger to these interests is "clear and present."

The advantage of "definitional" balancing is that it guarantees, by its *a priori* preference for the First Amendment value, that decisions in particular cases will be made in accord with that preference, without regard to the seemingly pressing demands of the particular case. It seems, therefore, thoroughly in accord with, and to provide a way to operationalize the "preferred position," that all First Amendment scholars, albeit in varying degrees, see as desirable. And because it is relatively precise, it is less likely that its application will result in a "chilling effect," under which allowing limitations on the exercise of First Amendment rights in some situations will lead others to forego exercising their rights. It has the additional advantage of being very much in accord with the general "common law" method of deciding cases, i.e. by reference to previously established norms.

"Definitional balancing" however, has the disadvantage that in individual cases it is less sensitive to the particular values involved, and cannot do as "fine" a job in weighing interests as can the *ad hoc* variety. In some cases this may lead to more protection for the alleged First Amendment interest than thought desirable even by dedicated libertarians.

Another problem which tends to temper the general approbation for "definitional balancing" is that in certain kinds of cases *ad hoc* balancing may be the only solution, perhaps because in these kinds of cases there is no preferred position for free communications claims. Situations in which there is a clash between the free communications values and those of the prohibition against establishment of religion or the right to a fair trial might present such a problem

Finally, there is the question of how useful "definitional balancing" really is in solving all or most free communications problems. The Court has not been at all consistent in its application. And the progression of libel and similar cases following Times may indicate that, although "definitional balancing" provides a good starting point, the resolution of concrete cases in at least this area requires a good deal of *ad hoc* balancing.

Ad hoc balancing means that free communications claims are to be weighed *in each particular case* against the other interest asserted, with the Courts determining which should prevail in the light of particular circumstances. The argument for *ad hoc* balancing, as well summarized by Shapiro (no friend of the technique), is roughly as follows: Speech cases involve the clashes of a number of rights. Definitional balancing forces the Court to concentrate on the free communication claim, and to discount the importance of other rights. But constitutional judgment requires impartial assessment of all competing claims present in the case. Only when the damage to free speech outweighs the other societal and individual interests served by the regulation at issue should the former be given preference.[27]

Ad hoc balancing thus defined does away with the idea of "preferred position" for free communication, counting it rather as only one among a number of competing values. And it is on the basis of an *ad hoc* approach that this book is organized. This, however, is not to say that *ad hoc* balancing is the preferable way for the Court to decide cases, but only that looking at cases in this way is a useful method for understanding what the Court has done.

The text does assert that balancing of one kind or another is the only way that the Court can deal with free communications questions. But the protection afforded by the Amendment cannot always be placed, as *ad hoc* balancing would have it, on the same level as other interests. The Court seemingly recognizes this in its insistence that the "vice of vagueness," where a statute is so imprecise that it cannot be understood by a person of common understanding, is particularly unacceptable where First Amendment values are affected. To the same effect is the "overbreadth" doctrine, which holds that a facially valid statute will be held to fail if it impinges on protected communication. In the same vein is the "least restrictive means" test, which states that a statute impinging on First Amendment values will be voided if it goes further than is necessary to deal with the particular problem involved.[28] These distinctions, like the Court's importation, from 14th Amendment "equal protection" analysis, of the doctrine that communication can be regulated only in pursuit of a "compelling state interest," all testify to the Court's unwillingness to accord to First Amendment rights only that status granted to other societal interests.

---

[1]Gitlow v. New York, (1925)

[2]The reference is to United States v. Carolene Products Co. (1938), in which Stone suggested that the presumption of constitutionality to be accorded legislation regulating commercial activities might be less appropriate in the case of that touching on the specific prohibitions "of the First Ten Amendments," that which "restricts . . . (the) . . . political processes," or that "directed at particular religious . . . or national . . . or racial minorities." As is apparent, each of these categories implicates, at least partially, First Amendment concerns.

[3]*Free Speech: A Philosophical Inquiry*, (Cambridge, England: Cambridge University Press, 1982), Ch. 1, 133.

[4] *Political Freedom: The Constitutional Powers of the People*, (New York, Oxford University Press, 1965), esp. Ch. 1. See also Schauer, Ch. 3. The discussion of the importance of "political speech" which follows largely follows Meiklejohn and Schauer. The comments on the limitations of the principle similarly follow Schauer.

[5]Among those who advance this justification for free speech are Schauer, Ch. 3; Thomas I. Emerson, *The System of Freedom of Expression* (New York: Random House Vintage Books (1971) Ch. 1, and Melville Nimmer, *Nimmer on Freedom of Speech*, (New York: Matthew Bender, 1984) Ch. 1.

[6]Emerson, *The System of Freedom of Expression*, 6, places "self-fulfillment" as first among the values justifying freedom of communication; as does Franklyn S. Haiman, *Speech and Law in a Free Society*, (Chicago, University of Chicago Press, 1981) 6.

[7]For a discussion of the Court's use of the "public-private" distinctions, see Chapter 10.

[8]Concurring in Brandenburg v. Ohio, (1969).

[9]Schauer, 26. The discussion of the "argument from truth" and its reformulation, in combination with "the argument from democracy" into an "argument from governmental incompetence" is based on Schauer, Ch. 2, and, with respect to the "reformulation", esp. Ch. 6.

continued on next page

[10]Haiman, Ch. 3, 34-35.

[11]The importance of distinguishing between the "scope" and the "protection" of the right of free communication is discussed by Schauer, Ch. 7, 89-91, using the metaphor of the "wearing of a suit of armor" which protects against some but not all projectiles. My own favorite metaphor is that of the "free speech umbrella," which may be wider or narrower and thus encompass a greater or lesser amount of "speech activity", and which may also be more or less "porous", and thus provide greater or less protection for that which is protected. Under this analogy one may not only conceive of some communication as being not at all protected, but also of some, "at the edges of the speech umbrella", receiving a lesser degree of protection. The Court has engaged in both of these kinds of categorization. See Chaplinsky v. New Hampshire, discussed herein, and Barnes v. Glen Theatre (1991).

[12]Justice Black's insistence on the "speech-action" distinction is made explicit in a number of cases, including Cohen v. California. Emerson's basis for distinction is suggested at 17-18, and more fully explored at 292-298 of *The System of Freedom of Expression*.

[13]Haiman's critique of the Emerson formulation is at 22-26 of *Speech and Law in a Free Society*.

[14]Haiman's own discussion revolves, as does that of Emerson, around "symbolic speech", and may be found at 25-38 of his book.

[15]In addition, Haiman asserts (37) in the case of "symbolic speech," that "in order for First Amendment considerations to come into play there must have been a *conscious intent* to communicate on the part of the actor at the time of the event. . . . It should be enough if, after the fact, he recognizes and claims that this is what he is doing." Courts must, he says, have some leeway in determining whether or not the claim is *bona fide.* How much leeway is, however, problematic, especially given the necessity, expressed by both Court and commentators, to err, if necessary, on the side of free communication.

Further, one must face the fact that *all* actions involve the communication of something. If I am shoveling manure I am, at the very least, conveying the desire that someone wishes to move the object of my efforts. How, then, is one to dispute my assertion that I *intended* to convey that message? Such a determination would, one would think, involve at least some consideration of Emerson's criterion of whether the "speech" or the "action" involved predominates.

[16]See the excellent and, in my opinion, persuasive discussion of "free expression" in Schauer, Ch. 4, especially 50-56.

[17]On the matter of the distinction between the "coverage" and the "protection" of the "free speech umbrella" see Schauer's discussion cited in fn. 11 above. On what should count as speech, see Schauer, Ch. 7. Schauer's theory is, of course, much more complex than as presented here. It will become obvious, if it is not already, that I not only believe that the Court has largely followed the path suggested by Schauer, but that I believe that is the path which, in most cases, should be followed.

[18] For the Court's initial attempt to place "commercial speech" beyond the protection of the First Amendment see Valentine v. Christiansen, 1942. For an example of its later "backtracking" on the issue see Virginia State Board of Pharmacy v. Virginia Citizens Consumer Council (1976). In Central Hudson Gas & Electric Corp. v. Public Service Commission (1980), the Court held that,

continued on next page

for commercial speech to be accorded a degree of First Amendment protection it must concern lawful activity and not be misleading. Given this, any restriction on such speech must further a "substantial governmental interest," must "directly advance" the interest asserted, and must not be more extensive than necessary to serve that interest.

[19]The Court's first discussion of the evils of prior restraint occurred in Near v. Minnesota (1931). Given the facts of Near it is at least arguable that the prior restraint at issue in that case was minimal. Near had, after all, published the types of allegations for which his newspaper was banned on a number of previous allegation. For a more recent example of the Court's distaste for prior restraint see New York Times Co. v. United States, discussed in Ch. 2.

[20]See the discussion of this point in the Introduction to this text.

[21]Brandenburg v. Ohio (1969). It is argued by some that the decision in Brandenburg effectively marked abandonment of the test. See David M. O'Brien, *Constitutional Law and Politics*, Vol. 2, *Civil Rights and Civil Liberties* (New York: W. W. Norton & Co., 1991) 354. While such a conclusion is certainly possible, my reading of Brandenburg indicates that the test was there only reformulated. Such an interpretation is supported Justice Douglas concurrence in that case, in which he argued that "I see no place in the regime of the First Amendment for any 'clear and present danger' test, whether strict and tight, or free-wheeling as the Court in Dennis rephrased it." And see Lawrence Tribe's discussion of "clear and present danger" in the context of incitement to illegal acts, in *American Constitutional Law*, 2nd ed., (Mineola, N.Y.: Foundation Press, 1988) 748-749.

[22]The genesis of the "preferred position" doctrine is usually traced to Chief Justice Stone's Carolene Products observation that the presumption of constitutionality accorded to economic legislation is not necessarily appropriate for legislation involving, *inter alia*, the "specific prohibitions" contained in the Bill of Rights. But if this is so, then the position that the First Amendment has its own special preference is somewhat untenable, for the Bill of Rights contains many other "specific prohibitions." But, of course, footnote 4 also indicates special solicitute for those rights thought essential to the governmental process, which certainly would include freedom of communication. (See above, fn. 2). At any rate, "preferred position" as applied to free communication apparently was first accepted by a Court majority in Thornhill v. Alabama (1940), in which the Court held labor picketing to be protected by the First Amendment. See Walter Berns, *Freedom, Virtue, and the First Amendment*, (Chicago: Henry Regnery Co., Gateway ed., 1965), 106-7.

[23]Berns position with respect to the result of the test is found at 120-121. His discussion of Prince v. Massachusetts (1944), in which he argues that "preferred position" was abandoned, is at 108-111. It should be noted, further, that Berns' definition of "preferred position" is somewhat suspect. He equates it, initially, with the reversal of the "presumption of constitutionality" mentioned in the Carolene Products footnote. (See above, fn.21). But he then argues that the adoption of "preferred position" necessarily means that, when it is applied, it must result in protection of the speech activity at issue. (Berns, 75) Such a result does not seem necessarily to follow from the adoption of the doctrine, nor in line with the meaning ordinarily assigned to it.

[24]See the discussion of "protection of the political process," and of the case of Buckley v. Valeo, in Ch. 6. On the conflict between press freedom and other interests see Chapters 5 and 10. And on recent attempts to limit speech in the interests of minorities, see Ch. 8.

continued on next page

24

on recent attempts to limit speech in the interests of minorities, see Ch. 8.

[26]Shapiro, *Freedom of Speech: The Supreme Court and Judicial Review* (Englewood Cliffs, NJ: Prentice-Hall Pub. Co., 1966) 115-121. In addition, application of this test, as Shapiro acknowledges, requires adoption of the speech/action distinction advocated by Thomas Emerson. As we have seen, the validity of this distinction is very much to be doubted.

[27]This discussion follows Melville Nimmer (See above, fn. 4), 9-24. Nimmer, along with most scholars, accepts "definitional" and criticizes "ad hoc" balancing.

[28]Shapiro, 76 .

[29]See, e.g. Papachristou v. City of Jacksonville (1972) - vagueness; Broadrick v. Oklahoma (1973) - overbreadth; Martin v. Struthers (1943) - least drastic means; First National Bank v. Bellotti (1978) - compelling state interest.

2

NATIONAL DEFENSE AND SECURITY

Issues of national security gave rise to the first cases on freedom of communication. And it seems natural for governments to believe in the necessity of their own self-preservation. Thus, when national security is threatened by direct action (i.e. by war), free speech, like other constitutional provisions, is likely to take a back seat. Even Abraham Lincoln, most revered of American presidents, interfered in wartime with constitutional liberties, and justified his actions on the basis that particular constitutional provisions could not be protected at the expense of the Constitution itself.

At the same time, government is likely to see threats to national security when they do not exist, and may use such supposed threats as a basis for actions which unjustifiably trample on individual rights. Thus the argument from "governmental incompetence" is particularly strong in the face of national security claims. It is no accident that the best known and generally most honored "definitional balance" in First Amendment jurisprudence, the "clear and present danger" test, was formulated in the context of national security considerations, and that it has been in the context of national security interests that it has been most severely tested.

The challenges to free communications presented by national security can be said to have occurred principally in three distinct periods. Very early in the history of the republic, the Federalists passed the Sedition Act, which made unlawful any "false, scandalous, and malicious" writing, uttering or publication "with intent to defame, bring into contempt, or incite popular hatred against the government, Congress or the President." The Act, however, occasioned no court challenges at the Supreme Court level, and thus no constitutional doctrine, and lapsed when the Jeffersonians came to power after the election of 1800.

Much more productive of doctrine was the second period, the time around and shortly after World War I, in which various "left-wing" individuals and ideologies ran afoul of state statutes against criminal syndicalism, and especially of the federal Espionage Act of 1917. The litigation which occurred in this period provided the basic First Amendment tenets which were to be employed in the third period, that of post-World War II and its perceived threat of Communism. That period, from approximately 1947 to 1960, was the time of McCarthyism, of presidential loyalty-security programs, and of major concern over the threat of Communism, foreign and domestic.

In the period of "glasnost," "perestroika," and the ending of the Cold War, it may be difficult for students to conceive of the danger thought to be presented by Communism in this era. On the international scene, the period saw such events as the expansion of the Soviet Union into all of Eastern Europe, the challenge to American rights in Germany which began with the Berlin Blockade and continued with the Berlin Wall, the loss of China to the Communists and, finally and most traumatically, the bitter and indecisive military struggle between the United States and the Communist allies of North Korea and the People's Republic of China. Internally, the existence of a fairly substantial Communist Party, loyal not to the United States but to the Soviet Union, had been presumed to be a fact since the late Thirties. That presumption was now fortified by disclosures of the betrayal of military and diplomatic secrets by citizens in places of importance, who turned such secrets over to Communist powers.

Under such circumstances political leaders of both parties, and both of the political branches of government, moved against domestic Communists in a variety of ways.[1] Of the various laws and regulations aimed at Communists, and tested in the Supreme Court, the best known were certainly the Smith Act provisions aimed at "advocacy of" and "conspiracy to advocate" violent overthrow of the government. Before considering, however, the cases in which these provisions were challenged, we will attempt to summarize the main threads of regulation and Court decisions in other areas.

The Smith Act also made criminal "membership" in the Communist Party, and the Court, in Scales v. United States and Noto v. United States (both 1961 and in fact decided on the same day) drew a line between the permissible and the prohibited under the membership clause. Knowing, active membership, said the Court in Scales, could properly be the basis for conviction. Membership without proof of knowledge or active intent to further the party's illegal aims, it held in Noto, could not. As to the registration of the Party required by the Subversive Activities Control Act of 1951, that requirement, said the Court in Communist Party v. Subversive Activities Control Board (1961), did not violate the First Amendment's "freedom of association."   Much earlier, in American Communications Association v. Douds (1950), the Court had upheld that part of the Taft-Hartley Act which required the National Labor Relations Board to refuse services to any union whose officers refused to sign a non-Communist affidavit, on the basis of Congress' interest in preventing strikes and the threat of strikes.[2] But the 1967 decision in Aptheker v. Secretary of State struck down a regulation permitting the revocation of the passports of Party members, on the grounds that no distinction was made between "knowing and active" and "unknowing and passive" Party membership. And in the same year the Court, in United States v. Robel, held invalid, on essentially the same ground, a provision that Party members could not work in defense facilities. Adding to the Court's disapproval in Robel was the fact that the regulation did not distinguish between "sensitive" and "nonsensitive" positions in defense establishments.

A second group of Cold War inspired regulations were directed at preventing the infiltration of Communists into certain "governmental" positions, or at "flushing out" those Communists already in such positions. Most of these took the form of loyalty oaths or disclaimers of Party membership. As in those discussed above, a survey of the cases reveal a pattern. In the "early days" of the Cold War, in the 1952 case of Adler v. Board of Education, the Court upheld New York's disqualification from the civil service, and from public teaching, of those who "advocated" or joined any group which advocated the forceful overthrow of the government. But in 1967, in Keyishian v. Board of Regents, the Court struck down the same law and overruled Adler, on the grounds that public employment could not be conditioned on the foregoing of constitutional rights. In between, loyalty oaths and related measures were sometimes invalidated on grounds of vagueness,[3] at other times on grounds of overbreadth, and at still other times were "saved" by a narrowing construction. In perhaps the best known of this last group of cases, Cole v. Richardson, the Court, as late as 1971, construed a Massachusetts oath to "uphold and defend" and to "oppose overthrow" of national and state governments to create no "specific responsibilities" but to "commit themselves to live by the constitutional processes of our system." Thus construed, said Chief Justice Burger, the requirement was neither vague nor violative of the First Amendment.

Also of note were the Court's decisions on the constitutionality of legislative investigations of "subversion." But here the timing was different. In Watkins v. United States (1957) the Court invalidated a "contempt of Congress" conviction for refusing to answer questions put by a Subcommittee of the House UnAmerican Activities Committee. The charge to HUAC by the House, said Chief Justice Warren, was impermissibly vague as to the "legislative purpose" served by the Committee's investigations. But, in Barenblatt v. United States (1959), while professing fidelity to the principle that legislative investigations could not be conducted merely "to expose," the Court held that "So long as Congress acts in pursuance of its constitutional power, the judiciary lacks authority to intervene on the basis of the motives which spurred the exercise of that power. . . ."

Important as these matters were, the central issue of the period was the attempt to punish, as criminal actions, Communist activity in organizing and in spreading their doctrine. The vehicle for such prosecution was the Smith Act, passed just prior to the Second World War, which made unlawful the intentional advocacy of overthrowing the government by force or violence, the printing and/or dissemination, with intent to cause such overthrow, of materials advocating such, and the organizing, or knowingly becoming a member, of any group engaged in such advocacy. The Act also made criminal the attempt to commit, or the conspiracy to commit, any of the acts which it prohibited.

The Smith Act cases presented, at least ostensibly, the same kinds of questions as had been at issue in the World War I Espionage Act cases and, to a lesser extent, in the "criminal syndicalism" prosecutions of the 1920s. For all were criminal prosecutions for actions thought to be threatening to the national security. In Schenck and in Abrams the threat had been to military conscription and to the prosecution of the First World War. In Gitlow and in Whitney it was the advocacy of anarchism which was said to present a danger of governmental overthrow. And, as we have seen, Justice Holmes, speaking for the Court in Schenck, had formulated the clear and present danger test and then, in cooperation with Justice Brandeis, had refined it in <u>Abrams</u>, <u>Gitlow</u>, and <u>Whitney</u>. Success in the Smith Act prosecutions, then, seemed likely to depend on whether the demands of clear and present danger could be satisfied.

But application of the test to the facts in <u>Dennis v. United States</u> (1951) presented problems. For one thing, the test was no longer what it had been originally. The Holmes-Brandeis "refinements," particularly that of Brandeis in <u>Whitney</u>, had transformed it from a formula for justifying convictions[4] to one likely to set free in all but the most extreme circumstances. Most importantly for the <u>Dennis</u> case, the formula required that the "danger" be imminent as well as serious. And, although the danger of Communist subversion was serious enough, the likelihood that it would lead *imminently* to overthrow of the government, or even to an attempt to overthrow the government was virtually nonexistent.

The danger test, it must be remembered, had been formulated and refined in the context of cases involving small, almost *ad hoc* groups of leftists and/or anarchists whose activity was limited to making impassioned speeches or distributing "incendiary" leaflets.[5] The Communist Party was not, however, of this ilk. Rather, it was relatively large, included members who were prominent in American society and adept at communication, had (or could have if it desired) the assistance of a foreign power, and was said to be highly disciplined. The evil to be feared from such an organization could not be limited to "imminent overthrow." Whatever danger there was from Communist activity was over the long haul.

That, at any rate, was the assumption on which the Supreme Court proceeded. The conviction of Eugene Dennis was upheld, along with those of the other "top Communists," for violation of the Smith Act's conspiracy provision. Dennis and his cohorts were not charged with advocating the desirability of governmental overthrow, or of printing materials toward that end, or even with organizing to do so, but rather with *conspiring* to do these things.

Six justices voted to uphold the convictions, with the plurality opinion being written by Chief Justice Fred Vinson, concurrences by Felix Frankfurter and Robert Jackson, and dissents by Hugo Black and William O. Douglas. Vinson's plurality opinion stressed that the Smith Act proscribed not the mere discussion of the desirability of overthrowing government forcefully, but the advocacy of such. Further, he applied the clear and present danger test in a substantially revised manner, as he had to do if its use was to result in conviction. Rejecting the view that the test allowed punishment for advocacy only if there was a substantial likelihood of successful accomplishment, Vinson argued that the "danger" which was relevant was not the overthrow of the government, but of the advocacy of such unlawful action. That being so, he reinterpreted "clear and present danger" to involve the consideration of "whether the gravity of the evil, discounted by its improbability" justified the interference with free speech. On this basis, he found the evidence to be persuasive that "the requisite danger existed."

Justice Frankfurter's concurring opinion ignored clear and present danger and, based on a frank and entirely *ad hoc* balancing of interests, agreed that the convictions did not unjustifiably interfere with free speech. The initial balancing, said Frankfurter, had been performed by Congress, and its decision was to be respected unless clearly wrong.

For Justice Robert Jackson, also concurring, clear and present danger had not been designed for cases involving nationwide and on-going conspiracy occurring in the context of pronounced international peril. Thus it should not be applied in this case. For Jackson, the danger posed by the act of *conspiracy*, coupled with the gravity of that which the conspirators intended, was dispositive.

Justice Black's dissenting opinion disagreed both with Vinson's reformulation (Black called it repudiation) of clear and present danger, and with Frankfurter's position of deference to Congressional judgement. Justice Douglas, also in dissent, argued that the defendants were being convicted for speech, rather than for actions directed toward governmental overthrow, and denied the existence of any realistic danger that overthrow itself could be accomplished by the convicted Communists.

The several opinions in Dennis, and especially Vinson's reformulation of the clear and present danger test, made the case unquestionably the most important and controversial decision of the era, and it is reproduced at the end of this chapter. Six years later, in Yates v. United States (1957), the Court reversed the conviction of ten "second line" Communist leaders on the basis that the trial judge's jury charge had permitted their conviction for mere "abstract advocacy" of the doctrine of forcible overthrow, "divorced from any effort to instigate action to that end." Dennis, the Court said, could not be interpreted to allow conviction for mere advocacy. With the decision in Yates, the attempt to control the threat of internal

Communism by employment of the Smith Act was largely brought to a close. Whether the "danger test" survived is a matter of dispute.

To the extent that there exist today entities which are even roughly comparable to the Communist Party in their willingness to use violence to achieve mostly illegal ends, such are probably to be found among the Ku Klux Klan, the Aryan Nations, and others of the same racist ilk. But such organizations are much closer in size, and perhaps in discipline, to the "criminal syndicalist" groups of the 1920s. And much of their activity seems similarly *ad hoc*. It might be supposed, therefore, and following the suggestion of Justice Jackson in Dennis, that "clear and present danger" would be useful in dealing with threats posed by such organizations. And so it was that, in the 1969 case of Brandenburg v. Ohio, the doctrine was once again employed. This time it was used to strike down the conviction of a KKK leader whose sentiments were reprehensible, but whose uttered threats were relatively mild. In a *per curiam* opinion, the Court expressly overruled Whitney v. California, adopting in doing so the Brandeis' formulation of "clear and present danger" in that case. The First Amendment, said the Court, does not permit a state to forbid advocacy of the use of force or violation of law, "except where such advocacy is directed to inciting or producing imminent lawless action and is likely to incite or produce such action."[6]

The Court's most consistent champions of a near absolutist approach to speech, Justices Black and Douglas, might have been expected to celebrate this vindication of the Holmes-Brandeis doctrine. Instead, reacting to the way in which "clear and present danger" had been employed during the "Communist era," they protested its resurrection in any form. "The line," said Douglas, "between what is permissible and not subject to control, and what may be made impermissible and subject to regulation, is the line between ideas and overt action," or those situations where "speech is brigaded with action . . . (and) . . . indeed inseparable."

The issue of national security, as applied to a Communist threat, raised its head once more in the Vietnam era. Here, however, the threat posed by Communism was conceded by virtually everyone to be entirely foreign in its genesis. And, though the government (and particularly the Nixon administration) raised the spectre of a danger to national security from the domestic dissent which accompanied that war, Vietnam produced few cases involving the First Amendment, and none implicating it in the manner of either the post-World War I or II eras. Indeed, the most celebrated "communications" case to come out of the Vietnam era did not involve organized groups of dissenters or the advocacy of unlawful actions. Rather, what was at stake in <u>New York Times Co. v. United States</u> (1971) was a battle between the government and a powerful newspaper over the validity of a classic prior restraint.

Daniel Ellsberg, a one-time Defense Department analyst who had become disenchanted with the Vietnam conflict, leaked to the *New York Times* and the *Washington Post* a secret and highly classified Pentagon study (*The Pentagon Papers*). The study severely criticized the conduct of the war, undermined official government claims as to its conduct, and cast grave doubt on the possibility of the conflict's success. When the newspapers began to print serial excerpts from the documents, the government sought an injunction against continued publication. Two district and one appellate court concluded that the material contained in the publication was not so threatening to national security as to justify a prohibition of its publication.

The Supreme Court, in a most uninformative *per curiam* opinion agreed, stating only that prior restraints require a very high level of justification, and that the government had not met that burden. Justice Black's concurrence argued that to hold "that the publication of news . . . [may]. . . sometimes be enjoined. . . would make a shambles of the First Amendment." He was joined in this view by Justice Douglas. Justice Brennan, also concurring, observed that the government's request for injunction had been premised upon dangers which "might" or "could" occur, and that the First Amendment permitted prior restraints only upon "governmental allegation and proof that publication must inevitably, directly, and immediately cause the occurrence of an event kindred to imperiling the safety of a transport already at sea. . . ." The three dissenters, Burger, Harlan, and Blackmun, contented themselves with protesting against the extraordinary speed with which the Court had moved to hear the case. (It had moved from the District to the Supreme Court in less than a week.) The case made no law, except to underscore once again the Court's distaste for prior restraint.

The same cannot be said for another "communications" case arising out of the Vietnam conflict. <u>United States v. O'Brien</u> (1968), reproduced herein, resulted in a decision which has been heavily and perhaps justly criticized.[7] But in announcing its decision, that war protester David P. O'Brien could be convicted and punished for burning his draft card, the Court announced a test which has had considerable influence in subsequent litigation concerning "speech plus" and which, because of that influence, is excerpted here. In upholding O'Brien's conviction the Court stated:

> . . . we think it clear that a government regulation is sufficiently justified if it is within the constitutional power of the Government; if it furthers an important or substantial governmental interest; if the governmental interest is unrelated to the suppression of free expression; and if the incidental restriction on alleged First Amendment freedoms is no greater than is essential for the furtherance of that interest.

Other cases arising from the Vietnam era typically involved the extent to which war protesters could be prevented from spreading their message on military bases, or using the flag in anti-war protests. Decided on grounds unrelated to national security, these cases will be considered in Chapters 4 and 7.

The recent case of Boos v. Barry (1988) presented the Court with that rarity, a case of virtually first impression. At issue in Barry, the final case to be excerpted in this chapter, were two questions. One was decided strictly on grounds related to "public order," and broke no new constitutional ground. The other, however, involved the question of whether the District of Columbia could forbid the displaying, adjacent to foreign embassies, of signs inimical to the dignity of foreign nations and their embassy personnel. It raised, therefore, considerations of national security as related to our relations with other countries. In a classic display of *ad hoc* balancing, the Court unanimously invalidated the statute, ultimately on the narrow grounds that there was readily available a "less restrictive means" for achieving the governmental purpose. Thus it was unnecessary for the Court to determine if the protection of "dignity," an interest almost certainly unjustified as applied to domestic politics and politicians, could override rights of free communication when applied to matters touching on foreign policy. Justice O'Connor's majority opinion seemed to indicate that the Court would be unlikely to sustain such an override.

---

[1]Whether or not the internal threat posed by Communism was sufficient to justify these measures was a hotly debated topic. For two contrasting views on the question see Berns, *Freedom, Virtue, and the First Amendment*, Ch. 5, and Shapiro, *Freedom of Speech: The Supreme Court and Judicial Review*, Ch. 4.

continued on next page

[2]But the practical effect of the registration requirement was largely nullified by the holding, in <u>Albertson v. SACB</u> (1965), that the Fifth Amendment shielded registration by members, either for the party or on their own behalf. And, in <u>United States v. Brown</u> (1965), that part of Taft-Hartley which made it a crime for a Communist to be an officer in a labor union was invalidated as a bill of attainder.

[3]See, e.g., <u>Baggett v. Bullitt</u> (1964), vagueness; <u>Elfbrandt v. Russell</u> (1966) overbreadth.

[4]Shenck had, after all, gone to prison as a result of Holmes' efforts in his behalf.

[5]This was not true in the case of Elizabeth Whitney, whose criminal action had been attending a convention of the Communist Party. But what happened to Ms. Whitney could itself be characterized as a crime, for the evidence seemed to establish that she at no time had advocated, or even agreed to participate in, forceful overthrow of government.

[6]This seems to me to be essentially the danger test "as refined." See the discussion of whether <u>Brandenburg</u> is properly interpreted as employing "clear and present danger" in Ch. 1, fn. 21.

[7]Thomas Emerson uses his critique of <u>O'Brien</u> to argue that the burning of a draft card, in the context of that case, should have been considered speech, rather than action; and, more generally, calls the decision a "serious setback for First Amendment theory." (Emerson, pp. 82-87.) For Lawrence Tribe the Court's principal failure in O'Brien was its incorrect assessment of the motive of Congress in passing the statute banning the burning of draft cards, and its consequent failure to subject the law to "clear and present danger" analysis. See Tribe, *American Constitutional Law*, 2nd ed. (Mineola N.Y.: Foundation Press, 1988), pp. 824-25.

DENNIS ET AL. V. UNITED STATES

341 U.S. 494 (1951)

MR. CHIEF JUSTICE VINSON announced the judgment of the Court and an opinion in which MR. JUSTICE REED, MR. JUSTICE BURTON and MR. JUSTICE MINTON join.

Petitioners were indicted in July, 1948, for violation of the conspiracy provisions of the Smith Act . . . A verdict of guilty as to all the petitioners was returned by the jury on October 14, 1949. The Court of Appeals affirmed the convictions. We granted certiorari, limited to the following two questions: (1) Whether either 2 or 3 of the Smith Act, inherently or as construed and applied in the instant case, violates the First Amendment and other provisions of the Bill of Rights: . . . Sections 2 and 3 of the Smith Act, (see present 18 U.S.C. 2385), provide as follows: "SEC. 2(a) It

shall be unlawful for any person— "(1) to knowingly or willfully advocate, abet, advise, or teach the duty, necessity, desirability, or propriety of overthrowing or destroying any government in the United States by force or violence, or by the assassination of any officer of any such government;" "(2) with intent to cause the overthrow or destruction of any government in the United States, to print, publish, edit, issue, circulate, sell, distribute, or publicly display any written or printed matter advocating, advising, or teaching the duty, necessity, desirability, or propriety of overthrowing or destroying any government in the United States by force or violence;" (3) to organize or help to organize any society, group, or assembly of persons who teach, advocate, or encourage the overthrow or destruction of any government in the United States by force or violence; or to be or become a member of, or affiliate with, any such society, group, or assembly of persons, knowing the purposes thereof." (b) For the purposes of this section, the term 'government in the United States' means the Government of the United States, the government of any State, Territory, or possession of the United States, the government of the District of Columbia, or the government of any political subdivision of any of them. "SEC. 3. It shall be unlawful for any person to attempt to commit, or to conspire to commit, any of the acts prohibited by the provisions of this title."

The indictment charged the petitioners with willfully and knowingly conspiring (1) to organize as the Communist Party of the United States of America a society, group and assembly of persons who teach and advocate the overthrow and destruction of the Government of the United States by force an violence, and (2) knowingly and willfully to advocate and teach the duty and necessity of overthrowing and destroying the Government of the United States by force and violence. The indictment further alleged that section 2 of the Smith Act proscribes these acts and that any conspiracy to take such action is a violation of section 3 of the Act. . . The obvious purpose of the statute is to protect existing Government, not from change by peaceable, lawful and constitutional means, but from change by violence, revolution and terrorism. That it is within the *power* of the Congress to protect the Government of the United States from armed rebellion is a proposition which requires little discussion. Whatever theoretical merit there may be to the argument that there is a "right" to rebellion against dictatorial governments is without force where the existing structure of the government provides for peaceful and orderly change. We reject any principle of governmental helplessness in the face of preparation for revolution, which principle, carried to its logical conclusion, must lead to anarchy. No one could conceive that it is not within the power of Congress to prohibit acts intended to overthrow the Government

by force and violence. The question with which we are concerned here is not whether Congress has such *power*, but whether the *means* which it has employed conflict with the First and Fifth Amendments to the Constitution. One of the bases for the contention that the means which Congress has employed are invalid takes the form of an attack on the face of the statute on the grounds that by its terms it prohibits academic discussion of the merits of Marxism—Leninism, that it stifles ideas and is contrary to all concepts of a free speech and a free press. . .The very language of the Smith Act negates the interpretation which petitioners would have us impose on that Act. It is directed at advocacy, not discussion. Thus, the trial judge properly charged the jury that they could not convict if they found that petitioners did "no more than pursue peaceful studies and discussions or teaching and advocacy in the realm of ideas." He further charged that it was not unlawful "to conduct in an American college or university a course explaining the philosophical theories set forth in the books which have been placed in evidence." Such a charge is in strict accord with the statutory language, and illustrates the meaning to be placed on those words. Congress did not intend to eradicate the free discussion of political theories, to destroy the traditional rights of Americans to discuss and evaluate ideas without fear of governmental sanction. Rather Congress was concerned with the very kind of activity in which the evidence showed these petitioners engaged. But although the statute is not directed at the hypothetical cases which petitioners have conjured, its application in this case has resulted in convictions for the teaching and advocacy of the overthrow of the Government by force and violence, which, even though coupled with the intent to accomplish that overthrow, contains an element of speech. For this reason, we must pay special heed to the demands of the First Amendment marking out the boundaries of speech. We pointed out in *Douds,* that the basis of the First Amendment is the hypothesis that speech can rebut speech, propaganda will answer propaganda, free debate of ideas will result in the wisest governmental policies. It is for this reason that this Court has recognized the inherent value of free discourse. An analysis of the leading cases in the Court which have involved direct limitations on speech, however, will demonstrate that both the majority of the Court and the dissenters in particular cases have recognized that this is not an unlimited, unqualified right, but that the societal value of speech must, on occasion, be subordinated to other values and considerations. No important case involving free speech was decided by this Court prior to *Schenck v. United States* (1919). Indeed, the summary treatment accorded an argument based upon an individual's claim that the First Amendment protected certain utterances indicates that the Court at earlier dates placed no unique emphasis upon that right. It was not until the classic dictum of Justice Holmes in the *Schenck* case that speech *per se* received that emphasis in a majority opinion. That case involved a conviction under the Criminal Espionage Act, 40 Stat. 217. The question the Court faced was whether the evidence was sufficient to sustain the conviction. Writing for a unanimous Court, Justice Holmes stated that the question in every case is whether the words used are used in such circumstances and are of such a nature as to create a clear and present danger that they will bring about the substantive evils that Congress has a right to prevent. . . .

The fact is inescapable, too, that the phrase bore no connotation that the danger was to be any threat to the safety of the Republic. The charge was causing and attempting to cause insubordination in the military forces and obstruct recruiting. The objectionable document denounced conscription and its most inciting sentence was, "You must do your share to maintain, support and uphold the rights of the people of this country." Fifteen thousand copies were printed and some circulated. This insubstantial gesture toward insubordination in 1917 during war was held to be a clear and present danger of bringing about the evil of military insubordination. In several later cases involving convictions under the Criminal Espionage Act, the nub of the evidence the Court held sufficient to meet the "clear and present danger" test enunciated in *Schenck* was as follows: *Frohwerk v. United States* (1919)—publication of twelve newspaper articles attacking the war; *Debs v. United States* (1919)—one speech attacking United States' participation in the war; *Abrams v. United States* (1919)—circulation of copies of two different socialist circulars attacking the war; *Schaefer v. United States* (1920)—publication of a German-language newspaper with allegedly false article, critical of capitalism and the war; *Pierce v. United States* (1920)—circulation of copies of a four-page pamphlet written by a clergyman, attacking the purposes of the war and United States' participation therein. . . .The rule we deduce from these cases is that where an offense is specified by a statute in non speech or non press terms, a conviction relying upon speech or press as evidence of violation may be sustained only when the speech or publication created a "clear and present danger" of attempting or accomplishing the prohibited crime, *e.g.,* interference with enlistment. . . . The next important case before the Court in which free speech was the crux of the conflict was *Gitlow v. New York* (1925). There New York had made it a crime to advocate "the necessity or propriety of overthrowing. . .organized government by force. . . ." The evidence of violation of the statute was that the defendant had published a Manifesto attacking the Government and capitalism. The convictions were sustained, Justices Holmes and Brandeis dissenting. The majority refused to apply the "clear and present danger" test to the specific utterance. Its reasoning was as follows: The "clear and present danger" test was applied to the utterance itself in *Schenck* because the question was merely one of sufficiency of evidence under an admittedly constitutional statute. *Gitlow,* however, presented a different question. There a legislature had found that a certain kind of speech was, itself, harmful and unlawful. The constitutionality of such a state statute had to be adjudged by this Court just as it determined the constitutionality of any state statute, namely, whether the statute was "reasonable." Since it was entirely reasonable for a state to attempt to protect itself from violent overthrow, the statute was perforce reasonable. The only question remaining in the case became whether there was evidence to support the conviction, a question which gave the majority no difficulty. Justices Holmes and Brandeis refused to accept this approach, but insisted that wherever speech was the evidence of the violation, it was necessary to show that the speech created the "clear and present danger" of the substantive evil which the legislature had the right to prevent. Justices Holmes and Brandeis, then, made no distinction between a federal statute which made certain acts unlawful, the evidence to support the conviction being speech, and a statute which made speech itself the crime. This approach was emphasized in *Whitney v. California* (1927), where the Court was confronted with a conviction under the California Criminal Syndicalist statute. The Court sustained the conviction, Justices Brandeis and Holmes concurring in the result. In their concurrence they repeated that even though the legislature had designated certain speech as criminal, this could not prevent the defendant from showing that there was no danger that the substantive evil would be brought about. Although no case subsequent to *Whitney* and *Gitlow* has expressly overruled the majority opinions in those cases, there is little doubt that subsequent opinions have inclined toward the Holmes-Brandeis rationale. . . . In this case we are squarely presented with the application of the "clear and present danger" test, and must decide what that phrase imports. We first note that many of the cases in which this Court has reversed convictions by use of this or similar tests have been based on the fact that the interest which the State was attempting to protect was itself too insubstantial to warrant restriction of speech. In this category we may put such cases as *Schneider v. State* (1939); *Cantwell v. Connecticut* (1940); *Martin v Struthers* (1943); *West Virginia Board of Education v. Barnette* (1943); *Thomas v. Collins* (1945); *Marsh v. Alabama* (1946); but cf. *Prince v. Massachusetts* (1944); *Cox v. New Hampshire* (1941).

Overthrow of the Government by force and violence is certainly a substantial enough interest for the Government to limit speech. Indeed, this is the ultimate value of any society, for if a society cannot protect its very structure from armed internal attack, it must follow that no subordinate value can be protected. If, then, this interest may be protected, the literal problem which is presented is what has been meant by the use of the phrase "clear and present danger" of the utterances bringing about the evil within the power of Congress to punish. Obviously, the words cannot mean that before the Government may act, it must wait until the *putsch* is about to be executed, the plans have been laid and the signal is awaited. If Government is aware that a group aiming at its overthrow is attempting to indoctrinate its members and to commit them to a course whereby they will strike when the leaders feel the circumstances permit, action by the Government is required. The argument that there is no need for Government to concern itself, for Government is strong, it possesses ample powers to put down a rebellion, it may defeat the revolution with ease needs no answer. For that is not the question. Certainly an attempt to overthrow the Government by force, even though doomed from the outset because of inadequate numbers or power of the revolutionists, is a sufficient evil for Congress to prevent. The damage which such attempts create both physically and politically to a nation makes it impossible to measure the validity in terms of the probability of success, or the immediacy of a successful attempt. In the instant case the trial judge charged the jury that they could not convict unless the found that petitioners intended to overthrow the Government "as speedily as circumstances would permit." This does not mean, and could not properly mean, that they would not strike until there was certainty of success. What was meant was that the revolutionists would strike when they thought the time was ripe. We must therefore reject the contention that success or probability of success is the criterion. . . . Chief Judge Learned Hand, writing for the majority below, interpreted the phrase as follows: "in each case [courts] must ask whether the gravity of the 'evil,' discounted by its improbability, justifies such invasion of free speech as is necessary to avoid the danger." 183 F. 2d at 212. We adopt this statement of the rule. As articulated by Chief Judge Hand, it is as succinct and inclusive as any other we might devise at this time. It takes into consideration those factors which we deem relevant, and relates their significances. More we cannot expect from words. Likewise, we are in accord with the court below, which affirmed the trial court's finding that the requisite danger existed. The mere fact that from the period 1945 to 1948 petitioners' activities did not result in an attempt to overthrow the Government by force and violence is of course no answer to the fact that there was a group that was ready to make the attempt. The formation by petitioners of such a highly organized conspiracy, with rigidly disciplined members subject to call when the leaders, these petitioners, felt that the time had come for action, coupled with the inflammable nature of world conditions, similar uprisings in other countries with whom petitioners were in the very least ideologically attuned, convince us that their convictions were justified on this score. And this analysis disposes of the contention that a conspiracy to advocacy itself, cannot be constitutionally restrained, because it comprises only the preparation. It is the existence of the conspiracy which creates the danger. *Pinkerton v. United States* (1946); *Goldman v. United States* (1918); *United States v. Rabinowich* (1915). If the ingredients of the reaction are present, we cannot bind the Government to wait until the catalyst is added. . . .

MR. JUSTICE CLARK took no part in the consideration or decision of this case. MR. JUSTICE FRANKFURTER, concurring in affirmance of the judgment. . . .

A survey of the relevant decisions indicates that the results which we have reached are on the whole those that would ensue from careful weighing of conflicting interests. The complex issues presented by regulation of speech in public places,

by picketing, and by legislation prohibiting advocacy of crime have been resolved by scrutiny of many factors besides the imminence and gravity of the evil threatened. The matter has been well summarized by a reflective student of the Court's work. "The truth is that the clear-and-present-danger test is an oversimplified judgment unless it takes account also of a number of other factors: the relative seriousness of the danger in comparison with the value of the occasion for speech or political activity; the availability of more moderate controls than those which the state has imposed; and perhaps the specific intent with which the speech or activity is launched. No matter how rapidly we utter the phrase 'clear and present danger,' or how closely we hyphenate the word, they are not a substitute for the weighing of values. They tend to convey a delusion of certitude when what is most certain is the complexity of the strands in the web of freedoms which the judge must disentangle" Freund, On Understanding the Supreme Court. . . .

MR. JUSTICE JACKSON, concurring. . . . The "clear and present danger" test was an innovation by Justice Holmes in the *Schenck* case, reiterated and refined by him and Mr. Justice Brandeis in later cases, all arising before the era of World War II revealed the subtlety and efficacy of modernized revolutionary techniques used by totalitarian parties. In those cases, they were faced with conviction under so-called criminal syndicalism statutes aimed at anarchists but which, loosely construed, had been applied to punish socialism, pacifism, and left-wing ideologies, the charges often resting on far-fetched inferences which, if true, would establish only technical or trivial violations. They proposed "clear and present danger" as a test for the sufficiency of evidence in particular cases. I would save it, unmodified, for application as a "rule of reason" in the kind of case for which it was devised. When the issue is criminality of a hot-headed speech on a street corner, or circulation of a few incendiary pamphlets, or parading by some zealots behind a red flag, or refusal of a handful of school children to salute our flag, it is not beyond the capacity of the judicial process to gather, comprehend, and weigh the necessary materials for decision whether it is a clear and present danger of substantive evil or a harmless letting off of steam. It is not a prophecy, for the danger in such cases has matured by the time of trial or it was never present. The test applies and has meaning where a conviction is sought to be based on a speech or writing which does not directly or explicitly advocate a crime but to which such tendency is sought to be attributed by construction or by implication from external circumstances. The formula in such cases favors freedoms that are vital to our society, and, even if sometimes applied too generously, the consequences cannot be grave. But its recent expansion has extended, in particular to Communists, unprecedented immunities. Unless we are to hold our Government captive in a judge-made verbal trap, we must approach the problem of a well-organized, nation-wide conspiracy, such as I have described, as realistically as our predecessors faced the trivialities that were being prosecuted until they were checked with a rule of reason. I think reason is lacking for applying that test to this case. . . What really is under review here is a conviction of conspiracy, after a trial for conspiracy, on an indictment charging conspiracy, brought under a statute outlawing conspiracy. With due respect to my colleagues, they seem to me to discuss anything under the sun except the law of conspiracy. One of the dissenting opinions even appears to chide me for "invoking the law of conspiracy." As that is the case before us, it may be more amazing that its reversal can be proposed without even considering the law of conspiracy. The Constitution does not make conspiracy a civil right. The Court has never before done so and I think it should not do so now. Conspiracies of labor unions, trade associations, and news agencies have been condemned, although accomplished, evidenced and carried out, like the conspiracy here, chiefly by letter-writing, meetings, speeches and organization. . . . The basic rationale of the law of conspiracy is that a conspiracy

may be an evil in itself, independently of any other evil it seeks to accomplish. . . . The reasons underlying the doctrine that conspiracy may be a substantive evil in itself, apart from any evil it may threatened, attempt, or accomplish, are peculiarly appropriate to conspiratorial Communism. "The reason for finding criminal liability in case of a combination to effect an unlawful end or to use unlawful means, where none would exist, even though the act contemplated were actually committed by an individual, is that a combination of persons to commit a wrong, either as an end or as a means to an end, is so much more dangerous, because of its increased power to do wrong, because it is more difficult to guard against and prevent the evil designs of a group of persons than of a single person, and because of the terror which fear of such a combination tends to create in the minds of people . . . . " Also, it is urged that since the conviction is for conspiracy to teach and advocate, and to organize the Communist Party to teach and advocate, the First Amendment is violated, because freedoms of speech and press protect teaching and advocacy regardless of what is taught or advocated. I have never thought that to be the law. I do not suggest that Congress could punish conspiracy to advocate something, the doing of which it may not punish. Advocacy or exposition of the doctrine of communal property ownership, or any political philosophy unassociated with advocacy of its imposition by force or seizure of government by unlawful means could not be reached through conspiracy prosecution. But it is not forbidden to put down force or violence, it is not forbidden to punish its teaching or advocacy, and the end being punishable, there is no doubt of the power to punish conspiracy for the purpose. . . .

MR. JUSTICE BLACK, dissenting . . . .

At the outset I want to emphasize what the crime involved in this case is, and what it is not. These petitioners were not charged with an attempt to overthrow the Government. They were not charged with overt acts of any kind designed to overthrow the Government. They were not even charged with saying anything or writing anything designed to overthrow the Government. The charge was that they agreed to assemble and to talk and publish certain ideas at a later date: The indictment is that they conspired to organize the Communist Party and to use speech or newspapers and other publications in the future to teach and advocate the forcible overthrow of the Government. No matter how it is worded, this is a virulent form of prior censorship of speech and press, which I believe the First Amendment forbids. I would gold *3 of the Smith Act authorizing this prior restraint unconstitutional on its face and as applied. But let us assume, contrary to all constitutional ideas of fair criminal procedure, that petitioners although not indicted for the crime of actual advocacy, may be punished for it. Even on this radical assumption, the other opinions in this case show that the only way to affirm these convictions is to repudiate directly or indirectly the established "clear and present danger" rule. This the Court does in a way which greatly restricts the protections afforded by the First Amendment. The opinions for affirmance indicate that the chief reason for jettisoning the rules the expressed fear that advocacy of Communist doctrine endangers the safety of the Republic. Undoubtedly, a governmental policy of unfettered communication of ideas does entail dangers. To the Founders of this Nation, however, the benefits derived from free expression were worth the risk. The embodied this philosophy in the First Amendment's command that "Congress shall make no law . . . abridging the freedom of speech, or of the press . . . ." I have always believed that the First Amendment is the keystone of our Government, that the freedoms it guarantees provide the best insurance against destruction of all freedom. At least as to speech in the realm of public matters, I believe that the "clear and present danger" test does not "mark the furthermost constitutional boundaries of protected expression" but does "no more than recognize a minimum compulsion of the Bill of Rights." *Bridges v. California.* So long as this Court exercises the power of judicial review of legislation, I cannot agree that the First Amendment permits us to sustain laws suppressing freedom of speech and press on the basis of Congress' or our own notions of mere "reasonableness." Such a doctrine waters down the First Amendment so that it amounts to little more than an admonition to Congress. The Amendment as so construed is not likely to protect any but those "safe" or orthodox views which rarely need its protection. . . . Public opinion being what it now is, few will protest the conviction of these Communist petitioners. There is hope, however, that in calmer times, when present pressures, passions and fears subside, this or some later Court will restore the First Amendment liberties to the high preferred place where they belong in a free society. . . .

MR. JUSTICE DOUGLAS, dissenting.

UNITED STATES v. O'BRIEN.

391 U.S. 367 (1968)

MR. CHIEF JUSTICE WARREN delivered the opinion of the Court.

On the morning of March 31, 1966, David Paul O'Brien and three companions burned their Selective Service registration certificates on the steps of the South Boston Courthouse. A sizable crowd, including several agents of the Federal Bureau of Investigation, witnessed the event. Immediately after the burning, members of the crowd began attacking O'Brien and his companions. An FBI agent ushered O'Brien to safety inside the courthouse. After he was advised of his right to counsel and to silence, O'Brien stated to FBI agents that he had burned his registration certificate because of his beliefs, knowing that he was violating federal law. He produced the charred remains of the certificate, which, with his consent, were photographed.

For this act, O'Brien was indicted, tried, convicted, and sentenced in the United States District Court for the District of Massachusetts. He did not contest the fact legitimate legislative purpose. The District Court rejected these arguments, holding that the statute on its face did not abridge First Amendment rights, that the court was not competent to inquire into the motives of Congress in enacting the 1965 Amendment, and that the Amendment was a reasonable exercise of the power of Congress to raise armies.

On appeal, the Court of Appeals for the First Circuit held the 1965 Amendment unconstitutional as a law abridging freedom of speech. At the time the Amendment was enacted, a regulation of the Selective Service System required registrants to keep their registration certificates in their "personal possession at all times." (1962). Wilful violations of regulations promulgated pursuant to the Universal Military Training and Service Act were made criminal by statute 462(b)(6). The Court of Appeals, therefore, was of the opinion that conduct punishable under the 1965 Amendment was already punishable under the nonpossession regulation, and consequently that the Amendment served no valid purpose; further, that in light of the prior regulation, the Amendment must have been "directed at public as distinguished from private destruction." On this basis, the court concluded that the 1965 Amendment ran afoul of the First Amendment by singling out persons engaged in protests for special treatment.

By the 1965 Amendment, Congress added to 12(b)(3) of the 1948 Act the provision here at issue, subjecting to criminal liability not only one who "forges, alters, or in any manner changes" but also one who "knowingly destroys, [or] knowingly mutilates" a certificate. We note at the outset that the 1965 Amendment plainly does not abridge free speech on its face, and we do not understand O'Brien to argue otherwise. Amended 12(b)(3) on its face deals with conduct having no connection with speech. It prohibits the knowing destruction of certificates issued by the Selective Service System, and there is nothing necessarily expressive about such conduct. The Amendment does not distinguish between public and private destruction, and it does not punish only destruction engaged in for the purpose of expressing views. Compare *Stromberg v. California* (1931). A law prohibiting destruction of Selective Service certificates no more abridges free speech on its face than a motor vehicle law prohibiting the destruction of drivers' licenses, or a tax law prohibiting the destruction of books and records. . . .

O'Brien nonetheless argues that the 1965 Amendment is unconstitutional in its application to him, and is unconstitutional as enacted because what he calls the "purpose" of Congress was "to suppress freedom of speech." We consider these arguments separately.

O'Brien first argues that the 1965 Amendment is unconstitutional as applied to him because his act of burning his registration certificate was protected "symbolic speech" within the First Amendment. His argument is that the freedom of expression which the First Amendment guarantees includes all modes of "communication of ideas by conduct," and that his conduct is within this definition because he did it in "demonstration against the war and against the draft."

We cannot accept the view that an apparently limitless variety of conduct can be labeled "speech" whenever the person engaging in the conduct intends thereby to express an idea. However even on the assumption that the alleged communicative element in O'Brien's conduct is sufficient to bring into play the First Amendment, it does not necessarily follow that the destruction of a registration certificate is constitutionally protected activity. This Court has held that when "speech" and "nonspeech" elements are combined in the same course of conduct, a sufficiently important governmental interest in regulating the nonspeech element can justify incidental limitations on First Amendment freedoms. To characterize the quality of the governmental interest which must appear, the Court has employed a variety of descriptive terms: compelling; substantial; subordinating; paramount; cogent; strong. Whatever imprecision inheres in these terms, we think it clear that a government regulation is sufficiently justified if it is within the constitutional power of the Government; if it furthers an important or substantial governmental interest; if the governmental interest is unrelated to the suppression of free expression; and if the incidental restriction on alleged First Amendment freedoms is no greater than is essential to the furtherance of that interest. We find that the 1965 Amendment to 12(b)(3) of the Universal Military Training and Service Act meets all of these requirements, and consequently that O'Brien can be constitutionally convicted for violating it.

We think it apparent that the continuing availability to each registrant of his Selective Service certificates substantially furthers the smooth and proper functioning of the system that Congress has established to raise armies. We think it also apparent that the Nation has a vital interest in having a system for raising armies that functions with maximum efficiency and is capable of easily and quickly responding to continually changing circumstances. For these reasons, the Government has a substantial interest in assuring the continuing availability of issued Selective Service certificates.

It is equally clear that the 1965 Amendment specifically protects this substantial governmental interest. We perceive no alternative means that would more precisely and narrowly assure the continuing availability of issued Selective Service certificates than a law which prohibits their wilful mutilation or destruction. Compare *Sherbert v. Verner* (1963), and the cases cited therein. The 1965 Amendment prohibits such conduct and does nothing more. In other words, both the governmental interest and the operation of the 1965 Amendment are limited to the noncommunicative aspect of O'Brien's conduct. The governmental interest and the scope of the 1965 Amendment are limited to preventing harm to the smooth and efficient functioning of the Selective Service System. When O'Brien deliberately rendered unavailable his registration certificate he wilfully frustrated this governmental interest. For this noncommunicative impact of his conduct, and for nothing else, he was convicted.

The case at bar is therefore unlike one where the alleged governmental interest in regulating conduct arises in some measure because the communication allegedly integral to the conduct is itself thought to be harmful. In *Stromberg v. California* (1931), for example, this Court struck down a statutory phrase which punished people who expressed their "opposition to organized government" by displaying "any flag, badge, banner, or device." Since the statute there was aimed at suppressing communication it could not be sustained as a regulation of noncommunicative conduct. See also, *NLRB v. Fruit & Vegetable Packers Union* (1964) (concurring opinion).

In conclusion, we find that because of the Government's substantial interest in assuring the continuing availability of issued Selective Service certificates, because amended 462(b) is an appropriately narrow means of protecting this interest and condemns only the independent noncommunicative impact of conduct within its reach, and because the noncommunicative impact of O'Brien's act of burning his registration certificate frustrated the Government's interest, a sufficient governmental interest has been shown to justify O'Brien's conviction.

O'Brien finally argues that the 1965 Amendment is unconstitutional as enacted because what he calls the "purpose" of Congress was "to suppress freedom of speech." We reject this argument because under settled principles the purpose of Congress, as O'Brien uses that term, is not a basis for declaring this legislation unconstitutional.

It is a familiar principle of constitutional law that this Court will not strike down an otherwise constitutional statute on the basis of an alleged illicit legislative motive. As the Court long ago stated:

"The decisions of this court from the beginning lend no support whatever to the assumption that the judiciary may restrain the exercise of lawful power on the assumption that a wrongful purpose or motive has caused the power to be exerted." *McCray v. United States* (1904).

This fundamental principle of constitutional adjudication was reaffirmed and the many cases were collected by Mr. Justice Brandeis for the Court in *Arizona v. California* (1931).

Inquiries into congressional motives or purposes are a hazardous matter. When the issue is simply the interpretation of legislation, the Court will look to statements by legislators for guidance as to the purpose of the legislature, because the benefit to sound decisionmaking in this circumstance is thought sufficient to risk the possibility of misreading Congress' purpose. It is entirely a different matter when we are asked to void a statute that is, under wellsettled criteria, constitutional on its face, on the basis of what fewer than a handful of Congressmen said about it. That motivates one legislator to make a speech about a statute is not necessarily what motivates scores of others to enact it, and the stakes are sufficiently high for us to eschew guesswork. We decline to void essentially on the ground that it is unwise legislation which Congress had the undoubted power to enact and which could be reenacted in its exact form if the same or another legislator made a "wiser" speech about it. . . .

We think it not amiss, in passing, to comment upon O'Brien's legislative-purpose argument. There was little floor debate on this legislation in either House. Only Senator Thurmond commented on its substantive features in the Senate. After his brief statement, and without any additional substantive comments, the bill,

H. R. 10306, passed the Senate. In the House debate only two Congressmen addressed themselves to the Amendment—Congressmen Rivers and Bray. The bill was passed after their statements without any further debate by a vote of 393 to 1. It is principally on the basis of the statements by these three Congressmen that O'Brien makes his congressional-"purpose" argument. We note that if we were to examine legislative purpose in the instant case, we would be obliged to consider not only these statements but also the more authoritative reports of the Senate and House Armed Services Committees. The portions of those reports explaining the purpose of the Amendment are reproduced in the Appendix in their entirety. While both reports make clear a concern with the "defiant" destruction of so-called "draft cards" and with "open" encouragement to others to destroy their cards, both reports also indicate that this concern stemmed from an apprehension that unrestrained destruction of cards would disrupt the smooth functioning of the Selective Service System. . . .

MR. JUSTICE MARSHALL took no part in the consideration or decision of these cases.

MR. JUSTICE HARLAN, concurring.

I, wish to make explicit my understanding that this does not foreclose consideration of First Amendment claims in those rare instances when an "incidental" restriction upon expression, imposed by a regulation which furthers an "important or substantial" governmental interest and satisfies the Court's other criteria, in practice has the effect of entirely preventing a "speaker" from reaching a significant audience with whom he could not otherwise lawfully communicate. This is not such a case, since O'Brien manifestly could have conveyed his message in many ways other than by burning his draft card.

MR. JUSTICE DOUGLAS, dissenting....

BOOS ET AL. V. BARRY, MAYOR OF THE DISTRICT OF COLUMBIA, ET AL.

485 U.S 312 (1987)

JUSTICE O'CONNOR delivered the opinion of the Court, except as to Part II-A.

The question presented in this case is whether a provision of the District of Columbia Code, 22-1115, violates the First Amendment. This section prohibits the display of any sign within 500 feet of a foreign embassy if that sign tends to bring that foreign government into "public odium" or "public disrepute." It also prohibits any congregation of three or more persons within 500 feet of a foreign embassy.

Petitioners are three individuals who wish to carry signs critical of the Governments of the Soviet Union and Nicaragua on the public sidewalks within 500 feet of the embassies of those Governments in Washington, D. C. Petitioners Bridget M. Brooker and Michael Boos, for example, wish to display signs stating "RELEASE SAKHAROV" and "SOLIDARITY" in front of the Soviet Embassy. Petitioner J. Michael Waller wishes to display a sign reading "STOP THE KILLING" within 500 feet of the Nicaraguan Embassy. All of the petitioners also wish to congregate with two or more other persons within 500 feet of official foreign buildings. . . .

Congress enacted 22-1115 in 1938, pursuant to its authority under Article I of the Constitution to "define and punish . . . Offenses against the Law of Nations." Section 22-1115 reads in pertinent part as follows: "It shall be unlawful to display any flag, banner, placard, or device designed or adapted to intimidate, coerce, or bring into public odium any foreign government, party, or organization, or any officer or officers thereof, or to bring into public disrepute political, social, or economic acts, views, or purposes of any foreign government, party or organization . . . within 500 feet of any building or premises within the District of Columbia used or occupied by any foreign government or its representative or representatives as an embassy, legation,

consulate, or for other official purposes . . . or to congregate within 500 feet of any such building or premises, and refuse to disperse after having been ordered so to do by the police authorities of said District."

The first portion of this statute, the "display" clause, applies to signs tending to bring a foreign government into public odium or public disrepute, such as signs critical of a foreign government or its policies. The display clause applies only to the display of signs, not to the spoken word. See *Zaimi v. United States* (1973). The second portion of the statute, the "congregation" clause, addresses a different concern. It prohibits congregation, which District of Columbia common law defines as an assemblage of three or more people. *District of Columbia v. Reed.*(1967) (reprinted in App. in *Kinoy* v. *District; of Columbia,* (1968)); *Hunter v. District of Columbia* (1918). Both of these prohibitions generally operate within a 500 foot zone surrounding embassies or consulates owned by foreign governments, but the statute also can extend to other buildings if foreign officials are inside for some official purpose.

The District Court granted respondents' motion for summary judgment, relying upon an earlier Court of Appeals decision, *Frend v. United States* (1938), denied (1939), that had sustained the statute against a similar First Amendment challenge. A divided panel of the Court of Appeals for the District of Columbia affirmed. *Finzer v. Barry* (1986). Although it found *Frend* "persuasive precedent," the Court of Appeals thought *Frend* was not binding because it "was decided almost a half century ago and in the interval the Supreme Court has developed constitutional law in ways that must be taken into account."

The Court of Appeals considered the two aspects of 22-1115 separately. First, the court concluded that the display clause was a content-based restriction on speech. Relying, however, upon our decisions in

Perry Education Assn. v. Perry Local Educators' Assn. (1983), and *Carey v. Brown* (1980), the court nonetheless found it constitutional because it was justified by a compelling governmental interest and was narrowly drawn to serve that interest. Second, the Court of Appeals concluded that the congregation clause should be construed to authorize an order to disperse "only when the police reasonably believe that a threat to the security or peace of the embassy is present," and that as construed, the congregation clause survived First Amendment scrutiny.

We granted certiorari, 479 U. S. 1083 (1987). We now reverse the Court of Appeals' conclusion as to the display clause, but affirm as to the congregation clause.

Analysis of the display clause must begin with several important features of that provision. First, the display clause operates at the core of the First Amendment by prohibiting petitioners from engaging in classically political speech. We have recognized that the First Amendment reflects a "profound national commitment" to the principle that "debate on public issues should be uninhibited, robust, and wide-open," *New York Times Co. v. Sullivan* (19G4), and have consistently commented on the central importance of protecting speech on public issues. See, *e. g., Connick v. Myers* (1983); *NAACP v. Claiborne Hardware Co.* (1982); *Carey v. Brown* (1980). This has led us to scrutinize carefully any restrictions on public issue picketing. See, *e. g., United States v. Grace*, (1983); *Carey v. Brown; Police Department of Chicago v. Mosley* (1972).

Second, the display clause bars such speech on public streets and sidewalks, traditional public for a that "time out of mind, have been used for purposes of assembly, communicating thoughts between citizens, and discussing public questions." *Hague v. CIO* (1939). In such places, which occupy a "special position in terms of First Amendment protection," *United States v. Grace* (1983),the government's ability to restrict expressive activity "is very limited."

Third, 22-1115 is content-based. Whether individuals may picket in front of a foreign embassy depends entirely upon whether their picket signs are critical of the foreign government or not. One category of speech has been completely prohibited within 500 feet of embassies. Other categories of speech, however, such as favorable speech about a foreign government or speech concerning a labor dispute with a foreign government, are permitted. See D. C. Code 22-1116 (1981).

Both the majority and dissent in the Court of Appeals accepted this common sense reading of the statute and concluded that the display clause was content-based. The majority indicated, however, that it could be argued that the I regulation was not content-based.

Both respondents and the United States have now made such an argument in this Court. They contend that the statute is not content-based because the government is not itself selecting between viewpoints; the permissible message on a picket sign is determined solely by the policies of a foreign government.

We reject this contention, although we agree the provision is not viewpoint-based. The display clause determines which viewpoint is acceptable in a neutral fashion by looking to the policies of foreign governments. While this prevents the display clause from being directly viewpoint-based, a label with potential First Amendment ramifications of its own, see, *e. g., Members of City Council of Los Angeles v. Taxpayers for Vincent* (1984); *Schacht v. United States* (1970), it does not render the statute content-neutral. Rather, we have held that a regulation that "does not favor either side of a political controversy" is nonetheless impermissible because the "First Amendment's hostility to content-based regulation extends . . . to prohibition of public discussion of an entire topic." *Consolidated Edison Co. v. Public Service Comm'n* (1980). Here the government has determined that an entire category of speech—signs or displays critical of foreign governments—is not to be permitted.

Respondents and the United States do not point to the "secondary effects" of-picket signs in front of embassies. They do not point to congestion, to interference with ingress or egress, to visual clutter, or to the need to protect the security of embassies. Rather, they rely on the need to protect the dignity of foreign diplomatic personnel by shielding them from speech that is critical of their governments. This justification focuses *only* on the content of the speech and the direct impact that speech has on its listeners. The emotive impact of speech on its audience is not a "secondary effect." Because the display clause regulates speech due to its potential primary impact, we conclude it must be considered content-based.

Our cases indicate that as a *content-based* restriction on *political speech* in a *public forum*, 22-1115 must be subjected to the most exacting scrutiny. Thus, we have required the State to show that the "regulation is necessary to serve a compelling state interest and that it is narrowly drawn to achieve that end." *Perry Education Assn. v. Perry Local Educators' Assn.* Accord, *Board of Airport Comm'rs of Los Angeles v. Jews for Jesus,* (1987); *Cornelius v. NAACP Legal Defense and Educational Fund, Inc.* (1985); *United States v. Grace.*

We first consider whether the display clause serves a compelling governmental interest in protecting the dignity of foreign diplomatic personnel. Since the dignity of foreign officials will be affronted by signs critical of their governments or governmental policies, we are told, these foreign diplomats must be shielded from such insults in order to fulfill own country's obligations under international law.

As a general matter, we have indicated that in public debate our own citizens must tolerate insulting, and even outrageous, speech in order to provide "adequate 'breathing space' to the freedoms protected by the First Amendment." *Hustler Magazine, Inc. v. Falwell* (1988). See also, *e. g., New York Times Co. v. Sullivan.* A "dignity" standard, like the "outrageousness" standard that we rejected in *Hustler, is so* inherently subjective that it would be inconsistent with "our longstanding refusal to [punish speech] because the speech in question may have an adverse emotional impact on the audience." *Hustler Magazine.*

We are not persuaded that the differences between foreign officials and American citizens require us to deviate from these principles here. The dignity interest is said to be compelling in this content primarily because its recognition and protection is part of the United States' obligations under international law. The Vienna Convention on Diplomatic Relations (1972), which all parties agree represents the current state of international law, imposes on host states "[the] special duty to take all appropriate steps to protect the premises of the mission against any intrusion or damage and to prevent any disturbance of the peace of the mission or impairment of its dignity."

The need to protect diplomats is grounded in our Nation's important interest in international relations. As a leading commentator observed in 1758, "[i]t is necessary that nations should treat and hold intercourse together, in order to promote their interests,—to avoid injuring each other,—and to adjust and terminate their disputes." E. Vattel, The Law of Nations 452 (J. Chitty ed. 1844) (translation). This observation is even more true today given the global nature of the economy and the extent to which actions in other parts of the world affect our own national security. Diplomatic personnel are essential to conduct the international affairs so crucial to the well-being of this Nation. In addition, in light of the concept of reciprocity that governs much of international law in this area, see C. Wilson, Diplomatic Privileges and Immunities (1967), we have a more parochial reason to protect foreign diplomats in this country. Doing so ensures that similar protections will be accorded those that we send abroad to represent the United States, and thus serves our national interest in protecting our own citizens. Recent history is replete with attempts, some unfortunately successful, to harass and harm our ambassadors and other diplomatic officials. These underlying purposes combine to make our national interest in protecting diplomatic personnel powerful indeed.

At the same time, it is well established that "no agreement with a foreign nation can confer power on the

Congress, or on any other branch of Government, which is free from the restraints of the Constitution. *Reid v. Covert* (1957)." See 1 Restatement of Foreign Relations Law of the United States (Apr. 12, 1985) ("[R]ules of international law and provisions of international agreements of the United States are subject to the Bill of Rights and other prohibitions, restrictions or requirements of the Constitution and cannot be given effect in violation of them").

Thus, the fact that an interest is recognized in international law does not automatically render that interest "compelling" for purposes of First Amendment analysis. We need not decide today whether, or to what extent, the dictates of international law could ever require that First Amendment analysis be adjusted to accommodate the interests of foreign officials. Even if we assume that international law recognizes a dignity interest and that it should be considered sufficiently "compelling" to support a content-based restriction on speech, we conclude that 22-1115 is not narrowly tailored to serve that interest.

The most useful starting point for assessing 22-1115 is to compare it with an analogous statute adopted by Congress, which is the body primarily responsible for implementing our obligations under the Vienna Convention. Title 18 U.S.C. 112(b)(2) subjects to criminal punishment willful acts or attempts to "intimidate, coerce, threaten, or harass a foreign official." In modifying 112, Congress was motivated by First Amendment concerns: "This language [of the original anti-picketing provision] raises serious Constitutional questions because it appears to include within its purview conduct and speech protected by the First Amendment."

Thus, after a careful balancing of our country's international obligations with our Constitution's protection of free expression, Congress has determined that 112 adequately satisfies the Government's interest in protecting diplomatic personnel outside the District of Columbia. It is the necessary, "appropriate" step that Congress has enacted to fulfill our international obligations.

Section 112 applies to all conduct "within the United States but outside the District of Columbia." In the legislative history, the exclusion of the District from the statute's reach is explained with reference to 22-1115; Congress was informed that a "similar" statute already applied inside the District (1972). The two statutes, however, are not identical, and the differences between them are constitutionally significant. In two obvious ways, 112 is considerably less restrictive than the display clause of 22-1115. First and foremost, 112 is not narrowly directed at the content of speech but at any activity, including speech, that has the prohibited effects. Moreover, 112, unlike 22-1115, does not prohibit picketing; it only prohibits activity undertaken to "intimidate, coerce, threaten, or harass." Indeed, unlike the display clause, even the repealed antipicketing portion of 112 permitted peaceful picketing.

Given this congressional development of a significantly less I restrictive statute to implement the Vienna Convention, there is little force to the argument that we should give deference to a supposed congressional judgment that the Convention demands the more problematic approach reflected in the display clause. . . . Relying on congressional judgment in this delicate area, we conclude that the availability of alternatives such as 112 amply demonstrates that the display clause is not crafted with sufficient precision to withstand First Amendment scrutiny. It may serve an interest in protecting the dignity of foreign missions, but it is not narrowly tailored; a less restrictive alternative is readily available. *Wygant v. Jackson Bd. of Ed.* (1986) (plurality opinion). Thus, even assuming for present purposes that the dignity interest is "compelling," we hold that the display clause of 22-1115 is inconsistent with the First Amendment.

Petitioners initially attack the congregation clause by arguing that it confers unbridled discretion upon the police. In addressing such a facial overbreadth challenge, a court's first task is to ascertain whether the enactment reaches a substantial amount of constitutionally protected conduct. *Houston v. Hill* (1987); *Hoffman Estates v. Flipside, Hoffman Estates, Inc.* (1982).

In making this assessment, we consider the actual text of the statute as well as any limiting constructions that have been developed. *Kolender v. Lawson* (1983).

The congregation clause makes it unlawful "to congregate within 500 feet of any [embassy, legation, or consulate] and refuse to disperse after having been ordered so to do by the police." 22-1115.

Standing alone, this text is problematic both because it applies to any congregation within 500 feet of an embassy for *any* reason and because it appears to place no limits at all on the dispersal authority of the police. The Court of Appeals, however, has provided a narrowing construction that alleviates both of these difficulties.

The Court of Appeals, we must first observe, read the congregation clause as distinct from the display clause, so the constitutional infirmity of the latter need not affect the former. Second, the Court of Appeals followed the lead of several earlier decisions, see, e. g., *United States v. Travers* (1970), and concluded that the statute permits the dispersal only of congregations that are directed at an embassy; it does not grant "police the power to disperse for reasons having nothing to do with the nearby embassy." Finally, the Court of Appeals further circumscribed police discretion by holding that the statute permits dispersal "only when the police reasonably believe that a threat to the security or peace of the embassy is present."

So narrowed, the congregation clause withstands First Amendment overbreadth scrutiny. It does not reach a substantial amount of constitutionally protected conduct; it merely regulates the place and manner of certain demonstrations. Unlike a general breach of the peace statute, see, e. g., *Cox v. Louisiana* (1965), the congregation clause is site-specific; it applies only within 500 feet of foreign embassies (ordinance prohibiting certain picketing "near" a courthouse upheld; 22-1115 cited with approval as being less

vague due to specification of 500 feet); *Grayned* (upholding ban on picketing near a school; special nature of place relevant in judging. reasonableness of restraint). Moreover, the congregation clause does not prohibit peaceful congregations; its reach is limited to groups posing a security threat. As we have noted, "where demonstrations turn violent, they lose their protected quality as expression under the First Amendment." *Grayned*. These two limitations prevent the congregation clause from reaching a substantial amount of constitutionally protected conduct and make the clause consistent with the First Amendment.

Petitioners argue that even as narrowed by the Court of Appeals, the congregation clause is invalid because it is impermissibly vague. In particular, petitioners focus on the word "peace," which is not further defined or limited. We rejected an identical argument in *Grayned*. *That* case concerned an ordinance that prohibited persons near schools from "disturb[ing] the peace" of the schools. We held that given the "particular context" of the ordinance it gave fair notice of its scope: "Although the prohibited quantum of disturbance is not specified in the ordinance, it is apparent from the statute's announced purpose that the measure is whether normal school activity has been or is about to be disrupted." Section 22-1115 presents the same situation. It is crafted for a particular context and given that context, it is apparent that the "prohibited quantum of disturbance" is whether normal embassy activities have been or are about to be disrupted. The statute communicates its reach in words of common understanding, *Cameron v. Johnson* (1968), and it accordingly withstands petitioners' vagueness challenge.

We conclude that the display clause of 22-1115 is unconstitutional on its face. It is a content-based restriction on political speech in a public forum, and it is not narrowly tailored to serve a compelling state interest. We also conclude that the congregation clause, as narrowed by the Court of Appeals, is not facially unconstitutional. Accordingly, the judgment of the Court of Appeals is reversed in part and affirmed in part. *It is so ordered.*

JUSTICE KENNEDY took no part in the consideration or decision of this case.

JUSTICE BRENNAN, with whom JUSTICE MARSHALL joins, concurring in part and concurring in the judgment.

CHIEF JUSTICE REHNQUIST, with whom JUSTICES WHITE and BLACKMUN join, concurring in part and dissenting in part.

For the reasons stated by Judge Bork in his majority opinion below, I would uphold that portion of 22-1115 of the District of Columbia Code that prohibits the display of any sign within 500 feet of a foreign embassy if that sign tends to bring that foreign government into "public odium" or "public disrepute." However, I agree with JUSTICE O'CONNOR that 22-1115's congregation clause is not unconstitutional and that the exemption for labor picketing does not violate the Equal Protection Clause, so I join in Parts III and IV of the majority opinion.

3
PUBLIC ORDER AND TRANQUILITY

If the maintenance of their own security is a function which all governments find necessary to undertake immediately upon coming into existence, the maintenance of public order is one which exists prior to, and is a major cause of the existence of government. Without a certain minimal degree of public order, civilized society would be impossible. The right to public order may be seen, then, as equal in importance to national security in the hierarchy of governmental functions.

In the United States the function of order maintenance differs significantly from that of the maintenance of national security. The latter, for the most part, is a function of the federal government. The former, except for those situations in which the federal government exercises the powers belonging to both nation and locality, is primarily a function of the states. For it is to the states and their constituent parts that the Constitution and constitutional practice have reserved the "police power." That power, though considerably larger than the power to maintain order, necessarily includes it.

A second significant difference between the concerns of this chapter and that of the preceding one is that, while the attempt to maintain the national security has often involved regulation of the content of communications, the regulations involved in maintaining order include chiefly those concerned with the "time, place, and manner" of communicative activity. For it is a cardinal principle of First Amendment doctrine that the state may not, except in narrowly defined circumstances, distinguish between the viewpoints advocated by those whose activity may threaten that order.

Finally, we may note by way of introduction that the concept of "public order" is extraordinarily difficult to conceptualize. First, "order" itself is hard to confine; it may include not only the absence of physical threat to person or property, but, as Emerson has noted, freedom from invasion of personality.[1] Second, what is "public" is not so easily determined. It may include not only the streets (the prototypical example of the "public forum"[2]), but at least for some purposes, areas which are "public" only in the sense that they are governmentally owned and open to citizens for the transaction of public business. We will concern ourselves in this chapter only with threats to order which take place in concededly "public" areas, i.e. those which have no other function but to facilitate the coming and goings, and the gathering of citizens. The problem of communicative activity in other "forums" will be dealt with in the following chapter, while that of "invasion of personality" will be considered in Chapter 11, under a different rubric.

Several factors, all interrelated, serve to complicate the "balancing of interests" between communications and order in the "public forum." First, much of the tension which arises occurs because the activity engaged in is one or another variety of "speech plus," i.e. it involves not only the use of words but also physical activity, including parades, demonstrations, mass meetings, leaflet distribution, etc. Such devices have been traditional methods for communicating viewpoints to the public. But, because of their physical component, they have a heightened potential for interference with what others see as their right to go about their business unhindered. It is no accident that much of the early doctrine on communication in public places arose in the context of religious proselytization and labor picketing, activities especially likely to interfere with the desire of others to act as they wish.

Additionally, such activity is likely to be engaged in by those whose views are outside the "mainstream." For people whose views are not quite "respectable" are less likely to command media attention, and thus to find it necessary to engage in "speech plus." And, of course, ideas not in the "mainstream" are more likely to be abrasive in themselves, and their expression to increase the potential for disorder. Finally, there is the fact that "speech plus" in the public forum, being directed at controversial matters, is likely to trigger response from those taking a different view of the matter at issue. Indeed, the sponsors of the activity may count on just such a reaction.

It is probable, therefore, that the attempts of state and local governments to deal with "speech plus" in the "public forum" have occasioned more litigation than any other single area of communicative activity. The very earliest attempts took the form of absolute prohibitions of such activity, and received initial Supreme Court approval in Davis v. Massachusetts (1897). In that case the Court held that, just as the private homeowner had the right to exclude people engaged in communication from his property, so also cities and towns could exclude communicative activity from their streets and parks. By 1938, however, a plurality of the Court, in Hague v. C.I.O., was ready to hold that streets and parks had from "time immemorial" been dedicated to the public expression of opinion, thus nullifying governmental attempts to solve the problem of public order by absolutely denying public access to those who wished to speak.

A second, more successful method of dealing with the problem has been through the application of licensing systems. Such systems usually require that, before an individual or group can hold a meeting, parade through the streets, or otherwise communicate their beliefs, they must procure a license from a responsible public official, usually the police chief. Where such systems give to the responsible official leeway to determine whether a license should issue on the basis of the views to be presented, the Court strikes them down. Typical of the kind of ordinance likely to be disapproved was that involved in Staub v. City of Baxley (1958), in which the required permit could be issued or denied on the basis of the "nature" of the organization involved or the "character" of the applicant.

Where no such discretion is involved, where the issuing official is limited to considerations of the time, place, and manner of the communicative activity, and where such considerations are handled in a manner not denying the applicants the opportunity to get their message across, such regulations will generally be upheld. The early case of Cox v. New Hampshire (1941) typifies the kind of licensing system likely to be approved by the Court. It is doubtful, however, that Cox's approval of a fee for the issuance of the license would today pass constitutional muster, particularly when applied, as it was there, to religious proselytization.

A recent example of the Court's reaction to a licensing system occurred in the 1988 case of City of Lakewood v. Cleveland Plain Dealer. In Lakewood, excerpted herein, the Court held that a system allowing official discretion could not be applied even if the activity affected, the placing of newspaper vending machines on public property, could be prohibited altogether.

Licensing systems, while not always raising issues of prior restraint, are nevertheless attempts to deal with the problem of public order by action precedent to the occurrence of communication. Where properly drawn, and where those subject to them demonstrate the good will to abide by their provisions, they are an effective manner of dealing with the problem of public order. Indeed, in the context of so emotional an issue as the controversy over abortion, they may be absolutely necessary in order to prevent those on the two sides of the controversy from harming each other.

Another, equally difficult issue arises in the absence of such systems, when speaker and audience do seem to present the danger of causing harm to others or to each other. What, then, of state attempts to prosecute those engaged in communicative activity for actual, or threatened, breach of the peace?

It was in the context of just such a situation that the Court made one of its few attempts to deal with problems of free communication by narrowing the coverage of the "First Amendment umbrella." In Chaplinsky v. New Hampshire (1942), petitioner, a member of the Jehovah's Witnesses, played recordings hostile to Roman Catholics on Sunday morning, outside a Catholic church. Warned by a City Marshall to "go slow" because his speech was upsetting some of his listeners, he later called that individual a "God damned racketeer" and a "damned Fascist." In upholding his conviction for violating a state statute forbidding the use of "any offensive, derisive, or annoying words to any other person who is lawfully in any public place, or calling him by any offensive or derisive name," the Court stated:

> There are certain well-defined and narrowly limited classes of speech, the prevention and punishment of which have never been thought to raise any Constitutional problem. These include the lewd and obscene, the profane, the libelous, and the insulting or 'fighting' words - those which by their very utterance inflict injury or tend to incite an immediate breach of the peace. Such utterances are no essential part of any exposition of ideas, and are of such slight social value as a step to truth that any benefit that may be derived from them is clearly outweighed by the social interest in order and morality.

Chaplinsky's categorization of the "lewd and obscene," the libelous, and the profane as outside the protection of the First Amendment has been substantially modified and, in the case of the "profane," probably negated by subsequent cases. As to "fighting words," the Court has moved very close to making that category a nullity. In Gooding v. Wilson (1972), a conviction for violating a statute prohibiting "without provocation, use to or of another, and in his presence . . . opprobrious words or abusive language, tending to cause a breach of the peace" was reversed. Appellee had, in the course of an anti-war demonstration, said to a policeman, "You white son of a bitch, I'll kill you"; You son of a bitch, I'll choke you to death." The statute, said the Court, was overbroad, in that it had not been limited to words that "have a direct tendency to cause acts of violence by the person to whom, individually, it is addressed," and thus was open to improper application.

More significantly, the Court, in Rosenfeld v. New Jersey (1972), summarily remanded a conviction for reconsideration, "in the light of Gooding . . ." The statute involved in Rosenfeld had been authoritatively construed to require that the language involved "be likely to incite the hearer to an immediate breach of the peace, or to be likely . . . to affect the sensibilities of a hearer," and the conviction rested on Rosenfeld's having, at a school board meeting, described the teachers and the school board as "mother fuckers." Thus it appears likely that words must be addressed to specific individuals before they can be considered "fighting," and the doctrine is not available in the circumstance, likely to present a greater problem for public order, where a speaker addresses a mass audience.

The problem of mass breach of the peace in response to the words of a speaker is complex. There may be, depending on the facts, two different questions involved. An individual may be charged with breach of the peace because of actions committed or threatened by his supporters. Or the charge may stem from deeds chargeable to opponents of the speaker. The latter situation is more difficult. It presents the problem of the "heckler's veto,"[3] i.e. that threats of breach of the peace by opponents of a speaker may be intended or employed simply as a device to justify silencing the speaker because of the content of the message involved. This is particularly true, it can be argued, because those responsible for enforcing the law are likely to be sympathetic to the views of the objecting audience. Whether or not that is so, it is likely always to be the case that administrative efficiency and considerations of economy, will argue for arrest of the speaker.

The case of Feiner v. New York (1951), an early attempt by the Court to deal with speech and breach of the peace, presented the issue of the heckler's veto in classic form. In that case Feiner, speaking in a public street, referred to President Truman and local officials as Fascists and urged, among other things, that Blacks "rise up" and demand their rights. Several individuals in the audience threatened to take action if the police did not, and Feiner was arrested. The decision of the Court upholding his conviction has been widely condemned and it is doubtful that the present day Court would reach the same conclusion.

In Feiner it appears obvious, with the benefit of hindsight, that the disturbance threatened was one that the police could easily have handled, probably by arresting those in the audience who threatened violence. Much more difficult was the situation in Terminiello v. Chicago (1949), a case in which both hostile and friendly audience reactions were present.

Father Terminiello, a suspended Catholic priest, addressed a meeting of his supporters in a packed Chicago auditorium. There he "vigorously" criticized government officials and various racial groups. Gathered outside the hall was a large group of those opposed to the speaker, who could be heard by his supporters to yell "Fascists, Hitlers" at those in attendance.[4] These opponents Terminiello characterized as "slimy scum," "snakes," "bedbugs," etc. The crowd outside tried to tear the clothes off those who entered, some 28 windows in the auditorium were broken, and numerous objects, including stink bombs, were thrown. In these conditions Terminiello was arrested and convicted of breach of the peace.

By a majority of five to four, the Court reversed Terminiello's conviction, on the grounds that in charging the jury the trial court had defined breach of the peace to include speech which "stirs the public to anger, invites dispute, or brings about a condition of unrest." This charge, said Justice Douglas , raised the possibility that Terminiello was convicted for protected speech, for:

> A function of free speech under our system is to invite dispute. It may indeed best serves its high purpose when it induces a condition of unrest, creates dissatisfaction with conditions as they are, or even stirs people to anger . . . That is why freedom of speech is nevertheless protected . . . unless shown likely to produce a clear and present danger of a serious substantive evil that rises far above public inconvenience, annoyance, or unrest.

One need not disagree with Douglas' view that speech should be protected except in cases rising "far above public inconvenience, annoyance or unrest" without wondering whether the situation faced by the police in this case did not fit the demands of his test. As Justice Jackson said in his dissenting opinion, to require that police do nothing in the face of a situation like that involved here was to require that police do nothing in the face of a situation like that involved here was to "invite rival groups to battle unchecked for control of the streets." In any event, it is unfortunate that the wording of the trial charge gave the majority the opportunity to dodge the substantive issue in <u>Terminiello</u>.

Are there any circumstances in which it is permissible for police to arrest the speaker who incites rather than to take action against those who listen to him? The answer one gives to this question depends, at least in part, on the view one has of the limits of human rationality. It is instructive, on this point, to compare the views of Franklyn Haiman, Thomas Emerson, and Walter Berns.[5] Haiman could never allow a speaker to be so punished. It is the listeners, he argues, who are moved to illegalities. They, whether supporters or opponents of the speaker's message, have minds and wills of their own and are not forced to take the illegal action. Thus, their intervening acts of will free the speaker from liability. Haiman would similarly do away with the "fighting words" doctrine, for if a word is a "fighting" one, it is only because of the interpretation put on it by the hearer.

Haiman's viewpoint is, of course, attractive to those who desire the absolute maximum of protection for communication. It is, further, appealing to those who believe that free will, and the ability to make decisions on the basis of that will, is a central and distinguishing characteristic of human beings. But one can at least question whether it is always reasonable to expect people to act according to strict rationality. This is particularly true, as Mr. Justice Jackson's <u>Terminiello</u> dissent notes, in the context of large groups of people, where mob psychology may be expected to take over.

Emerson, in partial contrast, would allow at least certain kinds of speech to be punished on the basis of the reaction of listeners. Some speech, he says, is so intertwined with action as to be a part of that action. Thus, for example, a speaker who gives specific instructions for the commission of immediate and particular acts of violence in the context of a riot actually in progress could be punished as if he had committed the violence himself. Emerson's theory, which takes into partial account the fact of human irrationality, would not, it would seem, allow punishment for words uttered before the beginning of violent action, nor would it allow the speaker to be punished for actions taken by those who disagree with him.

A third view of the problem is that offered by Walter Berns. Berns has long argued that the First Amendment should be interpreted in the light of the necessity so. He would hold incitation or provocation to illegal action punishable. This is so, says Berns, because incitation to violence or to the breaking of valid law is itself an evil, one which government may properly suppress.

The position taken by the Supreme Court is, perhaps, midway between these various prescriptions. The Court has never held that the provocation or advocacy of illegality is absolutely protected, regardless of the fact that others actually carry out that illegality. Nor has it held that incitation to unlawful acts is punishable only when it consists of actual instructions to commit the same, directed to those already engaged in illegal activity. Rather, as we noted in the previous chapter, such incitation may be punished if directed to "inciting or producing imminent lawless action and . . . likely to incite or produce such action." And, the Court noted in Hess v. Indiana (1973), the urging must be for immediate unlawful action; not action, that is contemplated only for the future.

Since Terminiello the Court has not had occasion to deal directly with the issue of the "heckler's veto." Had the factual situation been different, and had the Court chosen to hear the appeal, the celebrated case of the "Nazis in Skokie" might have presented such an opportunity. In that case an attempt by the American Nazi Party to hold a parade in the heavily Jewish town of Skokie, Illinois, was met by local ordinances, specifically designed to deal with their proposed appearance, which established a permit system by which the mayor was permitted to deny permission for such activity. Granting of the permit was premised on a finding that the message of a demonstration did not promote racial or religious violence or hatred, or be conducted for any unlawful purpose. Companion ordinances prohibited the dissemination of materials promoting or inciting such hatred, the wearing of symbols which promoted same, and the wearing of "military style uniforms" in such assemblies. Finally, any group of over 50 persons who were granted a permit were required to provide insurance against breach of the peace. On the basis of these ordinances the Nazi Party was denied a permit to parade in Skokie.

Collin, head of the party, appealed the city's decision to federal district court, which found in his favor. The Court of Appeals for the 8th Circuit affirmed,[6] and the Supreme Court denied *certiorari*. The majority opinion of Judge Pell reflected the general view as to the validity of discretionary permit systems and of the current reach of the "fighting words" doctrine, and canvassed a number of possible justifications for the kind of statute at issue here. The opinion of Judge Sprecher, concurring and dissenting, was particularly noteworthy for its argument that the Skokie situation presented a new and unique kind of threat, one which merited the rethinking of traditional First Amendment doctrines.

Neither of the final two cases reproduced in this chapter involve the issue the "heckler's veto." Heffron v. International Society for Krishna Consciousness (1981) concerned a regulation of the time, place, and manner of communication at a state fair, and is arguably not a pure "public forum" case. But the location involved was one in which more than 1400 groups, mostly commercial but also political and religious, had chosen to present themselves. Thus it was in only a minimal sense a "restricted environment." Further, although the Court does distinguished the fairgrounds from the classic "public forum" of the streets, it referred to it as a "limited public forum," and applied an analysis which seems wholly applicable to pure "forum" situations. Finally, although "forum analysis" is often indispensable for a consideration of the issue of public order," it is "order" that is decisive, and Heffron was clearly decided on the basis of threats to that interest.

Clark v. Committee for Creative Non-Violence (1984) is included for two principal reasons. In the first place, the desired *loci* of activity, two federal parks in Washington, D.C., are among the kinds of places which Hague v. C.I.O. identified as being "from time immemorial" dedicated to the dissemination of ideas. Secondly, Clark involved a kind of "speech plus" which, it would seem, was almost entirely "plus." For the question was not whether the appellants were free to communicate in the park. They were permitted to do so and were in fact doing so at the time they brought their lawsuit. Rather, the issue was whether the government could, in an admittedly public forum, prevent a certain type of "speech plus," (overnight sleeping) deemed useful to the communicative ends of the appellants. Clark, then, presents the issue of "speech plus" at what was, at least for the Supreme Court up to that time, its outer limits. In addition it, like Heffron, sparked a controversy reflected in the various opinions of the Justices. Thus it is admirably suited for the consideration of students attempting to do their own "balancing" of the issues involved.

[1]*The System of Freedom of Expression*, 285.

[2]The idea of the "public forum" had its genesis in the opinion of Mr. Justice Roberts in Hague v. C.I.O. Its analytical development owes much to an article by Harry Kalven, "The Concept of the Public Forum: Cox v. Louisiana," 1965 *Supreme Court Review* 1.

[3]The term "heckler's veto" was first employed in Harry Kalven, *The Negro and The First Amendment*, (Baton Rouge: Louisiana State University Press, 1965), 140-145.

[4]Terminiello, of course, gave his speech in a "private forum." But, given the facts of the case, it , would appear that principles applicable to the "public forum" should be applied.

5.See Haiman, *Speech and Law in a Free Society*, 258-260 and 276-283; Emerson, 328-342; and Berns, *Freedom Virtue, and the First Amendment*, 84-85, 93-94., and, generally, Ch. 10, The Problem of Virtue."

[6]Collin v. Smith, 578 F.2d 1197 (7th Cir. 1978), affirming 447 F. Supp. 676 (1978); cert. den. 439 U.S. 916 (1978). The case could, from another perspective, be treated in Ch. 11, "Freedom from Assaultive and Unwanted Stimuli". The challenges which the case posed to the "modern doctrine of free speech," are detailed in Donald Alexander Downs, *Nazis in Skokie,: Freedom, Community, and the First Amendment*, (South Bend, Ind.,: University of Notre Dame Press, 1985).

CITY OF LAKEWOOD V. PLAIN DEALER PUBLISHING CO.

486 U.S. 750 (1988)

JUSTICE BRENNAN delivered the opinion of the Court.

The city of Lakewood, a suburban community bordering Cleveland, Ohio, appeals a judgment of the Court of Appeals for the Sixth Circuit enjoining enforcement of its local ordinance regulating the placement of newsracks. The court's decision was based in part on its conclusion that the ordinance vests the Mayor with unbridled discretion over which publishers may place newsracks on public property and where. . . .

At the outset, we confront the issue whether the Newspaper may bring a facial challenge to the city's ordinance. We conclude that it may.

. . . . we have previously identified two major First Amendment risks associated with unbridled licensing schemes: self-censorship by speakers in order to avoid being denied a license to speak; and the difficulty of effectively detecting, reviewing, and correcting content-based censorship "as applied" without standards by which to measure the licensor's action. It is when statutes threaten these risks to a significant degree that courts must entertain an immediate facial attack on the law. Therefore, a facial challenge lies whenever a licensing law gives a government official or agency substantial power to discriminate based on the content or viewpoint of speech by suppressing disfavored speech or disliked speakers. This is not to say that the press or a speaker may challenge as censorship any law involving discretion to which it is subject. The law must have a close enough nexus to expression, or to conduct commonly associated with expression, to pose a real and substantial threat of the facial challenge. First, Lakewood's ordinance requires that the Newspaper apply annually for newsrack licenses. Thus, it is the sort of system in which an individual must apply for multiple licenses over time, or periodically renew a license. When such a system is applied to speech, or to conduct commonly associated with speech, the licensor does not necessarily view the text of the words about to be spoken, but can measure their probable content or viewpoint by speech already uttered. See *Saia v. New York*. A speaker in this position is under no illusion regarding the effect of the "licensed" speech on the ability to continue speaking in the future. Yet demonstrating the link between "licensed" expression and the denial of a later license might well prove impossible. While perhaps not as direct a threat to speech as a regulation allowing a licensor to view the actual content of the speech to be licensed or permitted, see *Cox v. Louisiana* (1965); *Bantam Books, Inc. v. Sullivan* (1963), a multiple or periodic licensing requirement is sufficiently threatening to invite judicial concern.

A second feature of the licensing system at issue here is that it is directed narrowly and specifically at expression or conduct commonly associated with expression: the circulation of newspapers. Such a framework creates an agency or establishes an official charged particularly with reviewing speech, or conduct commonly associated with it, breeding an "expertise" tending to favor censorship over speech. *Freedman.* Indeed, a law requiring the licensing of printers has historically been declared the archetypal censorship statute. Here again, without standards to bound the licensor, speakers denied a license will have no way of proving that the decision was unconstitutionally motivated, and, faced with that prospect, they will be pressured to conform their speech to the licensor's unreviewable preference.

Because of these features in the regulatory system at issue here, we think that a facial challenge is appropriate, and that standards controlling the Mayor's discretion must be required. Of course, the city may require periodic licensing, and may even have special licensing procedures for conduct commonly associated with expression; but he Constitution requires that the city establish neutral criteria to insure that the licensing decision is not based on-the content or viewpoint of the speech being considered.

In contrast to the type of law at issue in this case, laws of general application that are not aimed at conduct commonly associated with expression do not permit licensing determinations to be made on the basis of ongoing expression or the words about to be spoken, carry with them little danger of censorship. For example, a law requiring building permits is rarely effective as a means of censorship. To be sure, on rare occasion an opportunity for censorship will exist, such as when an unpopular newspaper seeks to build a new plant. But such laws provide too blunt a censorship instrument to warrant judicial intervention prior to an allegation of actual misuse. And if such charges are made, the general application of the statute to areas unrelated to expression will provide the courts a yardstick with which to measure the licensor's occasional speech-related decision.

The foregoing discussion explains why the dissent's analogy between newspapers and soda vendors is inapposite. Newspapers are in the business of expression, while soda vendors are in the business of selling soft drinks. Even if the soda vendor engages in speech, that speech is not related to the soda; therefore preventing it from installing its machines may penalize unrelated speech, but will not directly prevent that speech from occurring. In sum, a law giving the Mayor unbridled discretion to decide which soda vendors may place their machines on public property does not vest him with frequent opportunities to exercise substantial power over the content or viewpoint of the vendor's speech by suppressing the speech or directly controlling the vendor's ability to speak.

The proper analogy is between newspapers and leaflets. It is settled that leafletters may facially challenge licensing laws. See e. g., *Talley v. California* (1960); *Lovell v. Griffin* (1938). This settled law is based on the accurate premise that peaceful pamphleteering "is not fundamentally different from the function of a newspaper." *Organization for a Better Austin v. Keefe* (1971). The dissent's theory therefore would turn the law on its head.

The dissent reasons that if a particular manner of speech may be prohibited entirely, then no "activity protected by the First Amendment" can be implicated by a law imposing less than a total prohibition. It then finds that a total ban on newsracks would be constitutional. Therefore, the dissent concludes, the actual ordinance at issue involves no "activity protected by the First Amendment," and thus is not subject to facial challenge. However, that reasoning is little more than a legal sleight-of-hand, misdirecting the focus of the inquiry from a law allegedly vesting unbridled censorship discretion in a government official toward one imposing a blanket prohibition.

The key to the dissent's analysis is its "greater-includes-the-lesser" syllogism. But that syllogism is blind to the radically different constitutional harms inherent in the "greater" and "lesser" restrictions. Presumably in the case of an ordinance that completely prohibits a particular manner of expression, the law on its face is both content and viewpoint neutral. In analyzing such a hypothetical ordinance, the Court would apply the well-settled time, place, and manner test. The danger giving rise to the First Amendment inquiry is that the government is silencing or restraining a channel of speech; we ask whether some interest unrelated to speech justifies this silence. To put it another way, the question is whether "the manner of expression is basically incompatible with the normal activity of a particular place at a particular time." *Grayned v. Rockford* (1972).

In contrast, a law or policy permitting communication in a certain manner for some but not for others raises the specter of content and viewpoint censorship. This danger is at its zenith when the determination of who may speak and who may not is left to the unbridled discretion of a government official. As demonstrated above, we have often and uniformly held that such statutes or policies impose censorship on the public or the press, and hence are unconstitutional, because without standards governing the exercise of discretion, a government official may decide who may speak and who may not based upon the content of the speech or viewpoint of the speaker. Therefore, even if the government may constitutionally impose content-neutral prohibitions on a particular manner of speech, it may not *condition* that speech on obtaining a license or permit from a government official in that official's boundless discretion. It bears repeating that "[i]n the area of freedom of expression it is well established that one has standing to challenge a statute on the ground that it delegates overly broad licensing discretion to an administrative office, whether or not his conduct could be proscribed by a properly drawn statute, and whether or not he applied for a license." *Freedman.* Fundamentally, then, the dissent's proposal ignores the different concerns animating our test to determine whether an expressive activity may be banned entirely, and our test to determine whether it may be licensed in an official's unbridled discretion. . . .

Ultimately, then, the dissent's reasoning must fall of its own weight. As the preceding discussion demonstrates, this Court has long been sensitive to the special dangers inherent in a law placing unbridled discretion directly to license speech, or conduct commonly associated with speech, in the hands of a government official. In contrast, when the government is willing to prohibit a particular manner of speech entirely—the speech it favors along with the speech it disfavors—the risk of governmental censorship is simply not implicated. The "greater" power of outright prohibition raises other concerns, and we have developed tests to consider them. But we see no reason, and the dissent does not advance one, to ignore censorship dangers merely because other, unrelated concerns are satisfied.

The dissent compounds its error by defining an "activity protected by the First Amendment" by the time, place, or (in this case) manner by which the activity is exercised. The actual "activity" at issue here is the circulation of newspapers, which is constitutionally protected. After all, "[l]iberty of circulating is as essential to [freedom of expression] as liberty of publishing; indeed, without the circulation, the publication would be of little value." *Ex parte Jackson* (1878); *Lovell.*

The dissent's recharacterization of the issue is not merely semantic; substituting the time, place, or manner for the activity itself allows the dissent to define away a host of activities commonly considered to be protected. The right to demonstrate becomes the right to demonstrate at noise levels proscribed by law; the right to parade becomes the right to parade anywhere in the city 24 hours a day; and the right to circulate newspapers becomes the right to circulate newspapers by way of newsracks placed on public property. Under the dissent's analysis, ordinances giving the Mayor unbridled discretion over whether to permit loud demonstrations or evening parades would not be vulnerable to a facial challenge, since they would not "requir[e] a license to engage in activity protected by the First Amendment." But see *Grayned* (implying that a law banning excessively loud demonstrations was not facially invalid because its terms could not invite "subjective or discriminatory enforcement"). . . .

Having concluded that the Newspaper may facially challenge the Lakewood ordinance, we turn to the merits. Section 901.181, Codified Ordinances, City of Lakewood, provides: "The Mayor shall either deny the application [for a permit], stating the reasons for such denial or grant said permit subject to the following terms. . . ." Section 901.181 (c) sets out some of those terms, including: "such other terms and conditions deemed necessary and reasonable by the Mayor." It is apparent that the face of the ordinance itself contains no explicit limits on the Mayor's discretion. Indeed, nothing in the law as written requires the Mayor to do more than make the statement "it is not in the public interest" when denying a permit application.

The dissent is . . . comforted by the availability of judicial review. However, that review comes only after the Mayor and the City Council have denied the permit. Nowhere in the ordinance is either body required to act with reasonable dispatch. Rather, an application could languish indefinitely before the Council, with the Newspaper's only judicial remedy being a petition for mandamus. *Freedman.* Even if judicial review were relatively speedy, such review cannot substitute for concrete standards to guide the decisionmaker's discretion.

Finally, the dissent attempts to distinguish newsrack permits from parade permits in that the latter are often given for a particular event or time, whereas the former supposedly have no urgency. This overstates the proposition. We agree that in some cases there is exceptional force to the argument that a permit delayed is a permit denied. However, we cannot agree that newspaper publishers can wait indefinitely for a permit only because there will always be news to report. News is not fungible. Some stories may be particularly well covered by certain publications, providing that newspaper with a unique opportunity to develop readership. In order to benefit from that event, a paper needs public access at a particular time; eventual access would come "too little and too late." *Freedman.* The *Plain Dealer* has been willing to forgo this benefit for four years in order to bring and litigate this lawsuit. However, smaller publications may not be willing or able to make the same sacrifice.

We hold those portions of the Lakewood ordinance giving the Mayor unfettered discretion to deny a permit application and unbounded authority to condition the permit on any additional terms he deems "necessary and reasonable," to be unconstitutional.

THE CHIEF JUSTICE and JUSTICE KENNEDY took no part in the consideration or decision of this case.

JUSTICE WHITE, with whom JUSTICE STEVENS and JUSTICE O'CONNOR join, dissenting.

There are a few well-established contexts in which the Court has departed from its insistence on an as-applied approach to constitutional adjudication.

One of them is where a permit or license is required to engage in expressive activities protected by the First Amendment, and official discretion to grant or deny is not suitably confined. "In the area of freedom of expression it is well established that one has standing to challenge a statute on the ground that it delegates overly broad licensing discretion to an administrative office, whether or not his conduct could be proscribed by a properly drawn statute, and whether or not he applied for a license." *Freedman v. Maryland* (1965). It is this line of cases on which the majority draws to support its conclusion that the Lakewood ordinance is unconstitutional on its face.

The prevailing feature of these exceptional cases, however, is that each of them involved a law that required a license to engage in activity protected by the First Amendment. In each of the cases, the expressive conduct which a city sought to license was an activity which the locality could not prohibit altogether. Streets, sidewalks, and parks are traditional public fora; leafletting, pamphletting, and speaking in such places may be regulated, *Cox v. New Hampshire* (1941); *Cantwell v. Connecticut* (1940); but they may not be entirely forbidden, *Jamison v. Texas* (1943); *Lovell v. Griffin* (1938). Likewise, in *Freedman,* at issue was a license requirement that was a prerequisite for any exhibition of a film in the State of Maryland. In all of these cases, the scope of the local license requirement included expressive activity protected by the First Amendment.

. . . . the *Lovell-Freedman* line of cases would be applicable here if the city of Lakewood sought to license the distribution of all newspapers in the city, or if it required licenses for all stores which sold newspapers. These are obviously newspaper circulation activities which a municipality cannot prohibit and, therefore, any licensing scheme of this scope would have to pass muster under the *Lovell-Freedman* doctrine. But—and this is critical—Lakewood has not cast so wide a net. Instead, it has sought to license only the placement of newsracks (and other like devices) on city property. As I read our precedents, the *Lovell-Freedman*

line of cases is applicable here only if the Plain Dealer has a constitutional right to distribute its papers by means of dispensing devices or newsboxes, affixed to the public sidewalks. I am not convinced that this is the case. . . .

While there is a First Amendment right to publish newspapers, publishers have no right to force municipalities to turn over public property for the construction of a printing facility. There is a First Amendment right to sell books, but we would not accept an argument that a city must allow a book seller to construct a bookshop—even a small one—on a city sidewalk. The right to leaflet does not create a right to build a booth on city streets from which leafletting can be conducted. Preventing the "taking" of public property for these purposes does not abridge First Amendment freedoms. Just as there is no First Amendment right to operate a bookstore or locate a movie theater however or wherever one chooses notwithstanding local laws to the contrary, see *Arcara v. Cloud Books, Inc.* (1986); *Renton v. Playtime Theatres, Inc.* (1986), the First Amendment does not create a right of newspaper publishers to take city streets to erect structures to sell their papers.

It may be that newspaper distributors can sell more papers by placing their newsracks on city sidewalks. But those seeking to distribute materials protected by the First Amendment do not have a right to appropriate public property merely because it best facilitates their efforts. "We again reject the 'notion that First Amendment rights are somehow not fully realized unless they are subsidized by the State.'" *Regan v. Taxation with Representation of Wash.* (1983) (quoting *Cammarano v. United States* (1959) (Douglas, J., concurring)). Consequently, a city need not subsidize news distribution activities by giving, selling, or leasing a portion of city property for the erection of newsracks. "The State, no less than a private owner of property, has power to preserve the property under its control for the use to which it is lawfully dedicated." *Adderley v. Florida* (1966). Preserving public forum space for use by the public *generally*, as opposed to the exclusive use of one individual or corporation, is obviously one such "lawfully dedicated" use. "The streets belong to the public and are primarily for the use of the public in the ordinary way." *Packard v. Banton* (1924).

. . . . the Court asserts that I do not understand the nature of the conduct at issue here. It is asserted that "[t]he actual 'activity' at issue here is the circulation of newspapers, which is constitutionally protected." But of course, this is wrong. Lakewood does not, by its ordinance, seek to license the circulation of newspapers within the city. In fact, the Lakewood ordinance does not even require licenses of all newsracks within the jurisdiction—the many newsracks located within Lakewood on private property are *not* included within the scope of the city's ordinance. Thus, it is the majority—and not I—that is guilty of "recharacterizing" the activity that Lakewood licenses. The Lakewood ordinance must be considered for what it is: a license requirement for newsracks on city property. . . .

As I see it, the Court's new "nexus to expression, or to conduct commonly associated with expression" test is peculiarly troublesome, because it is of uncertain scope. . .

If the Court's treatment of the soda machine problem is not curious enough, it also "assures" us that its ruling does not invalidate local laws requiring, for example, building permits—even as they apply to the construction of newspaper printing facilities. These laws, we are told, provide "too blunt a censorship instrument to warrant judicial intervention." Thus, local "laws of general application that are not aimed at conduct commonly associated with expression" appear to survive the Court's decision today.

But what if Lakewood, following this decision, repeals local ordinance 901.181 (the detailed newsrack permit law) and simply left 901.18 (the general ordinance concerning "any . . . structure or device" on city property) on the books?

That section vests absolute discretion (without any of the guidelines found in 901.181) in the City Council to give or withhold permission for the erection of devices on city streets. Because this law is of "general application," it should survive scrutiny under the Court's opinion—even as applied to newsracks. If so, the Court's opinion takes on an odd "the-greater-but-not-the-lesser" quality: the more activities that are subjected to a discretionary licensing law, the more likely that law is to pass constitutional muster.

Seeking a way to limit its own expansive ruling, the Court provides two concrete examples of instances in which its newly crafted "nexus to expression" rule will *not* strike down local ordinances that permit discretionary licensing decisions. First, we are told that a law granting unbridled discretion to a mayor to grant licenses for soda machine placements passes constitutional muster because it does not give that official "frequent opportunities to exercise substantial power over the content or viewpoint of the vendor's speech." How the Court makes this empirical assessment, I do not know. It seems to me that the nature of a vendor's product—be it newspapers or soda pop—is not the measure of how potent a license law can be in the hands of local officials seeking to control or alter the vendor's speech. Of course, the newspaper vendor's speech is likely to be more public, more significant, and more widely known than the soda vendor's speech—and therefore more likely to incur the wrath of public officials. *But* in terms of the "usefulness" of the license power to exert control over a licensee's speech, there is no difference whatsoever between the situation of the soda vendor and the newspaper vendor. . . .

The Court mentions the risk of censorship, the ever-present danger of self-censorship, and the power of prior restraint to justify the result. Yet these fears and concerns have little to do with this case, which involves the efforts of Ohio's largest newspaper to place a handful of newsboxes in a few locations in a small suburban community. Even if one accepts the testimony of appellee's own expert, it seems unlikely that the newsboxes at issue here would increase the Plain Dealer's circulation within Lakewood by more than a percent or two; the paper's overall circulation would be affected only by about one one-hundredth of one percent (0.01%).

It is hard to see how the Court's concerns have any applicability here. And it is harder still to see how the Court's image of the unbridled local censor, seeking to control and direct the content of speech, fits this case. In the case before us, the city of Lakewood declined to appeal an adverse ruling against its ban on newsracks, and instead amended its local laws to permit appellee to place its newsboxes on city property. When the nature of this ordinance was not to the Plain Dealer's liking, Lakewood again amended its local laws to meet the newspaper's concerns. Finally, when the newspaper, still disgruntled, won a judgment against Lakewood from the Court of Appeals, the city once again amended its ordinance to address the constitutional issues. The Court's David and Goliath imagery concerning the balance of power between the regulated and the regulator in this case is wholly inapt—except, possibly, in reverse.

HEFFRON, SECRETARY AND MANAGER OF THE MINNESOTA STATE AGRICULTURAL SOCIETY BOARD OF MANAGERS, ET AL. V. INTERNATIONAL SOCIETY FOR KRISHNA CONSCIOUSNESS, INC., ET AL.

452 U.S. 640 (1981)

JUSTICE WHITE delivered the opinion of the Court.

The question presented for review is whether a State, consistent with the First and Fourteenth Amendments, may require a religious organization desiring to distribute and sell religious literature and to solicit donations at a state fair to conduct those activities only at an assigned location within the fairgrounds even though application of the rule limits the religious practices of the organization.

Each year, the Minnesota agricultural Society (Society), a public corporation organized under the laws of Minnesota, Statute 37.01 (1980), operates a State Fair on a 125-acre state-owned tract located in St. Paul Minn. The Fair is conducted for the purpose of "exhibiting . . . the agricultural, stock-breeding, horticultural, mining, mechanical, industrial, and other products and resources of the state, including proper exhibits and expositions of the arts, human skills, and sciences." The Fair is a major public event and attracts visitors from all over Minnesota as well as from other parts of the country. During the past five years, the average total attendance for the 12-day Fair has been 1,320,000 persons. The average daily attendance on weekdays has been 115,000 persons and on Saturdays and Sundays 160,000.

The Society is authorized to make all "bylaws, ordinances, and rules, not inconsistent with law, which it may deem necessary or proper for the government of the fair grounds. . . ." Under this authority, the Society promulgated Minnesota State Fair Rule 6.05 which provides in relevant part that

[s]ale or distribution of any merchandise, including printed or written material except under license issued by the Society and/or from a duly licensed location . shall be a misdemeanor.

As Rule 6.05 is construed and applied by the Society, "all persons, groups or firms which desire to sell, exhibit or distribute materials during the annual State Fair must do so only from fixed locations on the fairgrounds." Although the Rule does not prevent organizational representatives from walking about the fairgrounds and communicating the organization's views with fair patrons in face-to-face discussions, it does require that any exhibitor conduct its sales, distribution, and fund solicitation operations from a booth rented from the Society. Space in the fairgrounds is rented to all comers in a nondiscriminatory fashion on a first-come, first-served basis with the rental charge based on the size and location of the booth. The Rule applies alike to nonprofit charitable, and commercial enterprises. . . .

The issue here, as it was below, is whether Rule 6.05 is a permissible restriction the place and manner of communicating the views of the Krishna religion, more specifically whether the Society may require the members of ISKCON who desire to practice Sankirtan at the State Fair to confine their distribution, sales, and solicitation activities to a fixed location.

A major criterion for a valid time, place, and manner restriction is that the restriction "may not be based upon either the content or subject matter of speech." *Consolidated Edison Co. v. Public Service Comm'n.* Rule 6.05 qualifies in this respect, since, as the Supreme Court of Minnesota observed, the Rule applies evenhandedly to all who wish to distribute and sell written materials or to solicit funds. No person or organization, whether commercial or charitable, is permitted to engage in such activities except from a booth rented for those purposes.

Nor does Rule 6.05 suffer from the more covert forms of discrimination that may result when arbitrary discretion is vested in some governmental authority. The method of allocating space is a straightforward first-come, first-served system. The Rule is not open to the kind of arbitrary application that this Court has condemned as inherently inconsistent with a valid time, place, and manner regulation because such discretion has the potential for becoming a means of suppressing a particular point of view.

A valid time, place, and manner regulation must also "serve a significant governmental interest." *Virginia Pharmacy Board v. Virginia Citizens Consumer Council.* Here, the principal justification asserted by the State in support of Rule 6.05 is the need to maintain the orderly movement of the crowd given the large number of exhibitors and persons attending the Fair.

The fairgrounds comprise a relatively small area of 125 acres, the bulk of which is covered by permanent buildings, temporary structures, parking lots, and connecting thoroughfares. There were some 1,400 exhibitors and concessionaries renting space for the 1977 and 1978 Fairs, chiefly in permanent and temporary buildings. The Fair is designed to exhibit to the public an enormous variety of goods services, entertainment, and other matters of interest. This is accomplished by confining individual exhibitors to fixed locations, with the public moving to and among the booths or other attractions, using streets and open spaces provided for that purpose. Because the Fair attracts large crowds, it is apparent that the State's interest in the orderly movement and control of such an assembly of persons is a substantial consideration.

As a general matter, it is clear that a State's interest in protecting the "safety and convenience" of persons using a public forum is a valid governmental objective. See *Grayned v. City of Rockford; Cox v. New Hampshire.* Furthermore, consideration of a forum's special attributes is relevant to the constitutionality of a regulation since the significance of the governmental interest must be assessed in light of the characteristic nature and function of the particular forum involved. This observation bears particular import in the present case since respondents make a number of analogies between the fairgrounds and city streets, which have "immemorially been held in trust for the use of the public and . . . have been used for purposes of assembly, communicating thoughts between citizens, and discussing public questions." *Hague v. CIO.* See Kunz v. *New York* (1951). But it is clear that there are significant differences between a street and the fairgrounds. A street is continually open, often uncongested, and constitutes not only a necessary conduit in the daily affairs of a locality's citizens, but also a place where people may enjoy the open air or the company of friends and neighbors in a relaxed environment. The Minnesota Fair, as described above, is a temporary event attracting great numbers of visitors who come to the event for a short period to see and experience the host of exhibits and attractions at the Fair. The flow of the crowd and demands of safety are more pressing in the context of the Fair. As such, any comparisons to public streets are necessarily inexact. . . .

If Rule 6.05 is an invalid restriction on the activities of ISKCON, it is no more valid with respect to the other social, political or charitable organizations that have rented booths at the Fair and confined their distribution, sale, and fund solicitation to those locations. Nor would it be valid with respect to other organizations that did not rent booths, either because they were unavailable due to a lack of space or because they chose to avoid the expense involved, but that would in all probability appear in the fairgrounds to distribute, sell, and solicit if they could freely do so. The question would also inevitably arise as to what extent the First Amendment also gives commercial organizations a right to move among the crowd to distribute information about or to sell their wares as respondents claim they may do.

ISKCON desires to proselytize at the fair because it believes it can successfully communicate and raise funds. In its view, this can be done only by intercepting fair patrons as they move about, and if success is achieved, stopping them momentarily or for longer periods as money is given or exchanged for literature. This consequence would be multiplied many times over if Rule 6.05 could not be applied to confine such transactions by ISKCON and others to fixed locations. Indeed, the court below agreed that without Rule 6.05, there would be widespread disorder at the fairgrounds The court also recognized that some disorder would inevitably result from exempting the Krishnas from the Rule. Obviously, there would be a much larger threat to the State's interest in crowd control if all other religious, nonreligious, and noncommercial organizations could likewise move freely about the fairgrounds distributing and selling literature and soliciting funds at will.

Given these considerations, we hold that the State's interest in confining distribution, selling, and fund solicitation activities to fixed locations is sufficient to satisfy the requirement that a place or manner restriction must serve a substantial state interest. By focusing on the incidental effect of providing all exemption from Rule 6.05 to ISKCON, the Minnesota Supreme Court did not take into account the fact that any such exemption cannot be meaningfully limited to ISKCON, and as applied to similarly situated groups would prevent the State from furthering its important concern with managing the flow of the crowd. In our view, the Society may apply its Rule and confine the type of transactions at issue to designated locations without violating the First .Amendment.

For similar reasons, we cannot agree with the Minnesota Supreme Court that Rule 6.05 is an unnecessary regulation because the State could avoid the threat to its interest posed by ISKCON by less restrictive means, such as penalizing disorder or disruption, limiting the number of solicitors, or putting more narrowly drawn restrictions on the location and movement of ISKCON's representatives. As we have indicated, the inquiry must involve not only ISKCON, but also all other organizations that would be entitled to distribute, sell, or solicit if the booth rule may not be enforced with respect to ISKCON. Looked at in this way, it is quite improbable that the alternative means suggested by the Minnesota Supreme Court would deal adequately with the problems posed by the much larger number of distributors and solicitors that would be present on the fairgrounds if the judgment below were affirmed.

For Rule 6.05 to be valid as a place and manner restriction, it must also be sufficiently clear that alternative forums for the expression of respondents' protected speech exist despite the effects of the Rule. Rule 6.05 is not vulnerable on this ground. First, the Rule does not prevent ISKCON from practicing Sankirtan anywhere outside the fairgrounds. More importantly, the Rule has not been shown to deny access within the forum in question. Here, the Rule does not exclude ISKCON from the fairgrounds, nor does it deny that organization the right to conduct any desired activity at some point within the forum. Its members may mingle with the crowd and orally propagate their views. The organization may also arrange for a booth and distribute and sell literature and solicit funds from that location on the fairgrounds itself. The Minnesota State Fair is a limited public forum in that it exists to provide a means for a great number of exhibitors temporarily to present their products or views, be they commercial, religious, or political, to a large number of people in an efficient fashion. Considering the limited functions of the Fair and the combined area within which it operates, we are unwilling to say that Rule 6.05 does not provide ISKCON and other organizations with an adequate means to sell and solicit on the fairgrounds. The First Amendment protects the right of every citizen to "reach the minds of willing listeners and to do so there must be opportunity to in their attention." *Kovacs v. Cooper* (1949). Rule 6.05 does not unnecessarily limit that right within the fairgrounds.

The judgment of the Supreme Court of Minnesota is reversed, and the case is remanded for further proceeding not inconsistent with this opinion.

JUSTICE BRENNAN, with whom JUSTICE MARSHALL and JUSTICE STEVENS join, concurring in part and dissenting in part. . . .

I quite agree with the Court that the State has a significant interest in maintaining crowd control on its fairgrounds. I also have no doubt that the State has a significant interest in protecting its fairgoers from fraudulent or deceptive solicitation practices. Indeed, because I believe on this record that this latter interest is substantially furthered by a Rule that restricts sales and solicitation activities to fixed booth locations, where the State will have the greatest opportunity to police and prevent possible deceptive practices, I would hold that Rule 6.05's restriction on those particular forms of First Amendment expression is justified as an antifraud measure. Accordingly, I join the judgment of the Court insofar as it upholds Rule 6.05's restriction on sales and solicitations. However, because I believe that the booth Rule is an overly

intrusive means of achieving the State's interest in crowd control, and because I cannot accept the validity of the State's third asserted justification, I dissent from the Court's approval of Rule 6.05's restriction on the distribution of literature.

As our cases have long noted, once a governmental regulation is shown to impinge upon basic First Amendment rights, the burden falls on the government to show the validity of its asserted interest and the absence of less intrusive alternatives. The challenged "regulation must be narrowly tailored to further the State's legitimate interest." *Grayned v. City of Rockford*. Minnesota's Rule 6.05 does not meet this test. . . .

Because of Rule 6.05, as soon as a proselytizing member of ISKCON hands out a free copy of the Bhagavad-Gita to an interested listener, or a political candidate distributes his campaign brochure to a potential voter, he becomes subject to arrest and removal from the fairgrounds. This constitutes a significant restriction on First Amendment rights. By prohibiting distribution of literature outside the booths, the fair officials sharply limit the number of fairgoers to whom the proselytizers and candidates can communicate their messages. Only if a fairgoer affirmatively seeks out such information by approaching a booth does Rule 6.05 fully permit potential communicator to exercise their First Amendment rights. . . . If the State had a reasonable concern that distribution in certain parts of the fairgrounds—for example, entrances and exits—would cause disorder, it could have drafted its Rule to prohibit distribution of literature at those points. If the State felt it necessary to limit the number of persons distributing an organization's literature, it could, within reason, have done that as well. It had no right, however, to ban all distribution of literature outside the booths.

JUSTICE BLACKMUN, concurring in part and dissenting in part.

CLARK, SECRETARY OF THE INTERIOR V. COMMITTEE FOR CREATIVE NON-VIOLENCE

468 U.S. 288 (1984)

JUSTICE WHITE delivered the opinion of the Court.

The issue in this case is whether a National Park Service regulation prohibiting camping in certain parks violates the First Amendment when applied to prohibit demonstrators from sleeping in Lafayette Park and the Mall in connection with a demonstration intended to call attention to the plight of the homeless. We hold that it does not and reverse the contrary judgment of the Court of Appeals.

Under the regulations involved in this case, camping in National Parks is permitted only in campgrounds designated for that purpose. (1983). No such campgrounds have ever been designated in Lafayette Park or the Mall.

In 1982, the Park Service issued a renewable permit to respondent Community for Creative Non-Violence (CCNV) to conduct a wintertime demonstration in Lafayette Park and the Mall for the purpose of demonstrating the plight of the homeless. The permit authorized the erection of two symbolic tent cities: 20 tents in Lafayette Park that would accommodate 50 people and 40 tents in the Mall with a capacity of up to 100. The Park Service, however, relying on the above regulations, specifically denied CCNV's request that demonstrators be permitted to sleep in the symbolic tents.

CCNV and several individuals then filed an action to prevent the application of the no-camping regulations to the proposed demonstration, which, it was claimed, was not covered by the regulation. It was also submitted that the regulations were unconstitutionally vague, had been discriminatorily applied, and could not be applied to prevent sleeping in the tents without violating the First Amendment.

The District Court granted summary judgment in favor of the Park Service. The Court of Appeals, sitting *en banc*, reversed. . . .

We need not differ with the view of the Court of Appeals that overnight sleeping in connection with the demonstration is expressive conduct protected to some extent by the First Amendments We assume for present purposes, but do not decide, that such is the case, *United States v. O'Brien*, (1968), but this assumption only begins the inquiry. Expression, whether oral or written or symbolized by conduct, is subject to reasonable time, place, or manner restrictions. We have often noted that restrictions of this kind are valid provided that they are justified without reference to the content of the regulated speech, that they are narrowly tailored to serve a significant governmental interest, and that they leave open ample alternative channels for communication of the information.

The requirement that the regulation be content-neutral is clearly satisfied. The courts below accepted that view, and it is not disputed here that the prohibition on camping, and on sleeping specifically, is content-neutral and is not being applied because of disagreement with the message presented. Neither was the regulation faulted, nor could it be, on the ground that without overnight sleeping the plight of the homeless could not be communicated in other ways. The regulation otherwise left the demonstration intact, with its symbolic city, signs, and the presence of those who were willing to take their turns in a day-and-night vigil. Respondents do not suggest that there was, or is, any barrier to delivering to the media, or to the public by other means, the intended message concerning the plight of the homeless.

It is also apparent to us that the regulation narrowly focuses on the Government's substantial interest in maintaining the parks in the heart of our Capital in an attractive and intact condition, readily available to the millions of people who wish to see and enjoy them by their presence. To permit camping—using these areas as living accommodations—would be totally inimical to these purposes, as would be readily understood by those who have frequented the National Parks across the country and observed the unfortunate consequences of the activities of those ho refuse to confine their camping to designated areas.

It is urged by respondents, and the Court of Appeals was of this view, that if the symbolic city of tents was to be permitted and if the demonstrators did not in. end to cook, dig, or engage in aspects of camping other than sleeping, the incremental benefit to the parks could not justify the ban on sleeping, which was here an expressive activity said to enhance the message concerning the plight of the poor and homeless. We cannot agree. In the first place, we seriously doubt that the First Amendment requires the Park Service to permit a demonstration in Lafayette Park and the Mall involving a 24-hour vigil and the erection of tents to accommodate 150 people. Furthermore, although we have assumed for present purposes that the sleeping banned in this case would have an expressive element, it is evident that its major value to this demonstration would be facilitative. Without a permit to sleep, it would be difficult to get the poor and homeless to participate or to be present at all. This much is apparent from the permit application filed by respondents: "Without the incentive of sleeping space or a hot meal, the homeless would not come to the site." The sleeping ban, if enforced, would thus effectively limit the nature, extent, and duration of the demonstration and to that extent ease the pressure on the parks.

Beyond this, however, it is evident from our cases that the validity of this regulation need not be judged solely by reference to the demonstration at hand. Heffron v. International Society for Krishna Consciousness, Inc. Absent the prohibition on sleeping, there would be other groups who would demand permission to deliver an asserted message by camping in Lafayette Park. Some of them would surely have as credible a claim

in this regard as does CCNV, and the denial of permits to still others would present difficult problems for the Park Service. With the prohibition, however, as is evident in the case before us, at least some around-the-clock demonstrations lasting for days on end will not materialize, others will be limited in size and duration, and the purposes of the regulation will thus be materially served. Perhaps these purposes would be more effectively and not so clumsily achieved by preventing tents and 24-hour vigils entirely in the core areas. But the Park Service's decision to permit nonsleeping demonstrations does not, in our view, impugn the camping prohibition as a valuable, but perhaps imperfect, protection to the parks. If the Government has a legitimate interest in ensuring that the National Parks are adequately protected, which we think it has, and if the parks would be more exposed to harm without the sleeping prohibition than with it, the ban is safe from invalidation under the First Amendment as a reasonable regulation of the manner in which a demonstration may be carried out. As in City Council of Los Angeles v. Taxpayers for Vincent, the regulation "responds precisely to the substantive problems which legitimately concern the [Government]."

We have difficulty, therefore, in understanding why the prohibition against camping, with its ban on sleeping overnight, is not a reasonable time, place, or manner regulation that withstands constitutional scrutiny. Surely the regulation is not unconstitutional on its face. None of its provisions appears unrelated to the ends that it was designed to serve. Nor is it any less valid when applied to prevent camping in Memorial-core parks by those who wish to demonstrate and deliver a message to the public and the central Government. Damage to the parks as well as their partial inaccessibility to other members of the public can as easily result from camping by demonstrators as by nondemonstrators. In neither case must the Government tolerate it. All those who could resort to the parks must abide by otherwise valid rules for their use, just as they must observe the traffic laws, sanitation regulations, and laws to preserve the public peace. This is no more than a reaffirmation that reasonable time, place, or manner restrictions on expression are constitutionally acceptable and the social problem they seek to highlight. By using sleep as an integral part of their mode of protest, respondents "can express with their bodies the poignancy of their plight. They can physically demonstrate the neglect from which they suffer with an articulateness even Dickens could not match."

According to the majority, the significant Government interest advanced by denying respondents' request to engage in sleep-speech is the interest in "maintaining the parks in the heart of our Capital in an attractive and intact condition, readily available to the millions of people who wish to see and enjoy them by their presence." Ante, at 296. That interest is indeed significant. However, neither the Government nor the majority adequately explains how prohibiting respondents' planned activity will substantially further that interest.

The majority cites no evidence indicating that sleeping engaged in as symbolic speech will cause substantial wear and tear on park property. Furthermore, the Government's application of the .sleeping ban in the circumstances of this case is strikingly inclusive. The majority acknowledges that a proper time, place, and manner restriction must be "narrowly tailored." Here, however, the tailoring requirement is virtually forsaken inasmuch as the Government offers no justification - applying its absolute ban on sleeping yet is willing to allow respondents to engage in activities—such as feigned sleeping—that is no less burdensome.

In short, there are no substantial Government interests advanced by the Government's regulations as applied to respondents. All that the Court's decision advances are the prerogatives of a bureaucracy that over the years has shown an implacable hostility toward citizens' exercise of First Amendment rights.

The disposition of this case impels me to make two additional observations.

First, in this case, as in some others involving time, place, and manner restrictions, the Court has dramatically lowered its scrutiny of governmental regulations once it has determined that such regulations are content-neutral. The result has been the creation of a two-tiered approach to First Amendment cases: while regulations that turn on the content of the expression are subjected to a strict form of judicial review, regulations that are aimed at matters other than expression receive only a minimal level of scrutiny. The minimal scrutiny prong of this two-tiered approach has led to an unfortunate diminution of First Amendment protection. By narrowly limiting its concern to whether a given regulation creates a content-based distinction, the Court has seemingly overlooked the fact that content-neutral restrictions are also capable of unnecessarily restricting protected expressive activity. To be sure, the general prohibition against content-based regulations is an essential tool of First Amendment analysis. It helps to put into operation the well-established principle that "government may not grant the use of a forum to people whose views it finds acceptable, but deny use to those wishing to express less favored or more controversial views." Police Department of Chicago v. Mosley, (1972). The Court, however, has transformed the ban against content distinctions from a floor that offers all persons at least equal liberty under the First Amendment into a ceiling that restricts persons to the protection of First Amendment equality—but nothing more. The consistent imposition of silence upon all may fulfill the dictates of an evenhanded content-neutrality. But it offends our "profound national commitment to the principle that debate on public issues should be uninhibited. robust, and wide-open."

What the Court fails to recognize is that public officials have strong incentives to overregulate even in the absence of an intent to censor particular views. This incentive stems from the fact that of the two groups whose interests officials must accommodate—on the one hand, the interests of the general public and, on the other, the interests of those who seek to use a particular forum for First Amendment activity—the political power of the former is likely to be far greater than that of the latter.

Contrary to the conclusion of the Court of Appeals, the foregoing analysis demonstrates that the Park Service regulation is sustainable under the four-factor standard of United States v. O'Brien, (1968), for validating a regulation of expressive conduct, which, in the last analysis is little, if any, different from the standard applied to time, place, or manner restrictions. No one contends that aside from its impact on speech a rule against camping or overnight sleeping in public parks is beyond the constitutional power of the Government to enforce. And for the reasons we have discussed above, there is a substantial Government interest in conserving park property, an interest that is plainly served by, and requires for its implementation, measures such as the proscription of sleeping that are designed to limit the wear and tear on park properties. That interest is unrelated to suppression of expression.

Accordingly, the judgment of the Court of Appeals is Reversed.

CHIEF JUSTICE BURGER, concurring. . .

JUSTICE MARSHALL, with whom JUSTICE BRENNAN joins, dissenting.

The Court's disposition of this case is marked by two related failings. First, the majority is either unwilling or unable to take seriously the First Amendment claims advanced by respondents. Contrary to the impression given by the majority, respondents are not supplicants seeking to wheedle an undeserved favor from the Government. They are citizens raising issues of profound public importance who have properly turned to the courts for the vindication of their constitutional rights. Second, the majority misapplies the test for ascertaining whether a restraint on speech qualifies as a reasonable time, place, and manner regulation. In determining what constitutes a sustainable regulation, the majority fails to subject

the alleged interests of the Government to the degree of scrutiny required to ensure that expressive activity protected by the First Amendment remains free of unnecessary limitations.

The proper starting point for analysis of this case is a recognition that the activity in which respondents seek to engage in sleeping in a highly public place, outside, in the winter for the purpose of protesting homelessness—is symbolic speech protected by the First Amendment. The majority assumes, without deciding, that the respondents' conduct is entitled to constitutional protection. The problem with this assumption is that the Court thereby avoids examining closely the reality of respondents' planned expression. The majority's approach denatures respondents' assailed right and thus makes all too easy identification of a Government interest sufficient to warrant its abridgment. A realistic appraisal of the competing interests at stake in this case requires a closer look at the nature of the expressive conduct at issue and the context in which that conduct would be displayed.

The primary purpose for making sleep an integral part of the demonstration was "to re-enact the central reality of homelessness," and to impress upon public consciousness, in as dramatic a way as possible, that homelessness is a widespread problem, often ignored, that confronts its victims with life-threatening deprivations.

Nor can there be any doubt that in the surrounding circumstances the likelihood was great that the political significance of sleeping in the parks would be understood by those who viewed it. Certainly the news media understood the significance of respondents' proposed activity; newspapers and magazines from around the Nation reported their previous sleep-in and their planned display. Ordinary citizens, too, would likely understand the political message intended by respondents. This likelihood stems from the remarkably apt fit between the activity in which respondents seek to engage.

4

NECESSARY ACTIVITY IN CONTROLLED ENVIRONMENTS

The case of Edwards v. South Carolina (1963), which appears at the beginning of the "cases" section of this chapter, is one which could be (and often is) placed along with Feiner and Terminiello, and other cases dealing with public order. Given the fact that, in Edwards, the petitioners were convicted of breach of the peace, and that at least some of their activity took place on public sidewalks, such treatment is not surprising and may, indeed, be preferable. But from the perspective of this text, it is useful to view Edwards not as a simple breach of the peace case, but rather as one which provides a transition to, and is in some respects exemplary of the fundamental question with which this chapter deals. That question is whether, and to what extent communicative activity may be restricted so as to permit the continued normal functioning of entities which are publicly owned and which are in some sense dedicated to other uses. Although some of the activity in Edwards took place on public sidewalks, much of it also occurred on the grounds of the South Carolina statehouse, (i.e. the building where the state legislature meets). It thus had, or might have had, the potential to cause at least some disruption to the activity to which a statehouse is usually dedicated (i.e. the passing of laws).

The other cases that we consider in this chapter share the same characteristic of at least potential interference by communication, usually through "speech plus" rather than speech alone, with the normal usage of publicly owned property. They differ from the cases dealt with in the preceding chapter because, unlike those cases, they did not arise in settings (like the streets and parks in Hague v. C.I.O.)

dedicated to the dissemination of public views. But the degree to which they differ varies, depending on the particular governmental purposes to which the property in question was dedicated, and the consequent propriety, or lack thereof, of using it for communicative activity.

At the same time, the cases, or most of them, involve questions of considerable complexity. Arguing for a broad degree of freedom for those who wish to communicate in "controlled environments" is the fact that, in many cases, the place where the activity is to take place is, "controlled" or not, the best and perhaps the only effective place to make a particular point. But it is not easy to determine exactly the point at which the normal activity of the facility in question is sufficiently interfered with so that communicative activity must be limited or prohibited. Nor is it easy to overcome the feeling that, at least in certain circumstances, the only effective limitation is absolute prohibition.

Perhaps because of this, the Court, at least in the initial cases, did not deal with the matters at issue in the terms presented here. In Edwards it was able to reverse the conviction of the statehouse demonstrators because the breach of the peace statute was vague, and thus it was difficult for the demonstrators to know precisely what was forbidden. In Cox v. Louisiana I (1965) a conviction for obstructing public passageways was voided because the record disclosed that the ordinance had been discriminatorily enforced. And in Cox v. Louisiana II (1965), although a statute relating to "picketing near a courthouse" was upheld, the conviction was reversed on the basis of a sort of "entrapment" theory, the law enforcement officers having, in the view of the Court, first given the petitioners permission to picket and only later applied the law to conduct which they had at least impliedly permitted.

These cases are, nevertheless, valuable as introductions to the problem, and Edwards v. South Carolina, its "breach of the peace" aspects aside, seems particularly valuable. What was at issue in that case was not merely the generalized right to "communicate freely," but rather the specific First Amendment guarantees of freedom of assembly and petition. For the Edwards demonstrators chose as the locus of their activity the state house grounds. Their purpose was to protest the state's segregation laws, which were of course, the product of legislative action and could be changed by legislative action. They could, then, be viewed as having chosen not only an appropriate but the most appropriate place for airing their views.

And while the legislative arena may not be a "public forum" in the sense that it has been set aside "from time immemorial" for the expression of public views, "lobbying" the legislature is something of which our traditions approve. One may view attempts to influence other types of governmental agencies as inappropriate, but pressuring the legislature is entirely permissible.

Further, the activity engaged in by the Edwards demonstrators, whether or not it did indeed constitute a breach of the peace, in no sense interfered with the legislative activity of the state house. No one entered the legislative chambers, or even the rotunda. No one took possession of the Speaker's chair, or made it impossible for legislators to go back and forth unimpeded. There was, the record showed, a certain degree of noise, but not so much as to interrupt legislative activity. And the demonstrators' presence and activity did not and, in the context of the South Carolina politics of the time, could not have constituted the type of "intimidation" which might have prevented the performing of the legislative duty out of fear or apprehension.

On all counts, then, that which occurred in Edwards v. South Carolina was a classic example (the matter of breach of the peace once again aside) of permissible communicative activity at a public facility dedicated to other purposes. Not so the cases involving the courthouse, the jailhouse, the school, or the military installation. What seems to distinguish such cases from that of the statehouse, aside from the actual conduct of the demonstrators, is the fact that in none could it be fairly argued, as it could in Edwards, that the communicative activity was an adjunct to the principal activity to which the facility was dedicated.

In Cox v. Louisiana II the petitioners were picketing near a courthouse in which some of their friends were being tried for various alleged violations of law. That, indeed, was why the picketing was taking place. The conviction of the petitioners, as we have noted, was reversed. But while reversing the conviction, the Court expressly held that picketing near a courthouse could lawfully be prohibited. The right of free speech and assembly did not, said the Court, mean that everyone with opinions or beliefs was free to address any group in any public place and at any time. Here the activity of the petitioners, viewed without regard to the "entrapment" feature of the case, was inimical to the activity of the courthouse, and so could be prohibited. The courthouse might, by the same logic utilized in discussing the demonstration as the legislature in Edwards, be the most effective place to present views on what was going on in that courthouse. But such activity at or near a courthouse was contrary to its purpose, and therefore had to take a back seat to the realization of that purpose.

In Adderly v. Florida (1966) petitioners, college students like those in Cox II, were conducting a protest demonstration against the arrest and incarceration (in the jail where the demonstrators picketed) of some of their colleagues. The evidence indicated that their activity had spilled off the jail "lawn" and into a particular driveway, and the state alleged that they had interfered with the ingress and egress of jail officials, as well as suppliers, to the facility.

The opinion of the Court in Adderly was written by Justice Black and that fact did not bode well for the demonstrators. Though for most purposes a staunch friend of oppressed minorities, Black's absolutist view of the First Amendment caused him to make a sometimes unjustifiable distinction between "speech" and "action." In Brown v. Louisiana (1966) he had sharply dissented from a majority holding reversing the conviction of several Blacks who had "loitered" in a public library for the purpose of protesting library segregation, and who had thereby, in the eyes of local officials, caused a disturbance. And, concurring in Cox I, he had denied that "there is a constitutional right to engage in the conduct of picketing or patrolling, whether on publicly owned streets or on privately owned property," on the grounds that picketing "is not speech, and therefore is not of itself protected by the First Amendment."

In his Adderly opinion Justice Black began by making the distinction we have suggested: "In Edwards the demonstrators went to the South Carolina State Capital grounds to protest. In this case they went to the jail. Traditionally, state capital grounds are open to the public. Jails, built for security purposes, are not." Since Black did not say, and indeed the majority rejected the view that the demonstrators had interfered with jail activities, his opinion amounts to the position that, given the purpose of jails, any communicative activity can be proscribed. The minority, by contrast, argued that even in such an environment there must have been actual evidence of an inability to carry on jail functions.[1]

In the later and little noticed case of Cameron v. Johnson (1968), the Court dealt with the issue it was able to avoid in Cox v. Louisiana I, and stated in even broader fashion the right of the state to control property which it had dedicated to specific purposes. At issue was a Mississippi statute which prohibited "engaging in picketing or mass demonstrations in such a manner as to obstruct or unreasonably interfere with free ingress or egress to or from any public premises or the transaction of public business or the administration of justice therein; or so as to obstruct or reasonably interfere with the free use of public streets or sidewalks or other public ways adjacent or contiguous thereto."

Such a statute could, of course, be interpreted to mean not only interfering with going into and out of a place, but also interfering by noise or in any other way with the actual transaction of the business of the place. Its coverage extended not only to governmental premises, but to the streets adjacent to them. And the statute, passed when it was by the Mississippi legislature, was obviously motivated by the spectre of black demonstrations. Yet it was unanimously upheld by the Court, on the basis that the state can make reasonable regulations designed to "protect the integrity of the particular restricted environment."

The precise meaning of the Cameron holding has not been fully tested. Adderly seemed to say that, at least in the case of jails, protecting the integrity of *that* environment may permit absolute bans. What might be reasonable in the case of other, less restrictive environments is not so clear. Would, for example, the Court uphold all restrictions on communicative activity which "interfered with" ingress and egress to such facilities, even if the interference was only "psychological" as in the filling of the walkway into a governmental building with manure? Franklyn Haiman would assist that the only sanction for such an activity should be reimbursement for the cost of removal.[2] Others would argue that at least some "speech plus" might be prohibited in the interests of protecting the citizenry from "annoyance or unease."

In any event, if the holding in Adderly is as characterized, those involving communicative activity on military installations appear closely similar. This issue was directly faced by the Court in a series of Vietnam related cases. The most famous of these, Greer v. Spock (1976), involved the nationally famous "baby doctor" who became heavily involved in the anti-war protests of the time. As a part of his involvement, Spock attempted to give a speech and to distribute literature at Fort Dix, New Jersey. The commander of the base, General Greer, ruled it "off limits" to such activity on the basis of a military regulation which prohibited political speeches or demonstrations on military bases. Dr. Spock challenged the validity of the regulation.

The Court had little difficulty in upholding the General's action. First, the regulation was neutrally enforced. Dr. Spock was a prominent anti-Vietnam speaker and a candidate for president on an anti-war ticket. But there was no showing that any political candidate had been allowed to speak on the base. Second, military reservations, unlike streets and parks, are no part of the public forum. (It could, of course, be argued that if one is going to protest military activity, a military base might be the best place to do it.) Finally, the business of a military installation is not communication, but the training of military personnel. Just as in <u>Adderly</u> the business of the jail was security and the allowance of demonstrations would have been inimical to that security, so the allowance of demonstrations on military reservations would have been hostile to the military mission. And while Dr. Spock might have given his speech without interfering with that mission, that possibility was of no consequence. Discussion, being outside that mission, could be prohibited for that reason alone. Additionally, it was reasonable to keep the activities of military installations wholly separable from even the appearance of partisan activity.

This last argument would seem to have considerably merit, especially if one accepts the view (given great prominence by the Court in recent decisions on the "establishment" clause[3]) that what government does may be equally or more important for its symbolic rather than for its practical effect. While no one could conceivably have concluded, had Dr. Spock been allowed to speak at Ft. Dix, that General Greer must for that reason have been opposed to the Vietnam War, yet once Spock was allowed to speak, the rule of "equal access" would have allowed all candidates for president to give speeches on the base. But it is important that the military is not seen as involved in politics, for the Constitution subordinates it to political leaders. If the military fights, it does so because that is its job. This being the constitutional ideal, even the appearance of military involvement in politics must be avoided.

Also in <u>Greer v. Spock,</u> the Court upheld the considerably more controversial authority of a base commander to prohibit the distribution on his base of any materials which, in his judgment, created a clear and present danger of interfering with the mission of the base. It was the commander, and only the commander, said the Court, who was in a position to determine if such distribution would jeopardize his mission, and once he had made that judgment, so long as it applied evenhandedly, the courts could not question his judgment.

The provision for the education of youth is, particularly for the states, one of the major and necessary functions of government. And there would seem to be no doubt that outside influences, including communicative activity unrelated to the mission of the school, can make more difficult the achievement of that goal. From another perspective, however, it is less easy to justify restrictions on communication in this particular "restricted environment." For schools are designed for learning, and learning itself requires at least a modicum of freedom of inquiry.

On balance the Court's decisions on free communication in schools reflect a careful attempt to reconcile these sometimes conflicting goals. In the 1972 case of Chicago Police Department v. Mosely, the Court struck down a city's absolute ban on all picketing within 150 feet of a school building while classes were in session. The decision turned, however, not on the view that such a ban was unconstitutional, but rather on the fact that the statute in question explicitly exempted "the peaceful picketing of any school involved in a labor dispute." This, the Court said, was an impermissible distinction on the basis of content. But in the same year, in Grayned v. City of Rockford, an eight to one majority upheld a conviction for violation of an ordinance which prohibited anyone on school property from willfully making or assisting in the making of "any noise or diversion which disturbs or tends to disturb the peace or good order of such school session." The statute, said Justice Marshall for the Court, was neither vague nor overbroad, and:

> The nature of a place, the pattern of its normal activities, dictates the kind of regulations of time, place, and manner that are reasonable. . . . . The crucial question is whether the manner of expression is basically incompatible with the normal activity of a particular place at a particular time. . . . Rockford's anti-noise ordinance goes no further than . . . a municipality may go to prevent interference with its schools. It is narrowly tailored to further Rockford's compelling interest in having an undisrupted school session conducive to student learning. . . . Rockford punishes only conduct which disrupts or is about to disrupt normal school activities. That decision is made, as it should be, on an individualized basis, given the fact situation . . . . Rockford's modest restriction . . . reflects a considered and specific legislative judgment that some kinds of expressive activity should be restricted at a particular time and place, here in order to protect the schools. Such a reasonable regulation is not inconsistent with the First and Fourteenth Amendment.

The Grayned opinion is at pains to reconcile its holding with another, and probably the best known, Supreme Court decision on communicative activity affecting the schools, Tinker v. Des Moines Community School District (1969). The reconciliation is, however, only partly convincing.

Tinker involved a series of events which occurred at the height of protests against the Vietnam war, but in the unlikely setting of a public school in middle America. The children of the Tinker family were, perhaps due to the influence of their parents, opposed to the Vietnam war, and wanted to wear black armbands to school on a day when various anti-war groups around the nation would be wearing similar bands. The school principal, after a brief experience with the wearing of such symbols, banned them as disruptive of the learning environment. Whether there was actually any such disruption depends, for the reader of *United States Reports*, on whether one chooses to believe the majority opinion or the dissent. The majority seemed to assume that Mary Beth Tinker sat in class wearing her arm band and was received by the other students as if she had chosen an oddly colored hair ribbon. Justice Black, in dissent, saw it differently, noting that Mary Beth's mathematics teacher testified that the tension caused by the wearing of the band was so great that he could hardly conduct his class.

After first asserting that children do have constitutional rights, although perhaps not so extensive as adults, the majority struck down the ban on armbands on the grounds that the school district did not act on any reasonable fear of school disruption, but rather on the basis of "undifferentiated fear and apprehension, and the consequent desire to avoid *possible* problems." Further, said the majority, no such regulation had been applied in the many situations where students had worn other symbols, including the buttons of political candidates, iron crosses, etc. Thus, the regulation was not only not justified in this factual situation, but additionally violated the "equal protection" component of the First Amendment.[4] For Justice Black, given his acceptance of the reality of disruption, the regulation was merely an attempt to protect the learning process, not unlike that later legitimated by the Court in Grayned v. Rockford.

The Court in more recent cases has both expanded and sharply limited the application of Tinker. The expansion has taken place most notably in Widmar v. Vincent (1981), which dealt with the activities of college students. In that case the University of Missouri at Kansas City, fearful that any other action would violate the First Amendment's prohibition against "the establishment of religion," denied to a student religious group the right to meet on campus. The group challenged the denial as an infringement both on their right to "free exercise of religion" and to free speech. Justice Powell, for a seven person majority, decided the case on the basis of the communications clauses.

Agreeing with the state that its obligation to act in conformity with constitutional mandates constituted a "compelling state interest," Powell disagreed that such an obligation was involved in this case. Allowing the student religious group to meet on campus would not violate any of the three prongs of the "Lemon test" by which the Court decides establishment issues. That being so, it followed that "Having created a forum generally open to students, the University seeks to enforce a content-based exclusion of religious speech" which it was unable to justify. Cited in support of the majority position was, *inter alia*, Tinker.

In two later cases the Court, while professing fidelity to Tinker, limited considerably its usefulness as a precedent for the protection of "speech" in the context of the high school. In the second of these cases, Hazelwood School District v. Kuhlmeier (1988), the Court distinguished Tinker as involving whether a school might punish student expression which "happens to occur on school premises," rather than whether the school might "refuse to lend its name and resources to the dissemination of student expression." In the context of administrative censorship of a student newspaper only the second was at issue, and thus the restriction on expression at issue was upheld.

No such distinction was possible in Bethel School District v. Fraser (1986), which involved a sexually oriented speech by a high school student nominating a classmate for school office. Chief Justice Burger's opinion denying protection for the speech, and Justice Brennan's concurrence, set forth in considerable detail the varying views of the Court on the clash of free speech rights for high school students as opposed to the school's right to inculcate certain values. The Bethel opinions are reproduced in this chapter.

The cases that we have considered in this chapter depend in part on a distinction between communicative activity in "public" and other governmentally owned forums. The Court's recent attempts to utilize this distinction has created a three-tiered analysis. On the first level are "traditional public forums" of the type first recognized in Hague v. C.I.O., as well as those expressly created for the purpose of expression. "Limited public forums" are those which may have been opened to public debate for limited purposes, and "nonpublic forums" are those which have never been opened for communicative purposes and which, given their nature, probably could not be. Whether and to what extent government must accommodate communicative desires will depend on how any particular government "forum" is classified. In Perry Education Association v. Perry Local Educator's Association (1983) the issue was whether a school district, having opened its internal mail system to the organization recognized as exclusive bargaining agent for the district's teachers, had therefore to open that system to a competing labor union. The Court, finding that the mail system was a "limited public forum" whose purpose could be disrupted by opening the system, said no.[5]

"Forum analysis" and its consequences for the treatment of speech activity in "controlled environments" received, however, its most thorough canvassing in the majority and dissenting opinions of Justices O'Connor and Brennan, in Cornelius v. N.A.A.C.P. Legal Defense Fund. Those opinions, which also deal with the issue of the solicitation of contributions as an aspect of free speech, are reproduced herein. Students will wish to ask which of the two is more faithful to the logic of "forum" analysis, and to the concepts of "public" and "controlled" environments.

---

[1]With respect to the somewhat related matter of First Amendment freedoms in the context of prisons, most of the cases with which the Court has dealt have raised issues of "free exercise of religion." But in two cases involving the attempts of journalists to gain access to prisons and to prisoners, the Court has held that there is no right of such access for the media, so long as prisoners have alternative channels of communication, and so long as journalists can "access" prisons and prisoners in the same way as the general public. See Pell v. Procunier (1974) and Houchins v. KQED (1978), but see Turner v. Saffley (1987).

[2]Haiman, *Speech and Law in aFree Society*, 37.

[3]See the discussion of governmental "endorsement of religion" in Chapter's 17 and 18.

[4]The Court's "equal protection" analysis is at least open to question. For, if the reason for the instant ban had been a justified fear of conflict, and if no such fear could be demonstrated in the case of "other" political symbols, might it not be argued that the first could be prohibited while the second could not? The problem with this analysis is, of course, that it would inevitably lead to favoring symbols acceptable to the majority over those of the minority.

[5]In addition to its discussion of "forum analysis,' Perry also involves the issue of limitations on speech which derive from labor-management agreements, and for this reason is reproduced in Ch. 12.

EDWARDS ET AL. V. SOUTH CAROLINA

372 U.S. 229 (1963)

MR. JUSTICE STEWART delivered the opinion of the Court. . . .

It has been long established that these First Amendment freedoms are protected by the Fourteenth Amendment from invasion by the states. . . .

Circumstances in this case reflect an exercise of these basic constitutional rights in their most pristine and classic form. The petitioners felt aggrieved by laws of South Carolina which allegedly "prohibit Negro privileges in this State." They peaceably assembled at the site of the Capitol State Government and there peaceably expressed their grievance "to the citizens of South Carolina, along with the Legislative bodies of South Carolina." Not until they were told by police officials that they must disperse on pain of arrest did they do more. Even then, they but sang patriotic and religious songs after one of their leaders had delivered had delivered a "religious harangue." There was no violence or threat of violence on their part, or on the part of any member of the crowd watching them. Police protection was "ample."

This, therefore, was a far cry from the situation in *Feiner v. New York*, where two policemen were faced with the crowd which was "pushing, shoving, and milling around." Where at least one member of the crowd "threatened violence if the police did not act," where the crowd was pressing closer around petitioner and officer," and where "the speaker passes the bounds of argument or persuasion and undertakes incitement to riot." And the record is barren of any evidence of "fighting words."

We do not review in this case criminal convictions resulting from the evenhanded application of a precise and narrowly drawn regulatory statute invincing the legislative judgment that certain specific conduct be limited or proscribed. If, for example, the petitioners have been convicted upon evidence that they had violated a law regulating traffic, or had disobeyed a law reasonable limiting the periods during which the State House grounds were open to the public, this

would be a different case. . . .

These petitioners . . . were convicted upon evidence which showed no more than that the opinions which they were peaceably expressing were sufficiently opposed to the views of the majority of the community to attract a crowd and necessitate police protection.

The Fourteenth Amendment does not permit a State to make criminal the peaceful expression of unpopular views "[A] function of free speech under our system of government is to invite dispute. It may indeed best serve its high purpose when it induces a condition of unrest, creates dissatisfaction with conditions as they are, or even stirs people to anger. Speech is often provocative and challenging. It make strike at prejudices and preconceptions and have profound and unsettling effects as it presses for acceptance of an idea. That is why freedom of speech . . . is . . . protected against censorship or punishment, unless shown likely to produce a clear and present danger of a serious and substantial evil that rises far above public inconvenience, annoyance, or unrest. . . . There is no room under our Constitution for a more restrictive view. For the alternative would lead to standardization of ideas either by legislators, courts, or dominant political or community groups. *Terminiello v. Chicago*. As in the *Terminiello* case, the courts of South Carolina have defined a criminal offense so as to permit conviction of the petitioners if their speech "stirred people to anger, invited public dispute, or brought about a condition of unrest. A conviction resting on any of those grounds may not stand. . . ." *Reversed*

MR. JUSTICE CLARK, dissenting.

. . . . the petitioners arrested, as they apparently planned from the beginning, and convicted on evidence the sufficiency of which the Court does not challenge. The question thus seems to me whether a State is constitutionally prohibited from enforcing laws to prevent breach of the peace in a situation where city officials in good faith believe, and the record shows, that disorder and violence are imminent merely because the activities constituting that breach contain claimed elements of constitutionally protected speech and assembly. To me the answer under our cases is clearly in the negative.

Beginning, as did the South Carolina courts, with a premise that the petitioners were entitled to assemble and voice their dissatisfaction with segregation, the enlargement of constitutional protection for the conduct here is salacious as would be the conclusion that free speech necessary includes the right to broadcast from a sound truck in the public streets. *Kovacs v. Cooper* (1949).

This Court said in *Thornhill v. Alabama* (1940), that "[t]he power and the duty of the State to take adequate steps to preserve the peace and to protect the privacy, the lives, and the property of its residents cannot be doubted." Significantly, in holding that the petitioners picketing was constitutionally protected in that case, the Court took pains to differentiate it from "picketing *en masse.* or otherwise conducted which might occasion . . . imminent and aggravated danger. . ." Here the petitioners were permitted without hindrance to exercise their rights of free speech and assembly. The arrests occurred only after a situation arose in which the law-enforcement officials on the scene consider that a dangerous disturbance was imminent. The County Court found that "[t]he evidence is clear that the officers then motivated solely by a proper concern for the preservation of order and the protection of the general welfare in the face of an actual interference with traffic and an imminently threatened disturbance of the peace of the community." In affirming, the South Carolina Supreme Court said the action of the police was "reasonable and motivated solely by a proper concern for the preservation of order and prevention of further interference with traffic upon the public streets and sidewalks."

In *Cantwell v. Connecticut,* this Court recognized that "[w]hen clear and present danger of riot, disorder, interference with traffic upon the public streets or other immediate threat to public safety, peace, or order, appears, the power of the State to prevent or punish is obvious." And in *Feiner v. New York* (1951), we upheld a conviction for breach of the peace in a situation no more dangerous than that found here. There the demonstration was conducted by only one person and the crowd was limited to approximately 80, as compared with the present lineup of some 200 demonstrators and 300 onlookers. There the petitioner was "endeavoring to amuse the Negro people against whites, urging that they rise up in arms and fight for equal rights." Only one person—in a city having an entirely different historical background—was exhorting adults. Here 200 youthful Negro demonstrators were being aroused to a "fever pitch" before a crowd of some 300 people who undoubtedly were hostile. Perhaps their speech was not so animated but in this setting their actions, the placards, readings, "You may jail our bodies but not our souls" and their chanting of "I Shall Not Be Moved," accompanied by stamping feet and clapping hands, created a much greater danger of riot and disorder. It is my belief that anyone conversant with the almost spontaneous combustion in some southern communities in such a situation will agree that the City Manager's action may well have averted a major catastrophe.

The gravity of the danger here surely needs no further explication. The imminence of that danger has been emphasized at every stage of this proceeding, from the complaints charging that the demonstrations "tended directly to immediate violence" to the State Supreme Court's affirmance on the authority of *Feiner.* This record, then, shows no steps backward from a standard of "clear and present danger." But to say that the police may not intervene until the riot has occurred is like keeping out the doctor until the patient dies. I cannot subscribe to such a doctrine. I would affirm the convictions.

BETHEL SCHOOL DISTRICT NO. 403 ET AL. V. FRASER, A MINOR, ET AL.

478 U.S. 675 (1986)

CHIEF JUSTICE BURGER delivered the opinion of the Court.

On April 26, 1983, respondent Matthew N. Fraser, a student at Bethel High School in Pierce County, Washington, delivered a speech nominating a fellow student for student elective office. Approximately 600 high school students, many of whom were 14-year-olds, attended the assembly. Students were required to attend the assembly or to report to the study hall. The assembly was part of a school-sponsored educational program in self-government. Students who elected not to attend the assembly were required to report to study hall. During the entire speech, Fraser referred to his candidate in terms of an elaborate, graphic, and explicit sexual metaphor.

Two of Fraser's teachers, with whom he discussed the contents of his speech in advance, informed him that the speech was "inappropriate and that he probably should not deliver it," and that his delivery of the speech might have "severe consequences. "

During Fraser's delivery of the speech, a school counselor observed the reaction of students to the speech. Some students hooted and yelled; some by gestures graphically simulated the sexual activities pointedly alluded to in respondent's speech. Other students appeared to be bewildered and embarrassed by the speech. One teacher reported that on the day following the speech, she found it necessary to forgo a portion of the scheduled class lesson in order to discuss the speech with the class.

A Bethel High School disciplinary rule prohibiting the use of obscene language in the school provides: "Conduct which materially and substantially interferes with the educational process is prohibited, including the use of obscene, profane language or gestures." The morning after the assembly, the Assistant Principal called Fraser into her office and notified him that the school considered his speech to have been a violation of this rule.

Fraser was presented with copies of five letters submitted by teachers, describing his conduct at the assembly; he was given a chance to explain his conduct, and he admitted to having given the speech described and that he deliberately used sexual innuendo in the speech. Fraser was then informed that he would be suspended for three days, and that his name would be removed from the list of candidates for graduation speaker at the school's commencement exercises.

Fraser sought review of this disciplinary action through the School District's grievance procedures. The hearing officer determined that the speech given by respondent was "indecent, lewd, and offensive to the modesty and decency of many of the students and faculty in attendance at the assembly." The examiner determined that the speech fell within the ordinary meaning of "obscene," as used in the disruptive-conduct rule, and affirmed the discipline in its entirety. Fraser served two days of his suspension, and was allowed to return to school on the third day.

Respondent, by his father as guardian ad litem, then brought this action in the United States District Court for the Western District of Washington. Respondent alleged a violation of his First Amendment right to freedom of speech and sought both injunctive relief and monetary damages. The District Court held that the school's sanctions violated respondent's right to freedom of speech under the First Amendment to the United States Constitution, that the school's disruptive-conduct rule is unconstitutionally vague and overbroad, and that the removal of respondent's name from the graduation speaker's list violated the Due Process Clause of the Fourteenth Amendment because the disciplinary rule makes no mention of such removal as a possible sanction. The District Court awarded respondent $278 in damages, $12,750 in litigation costs and attorney's fees, and enjoined the School District from preventing respondent from speaking at the commencement ceremonies. Respondent, who had been elected graduation speaker by a write-in vote of his classmates, delivered a speech at the commencement ceremonies on June 8, 1983.

The Court of Appeals for the Ninth Circuit affirmed the judgment of the District Court (1985), holding that respondent's speech was indistinguishable from the protest armband in *Tinker v. Des Moines Independent Community School Dist.* (1969). The court explicitly rejected the School District's argument that the speech, unlike the passive conduct of wearing a black armband, had a disruptive effect on the educational process. The Court of Appeals also rejected the School District's argument that it had an interest in protecting an essentially captive audience of minors from lewd and indecent language in a setting sponsored by the school, reasoning that the School District's "unbridled discretion" to determine what discourse is "decent" would "increase the risk of cementing white, middle-class standards for determining what is acceptable and proper speech and behavior in our public schools." Finally, the Court of Appeals rejected the School District's argument that, incident to its responsibility for the school curriculum, it had the power to control the language used to express ideas during a school-sponsored activity.

We granted certiorari. We reverse.

This Court acknowledged in *Tinker v. Des Moines Independent Community School Dist*, that students do not "shed their constitutional rights to freedom of speech or expression at the schoolhouse gate." The Court of Appeals read that case as precluding any discipline of Fraser for indecent speech and lewd conduct in the school assembly. That court appears to have proceeded on the theory that the use of lewd and obscene speech in order to make what the speaker considered to be a point in a nominating speech for a fellow student was essentially the same as the wearing of an armband in *Tinker* as a form of protest or the expression of a political position.

The marked distinction between the political "message" of the armbands in *Tinker* and the sexual content of respondent's speech in this case seems to have been given little weight by the Court of Appeals. In upholding the students' right to engage in a nondisruptive, passive expression of a political viewpoint in *Tinker,* this Court was careful to note that the case did "not concern speech or action that intrudes upon the work of the schools or the rights of other students."

The role and purpose of the American public school system were well described by two historians, who stated: "[P]ublic education must prepare pupils for citizenship in the Republic. . . . It must inculcate the habits and manners of civility as values in themselves conducive to happiness and as indispensable to the practice of self-government in the community and the nation." In Ambach v. *Norwick* (1979), we echoed the essence of this statement of the objectives of public education as the "inculcat[ion of] fundamental values necessary to the maintenance of a democratic political system."

These fundamental values of "habits and manners of civility" essential to a democratic society must, of course, include tolerance of divergent political and religious views, even when the views expressed may be unpopular. But these "fundamental values" must also take into account consideration of the sensibilities of others, and, in the case of a school, the sensibilities of fellow students. The undoubted freedom to advocate unpopular and controversial views in schools and classrooms must be balanced against the society's countervailing interest in teaching students the boundaries of socially appropriate behavior. Even the most heated political discourse in a democratic society requires consideration for the personal sensibilities of the other participants and audiences. . . .

The First Amendment guarantees wide freedom in matters of adult public discourse. A sharply divided Court upheld the right to express an antidraft viewpoint in a public place albeit in terms highly offensive to most citizens. See *Cohen v. California* (1971). It does not follow, however, that simply because the use of an offensive form of expression may not be prohibited to adults making what the speaker considers a political point, the same latitude must be permitted to children in a public school. . . .

Surely it is a highly appropriate function of public school education to prohibit the use of vulgar and offensive terms in public discourse. Indeed, the "fundamental values necessary to the maintenance of a democratic political system" disfavor the use of terms of debate highly offensive or highly threatening to others. Nothing in the Constitution prohibits the states from insisting that certain modes of expression are inappropriate and subject to sanctions. The inculcation of these values is truly the "work of the schools." *Tinker*; see *Ambach v. Norwick*. The determination of what manner of speech in the classroom or in school assembly is inappropriate properly rests with the school board.

The process of educating our youth for citizenship in public schools is not confined to books, the curriculum, and the civics class; schools must teach by example the shared values of a civilized social order. Consciously or otherwise, teachers—and indeed the older students—demonstrate the appropriate form of civil discourse and political expression by their conduct and deportment in and out of class. Inescapably, like parents, they are role models. The schools, as instruments of the state, may determine that the essential lessons of civil, mature conduct cannot be conveyed in a school that tolerates lewd, indecent, or offensive speech and conduct such as that indulged in by this confused boy.

The pervasive sexual innuendo in Fraser's speech was plainly offensive to both teachers and students—indeed to any mature person. By glorifying male sexuality, and in its verbal content, the speech was acutely insulting to teenage girl students. The speech could well be seriously damaging to its less mature audience, many of whom were only 14 years old and on the threshold of awareness of human sexuality. Some students were reported as bewildered by the speech and the reaction of mimicry it provoked.

This Court's First Amendment jurisprudence has acknowledged limitations on the otherwise absolute interest of the speaker in reaching an unlimited audience where the speech is sexually explicit and the audience may include children.

In *Ginsberg v. New York* (1968), this Court upheld a New York statute banning the sale of sexually oriented material to minors, even though the material in question was entitled to First Amendment protection with respect to adults. And in addressing the question whether the First Amendment places any limit on the authority of public schools to remove books from a public school library, all Members of the Court, otherwise sharply divided, acknowledged that the school board has the authority to remove books that are vulgar. *Board of Education v. Pico* (1982) (plurality opinion); (BLACKMUN, J., concurring in part and in judgment); (REHNQUIST, J., dissenting). These cases recognize the obvious concern on the part of parents, and school authorities acting *in loco parentis,* to protect children—especially in a captive audience—from exposure to sexually explicit, indecent, or lewd speech. . . .

We hold that petitioner School District acted entirely within its permissible authority in imposing sanctions upon Fraser in response to his offensively lewd and indecent speech. Unlike the sanctions imposed on the students wearing armbands in *Tinker*, the penalties imposed in this case were unrelated to any political viewpoint. The First Amendment does not prevent the school officials from determining that to permit a vulgar and lewd speech such as respondent's would undermine the school's basic educational mission. A high school assembly or classroom is no place for a sexually explicit monologue directed towards an unsuspecting audience of teenage students. Accordingly, it was perfectly appropriate for the school to disassociate itself to make the point to the pupils that vulgar speech and lewd conduct is wholly inconsistent with the "fundamental values" of public school education. Justice Black, dissenting in *Tinker*, made a point that is especially relevant in this case: "I wish therefore, . . . to disclaim any purpose . . . to hold that the Federal Constitution compels the teachers, parents, and elected school officials to surrender control of the American public school system to public school students."

JUSTICE BLACKMUN concurs in the result.

JUSTICE BRENNAN, concurring in the judgment.

The Court today reaffirms the unimpeachable proposition that students do not "shed their constitutional rights to freedom of speech or expression at the schoolhouse gate." (quoting *Tinker v. Des Moines Independent Community School Dist.* 1969).

If respondent had given the same speech outside of the school environment, he could not have been penalized simply because government officials considered his language to be inappropriate, see *Cohen v. California* (1971); the Court's opinion does not suggest otherwise. Moreover, despite the Court's characterizations, the language respondent used is far removed from the very narrow class of "obscene" speech which the Court has held is not protected by the First Amendment. *Ginsberg v. New York* (1968); *Roth v. United States* (1957). It is true that the State has interests in teaching high school students how to conduct civil and effective public discourse and in avoiding disruption of educational school activities. . . .

Under the circumstances of this case, however, I believe that school officials did not violate the First Amendment in determining that respondent should be disciplined for the disruptive language he used while addressing a high school assembly. Thus, I concur in the judgment reversing the decision of the Court of Appeals.

JUSTICE MARSHALL, dissenting.

I agree with the principles that JUSTICE BRENNAN sets out in his opinion concurring in the judgment. I dissent from the Court's decision, however, because in my view the School District failed to demonstrate that respondent's remarks were indeed disruptive. . . .

JUSTICE STEVENS, dissenting.

"Frankly, my dear, I don't give a damn."

When I was a high school student, the use of those words in a public forum shocked the Nation. Today Clark Gable's four-letter expletive is less offensive than it was then. Nevertheless, I assume that high school administrators may prohibit the use of that word in classroom discussion and even in extracurricular activities that are sponsored by the school and held on school premises. For I believe a school faculty must regulate the content as well as the style of student speech in carrying out its educational mission. It does seem to me, however, that if a student is to be punished for using offensive speech, he is entitled to fair notice of the scope of the prohibition and the consequences of its violation. The interest in free speech protected by the First Amendment and the interest in fair procedure protected by the Due Process Clause of the Fourteenth Amendment combine to require this conclusion. . . .

CORNELIUS, ACTING DIRECTOR, OFFICE OF PERSONNEL MANAGEMENT V. NAACP LEGAL DEFENSE AND EDUCATIONAL FUND, INC., ET AL.

473 U.S. 788 (1985)

JUSTICE O'CONNOR delivered the opinion of the Court.

This case requires us to decide whether the Federal Government violates the First Amendment when it excludes legal defense and political advocacy organizations from participation in the Combined Federal Campaign (CFC or Campaign), a charity drive aimed at federal employees. The United States District Court for the District of Columbia held that the respondent organizations could not be excluded from the CFC, and the Court of Appeals affirmed. We granted certiorari (1984), and we now reverse.

The CFC is an annual charitable fundraising drive conducted in the federal workplace during working hours largely through the voluntary efforts of federal employees. . . .

Through the CFC, the Government employees contribute in excess of $100 million to charitable organizations each year.

Respondents in this case are the NAACP Legal Defense and Educational Fund, Inc., the Sierra Club Legal Defense Fund, the Puerto Rican Legal Defense and Education Fund, the Federally Employed Women Legal Defense and Education Fund, the Indian Law Resource Center, the Lawyers' Committee for Civil Rights under Law, and the Natural Resources Defense Council. Each of the respondents attempts to influence public policy through one or more of the following means: political activity, advocacy, lobbying, or litigation on behalf of others. In 1980, two of the respondents—the NAACP Legal Defense and Educational Fund, Inc., and the Puerto Rican Legal Defense and Education Fund (the Legal Defense Funds)—joined by the NAACP Special Contribution Fund, for the first time sought to participate in the CFC. The Office of Personnel Management (OPM), which in 1978 had assumed the duties of the Civil Service Commission, refused admission to the Legal Defense Funds. This action led to a series of three lawsuits, the third of which is before us today. In 1982, the President issued Executive Order No 12353, 3 CFR 139 (1983), to replace the 1961 Executive Order which had established the CFC. The new Order retained the original limitation to "national voluntary health and welfare agencies and such other national voluntary agencies as may be appropriate," and delegated to the Director of the Office of Personnel Management the authority to

establish criteria for determining appropriateness. Shortly thereafter, the President amended Executive Order No. 12353 to specify the purposes of the CFC and to identify groups whose participation would be consistent with those purposes. The CFC was designed to lessen the Government's burden in meeting human health and welfare needs by providing a convenient, nondisruptive channel for federal employees to contribute to nonpartisan agencies that directly serve those needs. The Order limited participation to "voluntary, charitable, health and welfare agencies that provide or support direct health and welfare services to individuals or their families," and specifically excluded those "[a]gencies that seek to influence the outcomes of elections or the determination of public policy through political activity or advocacy, lobbying, or litigation on behalf of parties other than themselves."

Respondents brought this action challenging their threatened exclusion under the new Executive Order. They argued that the denial of the right to seek designated funds violates their First Amendment right to solicit charitable contributions

In *Village of Schaumburg*, the Court struck down a local ordinance prohibiting solicitation in a public forum by charitable organizations that expended less than 75 percent of the receipts collected for charitable purposes. The plaintiff in that case was a public advocacy group that employed canvassers to distribute literature and answer questions about the group's goals and activities as well as to solicit contributions. The Court found that "charitable appeals for funds, on the street or door to door, involve a variety of speech interests—communication of information, the dissemination and propagation of views and ideas, and the advocacy of causes—that are within the protection of the First Amendment." The ordinance was invalid, the Court held, because it unduly interfered with the exercise of protected rights.

The conclusion that the solicitation which occurs in the CFC is protected speech merely begins our inquiry. Even protected speech is not equally permissible in all places and at all times. Recognizing that the Government, "no less than a private owner of property, has power to preserve the property under its control for the use to which it is lawfully dedicated," *Greer v. Spock* (1976), the Court has adopted a forum analysis as a means of determining when the Government's interest in limiting the use of its property to its intended purpose outweighs the interest of those wishing to use the property for other purposes. Accordingly, the extent to which the Government can control access depends on the nature of the relevant forum. Because a principal purpose of traditional public fora is the free exchange of ideas, speakers can be excluded from a public forum only when the exclusion is necessary to serve a compelling state interest and the exclusion is narrowly drawn to achieve that interest. See *Perry Education Assn. v Perry Local Educators' Assn.* Similarly; when the Government has intentionally designated a place or means of communication as a public forum speakers cannot be excluded without a compelling governmental interest. Access to a nonpublic forum, however, can be restricted as long as the restrictions are "reasonable and [are] not an effort to suppress expression merely because public officials oppose the speaker's view."

We agree with respondents that the relevant forum for our purposes is the CFC. Although petitioner is correct that as an initial matter a speaker must seek access to public property or to private property dedicated to public use to evoke First Amendment concerns, forum analysis is not completed merely by identifying the government property at issue. Rather, in defining the forum we have focused on the access sought by the speaker. When speakers seek general access to public property, the forum encompasses that property. See e. g., *Greer v. Spock*. In cases in which limited access is sought, our cases have taken a more tailored approach to ascertaining the perimeters of a forum within the confines of the government property....

Having identified the forum as the CFC, we must decide whether it is nonpublic or public in nature. Most relevant in this regard, of course, is *Perry Education Assn.* There the Court identified three types of fora: the traditional public forum, the public forum created by government designation, and the nonpublic forum. Traditional public fora are those places which "by long tradition or by government fiat have been devoted to assembly and debate." Public streets and parks fall into this category. See *Hague* v. *CIO* (1939). In addition to traditional public forum, a public forum may be created by government designation of a place or channel of communication for use by the public at large for assembly and speech, for use by certain speakers, or for the discussion of certain subjects. *Perry Education Assn.* Of course, the government "is not required to indefinitely retain the open character of the facility. . . ."

The government does not create a public forum by inaction or by permitting limited discourse, but only by intentionally opening a nontraditional forum for public discourse. Accordingly, the Court has looked to the policy and practice of the government to ascertain whether it intended to designate a place not traditionally open to assembly and debate as a public forum. The Court has also examined the nature of the property and its compatibility with expressive activity to discern the government's intent (For example, in *Widmar v. Vincent* (1981), we found that a state university that had an express policy of making its meeting facilities available to registered student groups had created a public forum for their use. . . .

Not every instrumentality used for communication, however, is a traditional public forum or a public forum by designation. *United States Postal Service v. Council of Greenburgh Civic Assns.* (1981). "[T]he First Amendment does not guarantee access to property simply because it is owned or controlled by the government." We will not find that a public forum has been created in the face of clear evidence of a contrary intent, nor will we infer that the government intended to create a public forum when the nature of the property is inconsistent with expressive activity. . . .

Here the parties agree that neither the CFC nor the federal workplace is a traditional public forum. Respondents argue, however, that the Government created a limited public forum for use by all charitable organizations to solicit funds from federal employees. Petitioner contends, and we agree, that neither its practice nor its policy is consistent with an intent to designate the CFC as a public forum open to all tax-exempt organizations.; In 1980, an estimated 850,000 organizations qualified for tax-exempt status. H. Godfrey Handbook on Tax Exempt Organizations 5 (1983). In contrast, only 237 organizations participated in the 1981 CFC of the National Capital Area. 1981 Combined Federal Campaign Contributor's Leaflet, National Capital Area. The government's consistent policy has been to limit participation in the CFC to "appropriate" voluntary agencies and to require agencies seeking admission to obtain permission from federal and local Campaign officials. Although the record does not show how many organizations have been denied permission throughout the 24-year history of the CFC, there is no evidence suggesting that the granting of the requisite permission is merely ministerial. . . . Such selective access, unsupported by evidence of a purposeful designation for public use, does not create a public forum. See *Greer v. Spock.*

Nor does the history of the CFC support a finding that the Government was motivated by an affirmative desire to provide an open forum for charitable solicitation in the federal workplace when it began the Campaign. The historical background indicates that the Campaign was designed to minimize the disruption to the workplace that had resulted from unlimited ad hoc solicitation activities by *lessening* the amount of expressive activity occurring on federal property. Indeed, the OPM stringently limited expression to the 30 word statement included in the Campaign literature. The decision of the Government to limit access to the CFC is not dispositive in itself; instead, it is relevant for what it suggests about the Government's intent in creating the forum. The Government did not create the CFC for purposes of providing a forum for expressive activity. That such activity occurs in the context of the forum created does not imply that the forum thereby becomes a public forum for First Amendment purposes. See *United States Postal Service v. Council of Greenburgh Civic Assns..*

An examination of the nature of the Government property involved strengthens the conclusion that the CFC is a nonpublic forum. *Greer v. Spock* ("[T]he business of a military installation [is] to train soldiers, not to provide a public forum"). The federal workplace, like any place of employment, exists to accomplish the business of the employer. *Connick v. Myers* (1983). "[T]he Government, as an employer, must have wide discretion and control over the management of its personnel and internal affairs." *Arnett v. Kennedy* (1974) (POWELL, J., concurring in part). It follows that the Government has the right to exercise control over access to the federal workplace in order to avoid interruptions to the performance of the duties of its employees. *United States Postal Service v. Council of Greenburgh Civic Assns..* In light of the Government policy in creating the CFC and its practice in limiting access, we conclude that the CFC is a nonpublic forum. . . .

Control over access to a nonpublic forum can be based on subject matter and speaker identity so long as the distinctions drawn are reasonable in light of the purpose served by the forum and are viewpoint neutral. *Perry Education Assn.* Although a speaker may be excluded from a nonpublic forum if he wishes to address a topic not encompassed within the purpose of the forum, see *Lehman v. City of Shaker Heights* (1974), or if he is not a member of the class of speakers for whose especial benefit the forum was created, see *Perry Education Assn.*, the government violates the First Amendment when it denies access to a speaker solely to suppress the point of view he espouses on an otherwise includible subject. Based on the present record, we . . . conclude that respondents may be excluded from the CFC. The Court of Appeals' conclusion to the contrary fails to reflect the nature of a nonpublic forum. The Government's decision to restrict access to a nonpublic forum need only be *reasonable;* it need not be the most reasonable or the only reasonable limitation. In contrast to a public forum, a finding of strict incompatibility between the nature of the speech or the identity of the speaker and the functioning of the nonpublic forum is not mandated. Cf. *Perry Education Assn. v. Perry Local Educators' Assn.* (1983); *Lehman v. City of Shaker Heights* (1974). Even if some incompatibility with general expressive activity were required, the CFC would meet the requirement because it would be administratively unmanageable if access could not be curtailed in a reasonable manner. Nor is there a requirement that the restriction be narrowly tailored or that the Government's interest be compelling. The First Amendment does not demand unrestricted access to a nonpublic forum merely because use of that forum may be the most efficient means of delivering the speaker's message. See *United States Postal Service v. Council of Greenburgh Civic Assns.* Rarely will a nonpublic forum provide the only means of contact with a particular audience. Here, as in *Perry Education Assn.*, the speakers have access to alternative channels, including direct mail and in-person solicitation outside the workplace, to solicit contributions from federal employees.

The reasonableness of the Government's restriction of access to a nonpublic forum must be assessed in the light of the purpose of the forum and all the surrounding circumstances. Here the President could reasonably conclude that a dollar directly spent on providing food or shelter to the needy is more beneficial than a dollar spent on litigation that might or might not result in aid to the needy. Moreover, avoiding the appearance of political favoritism is a valid justification for limiting speech in a nonpublic forum. Similarly, the exclusion of respondents may reasonably be considered a means of "insuring peace" in the federal workplace. . . .

Finally, the record amply supports an inference that respondents' participation in the CFC jeopardized the success of the Campaign. . . .

Although the avoidance of controversy is not a valid ground for restricting speech in a public forum, a nonpublic forum by definition is not dedicated to general debate or the free exchange of ideas. The First Amendment does not forbid a viewpoint-neutral exclusion of speakers who would disrupt a nonpublic forum and hinder its effectiveness for its intended purpose. On this record, the Government's posited justifications for denying respondents access to the CFC appear to be reasonable in light of the purpose of the CFC. The existence of reasonable grounds for limiting access to a nonpublic forum, however, will not save a regulation that is in reality a facade for viewpoint-based discrimination. See *Perry Education Assn. v. Perry Local Educators' Assn.*; cf. *City Council of Los Angeles v. Taxpayers for Vincent* (1984). . . .

Petitioner argues that a decision to exclude all advocacy groups, regardless of political or philosophical orientation, is by definition viewpoint neutral. Exclusion of groups advocating the use of litigation is not viewpoint-based, petitioner asserts, because litigation is a means of promoting a viewpoint, not a viewpoint in itself. While we accept the validity and reasonableness of the justifications offered by petitioner for excluding advocacy groups from the CFC, those justifications cannot save an exclusion that is in fact based on the desire to suppress a particular point of view . . .

We decline to decide in the first instance whether the exclusion of respondents was impermissibly motivated by a desire to suppress a particular point of view. Respondents are free to pursue this contention on remand . . . .

JUSTICE MARSHALL took no part in the consideration or decision of this case.

JUSTICE POWELL took no part in the decision of this case.

JUSTICE BLACKMUN, with whom JUSTICE BRENNAN joins, dissenting.

The Court's analysis transforms the First Amendment into a mere ban on viewpoint censorship, ignores the principles underlying the public forum doctrine, flies in the face of the decisions in which the Court has identified property as a limited public forum, and empties the limited-public-forum concept of all its meaning . . . . the public, limited-public-forum, and nonpublic forum categories are but analytical shorthand for the principles that have guided the Court's decisions regarding claims to access to public property for expressive activity. The interests served by the expressive activity must be balanced against the interests served by the uses for which the property was intended and the interests of all citizens to enjoy the property. Where an examination of all the relevant interests indicates that certain expressive activity is not compatible with the normal uses of the property, the First Amendment does not require the government to allow that activity.

The Court's analysis, it seems to me, turns these principles on end. Rather than recognize that a nonpublic forum is a place where expressive activity would be incompatible with the purposes the property is intended to serve, the Court states that a nonpublic forum is a place where we need not even be concerned about whether expressive activity is incompatible with the purposes of the property. Rather than taking the nature of the property into account in balancing the First Amendment interests of the speaker and society's interests in freedom of speech against the interests served by reserving the property to its normal use, the Court simply labels the property and dispenses with the balancing . . . .

Not only does the Court err in labeling the CFC a nonpublic forum without first engaging in a compatibility inquiry, but it errs as well in reasoning that the CFC is not a limited public forum because the Government permitted only "limited discourse," rather than "intentionally opening" the CFC for "public discourse." That reasoning is at odds with the cases in which the Court has found public property to be a limited public forum. Just as the Government's "consistent policy has been to limit participation in the CFC to 'appropriate' voluntary agencies and to require agencies seeking admission to obtain permission" from the relevant officials, *ante*, at 804,

the theater in *Southeastern Promotions, Ltd. v. Conrad* (1975), limited the use of its facilities to "clean, healthful entertainment which will make for the upbuilding of a better citizenship" and required productions wishing to use the theater to obtain permission of the relevant officials. Under the Court's reasoning, therefore, the theater in *Southeastern Promotions* would not have been a limited public forum. Similarly, the university meeting rooms in *Widmar v. Vincent* (1981), despite the Court's disclaimer, would not have been a limited public forum by the Court's reasoning, because the University had a policy of "selective access" whereby only registered nonreligious student groups, not religious student groups or the public at large were allowed to meet in the rooms . . .

The Court's analysis empties the limited-public-forum concept of meaning and collapses the three categories of public forum, limited public forum, and nonpublic forum into two. The Court makes it *virtually* impossible to prove that a forum restricted to a particular class of speakers is a limited public forum. If the Government does not create a limited public forum unless it intends to provide an "open forum" for expressive activity, and if the exclusion of some speakers is evidence that the Government did not intend to create such a forum, no speaker challenging denial of access will ever be able to prove that the forum is a limited public forum. The very fact that the Government denied access to the speaker indicates that the Government did not intend to provide an open forum for expressive activity, and under the Court's analysis that fact alone would demonstrate that the forum is not a limited public forum.

Further, the Court today explicitly redefines a limited public forum as a place which the Government intentionally opens "for public discourse." But traditional public forums are "places which by long tradition or by *government fiat* have been devoted to assembly and debate." *Perry* (emphasis added). I fail to see how the Court's new definition of limited public forums distinguishes them from public forums . . . .

The Court's strained efforts to avoid recognizing that the CFC is a limited public forum obscure the real issue in this case: what constraint does the First Amendment impose upon the Government's efforts to define the boundaries of a limited public forum? . . . . the Government did indeed adopt eligibility criteria in 1983 specifically designed to exclude respondents. Accordingly, the central question presented is whether those criteria need be anything more than rational.

The Court has said that access to a limited public forum extends only to "other entities of similar character." *Perry*. It never has indicated, however, that the First Amendment imposes no limits on the government's power to define which speakers are of "similar character" to those already allowed access. Obviously, if the government's ability to define the boundaries of a limited public forum is unconstrained, the limited-public-forum concept is meaningless. Under that reasoning, the defendants in *Widmar v. Vincent* (1981), would have been allowed to define the University's meeting places as limited to speakers of similar character to "nonreligious" groups; the defendants in *Southeastern Promotions, Ltd. v. Conrad* (1975) would have been allowed to define their theater as limited to plays of similar character to "clean, healthful entertainment"; and the school board in *Madison Joint School District v. Wisconsin Employment Relations Comm'n* (1976), would have been allowed to limit discussion of labor matters to persons similar in character to union representatives.

The constraints the First Amendment imposes upon the government's definition of the boundaries of a limited public forum follow from the principles underlying the public and limited-public-forum doctrine. As noted, the government's acquiescence in the use of property for expressive activity indicates that at least some expressive activity is compatible with the intended uses of the public property. If the government draws the boundaries of the forum to exclude expressive activity that is incompatible with the property, and to include that which is compatible, the boundaries will reflect precisely the balancing of interests the public forum doctrine was meant to encapsulate. If the government draws the line at a point which excludes speech that would be compatible with the intended uses of the property, however, then the government must explain how its exclusion of compatible speech is necessary to serve, and is narrowly tailored to serve, some compelling governmental interest other than preserving the property for its intended uses.

Petitioner does not even argue that the Government's exclusion of respondents from the CFC served any compelling governmental interest; she argues merely that the exclusion was "reasonable." The Court also implicitly concedes that the justifications petitioner offers would not meet anything more than the minimal "reasonable basis" scrutiny. I agree that petitioner's justifications for excluding respondents neither reserve the CFC for expressive activity compatible with the property nor serve any other compelling governmental interest . . . .

Even if I were to agree with the Court's determination that the CFC is a nonpublic forum, or even if I thought that the Government's exclusion of respondents from the CFC was necessary and narrowly tailored to serve a compelling governmental interest, I still would disagree with the Court's disposition, because I think the eligibility criteria, which exclude charities that "seek to influence . . . the determination of public policy," Executive Order No. 12404, 3 CFR 152 (1984), is on its face viewpoint based . . . .

Government employees may hear only from those charities that think that charitable goals can best be achieved within the confines of existing social policy and the status quo. The distinction is blatantly viewpoint based, so I see no reason to remand for a determination of whether the eligibility criteria are a facade for viewpoint-based discrimination.

I would affirm the judgment of the Court of Appeals.

JUSTICE STEVENS, dissenting . . . .

5

ASSURING THE FAIR ADMINISTRATION OF JUSTICE

The subject of this chapter is commonly known as the "free press–fair trial" controversy, and the conflict detailed is presented most sharply in the context of media publicity and criminal trials. For just as the First Amendment guarantees press freedom, so also does the Sixth Amendment guarantee the accused the right to a fair trial. And there are times when the achievement of the latter seems impossible without limits on the former. The existence of this conflict not only implies that the First Amendment cannot be regarded as an absolute but also casts doubt on some versions of the "preferred position" doctrine. For it is difficult to understand, when First and Sixth Amendment rights collide, why freedom of communication should always be given preference. The "free press–fair trial: controversy," then, provides one of the stronger arguments for a "balancing" approach to constitutional interpretation.[1]

It was not until 1961 that the Court first struck down a conviction on the basis of prejudicial pre-trial publicity. As early as 1941, however, it dealt with the underlying conflict, although in a case where trial had already been held. In Bridges v. California the Court reversed a contempt conviction against a labor leader for the sending of a telegram threatening a strike if a court decision were enforced. The companion case of Times-Mirror Co. v. California reversed a similar conviction against a newspaper which had printed an editorial warning a trial judge of the consequences to follow if he failed to impose a prison sentence on labor officials.

The Bridges decision was followed in the similar cases of Pennekamp v.

Florida (1946) and Craig v. Harney (1947). Lawrence Tribe has summarized the principles of this line of cases as follows: First, no clear and present danger can be posed by a publication which impugns the integrity of a judge or the administration of justice generally. Second, no sufficient danger can be held to arise from publication which criticizes a decision already made, or one which threatens future action. Rather, any danger which arises must relate to a pending or on-going judicial matter. And third, the Court will assume that judges will not be swayed in their decisions solely by public criticism.[2]

Wood v. Georgia (1962) involved a "pending or on-going judicial matter," but the Court nevertheless followed the teachings of Bridges. Wood, a county sheriff, harshly criticized a judge's instruction to a grand jury to investigate bloc voting and vote buying by and among the county's black citizens, publicly charging the judge with voter intimidation and racism. Chief Justice Warren's opinion reversing Wood's conviction recognized the importance of courts being able to conduct their business "in an untrammelled way," a right which, Warren said, "lies at the foundation of our system of government." But "consistent suppression of discussion likely to affect pending investigations would mean that some continuing public grievances could never be discussed at all, or at least not at the precise time when public discussion is most needed." Thus, ". . . in the absence of any showing of an actual interference with the undertakings of the grand jury, this record lacks persuasion in illustrating the serious degree of harm to the administration of law necessary to justify exercise of the contempt power. . . ."

The Court's opinion in Wood did not speak directly to the issue of "free press–fair trial." Chief Justice Warren carefully noted that "this case does not represent a situation where an individual is on trial" and that "the limitations on free speech assume a different proportion when expression is directed toward a trial as compared to a grand jury proceeding." Wood nevertheless, in its emphasis on the importance of public discussion of judicial matters, and its insistence on a showing of actual harm to judicial processes before First Amendment rights can be abridged, was a harbinger of things to come.

In Irvin v. Dowd (1961) the Court reversed a criminal conviction because of pre-trial publicity, but the majority opinion avoided any evaluation of the validity of restraints on the media. Reversal was on the ultimate grounds that, when eight of twelve jurors finally seated averred their belief in the accused's guilt, the conviction must be reversed. In such circumstances, said Justice Clark for the majority, the jurors' statements that they could nevertheless adjudge guilt or innocence fairly was entitled to little weight.

In Shephard v. Maxwell (1966) the petitioner was convicted of murdering his wife, allegedly in order to be free to marry his another. The case had all of the ingredients which some segments of the press, and of the public, find irresistible: the motive for the murder, the exposure of sexual promiscuity, and the social prominence of both victim and accused. Both the local and national press had a field day with the matter. Nationally known columnists adjudged Shephard guilty; the local press accused prosecutors and police of delay and delinquency in prosecution, and called for Shephard's conviction. The Ohio Supreme Court upheld the conviction, but referred to the atmosphere of the trial as a "three ring circus" and a "Roman holiday."

Twelve years after the trial, the Supreme Court reversed Shephard's conviction, on the grounds that extensive publicity had made impossible the achievement of a fair trial. The Court, however, avoided the potential clash of Sixth and First Amendment rights by laying the blame for the publicity on the trial judge's failure to exercise the proper control. Although Shephard made no First Amendment law, it foreshadowed the majority approach in Nebraska Press Association v. Stuart (1976), the first case reproduced in this chapter.

The trial judge in Nebraska Press, faced with a particularly gory multiple murder and massive media coverage of its aftermath, instituted a "gag order" which, as modified by the state Supreme Court, prohibited the media from divulging any of the confessions made by the defendant to the police or to other persons, or any other material "strongly implicative" of the defendant's guilt. The Nebraska Press Association sued to have the order rescinded and the Supreme Court complied.

Chief Justice Burger's majority opinion declined to establish priorities between the First and Sixth Amendments, and noted the "heavy burden" necessarily involved in justifying any prior restraint. The trial judge, Burger said, was correct in concluding that the pre-trial publicity might well have jeopardized the defendant's right to a fair trial. But the judge had found only that there was a clear and present danger that such an occurrence "could" result. Thus, the existence of such a danger was only "speculation." Further, other measures were available which might have mitigated the effects of unrestrained pre-trial publicity. The judge might have closed the preliminary hearing. He might have sequestered the jury. He might have moved the trial to another location, and/or postponed it to a later date. He might have employed "searching questioning" of prospective jurors. Finally, he could have used "emphatic and clear language" in instructing the jury to decide only on the facts presented at trial.

The concurring opinion of Justice Brennan asserted that there was no necessity for prior restraint in this case, for "judges possess adequate tools to resolve tensions between free press and fair trial," although "To be sure these alternatives may require greater sensitivity and effort on the part of judges . . . than would the stifling of publicity. . . ."

The Court's approach in Nebraska Press can be criticized on several grounds. In the first place, though Burger at the time rightly assumed the law to be different, the Court has virtually foreclosed the possibility of closing preliminary hearings. In Gannet Co. v. DiPasquale (1979) the Court did hold that suppression hearings could, with sufficient justification, be closed to the public. But, with Burger's partial cooperation, the Court has narrowed Gannet to involve only a Sixth Amendment right to access, and has made it all but impossible to close most preliminary hearings and other proceedings prefatory to trial.

Sequestration of the jury is a widely used method of controlling the effects of publicity which may occur during a trial. But its effect on pre-trial publicity, at stake in Nebraska Press, is problematic at best. Nor is "searching questioning" of prospective jurors necessarily an effective remedy. What the trial judge feared in the instant case was not that biased individuals would find their way onto the panel, but that widespread publicity would prevent the impaneling of any jury.

The alternatives of change of venue and postponement of the trial are commonly looked upon as effective methods of dealing with pre-trial publicity. But, it may be argued, each has a flaw which makes it objectionable as a method of mitigating the effects of pre-trial publicity. For each may conflict with another constitutional right. For the right to fair adjudication guaranteed by the Sixth Amendment includes a speedy trial, and one conducted by a jury "of the . . . district wherein the crime shall have been committed."[3]

It is true that the right is personal to the defendant and may be waived. But to "require" such waiver as an alternate to massive and prejudicial publicity is to elevate above it the right of the people to know, and the press to report, everything about a crime before guilt or innocence has been adjudicated. We may question the basis for preferring this latter "right" and the consequent validity of forcing a defendant to choose between the "vicinage" right and that of a fair trial. In the same vein is the alternative of trial delay, for such requires a defendant again to forego Sixth Amendment rights.

As to the alternative of "emphatic instructions" to the jury, the argument is that, since such instructions are generally used to cure the effects of various and possibly prejudicial missteps during the trial, they must be assumed to be equally effective in curing the effects of pre-trial publicity. As a matter of logic, this position seems correct. But it is somewhat unrealistic to expect that people can really discount the existence of that of which they have knowledge. We rely on jury instructions to cure the effects of trial misadventures because we have no alternative other than the granting of mistrials, not because we believe that jury instructions necessarily provide a cure commensurate with the disease. But in the case of pre-trial publicity, there is a readily available alternative, one which only a near absolutist view of the First Amendment, in which the "rights" of newspapers and the general public are viewed as always outweighing the defendant's rights, would reject.

One might also note that, besides the kind of prior restraints involved in Nebraska Press, there is also the possibility of previously enacted laws prohibiting the press from printing potentially prejudicial materials prior to the empaneling of the jury and/or the verdict in a criminal case. To uphold such laws would, of course, require recognition that there is usually little to be gained in the public's being informed as soon as such material becomes available.

In a series of cases decided since Nebraska Press the Court, with considerable unanimity, has explicitly recognized a First Amendment "right of access" for the general public and the press to be present at criminal trials. This right was first recognized in Richmond Newspapers v. Virginia (1980) where the Court reversed a Virginia decision upholding a closure order imposed, at the request of the defendant, at a trial for murder. The plurality opinion of Chief Justice Burger, joined by White and Stevens, based the "right of access" on the traditional openness of the criminal process, and the necessity to assure free communication on matters relating to the functions of government. This right, said Burger, though not absolute, was violated in the instant case in the absence of a showing that other alternatives would not have sufficed to secure the defendant's right to a fair trial.

In Globe Newspapers v. Superior Court (1982), Justice Brennan, with the support of five justices, held that the "right of access" was sufficient to invalidate a Massachusetts statute mandating the closure of trials for certain sexual offenses involving victims under 18. The right of access, said Brennan, exists to ensure that the constitutionally protected discussion of governmental affairs is an informed one. It is justified on the basis of the historical openness of criminal trials, and the significant role which the right of access to criminal trials plays in the "functioning of the judicial process and the government as a whole."

> Public scrutiny of a criminal trial enhances the quality and safeguards the integrity of the factfinding process, with benefits to both the criminal defendant and to society as a whole. Moreover, public access to the criminal trial fosters an appearance of fairness, thereby heightening public respect for the judicial process. And in the broadest terms, public access to criminal trials permits the public to participate in and serve as a check upon the judicial process.

This being so, though closure of trials on a case by case basis might be justified on a showing that "the State's legitimate concern for the well-being of the minor victim necessitates closure," the mandatory closure dictated by the statute in question was invalid.

Chief Justice Burger, author of the Richmond Newspapers plurality opinion, dissented along with Justice Rehnquist. For Burger the majority opinion had failed to follow Richmond Newspapers and its emphasis on the criterion of "historical openness." For the historical record demonstrated that trials of sex offenses, particularly those involving minor victims, had traditionally been closed. And, while the majority had questioned whether the statute could effectively prevent public knowledge of the identity of minor victims, for Burger the state's interest was not in preventing such identification, but in preventing the "severe psychological damage" involved in testifying in open court, before strangers.

Because it is the first case in which a majority of the Court agreed on a rationale for a "right to access" to criminal trials, and because that majority extended the right into an area, the protection of minors, traditionally regarded as worthy of special treatment, Globe Newspapers is excerpted in this chapter. Students will want to make their own judgments as to whether Justice Brennan or Chief Justice

Burger has the best of the argument over the values in conflict in that case.

The Court's insistence on "openness" has been extended not only to actual trials, but also to such prefatory activities as jury selection and preliminary hearings. In the case of jury selection a unanimous Court, in Press Enterprise Co. v. Superior Court (1984), rejected the view that either the right of the defendant to a fair trial or of prospective jurors to privacy justified the closure of *voir dire* examinations. In a 1985 case involving the same litigants, the defendant in a *cause celebre* child abuse trial requested that the court close the preliminary hearing in order to prevent publicity and preserve his right to a fair trial.

Chief Justice Burger, for a majority of seven, invalidated the closure, in part because of the "significant role" played by public access in the functioning of the particular process in question. Preliminary hearings, said Burger, were sufficiently like criminal trials that openness in their conduct could enhance "both the basic fairness of the criminal trial and the appearance of fairness so essential to public confidence in the system." Given this, closure was justified only if "essential to preserve higher values" and "narrowly tailored to serve that interest." Where the interest asserted, as here, was that of the defendant in a fair trial, it must be demonstrated that there was a "substantial probability" that these rights would be prejudiced, that closure could prevent them, and that reasonable alternatives could not adequately protect the defendant's rights.

In addition to its holdings on "rights of access," the Court has held that, even in the absence of such a right, the media cannot be prevented from publishing lawfully obtained information about judicial matters. Thus a state may not enjoin or punish the publication of a juvenile offender's name, or prevent the publication of information about proceedings before a state commission on judicial activity. And, despite the secrecy associated with the grand jury, a witness cannot be punished for making public his own testimony before such a body.[4]

Given the Court's insistence on the right of the media to publish, and its reluctance to allow limitations on pre-trial press activities in the context of sensational trials, the ability of the trial judge to control by the participants in criminal trials seems especially important. That ability, along with the trial judge's power to use the kinds of mitigating techniques described in Nebraska Press, was relied on in Shephard v. Maxwell, where much of the "circus atmosphere" surrounding the trial occurred because of a lack of restraint on the part of police and attorneys. Attorneys are, the Supreme Court observed in that case, court officers, and the trial judge could and should have restrained their statements, and that of police and other court personnel, with the press.

It does seem likely that such controls could go far to solve the problem of "free press–fair trial." But even this solution has its problems. For it is by no means certain that "gagging" court personnel can prevent media representatives from gaining information which is a part of the public record but which may nevertheless be prejudicial to a defendant. And the 6th Amendment right to a public trial, after all, belongs to the defendant, and seems rooted in the recognition that secrecy in criminal proceedings may be used to governmental advantage. Thus it is at least arguable that only the prosecution could effectively be presented from trying its case before the media.

Such a possibility was somewhat allayed by the very recent decision in Gentile v. State Bar of Nevada (1991), the final case excerpted in this chapter. In that case a majority of five to four reversed a Bar Association's imposition of discipline on the petitioner, on the grounds that the rule he was held to have violated was impermissibly vague and invited him to believe that he could give information to the press without fear of punishment. But a different five to four majority held that lawyers can be regulated under a standard not applicable to press publication of trial activities. Justice O'Connor voted with the first majority on the vagueness issue, and with the second on the issue of the standards applicable to attorney conduct in the context of pre-trial publicity. The difference in viewpoints on this issue are expressed in the majority opinion of Chief Justice Rehnquist, joined, in addition to O'Connor, by White, Scalia, and Souter, and the dissenting opinion of Kennedy, joined by Marshall, Blackmun, and Stevens. It is, again, for the student to determine which opinion best reconciles the interests at issue in the conflict between free press and fair trial.

---

[1]Lawrence Tribe argues that there is no real possibility of a conflict between the First Amendment and the defendant's rights. (*American Constitutional Law*, 2nd ed., 857. fn. 3). " . . . if pretrial publicity prevents the impaneling of an impartial jury, the defendant is entitled by the sixth amendment to a dismissal of the charges against him. The key conflict is therefore not between a defendant's . . . . rights and a publisher's . . . rights: the interests advanced to justify the suppression of prejudicial news are largely the state's interests - in putting guilty criminals in jail and in maintaining confidence in the jury system."

Professor Tribe's argument is not wholly convincing. It is certainly true that, in the extreme case, dismissal of charges will protect the defendant's rights. But it is not impossible, and seems very likely, that there will be cases in which a trial judge will conclude, erroneously, that publicity has not made impossible a fair trial. As a legal matter, his conclusion (subject to review) will stand. But if, as a matter of fact, publicity has caused the defendant to receive an unfair trial, and the trial judge's error is not corrected by an appellate court, then the defendant's conviction will stand, and the "publisher's rights" will have, indeed, triumphed over those of the defendant. It is, of course, true that errors of judgment are inherent in any system. But in this case the error could have been avoided had not the "public right to know" and the media's right to inform been given precedence.

In addition, Professor Tribe overlooks an important governmental (and public) interest in prosecuting the guilty. That interest is not only in "putting criminals in jail and in maintaining confidence in the fairness of the judicial system." It is also in removing dangerous people from our midst. Assuming, for example, that the person accused of the crimes which gave rise to Nebraska Press v. Stuart was indeed guilty, and that his ultimate conviction had been prevented by prejudicial publicity, a dismissal of charges would have vindicated his rights. But that would have been small comfort to those people cognizant of his factual guilt who might have been threatened by the fact of his freedom. Again, a risk would have been taken which, on any but an absolutist view of First Amendment rights, could have been avoided.

[2]Tribe, *American Constitutional Law*, lst ed. (Mineola, N.Y.: The Foundation Press, 1978), 624-625.

[3]Oklahoma Publishing Co. v. District Court (1977); Landmark Communications Co. v. Virginia (1978); Cohen v. Cowles Media Co. (1991). And see The Florida Star v. B.J.F., discussed in Ch. 10.

[4]This "vicinage" requirement, based initially on reaction to the British practice of removing colonial offenders for trial in England, is of more than historical importance. Imbedded in it is the belief that trial by one's neighbors may be crucially important as a way of preventing governmental tyranny.

NEBRASKA PRESS ASSN. ET AL. V. STUART, JUDGE, ET AL.

427 U.S 539 (1976)

MR. CHIEF JUSTICE BURGER delivered the opinion of the Court.

The respondent State District Judge entered an order restraining the petitioners from publishing or broadcasting accounts of confessions or admissions made by the accused or facts "strongly implicative" of the accused in a widely reported murder of six persons. We granted certiorari to decide whether the entry of suck an order on the showing made before the state court violated the constitutional guarantee of freedom of the press.

On the evening of October 18, 1975, local police found the six members of the Henry Kellie family murdered in their home in Sutherland, Neb., a town of about 850 people. Police released the description of a suspect, Erwin Charles Simants, to the reporters who had hastened to the scene of the crime. Simants was arrested and arraigned in Lincoln County Court the following morning, ending a tense night for this small rural community.

The crime immediately attracted widespread news coverage, by local, regional, and national newspapers, radio and television stations. Three days after the crime, the County Attorney and Simants' attorney joined in asking the County Court to enter a restrictive order relating to "matters that may or may not be publicly reported or disclosed to the public," because of the "mass coverage by news media" and the "reasonable likelihood of prejudicial news which would make difficult, if not impossible, the impaneling of an impartial jury and tend to prevent a fair trial." The County Court heard oral argument but took no evidence; no attorney for members of the press appeared at this stage. The County Court granted the prosecutor's motion for a restrictive order and entered it the next day, October 22. The order prohibited everyone in attendance from "releas[ing] or authoriz[ing] the release for public dissemination in any form or manner whatsoever any testimony given or evidence adduced."

Simants' preliminary hearing was held the same day, open to the public but subject to the order. The County Court bound over the defendant for trial to the State District Court. The charges, as amended to reflect the autopsy findings, were that Simants had committed the murders in the course of a sexual assault.

Petitioners—several press and broadcast associations, publishers, and individual reporters—moved on October 23 for leave to intervene in the District Court, asking that the restrictive order imposed by the County Court be vacated. The District Court conducted a hearing, at which the County Judge testified and newspaper articles about the *Simants* case were admitted in evidence. The District Judge granted petitioners' motion to intervene and, on October 27, entered his own restrictive order. The judge found "because of the nature of the crimes charged in the complaint that there is a clear and present danger that pre-trial publicity could impinge upon the defendant's right to a fair trial." The order applied only until the jury was impaneled, and specifically prohibited petitioners from reporting five subjects: (1) the existence or contents of a confession Simants had made to law enforcement officers, which had been introduced in open court at arraignment; (2) the fact or nature of statements Simants had made to other persons; (3) the contents of a note he had written the night of the crime; (4) certain aspects of the medical testimony at the preliminary hearing; and (5) the identity of the victims of the alleged sexual assault and the nature of the assault. It also prohibited reporting the exact nature of the restrictive order itself.

The Nebraska Supreme Court balanced the "heavy presumption against . . . constitutional validity" that an order restraining publication bears, *New York Times Co. v. United States* (1971), against the importance of the defendant's right to trial by an impartial jury. Both society and the individual defendant, the court held, had a vital interest in assuring that Simants be tried by an impartial jury. Because of the publicity surrounding the crime, the court determined that this right was in jeopardy. The court noted that Nebraska statutes required the District Court to try Simants within six months of his arrest, and that a change of venue could move the trial only to adjoining counties, which had been subject to essentially the same publicity as Lincoln County. The Nebraska Supreme Court held that "[u]nless the absolutist position of the relators was constitutionally correct, it would appear that the District Court acted properly."

The Nebraska Supreme Court rejected that "absolutist position," but modified the District Court's order to accommodate the defendant's right to a fair trial and the petitioners' interest in reporting pretrial events. The order as modified prohibited reporting of only three matters: (a) the existence and nature of any confessions or admissions made by the defendant to law enforcement officers, (b) any confessions or admissions made to any third parties, except members of the press, and (c) other facts "strongly implicative" of the accused.

. . . . prior restraints on speech and publication are the most serious and the least tolerable infringement on First Amendment rights. A criminal penalty or a judgment in a defamation case is subject to the whole panoply of protections afforded by deferring the impact of the judgment until all avenues of appellate review have been exhausted. Only after judgment has become final, correct or otherwise, does the law's sanction become fully operative.

A prior restraint, by contrast and by definition, has an immediate and irreversible sanction. If it can be said that a threat of criminal or civil sanctions after publication "chills" speech, prior restraint "freezes" it at least for the time.

The damage can be particularly great when the prior restraint falls upon the communication of news and commentary on current events. Truthful reports of public judicial proceedings have been afforded special protection against subsequent punishment. See *Cox Broadcasting Corp. v. Cohn* (1975); see also, *Craig v. Harney* (1947). For the same reasons the protection against prior restraint should have particular force as applied to reporting of criminal proceedings, whether the crime in question is a single isolated act or a pattern of criminal conduct.

Of course, the order at issue—like the order requested in *New York Times*—does not prohibit but only postpones publication. Some news can be delayed and most commentary can even more readily be delayed without serious injury, and there often is a self-imposed delay when responsible editors call for verification of information. But such delays are normally slight and they are self-imposed. Delays imposed by governmental authority are a different matter.

As a practical matter, moreover, the element of time is not unimportant if press coverage is to fulfill its traditional function of bringing news to the public promptly.

The authors of the Bill of Rights did not undertake to assign priorities as between First Amendment and Sixth Amendment rights, ranking one as superior to the other. In this case, the petitioners would have us declare the right of an accused subordinate to their right to publish in all circumstances. But if the authors of these guarantees, fully aware of the potential conflicts between them, were unwilling or unable to resolve the issue by assigning to one priority over the other, it is not for us to rewrite the Constitution by undertaking what they declined to do. It is unnecessary, after nearly two centuries, to establish a priority applicable in all circumstances. Yet it is nonetheless clear that the barriers

to prior restraint remain high unless we are to abandon what the Court has said for nearly a quarter of our national existence and implied throughout all of it.

We turn now to the record in this case to determine whether, as Learned Hand put it, "the gravity of the 'evil,' discounted by its improbability, justifies such invasion of free speech as is necessary to avoid the danger." *United States v. Dennis* (1950). To do so, we must examine the evidence before the trial judge when the order was entered to determine (a) the nature and extent of pretrial news coverage; (b) whether other measures would be likely to mitigate the effects of unrestrained pretrial publicity; and (c) how effectively a restraining order would operate to prevent the threatened danger. The precise terms of the restraining order are also important. We must then consider whether the record supports the entry of a prior restraint on publication, one of the most extraordinary remedies known to our jurisprudence.

Our review of the pretrial record persuades us that the trial judge was justified in concluding that there would be intense and pervasive pretrial publicity concerning this case. He could also reasonably conclude, based on common human experience, that publicity might impair the defendant's right to a fair trial. He did not purport to say more, for he found only "a clear and present danger that pre-trial publicity *could* impinge upon the defendant's right to a fair trial." His conclusion as to the impact of such publicity on prospective jurors was of necessity speculative, dealing as he was with factors unknown and unknowable.

We find little in the record that goes to another aspect of our task, determining whether measures short of an order restraining all publication would have insured the defendant a fair trial. Although the entry of the order might be read as a judicial determination that other measures would not suffice, the trial court made no express findings to that effect; the Nebraska Supreme Court referred to the issue only by implication.

Most of the alternatives to prior restraint of publication in these circumstances were discussed with obvious approval in *Sheppard v. Maxwell* (a) change of trial venue to a place less exposed to the intense publicity that seemed imminent in Lincoln County; (b) postponement of the trial to allow public attention to subside; (c) searching questioning of prospective jurors, as Mr. Chief Justice Marshall used in the *Burr* case, to screen out those with fixed opinions as to guilt or innocence; (d) the use of emphatic and clear instructions on the sworn duty of each juror to decide the issues only on evidence presented in open court. Sequestration of jurors is, of course, always available. Although that measure insulates jurors only after they are sworn, it also enhances the likelihood of dissipating the impact of pretrial publicity and emphasizes the elements of the jurors' oaths.

We have noted earlier that pretrial publicity, even if pervasive and concentrated, cannot be regarded as leading automatically and in every kind of criminal case to an unfair trial. The decided cases "cannot be made to stand for the proposition that juror exposure to information about a state defendant's prior convictions or to news accounts of the crime with which he is charged alone presumptively deprives the defendant of due process." *Murphy v. Florida.* Appellate evaluations as to the impact of publicity take into account what other measures were used to mitigate the adverse effects of publicity. The more difficult prospective or predictive assessment that a trial judge must make also call for a judgment as to whether other precautionary steps will suffice.

We have therefore examined this record to determine the probable efficacy of the measures short of prior restraint on the press and speech. There is no finding that alternative measures would not have protected Simants' rights, and the Nebraska Supreme Court did no more than imply that such measures might not be adequate. Moreover, the record is lacking in evidence to support such a finding

We must also assess the probable efficacy of prior restraint on publication as a workable method of protecting Simants' right to a fair trial, and we cannot ignore the reality of the problems of managing and enforcing pretrial restraining orders.

. . . . we note that the events disclosed by the record took place in a community of 850 people. It is reasonable to assume that, without any news accounts being printed or broadcast, rumors would travel swiftly by word of mouth. One can only speculate on the accuracy of such reports, given the generative propensities of rumors; they could well be more damaging than reasonably accurate news accounts. But plainly a whole community cannot be restrained from discussing a subject intimately affecting life within it.

Given these practical problems, it is far from clear that prior restraint on publication would have protected Simants' rights.

Finally, another feature of this case leads us to conclude that the restrictive order entered here is not supportable. At the outset the County Court entered a very broad restrictive order, the terms of which are not before us; it then held a preliminary hearing open to the public and the press. There was testimony concerning at least two incriminating statements made by Simants to private persons; the statement—evidently a confession—that he gave to law enforcement officials was also introduced. The State District Court's later order was entered after this public hearing and, as modified by the Nebraska Supreme Court, enjoined reporting of (1) "[c]onfessions or admissions against interest made by the accused to law enforcement officials"; (2) "[c]onfessions or admissions against interest, oral or written, if any, made by the accused to third parties, excepting any statements, if any, made by the accused to representatives of the news media"; and (3) all "[o]ther information strongly implicative of the accused as the perpetrator of the slayings."

To the extent that this order prohibited the reporting of evidence adduced at the open preliminary hearing, it plainly violated settled principles: "[T]here is nothing that proscribes the press from reporting events that transpire in the courtroom." *Sheppard v. Maxwell.*

The third prohibition of the order was defective in another respect as well. As part of a final order, entered after plenary review, this prohibition regarding "implicative" information is too vague and too broad to survive the scrutiny we have given to restraints on First Amendment rights.

The record demonstrates, as the Nebraska courts held, that there was indeed a risk that pretrial news accounts, true or false, would have some adverse impact on the attitudes of those who might be called as jurors. But on the record now before us it is not clear that further publicity, unchecked, would so distort the views of potential jurors that 12 could not be found who would, under proper instructions, fulfill their sworn duty to render a just verdict exclusively on the evidence presented in open court. We cannot say on this record that alternatives to a prior restraint on petitioners would not have sufficiently mitigated the adverse effects of pretrial publicity so as to make prior restraint unnecessary. Nor can we conclude that the restraining order actually entered would serve its intended purpose. Reasonable minds can have few doubts about the gravity of the evil pretrial publicity can work, but the probability that it would do so here was not demonstrated with the degree of certainty our cases on prior restraint require.

Of necessity our holding is confined to the record before us. But our conclusion is not simply a result of assessing the adequacy of the showing made in this case; it results in part from the problems inherent in meeting the heavy burden of demonstrating, in advance of trial, that without prior restraint a fair trial will be denied. The practical problems of managing and enforcing restrictive orders will always be present. In this sense, the record now before us is illustrative rather than exceptional. It is significant that when this Court has reversed a state conviction because of prejudicial publicity, it has carefully noted that some course of action short of prior restraint would have made a critical difference. See *Sheppard v. Maxwell.* However difficult it may be, we need not rule out the possibility of showing the kind of threat to fair trial rights that would possess the requisite degree of certainty to justify restraint. This Court has frequently denied

that First Amendment rights are absolute and has consistently rejected the proposition that a prior restraint can never be employed.

Our analysis ends as it began, with a confrontation between prior restraint imposed to protect one vital constitutional guarantee and the explicit command of another that the freedom to speak and publish shall not be abridged. We reaffirm that the guarantees of freedom of expression are not an absolute prohibition under all circumstances, but the barriers to prior restraint remain high and the presumption against its use continues intact. We hold that, with respect to the order entered in this case prohibiting reporting or commentary on judicial proceedings held in public, the barriers have not been overcome; to the extent that this order restrained publication of such material, it is clearly invalid. To the extent that it prohibited publication based on information gained from other sources, we conclude that the heavy burden imposed as a condition to securing a prior restraint was not met and the judgment of the Nebraska Supreme Court is therefore *Reversed.*

MR. JUSTICE BRENNAN, with whom MR. JUSTICE STEWART and MR. JUSTICE MARSHALL join, concurring in the judgment.

The question presented in this case is whether, consistently with the First Amendment, a court may enjoin the press, in advance of publication, from reporting or commenting on information acquired from public court proceedings, public court records, or other sources about pending judicial proceedings. The Nebraska Supreme Court upheld such a direct prior restraint on the press, issued by the judge presiding over a sensational state murder trial, on the ground that there existed a "clear and present danger that pretrial publicity could substantially impair the right of the defendant [in the murder trial] to a trial by an impartial jury unless restraints were imposed." *State v. Simants,* (1975). The right to a fair trial by a jury of one's peers is unquestionably one of the most precious and sacred safeguards enshrined in the Bill of Rights.

I would hold, however, that resort to prior restraints on the freedom of the press is a constitutionally impermissible method for enforcing that right; judges have at their disposal a broad spectrum of devices for ensuring that fundamental fairness is accorded the accused without necessitating so drastic an incursion on the equally fundamental and salutary constitutional mandate that discussion of public affairs in a free society cannot depend on the preliminary grace of judicial censors.

Respondents correctly contend that "the [First Amendment] protection even as to previous restraint is not absolutely unlimited." *Near v. Minnesota ex rel. Olson.* However, the exceptions to the rule have been confined to "exceptional cases." The Court in *Near,* the first case in which we were faced with a prior restraint against the press, delimited three such possible exceptional circumstances. The first two exceptions were that "the primary requirements of decency may be enforced against obscene publications," and that "[t]he security of the community life may be protected against incitements to acts of violence and the overthrow by force of orderly government [for] [t]he constitutional guaranty of free speech does not 'protect a man from an injunction against uttering words that may have all the effect of force. . . .'" These exceptions have since come to be interpreted as situations in which the "speech" involved is not encompassed within the meaning of the First Amendment.

And even in these situations, adequate and timely procedures are mandated to protect against any restraint of speech that does come within the ambit of the First Amendment. Thus, only the third category in *Near* contemplated the possibility that speech meriting and entitled to constitutional protection might nevertheless be suppressed before publication in the interest of some overriding countervailing interest: When a nation is at war many things that might be said in time of peace are such a hindrance to its effort that their utterance will not be endured so long as men fight and that no Court could regard them as protected by any constitutional right. *Schenck v. United States.* No one would

question but that a government might prevent actual obstruction to its recruiting service or the publication of the sailing dates of transports or the number and location of troops.

Even this third category, however, has only been adverted to in dictum and has never served as the basis for actually upholding a prior restraint against the publication of constitutionally protected materials. In *New York Times Co. v. United States,* we specifically addressed the scope of the "military security" exception alluded to in *Near* and held that there could be no prior restraint on publication of the "Pentagon Papers" despite the fact that a majority of the Court believed that release of the documents, which were classified "Top Secret-Sensitive" and which were obtained surreptitiously, would be harmful to the Nation and might even be prosecuted after publication as a violation of various espionage statutes. To be sure, our brief *per curiam* declared that " '[a]ny system of prior restraints of expression comes to this Court bearing a heavy presumption against its constitutional validity,'" quoting *Bantam Books, Inc. v. Sullivan,* and that the "Government 'thus carries a heavy burden of showing justification for the imposition of such a restraint." Organization *for a Better Austin v. Keefe* (1971) . This does not mean, as the Nebraska Supreme Court assumed, that prior restraints can be justified on an *ad hoc* balancing approach that concludes that the "presumption" must be overcome in light of some perceived "justification." Rather, this language refers to the fact that, as a matter of procedural safeguards and burden of proof, prior restraints even within a recognized exception to the rule against prior restraints will be extremely difficult to justify; but as an initial matter, the purpose for which a prior restraint is sought to be imposed "must fit within one of the narrowly defined exceptions to the prohibition against prior restraints."

It is thus clear that even within the sole possible exception to the prohibition against prior restraints on publication of constitutionally protected materials, the obstacles to issuance of such an injunction are formidable. What respondents urge upon us, however, is the creation of a new, potentially pervasive exception to this settled rule of virtually blanket prohibition of prior restraints. I would decline this invitation.

I unreservedly agree with Mr. Justice Black that "free speech and fair trials are two of the most cherished policies of our civilization, and it would be a trying task to choose between them." *Bridges v. California*. But I would reject the notion that a choice is necessary, that there is an inherent conflict that cannot be resolved without essentially abrogating one right or the other. To hold that courts cannot impose any prior restraints on the reporting of or commentary upon information revealed in open court proceedings, disclosed in public documents, or divulged by other sources with respect to the criminal justice system is not, I must emphasize, to countenance the sacrifice of precious Sixth Amendment rights on the altar of the First Amendment. For although there may in some instances be tension between uninhibited and robust reporting by the press and fair trials for criminal defendants, judges possess adequate tools short of injunctions against reporting for relieving that tension. To be sure, these alternatives may require greater sensitivity and effort on the part of judges conducting criminal trials than would the stifling of publicity through the simple expedient of issuing a restrictive order on the press; but that sensitivity and effort is required in order to ensure the full enjoyment and proper accommodation of both First and Sixth Amendment rights.

GLOBE NEWSPAPERS V. SUPERIOR COURT

457 U.S. 596 (1982)

JUSTICE BRENNAN delivered the opinion of the Court.

Section 16A of Chapter 278 of Massachusetts General Laws, as construed by the Massachusetts Supreme Judicial Court, requires trial judges, at trials for specified sexual offenses involving a victim under the age of 18, to exclude the press and general public from the courtroom during the testimony of that victim. The question presented is whether the statute thus construed violates the First Amendment as applied to the States through the Fourteenth Amendment.

The case began when appellant, Globe Newspaper Co. (Globe), unsuccessfully attempted to gain access to a rape trial conducted in the Superior Court for the County of Norfolk, Commonwealth of Massachusetts. The criminal defendant in that trial had been charged with the forcible rape and forced unnatural rape of three girls who were minors at the time of trial—two sixteen years of age and one seventeen. In April 1979, during hearings on several preliminary motions, the trial judge ordered the courtroom closed. Before the trial began, Globe moved that the court revoke this closure order, hold hearings on any future such orders, and permit appellant to intervene "for the limited purpose of asserting its rights to access to the trial and hearings on related preliminary motions." The trial court denied Globe's motions, relying on Mass. Gen. Laws Ann., and ordered the exclusion of the press and general public from the courtroom during the trial. The defendant immediately objected to that exclusion order, and the prosecution stated for purposes of the record that the order was issued on the court's "own motion" and not at the request of the Commonwealth. For the reasons that follow, and hold that the mandatory-closure rule contained in 16A violates the First Amendment.

The Court's recent decision in *Richmond Newspapers* firmly established for the first time that the press and general public have a constitutional right of access to criminal trials. . . . Underlying the First Amendment right of access to criminal trials is the common understanding that "a major purpose of that Amendment was to protect the free discussion of governmental affairs." *Miller v. Alabama* (1966). By offering such protection, the First Amendment serves to ensure that the individual citizen can effectively participate in and contribute to our republican system of self-government.

Thus to the extent that the First Amendment embraces a right of access to criminal trials, it is to ensure that this constitutionally protected "discussion of governmental affairs" is all informed one.

Two features of the criminal justice system, emphasized in the various opinions in Richmond Newspapers, together serve to explain why a right of access to *criminal trials* in particular is properly afforded protection by the First Amendment. First, the criminal trial historically has been open to the press and general public.

Second, the right of access to criminal trials plays a particularly significant role in the functioning of the judicial process and the government as a whole. Public scrutiny of a criminal trial enhances the quality and safeguards the integrity of the factfinding process, with benefits to both the defendant and to society as a whole." Moreover, public access to the criminal trial fosters an appearance of fairness, thereby heightening public respect for the judicial process. .And in the broadest terms, public access to criminal trials permits the public to participate in and serve as a check upon the judicial process—an essential component in our structure of self-government. In sum, the institutional value of the open criminal trial is recognized in both logic and experience.

The state interests asserted to support 16A, though articulated in various ways, are reducible to two: the protection of minor victims of sex crimes from further trauma and embarrassment; and the encouragement of such victims to come forward and testify in a truthful and credible manner. We consider these interests in turn.

We agree with respondent that the first interest—safe-guarding the physical and psychological well-being of a minor— is a compelling one. But as compelling as that interest is, it does not justify a *mandatory*-closure rule, for it is clear that the circumstances of the particular case may affect the significance of the interest. A trial court can determine on a case-by-case basis whether closure is necessary to protect the welfare of a minor victim. Among the factors to be weighed are the minor victim's age, psychological maturity, and understanding, the nature of the crime, the desires of the victim, and the interests of parents and relatives. Section 16A, in contrast, requires closure even if the victim does not seek the exclusion of the press and general public, and would not suffer injury by their presence. In the case before us, for example, the names of the minor victims were already in the public record and the record indicates that the victims may have been willing to testify despite the presence of the press. If the trial court had been permitted to exercise its discretion, closure might well have been deemed unnecessary. In short, 16A cannot be viewed as a narrowly tailored means of accommodating the State's asserted interest. That interest could be served just as well by requiring the trial court to determine on a case-by-case basis whether the State's legitimate concern for the well-being of the minor victim necessitates closure. Such an approach ensures that the constitutional right of the press and public to gain access to criminal trials will not be restricted except where necessary to protect the State's interest.

Nor can 16A be justified on the basis of the Commonwealth's second asserted interest—the encouragement of minor victims or sex crimes to come forward and provide accurate testimony. The Commonwealth has offered no empirical support for the claim that the rule of automatic closure contained in 16A will lead to an increase in the number of minor sex victims coming forward and cooperating with state authorities. Not only is the claim speculative in empirical terms, but it is also open to serious question as a matter of logic and common sense. Although 16A bars the press and general public from the courtroom during the testimony of minor sex victims, the press is not denied access to the transcript, court personnel, or any other possible source that could provide an account of the minor victim's testimony. Thus 16A cannot prevent the press from publicizing the substance of a minor victim's testimony, as well as his or her identity. If the Commonwealth's interest in encouraging minor victims to come forward depends on keeping such matters secret, 16A hardly advances that interest in an effective manner. And even if 16A effectively advanced the State's interest, it is doubtful that the interest would be sufficient to overcome the constitutional attack, for that same interest could be relied on to support an array of mandatory-closure rules designed to encourage victims to come forward: Surely it cannot be suggested that minor victims of sex crimes are the *only* crime victims who, because of publicity attendant to criminal trials, are reluctant to come forward and testify. The State's argument based on this interest therefore proves too much, and runs contrary to the very foundation of the right of access recognized in *Richmond Newspapers*: namely, "that a presumption of openness inheres in the very nature of a criminal trial under our system of justice. . . ."

JUSTICE O'CONNOR, concurring in the judgment. . . .

CHIEF JUSTICE BURGER, with whom JUSTICE REHNQUIST joins, dissenting.

Historically our Society has gone to great lengths to protect minors *charged* with crime, particularly by prohibiting the release or the names of offenders, barring the press and public from juvenile proceedings, and sealing the records of those proceedings. Yet today the Court holds unconstitutional a state statute designed to protect not the *accused*, but the minor *victims* of sex crimes. In doing so, it advances a disturbing paradox. Although states are permitted, for example, to mandate the closure of all proceedings in order to protect a 17-year-old charged with rape, they are not permitted to require the closing of part of criminal proceedings in older to protect an innocent child who has been raped or otherwise sexually abused. The Court seems to read our decision in *Richmond Newspapers*, as selling out a

First Amendment right of access to all aspects of all criminal trials under all circumstances. That is plainly incorrect. In *Richmond Newspapers*, we examined "the light of access to places traditionally open to the public" and concluded that criminal trials were generally open to the public throughout this country's history and even before that in England. The opinions of a majority of the Justices emphasized the historical tradition of open criminal trials. The proper mode of analysis to be followed in determining whether there is a light of access was emphasized by JUSTICE BRENNAN: "As previously noted, resolution of First Amendment public access claims in individual cases must be strongly influenced by the weight of historical practice and by an assessment, of the specific structural value of public access in the circumstances."

Today JUSTICE BRENNAN ignores the weight of historical practice. There is clearly a long history of exclusion of the public from trials involving sexual assaults, particularly those against minors. . . .

The purpose of the Commonwealth in enacting 16A was to give assurance to parents and minors that they would have this moderate and limited protection from the trauma, embarrassment and humiliation of having to reveal the intimate details of a sexual assault in front of a large group of unfamiliar spectators—and perhaps a television audience—and to lower the barriers to the reporting of such crimes which might come from the victim's dread of public testimony. . . .

Neither the purpose of the law nor its effect is primarily to deny the press or public access to information; the verbatim transcript is made available to the public and the media and may be used without limit. We therefore need only examine whether the restrictions imposed are reasonable and whether the interests of the Commonwealth override the very limited incidental effects of the law on First Amendment rights. See *Richmond v. Newspapers*. . . .

Our obligation in this case is to balance the competing interests: the interests of the media for instant access, against the interest of the state in protecting child rape victims from the trauma of public testimony. In more than half the states, public testimony will include television coverage.

For me, it seems beyond doubt, considering the minimal impact of the law on First Amendment rights and the overriding weight of the Commonwealth's interest in protecting child rape victims, that the Massachusetts law is not unconstitutional. The Court acknowledges that the press and the public have prompt and full access to all of the victims testimony. Their additional interest in actually being present during the testimony is minimal. While denying it the power to protect children, the Court admits that the Commonwealth's interest in protecting the victimized child is a compelling interest. This meets the test of *Richmond Newspaper*.

The law need not be precisely tailored so long as the state's interest overrides the law's impact on First Amendment rights and the restrictions imposed further that interest. Certainly this law, which excludes the press and public only during the actual testimony of the child victim of a sex crime, rationally serves the Commonwealth's overriding interest in protecting the child from the severe— possibly permanent—psychological damage. It is not disputed that such injury is a reality.

The law also seems a rational response to the undisputed problem of the underreporting of rapes and other sexual offenses. The Court rejects the Commonwealth's argument, that 16A is justified by its interest in encouraging minors to report sex crimes, finding the claim "speculative in empirical terms [and] open to serious question as a matter of logic and common sense." There is no basis whatever for this cavalier disregard of the reality of human experience. It makes no sense to criticize the Commonwealth for its failure to offer empirical data in support of its rule; only by allowing state experimentation may such empirical evidence be produced. . . .

The Court also concludes that the Commonwealth's assertion that the law might reduce underreporting of sexual offense fails "as a matter of logic and common sense." This conclusion is based on a misperception of the Commonwealth's argument and an overly narrow view of the protection the statute seeks to afford young victims. The Court apparently believes that the statute does not prevent any significant trauma, embarrassment or humiliation on the part of the victim simply because the press is not prevented from discovering and publicizing both the identity of the victim and the substance of the victim's testimony. Section 16A is intended not to preserve confidentiality, but to prevent the risk of severe psychological damage caused by having to relate the details of the crime in front of a crowd which inevitably will include voyeuristic strangers. In most states, that crowd may be expanded to include a live television audience, with reruns on the evening news. That ordeal could be difficult for an adult; to a child, the experience can be devastating and leave permanent scars.

The Commonwealth's interests are clearly furthered by the mandatory nature of the closure statute. Certainly if the law were discretionary, most judges would exercise that discretion soundly and would avoid unnecessary harm to the child, but victims and their families are entitled to assurance of such protection. The legislature did not act irrationally in deciding not to leave the closure determination to the idiosyncrasies of individual judges subject to the pressures available to the media. The victim might very well experience considerable distress prior to the court appearance, wondering, in the absence of such statutory protection, whether public testimony will be required. The mere possibility of public testimony may cause parents and children to decide not to report these heinous crimes. If, as psychologists report, the courtroom experience in such cases is almost as traumatic as the crime itself, a state certainly should be able to take whatever reasonable steps it believes are necessary to reduce that trauma. Furthermore, we cannot expect victims and their parents to be aware of all of the nuances of state law; a person who sees newspaper, or perhaps even television, reports of a minor victim's testimony may very well be deterred from reporting a crime on the belief that public testimony will be required. It is within the power of the state to provide for mandatory closure to alleviate such understandable fears and encourage the reporting of such crimes. . .

There is, of course, "a presumption of openness [that] inheres in the very nature of a criminal trial under our system of justice." But we have consistently emphasized that this presumption is not absolute or irrebutable. . . .

The Massachusetts statute has a relatively minor incidental impact on First Amendment rights and gives effect to the overriding state interest in protecting child rape victims. Paradoxically, the Court today denies the victims the kind of protection routinely given to juveniles who commit crimes. Many will find it difficult to reconcile the concern so often expressed for the rights of the accused with the callous indifference exhibited today for children who, having suffered the trauma of rape other sexual abuse, are denied the modest protection the Massachusetts legislature provided. . .

JUSTICE STEVENS, dissenting. . . .

GENTILE V. STATE BAR OF NEVADA

___U.S.___   (1991)

JUSTICE KENNEDY announced the judgment of the Court and delivered the opinion of the Court with respect to Parts III and VI, and an opinion with respect to Parts I, II, IV, and V in which JUSTICE MARSHALL, JUSTICE BLACKMUN and JUSTICE STEVENS join.

Hours after his client was indicted on criminal charges, petitioner Gentile, who is a member of the Bar of the State of Nevada, held a press conference. He made a prepared statement . . . and then he responded to questions.

Some six months later, the criminal case was tried to a jury and the client was acquitted on all counts. The State Bar of Nevada then filed a complaint against petitioner alleging a violation of Nevada Supreme Court Rule 177, a rule governing pretrial publicity almost identical to ABA Model Rule of Professional Conduct 3.6. Rule 177(1) prohibits an attorney from making "an extrajudicial statement that a reasonable person would expect to be disseminated by means of public communication if the lawyer knows or reasonably should know that it will have a substantial likelihood of materially prejudicing an adjudicative proceeding." Rule 177(2) lists a number of statements that are "ordinarily . . . likely" to result in material prejudice. Rule 177(3) provides a safe harbor for the attorney, listing a number of statements that can be made without fear of discipline notwithstanding the other parts of the rule.

Following a hearing, the Southern Nevada Disciplinary Board of the State Bar found that Gentile had made the statements in question and concluded that he violated Rule 177. The board recommended a private reprimand. Petitioner appealed to the Nevada Supreme Court, waiving the confidentiality of the disciplinary proceeding, and the Nevada court affirmed the decision of the Board.

Nevada's application of Rule 177 in this case violates the First Amendment. Petitioner spoke at a time and in a manner that neither in law nor in fact created any threat of real prejudice to his client's right to a fair trial or to the State's interest in the enforcement of its criminal laws. Furthermore, the Rule's safe harbor provision, Rule 177(3), appears to permit the speech in question, and Nevada's decision to discipline petitioner in spite of that provision raises concerns of vagueness and selective enforcement.

. . . this case involves punishment of pure speech in the political forum. Petitioner engaged not in solicitation of clients or advertising for his practice, as in our precedents from which some of our colleagues would discern a standard of diminished First Amendment protection.

His words were directed at public officials and their conduct in office.

There is no question that speech critical of the exercise of the State's power lies at the very center of the First Amendment. Nevada seeks to punish the dissemination of information relating to alleged governmental misconduct, which only last Term we described as "speech which has traditionally been recognized as lying at the core of the First Amendment." *Butterworth v. Smith* (1990).

The judicial system, and in particular our criminal justice courts, play a vital part in a democratic state, and the public has a legitimate interest in their operations. "[I]t would be difficult to single out any aspect of government of higher concern and importance to the people than the manner in which criminal trials are conducted" *Richmond Newspapers, Inc. v. Virginia. . . .*

Public awareness and criticism have even greater importance where, as here, they concern allegations of police corruption, see *Nebraska Press Assn. v. Stuart* (1976) (Brennan, J., concurring in judgment) "(commentary on the fact that there is strong evidence implicating a government official in criminal activity goes to the very core of matters of public concern)," or where, as is also the present circumstance, the criticism questions the judgment of an elected public prosecutor. Our system grants prosecutors vast discretion at all stages of the criminal process, see *Morrison v. Olson* (1988) (SCALIA, J., dissenting). The public has an interest in its responsible exercise. . . .

Even if one were to accept respondent's argument that lawyers participating in judicial proceedings may be subjected, consistent with the First Amendment, to speech restrictions that could not be imposed on the press or general public, the judgment should not be upheld. The record does not support the conclusion that petitioner knew or reasonably should have known his remarks created a substantial likelihood of material prejudice, if the Rule's terms are given any meaningful content. . . .

Neither the disciplinary board nor the reviewing court explain any sense in which petitioner's statements had a substantial likelihood of causing material prejudice. The only evidence against Gentile was the videotape of his statement and his own testimony at the disciplinary hearing. The Bar's whole case rests on the fact of the statement, the time it was made, and petitioner's own justifications.

Whether one applies the standard set out in *Landmark Communications* or the lower standard our colleagues find permissible, an examination of the record reveals no basis for the Nevada court's conclusion that the speech presented a substantial likelihood of material prejudice.

Petitioner is a Las Vegas criminal defense attorney . . . Through leaks from the police department, he had some advance notice of the date an indictment would be returned and the nature of the charges against Sanders. Petitioner had monitored the publicity surrounding the case, and prior to the indictment was personally aware of at least 17 articles in the major local newspapers, the Las Vegas Sun and Las Vegas Review-Journal, and numerous local television news stories which reported on the Western Vault theft and ensuing investigation.

Petitioner determined, for the first time in his career, that he would call a formal press conference. He did not blunder into a press conference, but acted with considerable deliberation.

1. Petitioner's Motivation.

As petitioner explained to the disciplinary board, his primary motivation was the concern that, unless some of the weaknesses in the State's case were made public, a potential jury venire would be poisoned by repetition in the press of information being released by the police and prosecutors, in particular the repeated press reports about polygraph tests and the fact that the two police officers were no longer suspects. Respondent distorts Rule 177 when it suggests this explanation admits a purpose to prejudice the venire and so proves a violation of the Rule. Rule 177 only prohibits the dissemination of information that one knows or reasonably should know has a "substantial likelihood of materially prejudicing an adjudicative proceeding." Petitioner did not indicate he thought he could sway the pool of potential jurors to form an opinion in advance of the trial, nor did he seek to discuss evidence that would be inadmissible at trial. He sought only to counter publicity already deemed prejudicial. . . .

Petitioner gave a second reason for holding the press conference, which demonstrates the additional value of his speech. Petitioner acted in part because the investigation had taken a serious toll on his client. Sanders was "not a man in good health," having suffered multiple open-heart surgeries prior to these events. And prior to indictment, the mere suspicion of wrongdoing had caused the closure of Western Vault and the loss of Sanders' ground lease on an Atlantic City, New Jersey property. . . .

2. Petitioner's Investigation of Rule 177.

Rule 177 is phrased in terms of what an attorney "knows or reasonably should know." On the evening before the press conference, petitioner and two colleagues spent several hours researching the extent of an attorney's obligations under Rule 177. He decided, as we have held, see *Patton v. Yount* (1984), that the timing of a statement was crucial in the assessment of possible prejudice and the Rule's application. . . .

In 1988, Clark County, Nevada had population in excess of 600,000 persons. Given the size of the community from which any potential jury venire would be drawn and the length of time before trial, only the most damaging of information could give rise to any likelihood of prejudice. The innocuous content of petitioner's statement reinforces my conclusion.

3. The Content of Petitioner's Statement.

Petitioner was disciplined for statements to the effect that (1) the evidence demonstrated his client's innocence, (2) the likely thief was a police detective, Steve Scholl, and (3) the other victims were not credible, as most were drug dealers or convicted money launderers, all but one of whom had only accused Sanders in response to police pressure, in the process of "trying to work

themselves out of something. . . ."

The stories mentioned not only Gentile's press conference but also a prosecution response and police press conference.

. . . . In the context of general public awareness, these police and prosecution statements were no more likely to result in prejudice than was petitioner's statement, but given the repetitive publicity from the police investigation, it is difficult to come to any conclusion but that the balance remained in favor of the prosecution.

Much of the information provided by petitioner had been published in one form or another, obviating any potential for prejudice. See ABA Annotated Model Rules of Professional Conduct 243 (1984) (extent to which information already circulated significant factor in determining likelihood of prejudice). The remainder, and details petitioner refused to provide, were available to any journalist willing to do a little bit of investigative work. Petitioner's statement lacks any of the more obvious bases for a finding of prejudice. Unlike the police, he refused to comment on polygraph tests except to confirm earlier reports that Sanders had not submitted to the police polygraph; he mentioned no confessions, and no evidence from searches or test results; he refused to elaborate upon his charge that the other so-called victims were not credible, except to explain his general theory that they were pressured to testify in an attempt to avoid drug-related legal trouble, and that some of them may have asserted claims in an attempt to collect insurance money.

As interpreted by the Nevada Supreme Court, the Rule is void for vagueness, in any event, for its safe harbor provision, Rule 177(3), misled petitioner into thinking that he could give his press conference without fear of discipline. Rule 177(3)(a) provides that a lawyer "may state without elaboration . . . the general nature of the . . . defense." Statements under this provision are protected "[n]otwithstanding subsection 1 and 2 (a-f)." By necessary operation of the word "notwithstanding," the Rule contemplates that a lawyer describing the "general nature of the . . . defense" "without elaboration" need fear no discipline, even if he comments on "[t]he character, credibility, reputation or criminal record of a . . . witness," and even if he "knows or reasonably should know that [the statement] will have a substantial likelihood of materially prejudicing an adjudicative proceeding. . . ."

Petitioner testified he thought his statements were protected by Rule 177(3). A review of the press conference supports that claim. . . . The fact Gentile was found in violation of the Rules after studying them and making a conscious effort at compliance demonstrates that Rule 177 creates a trap for the wary as well as the unwary. . . .

The analysis to this point resolves the case, and in the usual order of things the discussion should end here. Five members of the Court, however, endorse an extended discussion which concludes that Nevada may interpret its requirement of substantial likelihood of material prejudice under a standard more deferential than is the usual rule where speech is concerned. It appears necessary, therefore, to set forth my objections to that conclusion and to the reasoning which underlies it. . . .

At the very least, our cases recognize that disciplinary rules governing the legal profession cannot punish activity protected by the First Amendment, and that First Amendment protection survives even when the attorney violates a disciplinary rule he swore to obey when admitted to the practice of law. We have not in recent years accepted our colleagues' apparent theory that the practice of law brings with it comprehensive restrictions, or that we will defer to professional bodies when those restrictions impinge upon First Amendment freedoms. . . .

Only the occasional case presents a danger of prejudice from pretrial publicity. Empirical research suggests that in the few instances when jurors have been exposed to extensive and prejudicial publicity, they are able to disregard it and base their verdict upon the evidence presented in court. . . .

Voir dire can play an important role in reminding jurors to set aside out-of-court information, and to decide the case upon the evidence presented at trial. All of these factors weigh in favor of affording an attorney's speech about ongoing proceedings our traditional First Amendment protections. Our colleagues' historical survey notwithstanding, respondent has not demonstrated any sufficient state interest in restricting the speech of attorneys to justify a lower standard of First Amendment scrutiny.

Still less justification exists for a lower standard of scrutiny here, as this speech involved not the prosecutor or police, but a criminal defense attorney. . . .

The police, the prosecution, other government officials, and the community at large hold innumerable avenues for the dissemination of information adverse to a criminal defendant, many of which are not within the scope of Rule 177 or any other regulation. By contrast, a defendant cannot speak without fear of incriminating himself and prejudicing his defense, and most criminal defendants have insufficient means to retain a public relations team apart from defense counsel for the sole purpose of countering prosecution statements. These factors underscore my conclusion that blanket rules restricting speech of defense attorneys should not be accepted without careful First Amendment scrutiny. . . .

Because attorneys participate in the criminal justice system and are trained in its complexities, they hold unique qualifications as a source of information about pending cases. . .

If the dangers of their speech arise from its persuasiveness, from their ability to explain judicial proceedings, or from the likelihood the speech will be believed, these are not the sort of dangers that can validate restrictions. The First Amendment does not permit suppression of speech because of its power to command assent.

One may concede the proposition that an attorney's speech about pending cases may present dangers that could not arise from statements by a nonparticipant, and that an attorney's duty to cooperate in the judicial process may prevent him or her from taking actions with an intent to frustrate that process. The role of attorneys in the criminal justice system subjects them to fiduciary obligations to the court and the parties. An attorney's position may result in some added ability to obstruct the proceedings through well-timed statements to the press, though one can debate the extent of an attorney's ability to do so without violating other established duties. A court can require an attorney's cooperation to an extent not possible of nonparticipants. A proper weighing of dangers might consider the harm that occurs when speech about ongoing proceedings forces the court to take burdensome steps such as sequestration, continuance, or change of venue.

If as a regular matter speech by an attorney about pending cases raised real dangers of this kind then a substantial governmental interest might support additional regulation of speech. But this case involves the sanction of speech so innocuous, and an application of Rule 177(3)'s safe harbor provision so begrudging, that it is difficult to determine the force these arguments would carry in a different setting. The instant case is a poor vehicle for defining with precision the outer limits under the Constitution of a court's ability to regulate an attorney's statements about ongoing adjudicative proceedings. At the very least, however, we can say that the Rule which punished petitioner's statement represents a limitation of First Amendment freedoms greater than is necessary or essential to the protection of the particular governmental interest, and does not protect against a danger of the necessary gravity, imminence, or likelihood. . . .

The judgment of the Supreme Court of Nevada is *Reversed*.

CHIEF JUSTICE REHNQUIST delivered the opinion of the Court with respect to parts I and II, and delivered a dissenting opinion with respect to part III in which JUSTICE WHITE, JUSTICE SCALIA, and JUSTICE SOUTER have joined.

Petitioner was disciplined for making statements to the press about a pending case in which he represented a criminal defendant. The State Bar, and the Supreme Court of Nevada on review, found that petitioner knew or should have known that there was a substantial likelihood that his statements would materially prejudice the

trial of his client. Nonetheless, petitioner contends that the First Amendment to the United States Constitution requires a stricter standard to be met before such speech by an attorney may be disciplined: there must be a finding of "actual prejudice or a substantial and imminent threat to fair trial." We conclude that the "substantial likelihood of material prejudice" standard applied by Nevada and most other states satisfies the First Amendment.

Petitioner's client was the subject of a highly publicized case, and in response to adverse publicity about his client Gentile held a press conference on the day after Sanders was indicted. At the press conference, petitioner made, among others, the following statements: "When this case goes to trial, and as it develops, you're going to see that the evidence will prove not only that Grady Sanders is an innocent person and had nothing to do with any of the charges that are being leveled against him, but that the person that was in the most direct position to have stolen the drugs and the money, the American Express Travelers' checks, is Detective Steve Scholl."

"There is far more evidence that will establish that Detective Scholl took these drugs and took these American Express Travelers' checks than any other living human being. . . . the so-called other victims, as I sit here today I can tell you that one, two—four of them are known drug dealers and convicted money launderers and drug dealers; three of whom didn't say a word about anything until after they were approached by Metro and after they were already in trouble and are trying to work themselves out of something. Now, up until the moment, of course, that they started going along with what detectives from Metro wanted them to say, these people were being held out as being incredible and liars by the very same people who are going to say now that you can believe them." The following statements were in response to questions from members of the press: ". . . because of the stigma that attaches to merely being accused—okay—I know I represent an innocent man . . . . The last time I had a conference with you, was with a client and I let him talk to you and I told you that

that case would be dismissed and it was. Okay?

I don't take cheap shots like this. I represent an innocent guy. All right?

[The police] were playing very fast and loose . . . . We've got some video tapes that if you take a look at them, I'll tell you what, [Detective Scholl] either had a hell of a cold or he should have seen a better doctor."

Articles appeared in the local newspapers describing the press conference and petitioner's statements. The trial took place approximately six months later, and although the trial court succeeded in empaneling a jury that had not been affected by the media coverage and Sanders was acquitted on all charges, the state bar disciplined petitioner for his statements.

Gentile asserts that the same stringent standard applied in *Nebraska Press Assn. v. Stuart* (1976), to restraints on press publication during the pendency of a criminal trial should be applied to speech by a lawyer whose client is a defendant in a criminal proceeding. In that case, we held that in order to suppress press commentary on evidentiary matters, the state would have to show that "further publicity, unchecked, would so distort the views of potential jurors that 12 could not be found who would, under proper instructions, fulfill their sworn duty to render a just verdict exclusively on the evidence presented in open court." Respondent, on the other hand, relies on statements in cases such as *Sheppard v. Maxwell* (1966), which sharply distinguished between restraints on the press and restraints on lawyers whose clients are parties to the proceeding: "Collaboration between counsel and the press as to information affecting the fairness of a criminal trial is not only subject to regulation, but is highly censurable and worthy of disciplinary measures."

. . . . the outcome of a criminal trial is to be decided by impartial jurors, who know as little as possible of the case, based on material admitted into evidence before them in a court proceeding. Extrajudicial comments on, or discussion of, evidence which might never be admitted at trial and *ex parte* statements by counsel giving their version of the facts obviously threaten to undermine this basic tenet.

At the same time, however, the criminal justice system exists in a larger context of a government ultimately of the people, who wish to be informed about happenings in the criminal justice system, and, if sufficiently informed about those happenings might wish to make changes in the system. The way most of them acquire information is from the media. The First Amendment protections of speech and press have been held, in the cases cited above, to require a showing of "clear and present danger" that a malfunction in the criminal justice system will be caused before a State may prohibit media speech or publication about a particular pending trial. The question we must answer in this case is whether a lawyer who represents a defendant involved with the criminal justice system may insist on the same standard before he is disciplined for public pronouncements about the case, or whether the State instead may penalize that sort of speech upon a lesser showing.

It is unquestionable that in the courtroom itself, during a judicial proceeding, whatever right to "free speech" an attorney has is extremely circumscribed. An attorney may not, by speech or other conduct, resist a ruling of the trial court beyond the point necessary to preserve a claim for appeal.

. . . . Even outside the courtroom, a majority of the Court in two separate opinions in the case of *In re Sawyer* (1959), observed that lawyers in pending cases were subject to ethical restrictions on speech to which an ordinary citizen would not be. . . .

We think that the quoted statements from our opinions *In re Sawyer*, and *Sheppard* v. *Maxwell*, rather plainly indicate that the speech of lawyers representing clients in pending cases may be regulated under a less demanding standard than that established for regulation of the press in *Nebraska Press Assn. v. Stuart* (1976), and the cases which preceded it. Lawyers representing clients in pending cases are key participants in the criminal justice system, and the State may demand some adherence to the precepts of that system in regulating their speech as well as their conduct. As noted by Justice Brennan in his concurring opinion in *Nebraska Press,* which was joined by Justices Stewart and Marshall, "[a]s officers of the court, court personnel and attorneys have a fiduciary responsibility not to engage in public debate that will redound to the detriment of the accused or that will obstruct the fair administration of justice." Because lawyers have special access to information through discovery and client communications, their extrajudicial statements pose a threat to the fairness of a pending proceeding since lawyers' statements are likely to be received as especially authoritative. . . . We agree with the majority of the States that the "substantial likelihood of material prejudice" standard constitutes a constitutionally permissible balance between the First Amendment rights of attorneys in pending cases and the state's interest in fair trials.

When a state regulation implicates First Amendment rights, the Court must balance those interests against the State's legitimate interest in regulating the activity in question. The "substantial likelihood" test embodied in Rule 177 is constitutional under this analysis, for it is designed to protect the integrity and fairness of a state's judicial system, and it imposes only narrow and necessary limitations on lawyers' speech. The limitations are aimed at two principal evils: (1) comments that are likely to influence the actual outcome of the trial, and (2) comments that are likely to prejudice the jury venire, even if an untainted panel can ultimately be found. Few, if any, interests under the Constitution are more fundamental than the right to a fair trial by "impartial" jurors, and an outcome affected by extrajudicial statements would violate that fundamental right. See *Turner v. Louisiana* (1965) (evidence in criminal trial must come solely from witness stand in public courtroom with full evidentiary protections). Even if a fair trial can ultimately be ensured through *voir dire,* change of venue, or some other device, these measures entail serious costs to the system. Extensive *voir dire* may not be able to filter out all of the effects of pretrial publicity, and with increasingly widespread media coverage of criminal trials, a change of venue may not suffice to undo the effects of statements such as those made by petitioner. The State has a substantial interest in preventing officers of the court, such as lawyers, from imposing such costs on the judicial system and on the litigants.

The restraint on speech is narrowly tailored to achieve those objectives. The regulation of attorneys' speech is limited—it applies only to speech that is substantially likely to have a materially prejudicial effect; it is neutral as to points of view, applying equally to all attorneys' participating in a pending case; and it merely postpones the attorney's comments until after the trial. While supported by the substantial state interest in preventing prejudice to an adjudicative proceeding by those who have a duty to protect its integrity, the rule is limited on its face to preventing only speech having a substantial likelihood of materially prejudicing that proceeding.

The majority agrees with petitioner that he was the victim of unconstitutional vagueness in the regulations because of the relationship between 3 and 1 and 2 of rule 177. Section 3 allows an attorney to state "the general nature of the claim or defense" notwithstanding the prohibition contained in 1 and the examples contained in 2. It is of course true, as the majority points out, that the word "general" and the word "elaboration" are both terms of degree. But combined as they are in the first sentence of 3, they convey the very definite proposition that the authorized statements must not contain the sort of detailed allegations that petitioner made at his press conference. No sensible person could think that the following were "general" statements of a claim or defense made "without elaboration": "the person that was in the most direct position to have stolen the drugs and the money . . . is Detective Steve Scholl"; "there is far more evidence that will establish that Detective Scholl took these drugs and took these American Express travelers' checks than any other living human being;"

"[Detective Scholl] either had a hell of a cold, or he should have seen a better doctor"; and "the so-called other victims . . . one, two—four of them are known drug dealers and convicted money launderers." 3, as an exception to the provisions of 1 and 2, must be read in the light of the prohibitions and examples contained in the first two sections. It was obviously not intended to negate the prohibitions or the examples wholesale, but simply intended to provide a "safe harbor" where there might be doubt as to whether one of the examples covered proposed conduct. These provisions were not vague as to the conduct for which petitioner was disciplined; "[i]n determining the sufficiency of the notice a statute must of necessity be examined in the light of the conduct with which a defendant is charged." *United States v. National Dairy Products Corp.* (1963).

Petitioner's strongest arguments are that the statement was made well in advance of trial, and that the statements did not in fact taint the jury panel. But the Supreme Court of Nevada pointed out that petitioner's statements were not only highly inflammatory—they portrayed prospective government witnesses as drug users and dealers, and as money launderers—but the statements were timed to have maximum impact, when public interest in the case was at its height immediately after Sanders was indicted. Reviewing independently the entire record, see *Pennekamp v. Florida* (1946), we are convinced that petitioner's statements were "substantially likely to cause material prejudice" to the proceedings. While there is evidence pro and con on that point, we find it persuasive that, by his own admission, petitioner called the press conference for the express purpose of influencing the venire. It is difficult to believe that he went to such trouble, and took such a risk, if there was no substantial likelihood that he would succeed. . . .

Several *amici* argue that the First Amendment requires the state to show actual prejudice to a judicial proceeding before an attorney may be disciplined for extrajudicial statements, and since the Board and Nevada Supreme Court found no actual prejudice, petitioner should not have been disciplined. But this is simply another way of stating that the stringent standard of *Nebraska Press* should be applied to the speech of a lawyer in a pending case, and for the reasons heretofore given we decline to adopt it. . . .

JUSTICE O'CONNOR, concurring.

I agree with much of THE CHIEF JUSTICE'S opinion. In particular, I agree that a State may regulate speech by lawyers representing clients in pending cases more readily than it may regulate the press. Lawyers are officers of the court and, as such, may legitimately be subject to ethical precepts that keep them from engaging in what otherwise might be constitutionally protected speech. This does not mean, of course, that lawyers forfeit their First Amendment rights, only that a less demanding standard applies. I agree with THE CHIEF JUSTICE that the "substantial likelihood of material prejudice" standard articulated in Rule 177 passes constitutional muster. Accordingly, I join Parts I and II of THE CHIEF JUSTICE'S opinion.

For the reasons set out in Part III of JUSTICE KENNEDY'S opinion, however, I believe that Nevada's rule is void for vagueness. . . .

6

PROTECTION OF THE ELECTORAL PROCESS

The conflict between freedom of communication and the right to a fair trial provides, we have asserted, the clearest example of the need to balance First Amendment rights against competing governmental necessity. But the clash of interests involved in protecting the integrity of the electoral process is no less compelling, for elections are central to democracy and government must insure their integrity. And, it would seem, it has only slightly less interest in fostering the survival of entities such as political parties, without which a healthy democracy cannot exist.

As dealt with by the Court, five distinct types of issues have been involved with protection of the electoral process: whether government can restrict the political activity of certain of its employees; whether employment by government can be conditioned on adherence to a particular political party; to what extent government may regulate the operation of political parties; whether ballot access may be restricted for minority parties; and whether and to what extent government may regulate the contribution and expenditure of money in elections. Although the conditions giving rise to all of these issues have long been present, their formulation as judicial questions is of comparatively recent vintage and may be seen as a response to events which have made such questions seem particularly pressing, as well as a part of the willingness of the recent Court to try to solve such problems.

Before the rise of "big government," which in the United States had its origin in the New Deal, the issue of political activity by governmental employees was less urgent. Today, however, when almost twenty percent of non-military employment is in federal or state service, there is more reason to believe that at least some restrictions should be placed on the political activities of such employees. Fear that the sheer number of federal employees threatened to make possible the creation of a national political "machine"[1] led Congress, in the Hatch Act, to legislate limitations on such activity. Section 9 (a) of that Act forbade "an employee in any Executive agency or an individual employed by the government of the District of Columbia to . . . take an active part in political management or in political campaigns."

First upheld in United Public Workers v. Mitchell (1947), the Hatch Act received more recent consideration in Civil Service Commission v. National Association of Letter Carriers (1973). In that case several federal civil service workers challenged, as facially void, the Act and its amendments. The Court, upholding the Act by a six to three vote, first noted that it was content neutral and that it did not purport to control the opinions or beliefs of individuals, Federal employees were still free to vote and to express their political opinions privately. They were forbidden to do so only in formal and public ways.

Fundamentally, said the Court, such limitations arose from the need that governmental employees administer the law as Congress willed it to be, not in accordance with the views of political parties. Further, it was important not only that government employees practice "political justice," but that they "appear to be doing so . . . if confidence in the system of representative Government is not to be eroded . . ."

Additionally, employment and promotion in the public service should not be made dependent on political performance, and government employees should be free from pressure to vote in a certain way or to perform political acts to curry favor with their superiors. The Court was unwilling to disturb the judgment of Congress that this last goal could not be sufficiently achieved by the prohibition of coercion alone. Thus the Court agreed "with the basic holding of Mitchell that plainly identifiable acts of political management and political campaigning on the part of federal employees may constitutionally be prohibited." Further, said the Court, the Hatch Act's incorporation as a definition of "prohibited political acts" of those activities prohibited as such by the Civil Service Commission prior to a certain date did not make the act, as its challengers alleged, void for vagueness. For the purpose of that incorporation was merely to assure that no activities *other than* those which had then been prohibited were to come under the Act.

The dissenting opinion of Justice Douglas argued that the "incorporation" mentioned above did indeed make the Act impermissibly vague. (The regulations in question numbered more than eight hundred and were said to be inconsistent and even contradictory.) Additionally, the Act as a whole was an impermissible interference with First Amendment rights, for the sole allowable basis for limiting political activity by governmental employees should be whether such activity interfered with the particular employee's performance of the job.

The majority and minority opinions in Letter Carriers appear, as is not infrequent in such matters, to be talking past each other. Here, however, the crucial difference rests not in different perceptions of the facts, but rather in a different understanding as to their implications. For the majority surely did not disagree with Justice Douglas that improper performance of duties was the basic evil to be avoided. Rather, the dangers to which its opinion alluded outweighed any dangers to free communication presented by the Hatch Act.

Thus in Letter Carriers the Court, following the lead of Congress, recognized that partisan activity, and especially that engaged in by political parties, could create a threat to the fair and efficient functioning of the governmental service. More recent cases involving a somewhat different issue seem to have concluded that the governmental system, at least at the "civil service" level, must be purged of all vestiges of party influence. Somewhat ironically, those justices who were most defensive of the right to such activity in the context of government regulation have been most critical of it in the context of political patronage.

The seminal case on such patronage, Elrod v. Burns (1976), provides a good example of what might be called the Court's acceptance of the "goo goo" mentality. For the premises of the Elrod plurality are very similar to those accepted generally by early 20th century advocates of "good government," who saw the patronage system as incompatible with governmental efficiency and who succeeded, to a considerable extent, in rooting out that system. In doing so, of course, they made inevitable the rise of the very issue involved in Letter Carriers, the perceived necessity to prevent excessive political action by classified staff.

The first of the "patronage" cases arose in Cook County (Chicago) Illinois, one of the last bastions of machine politics. The vaunted Daley machine having several years earlier lost its grip on the office of County Sheriff (traditionally and throughout the United States one of the most patronage rich local offices), made a comeback. Led by the victorious Sheriff Elrod, it discharged or threatened to discharge a number of officials associated with the office of sheriff. The firings were based, not on any alleged inability of those affected to do their job, but rather on their inability or unwillingness to satisfy one of a number of traditional patronage criteria, including having a local leader of the "right" party as sponsor or indicating a willingness to contribute to the party. Those affected sued, alleging that the firings improperly interfered with their First Amendment rights.

The opinions in Elrod read somewhat like a seminar on the merits and demerits of the patronage system. Justice Brennan's plurality opinion, after defining the "general practice of political patronage," then asserted that "The cost of patronage is the restraint it places on freedoms of belief and association." Further:

> it is not only belief and association which are restricted where political patronage is the practice. The free functioning of the electoral process also suffers. Conditioning public employment prevents the support of competing political interests. Patronage thus tips the electoral process in favor of the incumbent party.

All of the interests said to justify the patronage system, said Brennan, were inadequate in the face of so direct an interference with First Amendment rights. Moreover, rather than promoting employee efficiency, the wholesale replacement of employees when political office changes hands actually made for inefficiency. The ability to discharge employees for cause, or to institute a merit system, would serve to make employees more accountable to the public than would any system which relies on the incentive of "machine reelection." The interest in ensuring the political loyalty of employees, while forceful, could be achieved by limiting patronage dismissals to policy positions, the holders of others not being in a position to thwart the goals of the in-party. And, contrary to the argument that patronage was necessary to preserve the democratic process and its concomitant, the political party: "Political parties existed . . . (prior to the Jacksonian period and its introduction of patronage) . . . and they have survived substantial reduction in their patronage power through the establishment of the merit system." More fundamentally, ". . . any contribution of patronage dismissals to the democratic process does not suffice to override their severe encroachment on First Amendment freedoms."

The dissenting opinion of Justice Powell took quite a different view.

Expressed in syllogistic form, Powell's argument was as follows: Parties are necessary to democracy; patronage is necessary to parties; thus patronage is necessary to democracy. Patronage increases involvement in elections, particularly in local elections. The lower one goes in the electoral system, the less likely it is that other stimuli for participation will be available. For issues are often mundane, and media coverage is slight. It is, therefore, naive to think that people will engage in politics at this level unless they see "what is in it" for them.

Justice Powell might have added, although he did not, that the lack of patronage motivations virtually assures that a *certain kind* of citizen will be most likely to be involved in politics. For if patronage is thrown out, the participation of ordinary people is, to a considerable extent, eliminated. Individuals who work an eight hour day are unlikely to get involved in politics unless they see some immediate benefit for themselves. To invalidate the incentive of patronage is, to a considerable extent, to leave the field to the upper-middle classes, or more accurately to those of any class who have the leisure to involve themselves without seriously harming their economic well-being.

The plurality opinion in Elrod reflected the views of only three members of the Court. Justice Stevens did not participate, and Justice Stewart and Blackmun concurred in the judgment only after confining the issue to whether a "nonpolicymaking, nonconfidential government employee can be discharged . . . from a job that he is satisfactorily performing upon the sole ground of his political beliefs." The distinction insisted upon by Stewart and Blackmun is akin to that made by Brennan in his argument about the relation of patronage to assuring that electorally sanctioned policies be faithfully implemented. It is attractive to the advocate of "balancing," representing as it does a "middle way" in the controversy. But it is at least arguable that the distinction between "policy" and "nonpolicy" positions is of little use. First, it seems very likely that the actions of "nonpolicy" personnel can affect implementation. Second, the distinction is almost necessarily vague, and one can be sure that a Court oriented to the Brennan viewpoint would resolve any matters of controversy to the detriment of patronage. And, of course, most of those likely to become involved in politics only in the presence of incentives are those who are likely to be qualified to fill only "nonpolicy" jobs.

The Elrod plurality opinion was confirmed in Branti v. Finkel (1980), in which the Court struck down the discharge by a politically elected public defender of two assistants who were members of "the other" political party. Branti is noteworthy not only for the majority's acceptance of the plurality position in Elrod, but also for its reformulation of Elrod's test of what politically-motivated discharges are constitutional. In Elrod this was said to depend on whether the position involved was "policy-making." But Justice Stewart, dissenting in Branti, rather conclusively demonstrated that the assistant public defenders at issue were precisely the kind of "confidential employees" said not to be covered by the Elrod test. Perhaps in recognition of this truth, the majority now stated the relevant criterion as to whether party membership was necessary to "continued efficient discharge of one's duties." Since few if any governmental positions would fulfill this criterion, the Branti formula significantly narrowed the degree to which party affiliation can be the basis for the selection of personnel. The dissenting opinion of Justice Powell once again emphasized the value of the patronage system to the health of political parties, and thus to democratic government.

In Rutan v. Republican Party of Illinois (1990), reproduced in this text, the Elrod-Branti line of cases resulted in the holding that patronage is an impermissible criterion for hiring, promotion, transfer, and return from layoff, except where it can be shown to be necessary to promote efficiency. The case contains, in Justice Brennan's majority opinion, an excellent example of the way in which the majority has dealt with the importance of patronage and, in Justice Scalia's dissent, an impassioned presentation of a different view. As such, Rutan presents an excellent opportunity for students themselves to weigh the contending issues and do their own "balancing."

Somewhat related to "patronage" is the right of the state to promote the creation of the type of political party system it deems best for its own citizens. This issue has been considered by the Court in two cases: Tashjian v. Republican Party of Connecticut (1986), and Eu v. San Francisco County Democratic Committee (1989). In both, the Court took the position, presaged by its holding in the Elrod-Branti line of cases, that the health of the parties is not of sufficient concern to justify state regulations superseding decisions of the parties themselves.

Thus in Tashjian the Court struck down a state regulation which prevented the Connecticut Republican party from opening its primary to persons not members of that party. Such a regulation, the Court said, burdened the right of the party and its members to free association. The interests said to justify the statute, that it ensured the ability to administer primary elections, prevented voter raiding, avoided confusion, and protected the integrity of the two-party system, were "insubstantial."

The Court's decision was made easier by the fact that, under applicable state law, individuals could register as late as the day before the election to vote in the primary of their choice. While this certainly undercut to a considerable extent Connecticut's asserted interest in discouraging "raiding," those who remember the lively debate among American political scientists over the desirability of "responsible party government"[2] will view with some discomfort the Court's rather cavalier disregard of that reputed state interest.

In a similar vein was the decision in Eu, which involved a California law that closely regulated the composition of the Democratic state committee (requiring, among other things, that the chairs of the state central committee be selected in alternate years from the northern and southern sections of the state), and imposed a ban on endorsement by the party's central committees of candidates in the party primary. (Individual committee members were free to make such endorsement.) All of this, said the Court, interfered with the rights of the party to make its own decisions as to what organization and leadership was best to secure its ends. In addition, the ban on committee endorsement interfered with the freedom of association of members of the party.

The Court's ultimate holding in Eu as in Tashjian was that the restrictions in question could not be justified in the absence of compelling state interests. The party, however, was free to make any such regulations as it deemed necessary. As to the ban on endorsement, the Court rejected the view that, where only one other state had such a ban, the necessity for it could be viewed as "compelling." The Court was careful to distinguish the instant cases from Smith v. Allwright (1944) and other cases where state regulation was in the service of another constitutionally required goal.[3] Taken together, however, Tashjian and Eu seem to back away from the long held judgment that political parties, because they conduct electoral activities which are governmental in nature, may be regulated to an extent not permissible in the private sector. Further, the Court, especially in its treatment of the "endorsement ban" and "rotating chairs" issues in Eu, seems to have foreclosed regulations which take into consideration the legitimate differences in the political, geographic, and economic makeup of the states. Thus, in so far as their political parties are concerned, the states seem to be foreclosed from acting as laboratories of experimentation, a function once regarded as primary for states in the federal system.

The decisions in Tashjian and Eu, as those in the "patronage" cases, can be said to rest on a formalistic view of what the First Amendment requires, and on a somewhat unrealistic perception of the realities of American politics. Something of the same may have influenced at least some of the Court's decisions on the issue of access to the ballot for minor parties.

The right of the states to limit minor party access to the electoral ballot is grounded in the need to foster efficiency in the administration of elections as well as to prevent confusion on the part of the voter. Such efforts have had a mixed reception in the Supreme Court. Restrictions operating in states in which the structure of elections make it virtually impossible for a minor party ever to have the opportunity to be on the ballot have been viewed with particular suspicion, although some have been upheld. By contrast, those restrictions which make it more difficult for a party to gain access to the general election ballot, but where they remain free to argue their case in primary elections, are less suspect. In general, Court majorities have held that states need only make a plausible case that the restrictions in question are related to a "compelling state interest," and that the laws in questions need not be narrowly tailored to the "least restrictive means" of achieving their goals.[4]

Court liberals, most notably Brennan and Marshall, have dissented from the Court's recent decisions in this area, arguing that a principal function of minor parties is voter education rather than electoral victory. Thus it is their access to the general election ballot, and the consequent ability to campaign when voters are most attentive, that should be protected. The answer given to this argument by Court majorities, both in the herein included case of Munro v. Socialist Party (1986) and in other cases, was that if voters are not as open to minority party persuasion in primaries as in general elections, that is not traceable to, and need not be remedied by the state. On balance, Brennan and Marshall seem to have the better of this argument, though there is irony in the fact that their view of the functions of minority parties displayed a sensitivity to political reality often absent in their approach to related issues.

To some extent at least, the reaction of the Court, and of most of its members to the most far-reaching and complex web of issues related to campaign financing may be said to suffer from the same insensitivity to political reality. The principal case in which these questions were addressed, Buckley v. Valeo (1976), is reproduced in some length at the end of the chapter, and we here consider its import only summarily.

At issue was the constitutionality of the Federal Elections Campaign Act of 1971, as amended in 1974. That law: 1) set limits on the amount of contributions by individuals both overall and to particular candidates; 2) limited independent expenditures by any individual or group for clearly identified candidates; 3) limited the amount of their own money that candidates for office could spend; 4) limited campaign spending by candidates for various offices, and 5) required that contributions and expenditures above certain levels be reported and publicly disclosed.

As indicated by its *per curiam* nature, and the fact that no less than five justices penned opinions "concurring and dissenting," Buckley v. Valeo was a difficult case, and certain of its holdings may be subjected to ready criticism. Chief Justice Burger was surely correct when he argued that applying the disclosure requirements to amounts as small as $10 and $100 is unnecessary, and that such requirements run a significant risk of "chilling" the exercise of First Amendment rights. Similarly, Justice Rehnquist seemed to make a valid point when he argued that the part of the public financing provision giving preference to long-established parties cannot be justified on the basis that "because no third party has posed a credible threat to the two major parties in Presidential elections since 1860, Congress may by law attempt to assure that this pattern will endure forever." And Justice Marshall's argument that limitations on personal campaign expenditures by the candidates themselves should be upheld on the basis of "the interest in promoting the reality and appearance of equal access among potential candidates" seems fully justified.

That part of the opinion which struck down overall campaign expenditures as interfering with the "quantity of speech" seems, along with that striking down limits on candidate expenditures, to be most out of line with reality. The Court attempted to justify its view by holding that such limits interfere with "deep and profound" discussion of the issues. But anyone familiar with American political campaigns knows that the result of unlimited spending is not weighty discussion, but overkill in the expression of the trivial. And it is not without significance that other democracies have successfully implemented limits on campaign expenditures.

One is tempted to argue that necessity provided, in a situation about which the Constitution speaks less than clearly, sufficient justification for upholding both the spending and contribution limits contained in the statute. In his opinion, Justice Blackmun contended that the distinction made by the Court between contributions and expenditures could not be made on a "principled, constitutional basis." And Justice Rehnquist was correct, in a sense, when he argued that contributions and expenditures are "two sides of the same coin." Yet, whatever it may lack in precision, the distinction suggested by the Court is not without value. Expenditure limits do seem to threaten more directly the exercise of free communication rights than do those on contributions. More importantly, limitations on contributions are a more direct, and one would think more effective, way of dealing with the overarching problem of corruption.

Thus, the core of Buckley may be seen as a delicate and perhaps effective balancing of competing interests. The validity of its central distinction, however, was called into question by a later case. At issue in Federal Election Commission v. National Conservative Political Action Committee (1985) was a section of the Presidential Election Campaign Fund Act. That Act offered major presidential candidates the option of having their campaigns financed by public funding, with consequent limitations on the amount which could be spent on the presidential campaign itself. Also limited, for those candidates who elected to receive such funds, was the spending of money on their behalf by independent political action committees.

Only the constitutionality of the latter issue was before the Court, which struck it down in language echoing that in Buckley. Limits on spending, said the Court, are a greater limitation on First Amendment freedoms than limits on contributions, and can be justified only in order to prevent corruption. But it is unlikely that presidential candidates will respond to, or that those spending money on their behalf will believe they will respond to, independent spending as a signal for *quid quo pros* on the part of government. Therefore such expenditures need not be limited to prevent either corruption or the appearance of corruption.

The dissent of Justice White, joined by Brennan and Marshall, stressed the Court's "credulous acceptance of the formal distinction between coordinated and independent expenditures," and urged that "it is pointless to limit the amount that can be contributed to a candidate or spent with his approval without also limiting the amounts that can be spent in his behalf." And Justice Marshall's dissent expressly recanted his agreement with the Buckley majority, on the grounds that he now viewed the effects of unlimited spending and contributions as the same, and that each implicated the same First Amendment interests.

---

[1]That this was not (and is not) an idle fear has been amply demonstrated in Mexico, where civil servants, the most important part of the "popular sector" of the ruling *Partido Revolucionario Institucional* contribute mightily and regularly to the success of national, state, and local segments of the PRI. Of course, such an outcome should be much less likely in a nation with a competitive party system.

[2]See Pendleton Herring, *The Politics of Democracy*, (N.Y.: W.W. Norton Co, 1965); Austin Ranney, *The Doctrine of Responsible Party Government* (Urbana, IL: The University of Illinois Press, 1962), and E.E. Schaatschneider, *Party Government*, (N.Y.: Holt, Rinehart, and Winston, 1942).

[3]Allwright was the definitive case in a series which finally succeeded in outlawing the "white primary," which device prevented Blacks from voting in Democratic party primaries, the only effective elections in what was then the "solid South." The key to this ultimately successful campaign was the Court's decision in United States v. Classic (1941), in which, overruling an earlier decision, it held that primary elections, "where the primary is by law made an integral part of the election machinery," were not merely "private." See also Terry v. Adams (1953), where even a "pre-primary primary" held by an ostensibly private organization was held subject to the requirements of the Constitution.

[4]See , e.g., Jenness v. Fortson (1971), American Party v. Texas (1974). And see, generally, Tribe, *American Constitutional Law,*, 2nd ed., 1101-1111.

RUTAN ET AL. V. REPUBLICAN PARTY OF ILLINOIS ET AL.

___U.S.___ (1990)

JUSTICE BRENNAN delivered the opinion of the Court.

To the victor belong only those spoils that may be constitutionally obtained. *Elrod v. Burns* (1976), and *Branti v. Finkel* (1980), decided that the First Amendment forbids government officials to discharge or threaten to discharge public employees solely for not being supporters of the political party in power, unless party affiliation is an appropriate requirement for the position involved. Today we are asked to decide the constitutionality of several related political patronage practices—whether promotion, transfer, recall, and hiring decisions involving low-level public employees may be constitutionally based on party affiliation and support. We hold that they may not.

The petition and cross-petition before us arise from a lawsuit protesting certain employment policies and practices instituted by Governor James Thompson of Illinois. On November 12, 1980, the Governor issued an executive order proclaiming a hiring freeze for every agency, bureau, board, or commission subject to his control. . . .

By means of the freeze, according to petitioners, the Governor has been using the Governor's Office to operate a political patronage system to limit state employment and beneficial employment-related decisions to those who are supported by the Republican Party. In reviewing an agency's request that a particular applicant be approved for a particular position, the Governor's Office has looked at whether the applicant voted in Republican primaries in past election years, whether the applicant has provided financial or other support to the Republican Party and its candidates, whether the applicant has promised to join and work for the Republican Party in the future, and whether the applicant has the support of Republican Party officials at state or local levels.

Five people (including the three petitioners) brought suit against various Illinois and Republican Party officials in the United States District Court for the Central District of Illinois. They alleged that they had suffered discrimination with respect to state employment because they had not been supporters of the State's Republican Party and that this discrimination violates the First Amendment.
. . . .

The same First Amendment concerns that underlay our decisions in *Elrod* and *Branti* are implicated here. Employees who do not compromise their beliefs stand to lose the considerable increases in pay and job satisfaction attendant to promotions, the hours and maintenance expenses that are consumed by long daily commutes, and even their jobs if they are not rehired after a "temporary" layoff. These are significant penalties and are imposed for the exercise of rights guaranteed by the First Amendment. Unless these patronage practices are narrowly tailored to further vital government interests, we must conclude that they impermissibly encroach on First Amendment freedoms.

We find, however, that our conclusions in *Elrod* and *Branti* are equally applicable to the patronage practices at issue here. A government's interest in securing effective employees can be met by discharging, demoting or transferring staffmembers whose work is deficient. A government's interest in securing employees who will loyally implement its policies can be adequately served by choosing or dismissing certain high-level employees on the basis of their political views. Likewise, the "preservation of the democratic process" is no more furthered by the patronage promotions, transfers, and rehires at issue here than it is by patronage dismissals. First, "political parties are nurtured by other, less intrusive and equally effective methods." Political parties have already survived the substantial decline in patronage employment practices in this century. Respondents, who include the Governor of Illinois and other state officials, do not suggest any other overriding government interest in favoring Republican Party supporters for promotion, transfer, and rehire.

We therefore determine that promotions, transfers, and recalls after layoffs based on political affiliation or support are an impermissible infringement on the First Amendment rights of public employees. . . .

Whether the employees were in fact denied promotions, transfers, or rehire for failure to affiliate with and support the Republican Party is for the District Court to decide in the first instance. What we decide today is that such denials are irreconcilable with the Constitution and that the allegations of the four employees state claims for violations of the First and Fourteenth Amendments. Therefore, although we affirm the Seventh Circuit's judgment to reverse the District Court's dismissal of these claims and remand them for further proceedings, we do not adopt the Seventh Circuit's reasoning.

JUSTICE STEVENS, concurring. . . .

JUSTICE SCALIA, with whom THE CHIEF JUSTICE and JUSTICE KENNEDY join, and with whom JUSTICE O'CONNOR joins as to Parts II and III, dissenting.

Today the Court establishes the

constitutional principle that party membership is not a permissible factor in the dispensation of government jobs, except those jobs for the performance of which party affiliation is an "appropriate requirement." It is hard to say precisely (or even generally) what that exception means, but if there is any category of jobs for whose performance party affiliation is not an appropriate requirement, it is the job of being a judge, where partisanship is not only unneeded but positively undesirable. It is, however, rare that a federal administration of one party will appoint a judge from another party. And it has always been rare. See *Marbury v. Madison* (1803). Thus, the new principle that the Court today announces will be enforced by a corps of judges (the Members of this Court included) who overwhelmingly owe their office to its violation. Something must be wrong here, and I suggest it is the Court. . . .

The restrictions that the Constitution places upon the government in its capacity as lawmaker, i. e., as the regulator of private conduct, are not the same as the restrictions that it places upon the government in its capacity as employer. We have recognized this in many contexts, with respect to many different constitutional guarantees. . . .

Once it is acknowledged that the Constitution's prohibition against laws "abridging the freedom of speech" does not apply to laws enacted in the government's capacity as employer the same way it does to laws enacted in the government's capacity as regulator of private conduct, it may sometimes be difficult to assess what employment practices are permissible and what are not. That seems to me not a difficult question, however, in the present context. The provisions of the Bill of Rights were designed to restrain transient majorities from impairing long-recognized personal liberties. They did not create by implication novel individual rights overturning accepted political norms. Thus, when a practice not expressly prohibited by the text ŏf the Bill of Rights bears the endorsement of a long tradition of open, widespread, and unchallenged use that dates back to the beginning of the Republic, we have no proper basis for

striking it down. Such a venerable and accepted tradition is not to be laid on the examining table and scrutinized for its conformity to some abstract principle of First-Amendment adjudication devised by this Court. To the contrary, such traditions are themselves the stuff out of which the Court's principles are to be formed. They are, in these uncertain areas, the very points of reference by which the legitimacy or illegitimacy of other practices are to be figured out. When it appears that the latest "rule," or "three-part test," or "balancing test" devised by the Court has placed us on a collision course with such a landmark practice, it is the former that must be recalculated by us, and not the latter that must be abandoned by our citizens. I know of no other way to formulate a constitutional jurisprudence that reflects, as it should, the principles adhered to, over time, by the American people, rather than those favored by the personal (and necessarily shifting) philosophical dispositions of a majority of this Court.

I will not describe at length the claim of patronage to landmark status as one of our accepted political traditions. Justice Powell discussed it in his dissenting opinions in *Elrod* and *Branti*. Suffice it to say that patronage was, without any thought that it could be unconstitutional, a basis for government employment from the earliest days of the Republic until *Elrod*—and has continued unabated since *Elrod*, to the extent still permitted by that unfortunate decision. Given that unbroken tradition regarding the application of an ambiguous constitutional text, there was in my view no basis for holding that patronage-based dismissals violated the First Amendment—much less for holding, as the Court does today, that even patronage hiring does so.

Even accepting the Court's own mode of analysis, however, and engaging in "balancing" a tradition that ought to be part of the scales, *Elrod*, *Branti*, and today's extension of them seem to me wrong. . . . .

Even laying tradition entirely aside, it seems to me our balancing test is amply met. I assume, as the Court's opinion assumes, that the balancing is to be done on a generalized basis, and not case-by-case. The Court holds that the governmental benefits of patronage cannot reasonably be thought to outweigh its "coercive" effects (even the lesser "coercive" effects of patronage hiring as opposed to patronage firing) not merely in 1990 in the State of Illinois, but at any time in any of the numerous political subdivisions of this vast country. It seems to me that categorical pronouncement reflects a naive vision of politics and an inadequate appreciation of the systemic effects of patronage in promoting political stability and facilitating the social and political integration of previously powerless groups. . . .

The Court simply refuses to acknowledge the link between patronage and party discipline, and between that and party success. It relies (as did the plurality in *Elrod*) on a single study of a rural Pennsylvania county by Professor Sorauf—a work that has been described as "more persuasive about the ineffectuality of Democratic leaders in Centre County than about the generalizability of [its] findings." *Wolfinger*. It is unpersuasive to claim, as the Court does, that party workers are now obsolete because campaigns are now conducted through media and other money-intensive means. Those techniques have supplemented but not supplanted personal contacts. Certainly they have not made personal contacts unnecessary in campaigns for the lower-level offices that are the foundations of party strength, nor have they replaced the myriad functions performed by party regulars not directly related to campaigning. And to the extent such techniques have replaced older methods of campaigning (partly in response to the limitations the Court has placed on patronage), the political system is not clearly better off. . . .

It is self-evident that eliminating patronage will significantly undermine party discipline; and that as party discipline wanes, so will the strength of the two-party system. But, says the Court, "[p]olitical parties have already survived the substantial decline in patronage employment practices in this century." This is almost verbatim what was said in *Elrod*. Fourteen years later it seems much less convincing.

. . . . Parties have assuredly survived—but as what? As the forges upon which many of the essential compromises of American political life are hammered out? Or merely as convenient vehicles for the conducting of national presidential elections?

The patronage system does not, of course, merely foster political parties in general; it fosters the two-party system in particular. When getting a job, as opposed to effectuating a particular substantive policy, is an available incentive for party-workers, those attracted by that incentive are likely to work for the party that has the best chance of displacing the "ins," rather than for some splinter group that has a more attractive political philosophy but little hope of success. Not only is a two-party system more likely to emerge, but the differences between those parties are more likely to be moderated, as each has a relatively greater interest in appealing to a majority of the electorate and a relatively lesser interest in furthering philosophies or programs that are far from the mainstream. The stabilizing effects of such a system are obvious. . . .

Patronage, moreover, has been a powerful means of achieving the social and political integration of excluded groups. By supporting and ultimately dominating a particular party "machine," racial and ethnic minorities have-- on the basis of their politics rather than their race or ethnicity—acquired the patronage awards the machine had power to confer. No one disputes the historical accuracy of this observation, and there is no reason to think that patronage can no longer serve that function. The abolition of patronage, however, prevents groups that have only recently obtained political power, especially blacks, from following this path to economic and social advancement.

"Every ethnic group that has achieved political power in American cities has used the bureaucracy to provide jobs in return for political support. It's only when Blacks begin to play the same game that the rules get changed. Now the use of such jobs to build political bases becomes an 'evil' activity, and the city insists on taking the control back "downtown.""

. . . . But when precedent is not only wrong, not only recent, not only contradicted by a long prior tradition, but also has proved unworkable in practice, then all reluctance ought to disappear. In my view that is the situation here. Though unwilling to leave it to the political process to draw the line between desirable and undesirable patronage, the Court has neither been prepared to rule that no such line exists (i. e., that all patronage is unconstitutional) nor able to design the line itself in a manner that judges, lawyers, and public employees can understand. *Elrod* allowed patronage dismissals of persons in "policymaking" or "confidential" positions. *Branti* retreated from that formulation, asking instead "whether the hiring authority can demonstrate that party affiliation is an appropriate requirement for the effective performance of the public office involved." What that means is anybody's guess. The Courts of Appeals have devised various tests for determining when "affiliation is an appropriate requirement." These interpretations of *Branti* are not only significantly at variance with each other; they are still so general that for most positions it is impossible to know whether party affiliation is a permissible requirement until a court renders its decision. . . . .

A few examples will illustrate the shambles *Branti* has produced. A city cannot fire a deputy sheriff because of his political affiliation but then again perhaps it can, especially if he is called the "police captain." A county cannot fire on that basis its attorney for the department of social services, nor its assistant attorney for family court, but a city can fire its solicitor and his assistants, or its assistant city attorney, or its assistant state's attorney, or its corporation counsel. A city cannot discharge its deputy court clerk for his political affiliation," but it can fire its legal assistant to the clerk on that basis. Firing a juvenile court bailiff seems impermissible, but it may be permissible if he is assigned permanently to a single judge. " A city cannot fire on partisan grounds its director of roads, but it can fire the second in command of the water department. A government cannot discharge for political reasons the senior vice president of its development bank, but it can discharge the regional director of its rural housing administration. . . .

The appropriate "mix" of party-based employment is a political question if there ever was one, and we should give it back to the voters of the various political units to decide, through civil-service legislation crafted to suit the time and place, which mix is best.

MUNRO, SECRETARY OF STATE OF WASHINGTON V. SOCIALIST WORKERS PARTY ET AL.

479 U.S. 189 (1986)

JUSTICE WHITE delivered the opinion of the Court.

The State of Washington requires that a minor-party candidate for partisan office receive at least 1% of all votes cast for that office in the State's primary election before the candidate's name will be placed on the general election ballot. The question for decision is whether this statutory requirement, as applied to candidates for statewide offices, violates the First and Fourteenth Amendments to the United States Constitution. The Court

of Appeals for the Ninth Circuit declared the provision unconstitutional. We reverse. . . . Restrictions upon the access of political parties to the ballot impinge upon the rights of individuals to associate for political purposes, as well as the rights of qualified voters to cast their votes effectively, *Williams v. Rhodes* (1968), and may not survive scrutiny under the First and Fourteenth Amendments. In *Williams v. Rhodes,* for example, we held unconstitutional the election laws of Ohio insofar as in combination they made it virtually impossible for a new political party to be placed on the ballot, even if the party had hundreds of thousands of adherents. These associational rights, however, are not absolute and are necessarily subject to qualification if elections are to be run fairly and effectively. *Storer v. Brown* (1974).

The Court of Appeals determined that Washington's interest in insuring that candidates had sufficient community support did not justify the enactment of 29.18.110 because "Washington's political history evidences no voter confusion from ballot overcrowding." We accept this historical fact, but it does not require invalidation of 29.18.110.

We have never required a State to make a particularized showing of the existence of voter confusion, ballot overcrowding, or the presence of frivolous candidacies prior to the imposition of reasonable restrictions on ballot access. In *Jenness v. Fortson*, we conducted no inquiry into the sufficiency and quantum of the data supporting the reasons for Georgia's 5% petition-signature requirement. In *American Party of Texas v. White*, we upheld the 1% petition-signature requirement, asserting that the "State's" admittedly vital interests are sufficiently implicated to insist that political parties appearing on the general ballot demonstrate a significant, measurable quantum of community support. And, in *Storer v. Brown*, we upheld California's statutory provisions that denied ballot access to an independent candidate if the candidate had been affiliated with any political party within one year prior to the immediately preceding primary election. We recognized that California had a "compelling" interest in maintaining the integrity of its political processes, and that the disaffiliation requirement furthered this interest and was therefore valid, even though it was an absolute bar to attaining a ballot position. We asserted that "[i]t appears obvious to us that the one-year disaffiliation provision furthers the State's interest in the stability of its political system." There is no indication that we held California to the burden of demonstrating empirically the objective effects on political stability that were produced by the 1-year disaffiliation requirement. . . .

In any event, the record here suggests that revision of 29.18.110 was, in fact, linked to the state legislature's perception that the general election ballot was becoming cluttered with candidates from minor parties who did not command significant voter support. In 1976, one year prior to revision of 29.18.110, the largest number of minor political parties in Washington's history—12—appeared on the general election ballot. The record demonstrates that at least part of the legislative impetus for revision of 29.18.110 was concern about minor parties having such easy access to Washington's general election ballot.

The primary election in Washington, like its counterpart in California, is "an integral part of the entire election process . . . [that] functions to winnow out and finally reject all but the chosen candidates." *Storer v. Brown*. We think that the State can properly reserve the general election ballot "for major struggles," by conditioning access to that ballot on a showing of a modicum of voter support. In this respect, the fact that the State is willing to have a long and complicated ballot at the primary provides no measure of what it may require for access to the general election ballot. The State of Washington was clearly entitled to raise the ante for ballot access, to simplify the general election ballot, and to avoid the possibility of unrestrained factionalism at the general election.

Appellees urge that this case differs substantially from our previous cases because requiring primary votes to qualify for a position on the general election ballot is qualitatively more restrictive than requiring signatures on a nominating petition. In effect, their submission would foreclose any use of the primary election to determine a minor party's qualification for the general ballot. We are unpersuaded, however, that the differences between the two mechanisms are of constitutional dimension. Because Washington provides a "blanket primary," minor-party candidates can campaign among the entire pool of registered voters. Effort and resources that would otherwise be directed at securing petition signatures can instead be channeled into campaigns to "get the vote out," foster candidate name recognition, and educate the electorate. To be sure, candidates must demonstrate, through their ability to secure votes at the primary election, that they enjoy a modicum of community support in order to advance to the general election. But requiring candidates to demonstrate such support is precisely what we have held States are permitted to do.

Appellees argue that voter turnout at primary elections is generally lower than the turnout at general elections, and therefore enactment of 29.18.110 has reduced the pool of potential supporters from which Party candidates can secure 1% of the vote. We perceive no more force to this argument than we would with an argument by a losing candidate that his supporters' constitutional rights were infringed by their failure to participate in the election. Washington has created no impediment to voting at the primary elections; every supporter of the Party in the State is free to cast his or her ballot for the Party's candidates. As was the case in *Jenness v. Fortson* (1971), candidates and members of small or newly formed political organizations are wholly free to associate, to proselytize, to speak, to write, and to organize campaigns for any school of thought they wish. . . . States are not burdened with a constitutional imperative to reduce voter apathy or to "handicap" an unpopular candidate to increase the likelihood that the candidate will gain access to the general election ballot. As we see it, Washington has done no more than to visit on a candidate a requirement to show a "significant modicum" of voter support, and it was entitled to require that showing in its primary elections. We also observe that 29.18.110 is more accommodating of First Amendment rights and values than were the statutes we upheld in *Jenness, American Party,* and *Storer.* Under each scheme analyzed in those cases, if a candidate failed to satisfy the qualifying criteria, the State's voters had no opportunity to cast a ballot for that candidate and the candidate had no ballot-connected campaign platform from which

to espouse his or her views; the unsatisfied qualifying criteria served as an absolute bar to ballot access. Undeniably, such restrictions raise concerns of constitutional dimension, for the exclusion of candidates . . . burdens voters' freedom of association, because an election campaign is an effective platform for the expression of views on the issues of the day . . . . *Anderson v. Celebrezze.*

Here, however, Washington virtually guarantees what the parties challenging the Georgia, Texas, and California election laws so vigorously sought—candidate access to a statewide ballot. This is a significant difference. Washington has chosen a vehicle by which minor-party candidates must demonstrate voter support that serves to promote the very First Amendment values that are threatened by overly burdensome ballot access restrictions. It can hardly be said that Washington's voters are denied freedom of association because they must channel their expressive activity into a campaign at the primary as opposed to the general election. It is true that voters must make choices as they vote at the primary, but there are no state-imposed obstacles impairing voters in the exercise of their choices. Washington simply has not substantially burdened the "availability of political opportunity." *Lubin v. Panish* (1974).

Jenness and *American Party* rejected challenges to ballot access restrictions that were based on a candidate's showing of voter support, notwithstanding the fact that the systems operated to foreclose a candidate's access to *any* statewide ballot. Here, because Washington affords a minor-party candidate easy access to the primary election ballot and the opportunity for the candidate to wage a ballot-connected campaign, we conclude that the magnitude of 29.18.110's effect on constitutional rights is slight when compared to the restrictions we upheld in *Jenness* and *American Party.* . . .

JUSTICE MARSHALL, with whom JUSTICE BRENNAN joins, dissenting.

Limitations on ballot access burden two fundamental rights: "the right of individuals to associate for the advancement of political beliefs, and the right of qualified voters, regardless of their political persuasion, to cast their votes effectively." *Williams v. Rhodes* (1968). These fundamental rights are implicated most clearly where minor-party access to the ballot is restricted. As we noted in *Illinois Board of Elections v. Socialist Workers Party* (1979), "[t]he States' interest in screening out frivolous candidates must be considered in light of the significant role that third parties have played in the political development of the Nation."

The minor party's often unconventional positions broaden political debate, expand the range of issues with which the electorate is concerned, and influence the positions of the majority, in some instances ultimately becoming majority positions. And its very existence provides an outlet for voters to express dissatisfaction with the candidates or platforms of the major parties. Notwithstanding the crucial role minor parties play in the American political arena, the Court holds today that the associational rights of minor parties and their supporters are not unduly burdened by a ballot access statute that, in practice, completely excludes minor parties from participating in statewide general elections. . . .

Appellant argues that there is no ballot access limitation here at all, and thus no need for the application of heightened scrutiny, because minor parties can appear on a *primary* ballot simply by meeting reasonable petition requirements. I cannot accept, however, as a general proposition, that access to *any* ballot is always constitutionally adequate. The Court, in concluding here that the State may reserve the general election ballot for "'major struggles,'" quoting *Storer v. Brown* (1974), appears to acknowledge that, because of its finality, the general election is the arena where issues are sharpened, policies are hotly debated, and the candidates' positions are clarified. Nonetheless, the Court deems access to the primary adequate to satisfy minor-party rights to ballot access, even though we have characterized the primary election principally as a "forum for continuing intraparty feuds," *Storer v. Brown*, rather than an arena for debate on the issues. Access to a primary election ballot is not, in my view, all the access that is due when minor parties are excluded entirely from the general election.

The Court's conclusion stems from a fundamental misconception of the role minor parties play in our constitutional scheme. To conclude that access to a primary ballot is adequate ballot access presumes that minor-party candidates seek only to get elected. But, as discussed earlier, minor-party participation in electoral politics serves to expand and affect political debate. Minor parties thus seek "influence, if not always electoral success." *Illinois Board of Elections v. Socialist Workers Party; Williams v. Rhodes* (States may not keep "all political parties off the ballot until they have enough members to win"). Their contribution to "diversity and competition in the marketplace of ideas," *Anderson v. Celebrezze* (1983), does not inevitably implicate their ability to *win* elections. That contribution cannot be realized if they are unable to participate meaningfully in the phase of the electoral process in which policy choices are most seriously considered. A statutory scheme that excludes minor parties entirely from this phase places an excessive burden on the constitutionally protected associational rights of those parties and their adherents. . . .

I am unconvinced that the Washington statute serves the asserted justification for the law: avoiding ballot overcrowding and voter confusion. The statute streamlines the general election, where overcrowding and confusion appear never to have been much of a problem before the 1977 amendments, at the expense of an already cumbersome primary ballot. Between 1907 and 1977, no more than six minor-party candidates ever appeared on the general election ballot for any statewide office, and no more than four ever ran for any statewide office other than Governor, suggesting that the ballot was never very crowded; *Williams v. Rhodes* (Harlan, J., concurring in result) ("[T]he presence of eight candidacies cannot be said, in light of experience, to carry a significant danger of voter confusion"). But in the 1983 special election that prompted this lawsuit, appellee Peoples, instead of being placed on the general election ballot with 2 other candidates, was placed on the primary ballot along with 32 other candidates: 18 Democrats and 14 Republicans.

The Court notes that we have not previously required a State seeking to impose reasonable ballot access restrictions to make a particularized showing that voter confusion in fact existed before those restrictions were imposed. But where the State's solution exacerbates the very problem it claims to solve, the State's means cannot be even rationally related to its asserted ends.

. . . . A minor party is not impermissibly burdened by ballot access restrictions when "a reasonably diligent independent candidate" could be expected to satisfy the ballot access requirement. *Storer v. Brown*; see *American Party of Texas*. We have therefore sustained restrictions on ballot access where they did not impose "insurmountable obstacles to fledgling political party efforts to generate support among the electorate and to evidence that support within the time allowed." In *American Party of Texas,* we sustained a 1% petition signature requirement because it was apparent that it was, in practice, neither "impossible nor impractical," for minor parties to demonstrate this level of support. Indeed, two of the minor parties that were plaintiffs in *American Party of Texas* qualified candidates for the general election ballot under the ballot access restrictions there at issue. Similarly, in *Jenness v. Fortson*, we approved Georgia's 5% petition requirement for ballot access, in part relying on the fact that "[t]he open

quality of the Georgia system [was] far from merely theoretical" because a candidate for Governor in 1966 and a candidate for President in 1966 had each gained access to the general election ballot through the nominating petition route.

Here, by contrast, Washington's primary law acts as an almost total bar to minor-party access to statewide general election ballots. Since the revision of Wash. Rev. Code 29.18.110 in 1977, minor-party candidates have been, in the words of the Court of Appeals, "substantially eliminated from Washington's general election ballot." The Court of Appeals found that by 1984, only one minor-party candidate had been able to surmount the 1% barrier and earn the right to participate in the general election. Ibid. The legislation leading to this substantial elimination of minor parties from the political arena in Washington's general elections should not be sustained as a legitimate requirement of a demonstration of significant support.

Since *Williams v. Rhodes*, this Court has recognized that state legislation may not ensure the continuing supremacy of the two major parties by precluding minor-party access to the ballot as a practical matter. Yet here the Court sustains a statute that does just that. In doing so, the Court permits a State to pre-empt meaningful participation by minor parties in the political process by requiring them to demonstrate their support in a crowded primary election. The Court thus holds that minor parties may be excised from the electoral process before they have fulfilled their central role in our democratic political tradition: to channel dissent into that process in a constructive fashion. Respectfully, I dissent.

JAMES L. BUCKLEY ET AL., V. FRANCIS R. VALEO, SECRETARY OF THE UNITED STATES SENATE, ET AL.

424 U.S. 1 (1976)

These appeals present constitutional challenges to the key provisions of the Federal Election Campaign Act of 1971 (Act), and related provisions of the Internal Revenue Code of 1954, all as amended in 1974.

The statutes at issue summarized in broad terms, contain the following provisions: (a) individual political contributions are limited $1,000 to any single candidate per election with an overall annual limitation of $25,000 by any contribution; independent expenditures by any contributor; independent expenditures by individuals and groups "relative to a clearly identified candidate" are limited to $1,000 a year; campaign spending by candidates for various federal offices and spending for national conventions by political parties are subject to prescribed limits; (b) contributions and expenditures above certain threshold levels must be reported and publicly disclosed.

The intricate statutory scheme adopted by Congress to regulate federal election campaigns includes restrictions on political contributions and expenditures that apply broadly to all phases of and all participants in the election process. The major contribution and expenditure limitations in the Act prohibit individuals from contribution more than $25,000 in a single candidate for an election campaign and from spending more than $1,000 a year "relative to a clearly identified candidate." Other provisions restrict a candidate's use of personal and family resources in his campaign and limit the overall amount that can be spent by a candidate in campaigning for federal office.

The Act's contribution and expenditure limitations operate in an area of the most fundamental First Amendment activities. Discussion of public issues and debate on the qualifications of candidates are integral to the operation of the system of government established by our Constitution. The First Amendment affords the broadest protection to such political expression in order "to assure [the] unfettered interchange of ideas for the bringing about of political and social changes desired by the people."

We cannot share the view that the present Act's contribution and expenditure limitations are comparable to the restrictions on conduct upheld in *O'Brien*. The expenditure of money simply cannot be equated with such conduct as destruction of a draft card. Some forms of communication made possible by the giving and spending of money involve speech alone, some involve conduct primarily, and some involve a combination of the two. Yet this Court has never suggested that the dependence of a communication on the expenditure of money operates itself to introduce a nonspeech element or to reduce the exaction scrutiny required by the First Amendment.

Even if the categorization of the expenditure of money as conduct were accepted, the limitations challenged here would not meet the *O'Brien* test because the governmental interests advanced in support of the Act involve "suppressing communication." The interests served by the Act include restricting the voices of people and interest groups who have money to spend and reducing the overall scope of federal election campaigns. Although the Act does not focus on the ideas expressed by persons or groups subject to its regulations it is aimed in part at equalizing the relative ability of all voters to affect electoral outcomes by placing a ceiling on expenditures for political expression by citizens and groups. Unlike *O'Brien*, where the Selective Service System's administrative interest in the preservation of draft cards was wholly unrelated to their use as a means of communication, it is beyond dispute that the interest in regulating the alleged "conduct" of giving or spending money "arises in some measure because the communication allegedly integral to the conduct is itself thought to be harmful."

Nor can the Act's contribution and expenditure limitations be sustained, as some of the parties suggest, by reference to the constitutional principles reflected in such decisions as *Cox v. Louisiana*; *Adderley v. Florida* (1966); and *Kovacs v. Cooper*, (1949) The critical difference between this case and those time, place, and manner cases is that the present Act's contribution and expenditure limitations impose direct quantity restrictions on political communication and association by persons, groups, candidates, and political parties in addition to any reasonable time, place, and manner regulations otherwise imposed.

A restriction on the amount of money a person or group can spend on political communication during a campaign necessarily reduces the quantity of expression by restricting the number of issues discussed, the depth of their exploration, and the size of the audience reached. This is because virtually every means of communicating ideas in today's mass society requires the expenditure of money. The distribution of the humblest handbill or leaflet entails printing, paper, and circulation costs. Speeches and rallies generally necessitate hiring a hall and publicizing the event. The electorate's increasing dependence on television, radio, and other mass media for news and information has made these expensive modes of communication indispensable instruments of effective political speech.

By contrast with a limitation upon expenditures for political expression, a limitation upon the amount that any one person or group may contribute to a candidate or political committee entails only a marginal restriction upon the contributor's ability to engage in free communication. A contribution serves as a general expression of support for the candidate and his views, but does not communicate the underlying basis for the support. The quantity of communication by the contributor does not increase perceptibly with the size of his contribution, since the expression rests solely on the undifferentiated, symbolic act of contributing. At most, the size of the contribution provides a very rough index of the intensity of the contributor's support for the candidate. A limitation on the amount of money a person may give to a candidate or campaign organization thus involves little direct restraint on his political communication, for it permits the symbolic expression of support evidenced by a contribution but does not in any way infringe the contributor's freedom to discuss candidates and issues. While contributions may result in political expression if spent by a candidate or an association to present views to the voters, the transformation of contributions into political debate involves speech by someone other than the contributor.

Given the important role of contributions in financing political campaigns, contribution restrictions could have a severe impact on political dialogue if the limitations prevented candidates and political committees from amassing the resources necessary for effective advocacy. There is no indication, however, that the contribution limitations imposed by the Act would have any dramatic adverse effect on the funding of campaigns and political associations. The overall effect of the Act's contribution ceilings is merely to require candidates and political committees to raise funds from a greater number of persons and to compel people who would otherwise contribute amounts greater than the statutory limits to expend such funds on direct political expression, rather than to reduce the total amount of money potentially available to promote political expression.

The Act's contribution and expenditure limitations also impinge on protected associational freedoms. Making a contribution, like joining a political party, serves to affiliate a person with a candidate. In addition, it enables like-minded persons to pool their resources in furtherance of common political goals. The Act's contribution ceilings thus limit one important means of associating with a candidate or committee, but leave the contributor free to become a member of any political association and to assist personally in the association's efforts on behalf of candidates. And the Act's contribution limitations permit associations and candidates to aggregate large sums of money to promote effective advocacy. By contrast, the Act's $1,000 limitation on independent expenditures "relative to a clearly identified candidate" precludes most associations from effectively amplifying the voice of their adherents, the original basis for the recognition of First Amendment protection of the freedom of association. See NAACP v. Alabama,. The Act's constraints on the ability of independent associations and candidate campaign organizations to expend resources on political expression "is simultaneously an interference with the freedom of their adherents. . . ."

In sum although the Act's contribution and expenditure limitations both implicate fundamental First Amendment interests, its expenditure ceilings impose significantly more severe restrictions on protected freedoms of political expression and association than do its limitations on financial contributions.

The $1,000 Limitation on Contributions by Individuals and Groups to Candidates and Authorized Campaign Committees. . . .

It is unnecessary to look beyond the Act's primary purpose—to limit the actuality and appearance of corruption resulting from large individual financial contributions—in order to find a constitutionally sufficient justification for the $1,000 contribution limitation. Under a system of private financing of elections, a candidate lacking immense personal or family wealth must depend on financial contributions from others to provide the resources necessary to conduct a successful campaign. The increasing importance of the communications media and sophisticated mass-mailing and polling operations to effective campaigning make the raising of large sums of money an ever more essential ingredient of an effective candidacy. To the extent that large contributions are given to secure a political *quid pro quo* from current and potential office holders, the integrity of our system of representative democracy is undermined. although the scope of such pernicious practices can never be reliably ascertained, the deeply disturbing examples surfacing after the 1972 election

demonstrate that the problem is not an illusory one.

Of almost equal concern as the danger of actual quid pro quo arrangements is the impact of the appearance of corruption stemming from public awareness of the opportunities for abuse inherent in a regime of large individual financial contributions.

The Act's $1,000 contribution limitation focuses precisely on the problem of large campaign contributions—the narrow aspect of political association where the actuality and potential for corruption have been identified—while leaving persons free to engage in independent political expression to associate actively through volunteering their services, and to assist to a limited but nonetheless substantial extent in supporting candidates and committees with financial resources. Significantly, the Act's contribution limitations in themselves do not undermine to any material degree the potential for robust and effective discussion of candidates and campaign issues by Individual citizens, associations, the institutional press, candidates, and political parties. . . .

The $25,000 Limitation on Total Contributions During any Calendar Year

. . . this quite modest restraint upon protected political activity serves to prevent evasion of the $1,000 contribution limitation by a person who might otherwise contribute massive amounts of money to a particular candidate through the use of unearmarked contributions to political committees likely to contribute to that candidate, or huge contributions to the candidate's political party. The limited, additional restriction on associational freedom imposed by the overall ceiling is thus no more than a corollary of the basic individual contribution limitation that we have found to be constitutionally valid. . .
.

The Act's expenditure ceilings impose direct and substantial restraints on the quantity of political speech. The most drastic of the limitations restricts individuals and groups, including political parties that fail to place a candidate on the ballot, to an expenditure of .$1,000 "relative to a clearly identified candidate during a calendar year." Other expenditure ceilings limit spending by candidates, their campaigns, and political parties in connection with election campaigns. It is clear that a primary effect of these expenditure limitations is to restrict the quantity of campaign speech by individuals, groups and candidates. The restrictions, while neutral as to the ideas expressed, limit political expression "at the core of our electoral process and of the First Amendment freedoms."

The $1,000 Limitation on Expenditures "Relative to a Clearly Identified Candidate" Section (l) provides that "[n]o person may make any expenditure . . . relative to a clearly identified candidate during a calendar year which, when added to all other expenditures made by such person during the year advocating the election or defeat of such candidate exceeds $1,000. . . ."

The discussion in Part 1-A, explains why the Act's expenditure limitations impose far greater restraints on the freedom of speech and association than do its contribution limitations. The markedly greater burden on basic freedoms caused by 608(e)(l) thus cannot be sustained simply by invoking the interest in maximizing the effectiveness of the less intrusive contribution limitations. Rather, the constitutionality of 608(e)(l) turns on whether the governmental interests advanced in its support satisfy the exacting scrutiny applicable to limitations on core First Amendment rights of political expression.

We find that the governmental interest in preventing corruption and the appearance of corruption is inadequate to justify 608(e)(l)'s ceiling on independent expenditures. First, assuming, arguendo, that large independent expenditures pose the same dangers of actual or apparent quid pro quo arrangements as do large Contributions, 608(e)(l) does not provide an answer that sufficiently relates to the elimination of those dangers. Unlike the contribution limitations' total ban on the giving of large amounts of money to candidates, 608(e)(l) prevents only some large expenditures. So long as persons and groups eschew expenditures that in express terms advocate the election or defeat of a

clearly identified candidate, they are free to spend as much as they want to promote the candidate and his views.

Second, quite apart from the shortcomings of 608 (e)(l) in preventing any abuses generated by large independent expenditures, the independent advocacy restricted by the provision does not presently appear to pose dangers of real or apparent corruption comparable to those identified with large campaign contributions. The parties defending 608(e)(1) contend that it is necessary to prevent would-be contributors from avoiding the contribution limitations by the simple expedient of paying directly for media advertisements or for other portions of the candidate's campaign activities. They argue that expenditures controlled by or coordinated with the candidate and his campaign might well have virtually the same value to the candidate as a contribution and would pose similar dangers of abuse. Yet such controlled or coordinated expenditures are treated as contributions rather than expenditures under the Act. Section 608(b)'s contribution ceilings rather than 608(e)(l)'s independent expenditure limitation prevent attempts to circumvent the Act through prearranged or coordinated expenditures amounting to disguised contributions. By contrast, 608(e)(1) limits expenditures for express advocacy of candidates made totally independently of the candidate and his campaign. Unlike contributions, such independent expenditures may well provide little assistance to the candidate's campaign and indeed may prove counterproductive. The absence of prearrangement and coordination of an expenditure with the candidate or his agent not only undermines the value of the expenditure to the candidate, but also alleviates the danger that expenditures will be given as a quid pro quo for improper commitments from the candidate. Rather than preventing circumvention of the contribution limitations, 608(e)(1) severely restricts all independent advocacy despite its substantially diminished potential for abuse.

While the independent expenditure ceiling thus fails to serve any substantial governmental interest in stemming the reality or appearance of corruption in the electoral process, it heavily burdens core First Amendment expression. For the First Amendment right to "'speak one's mind . . . on all public institutions'" includes the right to engage in "'vigorous advocacy' no less than 'abstract discussion. . . .'"

It is argued, however, that the ancillary governmental interest in equalizing the relative ability of individuals and groups to influence the outcome of elections serves to justify the limitation on express advocacy of the election or defeat of candidates imposed by 608(e)(l)'s expenditure ceiling. But the concept that government may restrict the speech of some elements of our society in order to enhance the relative voice of others is wholly foreign to the First Amendment, which was designed "to secure 'the widest possible dissemination of information from diverse and antagonistic sources,'" and "'to assure unfettered interchange of ideas for the bringing about of political and social changes desired by the people. . . .'"

The First Amendment's protection against governmental abridgment of free expression cannot properly be made to depend on a persons financial ability to engage in public discussion. For the reasons stated we conclude that 608(e)(l)'s independent expenditure limitation is unconstitutional under the First Amendment.

Limitation on Expenditures by Candidates from Personal or Family Resources

The Act also sets limits on expenditures by a candidate "from his personal funds, or the personal funds of his immediate family, in connection with his campaigns during any calendar year." 608(a)(1). These ceilings vary from $50,000 for Presidential or Vice Presidential candidates to $35,000 for senatorial candidates, and $25,000 for most candidates for the House of Representatives.

The ceiling on personal expenditures by candidates on their own behalf, like the limitations on independent expenditures contained in 608(e)(1), imposes a substantial restraint on the ability of persons to engage in protected First Amendment expression. The candidate, no less than any other person, has a First Amendment right to engage in the discussion of public issues and vigorously and tirelessly to advocate his own election and the election of other candidates. Indeed, it is of particular importance that candidates have the unfettered opportunity to make their views known so that the electorate may intelligently evaluate the candidates personal qualities and their positions on vital public issues before choosing among them on election day.

The primary governmental interest served by the Act—the prevention of actual and apparent corruption of the political process—does not support the limitation on the candidate's expenditure of his own personal funds. As the Court of Appeals concluded: "Manifestly the core problem of avoiding undisclosed and undue influence on candidates from outside interests has lesser application when the monies involved come from the candidate himself or from his immediate family." Indeed, the use of personal funds reduces the candidates dependence on outside contributions and thereby counteracts the coercive pressures and attendant risks of abuse to which the Act's contribution limitations are directed.

The ancillary interest in equalizing the relative financial resources of candidates competing for elective office, therefore, provides the sole relevant rationale for 608(a)'s expenditure ceiling. That interest is clearly not sufficient to justify the provision's infringement of fundamental First Amendment rights. First, the limitation may fail to promote financial equality among candidates. A candidate who spends less of his personal resources on his campaign may nonetheless outspend his rival as a result of more successful fundraising efforts. Indeed, a candidate's personal wealth may impede his efforts to persuade others that he needs their financial contributions or volunteer efforts to conduct an effective campaign. Second, and more fundamentally, the First Amendment simply cannot tolerate 608(a)'s restriction upon the freedom of a candidate to speak without legislative limit on behalf of his own candidacy. We therefore hold that 608(a)'s restriction on a candidate's personal expenditures is unconstitutional.

Limitations on Campaign Expenditures

Section 608(c) places limitations on overall campaign expenditures by candidates seeking nomination for election and election to federal office. Presidential candidates may spend $10,000,000 in seeking nomination for office and an additional $20,000,000 in the general election campaign.

The ceiling on senatorial campaigns is pegged to the size of the voting-age population of the State with minimum dollar amounts applicable to campaigns in States with small populations. In senatorial primary elections, the limit is the greater of eight cents multiplied by the voting-age population or $100,000, and in the general election the limit is increased to 12 cents multiplied by the voting-age population or $150,000. The Act imposes blanket $70,000 limitations on both primary campaigns and general election campaigns for the House of Representatives with the exception that the senatorial ceiling applies to campaigns in States entitled to only one Representative. These ceilings are to be adjusted upwards at the beginning of each calendar year by the average percentage rise in the consumer price index for the 12 preceding months. No governmental interest that has been suggested is sufficient to justify the restriction on the quantity of political expression imposed by 608(c)'s campaign expenditure limitations. The major evil associated with rapidly increasing campaign expenditures is the danger of candidate dependence on large contributions. The interest in alleviating the corrupting influence of large contributions is served by the Act's contribution limitations and disclosure provisions rather than by 608(c)'s campaign expenditure ceilings. . . .

There is no indication that the substantial criminal penalties for violating the contribution ceilings combined with the political repercussion of such violations will be insufficient to police the contribution provisions. Extensive reporting, auditing and disclosure requirements applicable to both contributions and expenditures by political campaigns are designed to facilitate the detection of illegal contributions. Moreover, as the Court of Appeals noted, the Act permits an officeholder or successful candidate to retain contributions in excess of the expenditure ceiling and to use these funds for "any other lawful purpose."(1970). This provision undercuts whatever marginal role the expenditure limitations might otherwise play in enforcing the contribution ceilings.

The interest in equalizing the financial resources of candidates competing for federal office is no more convincing a justification for restricting the scope of federal election campaigns. Given the limitation on the size of outside contributions, the financial resources available to a candidate's campaign, like the number of volunteers recruited, will normally vary with the size and intensity of the candidate's support. There is nothing invidious, improper, or unhealthy in permitting such funds to be spent to carry the candidate's message to the electorate. Moreover, the equalization of permissible campaign expenditures might serve not to equalize the opportunities of all candidates, but to handicap a candidate who lacked substantial name recognition or exposure of his views before the start of the campaign.

The campaign expenditure ceilings appear to be designed primarily to serve the governmental interests in reducing the allegedly skyrocketing costs of political campaigns.

. . . . the mere growth in the cost of federal election campaigns in and of itself provides no basis for governmental restrictions on the quantity of campaign spending and the resulting limitation on the scope of federal campaigns. The First Amendment denies government the power to determine that spending to promote one's political views is wasteful, excessive, or unwise. In the free society ordained by our Constitution it is not the government, but the people—individually as citizens and candidates and collectively as associations and political committees—who must retain control over the quantity and range of debate on public issues in a political campaign.

Unlike the limitations on contributions and expenditures, the disclosure requirements of the Act are not challenged by appellants as per se unconstitutional restrictions on the exercise of First Amendment freedoms of speech and association. Indeed, appellants argue that "narrowly drawn disclosure requirements are the proper solution to virtually all of the evils Congress sought to remedy." The particular requirements embodied in the Act are attacked as overbroad—both in their application to minor-party and independent candidates and in their extension to contributions as small as $11 or $101. Appellants also challenge the provision for disclosure by those who make independent contributions and expenditures. The Court of Appeals found no constitutional infirmities in the provisions challenged here. We affirm the determination on overbreadth and hold that 434(e), if narrowly construed also is within constitutional bounds. . . .

The Act presently under review replaced all prior disclosure laws. Its primary disclosure provisions impose reporting obligations on "political committees" and candidates. "Political committee" is defined in 431(d) as a group of persons that receives "contributions" or makes "expenditures" of over $1,000 in a calendar year. "Contributions" and "expenditures" are defined in lengthy parallel provisions similar to those in Title 18, discussed above. Both definitions focus on the use of money or other objects of value "for the purpose of . . . influencing" the nomination or election of any person to federal office. . .

Each political committee is required to register with the Commission, and to keep detailed records of both contributions and expenditures. . . .

Every individual or group, other than a political committee or candidate, who makes "contributions" or "expenditures" of over $100 in a calendar year "other than by contribution to a political committee or candidate" is required to file a statement with the Commission. . . .

We long have recognized that significant encroachments on First Amendment rights of the sort that compelled disclosure imposes cannot be justified by a mere showing of some legitimate governmental interest. Since *NAACP v. Alabama* we have required that the subordinating interests of the State must survive exacting scrutiny. We also have insisted that there be a "relevant correlation" or "substantial relation" between the governmental interest and the information required to be disclosed. . . .

The governmental interests sought to be vindicated by the disclosure requirements are of this magnitude. They fall into three categories. First, disclosure provides the electorate with information "as to where political campaign money comes from and how it is spent by the candidate" in order to aid the voters in evaluating those who seek federal office. It allows voters to place each candidate in the political spectrum more precisely than is often possible solely on the basis of party labels and campaign speeches. The sources of a candidate's financial support also alert the voter to the interests to which a candidate is most likely to be responsive and thus facilitate predictions of future performance in office.

Second, disclosure requirements deter actual corruption and avoid the appearance of corruption by exposing large contributions and expenditures to the light of publicity. This exposure may discourage those who would use money for improper purposes either before or after the election. A public armed with information about a candidate's most generous supporters is better able to detect any post-election special favors that may be given in return. . . .

Third, and not least significant, recordkeeping, reporting, and disclosure requirements are an essential means of gathering the data necessary to detect violations of the contribution limitations described above. . . .

Appellants contend that the Act's requirements are overbroad insofar as they apply to contributions to minor parties and independent candidates because the governmental interest in this information is minimal and the danger of significant infringement on First Amendment rights is greatly increased. . . .

It is true that the governmental interest in disclosure is diminished when the contribution in question is made to a minor party with little chance of winning an election. As minor parties usually represent definite and publicized viewpoints, there may be less need to inform the voters of the interests that specific candidates represent. Major parties encompass candidates of greater diversity. In many situations the label "Republican" or "Democrat" tells a voter little. The candidate who bears it may be supported by funds from the far right, the far left, or any place in between on the political spectrum. It is less likely that a candidate of, say, the Socialist Labor Party will represent interests that cannot be discerned from the party's ideological position.

The Government's interest in deterring the "buying" of elections and the undue influence of large contributors on officeholders also may be reduced where contributions to a minor party or an independent candidate are concerned, for it is less likely that the candidate will be victorious. But a minor party sometimes can play a significant role in an election. Even when a minor-party candidate has little or no chance of winning, he may be encouraged by major-party interests in order to divert votes from other major-party contenders.

We are not unmindful that the damage done by disclosure to the associational interests of the minor parties and their members and to supporters of independents could be significant. These movements are less likely to have a sound financial base and thus are more vulnerable to falloffs in contributions. In some instances fears of reprisal may deter contributions to the point where the movement cannot survive. The public interest also suffers if that result comes to pass, for there is a consequent reduction in the free circulation of ideas both within and without the political arena.

There could well be a case, similar to those before the Court in *NAACP v. Alabama* and *Bates*, where the threat to the exercise of First Amendment rights is so serious and the state interest furthered by disclosure so insubstantial that the Act's requirements cannot be constitutionally applied. But no appellant in this case has tendered record evidence of the sort proffered in *NAACP v. Alabama*. Instead, appellants primarily rely on "the clearly articulated fears of individuals, well experienced in the political process." At best they offer the testimony of several minor-party officials that one or two persons refused to make contributions because of the possibility of disclosure. On this record, the substantial public interest in disclosure identified by the legislative history of this Act outweighs the harm generally alleged. . . .

Section 434(e) requires "[e]very person (other than a political committee or candidate) who makes contributions or expenditures" aggregating over $100 in a calendar year "other than by contribution to a political committee or candidate" to file a statement with the Commission. Unlike the other disclosure provisions, this section does not seek the contribution list of any association. Instead, it requires direct disclosure of what an individual or group contributes or spends. . . .

Appellants attack 434(e) as a direct intrusion on privacy of belief, . . . and as imposing "very real; practical burdens . . . certain to deter individuals from making expenditures for their independent political speech."

We have found that 608(e)(1) unconstitutionally infringes upon First Amendment rights. If the sole function of 434(e) were to aid in the enforcement of that provision, it would no longer serve any governmental purpose.

But the two provisions are not so intimately tied. . . .

Like the other disclosure provisions, 434(e) could play a role in the enforcement of the expanded contribution and expenditure limitations included in the 1974 amendments, but it also has independent functions. Section 434(e) is part of Congress' effort to achieve "total disclosure" by reaching "every kind of political activity" in order to insure that the voters are fully informed and to achieve through publicity the maximum deterrence to corruption and undue influence possible. The provision is responsive to the legitimate fear that efforts would be made, as they had been in the past, to avoid the disclosure requirements by routing financial support of candidates through avenues not explicitly covered by the general provisions of the Act . . . . To insure that the reach of 434(e) is not impermissibly broad, we construe "expenditure" for purposes of that section in the same way we construed the terms of 608(e)—to reach only funds used for communications that expressly advocate the election or defeat of a clearly identified candidate. This reading is directed precisely to that spending that is unambiguously related to the campaign of a particular federal candidate.

In summary, 434(e), as construed, imposes independent reporting requirements on individuals and groups that are not candidates or political committees only in the following circumstances: (1) when they make contributions earmarked for political purposes or authorized or requested by a candidate or his agent, to some person other than a candidate or political committee, and (2) when they make expenditures for communications that expressly advocate the election or defeat of a clearly identified candidate. . . .

434(e), as construed, bears a sufficient relationship to a substantial governmental interest. As narrowed, 434(e), like 608(e)(1), does not reach all partisan discussion for it only requires disclosure of those expenditures that expressly advocate a particular election result. This might have been fatal if the only purpose of 434(e) were to stem corruption or its appearance by closing a loophole in the general disclosure requirements. But the disclosure provisions, including 434(e) increases the fund of information concerning those who support the candidates. It goes beyond the general disclosure requirements to shed the light of publicity on spending that is unambiguously campaign related but would not otherwise be reported because it takes the form of independent expenditures or of contributions to an individual or group not itself required to report the names of its contributors. By the same token, it is not fatal that 434(e) encompasses purely independent expenditures uncoordinated with a

particular candidate or his agent. The corruption potential of these expenditures may be significantly different, but the informational interest can be as strong as it is in coordinated spending, for disclosure helps voters to define more of the candidates' constituencies.

Appellants' third contention, based on alleged overbreadth, is that the monetary thresholds in the recordkeeping and reporting provisions lack a substantial nexus with the claimed governmental interests, for the amounts involved are too low even to attract the attention of the candidate, much less have a corrupting influence.

The provisions contain two thresholds. Records are to be kept by political committees of the names and addresses of those who make contributions in excess of $10, and these records are subject to Commission audit. If a person's contributions to a committee or candidate aggregate more than $100, his name and address, as well as his occupation and principal place of business, are to be included in reports filed by committees and candidates with the Commission, and made available for public inspection.

The Court of Appeals rejected appellants' contention that these thresholds are unconstitutional. It found the challenge on First Amendment grounds to the $10 threshold to be premature, for it could "discern no basis in the statute for authorizing disclosure outside the Commission . . ., and hence no substantial 'inhibitory effect' operating upon" appellants. The $100 threshold was found to be within the "reasonable latitude" given the legislature "as to where to draw the line." We agree.

The $10 and $100 thresholds are indeed low. Contributors of relatively small amounts are likely to be especially sensitive to recording or disclosure of their political preferences. These strict requirements may well discourage participation by some citizens in the political process, a result that Congress hardly could have intended.

But we cannot require Congress to establish that it has chosen the highest reasonable threshold. The line is necessarily a judgmental decision, best left in the context of this complex legislation to congressional discretion. We cannot say, on this bare record, that the limits designated are wholly without rationality.

We are mindful that disclosure serves informational functions, as well as the prevention of corruption and the enforcement of the contribution limitations. Congress is not required to set a threshold that is tailored only to the latter goals. In addition, the enforcement goal can never be well served if the threshold is so high that disclosure becomes equivalent to admitting violation of the contribution limitations.

The $10 recordkeeping threshold, in a somewhat similar fashion, facilitates the enforcement of the disclosure provisions by making it relatively difficult to aggregate secret contributions in amounts that surpass the $100 limit. We agree with the Court of Appeals that there is no warrant for assuming that public disclosure of contributions between $10 and $100 is authorized by the Act. Accordingly, we do not reach the question whether information concerning gifts of this size can be made available to the public without trespassing impermissibly on First Amendment rights. . . .

A series of statutes for the public financing of presidential election campaigns produced the scheme now found in 6096 and Subtitle H of the Internal Revenue Code of 1954, . . . Appellants . . . [contend] . . . that the legislation violates the First and Fifth Amendments. We find no merit in their claims . . . Although "Congress shall make no law . . . abridging the freedom of speech, or of the press," Subtitle H is a congressional effort, not to abridge, restrict, or censor speech, but rather to use public money to facilitate and enlarge public discussion and participation in the electoral process, goals vital to a self-governing people. Thus, Subtitle H furthers, not abridges, pertinent First Amendment values.
In summary, we sustain the individual contribution limits, the disclosure and reporting provisions, and the public financing scheme. We conclude, however, that the limitations on campaign expenditures, on independent expenditures by individuals and groups, and on

expenditures by a candidate, from his personal funds are constitutionally infirm.

MR. JUSTICE STEVENS took no part in the consideration or decision of these cases. . . .

MR. CHIEF JUSTICE BURGER, concurring in part and dissenting in part.

For reasons set forth more fully later, I dissent from those parts of the Court's holding sustaining the statutory provisions (a) for disclosure of small contributions, (b) for limitations on contributions and (c) for public financing of Presidential campaigns. In my view the Act's disclosure scheme is impermissibly broad and violative of the First Amendment as it relates to reporting contributions in excess of $10 and $100. The contribution limitations infringe on First Amendment liberties and suffer from the same infirmities that The Court correctly sees in the expenditure ceilings. The system for public financing of Presidential campaigns is in my judgment, an impermissible intrusion by the Government into the traditionally private political process. . . .

Disclosure is, in principle, the salutary and constitutional remedy for most of the ills Congress was seeking to alleviate. I therefore agree fully with the broad proposition that public disclosure of contributions by individuals and by entities—particularly corporations and labor unions—is an effective means of revealing the type of political support that is sometimes coupled with expectations of special favors or rewards. That disclosure impinges on First Amendment rights is conceded by the Court, but given the objectives to which disclosure is directed, I agree that the need for disclosure outweighs individual constitutional claims.

Disclosure is, however, subject to First Amendment limitations which are to be defined by looking to the relevant public interests. The legitimate public interest is the elimination of the appearance and reality of corrupting influences. Serious dangers to the very processes of government justify disclosure of contributions of such dimensions reasonably thought likely to purchase special favors. . . .

The public right to know ought not to be absolute when its exercise reveals private political convictions. Secrecy, like privacy, is not per se criminal. On the contrary, secrecy and privacy as to political preferences and convictions are fundamental in a free society. . . .

To argue that a 1976 contribution of $10 or $100 entails a risk of corruption or its appearance is simply too extravagant to be maintained. No public right to know justifies the compelled disclosure of such contributions, at the risk of discouraging them. There is, in short no relation whatever between the means used and the legitimate goal of ventilating possible undue influence. Congress has used a shotgun to kill wrens as well as hawks. . .

I agree fully with that part of the Court's opinion that holds unconstitutional the limitations the Act puts on campaign expenditures which "place substantial and direct restrictions on the ability of candidates, citizens, and associations to engage in protected political expression restrictions that the First Amendment cannot tolerate." Yet when it approves similarly stringent limitations on contributions, the Court ignores the reasons it finds so persuasive in the context of expenditures. For me contributions and expenditures are two sides of the same First Amendment coin. . . .

The Court's attempt to distinguish the communication inherent in political *contributions* from the speech aspects of political *expenditures* simply "will not wash." We do little but engage in word games unless we recognize that people—candidates and contributors—spend money on political activity because they wish to communicate ideas, and their constitutional interest in doing so is precisely the same whether they or someone else utters the words. . . .

After a bow to the "weighty interests" Congress meant to serve, the Court then forsakes this analysis in one sentence: "Congress was surely entitled to conclude that disclosure was only a partial measure, and that contribution ceilings were a necessary legislative concomitant to deal

with the reality or appearance of corruption . . . ." In striking down the limitations on campaign expenditures, the Court relies in part on its conclusion that other means—namely, disclosure and contribution ceilings—will adequately serve the statutes aim. It is not clear why the same analysis is not also appropriate in weighing the need for contribution ceilings in addition to disclosure requirements. Congress may well be entitled to conclude that disclosure was a "partial measure," but I had not thought until today that Congress could enact its conclusions in the First Amendment area into laws immune from the most searching review by this Court. . . .

I dissent from Part III sustaining the constitutionality of the public financing provisions of Subtitle H.

Since the turn of this century when the idea of Government subsidies for political campaigns first was broached, there has been no lack of realization that the use of funds.

Recent history shows dangerous examples of systems with a close "incestuous" relationship between "government" and "politics"; . . . . once the Government finances these national conventions by the expenditure of millions of dollars from the public treasury, we may be providing a springboard for later attempts to impose a whole range of requirements on delegate selection and convention activities. Does this foreshadow judicial decisions allowing the federal courts to "monitor" these conventions to assure compliance with court orders or regulations? . . . .

I would also find unconstitutional the system of matching grants which makes a candidate's ability to amass private funds the sole criterion for eligibility for public funds. Such an arrangement can put at serious disadvantage a candidate with a potentially large, widely diffused—but poor—constituency. The ability of a candidate's supporters to help pay for his campaign cannot be equated with their willingness to cast a ballot for him. . . .

MR. JUSTICE WHITE, concurring in part and dissenting in part.

Concededly, neither the limitations on

contributions nor those on expenditures directly or indirectly purport to control the content of political speech by candidates or by their supporters or detractors. What the Act regulates is giving and spending money, acts that have First Amendment significance not because they are themselves communicative with respect to the qualifications of the candidate, but because money may be used to defray the expenses of speaking or otherwise communicating about the merits or demerits of federal candidates for election. The act of giving money to political candidates, however, may have illegal or other undesirable consequences: it may be used to secure the express or tacit understanding that the giver will enjoy political favor if the candidate is elected. Both Congress and this Court's cases have recognized this as a mortal danger against which effective preventive and curative steps must be taken.

Since the contribution and expenditure limitations are neutral as to the content of speech and are not motivated by fear of the consequences of the political speech of particular candidates or of political speech in general, this case depends on whether the nonspeech interests of the Federal Government in regulating the use of money in political campaigns are sufficiently urgent to justify the incidental effects that the limitations visit upon the First Amendment interests of candidates and their supporters.

Proceeding from the maxim that "money talks," the Court finds that the expenditure limitations will seriously curtail political expression by candidates and interfere substantially with their chances for election. The Court concludes that the Constitution denies Congress the power to limit campaign expenses; federal candidates—and I would suppose state candidates, too—are to have the constitutional right to raise and spend unlimited amounts of money in quest of their own election. . . .

The record before us no more supports the conclusion that the communicative efforts of congressional and Presidential candidates will be crippled by the expenditure limitations than it supports the contrary. The judgment of Congress was that reasonably effective campaigns could be conducted within the limits established by the Act and that the communicative efforts of these campaigns would not seriously suffer. In this posture of the case, there is no sound basis for invalidating the expenditure limitations, so long as the purposes they serve are legitimate and sufficiently substantial, which in my view they are.

In the first place, expenditure ceilings reinforce the contribution limits and help eradicate the hazard of corruption. The Court upholds the overall limit of $25,000 on an individual's political contributions in a single election year on the ground that it helps reinforce the limits on gifts to a single candidate. By the same token, the expenditure limit imposed on candidates plays its own role in lessening the chance that the contribution ceiling will be violated. Without limits on total expenditures, campaign costs will inevitably and endlessly escalate. Pressure to raise funds will constantly build and with it the temptation to resort in "emergencies" to those sources of large sums, who, history shows, are sufficiently confident of not being caught to risk flouting contribution limits.

I have little doubt in addition that limiting the total that can be spent will ease the candidate's understandable obsession with fundraising, and so free him and his staff to communicate in more places and ways unconnected with the fundraising function. There is nothing objectionable—indeed it seems to me a weighty interest in favor of the provision—in the attempt to insulate the political expression of federal candidates from the influence inevitably exerted by the endless job of raising increasingly large sums of money. I regret that the Court has returned them all to the treadmill.

It is also important to restore and maintain public confidence in federal elections. It is critical to obviate or dispel the impression that federal elections are purely and simply a function of money, that federal offices are bought and sold or that political races are reserved for those who have the facility—and the stomach—

for doing whatever it takes to bring together those interests, groups, and individuals that can raise or contribute large fortunes in order to prevail at the polls.

The ceiling on candidate expenditures represents the considered judgment of Congress that elections are to be decided among candidates none of whom has overpowering advantage by reason of a huge campaign war chest. At least so long as the ceiling placed upon the candidates is not plainly too low, elections are not to turn on the difference in the amounts of money that candidates have to spend. This seems an acceptable purpose and the mean chosen a commonsense way to achieve it.
. . .

I also disagree with the Court's judgment that 608 (a), which limits the amount of money that a candidate or his family may spend on his campaign, violates the Constitution. Although it is true that this provision does not promote any interest in preventing the corruption of candidates, the provision does, nevertheless, serve salutary purposes related to the integrity of federal campaigns. By limiting the importance of personal wealth, 608(a) helps to assure that only individuals with a modicum of support from others will be viable candidates. This in turn would tend to discourage any notion that the outcome of elections is primarily a function of money. Similarly, 608(a) tends to equalize access to the political arena, encouraging the less wealthy, unable to bankroll their own campaigns, to run for political office.

As with the campaign expenditure limits, Congress was entitled to determine that personal wealth ought to play a less important role in political campaigns than it has in the past. Nothing in the First Amendment stands in the way of that determination.

MR. JUSTICE MARSHALL, concurring in part and dissenting in part.

I join in all of the Court's opinion except Part I-C-2, which deals with 608 (a). That section limits the amount a candidate may spend from his personal funds, or family funds under his control, in connection with his campaigns during any calendar year. . . .

To be sure, 608(a) affects the candidate's exercise of his First Amendment rights. But unlike the other expenditure limitations contained in the Act and invalidated by the Court—the limitation on independent expenditures relative to a clearly identified candidate, 608(e), and the limitations on overall candidate expenditures, 608(c)—the limitations on expenditures by candidates from personal resources contained in 608(a) need never prevent the speaker from spending another dollar to communicate his ideas. Section 608(a) imposes no overall limit on the amount a candidate can spend; it simply limits the "contribution" a candidate may make to his own campaign. The candidate remains free to raise an unlimited amount in contributions from others. . . .

The Court views "[t]he ancillary interest in equalizing the relative financial resources of candidates" as the relevant rationale for 608(a), and deems that interest insufficient to justify 608(a). In my view the interest is more precisely the interest in promoting the reality and appearance of equal access to the political arena. . . .

In view of 608(b)'s limitations on contributions, then, 608(a) emerges not simply as a device to reduce the natural advantage of the wealthy candidate, but as a provision providing some symmetry to a regulatory scheme that otherwise enhances the natural advantage of the wealthy. Regardless of whether the goal of equalizing access would justify a legislative limit on personal candidate expenditures standing by itself, I think it clear that that goal justifies 608(a)'s limits when they are considered in conjunction with the remainder of the Act. I therefore respectfully dissent from the Court's invalidation of 608(a).

MR. JUSTICE BLACKMUN, concurring in part and dissenting in part.

I am not persuaded that the Court makes, or indeed is able to make, a principled constitutional distinction between the contribution limitations, on the one hand, and the expenditure limitations, on the other, that are involved here. . . .

MR. JUSTICE REHNQUIST, concurring in part and dissenting in part.

I . . . dissent from Part III-B-l of the Court's opinion, which holds that certain aspects of the statutory treatment of minor parties and independent candidates are constitutionally valid. . . .

Congress, of course, does have an interest in not "funding hopeless candidacies with large sums of public money," and may for that purpose legitimately require "some preliminary showing of a significant modicum of support, *Jenness v. Fortson* (1971), as an eligibility requirement for public funds." But Congress in this legislation has done a good deal more than that. It has enshrined the Republican and Democratic Parties in a permanently preferred position, and has established requirements for funding minor-party and independent candidates to which the two major parties are not subject. Congress would undoubtedly be justified in treating the Presidential candidates of the two major parties differently from minor-party or independent Presidential candidates, in view of the long demonstrated public support of the former. But because of the First Amendment overtones of the appellants' Fifth Amendment equal protection claim, something more than a merely rational basis for the difference in treatment must be shown, as the Court apparently recognizes. I find it impossible to subscribe to the Court's reasoning that because no third party has posed a credible threat to the two major parties in Presidential elections since 1860, Congress may by law attempt to assure that this pattern will endure forever.

I would hold that, as to general election financing, Congress has not merely treated the two major parties differently from minor parties and independents, but has discriminated in favor of the former in such a way as to run afoul of the Fifth and First Amendments to the United States Constitution.

7

THE ADVANCEMENT OF PATRIOTISM

For this and the next five chapters, we are concerned with the clash between freedom of communication and governmental desire to advance certain values which are thought useful, if not indispensable, in our society. It is possible, of course, to maintain that it is not the business of government to be concerned with values, but rather that such things are best left to the individual. There is some force to this argument, but it should not prevent discussion of the clash between such governmental activity and the First Amendment.[1]

The belief that advancing values is a proper concern of government has traditionally been associated with conservatism, but the recent controversy over "political correctness" in and out of *academia* demonstrates that the political left is no less anxious to use government to promote that which it sees as desirable. And it is obvious that government does quite often attempt to advance values. Finally, at least in so far as the Supreme Court is concerned, there does not seem to be any serious argument over the mere attempt by government to do so. A case can be made that merely by participating in such activity, government poses a threat to freedom; for the weight which it can bring to bear is heavy, and may pose the danger of overpowering those who would advance other and contradictory values.

The problem however, has not been seen in these terms. The government, the Court has said, is free to advance the values it chooses, so long as it does not do so by methods which implicate the individual exercise of constitutionally protected rights. The individual may be free, as the Court recently held, to dishonor the flag. That does not mean, however, that government must halt its many attempts to foster reverence for this national symbol.[2]

There may be a number of reasons for the distinction thus made, but one is tempted to believe that its existence is largely due to the Court's intuitive recognition that the continued existence of society and government presupposes the existence of certain shared values, and that government must, then, engage in activity directed to their preservation and advancement. And, while it may be argued that the only value which government is free to advance is the value of individual choice, at least as applied to the situation at hand that seems only a variation on the previously rejected doctrine of First Amendment absolutism.

The recognition that government has at least some proper role in advancing societal values necessitates the similar recognition that, at least from the perspective of government and society, speech can be classified as "good" and "bad." In other words, some speech, merely because of its existence, can be seen as dysfunctional to the values that society holds. That was at least part of the message of <u>Chaplinsky v. New Hampshire</u>, in which the Court held not only that "fighting words," but also the libelous and obscene, were outside the scope of the First Amendment. Although the <u>Chaplinsky</u> formulation held that all three could be banned as "playing no part in the exposition of ideas," there is a fundamental distinction between "fighting words" and the other types of speech mentioned in that decision. For "fighting words" might easily be banned simply on a fair application of the "clear and present danger" test. Not so, it would seem, for that which is libelous or obscene. For it is impossible to argue that social values will be destroyed if they are flouted in any single instance. Thus the determination of whether limitation is proper must, in these matters, depend on the application of different kinds of tests.

First among the "values" which we will weigh against the command of the First Amendment is that of patriotism (i.e. the promotion of a certain respect and love for our country). The first question that the Court has considered regarding the advancement of patriotism is whether and to what extent such advancement can be promoted by forcing individuals to avow "patriotic" attitudes that they either do not feel, or for one reason or another do not wish to affirm. Most numerous of these, perhaps, were the series of "test oath" cases, in which individuals, as a condition of employment, were required to take an oath disavowing belief in the violent overthrow of the government. As we observed in Chapter 2, these oaths, when construed as requiring some positive action on the part of the individual, were uniformly struck down, and were otherwise legitimized only on very narrow bases. Predating the decisions in these cases however, the issue of compulsory affirmation had been faced in two cases involving the Pledge of Allegiance, as that practice collided with the religious beliefs of Jehovah's Witnesses.

The facts of the two cases were essentially similar. Both involved laws requiring that children in the public schools recite the Pledge at the beginning of the school day, and children of the Jehovah's Witness faith who refused to participate in the ceremony. For this action, the children were suspended or expelled from school, and their parents threatened with the application of truancy laws.

The outcomes of the cases were, however, very different. In Minersville School District v. Gobitis (1940) an eight to one majority upheld the law. Justice Frankfurter's majority opinion saw the constitutional issue as one of free exercise of religion, and finally rested on the assertion that:

> The ultimate foundation of a free society is the binding tie of cohesive sentiment. Such a sentiment is fostered by all those agencies of the mind and spirit which may serve to gather up the traditions of a people, transmit them from generation to generation, and thereby create that continuity of a treasured common life which constitutes a civilization. "We live by symbols." The flag is the symbol of our national unity, transcending all internal differences, however large, within the framework of the Constitution. The influences which help toward a common feeling for the common country are manifold. Some may seem harsh and others no doubt are foolish. Surely, however, the end is legitimate. And the effective means are still so uncertain and so unauthenticated by science as to preclude us from putting the widely prevalent belief in flag-saluting beyond the pale of legislative power.

Only three years later the Court, by a vote of six to three, struck down the compulsory flag salute in West Virginia Board of Education v. Barnette (1943). The majority included three justices, Black, Douglas, and Murphy, who had formed a part of the Gobitis majority and who had indicated in a later case that they believed their initial vote to have been in error. Also included were Chief Justice Stone, the lone dissenter in Gobitis, and Justices Rutledge and Jackson, who came to the Court after that case was decided. The majority opinion was written by Jackson. Justice Frankfurter, faithful to the view he had expressed in Gobitis, wrote for the three dissenters.

It is conventional to classify "flag salute" cases as relating to the "free exercise of religion." Gobitis certainly treated the issue in that way, and such treatment was perhaps necessary to Frankfurter's opinion in that case. But Barnette seems quintessentially to involve the freedom to communicate, or rather, the freedom *not* to communicate when doing so would violate one's conscience. Jackson's majority opinion, a superb example of his rhetorical skills, and Frankfurter's dissent, are excerpted in this chapter.

Jackson treated the flag salute as "a form of utterance" which "requires affirmation of a belief and an attitude of mind." He also addressed the issue of the proper means for advancing patriotism, which the Gobitis majority had held to be a matter for legislative judgment:

> Struggles to coerce uniformity of sentiment in support of some end thought essential to their time and country have been waged by many good as well as by evil men. Nationalism is a relatively recent phenomenon, but at other times and places the ends have been racial or territorial security, support of a dynasty or regime, or particular plans for saving souls. As first and moderate methods to attain unity have failed, those bent on its accomplishment must resort to an ever-increasing severity. . . . Those who begin coercive elimination of dissent soon find themselves exterminating dissenters. Compulsory unification of opinion achieves only the unanimity of the graveyard.

And he concluded, in words that have become justly famous:

> If there is any fixed star in our constitutional constellation, it is that no official, high or petty, can prescribe what shall be orthodox in politics, nationalism, religion, or other matters of opinion or force citizens to confess by word or act their faith therein. If there are any circumstances which permit an exception, they do not now occur to us.

Barnette provides the touchstone for dealing with other matters relating to the advancement of patriotism. Since that case, the power of the state to compel the expression of beliefs has been thought to be virtually nil. Indeed, with the exception of the loyalty oath controversies of the 1950s, no cases raising the issue came to the Court from 1943 until the decision, in 1977, in Wooley v. Maynard.

At issue in Maynard was a state statute which mandated that the license plates on a vehicle licensed in New Hampshire carry a particular legend. The presence of such legends on license plates is commonplace, such slogans usually invoking the spectacular beauties of the particular state (New Mexico, Land of Enchantment), one of its well known natural features (Arizona, the Grand Canyon State), or a product for which it is famous, (Idaho, Famous Potatoes). The state of New Hampshire however, had deviated from the norm and, reflecting the views of its then very conservative governor and legislature, mandated that its license plates carry the legend "Live Free or Die." Petitioner, a Jehovah's Witness, argued successfully that he, like the children in Barnette, could not be forced to avow a viewpoint he found objectionable.

Whether Maynard was decided correctly is, one supposes, a matter of opinion. But there is little doubt that it extended Barnette's principle further than fidelity to that decision required. The state, said the majority, by the imprinting of this legend, was seeking to communicate an official view as to the proper appreciation of its history, the objects of its pride, or the particular characteristics of its citizens. This contention is obviously correct, but it does not follow that such an attempt is prohibited under Barnette. For, as Justice Rehnquist noted in caustic dissent, the petitioners in this case were not forced to avow anything. Unlike the Barnette children, they could not have reasonably been thought by those who viewed their license plates necessarily to have agreed with it. Such legends, as we all know, are chosen by the state, not by those on whose license plates they are imprinted. Further, petitioners were free to put on their vehicles bumper stickers of whatever kind they chose, so long as the placement of such devices did not obscure the license plate itself. And, one might also note, the practice struck down in Maynard seems indistinguishable from that of at least some other states. How, for example, is the New Hampshire slogan different from the assertion, by Missouri, that it is the "Show Me" state. Surely that, as most Missourians would agree readily and with pride, asserts something about "the particular characteristics" of Missourians.

Maynard seems destined to remain a relatively unimportant decision on a perhaps idiosyncratic matter, although logically it raises the question of how the Court would deal with a challenge, on similar grounds, to such practices as the imprinting on United States' coins of the legend "In God We Trust." In the absence of such challenges, its importance may lie in the bridge it might have provided between the principle established in Barnette and a series of cases dealing with the use, abuse, and ultimately the destruction of the United States flag. Justice Rehnquist's Maynard dissent argued that individual ownership of license plates is limited in a way that ownership of other things is not. This limitation can be justified, he said, on the grounds that they have a state function to perform. And the performance of such a function presupposes the states' right to limit the manner in which such plates are used. Can the same principle be applied to the right of government to regulate use of the United States flag?

The flag, as Justices Frankfurter and Jackson agreed, is one of the symbols by which we live. Indeed, for most Americans it is probably the most visible and powerful symbol of the nation. It is for this reason, and the accompanying desire to protect that symbol of unity, that Congress has prescribed regulations as to how it is to be raised, flown, struck, and disposed of. For the same reason there have existed for many years a number of state statutes intended to protect the flag from dishonor or inappropriate use.

Such statutes were repeatedly questioned in the turbulent 1960s, for the most part in the context of racial protests or protests against the Vietnam War. In the first such case, Street v. New York (1969), the Court avoided the issue of flag abuse or destruction by ruling that petitioner's conviction might have been based not on his actions, but on the words which he uttered. Street, at the time he was arrested, was publicly burning a flag to protest the shooting of civil rights activist James Meredith. Simultaneously he was uttering words perhaps derisive of the flag. And the New York statute forbade not only the destruction of the flag, but also the utterance of contemptuous words about it. Since Street's conviction might have rested on the speaking of mere words, said Justice Harlan, the conviction must be reversed. Chief Justice Warren, and Justices Black and Fortas, rejected the view that Street's conviction had rested on his words, and would have upheld his conviction. The fact that such staunch defenders of First Amendment freedom as Black and Warren saw no constitutional bar to the prevention of flag burning is worthy of note, but it was the opinion of Fortas which provided justification for that position:

> ... the flag is a special kind of personality. Its use is traditionally and universally subject to special rules and regulations. As early as 1907 the Court affirmed the constitutionality of a state statute making it a crime to use a representation of the United States flag for purposes of advertising. ... Statutes prescribe how the flag may be displayed; how it may lawfully be disposed of; when, how, and for what purposes it may and may not be used. ... A person may "own" a flag but ownership is subject to special burdens and responsibilities. A flag may be property, in a sense; but it is property burdened with peculiar obligations and restrictions. ... Certainly ... these special conditions are not *per se* arbitrary or beyond governmental power ...

In the 1974 case of <u>Smith v. Goguen</u>, petitioner wore a small cloth version of the flag on the seat of his pants. He was convicted of violating a state statute prohibiting public mutilation, trampling, defacing or treating the flag contemptuously. The Court was able to decide the case by holding that, since petitioner was not charged with physical abuse of the flag, the conviction must have been on the impermissible ground of treating it "contemptuously." And, in <u>Schacht v. United States</u> (1970), it held that a federal statute prohibiting use of the flag in dramatic presentations, except in the context of presentations honoring the flag or the nation, was an impermissible discrimination on the basis of viewpoint.

Until recently, the case of <u>Spence v. Washington</u> (1974) raised most directly the issue of governmental power to protect the integrity of the flag. Spence, an opponent of the Vietnam War, displayed an American flag upside down in his apartment window, taping to it a "peace symbol." He was convicted of violating a state statute forbidding the exhibition of a United States flag to which was attached or superimposed figures, symbols, or other extraneous materials.

On its face this law, unlike those involved in other cases, was neither vague nor based on content. It forbade not the treating of the flag in a "contemptuous" manner, but the exhibition of a flag on which anything, whether an overlay of the Statute of Liberty or of a Swastika, was superimposed. Thus the basis for prohibition seemed wholly unrelated to viewpoint, and was concerned only with the issue of assuring that the flag be presented as "the flag." Indeed, it seemed directed more at commercial use of the flag than at its use for disfavored political purposes.

The Court, nevertheless, struck down the conviction, in a *per curiam* opinion based in part on the fact that Spence owned the flag and his action caused it no permanent harm. Justice Rehnquist, dissenting, argued that the majority's treatment of the temporary nature of the act indicated that all that was at stake was an interest in protecting the flag's resale value. Because <u>Spence</u> was the first case in which the Court squarely dealt with the issue of flag "desecration" as "symbolic speech," and because majority and minority opinions foreshadow recent controversies, it is excerpted herein.

The above was, of course, mere prelude to what has lately occurred. In the 1989 case of <u>Texas v. Johnson</u>, the validity of governmental protection of the integrity of the flag as a symbol of national unity was, at last, squarely faced. In the course of a protest demonstration outside the Republican National Convention of 1984, Gregory Johnson burned a flag. He was arrested for violation of a Texas statute which prohibited physical mistreatment of the flag "in a way that the actor knows will seriously offend one or more persons likely to observe and discover his action". The Texas Court of Criminal Appeals reversed his conviction and the Supreme Court, by a vote of five to four, affirmed.

Application of the Texas statute to Johnson's action, said Brennan's majority opinion, could be justified neither by the state's asserted interested in preventing breach of the peace nor in preserving the flag as an instrument of "nationhood and national unity." As to the former, there was no evidence of any threat to the peace for, at most, observers had been "offended" by the burning. As to the latter, prohibition of flag burning on such a basis was inevitably a content-based limitation on expressive activity.

The opinion of the Court in Johnson, as well as the dissenting opinions of Chief Justice Rehnquist (joined by O'Connor and White) and Justice Stevens, is excerpted at the end of this chapter. The decision in that case occasioned a furor or protest. George Bush, not above using a "flag issue" reminiscent of that in Barnette in his campaign for the presidency,[3] recommended a constitutional amendment. And Congress, while rejecting constitutional change, quickly and overwhelmingly passed a federal flag protection statute which, its supporters argued, might pass constitutional muster.

Unlike the invalidated Texas law, the Flag Protection Act of 1989 made, at least on its face, no attempt to distinguish between the messages which "flag desecrators" might seek to convey. It subjected to criminal penalties anyone who "knowingly mutilates, defaces, physically defiles, burns, maintains on the floor or ground, or tramples upon" a United States flag, except when such conduct related to the disposal of a "worn or soiled" flag. Nor did its violation depend on whether others were offended by the conduct at issue.

The constitutionality of the Act was soon tested and, in United States v. Eichman (1990) the Court struck it down. Again the decision was by a five to four margin, and again Justice Brennan spoke for the majority. Conceding that the statute contained "no explicit content-based limitation on the scope of prohibited conduct," Brennan found it "nevertheless clear" that the Government's asserted interested was concerned with the content, and related to the suppression, of expression.

The government's interest in protecting the "physical integrity" of a privately owned flag rests upon a perceived need to preserve the flag's status as a symbol of our Nation and certain national ideals. But the mere destruction or disfigurement of a particular physical manifestation of the symbol, without more, does not diminish or otherwise affect the symbol itself in any way. For example, the secret destruction of a flag in one's own basement would not threaten the flag's recognized meaning. Rather, the Government's desire to preserve the flag as a symbol for certain national ideals is implicated "only when a person's treatment of the flag communicates . . . [a] message that is inconsistent with those ideals.

In support of his view, Brennan pointed to the fact that most of the words used in describing the prohibited conduct "unmistakably connote disrespectful treatment of the flag and suggest a focus on those acts likely to damage the flag's symbolic value." And "the explicit exemption for disposal of 'worn or soiled' flags protects certain acts traditionally associated with respect for the flag." Thus the Act's restriction on expression could not be "justified without reference to the content of the regulated speech" and, for the reasons stated in Johnson, the government's interest could not justify the Act's interference with First Amendment rights.

Justice Stevens, now joined by Rehnquist, White, and O'Connor, again dissented. For Steven's the Court's opinion ended where it should have begun. And

The Government's legitimate interest in preserving the symbolic value of the flag is, however, essentially the same regardless of which of many different ideas may have motivated a particular act of flag burning. . . . the flag uniquely symbolizes the ideas of liberty, equality, and tolerance–ideas that Americans have passionately defended and debated throughout our history. The flag embodies the spirit of our national committment to those ideals. The message thereby transmitted does not take a stand upon our disagreements.

Thus, said Stevens, the Government "may–indeed it should–protect the symbolic value of the flag without regard to the specific content of the flag burner's speech.

As noted, Justice Stevens makes reference to the ideal of "tolerance" as one to which we as a nation are committed. It is perhaps in consideration of that ideal, and in the fact that we are primarily talking about symbols, that a resolution of the conflict over flag desecration may be found. As seems likely with Barnette, recent decisions may be most valuable as "beacons of freedom" and "teachings of "tolerance." One need only recall the persecution of Jehovah's Witnesses which followed Gobitis to appreciate the necessity for Barnette's reaffirmation of the "fixed star" in our constitutional constellation.[4] Perhaps Johnson and Eichman help to prevent similarly intolerant reactions to dissent. And it may be in this manner that even Maynard, a decision which on its face seems illogical, can be applauded, as a recognition of the right of the most idiosyncratic to protection from even the *perception* of governmental compulsion.

---

[1] The "values" of reputation and privacy, of protection from "assaultive and unwanted stimuli," and of private property, discussed in Chapters 10, 11, and 12, are relatively noncontroversial. Not so those dealing with the advancement of patriotism, equality, and decency, the subjects of Chapters 7, 8, and 9. Indeed, some would argue that government is mistaken in what it considers to be patriotic, equal, and decent. Such positions may, of course, be correct. But the legislatures who passed the statutes at issue in the cases to be discussed certainly thought that they were advancing patriotism, equality, and decency. Thus it is that I have employed their terminology, as well as the conceptualizations which underlie their efforts.

[2] See the discussion of the government's right to advocate "values" and political positions, and the dangers associated with such a right, in Tribe, *American Constitutional Law*, 2nd ed., 1988, 807-14.

[3] Bush made political capital of the fact that his Democratic opponent, while Governor of Massachusetts, vetoed a law requiring teachers to lead the Pledge of Allegiance in the state's schools. The Court has not yet decided whether such a law would be valid, and the decision in Barnette would not, contrary to numerous assertions during the campaign, necessarily be dispositive. It is one thing to force a child to say the Pledge when doing so violates his or her conscience. It is another, perhaps, to require a teacher, as a part of the normal duties of the position, to lead children in their voluntary recitation of the Pledge.

[4] On the aftermath of Gobitis and its tragic consequences for Jehovah's Witnesses, see David Manwaring, *Render Unto Caesar: the Flag-Salute Controversy* (Chicago: University of Chicago Press, 1962).

WEST VIRGINIA BOARD OF EDUCATION V. BARNETTE.

319 U.S. 624 (1943)

MR. JUSTICE JACKSON delivered the opinion of the Court.

Following the decision by this Court on June 3,1940, in Minersville School District v. Gobitis, the West Virginia legislature amended its statutes to require all schools therein to conduct courses of instruction in history, civic, and in the Constitutions of the United States and of the State "for the purpose of teaching, fostering and perpetuating the ideals, principles and spirit of Americanism, and increasing the knowledge of the organization and machinery of the government." Appellant Board of Education was directed, with advice of the State Superintendent of Schools, to "prescribe the courses of study covering these subjects" for public schools. The Act made it the duty of private, parochial and denominational schools to prescribe courses of study "similar to those required for the public schools."

The Board of Education on January 9, 1942, adopted a resolution containing recitals taken largely from the Court's Gobitis opinion and ordering that the Salute to the flag become "a regular part of the program of activities in the public schools," that all teachers and pupils "shall be required to participate in the salute honoring the Nation represented by the Flag; provided, however, that refusal to salute the Flag be regarded as an act of insubordination, and shall be dealt with accordingly."

The Witnesses are an unincorporated body teaching that the obligation imposed by law of God is superior to that of laws enacted by temporal government. Their religious beliefs include a literal version of Exodus, Chapter 20, verses 4 and 5, which says: "Thou shalt not make unto thee any graven image, or any likeness of anything that is in heaven above, or that is in the earth beneath, or that is in the water under the earth; thou shalt not bow down thyself to them nor serve them." They consider that the flag is an "image" within this command. For this reason they refuse to salute it.

Officials threaten to send them to reformatories maintained for criminally inclined juveniles. Parents of such children have been prosecuted and are threatened with prosecutions for causing delinquency.

At the present, CHIEF JUSTICE said in dissent in the Gobitis case, the State may "require teaching by instruction and study of all in our history and in the structure and organization of our government, including the guaranties of civil liberty, which tend to inspire patriotism and love of country." Here, however, we are dealing with a compulsion of students to declare a belief. They are not merely made acquainted with the flag salute so that they may be informed as to what it is or even what it means. The issue here is whether this slow and easily neglected route to aroused loyalties constitutionally may be short-cut by substituting a compulsory salute and slogan."

This issue is not prejudiced by pledge requires affirmation of a belief and an attitude of mind. It is not clear whether the regulation contemplates that pupils forego any contrary convictions of their own and become unwilling converts to the prescribed ceremony or whether it will be acceptable if they simulate assent by words without belief and by a gesture barren of meaning. It is now a commonplace that censorship or suppression of expression of opinion is tolerated by our Constitution only when the expression presents a clear and present danger of action of a kind the State is empowered to prevent and punish. It would seem that involuntary affirmation could be commanded only on even more immediate and urgent grounds than silence. But here the power of compulsion is invoked without any allegation that remaining passive during a flag salute ritual creates a clear and present danger that would justify an effort even to muffle expression. To sustain the compulsory flag salute we are required to say that a Bill of Rights which guards the individual's right to speak his own mind, left it open to public authorities to compel him to utter what is not in his mind.

The very purpose of a Bill of Rights was to withdraw certain subjects from the vicissitudes of political controversy, to place them beyond the reach of majorities and officials and to establish them as legal principles to be applied by the courts. One's right to life, liberty, and property, to free speech, a free press, freedom of worship and assembly, and other fundamental rights may not be submitted to vote; they depend on the outcome of no elections.

National unity as an end with officials may foster by persuasion and example is not in question. The problem is whether under our Constitution compulsion as here employed is a permissible means for its achievement.

Struggles to coerce uniformity of sentiment in support of some end thought essential to their time and country have been waged by many good as well as by evil men. Nationalism is a relatively recent phenomenon but at other times and places the ends have been racial or territorial security, support of a dynasty or regime, and particular plans for saving souls. As first and moderate methods to attain unity have failed, those bent on its accomplishment must resort to an ever-increasing severity.

As governmental pressure toward unity becomes greater, so strife becomes more bitter as to whose unity it shall be. Probably no deeper division of our people could proceed from any provocation than from finding it necessary to choose what doctrine and whose program public educational officials shall compel youth to unite in embracing. Ultimate futility of such attempts to compel coherence in the lesson of every such effort from the Roman drive to stamp out Christianity as a disturber of its pagan unity, the Inquisition, as a means to religious and dynastic unity, the Siberian exiles as a means to Russian unity, down to the fast failing efforts of our present totalitarian enemies. Those who begin coercive elimination of dissent soon find themselves exterminating dissenters. Compulsory unification of opinion achieves only the unanimity of the graveyard.

It seems trite but necessary to say that the First Amendment to our Constitution was designed to avoid these ends by avoiding these beginnings. There is no mysticism in the American concept of the State or of the nature or origin of its authority. We set up government by consent of the governed, and the Bill of Rights denies those in power any legal opportunity to coerce that consent. Authority here is to be controlled by public opinion, not public opinion by authority.

The case is made difficult not because the principles of its decision are obscure but because the flag involved is our own. Nevertheless, we apply the limitations of the Constitution with no fear that freedom to be intellectually and spiritually diverse or even contrary will disintegrate the social organization. To believe that patriotism will not flourish if patriotic ceremonies are voluntary and spontaneous instead of a compulsory routine is to make an unflattering estimate of the appeal of our institutions to free minds. We can have intellectual individualism and the rich cultural diversities that we owe to exception minds only at the price of occasional eccentricity and abnormal attitudes. When they are both harmless to others or to the State as those we deal with here, the price is not too great. But freedom to differ is not limited to things that do not matter much. That would be a mere shadow of freedom. The test of its substance is the right to differ as to things that touch the heart of the existing order.

If there is any fixed star in our constitutional constellation, it is that no official, high or petty, can prescribe what shall be orthodox in politics, nationalism, religion, or other matters of opinion or force citizens to confess by word or act their faith therein. If there are any circumstances which permit an exception, they do not now occur to us.

We think the action of the local authorities in compelling the flag salute and pledge transcends constitutional limitations on their power and invades the sphere of intellect and spirit which it is the purpose of the First Amendment to our Constitution to reserve from all official control.

The decision of this Court in *Minersville School District v. Gobitis* and the holdings of those few per curiam decisions which preceded and foreshadowed it are overruled, and the judgment enjoining enforcement of the West Virginia Regulation is Affirmed.

MR. JUSTICE FRANKFURTER, dissenting:

One who belongs to the most vilified and persecuted minority in history is not likely to be insensible to the freedoms guaranteed by our Constitution. Were my purely personal attitude relevant I should wholeheartedly associate myself with the general libertarian views in the Court's opinion, representing as they do the thought and action of a lifetime. But as judges we are neither jew nor gentile, neither Catholic nor agnostic. We owe equal attachment to the Constitution and are equally bound by our judicial obligations whether we derive our citizenship from the earliest or the latest immigrants to these shores. As a member of this Court I am not justified in writing my private notions of policy into the Constitution, no matter how deeply I may cherish them or how mischievous I may deem their disregard. The duty of a judge who must decide which of two claims before the Court shall prevail, that of a State to enact and enforce laws within its general competence or that of an individual to refuse obedience because of the demands of his conscience, is not that of the ordinary person. It can never be emphasized too much that one's own opinion about the wisdom or evil of a law should be excluded altogether when one is doing one's duty on the bench. The only opinion of our own even looking in that direction that is material is our opinion whether legislators could in reason have enacted such a law. In the light of all the circumstances, including the history of this question in this Court, it would require more daring than I possess to deny that reasonable legislators could have taken the action which is before us for review. Most unwillingly, therefore, I must differ from my brethren with regard to legislation like this. I cannot bring my mind to believe that the "liberty" secured by the Due Process Clause gives this Court authority to deny to the State of West Virginia the attainment of that which we all recognize as a legitimate legislative end, namely, the promotion of good citizenship, by employment of the means here chosen.

Consciencious scruples, all would admit, cannot stand against every legislative compulsion to do positive acts in conflict with such scruples. We have been told that such compulsions override religious scruples only as to major concerns of the state. But the determination of what is major and what is minor itself raises questions of policy. For the way in which men equally guided by reason appraise importance goes to the very heart of policy. Judges should be very diffident in setting their judgment against that of a state in determining what is and what is not a major concern, what means are appropriate to proper ends, and what is the total social cost in striking the balance of imponderables.

The constitutional protection of religious freedom, terminated disabilities, it did not create new privileges. It gave religious equality, not civil immunity. Its essence is freedom from conformity to religious dogma, not freedom from conformity to law because of religious dogma. Religious loyalties may be exercised without hinderance from the state, not the state may not exercise that which except by leave of religious loyalties is within the domain of temporal power. Otherwise each individual could set up his own censor against obedience to laws conscienciously deemed for the public, good by those whose business it is to make laws.

Though prohibited by the variety of religious beliefs, otherwise the constitutional guaranty would be not a protection of the free exercise of religion but a denial of the exercise of legislation.

The essence of the religious freedom guaranteed by our Constitution is therefore this: no religion shall either receive the state's support or incur its hostility. Religion is outside the sphere of political government. This does not mean that all matters on which religious organizations or beliefs may pronounce are outside the sphere of government. Were this 80, instead of the separation of church and state, there would be the subordination of the state on any matter deemed within the sovereignty of the religious conscience. Much that is the concern of temporal authority affects the spiritual interests of men. But it is not enough to strike down a non-discriminatory law that it may hurt or offend some dissident view. It would be too easy to cite numerous prohibitions and injunctions to which laws run counter if the variant interpretations of the Bible were made the tests of obedience to law. The validity of secular laws cannot be measured by their conformity to religious doctrines. It is only in a theocratic state that ecclesiastical doctrines measure legal right or wrong.

We are told that a flag salute is a doubtful substitutefor adequate understanding of our institutions. The states that require such a school exercise do not have to justify it as the only means for promoting good citizenship m children, but merely as one of diverse means for accomplishing a worthy end. We may deem it a foolish measure, but the point is that this Court is not the organ of government to resolve doubts as to whether it will fulfill Its purpose. Only if there be no doubt that any reasonable mind could entertain can we deny to the states the right to resolve doubts their way and not ours.

That which to the majority may seem essential for the welfare of the state may offend the consensus of a minority. But, so long as no inroads are made upon the actual exercise of religion by the minority, to deny the political power of the majority to enact laws concerned with civil matters simply because they may offend the consciences of a minority, really means that the consciences of a minority are more sacred and more enshrined in the Constitution than the consciences of the majority.

SPENCE V. WASHINGTON

418 U.S. 405 (1974)

PER CURIAM.

Appellant displayed a United States flag, which he owned, out of the window of his apartment. Affixed to both surfaces of the flag was a large peace symbol fashioned of removable tape. Appellant was convicted under a Washington statute forbidding the exhibition of a United States flag to which is attached or superimposed figures, symbols, or other extraneous material. The Supreme Court of Washington affirmed appellant's

A number of factors are important in the instant case. First, this was a privately owned flag. In a technical property sense it was the property of any government. We have no doubt that the State or National Governments constitutionally may forbid anyone from mishandling in any manner a flag that is public property. But this is a different case. Second, appellant displayed his flag on private property. He engaged in no trespass or disorderly conduct. Nor is this a case that might be analyzed in terms of reasonable time, place, or manner restraints on access to a public area. Third, the record is devoid of proof of any risk of breach of the peace. It was not appellant's purpose to incite violence or even stimulate a public demonstration. There is no evidence that any crowd gathered or that appellant made any effort to attract attention beyond hanging the flag out of his own window. Indeed, on the facts stipulated by the parties there is no evidence that anyone other than the three police officers observed the flag.

Fourth, the State concedes, as did the Washington Supreme Court, that appellant engaged in a form of communication. Although the stipulated facts fail to show that any member of the general public viewed the flag, the State's concession is inevitable on this record. The undisputed facts are that appellant "wanted people to know that I thought America stood for peace." To be sure, appellant did not choose to articulate his views through printed or spoken words. It is therefore necessary to determine whether his activity was sufficiently imbued with elements of communication to fall within the scope of the First and Fourteenth Amendments for as the Court noted in *United States* v. *O'Brien*, (1968), "[w]e cannot accept the view that an apparently limitless variety of conduct can be labeled 'speech' whenever the person engaging in the conduct intends thereby to express an idea." But the nature of appellant's activity, combined with the factual context and environment in which it was undertaken, lead to the conclusion that he engaged in a form of protected expression.

The Court for decades has recognized the communicative connotations of the use of flags. e. g., *Stromberg* v. *California* (1931). In many of their uses flags are a form of symbolism comprising a "primitive but effective way of communicating ideas . . .," and "a short cut from mind to mind." *Board of Education, v. Barnette* (1943). On this record there can be little doubt that appellant communicated through the use of symbols. The symbolism included not only the flag but also the superimposed peace symbol.

Moreover, the context in which a symbol is used for purposes of expression is important, for the context may give meaning to the symbol. See *Tinker* v. *Des Moines School District* (1969). In *Tinker*, the wearing of black armbands in a school environment conveyed an unmistakable message about a contemporaneous issue of intense public concern—the Vietnam hostilities. In this case, appellant's activity was roughly simultaneous with and concededly triggered by the Cambodian incursion and the Kent State tragedy, also issues of great public moment. Cf. *Scheuer* v. *Rhodes*, (1974). A flag bearing a peace symbol and displayed upside down by a student today might be interpreted as nothing more than bizarre behavior, but it would have been difficult for the great majority of citizens to miss the drift of appellant's point at the time that he made it.

We think it appropriate to review briefly the range of various state interests that might be thought to support the challenged conviction, drawing upon the arguments before us, the opinions below, and the Court's opinion in *Street* v. *New York* (1969). The first interest at issue is prevention of breach of the peace. In our view, the Washington Supreme Court correctly rejected this notion. It is totally without support in the record.

We are also unable to affirm the judgment below on the ground that the State may have desired to protect the sensibilities of passersby. "It is firmly settled that under our Constitution the public expression of ideas may not be prohibited merely because the ideas are themselves offensive to some of their hearers." *Street* v. *New York*. Moreover, appellant did not impose his ideas upon a captive audience. Anyone who might have been offended could easily have avoided the display. See *Cohen* v.

California (1971). Nor may appellant be punished for failing to show proper respect for our national emblem. *Street* v. *New York*; *Board of Education* v. *Barnette*.

We are brought, then, to the state court's thesis that Washington has an interest in preserving the national flag as an unalloyed symbol of our country. The court did not define this interest; it simply asserted it. MR. JUSTICE REHNQUIST'S dissenting opinion today, adopts essentially the same approach. Presumably, this interest might be seen as an effort to prevent the appropriation of a revered national symbol by an individual, interest group, or enterprise where there was a risk that association of the symbol with a particular product or viewpoint might be taken erroneously as evidence of governmental endorsement. Alternatively, it might be argued that the interest asserted by the state court is based on the uniquely universal character of the national flag as a symbol. For the great majority of us, the flag is a symbol of patriotism, of pride in the history of our country, and of the service, sacrifice, and valor of the millions of Americans who in peace and war have joined together to build and to defend a Nation in which self-government and personal liberty endure. It evidences both the unity and diversity which are America. For others the flag carries in varying degrees a different message. "A person gets from a symbol the meaning he puts into it, and what is one man's comfort and inspiration is another's jest and scorn." *Board of Education* v. *Barnette*. It might be said that we all draw something from our national symbol, for it is capable of conveying simultaneously a spectrum of meanings. If it may be destroyed or permanently disfigured, it could be argued that it will lose its capability of mirroring the sentiments of all who view it.

But we need not decide in this case whether the interest advanced by the court below is valid. We assume, *arguendo*, that it is. The statute is nonetheless unconstitutional as applied to appellant's activity. There was no risk that appellant's acts would mislead viewers into assuming that the Government endorsed his viewpoint. To the contrary, he was plainly and peacefully protesting the fact that it did not. Appellant was not charged under the desecration statute, nor did he permanently disfigure the flag or destroy it. He displayed it as a flag of his country in a way closely analogous to the manner in which flags have always been used to convey ideas. Moreover, his message was direct, likely to be understood, and within the contours of the First Amendment. Given the protected character of his expression and in light of the fact that no interest the State may have in preserving the physical integrity of a privately owned flag was significantly impaired on these facts, the conviction must be invalidated.

The judgment is reversed.

MR. JUSTICE REHNQUIST, with whom THE CHIEF JUSTICE and MR. JUSTICE WHITE join, dissenting.

The Court holds that a Washington statute prohibiting persons from attaching material to the American flag was unconstitutionally applied to appellant. Although I agree with the Court that appellant's activity was a form of communication, I do not agree that the First Amendment prohibits the State from restricting this activity in furtherance of other important interests. And I believe the rationale by which the Court reaches its conclusion is unsound.

"[T]he right of free speech is not absolute at all times and under all circumstances," *Chaplinsky* v. *New Hampshire* (1942). This Court has long recognized, for example, that some forms of expression are not entitled to any protection at all under the First Amendment, despite the fact that they could reasonably be thought protected under its literal language. See *Roth* v. *United States* (1957). The Court has further recognized that even protected speech may be subject to reasonable limitation when important countervailing interests are involved. Citizens are not completely free to commit perjury, to libel other citizens, to infringe copyrights, to incite riots, or to interfere unduly with passage through a public thoroughfare. The right of free speech, though precious, remains subject to reasonable accommodation to other valued interests.

Since a State concededly may impose some limitations on speech directly, it would seem to follow *a fortiori* that a State may legislate to protect important state interests even though an incidental limitation on free speech results. Virtually any law enacted by a State, when viewed with sufficient ingenuity, could be thought to interfere with some citizen's preferred means of expression. But no one would argue, I presume, that a State could not prevent the painting of public buildings simply because a particular class of protesters believed their message would best be conveyed through that medium. Had appellant here chosen to tape his peace symbol to a federal courthouse, I have little doubt that he could be prosecuted under a statute properly drawn to protect public property.

Yet the Court today holds that the State of Washington cannot limit use of the American flag, at least insofar as its statute prevents appellant from using a privately owned flag to convey his personal message. Expressing its willingness to assume, *arguendo*, that Washington has a valid interest in preserving the integrity of the flag, the Court nevertheless finds that interest to be insufficient in this case. To achieve this result the Court first devalues the State's interest under these circumstances, noting that "no interest the State may have in preserving the physical integrity of a privately owned flag was significantly impaired on these facts. . . ." The Court takes pains to point out that appellant did not "permanently disfigure the flag or destroy it," and emphasizes that the flag was displayed "in a way closely analogous to the manner in which flags have always been used to convey ideas." The Court then restates the notion that such state interests are secondary to messages which are "direct, likely to be understood, and within the contours of the First Amendment.

Turning to the question of the State's interest in the flag it seems to me that the Court's treatment lacks all substance. The suggestion that the State's interest somehow diminishes when the flag is decorated with *removable* tape trivializes something which is not trivial. The State of Washington is hardly seeking to protect the flag's resale value, and yet the Court's emphasis on the lack of actual damage to the flag suggests that this is a significant aspect of the State's interest. Surely the Court does not mean to imply that appellant *could* be prosecuted if he subsequently tore the flag in the process of trying to take the tape off. Unlike flag-desecration statutes, which the Court correctly notes are not at issue in this case, the Washington statute challenged here seeks to prevent personal *use* of the flag, not simply particular forms of *abuse*. The State of Washington has chosen to set the flag apart for a special purpose, and has directed that it not be turned into a common background for an endless variety of superimposed messages. The physical condition of the flag itself is irrelevant to that purpose.

The true nature of the State's interest in this case is not only one of preserving "the physical integrity of the flag," but also one of preserving the flag as "an important symbol of nationhood and unity."

The value of this interest has been emphasized in recent as well as distant times. Mr. Justice Fortas, for example noted in *Street* v. *New York* (1969), that "the flag is a special kind of personalty," a form of property "burdened with peculiar obligations and restrictions." MR. JUSTICE WHITE has observed that "[t]he flag is a national property, and the Nation may regulate those who would make, imitate, sell, possess, or use it." *Smith* v. *Goguen* (concurring in judgment). I

agree. What appellant here seeks is simply license to use the flag however he pleases, so long as the activity can be tied to a concept of speech, regardless of any state interest in having the flag used only for more limited purposes. I find no reasoning in the Court's opinion which convinces me that the Constitution requires such license to be given.

The fact that the State has a valid interest in preserving the character of the flag does not mean, of course, that it can employ all conceivable means to enforce it. It certainly could not require all citizens to own the flag or compel citizens to salute one. *Board of Education* v. *Barnette* (1943). It presumably cannot punish criticism of the flag, or the principles for which it stands, any more than it could punish criticism of this country's policies or ideas. But the statute in this case demands no such allegiance. Its operation does not depend upon whether the flag is used for communicative or noncommunicative purposes; upon whether a particular message is deemed commercial or political; upon whether the use of the flag is respectful or contemptuous; or upon whether any particular segment of the State's citizenry might applaud or oppose the intended message. It simply withdraws a unique national symbol from the roster of materials that may be used as a background for communications. Since I do not believe the Constitution prohibits Washington from making that decision, I dissent.

TEXAS, PETITIONER V. GREGORY LEE JOHNSON ON WRIT OF CERTIORARI TO THE COURT OF CRIMINAL APPEALS OF TEXAS

491 U.S. 397 (1989)

JUSTICE BRENNAN delivered the opinion of the Court.

After publicly burning an American flag as a means of political protest, Gregory Lee Johnson was convicted of desecrating a flag in violation of Texas law. This case presents the question

whether his conviction is consistent with the First Amendment. We hold that it is not.

While the Republican National Convention was taking place in Dallas in 1984, respondent Johnson participated in a political demonstration dubbed the

"Republican War Chest Tour." As explained in literature distributed by the demonstrators and in speeches made by them, the purpose of this event was to protest the policies of the Reagan administration and of certain Dallas-based corporations. The demonstrators marched through the Dallas streets, chanting political slogans and stopping at several corporate locations to stage "die-ins" intended to dramatize the consequences of nuclear war. On several occasions they spray-painted the walls of buildings and overturned potted plants, but Johnson himself took no part in such activities. He did, however, accept an American flag handed to him by a fellow protester who had taken it from a flag pole outside one of the targeted buildings.

The demonstration ended in front of Dallas City Hall, where Johnson unfurled the American flag, doused it with kerosene, and set it on fire. While the flag burned, the protesters chanted, "America, the red, white, and blue, we spit on you." After the demonstrators dispersed, a witness to the flag-burning collected the flag's remains and buried them in his backyard. No one was physically injured or threatened with injury, though several witnesses testified that they had been seriously offended by the flag-burning. the approximately 100 demonstrators, Johnson a was charged with a crime. The only criminal offense with which he was charged was the desecration of a venerated object in violation of Tex. Penal Code Ann. 42.09(a)(3) (1989). After a trial, he was convicted, sentenced to one year in prison, and fined $2,000. The Court of Appeals for the Fifth District of Texas at Dallas affirmed Johnson's conviction, but the Texas Court of Criminal Appeals reversed, holding that the State could not, consistent with the First Amendment, punish Johnson for burning the flag in these circumstances.

Johnson was convicted of flag desecration for harming the flag rather than for uttering insulting words. This fact somewhat complicates our consideration of his conviction under the First Amendment. We must first determine whether Johnson's burning of the flag constituted expressive conduct, permitting him to invoke the First Amendment in challenging his conviction.

The State of Texas conceded for purposes of its oral argument in this case that Johnson's conduct was expressive conduct and this concession seems to us as prudent as was Washington's in *Spence*. Johnson burned an American flag as part—indeed, as the culmination—of a political demonstration that coincided with the convening of the Republican Party and its renomination of Ronald Reagan for President. The expressive, overtly political nature of this conduct was both intentional and overwhelmingly apparent. At his trial, Johnson explained his reasons for burning the flag as follows: "The American Flag was burned as Ronald Reagan was being renominated as President. And a more powerful statement of symbolic speech, whether you agree with it or not, couldn't have been made at that time. It's quite a just position [juxtaposition]. We had new patriotism and no patriotism." In these circumstances, Johnson's burning of the flag was conduct "sufficiently imbued with elements of communication," *Spence*, to implicate the First Amendment, although we have recognized that where "'speech' and 'nonspeech' elements are combined in the same course of conduct, a sufficiently important governmental interest in regulating the nonspeech element can justify incidental limitations on First Amendment freedoms," *O'Brien*, we have limited the applicability of *O'Brien's* relatively lenient standard to those cases in which "the governmental interest is unrelated to the suppression of free expression." In stating, moreover, that *O'Brien's* test "in the last analysis is little, if any, different from the standard applied to time, place, or manner restrictions," *Clark*, we have highlighted the requirement that the governmental interest in question be unconnected to expression in order to come under *O'Brien's* less demanding rule.

In order to decide whether *O'Brien's* test applies here, therefore, we must decide whether Texas has asserted an interest in support of Johnson's conviction that is unrelated to the suppression of expression.

Texas claims that its interest in preventing breaches of the peace justifies

Johnson's conviction for flag desecration. However, no disturbance of the peace actually occurred or threatened to occur because of Johnson's burning of the flag. Although the State stresses the disruptive behavior of the protesters during their march toward City Hall, it admits that "no actual breach of the peace occurred at the time of the flag-burning or in response to the flag-burning." The State's emphasis on the protestors' disorderly actions prior to arriving at City Hall is not only somewhat surprising given that no charges were brought on the basis of this conduct, but it also fails to show that a disturbance of the peace was a likely reaction to Johnson's conduct. The only evidence offered by the State at trial to show the reaction to Johnson's actions was the testimony of several persons who had been seriously offended by the flag-burning.

The State's position, therefore, amounts to a claim that an audience that takes serious offense at particular expression is necessarily likely to disturb the peace and that the expression may be prohibited on this basis. our precedents not countenance such a presumption. On the contrary, they recognize that a principal "function of free speech under our system of government is to invite dispute. It may indeed best serve its high purpose when it induces a condition of unrest, creates dissatisfaction with conditions as they are, or even stirs people to anger." *Terminiello v. Chicago.*

Thus, we have not permitted the (government to assume that every expression of a provocative idea will incite a riot, but have instead required careful consideration of the actual circumstances surrounding such expression, asking whether the expression is directed to inciting or producing imminent lawless action and is likely to incite or produce such action." *Brandenburg v. Ohio* (1969) (reviewing circumstances surrounding rally and speeches by Ku Klux Klan). To accept Texas' arguments that it need only demonstrate "the potential for a breach of the peace," and that every flag-burning necessarily possesses that potential, would be to eviscerate our holding in *Brandenburg.* This we decline to do.

Nor does Johnson's expressive

conduct fall within that small class of "fighting words" that are "likely to provoke the average person to retaliation, and thereby cause a breach of the peace." *Chaplinsky* v. *New Hampshire* (1942). No reasonable onlooker would have regarded Johnson's generalized expression of dissatisfaction with the policies of the Federal Government as a direct personal insult or an invitation to exchange fisticuffs. See *Cantwell v. Connecticut* (1940); *FCC v. Pacifica Foundation* (opinion of STEVENS, J.).

We thus conclude that the State's interest in maintaining order is not implicated on these facts.

The State also asserts an interest in preserving the flag as a symbol of nationhood and national unity. In *Spence,* we acknowledged that the Government's interest in preserving the flag's special symbolic value "is directly related to expression in the context of activity" such as affixing a peace symbol to a flag. We are equally persuaded that this interest is related to expression in the case of Johnson's burning of the flag. The State, apparently, is concerned that such conduct will lead people to believe either that the flag does not stand for nationhood and national unity, but instead reflects other, less positive concepts, or that the concepts reflected in the flag do not in fact exist, that is, we do not enjoy unity as a Nation. These concerns blossom only when a person's treatment of the flag communicates some message, and thus are related "to the suppression of free expression" within the meaning of *O'Brien.* We are thus outside of *O'Brien's* test altogether.

It remains to consider whether the State's interest in preserving the flag as a symbol of nationhood and national unity justifies Johnson's conviction.

As in *Spence,* "[w]e are confronted with a case of prosecution for the expression of an idea through activity," and "[a]ccordingly, we must examine with particular care the interests advanced by [petitioner] to support its prosecution." Johnson was not, we add, prosecuted for the expression of just any idea; he was prosecuted for his expression of dissatisfaction with the policies of this country, expression situated at the core of our First Amendment values. Moreover, Johnson was prosecuted because he knew that his politically charged expression would cause "serious offense." If he had burned the flag as a means of disposing of it because it was dirty or torn, he would not have been convicted of flag desecration under this Texas law: federal law designates burning as the preferred means of disposing of a flag "when it is in such condition that it is no longer a fitting emblem for display," and Texas has no quarrel with this means of disposal. The Texas law is thus not aimed at protecting the physical integrity of the flag in all circumstances, but is designed instead to protect it only against impairments that would cause serious offense to others. Texas concedes as much: "Section 42.09(b) reaches only those severe acts of physical abuse of the flag carried out in a way likely to be offensive. The statute mandates intentional or knowing abuse, that is, the kind of mistreatment that is not innocent, but rather is intentionally designed to seriously offend other individuals."

Johnson's political expression was restricted because of the content of the message he conveyed. We must therefore subject the State's asserted interest in preserving the special symbolic character of the flag to the most exacting scrutiny." *Boos v. Barry.*

Texas argues that its interest in preserving the flag as a symbol of nationhood and national unity survives this close analysis. Quoting extensively from the writings of this Court chronicling the flag's historic and symbolic role in our society, the State emphasizes the "special place" reserved for the flag in own Nation. The State's argument is not that it has an interest simply in maintaining the flag as a symbol of *something*, no matter what it symbolizes; indeed, if that were the State's position, it would be difficult to see how that interest is endangered by highly symbolic conduct such as Johnson's. Rather, the State's claim is that it has an interest in preserving the flag as a symbol of *nationhood* and *national unity*, a symbol with a determinate range of meanings. According to Texas, if one

physically treats the flag in a way that would tend to cast doubt on either the idea that nationhood and national unity are the flag's referents or that national unity actually exists, the message conveyed thereby is a harmful one and therefore may be prohibited.

If there is a bedrock principle underlying the First Amendment, it is that the Government may not prohibit the expression of an idea simply because society finds the idea itself offensive or disagreeable.

We never before have held that the Government may ensure that a symbol be used to express only one view of that symbol or its referents. Indeed, in *Schacht v. United States,* we invalidated a federal statute permitting an actor portraying a member of one of our armed forces to " 'wear the uniform of that armed force if the portrayal does not tend to discredit that armed force." This proviso, we held, "which leaves Americans free to praise the war in Vietnam but can send persons like Schacht to prison for opposing it, cannot survive in a country which has the First Amendment."

We perceive no basis on which to hold that the principle underlying our decision in *Schacht* does not apply to this case. To conclude that the Government may permit designated symbols to be used to communicate only a limited set of messages would be to enter territory having no discernible or defensible boundaries. Could the Government, on this theory, prohibit the burning of state flags? Of copies of the Presidential seal? Of the Constitution? In evaluating these choices under the First Amendment, how would we decide which symbols were sufficiently special to warrant this unique status? To do so, we would be forced to consult our own political preferences, and impose them on the citizenry, in the very way that the First Amendment forbids us to do.

The First Amendment does not guarantee that other concepts virtually sacred to our Nation as a whole—such as the principle that discrimination on the basis of race is odious and destructive—will go unquestioned in the marketplace of ideas. See *Brandenburg v. Ohio* (1969).

We decline, therefore, to create for the flag an exception to the joust of principles protected by the First Amendment.

It is not the State's ends, but its means, to which we object. It cannot be gainsaid that there is a special place reserved for the flag in this Nation, and thus we do not doubt that the Government has a legitimate interest in making efforts to "preserv[e] the national flag as an unalloyed symbol of our country." *Spence.* We reject the suggestion, urged at oral argument by counsel for Johnson, that the Government lacks "any state interest whatsoever" in regulating the manner in which the flag may be displayed. Congress has, for example, enacted precatory regulations describing the proper treatment of the flag, and we cast no doubt on the legitimacy of its interest in making such recommendations.

To say that the Government has an interest in encouraging proper treatment of the flag, however, is not to say that it may criminally punish a person for burning a flag as a means of political protest. "National unity as an end which officials may foster by persuasion and example is not in question. The problem is whether under our Constitution compulsion here employed is a permissible means for its achievement." *Barnette.*

CHIEF JUSTICE REHNQUIST, with whom JUSTICE WHITE and JUSTICE O'CONNOR join, dissenting. . . .

The American flag, then, throughout more than 200 years of our history, has come to be the visible symbol embodying our Nation. It does not represent the views of any particular political party, and it does not represent any particular political philosophy. The flag is not simply another "idea" or "point of view" competing for recognition in the marketplace of ideas. Millions and millions of Americans regard it with an almost mystical reverence regardless of what sort of social, political, or philosophical beliefs they may have. I cannot agree that the First Amendment invalidates the Act of Congress, and the laws of 48 of the 50 States, which make criminal the public burning of the flag.

More than 80 years ago in *Halter v. Nebraska* (1907), this Court upheld the constitutionality of a Nebraska statute that forbade the use of representations of the American flag for advertising purposes upon articles of merchandise. The Court there said:

For that flag every true American has not simply an appreciation but a deep affection. . . . Hence, it has often occurred that insults to a flag have been the cause of war, and indignities put upon it, in the presence of those who revere it, have often been resented and sometimes punished on the spot.

Only two Terms ago, in *San Francisco Arts & Athletics, Inc. v. United States Olympic Committee* (1987), the Court held that Congress could grant exclusive use of the word "Olympic" to the United States Olympic Committee. The Court thought that this "restrictio[n] on expressive speech properly [was] characterized as incidental to the primary congressional purpose of encouraging and rewarding the USOC's activities." As the Court stated, "when a word [or symbol] acquires value as the result of organization and the expenditure of labor, skill, and money by an entity, that entity constitutionally may obtain a limited property right in the word [or symbol]." Quoting *International News Service v. Associated Press* (1918). Surely Congress or the States may recognize a similar interest in the flag.

But the Court insists that the Texas statute prohibiting the public burning of the American flag infringes on respondent Johnson's freedom of expression. Such freedom, of course, is not absolute. See *Schenck v. United States* (1919). In *Chaplinsky* v. *New Hampshire* (1942), a unanimous Court said:

Allowing the broadest scope to the language and purpose of the Fourteenth Amendment, it is well understood that the right of free speech is not absolute at all times and under all circumstances. There are certain well-defined and narrowly limited classes of speech, the prevention and punishment of which have never been thought to raise any Constitutional problem. These include the lewd and obscene, the profane, the libelous, and the insulting or 'fighting' words—those which by their very utterance inflict injury or tend to incite an immediate breach of the peace. It has been well observed that such utterances are no essential part of any exposition of ideas, and are of such slight social value as a step to truth that any benefit that may be derived from them is clearly outweighed by the social interest in order and morality.

The Court upheld *Chaplinsky's* conviction under a state statute that made it unlawful to "address any offensive, derisive or annoying word to any person who is lawfully in any street or other public place." Chaplinsky had told a local Marshal, "You are a God damned racketeer" and a "damned Fascist and the whole government of Rochester are Fascists or agents of Fascists."

Here it may equally well be said that the public burning of the American flag by Johnson was no essential part of any exposition of ideas, and at the same time it had a tendency to incite a breach of the peace. Johnson was free to make any verbal denunciation of the Hag that he wished; indeed, he was free to burn the flag in private. He could publicly burn other symbols of the Government or effigies of political leaders. He did lead a march through the streets of Dallas, and conducted a rally in front of the Dallas City Hall. He engaged in a "die-in" to protest nuclear weapons. He shouted out various slogans during the march, including: "Reagan, Mondale which will it be? Either one means World War III"; "Ronald Reagan, killer of the hour, Perfect example of U. S. power"; and "red, white and blue, we spit on you, you stand for plunder, you will go under." For none of these acts was he arrested or prosecuted; it was only when he proceeded to burn publicly an American flag stolen from its rightful owner that he violated the Texas statute.

The Court could not, and did not, say that Chaplinsky's utterances were not expressive phrases—they clearly and succinctly conveyed an extremely low opinion of the addressee. The same may be said of Johnson's public burning of the flag in this case; it obviously did convey Johnson's bitter dislike of his country. But his act, like Chaplinsky's provocative words, conveyed nothing that could not have been conveyed and was not conveyed just as forcefully in a dozen different ways. As with "fighting words," so with flag burning. for purposes of the First Amendment: It is "no essential part of any exposition of ideas, and [is] of such slight social value as a step to truth that any benefit that may be derived from [it] is clearly outweighed" by the public interest in avoiding a probable breach of the peace.

The result of the Texas statute is obviously to deny one in Johnson's frame of mind one of many means of "symbolic speech." Far from being a case of "one picture being worth a thousand words," flag burning is the equivalent of an inarticulate grunt or roar that, it seems fair to say, is most likely to be indulged in not to express any particular idea, but to antagonize others. Only five years ago we said in *Los Angeles City Council v. Taxpayers for Vincent* (1984), that "the First Amendment does not guarantee the right to employ every conceivable method of communication at all times and in all places." The Texas statute deprived Johnson of only one rather inarticulate symbolic form of protest—a form of protest that was profoundly offensive to many—and left him with a full panoply of other symbols and every conceivable form of verbal expression to express his deep disapproval of national policy. Thus, in no way can it be said that Texas is punishing him because his hearers—or any other group of people—were profoundly opposed to the message that he sought to convey. Such opposition is not a proper basis for restricting speech or expression under the First Amendment. It was Johnson's use of this particular symbol, and not the idea that he sought to convey by it or by his many other expressions, for which he was punished.

JUSTICE STEVENS, dissenting.

The value of the flag as a symbol cannot be measured. Even so, I have no doubt that the interest in preserving that value for the future is both significant and legitimate. Conceivably that value will be enhanced by the Court's conclusion that our national commitment to free expression is so strong that even the United States as ultimate guarantor of that freedom is without power to prohibit the desecration of its unique symbol. But I am unpersuaded. The creation of a federal right to post bulletin boards and graffiti on the Washington Monument might enlarge the market for free expression, but at a cost I would not pay. Similarly, in my considered judgment, sanctioning the public desecration of the flag will tarnish its value—both for those who cherish the ideas for which it waves and for those who desire to don the U. S. 50, 70 (1976) (plurality opinion). The content of respondent's message has no relevance whatsoever to the case. The concept of "desecration" does not turn on the substance of the message the actor intends to convey, but rather on whether those who view the *act* will take serious offense. Accordingly, one intending to convey a message of respect for the flag by burning it in a public square might nonetheless be guilty of desecration if he knows that others—perhaps simply because they misperceive the intended message—will be seriously offended. Indeed, even if the actor knows that all possible witnesses will understand that he intends to send a message of respect, he might still be guilty of desecration if he also knows that this understanding does not lessen the offense taken by some of those witnesses. Thus, this is not a case in which the fact that "it is the speaker's opinion that gives offense" provides a special "reason for according it constitutional protection," *FCC v. Pacifica Foundation* (1978) (plurality opinion). The case has nothing to do with "disagreeable ideas." It involves disagreeable conduct that, in my opinion, diminishes the value of an important national asset.

The Court is therefore quite wrong in blandly asserting that respondent "was prosecuted for his expression of dissatisfaction with the policies of this country, expression situated at the core of our First Amendment values." Respondent was prosecuted because of the method he chose to express his dissatisfaction with those policies. Had he chosen to spray paint—or perhaps convey with a motion picture projector—his message of dissatisfaction on the facade of the Lincoln Memorial, there would be no question about the power of the Government to prohibit his means of expression. The prohibition would be supported by the legitimate interest in preserving the quality of an important national asset. Though the asset at stake in this case is intangible, given its unique value, the same interest supports a prohibition on the desecration of the American flag.

8

THE ADVANCEMENT OF EQUALITY

By the "advancement of equality," we mean, for the purpose of this chapter, governmental attempts to prevent communicative activity[1] which denigrates the status or self-esteem of members of certain groups in society, or which interferes with their enjoyment of equal rights. Such attempts, commonly although not inevitably, have as their long range goal not merely equal treatment but the fostering of the "idea" of equality.

The idea of equality has long and rightfully been a concern of the government. Of particular concern are matters related to race and ethnicity, and more recently, to sex. The reasons for this governmental concern are easy to grasp. They include the fact that distinctions based on irrelevancies are contrary to the democratic idea itself, and that, though our society's ideals have long held this to be true, our practice regarding Blacks, Indians, Hispanics, women, and other groups has diverged widely from the democratic ideal. It is considerations such as these, along with the reactions of unfavored groups to unequal treatment, that have caused government to attempt to redress not only the balance of unequal treatment, but also to adopt policies designed to foster equal perception as well as equal action.

On the other hand, First Amendment values argue for great care in the making of such attempts; for most of them implicate not only speech, but "political speech," which is at the core of the First Amendment. As Justice Jackson said in his Barnette opinion, "If there is any fixed star in our constitutional constellation, it is that no official, high or petty, can prescribe what shall be orthodox in politics, nationalism, religion, or other matters of opinion . . ." If this statement is not an accurate description of the current state of affairs, it is probably because of the pull of equality.

Thus we have recently seen attempts to circumscribe the range of permissible speech in colleges and universities, on the grounds that communications contrary to the idea of equality create an unfavorable atmosphere for learning. And we have seen some elements of the women's movement join conservative groups in an attempt to stamp out pornography, thought to contribute to the perception of women as inferior or to stimulate violence against women.

The tension that exists between freedom of communication and the advancement of equality can be seen most sharply in a Supreme Court decision that, although 40 years old and largely superseded, still remains at least technically the law of the land. Beauharnais v. Illinois, reproduced herein, involved violation of a group libel statute that forbade the communication of words which portrayed "depravity, criminality, unchastity, or lack of virtue of a class of citizens," or which exposed such citizens to "contempt, derision, or obloquy, or is productive of breach of the peace or riots." Petitioner was convicted for distributing leaflets on the streets of Chicago asking city officials to "halt the further encroachment, harassment, and invasion of white people, their property, neighborhoods, and persons by the Negro," and calling for Chicago's white citizens to unite, warning that "if the need to prevent the white race from becoming mongrelized by the Negro will not unite us, then the aggressions. . . .rapes, robberies, knives, guns, and marijuana of the Negro surely will." The Court, by a five to four margin, upheld the Beauharnais conviction.[2]

Both the majority and minority concluded that Beauharnais was circulating a petition to city officials, an activity that the First Amendment specifically protects. The majority opinion avoided this problem by seeing the statute as a type of libel law. Surely, argued Justice Frankfurter, accusing individuals or groups of such crimes could be punished as libel "unless we can say that this is a willful and purposeless restriction unrelated to the peace and welfare of the state." But such a motivation could not, in view of Illinois' long history of racial tension and race riots, be ascribed to the legislature. Further, Frankfurter argued in what is perhaps the most persuasive section of his opinion, it is not merely the interest of Blacks as a group that is at issue, it is the interests of individual Blacks. For a man's job, his educational opportunities, and the dignity accorded him may depend as much on the reputation of the racial group to which he belongs, as it does on his own reputation.

Frankfurter's opinion has, to anyone interested in racial harmony and cognizant of the realities of prejudice, considerable persuasive power. The problem is, as the dissenting opinions of Justices Black and Douglas noted, that the statute as written clearly infringed on what is normally considered to be political speech, which the Court has repeatedly held is at the "core" of the First Amendment. Additionally, the test which Frankfurter applied to the statute, that it not be a "willful and purposeless" restriction on speech, is much less demanding than the requirement currently applied in the First Amendment context, that the restriction be justified by a "compelling state interest," and be narrowly drawn so as to constitute the "least restrictive means" to accomplish its object.

At one time one might have argued that the Beauharnais problem could be solved by application of the "fighting words" doctrine, for petitioner distributed his leaflets in an area of Chicago where Blacks were certain to see them and take offense. But the concept of "fighting words" has, as we have noted, been limited to situations in which words are addressed to individuals in one-on-one situations. One may wish that the Court had left a little "play in the joints" for the doctrine, thus making it available for this kind of case. The fundamental problem, however, would remain. For the evil which the state sought to alleviate was not simply the danger to the peace which the distribution of Beauharnais' message could be expected to cause, but the long term evil which was thought to flow from his message.

Long term evil and the possibility that it might be caused by a particular message, were also the concerns in two more recent cases. Pittsburgh Press Company v. Pittsburgh Commission on Human Relations (1973) was the first case in which the Court attempted to balance the First Amendment against the advancement of gender equality. In that case, a Pittsburgh, Pennsylvania, ordinance forbade newspapers to carry "help wanted" ad in columns which were gender-specific. The statute, as construed by the state courts, did not apply to those positions for which sex was a *bona fide* occupational qualification, or those which were otherwise exempt from statutes relating to gender discrimination. The Pittsburgh Press appealed a conviction for carrying such advertisements. Its chief argument was that the ordinance interfered impermissibly with its editorial judgment as to where in the paper materials should be placed.

The case was decided before the Court's extension of First Amendment protection to commercial speech, a fact which played a large part in the six to three decision upholding the ordinance. Justice Powell's majority opinion emphasized that the kind of information involved related solely to the availability of jobs and was thus a classic example of unprotected commercial speech. The employer's desire to place an advertisement in a specific, gender-designated column, indicated likely discrimination. Thus, the placing of the advertisement not only involved an editorial judgment about where commercial messages should be placed, but in practice fostered discrimination forbidden by law. Just as an advertiser would not be free to advertise the availability of heroin or prostitution, the newspaper's editorial judgment, in the face of the illegality involved, could not be determinative as to the proper location for the advertisement.

Justice Stewart, dissenting, "saw no reason . . .(after this decision). . . why government cannot force a newspaper publisher to conform in the same way in order to achieve other goals thought socially desirable." And, although "those who think the First Amendment can and should be subordinated to other socially desirable interests, will hail today's decision," Stewart found it frightening.

Justice Douglas, also dissenting, sought to distinguish between the publishing of the ad and the carrying through by the employer of the discrimination evidenced by its placement. The employer could, said Douglas, be punished for the second, but neither he nor the newspaper could be punished for the first, particularly in view of the fact that he would be entirely free to write a letter to the newspaper, which letter it would be free to print, denouncing the law mandating equality in hiring.

The observation of Justice Stewart, that newspapers should not be forced to bend their judgment to what may be regarded as socially desirable goals, seems on its face, both unremarkable and very attractive. Yet reflection will reveal that, at least in so far as the premises of this book are concerned, it will not stand analysis. For the essence of "balancing" is the idea that, at least in some cases, First Amendment values must give way to socially desirable goals.

The argument of Justice Douglas is even less persuasive. It is, in the first place, a *non-sequitur* to hold that because one may object to the contents of a law, one is free to participate in an agreement designed to make it easier to break that law. Second, the adoption of Douglas' distinction between the publishing of the ad and the violating of the statute would sweep away all laws prohibiting the advertising of illegal products or activity. Finally, the evil of gender discrimination is served very nearly as much by the placing of such an ad as it is by the refusal to hire a female. If a woman looking for a position saw an ad placed in the "males only" column, surely the very placement of the ad would inhibit and perhaps prevent her from attempting to seek the position. Thus, the illegal goal of the employer would be at least partially fulfilled.

It is perhaps doubtful that the decision in Pittsburgh Press will survive the Court's more recent rejection of the position that commercial speech is unprotected by the First Amendment. In a more recent case also involving such speech, as well as a governmental attempt to foster racial integration, the Court unanimously struck down the challenged statute.

In Linmark Associates v. Willingboro (1977), the issue was whether government could prohibit the placement of "For Sale" signs on private property which the owners wished to sell. The Township of Willingboro, N.J., in order to discourage panic selling, "blockbusting," and "white flight," all actions thought likely to follow if it became known that blacks were moving into an area, had prohibited real estate agencies and private citizens from displaying such signs.

The Supreme Court, following its decision in Virginia Board of Pharmacy v. Virginia Consumers Group (which held commercial speech to be entitled to First Amendment protection), ruled the ordinance invalid. Justice Marshall, writing for a unanimous Court, first noted that people have as much interest in the availability of information for commercial decisions as for decisions in other areas of life. As to the Township's argument that since other alternatives were available to those who wished to sell their homes, this was a "time, place, and manner" regulation. Marshall was unconvinced. In the first place, the activity involved here was one that was central, rather than peripheral, to the business of selling homes. And it was a way, perhaps the only way, for the householder himself to convey the fact that the property was for sale.

More fundamentally, the city was not really concerned with the manner of communicating the message in question. Rather, it did not wish the fact that houses were for sale to be communicated at all. The goal, according to the city, was to promote stable, racially integrated housing. But the presence of a laudable goal could not justify limiting the dissemination of truthful and wholly legal information on the basis of its content.

The activity thought to be fostered by the gender specific ads in Pittsburgh Press had been declared to be illegal. The communications which the Township had sought to suppress were legal, and were themselves devoid of any specific racial context. Thus it is unlikely that either of these cases can be regarded as dispositive of the issues raised by the movement for "political correctness." Although "PC" has had its major impact on college campuses, the viewpoint it represents is similar to that underlying statutes directed at insuring "correctness" in the treatment of women in sexually explicit motion pictures. Such ordinances have been considered by at least two cities.[3]

Spurred on by feminist groups, and with the assistance of attorneys associated with the feminist cause, local governing bodies in Hennepin County, Minnesota (Minneapolis), and in Indianapolis, Indiana adopted ordinances which proscribed the showing, in any pictorial form, of women as victims in scenes of sexual violence, or as subservient to men in sexual scenes. The rationale of the ordinances was that such depictions led to the rape of women, or to a more generalized male tendency to regard women as objects to be dealt with violently and to be subdued. The ordinances did not purport to reach other sexual depictions of women (i.e. those which pictured women as being assertive and dominant in sexual matters), and thus cannot be seen as directed at "obscenity" in the traditional sense. They were also, as is obvious from the description above, neither "content" nor "viewpoint" neutral. It was principally on these bases that the Federal District Court for the Eastern District of Indiana, and the Federal Court of Appeals for the 6th Circuit held the Indianapolis ordinances unconstitutional.[4]

It is difficult for anyone interested in defending First Amendment values to disagree with the Courts' conclusions in the two cases. The feminist contention that sexual violence and the subordination of women is promoted by depictions of women in degrading positions is probably well-taken. But distinguishing, as the ordinances in question did, on the basis of such "viewpoints," is not only "content-based" but seems based on "political" content.

In the same vein, those who argue for restrictions on campus speech directed against blacks, Hispanics, women, and gays are probably correct in their assessment of the consequences of such speech. Here, the danger is not only that some will accept the viewpoints presented in such a speech, but that at least to some extent, the presence of such speech will create a "hostile learning environment" for the members of affected groups. It is this argument, following the lead of cases upholding statutes directed against sexual harassment in the workplace,[5] that has been the basis for many campus regulations. Two federal district courts, in cases coming from the Universities of Michigan and Wisconsin-Madison, have held such regulations unconstitutional.[6]

The Supreme Court has yet to make a decision in this matter. But in R.A.V. v. City of St. Paul, decided in 1992 and reproduced herein, it unanimously struck down an ordinance prohibiting "bias motivated fighting words." Justice White's concurrance held the law overbroad, but indicated general approval for its selection of biased communications as especially intolerable. But Justice Scalia, for the majority, held that not even "fighting words" could be prohibited on a selected basis. Students shold ponder which approach, that of Scalia or White, accords with First Amendment tradition and and best accomodates the conflicting values of liberty and equality.

A final class of cases on the issue of First Amendment values versus the advancement of equality involves attempts to regulate the admission policies of "private clubs," so as to prohibit discrimination in such clubs. As they have come to the Court, such issues have involved discrimination, not on the basis of race, but rather that of gender. In the seminal case of Roberts v. United States Jaycees, the Court recognized two different bases for the constitutional right of association: one flowing from the freedom of association long held to be implicit in the First Amendment, and a more general right to "intimate association" said to issue from the constitutional "right of privacy." The Court has had little difficulty in concluding that state efforts to promote nondiscrimination in quasi-business organizations (such as the Rotary and the Junior Chamber of Commerce) do not impact impermissibly on "intimacy." More directly challenging to First Amendment freedoms is the right to join for expressive or communicative purposes. Once again the Court has found that such a right, as enjoyed by organizations such as those mentioned above, is only minimally implicated by equal access laws. At the same time the Court has been careful to leave open the possibility that laws in fact interfering with a group's ability to present its message would be more closely scrutinized. Perhaps the best example of the Court's sensitivity to both of these values can be found in its recent decision in New York State Club Association v.

City of New York. That case involved a challenge "on its face" to a New York City ordinance forbidding discrimination in places of public accommodation. The Court's opinion is thus additionally valuable for its treatment of facial challenges based on the First Amendment, and is the final case excerpted herein.

---

[1]With but a single exception, it is ideas and their communication that is at issue. The exception occurs with respect to laws which ban "association" on the basis of principles of racial or sexual exclusion. Both matters, obviously, directly implicate First Amendment values.

[2]A much noted later case in which the justifications for a law were somewhat similar to those in Beauharnais, is Collin v. Smith, 578 F.Ed. 1197 (1978), in which the Court of Appeals for the 7th Circuit invalidated a measure passed by the City Council of Skokie, Illinois. The ordinance governed the conditions under which groups preaching race hatred would be allowed to march in Skokie, and was intended to prevent the appearance of the American Nazi Party in a village in which a large percentage of the population was Jewish, and included some survivors of the Holocaust. As we noted in Chapter 3, the story of this case has been chronicled in Donald Alexander Downs, *Nazis in Skokie: Freedom, Community, and the First Amendment*.

[3]This account of the events in Minneapolis and Indianapolis is based on Donald Alexander Downs, The New Politics of Pornography, (Chicago: University of Chicago Press, 1989) Professor Downs gives a full account of the controversy, the political forces behind adoption of the two ordinances, and the reaction of the judiciary. In addition, it places the ordinances in the context of the general controversy over pornography.

[4]See American Booksellers Association v. Hudnut, 771 F. 2ed 323 (1985), affirming 598 F. Supp. 1316 (1984). The Minneapolis proposal was vetoed by the mayor.

[5]See, inter alia, Ways v. City of Lincoln, 705 F. Supp. 1420 (1988).

[6]See Doe v. University of Michigan, 721 F. Supp. 852 (1989), and UWM Post v. Bd. of Regents of University of Wisconsin, 774 F. Supp. 1163 (1991).

BEAUHARNAIS V. ILLINOIS

343 U.S. 250 (1952)

MR. JUSTICE FRANKFURTER delivered the opinion of the Court.

The information, cast generally in the terms of the statute, charged that Beauharnais "did unlawfully . . . exhibit in public places lithographs, which publications portray depravity, criminality, unchastity or lack of virtue of citizens of Negro race and color and which exposes *[sic]* citizens of Illinois of the Negro race and color to contempt, derision, obloquy. . . ." The lithograph complained of was a leaflet setting forth a petition calling on the Mayor and City Council of Chicago "to halt the further encroachment, harassment and invasion of white people, their property, neighborhoods and persons, by the Negro. . . ." Below was a call for "One million self respecting white people in Chicago to unite. . . ." with the statement added that "If persuasion and the need to prevent the white race from becoming mongrelized by the Negro will not unite us, then the aggressions . . . rapes, robberies, knives, guns and marijuana of the negro, surely will." This, with more language, similar if not so violent, concluded with an attached application for membership in the White Circle League of America, Inc. . . .

The Illinois Supreme Court tells us that 224a "is a form of criminal libel law." The defendant, the trial court and the Supreme Court consistently treated it as such. . . .

No one will gainsay that it is libelous falsely to charge another with being a rapist, robber, carrier of knives and guns, and user of marijuana. The precise question before us, then, is whether the protection of "liberty" in the Due Process Clause of the Fourteenth Amendment prevents a state from punishing such libels—as criminal libel has been defined, limited and constitutionally recognized time out of mind—directed at designated collectivities and flagrantly disseminated...

If an utterance directed at an individual may be the object of criminal sanctions, we cannot deny to State power to punish the same utterance directed at a defined group, unless we can say that this is a willful and purposeless restriction unrelated to the peace and well-being of the State.

Illinois did not have to look beyond her own borders or await the tragic experience of the last three decades to conclude that willful purveyors of falsehood concerning racial and religious groups promote strife and tend powerfully to obstruct the manifold adjustments required for free, ordered life in a metropolitan, polyglot community. From the murder of the abolitionist Lovejoy in 1837 to the Cicero riots of 1951, Illinois has been the scene of exacerbated tension between races, often flaring into violence and destruction. In many of these outbreaks, utterances of the character here in question, so the Illinois legislature could conclude, played a significant part....

. . . . the Illinois legislature may warrantably believe that a man's job and his educational opportunities and the dignity accorded him may depend as much on the reputation of the racial and religious group to which he willy-nilly belongs, as on his own merits. This being

so, we are precluded from saying that speech concededly punishable when immediately directed at individuals cannot be outlawed if directed at groups with whose position and esteem in society the affiliated individual may be inextricably involved. . . . *Affirmed.*

MR. JUSTICE BLACK with whom MR. JUSTICE DOUGLAS concurs, dissenting.

This case is here because Illinois inflicted criminal punishment on Beauharnais for causing the distribution of leaflets in the city of Chicago. The conviction rests on the leaflet's contents, not on the time, manner or place of distribution. Beauharnais is head of an organization that opposes amalgamation and favors segregation of white and colored people. After discussion, an assembly of his group decided to petition the mayor and council of Chicago to pass laws for segregation. Volunteer members of the group agreed to stand on street corners, solicit signers to petitions addressed to the city authorities, and distribute leaflets giving information about the group, its beliefs and its plans. In carrying out this program a solicitor handed out a leaflet which was the basis of this prosecution. . .

That Beauharnais and his group were making a genuine effort to petition their elected representatives is not disputed. . . .

The Court condones this expansive state censorship by painstakingly analogizing it to the law of criminal libel. As a result of this refined analysis, the Illinois statute emerges labeled a "group libel law." This label may make the Court's holding more palatable for those who sustain it, but the sugar-coating does not make the censorship deadly. However tagged, the Illinois law is not that criminal libel which has been "defined, limited and constitutionally recognized time out of mind." For as "constitutionally recognized" that crime provided for" punishment of false, malicious, scurrilous charges against individuals, not against huge groups. This limited scope of the law of criminal libel is of no small importance. It has confined state punishment of speech and expression to the narrowest of areas involving nothing more than purely private feuds.

Every expansion of the law of criminal libel so as to punish discussions of matters of public concern means a corresponding invasion of the area dedicated to free expression by the First Amendment. . . .

The Court's reliance on *Chaplinsky v. New Hampshire.*is also misplaced. New Hampshire had a state law making it an offense to direct insulting words at *an individual* on a public street. Chaplinsky had violated that law by calling a man vile names "face-to-face." We pointed out in that context that the use of which "fighting" words was not an essential part of exposition of ideas. Whether the words used in their context here are "fighting" words in the same sense is doubtful but whether so or not they not addressed to or about *individuals.* Moreover, the leaflet used here was also the means adopted by an assembled group to enlist interest in their efforts to have legislation enacted. And the fighting words were but a part of arguments on questions of wide public interest and importance. Freedom of petition, assembly, speech and press could be greatly abridged by a practice of meticulously scrutinizing every editorial, speech, sermon or other printed matter to extract two or three naughty words on which to hang charges of "group libel."

The *Chaplinsky* case makes no such broad inroads on

MR. JUSTICE REED, with whom MR. JUSTICE DOUGLAS joins, dissenting. . .

MR. JUSTICE DOUGLAS, dissenting.

Hitler and his Nazis showed how evil a conspiracy could be which was aimed at destroying a race by exposing it to contempt, derision, and obloquy. I would be willing to concede that such conduct directed at a race or group in this country could be made an indictable offense. For such a project would be more than the exercise of free speech. Like picketing, it would be free speech plus.

I would also be willing to concede that even without, the element of conspiracy there might be times and occasions which the legislative or executive branch might call a halt to inflammatory talk, such as the shouting of "fire" in a school or a theatre.

My view is that if in any case other public interests are to override the plain command of the First Amendment, the peril of speech must be clear and present, leaving no room for argument, raising no doubts as to the necessity of curbing speech in order to prevent disaster. . . .

MR. JUSTICE JACKSON, dissenting. . .

R.A.V. v. CITY OF ST. PAUL

___U.S ___ (1992)

JUSTICE SCALIA delivered the opinion of the court.

In the predawn hours of June 21, 1990, petitioner and several other teenagers allegedly assembled a crudely-made cross by taping together broken chair legs. They then allegedly burned the cross inside the fenced yard of a black family that lived across the street from the house where petitioner was staying. Although this conduct could have been punished under any of a number of laws, one of the two provisions under which respondent city of St. Paul chose to charge petitioner (then a juvenile) was the St. Paul Code which provides: "Whoever places on public or private property a symbol, object, appellation, characterization or graffiti including, but not limited to, a

burning cross or Nazi swastika, which one knows or has reasonable grounds to know arouses anger, alarm or resentment in others on the basis of race, color, creed, religion or gender commits disorderly conduct and shall be guilty of a misdemeanor."

Petitioner moved to dismiss this count on the ground that the St. Paul ordinance was substantially overbroad and impermissibly content-based and therefore facially invalid under the First Amendment. The trial court granted this motion, but the Minnesota Supreme Court reversed. That court rejected petitioner's overbreadth claim because, as construed in prior Minnesota cases, the modifying phrase "arouses anger, alarm or resentment in others" limited the reach of the ordinance to conduct that amounts to "fighting words," *i.e.,* "conduct that itself inflicts injury or tends to incite immediate violence . . .," and therefore the ordinance reached only expression "that the first amendment does not protect." The court also concluded that the ordinance was not impermissibly content-based because, in its view, "the ordinance is a narrowly tailored means toward accomplishing the compelling governmental interest in protecting the community against bias-motivated threats to public safety and order."

I

. . . . Assuming, *arguendo,* that all of the expression reached by the ordinance is proscribable under the "fighting words" doctrine, we nonetheless conclude that the ordinance is facially unconstitutional in that it prohibits otherwise permitted speech solely on the basis of the subjects the speech addresses.

The First Amendment generally prevents government from proscribing speech, or even expressive conduct, because of disapproval of the ideas expressed. Content-based regulations are presumptively invalid. . .

From 1791 to the present, however, our society, like other free but civilized societies, has permitted restrictions upon the content of speech in a few limited areas, which are "of such slight social value as a step to truth that any benefit that may be derived from them is clearly outweighed by the social interest in order and morality."

. . . We have sometimes said that these categories of expression are "not within the area of constitutionally protected speech," or that the "protection of the First Amendment does not extend" to them. Such statements must be taken in context, however, and are no more literally true than is the occasionally repeated shorthand characterizing obscenity "as not being speech at all." What they mean is that these areas of speech can, consistently with the First Amendment, be regulated *because of their constitutionally proscribable content* (obscenity, defamation, etc.)—not that

they are categories of speech entirely invisible to the Constitution, so that they may be made the vehicles for content discrimination unrelated to their distinctively proscribable content. Thus, the government may proscribe libel; but it may not make the further content discrimination of proscribing *only* libel critical of, the government. . . .

In our view, the First Amendment imposes not an "underinclusiveness" limitation but a "content discrimination" limitation upon a State's prohibition of proscribable speech. There is no problem whatever, for example, with a State's prohibiting obscenity (and other forms of proscribable expression) only in certain media or markets, for although that prohibition would be "underinclusive," it would not discriminate on the basis of content.

Even the prohibition against content discrimination that we assert the First Amendment requires is not absolute. It applies differently in the contest of proscribable speech than in the area of fully protected speech. The rationale of the general prohibition, after all, is that content discrimination "rais[es] the specter that the Government may effectively drive certain ideas or viewpoints from the marketplace." But content discrimination among various instances of a class of proscribable speech often does not pose this threat.

When the basis for the content discrimination consists entirely of the very reason the entire class of speech at issue is proscribable, no significant danger of idea or viewpoint discrimination exists. Such a reason, having been adjudged neutral enough to support exclusion of the entire class of speech from First Amendment protection, is also neutral enough to form the basis of distinction within the class. To illustrate: A State might choose to prohibit only that obscenity which is the most patently offensive *in its prurience—i. e.,* that which involves the most lascivious displays of sexual activity. But it may not prohibit, for example, only that obscenity which includes offensive *political* messages.

Another valid basis for according differential treatment to even a content-defined subclass of proscribable speech is that the subclass happens to be associated with particular "secondary effects" of the speech, so that the regulation is *"justified* without reference to the content of the . . . speech."

Where the government does not target conduct on the basis of its expressive content, acts are not shielded from regulation merely because they express a discriminatory idea or philosophy.

These bases for distinction refute the proposition that the selectivity of the restriction is "even arguably 'conditioned upon the sovereign's agreement with what a speaker may intend to say.'" There may be other such bases as well. Indeed, to validate such selectivity (where totally proscribable speech is at issue) it may not even be necessary to identify any particular "neutral" basis, so long as the nature of the content discrimination is such that there is no realistic possibility that official suppression of ideas is afoot. (We cannot think of any First Amendment interest that would stand in the way of a State's prohibiting only those obscene motion pictures with blue-eyed actresses.) Save for that limitation, the regulation of "fighting words," like the regulation of noisy speech, may address some offensive instances and leave other, equally offensive, instances alone.

II

Applying these principles to the St. Paul ordinance, we conclude that, even as narrowly construed by the Minnesota Supreme Court, the ordinance is facially unconstitutional. Although the phrase in the ordinance, "arouses anger, alarm or resentment in others," has been limited by the Minnesota Supreme Court's construction to reach only those symbols or displays that amount to "fighting words," the remaining, unmodified terms make clear that the ordinance applies only to "fighting words" that insult, or provoke violence, "on the basis of race, color, creed, religion or gender." Displays containing abusive invective, no matter how vicious or severe, are permissible unless they are addressed to one of the specified disfavored topics. Those who wish to use "fighting words" in connection with other ideas—to express

hostility, for example, on the basis of political affiliation, union membership, or homosexuality—are not covered. The First Amendment does not permit St. Paul to impose special prohibitions on those speakers who express views on disfavored subjects.

In its practical operation, moreover, the ordinance goes even beyond mere content discrimination, to actual viewpoint discrimination. Displays containing some words—odious racial epithets, for example—would be prohibited to proponents of all views. But "fighting words" that do not themselves invoke race, color, creed, religion, or gender—aspersions upon a person's mother, for example—would seemingly be usable *ad libitum* in the placards of those arguing *in favor* of racial, color, etc. tolerance and equality, but could not be used by that speaker's opponents. One could hold up a sign saying, for example, that all "antiCatholic bigots" are misbegotten; but not that all "papists" are, for that would insult and provoke violence "on the basis of religion." St. Paul has no such authority to license one side of a debate to fight freestyle, while requiring the other to follow Marquis of Queensbury Rules.

What we have here, it must be emphasized, is not a prohibition of fighting words that are directed at certain persons or groups (which would be *facially* valid if it met the requirements of the Equal Protection Clause); but rather, a prohibition of fighting words that contain (as the Minnesota Supreme Court repeatedly emphasized) messages of "bias-motivated" hatred and in particular, as applied to this case, messages "based on virulent notions of racial supremacy."

Despite the fact that the Minnesota Supreme Court and St. Paul acknowledge that the ordinance is directed at expression of group hatred, JUSTICE STEVENS suggests that this "fundamentally misreads" the ordinance. It is directed, he claims, not to speech of a particular content, but to particular "injur[ies]" that are "qualitatively different" from other injuries. This is word-play. What makes the anger, fear, sense of dishonor, etc. produced by violation of this ordinance distinct from the anger, fear, sense of dishonor, etc. produced by other fighting words is nothing other than the fact that it is caused by a distinctive idea, conveyed by a distinctive message. The First Amendment cannot be evaded that easily. It is obvious that the symbols which will arouse "anger, alarm or resentment in others on the basis of race, color, creed, religion or gender" are those symbols that communicate a message of hostility based on one of these characteristics.

The content-based discrimination reflected in the St. Paul ordinance comes within neither any of the specific exceptions to the First Amendment prohibition we discussed earlier, nor within a more general exception for content discrimination that does not threaten censorship of ideas. It assuredly does not fall within the exception for content discrimination based on the very reasons why the particular class of speech at issue (here, fighting words) is proscribable. As explained earlier, the reason why fighting words are categorically excluded from the protection of the First Amendment is not that their content communicates any particular idea, but that their content embodies a particularly intolerable (and socially unnecessary) *mode* of expressing *whatever* idea the speaker wishes to convey. St. Paul has not singled out an especially offensive mode of expression—it has not, for example, selected for prohibition only those fighting words that communicate ideas in a threatening (as opposed to a merely obnoxious) manner. Rather, it has proscribed fighting words of whatever manner that communicate messages of racial, gender, or religious intolerance. Selectivity of this sort creates the possibility that the city is seeking to handicap the expression of particular ideas. That possibility would alone be enough to render the ordinance presumptively invalid, but St. Paul's comments and concessions in this case elevate the possibility to a certainty.

St. Paul argues that the ordinance comes within another of the specific exceptions we mentioned, the one that allows content discrimination aimed only at the "secondary effects" of the speech.

. . . it is clear that the St. Paul ordinance is not directed to secondary effects within the meaning of *Renton*. As we said in *Boos v. Barry*, "[l]isteners' reactions to speech are not the type of 'secondary effects' we referred to in *Renton*.". The emotive impact of speech on its audience is not a 'secondary effect.'"

It hardly needs discussion that the ordinance does not fall within some more general exception permitting *all* selectivity that for any reason is beyond the suspicion of official suppression of ideas. The statements of St. Paul in this very case afford ample basis for, if not full confirmation of, that suspicion.

Finally, St. Paul and its *amici* defend the conclusion of the Minnesota Supreme Court that, even if the ordinance regulates expression based on hostility towards its protected ideological content, this discrimination is nonetheless justified because it is narrowly tailored to serve compelling state interests. Specifically, they assert that the ordinance helps to ensure the basic human rights of members of groups that have historically been subjected to discrimination, including the right of such group members to live in peace where they wish. We do not doubt that these interests are compelling, and that the ordinance can be said to promote them. But the "danger of censorship" presented by a facially content-based statute, requires that that weapon be employed only where it is *"necessary* to serve the asserted [compelling] interest." The existence of adequate content-neutral alternatives thus "undercut[s] significantly" any defense of such a statute, casting considerable doubt on the government's protestations that "the asserted justification is in fact an accurate description of the purpose and effect of the law." The dispositive question in this case, therefore, is whether content discrimination is reasonably necessary to achieve St. Paul's compelling interests; it plainly is not. An ordinance not limited to the favored topics, for example, would have precisely the same beneficial effect. In fact the only interest distinctively served by the content limitation is that of displaying the city council's special hostility towards the particular biases thus singled out. That is precisely what the First Amendment forbids. The politicians of St. Paul are entitled to express that hostility—but not through the means of imposing unique limitations upon speakers who (however benightedly) disagree. . .

JUSTICE WHITE, with whom JUSTICE BLACKMUN and JUSTICE O'CONNOR join, and with whom JUSTICE STEVENS joins except as to Part I(A), concurring in the judgment.

I agree with the majority that the judgment of the Minnesota Supreme Court should be reversed. However, our agreement ends there.

This case could easily be decided within the contours of established First Amendment law by holding, as petitioner argues, that the St. Paul ordinance is fatally overbroad because it criminalizes not only unprotected expression but expression protected by the First Amendment.

. . . as the majority concedes, this Court has long held certain discrete categories of expression to be proscribable on the basis of their content. For instance, the Court has held that the individual who falsely shouts "fire" in a crowded theatre may not claim the protection of the First Amendment. The Court has concluded that neither child pornography, nor obscenity, is protected by the First Amendment. And the Court has observed that, "[l]eaving aside the special considerations when public officials [and public figures] are the target, a libelous publication is not protected by the Constitution."

All of these categories are content based. But the Court has held that First Amendment does not apply to them because their expressive content is worthless or of *de minimis* value to society. We have not departed from this principle, emphasizing repeatedly that, "within the confines of [these] given classification[s], the evil to be restricted so overwhelmingly outweighs the expressive interests, if any, at stake, that no process of case-by-case adjudication is required." This categorical approach has provided a principled and narrowly focused means for distinguishing between expression that the government may regulate freely and that

which it may regulate on the basis of content only upon a showing of compelling need. . . .

Nevertheless, the majority holds that the First Amendment protects those narrow categories of expression long held to be undeserving of First Amendment protection—at least to the extent that lawmakers may not regulate some fighting words more strictly than others because of their content. The Court announces that such content-based distinctions violate the First Amendment because "the government may not regulate use based on hostility—or favoritism—towards the underlying message expressed." Should the government want to criminalize certain fighting words, the Court now requires it to criminalize all fighting words.

To borrow a phrase, "Such a simplistic, all-or-nothing-at-all approach to First Amendment protection is at odds with common sense and with our jurisprudence as well." It is inconsistent to hold that the government may proscribe an entire category of speech because the content of that speech is evil; but that the government may not treat a subset of that category differently without violating the First Amendment; the content of the subset is by definition worthless and undeserving of constitutional protection....

In a second break with precedent, the Court refuses to sustain the ordinance even though it would survive under the strict scrutiny applicable to other protected expression. Assuming, *arguendo*, that the St. Paul ordinance is a content-based regulation of protected expression, it nevertheless would pass First Amendment review under settled law upon a showing that the regulation "is necessary to serve a compelling state interest and is narrowly drawn to achieve that end."

St. Paul has urged that its ordinance, in the words of the majority, "helps to ensure the basic human rights of members of groups that have historically been subjected to discrimination. . . ." The Court expressly concedes that this interest is compelling and is promoted by the ordinance. Nevertheless, the Court treats strict scrutiny analysis as irrelevant to the constitutionality of the legislation. . .

Under the majority's view, a narrowly

drawn, content-based ordinance could never pass constitutional muster if the object of that legislation could be accomplished by banning a wider category of speech. This appears to be a general renunciation of strict scrutiny review, a fundamental tool of First Amendment analysis. . . .

As with its rejection of the Court's categorical analysis, the majority offers no reasoned basis for discarding our firmly established strict scrutiny analysis at this time. The majority appears to believe that its doctrinal revisionism is necessary to prevent our elected lawmakers from prohibiting libel against members of one political party but not another and from enacting similarly preposterous laws. The majority is misguided.

Although the First Amendment does not apply to categories of unprotected speech, such as fighting words, the Equal Protection Clause requires that the regulation of unprotected speech be rationally related to a legitimate government interest. A defamation statute that drew distinctions on the basis of political affiliation or "an ordinance prohibiting only those legally obscene works that contain criticism of the city government," would unquestionably fail rational basis review.

Turning to the St. Paul ordinance and assuming *arguendo*, as the majority does, that the ordinance is not constitutionally overbroad (but see Part II), there is no question that it would pass equal protection review. The ordinance proscribes a subset of "fighting words," those that injure "on the basis of race, color, creed, religion or gender." This selective regulation reflects the City's judgment that harms based on race, color, creed, religion, or gender are more pressing public concerns than the harms caused by other fighting words. In light of our Nation's long and painful experience with discrimination, this determination is plainly reasonable. Indeed, as the majority concedes, the interest is compelling. . . .

III

. . . . I agree with petitioner that the ordinance is invalid on its face. Although the ordinance as construed reaches categories of speech that are constitutionally unprotected, it also criminalizes a substantial amount of expression that—however repugnant—is shielded by the First Amendment.

In attempting to narrow the scope of the St. Paul antibias ordinance, the Minnesota Supreme Court relied upon two of the categories of speech and expressive conduct that fall outside the First Amendment's protective sphere: words that incite "imminent lawless action," and "fighting" words. The Minnesota Supreme Court erred in its application of the *Chaplinsky* fighting words test and consequently interpreted the St. Paul ordinance in a fashion that rendered the ordinance facially overbroad.

In construing the St. Paul ordinance, the Minnesota Supreme Court drew upon the definition of fighting words that appears in *Chaplinsky*—words "which by their very utterance inflict injury or tend to incite an immediate breach of the peace." However, the Minnesota court was far from clear in identifying the "injur[ies]" inflicted by the expression that St. Paul sought to regulate. Indeed, the Minnesota court emphasized (tracking the language of the ordinance) that "the ordinance censors only those displays that one knows or should know will create anger, alarm or resentment based on racial, ethnic, gender or religious bias." I therefore understand the court to have ruled that St. Paul may constitutionally prohibit expression that "by its very utterance" causes "anger, alarm or resentment."

Our fighting words cases have made clear, however, that such generalized reactions are not sufficient to strip expression of its constitutional protection. The mere fact that expressive activity causes hurt feelings, offense, or resentment does not render the expression unprotected.

JUSTICE BLACKMUN, concurring in the judgment.

JUSTICE STEVENS, with whom JUSTICE *WHITE* and JUSTICE BLACKMUN join as to Part I, concurring in the judgment.

Looking to the content and character of the regulated activity, two things are clear. First, by hypothesis the ordinance bars only low-value speech, namely, fighting words. By definition such expression constitutes "no essential part of any exposition of ideas, and [is] of such slight social value as a step to truth that any benefit that may be derived from [it] is clearly outweighed by the social interest in order and morality." Second, the ordinance regulates "expressive conduct [rather] than . . . the written or spoken word."

Looking to the context of the regulated activity, it is again significant that the statute (by hypothesis) regulates *only* fighting words. Whether words are fighting words is determined in part by their context. Fighting words are not words that merely cause offense; fighting words must be directed at individuals so as to "by their very utterance inflict injury." By hypothesis, then, the St. Paul ordinance restricts speech in confrontational and potentially violent situations. The case at hand is illustrative. The crossburning in this case—directed as it was to a single African-American family trapped in their home—was nothing more than a crude form of physical intimidation. That this crossburning sends a message of racial hostility does not automatically endow it with complete constitutional protection.'

Significantly, the St. Paul ordinance regulates speech not on the basis of its subject matter or the viewpoint expressed, but rather on the basis of the *harm* the speech causes. In this regard, the Court fundamentally misreads the St. Paul ordinance. The Court describes the St. Paul ordinance as regulating expression "addressed to one of [several] specified disfavored *topics*," as policing "disfavored *subjects*," and as "prohibit[ing] . . . speech solely on the basis of the *subjects* the speech addresses." Contrary to the Court's suggestion, the ordinance regulates only a subcategory of expression that causes *injuries based on* "race, color, creed, religion or gender," not a subcategory that involves *discussions* that concern those characteristics. The ordinance, as construed by the Court, criminalizes expression that "one knows . . . [by its very utterance inflicts injury on] others on the basis of race, color, creed, religion or gender." In this regard, the ordinance resembles the child pornography law at issue in *Ferber*, which in effect singled out child

pornography because those publications caused far greater harms than pornography involving adults.

Moreover, even if the St. Paul ordinance did regulate fighting words based on its subject matter, such a regulation would, in my opinion, be constitutional. As noted above, subject-matter based regulations on commercial speech are widespread and largely unproblematic. As we have long recognized, subject-matter regulations generally do not raise the same concerns of government censorship and the distortion of public discourse presented by viewpoint regulations. Thus, in upholding subject-matter regulations we have carefully noted that viewpoint-based discrimination was not implicated. . . .

St. Paul ordinance is evenhanded. In a battle between advocates of tolerance and advocates of intolerance, the ordinance does not prevent either side from hurling fighting words at the other on the basis of their conflicting ideas, but it does bar *both* sides from hurling such words on the basis of the target's "race, color, creed, religion or gender." To extend the Court's pugilistic metaphor, the St. Paul ordinance simply bans punches "below the belt"—*by either party*. It does not, therefore, favor one side of any debate.

Finally, it is noteworthy that the St. Paul ordinance is, as construed by the Court today, quite narrow. The St. Paul ordinance does not ban an "hate speech," nor does it ban, say, all cross-burnings or all swastika displays. Rather it only bans a subcategory of the already narrow category of fighting words. Such a limited ordinance leaves open and protected a vast range of expression on the subjects of racial, religious, and gender equality. As construed by the Court today, the ordinance certainly does not "raise the specter that the Government may effectively drive certain ideas or viewpoints from the marketplace." Petitioner is free to burn a cross to announce a rally or to express his views about racial supremacy, he may do so on private property or public land, at day or at night, so long as the burning is not so threatening and so directed at an individual as to "by its very [execution] inflict injury." Such a limited proscription scarcely offends the First Amendment.

NEW YORK STATE CLUB ASSOCIATION, INC. V. CITY OF NEW YORK ET AL.

487 U.S. 1 (1988)

JUSTICE WHITE delivered the opinion of the Court.

In 1984, New York City amended its Human Rights Law. The basic purpose of the amendment is to prohibit discrimination in certain private clubs that are determined to be sufficiently "public" in nature that they do not fit properly within the exemption for "any institution, club or place of accommodation which is in its nature distinctly private. . . ."

The specific change wrought by the amendment is to extend the antidiscrimination provisions of the Human Rights Law to any "institution, club or place of accommodation that has more than four hundred members, provides regular meal service and regularly receives payment for dues, fees, use of space, facilities, services, meals or beverages directly or indirectly from or on behalf of nonmembers for the furtherance of trade or business." N. Y. C. Admin. Code 8-102(9) (1986). Any such club "shall not be considered in its nature distinctly private." . . . The City Council explained that it drafted the amendment in this way so as to meet the specific problem confronting women and minorities in the city's business and professional world. . . .

. . . . appellant brought this suit challenging the constitutionality of the 1984 Law on its face before any enforcement proceedings were initiated against any of its member associations. Although such facial challenges are sometimes permissible and often have been entertained, especially when speech protected by the First Amendment is at stake, to prevail on a facial attack the plaintiff must demonstrate that the challenged law either "could never be applied in a valid manner" or that even though it may be validly applied to the plaintiff and others, it nevertheless is so broad that it "may inhibit the

constitutionally protected speech of third parties." *City Council v. Taxpayers for Vincent.*

Both exceptions are narrow ones: the first kind of facial challenge will not succeed unless the court finds that "every application of the statute created an impermissible risk of suppression of ideas," *Taxpayers for Vincent,* and the second kind of facial challenge will not succeed unless the statute is "substantially" overbroad, which requires the court to find "a realistic danger that the statute itself will significantly compromise recognized First Amendment protections of parties not before the Court."

We are unpersuaded that appellant is entitled to make either one of these two distinct facial challenges. Appellant conceded at oral argument, understandably we think, that the antidiscrimination provisions of the Human Rights Law certainly could be constitutionally applied at least to some of the large clubs, under this Court's decisions in *Rotary* and *Roberts.* The clubs that are covered under the Law contain at least 400 members. They thus are comparable in size to the local chapters of the Jaycees that we found not to be protected private associations in *Roberts,* and they are considerably larger than many of the local clubs that were found to be unprotected in *Rotary,* some which included as few as 20 members. . .

The clubs covered by Local Law 63 also provide "regular meal service" and receive regular payments "directly or indirectly from or on behalf of nonmembers for the furtherance of trade or business." N. Y. C. Admin. Code 8-102(9) (1986). The city found these two characteristics to be significant in pinpointing organizations which are "commercial" in nature, "where business deals are often made and personal contacts valuable for business purposes, employment and professional advancement are formed." Local Law 63.

These characteristics are at least as significant in defining the nonprivate nature of these associations, because of the kind of role that strangers play in their ordinary existence, as is the regular participation of strangers at meetings, which we emphasized in *Roberts* and *Rotary.* See *Roberts.* It may well be that a considerable amount of private or intimate association occurs in such a setting, as is also true in many restaurants and other places of public accommodation, but that fact alone does not afford the entity as a whole any constitutional immunity to practice discrimination when the government has barred it from doing so.

Although there may be clubs that would be entitled to constitutional protection despite the presence of these characteristics, surely it cannot be said that Local Law 63 is invalid on its face because it infringes the private associational rights of each and every club covered by it. . . .

The same may be said about the contention that the Law infringes upon every club member's right of expressive association. The ability and the opportunity to combine with others to advance one's views is a powerful practical means of ensuring the perpetuation of the freedoms the First Amendment has guaranteed to individuals as against the government.

On its face, Local Law 63 does not affect "in any significant way" the ability of individuals to form associations that will advocate public or private viewpoints. *Rotary.* It does not require the clubs "to abandon or alter" any activities that are protected by the First Amendment. If a club seeks to exclude individuals who do not share the views that the club's members wish to promote, the Law erects no obstacle to this end. Instead, the Law merely prevents an association from using race, sex, and the other specified characteristics as shorthand measures in place of what the city considers to be more legitimate criteria for determining membership. It is conceivable, of course, that an association might be able to show

that it is organized for specific expressive purposes and that it will not be able to advocate its desired viewpoints nearly as effectively if it cannot confine its membership to those who share the same sex, for example, or the same religion. In the case before us, however, it seems sensible enough to believe that many of the large clubs covered by the Law are not of this kind. We could hardly hold otherwise on the record before us, which contains no specific evidence on the characteristics of *any* club covered by the Law.

The facial attack based on the claim that Local Law 63 is invalid in all of its applications must therefore fail. Appellant insists, however, that there are some clubs within the reach of the Law that are "distinctively private" and that the Law is therefore overbroad and invalid on its face. But as we have indicated, this kind of facial challenge also falls short.

The overbreadth doctrine is "strong medicine" that is used "sparingly and only as a last resort." *Broadrick* v. *Oklahoma* (1973). A law is constitutional unless it is "substantially overbroad." To succeed in its challenge, appellant must demonstrate from the text of Local Law 63 and from actual fact that a substantial number of instances exist in which the Law cannot be applied constitutionally. Yet appellant has not identified those clubs for whom the antidiscrimination provisions will impair their ability to associate together or to advocate public or private viewpoints. No record was made in this respect, we are not informed of the characteristics of any particular clubs, and hence we cannot conclude that the Law threatens to undermine the associational or expressive purposes of any club, let alone a substantial number of them. We therefore cannot conclude that the Law is substantially overbroad and must assume that "whatever overbreadth may exist should be cured through case-by-case analysis of the fact situations to which its sanctions, assertedly, may not be applied." JUSTICE O'CONNOR, with whom JUSTICE KENNEDY joins, concurring. JUSTICE SCALIA, concurring in part and concurring in the Judgment.

9

TOWARD A DECENT SOCIETY

Earl Warren called the issue of obscenity[1] the most difficult of his tenure on the Supreme Court. Scholars have said that Warren Court decisions on the matter created a "constitutional disaster area" and "hard core confusion."[2] The issue is both difficult and controversial, not the least because the meaning of "obscenity" eludes precise definition. In addition, many who would allow government activity to advance equality or patriotism would deny that government has any proper role to play as to the obscene. For others, the regulation of such matters is a necessity.[3]

Those who would regulate or prohibit obscenity advance, ordinarily, one or both of two arguments. One, popular with police chiefs and crime commissions, views obscenity as a causative factor leading directly and immediately to the commission of rape and other sex crimes. Until fairly recently, most students of the matter would have dismissed this argument as unpersuasive. But some feminists, supported by recent research, believe that violent pornography *can* lead directly to crimes against women.

A more traditional argument, widely accepted by scholars who favor limits on obscenity, asserts that such material will have long term and counterproductive effects on people and society. In a similar and more recent vein, some feminists argue that obscenity, because it reduces women to objects, will lead eventually to the exploitation of women. In support of this argument they point to the fact that virtually all pornographic materials have as a dominant theme women in a submissive position, acting as devices of pleasure for men, and further, as enjoying such treatment.

Another variation of the same argument ties limitations on obscenity to the kind of society in which we live, and thus to the matter of democracy. A democratic society, it is argued, requires people who are cooperative and who are capable of practicing self-restraint. Pornography, however, preaches not cooperation but dominance, and a complete lack of restraint.

There would seem to be three principal arguments against the regulation of obscenity. One is that it may in itself be a positive good. This argument may be made in two ways. Some hold that constant exposure to obscenity will be a plus for everyone, enabling us to "act out" our sexual fantasies vicariously. A larger number contend that the use of obscenity, under the direction of skilled mental health professionals, can be useful in treating specific individuals and couples. The second contention seems beyond dispute, although it says little or nothing about whether obscene materials should be generally banned. The first rests on the somewhat dubious premise that self-restraint is itself evil, and argues that obscenity contributes to our "letting it all hang out."

A second argument directly confronts the issue of the supposed "harm" of obscenity. No harm, it is asserted, can be shown to come from pornographic materials. If that is so, there is no adequate basis for its regulation. Proponents of this view rely for support on the conclusions of the Lockhart Commission. That group, however, did not conclude that pornography does no harm, but rather that the fact of such harm cannot be shown empirically. Whether one supports its position depends partly, therefore, on the degree to which one believes the studies sponsored by the Commission to be both valid and persuasive. But, although the Commission's findings were widely praised, it is acknowledged that they rested heavily on short term-experiments. Proponents of regulation would argue that they have little relevance to the question of the long-term effects of exposure to obscenity.

From a First Amendment perspective, the most important argument against restrictions on obscenity is one which asserts that, given the lack of empirical evidence of harm, attempts to deal with it present too great a risk of the banning of worthwhile material. This "slippery slope" argument posits the impossibility of drawing lines with sufficient precision to save that which is of value, and its proponents have considerable history to support them. At various times any number of works which most would consider worthwhile have been banned as obscene, among them Theodore Dreiser's Sister Carrie and An American Tragedy, and James Joyce's Ulysses.

Until recently, the Court's attempt to deal with the obscenity problem revolved around the question of definition. But it is useful to begin by noting that certain aspects of the debate have been largely settled. In Butler v. Michigan (1957) the Court unanimously concluded that a state could not prohibit sexually oriented materials on the basis of their harm to children. To do so, said Justice Frankfurter for the majority, would be to "burn down the house to roast the pig."

Conversely the Court, in Ginsberg v. New York (1968), held that materials not considered obscene for adults might nevertheless be regulated to prevent children from obtaining them. And the Court has been emphatic in its rejection of a constitutional right to produce and even to possess "child pornography" (i.e. that which employs children in sexual activity and as sexual objects). Such activity, the Court said in New York v. Ferber (1982) and Osborne v. Ohio (1990), might be prohibited on the grounds that allowing the use of "child pornography" would inevitably lead to the abuse of children by those producing such material. Finally, the Court, in the 1964 case of Jacobellis v. Ohio, decided that whatever regulation was permissible did not include the prohibition of so-called "thematic obscenity" (i.e. non-explicit material which suggested and indicated approval of unconventional sexual relationships and activities).

In general the Court, following its assertion in Chaplinsky that obscenity is not protected by the First Amendment, has accepted in principal the arguments of those who would limit or prohibit the availability of pornography. At the same time, the practical effect of its attempts at definition has been to protect all but a very narrow spectrum of materials, usually denominated "hard core," from prohibition.

The Court's first attempt to define obscenity came in the 1957 case of Roth v. United States, in which it held that the obscenity of a work depended upon "whether to the average person, applying contemporary community standards, the dominant theme of the material, taken as a whole, appeals to the prurient interest." The Roth definition, though often criticized, contained features highly protective of threatened material. First, its "average person" feature removed any possibility that material could be deemed obscene for its effect on those of unusual susceptibility. Second, the application of "contemporary community standards" meant that obscenity must be judged from a contemporary perspective, not from that of a past and perhaps more repressive time. Finally, the necessity that the material be judged by its "dominant theme, taken as a whole" ensured that material could not be deemed obscene because of isolated passages.

In a series of later cases, Roth was refined to require that material deemed obscene must be "patently offensive," that in appropriate cases it could be judged by its affect on "the average person of its probable recipient group," that one accused of selling such material must have knowledge of its character, and that a conviction for the sale of "borderline" material was justified if the salaciousness of the material had been the subject of "pandering." Most importantly, the decision in Memoirs v. Massachusetts (1966) altered Roth in a substantial and crucial way. Roth had followed Chaplinsky in holding that obscenity was beyond constitutional protection *because* it had no "redeeming social importance." The Memoirs plurality, by contrast, made "redeeming social importance" a part of the test of obscenity, holding that material could not be banned unless it was "utterly without redeeming social importance."

This fundamental modification of Roth occasioned a considerable degree of almost comedic effects in some allegedly obscene materials, as appropriate commentary was introduced to provide "social importance." It also made much more difficult the task of prosecutors. The prosecutorial difficulty was occasioned by the fact that, as in Memoirs itself, the issue of social importance was usually dealt with by testimony from experts. And, as Berns has observed, there has seemingly been nothing produced for which it is impossible to find an "expert" to testify to its "redeeming social importance." Such expertise has not, however, been equally available to prosecutors, at least sometimes because of "peer pressure" operating against those who might have so testified.[4]

The growing fragmentation of the Court on the issue led, for a number of years following Memoirs, to an increasing disposition of such cases by *per curiam* reversals of lower court decisions. These Redrup reversals (so-called because the authority usually cited in them was the Court's 1967 decision in Redrup v. New York) occurred almost inevitably unless it could be shown that the material had been distributed to minors or that it had been imposed on those who did not wish to receive it. Such summary dispositions were of little assistance to lower courts and, coupled with the necessity of the justices viewing each product at issue, were a major burden on an already overworked Court. And the spectacle of the nation's highest jurists solemnly perusing the latest products of the purveyors of obscenity was hardly edifying.

It was, perhaps, in response to these concerns that the Court, in the 1973 cases of Miller v. California and Paris Adult Theatre v. Slaton, assayed one more attempt to deal with the definition of obscenity. The results of that attempt have been the basis of obscenity law for almost 20 years, and for that reason the majority opinions of Chief Justice Burger, and Justice Brennan's principal dissent are excerpted at the end of this chapter.[5]

In Miller, the Court substantially revised the Roth-Memoirs definition, simultaneously attempting to make easier the prosecution of purveyors and to deal with the vagueness inherent in the Roth formulation. Miller established that the "community" whose standards were at issue in defining "patent offensiveness" did not have to be the national community. (Although the case itself was vague about whether local or state standards were to be preferred, later refinements indicated that the states themselves were free to make this choice.) It required that the material deemed obscene be specifically defined beforehand by the applicable state law, and gave a "few plain examples" of the kind of materials which could lawfully be considered obscene. Finally, it rejected Memoirs' "utterly without redeeming social value" formulation, substituting one which required that the material be without "serious literary, artistic, political or scientific value."

In his Miller opinion the Chief Justice met head on the argument of those who argue for complete freedom from restriction on the grounds that the linkage between obscenity and harm is not proven. In a passage which could be a byword for those who would limit such material, Burger argued:

> If we accept the unprovable assumption that a complete education requires certain books, and the well nigh universal belief that good books, plays, and art lift the spirit, improve the mind, enrich the human personality and develop character, can we then say that a state legislature may not act on the corollary assumption that commerce in obscene books, or public exhibitions focused on obscene conduct, have a tendency to assert a corrupting and debasing impact leading to anti-social behavior?

This is, of course, to accept the argument made by proponents of regulation who argue for such regulation on the basis of long-term effects.

The dissenting opinion of Justice Brennan is also noteworthy. Brennan wrote the original <u>Roth</u> opinion, was one of the chief architects of the developing constitutional doctrine of obscenity, and penned the plurality opinion in <u>Memoirs</u>. But in <u>Miller</u> he retreated from his original position and adopted the view that there should be no regulation of obscenity except in the case of distribution to juveniles or unwilling adults. He did so for two principal and related reasons. First, the problem of the vagueness of definition had been shown to his satisfaction to be unsolvable. Vagueness, of course, raises fundamental issues of due process for those who are accused of violating the law. Second, the vagueness of the Court's definition, Brennan said, must have serious institutional effects, including the "chilling" of the publication of protected materials, the prosecution of non-obscene products, and the waste of valuable Court time.

Justice Brennan to the contrary, there seem to have been few instances of unwarranted obscenity prosecutions since <u>Miller</u>,[6] and the Court was able to use the first of these to establish firmly that states were not free to engage in such prosecutions. The case was <u>Jenkins v. Georgia</u> (1974), in which the Court reiterated its <u>Miller</u> determination that only "patently offensive representations" of "ultimate sexual acts" could be considered obscene. In <u>Pope v. Illinois</u> (1987) the Court did find it necessary to overturn a conviction in which the "value" test of <u>Miller</u> was determined by reference to the "average person" rather than the "reasonable person." But, in general, it does not seem to have found it necessary to markedly increase its supervision of anti-obscenity activity.

One reason for this may be that prosecutors are less interested in trying obscenity cases. Such cases are enormously difficult and expensive to prosecute and to win, in part because juries are, in effect, required to find that the material prosecuted appeals to their own "prurient interest" in order to convict, a conclusion they may be reluctant to reach. Another reason may be that social standards themselves have so changed, perhaps under the impetus of our experience under <u>Memoirs</u>, that things formerly thought to qualify as obscene are now generally accepted. At any rate, the obscenity issue in the post-<u>Miller</u> years has been largely one, not of defining what may be prohibited, but rather of determining the permissible scope of regulation.

Thus in <u>Young v. American Mini-Theatres</u> (1976), the Court had before it the validity of a Detroit zoning ordinance which provided that so-called "adult" enterprises could not be established closer than within 3000 yards of each other.

The intent of the ordinance was to prevent the clustering of such establishments in a way which, in the city's view, would inevitably lead to the destruction of commercial and other values. (The city of Boston, by contrast, has concluded that all such establishments should be congregated together, along with other sexually-oriented businesses, in an area popularly known as the "combat zone.")

The Court upheld the Detroit ordinance as a valid exercise of the zoning power, even though the places to which it applied sold materials not "obscene," and therefore constitutionally protected. The city's interest in its "quality of life," as well as in the continued health of its commercial section, was deemed sufficient to allow such regulation. Subsequent decisions have reaffirmed this holding, requiring only that zoning ordinances not be used as a basis for absolute prohibition. One of them, City of Renton v. Playtime Theatres, is excerpted in this chapter.

It is perhaps significant that the most recent decision on the obscenity issue does not even mention the Miller definition. In Barnes v. Glen Theatre (1991), the Court had before it an Indiana statute prohibiting public nudity as applied to an "adult" establishment wishing to feature totally nude dancing. A related issue had been before the Court in California v. LaRue (1972) in which a ban on sexually explicit entertainment was upheld on the basis of the state's power to regulate the sale of liquor under the 21st Amendment. And though holding, in Schad v. Borough of Mount Ephraim (1981), that nude dancing could not be proscribed in places of "adults only" entertainment, the Court had also held, in New York State Liquor Authority v. Bellanco (1981) that such activity could be prohibited in bars.

Chief Justice Rehnquist's plurality opinion in Barnes applied not Miller, but the four-part test of United States v. O'Brien, finding the "incidental effect" on expression protected "at the outer perimeters of the First Amendment" to be justified by the state's substantial interest in prohibiting public nudity. Said the Chief Justice:

> ". . . we do not think that when Indiana applies its statute to the nude dancing in these nightclubs it is proscribing nudity because of the erotic message conveyed by the dancers. Presumably numerous other erotic performances are presented at these establishments and similar clubs without any interference from the state. Likewise, the requirement . . . does not deprive the dance of whatever erotic message it conveys; it simply makes the message slightly less graphic. The perceived evil that Indiana seeks to address is not erotic dancing, but public nudity.

One is tempted to conclude that the Chief Justice regarded the state's requirement that the dancers "don pasties and a G-string" as *de minimis*. Justice

Souter's opinion concurring in the judgment almost says as much. But Justice White, for himself, Marshall, Blackmun, and Stevens, viewed the distinction suggested by Rehnquist as "transparently erroneous:"

> ... the Court concedes that nude dancing conveys an erotic message and concedes that the message would be muted if the dancers wore pasties and G-strings. Indeed, the emotional or erotic impact of the dance is intensified by the nudity of the performers. . . . The sight of a fully clothed, or even a partially clothed, dancer generally will have a far different impact on a spectator than that of a nude dancer, even if the same dance is performed. The nudity is itself an expressive component of the dance, not merely incidental "conduct."

Justice White's analysis would seem to be correct, but one may query whether the fact that something is an "expressive component" of communication should always be enough to bring it under the First Amendment umbrella? For could not the same be said of almost any "conduct" associated with communication? And, that issue aside, it seems appropriate to ask what, if anything, the activity in question had to do with either "self-government" or with the "search for truth," the goals most closely associated with the First Amendment.

Barnes, as well as other cases previously noted, suggests that the current Court will countenance a broader range of peripheral regulations of allegedly obscene "communication." But it would appear that the conflict over verbal or pictorial representations of sexual activity has been won by the opponents of regulation. Not only do "adult" book stores flourish in every part of the country, but videos of explicit sexual activity are available, and in demand, at most general purpose video stores. With respect to these materials then, we may have seen, as Charles Rembar once predicted with respect to the purely verbal, "the end of obscenity."[7] Future battles are likely to be waged on the regulatory periphery.

One battle over regulation however, which cannot be regarded as "peripheral" involves the extent to which the Miller formula, particularly that related to "contemporary community standards" can be applied to sexually explicit entertainment transmitted electronically. Miller, it will be recalled, held that material could be judged obscene by something other than national standards. And later cases made clear that the standard applied could be local as well as statewide. In Sable Communications v. Federal Communications Commission (1989), the Court had before it the issue of whether non-national standards could be applied to the regulation of obscene telephone messages, as well as whether the FCC could ban "indecent but not obscene" messages on a national basis. Though holding unanimously that the ban on the "indecent" could not stand, the Court divided, five to four, on the constitutionality of requiring the transmitters of telephonic messages to "tailor" such messages according to the standards of the "localities in which they . . . (chose) to do business." While such "tailoring" may be possible in the case of telephonic and even cable television transmissions, whether the same requirement can or should be applied to satellite television is much more problematic. Because it is represents what, in the future, seems likely to become the "core constitutional question" in the matter of obscenity, Sable is the final case excerpted.

---

[1]The terms "obscenity" and "pornography" have somewhat different connotations, but they are commonly, and in this text, used synonymously.

[2]The quotation from Chief Justice Warren is in Charles H. Sheldon, *The Supreme Court: Politicians in Robes*, (Beverly Hills, CA: Glencoe Press, 1970, xix.) The "disaster area" characterization, which refers explicitly to the Court's 1966 decisions in Memoirs v. Massachusetts, Mishkin v. New York, and Ginzburg v. United States, is in C. Peter Magrath, "The Obscenity Cases: Grapes of Roth," 1966 *Supreme Court Review* 7, 59. The references to "confusion" are in my unpublished papers, "Hard Core Confusion: The Warren Court and Obscenity," (1970), and "Confusion Compounded: The Burger Court and Obscenity" (1975).

[3]The literature on obscenity and its regulation is extensive. Students will find most accessible, and containing samples of the relevant literature as well as data and opinions on the effects of obscenity, the *Reports* of the Lockhart Commission (The Commission on Obscenity and Pornography, 1970), and the Meese Commission (Attorney General's Commission on Pornography, 1986).

[4]On the vagaries of expert testimony see Walter Berns, "Beyond the (Garbage) Pale," in Harry M. Clor, ed., *Censorship and Freedom of Expression*, (Chicago: Rand McNally Pub. Co., 1971). On the difficulties associated with governmental use of experts see Richard Kuh, *Foolish Figleaves: Pornography In and Out of Court*, (New York: The Macmillan Co., 1967) 204-207).

[5]Because Miller and Paris Adult each contains important elements of the Court's revised view on the obscenity question, and because the most cogent dissent is that of Justice Brennan in the latter case, both Miller and Paris Adult are reproduced.

[6]Donald Alexander Downs, *The New Politics of Pornography*, (Chicago: University of Chicago Press, 1989), 18-22. Downs book includes an excellent summary of the development of the law, and the data on the effects, of pornography. He concludes that prohibition should be limited to "violent and degrading sexual materials . . ."

The feminist attack on pornography, which is the chief focus of Downs' book is, from the perspective of this book, best seen as a part of the movement for "advancing equality" and has, therefore, been discussed in Chapter 8.

[6]Rembar, *The End of Obscenity*, (New York: Random House Pub. Co, 1968), 490.

continued on next page

MILLER V. CALIFORNIA

413 U.S 15 (1973)

MR. CHIEF JUSTICE BURGER delivered the opinion of the Court.

Apart from the initial formulation in the *Roth* case, no majority of the Court has at any given time been able to agree on a standard to determine what constitutes obscene pornographic material subject to regulation under the States' police power. We have seen "a variety of views among the members of the Court unmatched any other course of constitutional adjudication." *Interstate Circuit, Inc. v. Dallas* (Harlan, J., concurring and dissenting). This is not remarkable, for in the area of freedom of speech and press the courts must always remain sensitive to any infringement on genuinely serious literary, artistic, political, or scientific expression. This is an area in which there are few eternal verities.

The case we now review was tried on the theory that the California Penal Code 311 approximately incorporates the three-stage *Memoirs* test. But now the *Memoirs* test has been abandoned as unworkable by its author, and no Member of the Court today supports the *Memoirs* formulation. . . .

This much has been categorically settled by the Court, that obscene material is unprotected by the First Amendment. . .

We acknowledge, however, the inherent dangers of undertaking to regulate any form of expression. State statutes designed to regulate obscene materials must be carefully limited. See *Interstate Circuit, Inc. v. Dallas.* As a result, we now confine the permissible scope of such regulation to works which depict or describe sexual conduct. That conduct must be specifically defined by the applicable state law, as written or authoritatively construed." A state offense must also be limited to works which, taken as a whole appeal to the prurient interest in sex, which portray sexual conduct in a patently offensive way, and which taken as a whole, do not have serious literary, artistic, political, or scientific value.

The basic guidelines for the trier of fact must be: (a) whether "the average person, applying contemporary community standards" would find that the work, taken as a whole, appeals to the prurient interest, *Kois v. Wisconsin,* quoting *Roth v. United States* ; (b) whether the work depicts or describes in a patently offensive way, sexual conduct specifically defined by the applicable state law; and (c) whether the work, taken as a whole, lacks serious literary, artistic, political, or scientific value.

We emphasize that it is not our function to propose regulatory schemes for the States. That must await their concrete legislative efforts. It is possible, however, to give a few plain examples of what a state statute could define for regulation under part (b) of the standard announced in this opinion:

(a) Patently offensive representations or descriptions of ultimate sexual acts, normal or perverted, actual or simulated.

(b) Patently offensive representations or descriptions of masturbation, excretory functions, and lewd exhibition of the genitals.

Sex and nudity may not be exploited without limit by films or pictures exhibited or sold in places of public accommodation any more than live sex and nudity can exhibited or sold without limit in such public places. At a minimum, prurient, patently offensive depiction or description of sexual conduct must have serious literary, artistic, political, or scientific value to merit First Amendment protection. . . .

Under the holdings announced today, no one will be subject to prosecution for the sale or exposure of obscene materials unless these materials depict or describe patently offensive "hard core" sexual conduct specifically defined by the regulating state law, as written or construed. We are satisfied that these specific prerequisites will provide fair notice to a dealer in such materials that his public and commercial activities may bring prosecution.

. . . . today, for the first time since *Roth* was decided in 1957, a majority of this Court has agreed on concrete guidelines to isolate "hard core" pornography from expression protected by the First Amendment. Now we may abandon the casual practice of *Redrup v. New York* (1967), and attempt to provide positive guidance to federal and state courts alike.

This may not be an easy road, free from difficulty. But no amount of "fatigue" should lead us to adopt a convenient "institutional" rationale—an absolutist, "anything goes" view of the First Amendment—because it will lighten our burdens." Such an abnegation of judicial supervision in this field would be inconsistent with our duty to uphold the constitutional guarantees." *Jacobellis v. Ohio* (opinion of BRENNAN, J.). Nor should we remedy "tension between state and federal courts" by arbitrarily depriving the States of a power reserved to them under the Constitution, a power which they have enjoyed and exercised continuously from before the adoption of the First Amendment to this day. See *Roth v. United States.*

Under a National Constitution, fundamental First Amendment limitations on the powers of the States do not vary from community to community, but this does not mean that there are, or should or can be, fixed, uniform national standards of precisely what appeals to the "prurient interest" or is "patently offensive." These are essentially questions of fact, and our Nation is simply too big and too diverse for this Court to reasonably expect that such standards could be articulated for all 50 States in a single formulation, even assuming the prerequisite consensus exists. When triers of fact are asked to decide whether "the average person, applying contemporary community standards" would consider certain materials "prurient," it would be unrealistic to require that the answer be based on some abstract formulation. The adversary system, with lay jurors as the usual ultimate factfinders in criminal prosecutions, has historically permitted triers of fact to draw on the standards of their community, guided always by limiting instructions on the law. To require a State to structure obscenity proceedings around evidence of a *national* "community standard" would be an exercise in futility. . . .

We conclude that neither the State's alleged failure to offer evidence of "national standards," nor the trial court's charge that the jury consider state community standards, were constitutional errors. Nothing in the First Amendment requires that a jury must consider hypothetical and unascertainable "national standards" when attempting to determine whether certain materials are obscene as a matter of fact. . . .

It is neither realistic nor constitutionally sound to read the First Amendment as requiring that the people of Maine or Mississippi accept public depiction of conduct found tolerable in La Vegas, or New York City.

In sum, we (a) reaffirm the *Roth* holding that obscene material is not protected by the First Amendment; (b) hold that such material can be regulated by the States, subject to the specific safeguards enunciated above, without a showing that the material is *"utterly* without redeeming social value"; and (c) hold that obscenity is to be determined by applying "contemporary community standards."

MR. JUSTICE DOUGLAS, dissenting. . . .

Today the Court retreats from the earlier formulations of the constitutional test and undertakes to make new definitions. This effort, like the earlier ones, is earnest and well intentioned. The difficulty is that we do not deal with constitutional terms, since "obscenity" is not mentioned in the Constitution or Bill of Rights. And the First Amendment makes no such exception from "the press" which it undertakes to protect nor, as I have said on other occasions, is an exception necessarily implied, for there was no recognized exception to the free press at the time the Bill of Rights was adopted which treated "obscene" publications differently from other types of papers, magazines, and books. So there are no constitutional guidelines for deciding what is and what is not "obscene." The Court is at large because we deal with tastes and standards of literature. What shocks me may be sustenance for my neighbor. What causes one person to boil up in rage over one pamphlet or movie may reflect only his neurosis, not shared by others. We deal here with a regime of censorship which, if adopted, should be done by constitutional amendment after full debate by the people.

The idea that the First Amendment permits government to ban publications that are "offensive" to some people puts an ominous gloss on freedom of the press. That test would make it possible to ban any paper or any journal or magazine in some benighted place. The First Amendment was designed "to invite dispute," to induce "a condition of unrest," to "create dissatisfaction with conditions as they are," and even to stir "people to anger." *Terminiello v. Chicago*. The idea that the First Amendment permits punishment for ideas that are "offensive" to the particular judge or jury sitting in judgment is astounding. No greater leveler of speech or literature has ever been designed. To give the power to the censor, as we do today, is to make a sharp and radical break with the traditions of a free society. . . .

If there are to be restraints on what is obscene, then a constitutional amendment should be the way of achieving the end. There are societies where religion and mathematics are the only free segments. It would be a dark day for America if that were our destiny. But the people can make it such if they choose to write obscenity into the Constitution and define it. . . .

MR. JUSTICE BRENNAN with whom MR. JUSTICE STEWART and MR. JUSTICE MARSHALL join, dissenting.

PARIS ADULT THEATRE I ET AL. V. SLATON, DISTRICT ATTORNEY, ET AL.

413 U.S. 49 (1973)

MR. CHIEF JUSTICE BURGER delivered the opinion of the Court. . . .

We categorically disapprove the theory, apparently adopted by the trial judge, that obscene, pornographic films acquire constitutional immunity from state regulation simply because they are exhibited for consenting adults only. . . . The States have a long recognized legitimate interest in regulating the use of obscene material in local commerce and in all places of public accommodation, as long as these regulations do not run afoul of specific constitutional prohibitions. . .

In particular, we hold that there are legitimate state interests at stake in stemming the tide of commercialized obscenity, even assuming it is feasible to enforce effective safeguards against exposure to juveniles and to passersby. Rights and interests "other than those of the advocates are involved." *Breard v. Alexandria* (1951). These include the interest of the public in the quality of life and the total community environment, the tone of commerce in the great city centers, and, possibly, the public safety itself. The Hill-Link Minority Report of the Commission on Obscenity and Pornography indicates that there is at least an arguable correlation between obscene material and crime. Quite apart from sex crimes, however, there remains one problem of large proportions aptly described by Professor Bickel:

"It concerns the tone of the society, the mode, or to use terms that have perhaps greater currency, the style and quality of life, now and in the future. A man may be entitled to read an obscene book in his room, or expose himself indecently there . . . . We should protect his privacy. But if he demands a right to obtain the books and pictures he wants in the market, and to foregather in public places—discreet, if you will, but accessible to all—with others who share his tastes, *then to grant him his right is to affect the world about the rest of us, and to impinge on other privacies.* Even supposing that each of us can, if he wishes, effectively avert the eye and stop the ear (which, in truth, we cannot), what is commonly read and seen and heard and done intrudes upon us all, want it or not." The Public Interest 25-26 (Winter 1971).

As Mr. Chief Justice Warren stated, there is a "right" of the Nation and of the States to maintain a decent society.

But, it is argued, there are no scientific data which conclusively demonstrate that exposure to obscene material adversely affects men and women or their society. It is urged on behalf of the petitioners that, absent such a demonstration, any kind of state regulation is "impermissible." We reject this argument. It is not for us to resolve empirical uncertainties underlying state legislation, save in the exceptional case where that legislation plainly impinges upon rights protected by the Constitution itself.

From the beginning of civilized societies, legislators and judges have acted on various unprovable assumptions. Such assumptions underlie much lawful state regulation of commercial and business affairs. . . .

On the basis of these assumptions both Congress and state legislatures have, for example, drastically restricted associational rights by adopting antitrust laws, and have strictly regulated public expression by issuers of and dealers in securities, profit sharing "coupons," and "trading stamps," commanding what they must and must not publish and announce. . . .

Understandably those who entertain an absolutist view of the First Amendment find it uncomfortable to explain why rights of association, speech, and press should be severely restrained in the marketplace of goods and money, but not in the marketplace of pornography.

Likewise, when legislatures and administrators act to protect the physical environment from pollution and to preserve our resources of forests, streams, and parks, they must act on such imponderables as the impact of a new highway near or through an existing park or wilderness area. . . . The fact that a congressional directive reflects unprovable assumptions about what is good for the people, including imponderable aesthetic assumptions, is not a sufficient reason to find that statute unconstitutional.

If we accept the unprovable assumption that a complete education requires the reading of certain books . . . and the will nigh universal belief that good books, plays, and art lift the spirit, improve the mind, enrich the human personality and develop character, can we then say that a state legislature may not act on the corollary assumption that commerce in obscene books, or public exhibitions focused on obscene conduct, have a tendency to exert a corrupting and debasing impact leading to antisocial behavior?

. . . . The sum of experience, including that of the past two decades, affords an ample basis for legislatures to conclude that a sensitive, key relationship of human existence, central to family life, community welfare, and the development of human personality, can be debased and distorted by crass commercial exploitation of sex. Nothing in the Constitution prohibits a State from reaching such a conclusion and acting on it legislatively simply because there is no conclusive evidence or empirical data. . . .

- If obscene material unprotected by the First Amendment in itself carried with it a "penumbra" of constitutionally protected privacy, this Court would not have found it necessary to decide *Stanley* on the narrow basis of the "privacy of the home," which was hardly more than a reaffirmation that "a man's home is his castle." *Stanley* v. *Georgia*. Moreover, we have declined to equate the privacy of the home relied on in *Stanley* with a "zone" of "privacy" that follows a distributor or a consumer of obscene materials wherever he goes. . . .

The idea of a "privacy" right and a place of public accommodation are, in this context, mutually exclusive. Conduct or depictions of conduct that the state police power can prohibit on a public street do not become automatically protected by the Constitution merely because the conduct is moved to a bar or a "live" theater stage, any more than a "live" performance of a man and woman locked in a sexual embrace at high noon in Times Square is protected by the Constitution because they simultaneously engage in a valid political dialogue.

It is also argued that the State has no legitimate interest in "control [of] the moral content of a person's thoughts," *Stanley* v. *Georgia*, and we need not quarrel with this. But we reject the claim that the State of Georgia is here attempting to control the minds or thoughts of those who patronize theaters. Preventing unlimited display or distribution of obscene material, which by definition lacks any serious literary, artistic, political, or scientific value as communication, *Miller* v. *California*, is distinct from a control of reason and the intellect. Where communication of ideas, protected by the First Amendment, is not involved, or the particular privacy of the home protected by *Stanley*, or any of the other "areas or zones" of constitutionally protected privacy, the mere fact that, as a consequence, some human "utterances" or "thoughts" may be incidentally affected does not bar the State from acting to protect legitimate state interests. The fantasies of a drug addict are his own and beyond the reach of government, but government regulation of drug sales is not prohibited by the Constitution. . .

Finally, petitioners argue that conduct which directly involves "consenting adults" only has, for that sole reason, a special claim to constitutional protection. Our Constitution establishes a broad range of conditions on the exercise of power by the States, but for us to say that our Constitution incorporates the proposition that conduct involving consenting adults only is always beyond state regulation, is a step we are unable to take. Commercial exploitation of depictions, descriptions, or exhibitions of obscene conduct on commercial premises open to the adult public falls within a State's broad power to regulate commerce and protect the public environment. The issue in this context goes beyond whether someone, or even the majority, considers the conduct depicted as "wrong" or "sinful." The States have the power to make a morally neutral judgment that public exhibition of obscene material, or commerce in such material, has a tendency to injure the community as a whole, to endanger the public safety, or to jeopardize, in Mr. Chief Justice Warren's words, the State's "right . . . to maintain a decent society." *Jacobellis* v. *Ohio*.

To summarize, we have today reaffirmed the basic holding of *Roth* v. *United States*, that obscene material has no protection under the First Amendment. See *Miller* v. *California*, and *Kaplan* v. *California*. We have directed our holdings, not at thoughts or speech, but at depiction and description of specifically defined sexual conduct that States may regulate within limits designed to prevent infringement of First Amendment rights. We have also reaffirmed the holdings of *United States* v. *Reidel*, and *United States* v. *Thirty-seven Photographs*, that commerce in obscene material is unprotected by any constitutional doctrine of privacy. In this case we hold that the States have a legitimate interest in regulating commerce in obscene material and in regulating exhibition of obscene material in places of public accommodation, including so-called "adult" theaters from which minors are excluded. In light of these holdings, nothing precludes the State of Georgia from the regulation of the allegedly obscene material exhibited in Paris Adult Theatre I or II, provided that the applicable Georgia law, as written or authoritatively interpreted by the Georgia courts, meets the First Amendment standards set forth in *Miller* v. *California*. . . .

MR. JUSTICE DOUGLAS, dissenting. . . .

MR. JUSTICE BRENNAN, with whom MR. JUSTICE STEWART and MR.

JUSTICE MARSHALL join, dissenting.

This case requires the Court to confront once again the vexing problem of reconciling state efforts to suppress sexually oriented expression with the protections of the First Amendment, as applied to the States through the Fourteenth Amendment. No other aspect of the First Amendment has, in recent years, demanded so substantial a commitment of our time, generated such disharmony of views, and remained so resistant to the formulation of stable and manageable standards. I am convinced that the approach initiated 16 years ago in *Roth v. United States* (1957), and culminating in the Court's decision today, cannot bring stability to this area of the law without jeopardizing fundamental First Amendment values and I have concluded that the time has come to make a significant departure from that approach.
. . . .

Our experience with the *Roth* approach has certainly taught us that the outright suppression of obscenity cannot be reconciled with the fundamental principles of the First and Fourteenth Amendments. For we have failed to formulate a standard that sharply distinguishes protected from unprotected speech, and out of necessity, we have resorted to the *Redrup* approach, which resolves cases as between the parties, but offers only the most obscure guidance to legislation, adjudication by other courts, and primary conduct. By disposing of cases through summary reversal or denial of certiorari we have deliberately and effectively obscured the rationale underlying the decisions. It comes as no surprise that judicial attempts to follow our lead conscientiously have often ended in hopeless confusion.

Of course, the vagueness problem would be largely of our own creation if it stemmed primarily from our failure to reach a consensus on any one standard. But after 16 years of experimentation and debate I am reluctantly forced to the conclusion that none of the available formulas, including the one announced today, can reduce the vagueness to a tolerable level while at the same time striking an acceptable balance between the protections of the First and Fourteenth Amendments, on the one hand, and on the other the asserted state interest in regulating the dissemination of certain sexually oriented materials. Any effort to draw a constitutionally acceptable boundary on state power must resort to such indefinite concepts as "prurient interest," "patent offensiveness," "serious literary value," and the like. The meaning of these concepts necessarily varies with the experience, outlook, and even idiosyncrasies of the person defining them. Although we have assumed that obscenity does exist and that we "know it when [we] see it," *Jacobellis v. Ohio*, we are manifestly unable to describe it in advance except by reference to concepts so elusive that they fail to distinguish clearly between protected and unprotected speech.
. . .

The vagueness of the standards in the obscenity area produces a number of separate problems, and any improvement must rest on an understanding that the problems are to some extent distinct. First, a vague statute fails to provide adequate notice to persons who are engaged in the type of conduct that the statute could be thought to proscribe. The Due Process Clause of the Fourteenth Amendment requires that all criminal laws provide fair notice of "what the State commands or forbids. . . ."

In addition to problems that arise when any criminal statute fails to afford fair notice of what it forbids, a vague statute in the areas of speech and press creates a second level of difficulty. We have indicated that "stricter standards of permissible statutory vagueness may be applied to a statute having a potentially inhibiting effect on speech; a man may the less be required to act at his peril here, because the free dissemination of ideas may be the loser."

Similarly, we have held that a State cannot impose criminal sanctions for the possession of obscene material absent proof that the possessor had knowledge of the contents of the material. *Smith v. California.* "Proof of scienter" is necessary "to avoid the hazard of self-censorship of constitutionally protected material and to compensate for the ambiguities inherent in the definition of obscenity. . . ." "The problems of fair notice and chilling protected speech are very grave standing alone. But it does not detract from their importance to recognize that a vague statute in this area creates a third, although admittedly more subtle, set of problems. These problems concern the institutional stress that inevitably results where the line separating protected from unprotected speech is excessively vague. In *Roth* we conceded that "there may be marginal cases in which it is difficult to determine the side of the line on which a particular fact situation falls. . . ." Our subsequent experience demonstrates that almost every case is "marginal." And since the "margin" marks the point of separation between protected and unprotected speech, we are left with a system in which almost every obscenity case presents a constitutional question of exceptional difficulty. "The suppression of a particular writing or other tangible form of expression is . . . an *individual* matter, and in the nature of things every such suppression raises an individual constitutional problem, in which a reviewing court must determine for *itself* whether the attacked expression is suppressible within constitutional standards. . . ."

As a result of our failure to define standards with predictable application to any given piece of material, there is no probability of regularity in obscenity decisions by state and lower federal courts. That is not to say that these courts have performed badly in this area or paid insufficient attention to the principles we have established. The problem is, rather, that one cannot say with certainty that material is obscene until at least five members of this Court, applying inevitably obscure standards, have pronounced it so. The number of obscenity cases on our docket gives ample testimony to the burden that has been placed upon this Court.

Moreover, we have managed the burden of deciding scores of obscenity cases by relying on *per curiam* reversals or denials of certiorari—a practice which conceals the rationale of decision and gives at least the appearance of arbitrary action by this Court. More important, no less than the procedural schemes struck down in such cases as *Blount v. Rizzi, and Freedman v. Maryland,* the practice effectively censors protected expression by leaving lower court determinations of obscenity intact even though the status of the allegedly obscene material is entirely unsettled until final review here. In addition, the uncertainty of the standards creates a continuing source of tension between state and federal courts, since the need for an independent determination by this Court seems to render superfluous even the most conscientious analysis by state tribunals. And our inability to justify our decisions with a persuasive rationale— or indeed, any rationale at all—necessarily creates the impression that we are merely second-guessing state court judges. . . .

Of course, the Court's restated *Roth* test does limit the definition of obscenity to depictions of physical conduct and explicit sexual acts. And that limitation may seem, at first glance, a welcome and clarifying addition to the *Roth-Memoirs* formula. But, just as the agreement in *Roth* on an abstract definition of obscenity gave little hint of the extreme difficulty that was to follow in attempting to apply that definition to specific material, the mere formulation of a "physical conduct" test is no assurance that it can be applied with any greater facility. The Court does not indicate how it would apply its test to the materials involved in *Miller v. California,* and we can only speculate as to its application. But even a confirmed optimist could find little realistic comfort in the adoption of such a test. Indeed, the valiant attempt of one lower federal court to draw the constitutional line at depictions of explicit sexual conduct seems to belie any suggestion that this approach marks the road to clarity. The Court surely demonstrates little sensitivity to our own institutional problems, much less the other vagueness-related difficulties, in establishing a system that requires us to consider whether a description of human genitals is sufficiently "lewd" to deprive it of constitutional protection; whether a sexual act is "ultimate"; whether the conduct depicted in materials before us fits within one of the categories of conduct whose depiction the State and Federal Governments have attempted to suppress; and a host of equally pointless inquiries. In addition, adoption of such a test does not presumably, obviate the need for consideration of the nuances of presentation of sexually oriented material, yet it hardly clarifies the application of those opaque but important factors.

If the application of the "physical conduct" test to pictorial material is fraught with difficulty, its application to textual material carries the potential for extraordinary abuse. Surely we have passed the point where the mere written description of sexual conduct is deprived of First Amendment protection. Yet the test offers no guidance to us, or anyone else, in determining which written descriptions of sexual conduct are protected, and which are not.

Ultimately, the reformulation must fail because it still leaves in this Court the responsibility of determining in each case whether the materials are protected by the First Amendment.

Our experience since *Roth* requires us not only to abandon the effort to pick out obscene materials on a case-by-case basis, but also to reconsider a fundamental postulate of *Roth:* that there exists a definable class of sexually oriented expression that may be totally suppressed by the Federal and State Governments. Assuming that such a class of expression in fact exist, I am forced to conclude that the concept of "obscenity" cannot be defined with sufficient specificity and clarity to provide fair notice to persons who create and distribute sexually oriented materials, to prevent substantial erosion of protected speech as a byproduct of the attempt to suppress unprotected speech, and to avoid very costly institutional harms. Given these inevitable side effects of state efforts to suppress what is assumed to be *unprotected* speech, we must scrutinize with care the state interest that is asserted to justify the suppression. For in the absence of some very substantial interest in suppressing such speech, we can hardly condone the ill effects that seem to flow inevitably from the effort. . . .

The opinions in *Redrup* and *Stanley* reflected our emerging view that the state interests in protecting children and in protecting unconsenting adults may stand on different footing from the other asserted state interests. It may well be, as one commentator has argued, that "exposure to [erotic material] is for some persons an intense emotional experience. A communication of this nature, imposed upon a person contrary to his wishes, has all the characteristics of a physical assault. . . [And it constitutes an invasion of his privacy . . . ." Similarly, if children are "not possessed of that full capacity for individual choice which is the presupposition of the First Amendment guarantees," *Ginsberg v. New York* (STEWART, J., concurring), then the State may have a substantial interest in precluding the flow of obscene materials even to consenting juveniles.

But, whatever the strength of the state interests in protecting juveniles and unconsenting adults from exposure to sexually oriented materials, those interests cannot be asserted in defense of the holding of the Georgia Supreme Court in this case. That court assumed for the purposes of its decision that the films in issue were exhibited only to persons over the age of 21 who viewed them willingly and with prior knowledge of the nature of their contents. And on that assumption the state court held that the films could still be suppressed. The justification for the suppression must be found, therefore, in some independent interest in regulating the reading and viewing habits of consenting adults. . . .

In short, while I cannot say that the interests of the state—apart from the question of juveniles and unconsenting adults—are trivial or nonexistent, I am compelled to conclude that these interests cannot justify the substantial damage to constitutional rights and to this Nation's judicial machinery that inevitably results from state efforts to bar the distribution even of unprotected material to consenting adults. *NAACP v Alabama* (1964). I would hold therefore, that at least in the absence of distribution to juveniles or obtrusive exposure to unconsenting adults, the First and Fourteenth Amendments prohibit the State and Federal Governments from attempting wholly to suppress sexually oriented materials on the basis of their allegedly "obscene" contents.

Nothing in this approach precludes those governments from taking action to serve what may be strong and legitimate interests through regulation of the manner of distribution of sexually oriented material. . .

CITY OF RENTON ET AL. V. PLAYTIME THEATRES, INC., ET AL.

475 U.S. 41 (1986)

JUSTICE REHNQUIST delivered the opinion of the Court.

This case involves a constitutional challenge to a zoning ordinance, enacted by appellant city of Renton, Washington, that prohibits adult motion picture theaters from locating within 1,000 feet of any residential zone, single- or multiple-family dwelling, church, park, or school. Appellees, Playtime Theatres, Inc., and Sea-First Properties, Inc., filed an action in the United States District Court for the Western District of Washington seeking a declaratory judgment that the Renton ordinance violated the First and Fourteenth Amendments and a permanent injunction against its enforcement. The District Court ruled in favor of Renton and denied the permanent injunction, but the Court of Appeals for the Ninth Circuit reversed and remanded for reconsideration. We noted probable jurisdiction, and now reverse the judgment of the Ninth Circuit. . . .

In our view, the resolution of this case is largely dictated by our decision in *Young v. American Mini Theatres, Inc.* There, although five Members of the Court did not agree on a single rationale for the decision, we held that the city of Detroit's zoning ordinance, which prohibited locating an adult theater within 1,000 feet of any two other "regulated uses" or within 500 feet of any residential zone, did not violate the First and Fourteenth Amendments. The Renton ordinance, like the one in *American Mini Theatres,* does not ban adult theaters altogether, but merely provides that such theaters may not be located within 1,000 feet of any residential zone, single- or multiple-family dwelling, church, park, or

school. The ordinance is therefore properly analyzed as a form of time, place, and manner regulation.

Describing the ordinance as a time, place, and manner regulation is, of course, only the first step in our inquiry. This Court has long held that regulations enacted for the purpose of restraining on the basis of its content presumptively violate the First Amendment. . . On the other hand, so-called "content-neutral" time, place and manner regulations are acceptable so long as they are designed to serve a substantial governmental interest and do not unreasonably limit alternative avenues of communication.

At first glance, the Renton ordinance, like the ordinance in *American Mini Theatres,* does not appear to fit neatly into either the "content-based" or the "content-neutral" category. To be sure, the ordinance treats theaters that specialize in adult films differently from other kinds of theaters. Nevertheless, as the District Court concluded, the Renton ordinance is aimed not at the *content* of the films shown at "adult motion picture theatres," but rather at the *secondary effects* of such theaters on the surrounding community. The District Court found that the City Council's *"predominate* concerns" were with the secondary effects of adult theaters, and not with the content of adult films themselves. . . .

The District Court's finding as to "predominate" intent, left undisturbed by the Court of Appeals, is more than adequate to establish that the city's pursuit of its zoning interests here was unrelated to the suppression of free expression. The ordinance by its terms is designed to prevent crime, protect the city's retail trade, maintain property values, and generally "protec[t] and preserv[e] the quality of [the city's] neighborhoods, commercial districts, and the quality of urban life," not to suppress the expression of unpopular views. As JUSTICE POWELL observed in *American Mini Theatres*, "[i]f [the city] had been concerned with restricting the message purveyed by adult theaters, it would have tried to close them or restrict their number rather than circumscribe their choice as to location."

In short, the Renton ordinance is completely consistent with our definition of "content-neutral" speech regulations as those that "are *justified* without reference to the content of the regulated speech. . . ."

The appropriate inquiry in this case, then, is whether the Renton ordinance is designed to serve a substantial governmental interest and allows for reasonable alternative avenues of communication. . . It is clear that the ordinance meets such a standard. As a majority of this Court recognized in *American Mini Theatres*, a city's "interest in attempting to preserve the quality of urban life is one that must be accorded high respect. . . ."

The Court of Appeals ruled, however, that because the Renton ordinance was enacted without the benefit of studies specifically relating to "the particular problems or needs of Renton," the city's justifications for the ordinance were "conclusory and speculative." We think the Court of Appeals imposed on the city an unnecessarily rigid burden of proof. The record in this case reveals that Renton relied heavily on the experience of, and studies produced by, the city of Seattle. In Seattle, as in Renton, the adult theater zoning ordinance was aimed at preventing the secondary effects caused by the presence of even one such theater in a given neighborhood.

We also find no constitutional defect in the method chosen by Renton to further its substantial interests. Cities may regulate adult theaters by dispersing them, as in Detroit, or by effectively concentrating them, as in Renton. . . .

Respondents contend that the Renton ordinance is "under-inclusive," in that it fails to regulate other kinds of adult businesses that are likely to produce secondary effects similar to those produced by adult theaters. On this record the contention must fail. There is no evidence that, at the time the Renton ordinance was enacted, any other adult business was located in, or was contemplating moving into, Renton. . . .

Finally, turning to the question whether the Renton ordinance allows for reasonable alternative avenues of communication, we note that the ordinance leaves some 520 acres, or more than five percent of the entire land area of Renton, open to use as adult theater sites. The District Court found, and the Court of Appeals did not dispute the finding, that the 520 acres of land consists of "[a]mple, accessible real estate," including "acreage in all stages of development from raw land to developed, industrial, warehouse, office, and shopping space that is criss-crossed by freeways, highways, and roads." Respondents argue, however, that some of the land in question is already occupied by existing businesses, that "practically none" of the undeveloped land is currently for sale or lease, and that in general there are no "commercially viable" adult theater sites within the 520 acres left open by the Renton ordinance. The Court of Appeals accepted these arguments, concluded that the 520 acres was not truly "available" land, and therefore held that the Renton ordinance "would result in a substantial restriction" on speech.

We disagree with both the reasoning and the conclusion of the Court of Appeals. That respondents must fend for themselves in the real estate market, on an equal footing with other prospective purchasers and lessees, does not give rise to a First Amendment violation. And although we have cautioned against the enactment of zoning regulations that have "the effect of suppressing, or greatly restricting access to, lawful speech," *American Mini Theatres* (plurality opinion), we have never suggested that the First Amendment compels the Government to ensure that adult theaters, or any other kinds of speech-related businesses for that matter, will be able to obtain sites at bargain prices. (POWELL, J., concurring) ("The inquiry for First Amendment purposes is not concerned with economic impact"). In our view, the First Amendment requires only that Renton refrain from effectively denying respondents a reasonable opportunity to open and operate an adult theater within the city, and the ordinance before us easily meet this requirement.

JUSTICE BLACKMUN concurs in the result.

JUSTICE BRENNAN, with whom JUSTICE MARSHALL joins, dissenting.

Renton's zoning ordinance selectively imposes limitations on the location of a movie theater based exclusively on the content of the films shown there. The constitutionality of the ordinance is therefore not correctly analyzed under standards applied to content-neutral time, place, and manner restrictions. But even assuming that the ordinance may fairly be characterized as content-neutral, it is plainly unconstitutional under the standards established by the decisions of this Court. . . .

The fact that adult movie theaters may cause harmful "secondary" land-use effects may arguably give Renton a compelling reason to regulate such establishments; it does not mean, however, that such regulations are content neutral.

The ordinance discriminates on its face against certain forms of speech based on content. Movie theaters specializing in "adult motion pictures" may not be located within 1,000 feet of any residential zone, single- or multiple-family dwelling, church, park, or school. Other motion picture theaters, and other forms of "adult entertainment," such as bars, massage parlors, and adult bookstores, are not subject to the same restrictions. This selective treatment strongly suggests that Renton was interested not in controlling the "secondary effects" associated with adult businesses, but in discriminating against adult theaters based on the content of the films they exhibit. The Court ignores this discriminatory treatment, declaring that Renton is free "to address

the potential problems created by one particular kind of adult business," and to amend the ordinance in the future to include other adult enterprises.

In this case, the city has not justified treating adult movie theaters differently from other adult entertainment businesses. The ordinance's underinclusiveness is cogent evidence that it was aimed at the *content* of the films shown in adult movie theaters. . . .

The Court holds that Renton was entitled to rely on the experiences of cities like Detroit and Seattle, which had enacted special zoning regulations for adult entertainment businesses after studying the adverse effects caused by such establishments. However, even assuming that Renton was concerned with the same problems as Seattle and Detroit, it never actually reviewed any of the studies conducted by those cities. Renton had no basis for determining if any of the "findings" made by these cities were relevant to *Renton's* problems or needs. Moreover, since Renton ultimately adopted zoning regulations different from either Detroit or Seattle, these "studies" provide no basis for assessing the effectiveness of the particular restrictions adopted under the ordinance. Renton cannot merely rely on the general experiences of Seattle of Detroit, for it must "justify its ordinance in the context of *Renton's* problems—not Seattle's or Detroit's problems." In sum, the circumstances here strongly suggest that the ordinance was designed to suppress expression, even that constitutionally protected, and thus was not to be analyzed as a content-neutral time, place, and manner restriction. The Court allows Renton to conceal its illicit motives, however, by reliance on the fact that other communities adopted similar restrictions. The Court's approach largely immunizes such measures from judicial scrutiny, since a municipality can readily find other municipal ordinances to rely upon, thus always retrospectively justifying special zoning regulations for adult theaters. Rather than speculate about Renton's motives for adopting such measures, our cases require the conclusion that the ordinance, like any other content-based restriction on speech, is constitutional "only if the [city] can show that [it] is a precisely drawn means of serving a compelling [governmental] interest. . . ."

Even assuming that the ordinance should be treated like a content-neutral time, place, and manner restriction, I would still find it unconstitutional. "[R]estrictions of this kind are valid provided . . . that they are narrowly tailored to serve a significant governmental interest, and that they leave open ample alternative channels for communication of the information. . . ."

The Court finds that the ordinance was designed to further Renton's substantial interest in "preserv[ing] the quality of urban life." As explained above, the record here is simply insufficient to support this assertion. The city made no showing as to how uses "protected" by the ordinance would be affected by the presence of an adult movie theater. Thus, the Renton ordinance is clearly distinguishable from the Detroit zoning ordinance upheld in *Young v. American Mini Theatres, Inc. (1976)*. The Detroit ordinance, which was designed to disperse adult theaters throughout the city, was supported by the testimony of urban planners and real estate experts regarding the adverse effects of locating several such businesses in the same neighborhood. . .

Here, the Renton Council was aware only that some residents had complained about adult movie theaters, and that other localities had adopted special zoning restrictions for such establishments. These are not "facts" sufficient to justify the burdens the ordinance imposed upon constitutionally protected expression. . . .

Finally, the ordinance is invalid because it does not provide for reasonable alternative avenues of communication. The District Court found that the ordinance left 520 acres in Renton available for adult theater sites, an area comprising about five percent of the city. However, the Court of Appeals found that because much of this land was already occupied, "[l]imiting adult theater uses to these areas is a substantial restriction on speech." Many "available" sites are also largely unsuited for use by movie theaters. Again, these facts serve to distinguish this case from *American Mini Theatres*, where there was no indication that the Detroit zoning ordinance seriously limited the locations available for adult businesses. See *American Mini Theatres* (plurality opinion) ("The situation would be quite different if the ordinance had the effect of . . . greatly restricting access to . . . lawful speech").

Despite the evidence in the record, the Court reasons that the fact "[t]hat respondents must fend for themselves in the real estate market, on an equal footing with other prospective purchasers and lessees, does not give rise to a First Amendment violation." However, respondents are not on equal footing with other prospective purchasers and lessees, but must conduct business under severe restrictions not imposed upon other establishments. The Court also argues that the First Amendment does not compel "the government to ensure that adult theaters, or any other kinds of speech-related businesses for that matter, will be able to obtain sites at bargain prices." However, respondents do not ask Renton to guarantee low-price sites for their businesses, but seek only a reasonable opportunity to operate adult theaters in the city. By denying them this opportunity, Renton can effectively ban a form of protected speech from its borders. The ordinance "greatly restrict[s] access to . . . lawful speech," *American Mini Theatres*, (plurality opinion), and is plainly unconstitutional.

SABLE COMMUNICATIONS OF CALIFORNIA, INC. V. FEDERAL COMMUNICATIONS COMMISSION ET AL.

492 U.S. 115 (1989)

JUSTICE WHITE delivered the opinion of the Court.

The issue before us is the constitutionality of 223(b) of the

Communications Act of 1934. The statute, as amended in 1988, imposes an outright ban on indecent as well as obscene interstate commercial telephone messages. The District Court upheld the prohibition against obscene interstate telephone communications for commercial purposes, but enjoined the enforcement of the statute insofar as it applied to indecent messages. We affirm the District Court in both respects. . . . In contrast to the prohibition on indecent communications; there is no constitutional barrier to the ban on obscene dial-a-porn recordings. We have repeatedly held that the protection of the First Amendment does not extend to obscene speech. See, e. g., *Paris Adult Theatre I v. Slaton* (1973). The case before us today does not require us to decide what is obscene or what is indecent but rather to determine whether Congress is empowered to prohibit transmission of obscene telephonic communications.

In its facial challenge to the statute, Sable argues that the legislation creates an impermissible national standard of obscenity, and that it places message senders in a "double bind" by compelling them to tailor all their messages to the least tolerant community.

We do not read 223(b) as contravening the "contemporary community standards" requirement of *Miller v. California* (1973). Section 223(b) no more establishes a "national standard" of obscenity than do federal statutes prohibiting the mailing of obscene materials. . . .

In *United States v. Reidel* (1971), we said that Congress could prohibit the use of the mails for commercial distribution of materials properly classifiable as obscene, even though those materials were being distributed to willing adults who stated that they were adults. Similarly, we hold today that there is no constitutional stricture against Congress' prohibiting the interstate transmission of obscene commercial telephone recordings.

We stated in *United States v. 12 200-ft. Reels of Film* (1973), that the *Miller* standards, including the "contemporary community standards" formulation, apply to federal legislation. As we have said before, the fact that "distributors of allegedly obscene materials may be subjected to varying community standards in the various federal judicial districts into which they transmit the materials does not render a federal statute unconstitutional because of the failure of application of uniform national standards of obscenity." *Hamling v. United States.*

Furthermore, Sable is free to tailor its messages, on a selective basis, if it so chooses, to the communities it chooses to serve. While Sable may be forced to incur some costs in developing and implementing a system for screening the locale of incoming calls, there is no constitutional impediment to enacting a law which may impose such costs on a medium electing to provide these messages. Whether Sable chooses to hire operators to determine the source of the calls or engages with the telephone company to arrange for the screening and blocking of out-of-area calls or finds another means for providing messages compatible with community standards is a decision for the message provider to make. There is no constitutional barrier under *Miller* to prohibiting communications that are obscene in some communities under local standards even though they are not obscene in others. If Sable's audience is comprised of different communities with different local standards, Sable ultimately bears the burden of, complying with the prohibition on obscene messages.

 . . . . the District Court concluded that while the government has a legitimate interest in protecting children from exposure to indecent dial-a-porn messages, 223(b) was not sufficiently narrowly drawn to serve that purpose and thus violated the First Amendment. We agree.

Sexual expression which is indecent but not obscene is protected by the First Amendment; and the government does not submit that the sale of such materials to adults could be criminalized solely because they are indecent. The government may, however, regulate the content of constitutionally protected speech in order to promote a compelling interest if it chooses the least restrictive means to further the articulated interest. We have recognized that there is a compelling interest in protecting the physical and psychological well-being of minors. This interest extends to shielding minors from the influence of literature that is not obscene by adult standards. The government may serve this legitimate interest, but to withstand constitutional scrutiny, "it must do so by narrowly drawn regulations designed to serve those interests without unnecessarily interfering with First Amendment freedoms. It is not enough to show that the government's ends are compelling; the means must be carefully tailored to achieve those ends.

In attempting to justify the complete ban and criminalization of the indecent commercial telephone communications with adults as well as minors, the government relies on *FCC v. Pacifica Foundation* (1978), a case in which the Court considered whether the FCC has the power to regulate a radio broadcast that is indecent but not obscene. In an emphatically narrow holding, the *Pacifica* Court concluded that special treatment of indecent broadcasting was justified.

Pacifica is readily distinguishable from this case, most obviously because it did not involve a total ban on broadcasting indecent material. The FCC rule was not "'intended to place an absolute prohibition on the broadcast of this type of language, but rather sought to channel it to times of day when children most likely would not be exposed to it." *Pacifica.* The issue of a total ban was not before the Court.

The *Pacifica* opinion also relied on the "unique" attributes of broadcasting, noting that broadcasting is "uniquely pervasive," can intrude on the privacy of the home without prior warning as to program content, and is "uniquely accessible to children, even those too young to read." The private commercial telephone communications at issue here are substantially different from the public radio broadcast at issue in *Pacifica.* In contrast to public displays, unsolicited mailings and other means of expression which the recipient has no meaningful opportunity to avoid, the dial-it medium requires the listener to take affirmative steps to receive the communication. There is no "captive audience" problem here; callers will generally not be unwilling listeners. The context of dial-in services, where a caller seeks and is willing to pay

for the communication, is manifestly different from a situation in which a listener does not want the received message. Placing a telephone call is not the same as turning on a radio and being taken by surprise by an indecent message. Unlike an unexpected outburst on a radio broadcast, the message received by one who places a call to a dial-a-porn service is not so invasive or surprising that it prevents an unwilling listener from avoiding exposure to it.

The Government nevertheless argues that the total ban on indecent commercial telephone communications is justified because nothing less could prevent children from gaining access to such messages. We find the argument quite unpersuasive. The FCC, after lengthy proceedings, determined that its credit card, access code, and scrambling rules were a satisfactory solution to the problem of keeping indecent dial-a-porn messages out of the reach of minors. The Court of Appeals, after careful consideration, agreed that these rules represented a "feasible and effective" way to serve the Government's compelling interest in protecting children. The Government now insists that the rules would not be effective enough—that enterprising youngsters could and would evade the rules and gain access to communications from which they should be shielded. There is no evidence in the record before us to that effect, nor could there be since the FCC's implementation of 223(b) prior to its 1988 amendment has never been tested over time. . . .

There is no doubt Congress enacted a total ban on both obscene and indecent telephone communications. But aside from conclusory statements during the debates by proponents of the bill, as well as similar assertions in hearings on a substantially identical bill the year before, that under the FCC regulations minors could still have access to dial-a-porn messages, the Congressional record presented to us contains no evidence as to *how* effective or ineffective the FCC's most recent regulations were or might prove to be. . . .

For all we know from this record, the FCC's technological approach to restricting dial-a-porn messages to adults who seek them would be extremely effective, and only a few of the most enterprising and disobedient young people will manage to secure access to such messages. If this is the case, it seems to us that 223(b) is not a narrowly tailored effort to serve the compelling interest of preventing minors from being exposed to indecent telephone messages. Under our precedents, 223(b), in its present form, has the invalid effect of limiting the content of adult telephone conversations to that which is suitable for children to hear. It is another case of "burn[ing] up the house to roast the pig." *Butler* v. *Michigan.*

Because the statute's denial of adult access to telephone messages which are indecent but not obscene far exceeds that which is necessary to limit the access of minors to such messages, we hold that the ban does not survive constitutional scrutiny. . . .

JUSTICE SCALIA, concurring. . . .

I join the Court s opinion because I think it correct that a wholesale prohibition upon adult access to indecent speech cannot be adopted merely because the FCC's alternate proposal could be circumvented by as few children as the evidence suggests. But where a reasonable person draws the line in this balancing process—that is, how few children render the risk unacceptable—depends in part upon what mere "indecency" (as opposed to "obscenity") includes. The more narrow the understanding of what is "obscene," and hence the more pornographic what is embraced within the residual category of "indecency," the more reasonable it becomes to insist upon greater assurance of insulation from minors. So while the Court is unanimous on the reasoning of Part IV, I am not sure it is unanimous on the assumptions underlying that reasoning. I do not believe, for example, that any sort of sexual activity portrayed or enacted over the phone lines would fall outside of the obscenity portion of the statute that we uphold, and within the

indecency portion that we strike down, so long as it appeals only to "normal, healthy sexual desires" as opposed to "shameful or morbid" ones. . . .

JUSTICE BRENNAN, with whom JUSTICE MARSHALL, and JUSTICE STEVENS join, concurring in part and dissenting in part.

I agree that a statute imposing criminal penalties for making, or for allowing others to use a telephone under one's control to make, any indecent telephonic communication for a commercial purpose is patently unconstitutional. . . .

The very evidence the Court adduces to show that denying adults access to all indecent commercial messages "far exceeds that which is necessary to limit the access of minors to such messages," also demonstrates that forbidding the transmission of all obscene messages is unduly heavy-handed. After painstaking scrutiny, both the FCC and the Second Circuit found that "a scheme involving access codes, scrambling, and credit card payment is a feasible and effective way to serve this compelling state interest" in safe-guarding children. . . . In addition, no contrary evidence was before Congress when it voted to impose a total prohibition on obscene telephonic messages for profit. Hence, the Government cannot plausibly claim that its legitimate interest in protecting children warrants this draconian restriction on the First Amendment rights of adults who seek to hear the messages that Sable and others provide.

Section 223(b)(1)(A) unambiguously proscribes all obscene commercial messages, and thus admits of no construction that would render it constitutionally permissible. Because this criminal statute curtails freedom of speech far more radically than the Government's interest in preventing harm to minors could possibly license on the record before us, I would reverse. . . .

10

PROTECTION FROM LIBEL AND INVASION OF PRIVACY

"Who steals my purse steals trash. . . . But he that filches from me my good name robs me of that which not enriches him, and makes me poor indeed."[1] The truth of this sentiment, which Shakespeare put into the mouth of Iago, is recognized historically by the long existence of libel law in the United States and England, and constitutionally by Chaplinsky's view of libel as unprotected by the First Amendment. Such was the law, simply and clearly, until New York Times v. Sullivan (1964), the preeminent case on the constitutional law of libel, and excerpted at the end of this chapter. In Times the Court had before it, for the first time, the issue of whether the First Amendment barred recovery for libel when the alleged libel was of a public official for actions related to his public duty.

It is clear from the facts of Times that some of the allegations allegedly made about Public Safety Commissioner Sullivan of Birmingham, Alabama, were indeed false, some of them seriously so. The advertisement which was the basis for the suit stated that the dining room of the college where protesting black students were enrolled was padlocked in retaliation for their protests. This was not true; the dining room was never closed. Other misstatements of fact also appeared in the ad. And the trial court determined as a factual matter that all of the allegations of misconduct in the ad might have been read as referring to Sullivan.

For the Times Court, however, none of this made any difference. The damage award was reversed on the fundamental ground that it was inconsistent with the "widespread, robust" discussion of public issues that is a part of the national commitment, and which the First Amendment was designed to protect.

The fact that some falsity was contained in the advertisement did not dictate a different result, for "erroneous statement is inevitable in free debate, and . . . it must be protected if the freedoms of expression are to have the 'breathing space' that they need to survive."

Further, the fact that official reputation might be injured afforded no warrant for suppressing speech. "Criticism of . . . official conduct does not lose its constitutional protection merely because it is effective criticism and hence diminishes . . . official reputation." And, if neither of the above was sufficient "to remove the constitutional shield from criticism of official conduct, the combination of the two elements is no less inadequate."

What was needed was a rule explicating the constitutional guarantee in matters of libel, which the Court provided as follows:

> The . . .[First Amendment requires] . . ., we think a federal rule that prohibits a public official from recovering damages for a defamatory falsehood relating to his official conduct unless he proves that the statement was made with "actual malice" - that is, with knowledge that it was false or with reckless disregard of whether it was false or not.

The Sullivan rule has been widely approved, and appears to draw both an acceptable and a necessary line which protects the freedom to comment on governmental affairs which is "at the core" of the First Amendment. Although the rule, in the hands of the unscrupulous, can lead to melancholy and unfair results,[2] that is the price we must pay for necessary media freedom. Much more controversial than the rule as initially stated is the modification which Times underwent after its inception.

Sullivan was a sitting public official, the elected Public Safety Commissioner of a major city. But the Court soon extended the rule to those who were candidates for public office. Further, protection of such criticism was broadened to include not only "official conduct," a record of which a candidate may not have, but also any matter relating to "fitness for public office." Since the individual citizen may, and would seemingly have every right to judge such "fitness" on the basis of any criterion thought relevant, the result seems to establish a lesser degree of protection for candidates for elective office than for sitting officials. Again, the rule is probably justified. But the potential for abuse is even broader.

In Associated Press v. Walker and Curtiss Publishing Co. v. Butts (1967), the Court had before it the issue of whether the extended _Times_ standard should be applied to "public figures." While deciding that criticism of such persons merited First Amendment protection, a Court plurality temporarily lowered the bar to damages for those involved in public controversies who were neither public officials nor candidates for official positions. The plurality held that mere "public figures" could recover damages on a showing of "highly unreasonable conduct constituting an extreme departure from the standards of investigation and reporting ordinarily adhered to by responsible publishers."[3] The _Saturday Evening Post_, alleged libelers of Wally Butts, had as a monthly magazine sufficient time to check out the allegations made in its story and, failing that, could be held to have violated the new standard. The Associated Press, reporting on events as they occurred, and relying on the reputation of the "stringer" who reported falsely the activities of General Walker in connection with the integration crisis at the University of Mississippi, could not.

The "public figure" category was broadened, and the expansion of media protection made most extensive, in _Time, Inc. v. Hill_ (1967). _Hill_ involved a "false light" claim against _Life_ magazine by a family whom events, rather than their own actions, had propelled into the limelight. It was the misfortune of the Hill family to have its home invaded and to be held captive for some three days by a group of escaped convicts. The story became notorious and eventually was fictionalized by Joseph Hayes in his novel _The Desperate Hours_. That novel was then made into a play (and later into a motion picture starring Humphrey Bogart). When the play made its debut, _Life_ used it as the basis for an article about the Hill family, and in that article asserted that the Hill's had been brutalized by the convicts, and that the father had shown cowardice in responding to the threat to his family. None of this was true, although it faithfully reflected the fictionalized version. A trial court awarded damages to the Hill's, but the Supreme Court, applying the "public person" standard even to those who had taken no action to involve themselves in such matters, reversed. Seemingly forgotten was the relative inability of the Hills (as compared to nationally known football coach Wally Butts), to effectively counter the untruths told about them. It was enough for the Court that the matter was one of "public concern."

Such a position, carried to its logical conclusion, could have all but wiped out the protection against libel and false light when perpetrated by the news media. For the mere fact that the media chooses to focus on particular persons may in itself be enough to demonstrate that they are of "public concern." Perhaps recognizing this fact, the Court soon retreated and, in Gertz v. Robert Welch, Inc. (1974), all but overruled Hill.

Robert Welch was the millionaire candy maker and founder of the John Birch society who had first gained notoriety by claiming that Dwight Eisenhower was a "conscious and dedicated agent of the Communist Party." Welch made false and derogatory statements about Elmer Gertz, a Chicago lawyer who had been involved, on the liberal side, in a number of controversies. Gertz represented a family whose son was killed by a Chicago police officer in a civil suit based on that event, and the statements damaging to his reputation were made in the criticizing him for acting in that capacity. Gertz was awarded damages by a trial court, but an appellate court reversed on the grounds of Hill and previous cases.

The Supreme Court reversed and reinstated the judgment. In doing so, it recognized that a person might be a public figure for some purposes but not for others. And, since Gertz himself had done nothing to invite controversy, other than agreeing to act for a party in a lawsuit, he could not be considered a "public person." Thus, so long as damages were not awarded without fault, it was proper in his case to apply ordinary rules of liability. The possibility that such a standard could chill the media's exercise of its reportial function could be adequately forestalled, said the Court, by a prohibition (which it held to be constitutionally required) of presumed or punitive damages in such cases.

The Gertz holding, and its seeming overruling of Hill, was made even more explicit in Time, Inc. v. Firestone. Harvey Firestone and his wife Mary were socially prominent citizens of Miami, Florida, who divorced after many years of marriage. The legal ground stated in the courts was mental cruelty, although actually Firestone had discovered his wife in an adulterous situation. Time, in its "Milestone's" column, recorded the fact of the divorce, and reported the legal grounds as being "adultery." Mrs. Firestone then sued and collected substantial damages. Here there was no question of the "public figure" status of the Firestones, and there was also the fact that they had placed their marital difficulties on the public record by the divorce action. But, said the Court, this alone did not make them "public figures" for purposes of the controversy, since they had had no choice but to make such a "public record" in order to avail themselves of the relief which only a court could grant. Thus, as in Gertz, there was no justification for any special protection for the magazine's perpetration of the alleged libel.

If Gertz and Firestone are taken together, and despite the failure to explicitly overrule Hill, it would seem that current doctrine allows those who are neither public officials nor candidates for such positions, and who have become "public figures" in a particular context by other than their own choice, to sue for libel without being held to either the Times or any intermediate standard. And such would seem to be the good sense of the matter. The original Times standard was formulated in order to protect robust and widespread commentary on matters of political concern. To apply it, or any version of it, to people who willy-nilly find themselves in the public eye would seem, given that purpose, to be unjustified.[4]

However, this differentiation may itself lead, as may also the expansion of the Times rule to those who are mere candidates for public office, to an actual restriction of free, open, and robust debate. It will be recalled that the Court, in extending the rule to candidates, did so on the grounds that all matters which may be of concern to the voters are of proper public concern. And we have noted that such a standard opens up virtually everything in the life of a potential candidate to scrutiny, with libelous statements on any matter being punishable only on a showing of "actual malice." This being the case, it would appear that the application of Times in those situations, and its limitation to only those kinds of cases, could effectively deter qualified individuals from seeking public office, or from participating in public controversies. A citizen with a nongovernmentally related "skeleton in his closet" could be fairly certain that so long as he stayed out of the public eye the media would ignore him, or that if it did not and he was libeled, he could recover under conventional standards. But if he became a candidate for public office, or injected himself purposefully into a public controversy, any errors made by the media in reporting his history would be virtually unpunishable. In such circumstances, the cautious person, at least, might well opt for uninvolvement and anonymity.

The answer to this dilemma does not lie in abandoning the Times rule, for the Court was surely correct in its assertion that any other rule would overly insulate public officials (and candidates) from criticism. And, just as assuredly, it does not lie in making the risk for all citizens equal. As we have seen, the purposes of Times would not be served by such an extension, and much harm and injustice could be done to citizens whose privacy and reputation should be protected. Perhaps the answer, if there is one, is for the Court to back away from its blanket extension of Times to all comments about candidates for election and other public, nongovernmental officials. The issue of the liability to be assessed in the case of candidates and other public figures could be perhaps be left open, to be determined at least in part by the logical relevance of the information purveyed to the current controversy. To do so, however, would involve judgments which the Court is not likely to be eager to make.

New York Times v. Sullivan was decided almost 30 years ago, at the height of Warren Court "activism" in the pursuit of liberal goals. But the principle which it established, that debate on public matters must be given the widest "breathing space" even in the context of libel, has been consistently followed. Indeed, in Philadelphia Newspapers v. Hepps (1986), the second case excerpted in this chapter, a very different Court once more *extended* the reach of the Times standard. In Hepps the Court had before it the issue of whether the burden of proving truth or falsity could, in a libel action involving matters of public interest, be properly placed on the defense. In reversing the Pennsylvania Supreme Court's decision which upheld such an assignment, Justice O'Connor, for a majority of five, observed:

> There will always be instances when the factfinding procedure will be unable to resolve conclusively whether the speech is true or false; it is in those cases that the burden of proof is dispositive. Under a rule forcing the plaintiff to bear the burden of showing falsity, there will be some cases in which plaintiffs cannot meet their burden despite the fact that the speech is in fact false. Under an alternative rule placing the burden of showing truth on defendants, there would be some cases in which defendants could not bear their burden despite the fact that the speech is in fact true. . . . Under either rule, then, the outcome of the suit will sometimes be at variance with the outcome that we would desire if all speech were either demonstrably true or false.

But, said O'Connor, in a case involving such an "uncertain balance," the scales must be tipped to favor protecting true speech. And thus "we hold that the common-law presumption that defamatory speech is false cannot stand when a plaintiff seeks damages against a media defendant for speech of public concern." Justice Stevens, for four dissenters, saw things differently:

The issue the Court resolves today will make a difference in only one category of cases - those in which a private individual can prove that he was libeled by a defendant who was at least negligent. For unless such a plaintiff can overcome the burden imposed by (Gertz). . . he cannot recover regardless of how the burden of proof on the issue of truth or falsity is allocated. By definition, therefore, the only litigants - and the only publishers who will benefit from today's decision are those who act negligently or maliciously.

Both O'Connor's opinion and Stevens' dissent emphasize the length to which the Court, in its libel decisions, goes to protect First Amendment interests. To the same effect was the decision in the recent case of Masson v. New Yorker Magazine (1991). In Masson the issue was whether the knowing and deliberate misquotation of a person's words could, when the "quotation" was surrounded by the appropriate marks, suffice to satisfy the Times standard of "deliberate or reckless falsification." Justice Kennedy, for a majority of seven, held that it could not.

Conceding that "in some sense" any alteration of a verbatim quotation is false, Kennedy nevertheless concluded that "if every alteration constituted the falsity required to prove actual malice," journalism would change in a manner inconsistent with First Amendment principles. For interviewers write from notes, and often reconstruct statements knowing they are using words different than those actually used. And even tape recorded conversations may not be complete and will require "translation." Thus "a deliberate alteration of the words uttered by a plaintiff does not equate with knowledge of falsity for purposes of" the Times standard.

Justice White, with Justice Scalia, concurring and dissenting, stressed the fact that the reporter involved in the instant case "wrote that Masson said certain things that she knew he did not say." This, he argued, was "knowing falsehood." Thus the Court's holding established the principle that the "falsehood must be substantial; the reporter may lie a little, but not too much." That standard, unjustified in the present case, was also "less manageable" than the traditional approach, and assigned to the courts issues that are for the jury.

> For a court to ask whether a misquotation substantially alters the meaning of spoken words in a defamatory manner is a far different inquiry than whether reasonable jurors could find that the misquotation was different enough to be libelous. In the one case, the court is measuring the difference from its own point of view; in the other it is asking how the jury would or could view the erroneous attribution.

Justice White, it would seem, is correct in his assertion that Masson's modification of the _Times_ rule substitutes, in part, the judgment of courts for that of juries. He also seems correct on the facts of the instant case, where the deliberate alteration of words was admitted. But the majority opinion, directed as it was to the generality of situations involving misquotations, also has validity. And, it should be noted, the Court properly rejected the suggestion, accepted in part by the lower court, that a "quotation" could not be judged "false under _Times_" so long as is a "rational interpretation" of an actual statement. Such a rule, said Kennedy, would "give journalists the freedom to place statements in their subjects' mouths without fear of liability," and would ill serve the goals of the First Amendment:

> By eliminating any method of distinguishing between the statements of the subject and the interpretation of the author, we would diminish . . . the trustworthiness of the printed word . . . Not only public figures but the press doubtless would suffer under such a rule. Newsworthy figures might become more wary of journalists, knowing that any comment could be transmuted and attributed to the subject, so long as some bounds of rational interpretation were not exceeded.

Thus the majority in _Masson_ took a middle ground on the issue before it, and rejected a rule which could have given constitutional protection to deliberate deceit. But there is no doubt that its opinion extended the _Times_ ruling far beyond its original boundaries. In doing so, it reflected the same concern for "uninhibited, robust debate" that was the basis for _Times_.

By and large, this solicitude has been necessary and salutary. But, as Justice Stevens made clear in his _Hepps_ dissent, it has also been costly. And the costs are not limited to the libel area, for the Court has in large part extended the principle, if not the precise holding, of _Times_ to areas other than libel.

Perhaps the clearest example, in a non-libel context, of the court's devotion to the principle of "robust debate" occurred in the case of _Hustler Magazine v. Falwell_ (1988). The Rev. Jerry Falwell, prominent Baptist minister with a long-standing record of political activity, obtained and sought to have the Court protect an award of damages for "intentional infliction of emotional distress." The occasion of that distress was _Hustler's_ publication of a satirical piece, a parody on advertisements for a liqueur, in which Falwell was depicted as having enjoyed his "first time" with his mother. The parody's sexual innuendo clearly implied that that "first time" referred to sexual intercourse. No one, the Court observed, could have believed either that the incident implied had actually occurred, or that _Hustler_ intended that it be so believed. Thus, and resting its holding squarely on the need to protect political commentary, the Court reversed the award, holding that this necessity precluded the awarding of damages for "intentional infliction of emotional distress" unless accompanied by a falsehood made with "actual malice." Which is to say, it would seem, unless *libel* could simultaneously be proven, and under the Times standard.

Falwell was, of course, a "public person" by his own choice. But, and despite Gertz, those who are in no sense "public" can also be harmed by the Court's fidelity to the "public discussion" standard. In the case of "invasion of privacy" suits stemming from the printing of the name of a rape victim, the Court has viewed such publication as a part of the media's general obligation to report truthfully and completely the workings of the criminal justice system, and has disallowed damages. Of no interest, at least so long as the name was obtained from public records, has been the question of how the addition to the story of a victim's name reveals anything particularly relevant to the self-governing function. In the most recent such decision, The Florida Star v. B.J.F. (1989), none of the three opinions even adverted to this factor. But Justice Marshall's majority and Justice White's dissenting opinions do engage the issue of the appropriate balance to be struck when the Court must reconcile the demands of a free press with the right to privacy. Because of this, and because continuing pressures for "rape shield" laws could very well cause a now reconstituted Court to reconsider its position, The Florida Star is the final case included in this chapter.

---

[1]William Shakespeare, Othello, Act III, Scene iii.

[2]A case can be made that a result which was both "melancholy and unfair" occurred in the settlement of General William Westmoreland's libel suit against the Columbia Broadcasting System. The facts showed, inter alia, that CBS's allegation that the General had falsified "body counts" in Vietnam were false, and that the network was more than minimally negligent in so reporting. Because, however, of his status as a "public figure", and the consequent application of the Times actual malice rule, Westmoreland was forced to settle for the most general of apologies. See Westmoreland v. Columbia Broadcasting System, 752 F. 2d (1984).

[3]But in Harte-Hanks Publishing Co. v. McNaughton (1991) the Court, though upholding a libel judgment, made clear that the lower standard for "public persons" applied in Walker and Butts had never commanded a Court majority, and expressly disapproved it.

[4]It is tempting to propose that "private persons" who, even without any action on their part, became embroiled in a matter of "governmental" or "political" concern should be subject to the

continued on next page

Times standard. For it can be argued that the same reasoning which required the Times standard in the case of public persons, the need for "wide open and robust debate" on public matters, would be equally compelling in the case of private ones embroiled in public controversies. But, of course, virtually any matter could be considered "of public concern."

NEW YORK TIMES CO. V. SULLIVAN

376 U.S. 254 (1964)

MR. JUSTICE BRENNAN delivered the opinion of the Court.

We are required in this case to determine for the first time the extent to which the constitutional protections for speech and press limit a State's power to award damages in a libel action brought by a public official against critics of his official conduct. . . .

Respondent's complaint alleged that he had been libeled by statements in a full-page advertisement that was carried in the New York Times on March 29, 1960. . . .

Of the 10 paragraphs of text in the advertisement, the third and a portion of the sixth were the basis of respondent's claim of libel. They read as follows:

Third paragraph: "In Montgomery, Alabama, after students sang 'My Country, 'Tis of Thee' on the State Capitol steps, their leaders were expelled from school, and truckloads of police armed with shotguns and tear-gas ringed the Alabama State College Campus. When the entire student body protested to state authorities by refusing to re-register, their dining hall was padlocked in an attempt to starve them into submission."

Sixth paragraph: "Again and again the Southern violators have answered Dr. King's peaceful protests with intimidation and violence. They have bombed his home almost killing his wife and child. They have assaulted his person. They have arrested him seven times—for 'speeding,' 'loitering' and similar 'offenses.' And now they have charged him the 'perjury'—a *felony* under which they could imprison him for *ten years*. . . ."

Although neither of these statements mentions respondent by name, he contended that the word "police" in the third paragraph referred to him as the Montgomery Commissioner who supervised the Police Department, so that he was being accused of "ringing" the campus with police. He further claimed that the paragraph would be read as imputing to the police, and hence to him, the padlocking of the dining hall in order to starve the students into submission. As to the sixth paragraph, he contended that since arrests are ordinarily made by the police, the statement "They have arrested [Dr. King] seven times" would be read as referring to him; he further contended that the "They" who did the arresting would be equated with the "they" who committed the other described acts and with the "southern violators." Thus, he argued, the paragraph would be read as accusing the Montgomery police, and hence him, of answering Dr. King's protests with "intimidation and violence," bombing his home, assaulting his person, and charging him with perjury. Respondent and six other Montgomery residents testified that they read some or all of the statements as referring to him in his capacity as Commissioner.

It is uncontroverted that some of the statements contained in the two paragraphs were not accurate descriptions of events which occurred in Montgomery. Although Negro students staged a demonstration on the State Capitol steps, they sang the National Anthem and not "My Country, 'Tis of Thee." Although nine students were expelled by the State Board of Education, this was not for leading the demonstration at the Capitol, but for demanding service at a lunch counter in the Montgomery County Courthouse on another day. Not the entire student body, but most of it, had protested the expulsion, not by refusing to register, but by boycotting classes on a single day; virtually all the students did register for the ensuing semester. The campus dining hall was not padlocked on any occasion, and the only students who may have been barred from eating there were the few who had neither signed a preregistration application nor requested temporary meal tickets. Although the police were deployed near the campus in large numbers on three occasions, they did not at any time "ring" the campus, and they were not called to the campus in connection with the demonstration on the State Capitol steps, as the third paragraph implied. Dr. King had not been arrested seven times, but only four; and although he claimed to have been assaulted some years earlier in connection with his arrest for loitering outside a courtroom, one of the officers who made the arrest denied that there was such an assault.

On the premise that the charges in the sixth paragraph could be read as referring to him, respondent was allowed to prove that he had not participated in the events described. Although Dr. King's home had in fact been bombed twice when his wife and child were there, both of these occasions antedated respondent's tenure as Commissioner, and the police were not only not implicated in the bombings, but had made every effort to apprehend those who were. Three of Dr. King's four arrests took place before respondent became Commissioner. Although Dr. King had in fact been indicted (he was subsequently acquitted) on two counts of perjury, each of which carried a possible five-year sentence, respondent had nothing to do with procuring the indictment.

Under Alabama law as applied in this case, a publication is "libelous per se" if the words "tend to injure a person . . . in his reputation" or to "bring [him] into public contempt"; the trial court stated that the standard was met if the words are such as to "injure him in his public office, or impute misconduct to him in his office, or want of official integrity, or want of fidelity to a public trust. . . ." The jury must find that the words were published "of and concerning" the plaintiff, but

where the plaintiff is a public official his place in the governmental hierarchy is sufficient evidence to support a finding that his reputation has been affected by statements that reflect upon the agency of which he is in charge. Once "libel per se" has been established, the defendant has no defense as to stated facts unless he can persuade the jury that they were true in all their particulars. . . . His privilege of "fair comment" for expression of opinion depends on the truth of the facts upon which the comment is based. . . . Unless he can discharge the burden of proving truth, general damages are presumed, and may be awarded without proof of pecuniary injury. A showing of actual malice is apparently a prerequisite to recovery of punitive damages, and the defendant may in any event forestall a punitive award by a retraction meeting the statutory requirements. Good motives and belief in truth do not negate any inference of malice, but are relevant only in mitigation of punitive damages if the jury chooses to accord them weight.

The question before us is whether this rule of liability, as applied to an action brought by a public official against critics of his official conduct abridges the freedom of speech and of the press that is guaranteed by the First and Fourteenth Amendments.

. . . we consider this case against the background of a profound national commitment to the principle that debate on public issues should be uninhibited, robust, and wide-open, and that it may well include vehement, caustic, and sometimes unpleasantly sharp attacks on government and public officials. See *Terminiello* v. *Chicago, De Jonge* v. *Oregon.* The present advertisement, as an expression of grievance and protest on one of the major public issues of our time, would seem clearly to qualify for the constitutional protection. The question is whether it forfeits that protection by the falsity of some of its factual statements and by its alleged defamation of respondent.

Authoritative interpretations of the First Amendment guarantees have consistently refused to recognize an exception for any test of truth—whether administered by judges, juries, or administrative officials—and especially one that puts the burden of proving truth on the speaker. The constitutional protection does not turn upon "the truth, popularity, or social utility of the ideas and beliefs which are offered." *N.A.A.C.P.* v. *Button.* As Madison said, "Some degree of abuse is inseparable from the proper use of every thing; and in no instance is this more true than in that of the press."

. . . erroneous statement is inevitable in free debate, and it must be protected if the freedoms of expression are to have the "breathing space" that they "need . . . to survive. . . ."

Injury to official reputation affords no more warrant for repressing speech that would otherwise be free than does factual error. Where judicial officers are involved, this Court has held that concern for the dignity and reputation of the courts does not justify the punishment as criminal contempt of criticism of the judge or his decision. *Bridges* v. *California.* This is true even though the utterance contains "half-truths" and "misinformation." *Pennekamp* v. *Florida.* Such repression can be justified, if at all, only by a clear and present danger of the obstruction of justice. See also *Craig* v. *Harney, Wood* v. *Georgia.* If judges are to be treated as "men of fortitude, able to thrive in a hardy climate," *Craig* V. *Harney*, surely the same must be true of other government officials, such as elected city commissioners. Criticism of their official conduct does not lose its constitutional protection merely because it is effective criticism and hence diminishes their official reputations.

If neither factual error nor defamatory content suffices to remove the constitutional shield from criticism of official conduct, the combination of the two elements is no less inadequate.

A rule compelling the critic of official conduct to guarantee the truth of all his factual assertions—and to do so on pain of libel judgments virtually unlimited in amount—leads to a comparable "self-censorship." Allowance of the defense of truth, with the burden of proving it on the defendant, does not mean that only false

speech will be deterred. . . . Under such a rule, would-be critics of official conduct may be deterred from voicing their criticism, even though it is believed to be true and even though it is in fact true, because of doubt whether it can be proved in court or fear of the expense of having to do so. They tend to make only statements which "steer far wider of the unlawful zone." *Speiser* v. *Randall.* The rule thus dampens the vigor and limits the variety of public debate. It is inconsistent with the First and Fourteenth Amendments.

The constitutional guarantees require, we think, a federal rule that prohibits a public official from recovering damages for a defamatory falsehood relating to his official conduct unless he proves that the statement was made with "actual malice"—that is, with knowledge that it was false or with reckless disregard of whether it was false or not. . . .

We hold today that the Constitution delimits a State's power to award damages for libel in actions brought by public officials against critics of their official conduct. Since this is such an action, the rule requiring proof of actual malice is applicable. While Alabama law apparently requires proof of actual malice for an award of punitive damages, where general damages are concerned malice is "presumed." Such a presumption is inconsistent with the federal rule. . . .

. . . Since the trial judge did not instruct the jury to differentiate between general and punitive damages, it may be that the verdict was wholly an award of one or the other. But it is impossible to know, in view of the general verdict returned. Because of this uncertainty, the judgment must be reversed and the case remanded.

Since respondent may seek a new trial, we deem that considerations of effective judicial administration require us to review the evidence in the present record to determine whether it could constitutionally support a judgment for respondent. . . . we consider that the proof presented to show actual malice lacks the convincing clarity which the constitutional standard demands, and hence that it would not constitutionally sustain the judgment for respondent under the proper rule of law. The case of the individual petitioners requires little discussion. Even assuming that they could constitutionally be found to have authorized the use of their names on the advertisement, there was no evidence whatever that they were aware of any erroneous statements of were in any way reckless in that regard. The judgment against them is thus without constitutional support.

As to the Times, we similarly conclude that the facts do not support a finding of actual malice. The statement by the Times' Secretary that, apart from the padlocking allegation, he thought the advertisement was "substantially correct," affords no constitutional warrant for the Alabama Supreme Court's conclusion that it was a "cavalier ignoring of the falsity of the advertisement [from which] the jury could not have but been impressed with the bad faith of The Times, and its maliciousness inferable therefrom." The statement does not indicate malice at the time of the publication; even if the advertisement was not "substantially correct"—although respondent's own proofs tend to show that it was—that opinion was at least a reasonable one, and there was no evidence to impeach the witness' good faith in holding it. The Times' failure to retract upon respondent's demand, although it later retracted upon the demand of Governor Patterson, is likewise not adequate evidence of malice for constitutional purposes. Whether or not a failure to retract may ever constitute such evidence, there are two reasons why it does not here. *First*, the letter written by the Times reflected a reasonable doubt on its part as to whether the advertisement could reasonably be taken to refer to respondent at all. *Second*, it was not a final refusal, since it asked for an explanation on this point—a request that respondent chose to ignore. Nor does the retraction upon the demand of the Governor supply the necessary proof. It may be doubted that a failure to retract which is not itself evidence malice can retroactively become such by virtue of a retraction subsequently made to another party. But in any event that did not happen here, since the explanation given

by the Times' Secretary for the distinction drawn between respondent and the Governor was a reasonable one, the good faith of which was not impeached.

Finally, there is evidence that the Times published the advertisement without checking its accuracy against the news stories in the Times' own files. The mere presence of the stories in the files does not, of course, establish that the Times "knew" the advertisement was false, since the state of mind required for actual malice would have to be brought home to the persons in the Times' organization having responsibility for the publication of the advertisement. With respect to the failure of those persons to make the check, the record shows that they relied upon their knowledge of the good reputation of many of those who names were listed as sponsors of the advertisement, and upon the letter from A. Philip Randolph, known to them as a responsible individual, certifying that the use of the names was authorized. There was testimony that the persons handling the advertisement saw nothing in it that would render it unacceptable under the Times' policy of rejecting advertisements containing "attacks of a personal character"; their failure to reject it on this ground was not unreasonable. We think the evidence against the Times supports at most a finding of negligence in ailing to discover the misstatements, and is constitutionally insufficient to show the recklessness that is required for a finding of actual malice.

We also think the evidence was constitutionally defective in another respect: it was incapable of supporting the jury's finding that the allegedly libelous statements were made "of and concerning" respondent. . . . There was no reference to respondent in the advertisement, either by name or official position. A number of the allegedly libelous statements—the charges that the dining hall was padlocked and that Dr. King's home was bombed, his person assaulted, and a perjury prosecution instituted against him—did not even concern the police.

. . . The statements upon which respondent principally relies as referring to him are the two allegations that did concern the police or police functions: that "truckloads of police . . . ringed the Alabama State College Campus" after the demonstration on the State Capitol steps, and that Dr. King had been "arrested . . . seven times." . . . Although the statements may be taken as referring to the police, they did not on their face make even an oblique reference to respondent as an individual. . . . to the extent that some of the witnesses thought respondent to have been charged with ordering or approving the conduct or otherwise being personally involved in it, they based this notion not on any statements in the advertisement, and not on any evidence that he had in fact been so involved, but solely on the unsupported assumption that, because of his official position, he must have been. This reliance on the bare fact of respondent's official position was made explicit by the Supreme Court of Alabama. . . .

This proposition has disquieting implications for criticism of governmental conduct. For good reason, "no court of last resort in this country has ever held, or even suggested, that prosecutions for libel on government have any place in the American system of jurisprudence."

. . . The present proposition would sidestep this obstacle by transmuting criticism of government, however impersonal it may seem on its face, into personal criticism, and hence potential libel, of the officials of whom the government is composed. There is no legal alchemy by which a State may thus create the cause of action that would otherwise be denied for a publication which, as respondent himself said of the advertisement, "reflects not only on me but on the other Commissioners and the community." Raising as it does the possibility that a good-faith critic of government will be penalized for his criticism, the proposition relied on by the Alabama courts strikes at the very center of the constitutionally protected area of free expression. We hold that such a proposition may not constitutionally be utilized to establish that an otherwise impersonal attack on government operations was a libel of an official

responsible for those operations. Since it was relied on exclusively here, and there was no other evidence to connect the statements with respondent, the evidence was constitutionally insufficient to support a finding that the statements referred to respondent.

The judgment of the Supreme Court of Alabama is reversed and the case is remanded to that court for further proceedings not inconsistent with this opinion.

Reversed and remanded.

MR. JUSTICE BLACK, with whom MR. JUSTICE DOUGLAS joins, concurring.

I concur in reversing this half-million-dollar judgment against the New York Times Company and the four individual defendants. In reversing the Court holds that "the Constitution delimits a State's power to award damages for libel in actions brought by public officials against critics of their official conduct." I base my vote to reverse on the belief that the First and Fourteenth Amendments not merely "delimit" a State's power to award damages to "public officials against critics of their official conduct" but completely prohibit a State from exercising such a power. The Curt goes on to hold that a State can subject such critics to damages if "actual malice" can be proved against them. "Malice," even as defined by the Court, is an elusive, abstract concept, hard to prove and hard to disprove. The requirement that malice be proved provides at best an evanescent protection for the right critically to discuss public affairs and certainly does not measure up to the sturdy safeguard embodied in the First Amendment. Unlike the Court, therefore, I vote to reverse exclusively on the ground that the Times and the individual defendants had an absolute, unconditional constitutional right to publish in the Times advertisement their criticisms of the Montgomery agencies and officials.

In my opinion the Federal Constitution has dealt with this deadly danger to the press in the only way possible without leaving the free press open to destruction—by granting the press an absolute immunity for criticism of the way public officials do their public duty. Compare *Barr* v. *Matteo*. Stopgap measures like those the Court adopts are in my judgment not enough. This record certainly does not indicate that any different verdict would have been rendered here whatever the Court had charged the jury about "malice," "truth," "good motives," "justifiable ends," or any other legal formulas which in theory would protect the press. Nor does the record indicate that any of these legalistic words would have cause the courts below to set aside or to reduce the half-million-dollar verdict in any amount.

I regret that the Court has stopped short of this holding indispensable to preserve our free press from destruction.

MR. JUSTICE GOLDBERG, with whom MR. JUSTICE DOUGLAS joins, concurring in the result.

PHILADELPHIA NEWSPAPERS, INC., ET AL. V. HEPPS ET AL.

475 U.S 767 (1986)

JUSTICE O'CONNOR delivered the opinion of the Court.

This case requires us once more to "struggl[e] . . . to define the proper accommodation between the law of defamation and the freedoms of speech and press protected by the First Amendment." *Gertz v. Robert Welch*, Inc. (1974). In *Gertz*, the Court held that a private figure who brings a suit for defamation cannot recover without some showing that the media defendant was at fault in publishing the statements at issue. Here, we hold that, at least where a newspaper publishes speech of public concern, a private-figure plaintiff cannot recover damages without also showing that the statements at issue are false. . . .

Maurice S. Hepps is the principal stockholder of General Programming, Inc. (GPI), a corporation that franchises a chain of stores—known at the relevant time as "Thrifty" stores—selling beer, soft drinks, and snacks. Mr. Hepps, GPI, and a number of its franchisees are the appellees here. Appellant Philadelphia Newspapers, Inc., owns the Philadelphia Inquirer (Inquirer). The Inquirer published a series of articles, authored by appellants William Ecenbarger and William Lambert, containing the statements at issue here. The general theme of the five articles, which appeared in the Inquirer between May 1975 and May 1976, was that appellees had links to organized crime and used some of those links to influence the State's governmental processes, both legislative and administrative. The articles discussed a state legislator, described as "a Pittsburgh Democrat and convicted felon," whose actions displayed "a clear pattern of interference in state government by [the legislator] on behalf of Hepps and Thrifty." The stories reported that federal "investigators have found connections between Thrifty and underworld figures,"; that "the Thrifty Beverage beer chain . . . had connections . . . with organized crime,"; and that Thrifty had "won a series of competitive advantages through rulings by the State Liquor Control Board." A grand jury was said to be investigating the "alleged relationship between the Thrifty chain and known Mafia figures," and "[w]hether the chain received special treatment from the [state Governor's] administration and the Liquor Control Board."

Appellees brought suit for defamation against appellants in a Pennsylvania state court. Consistent with *Gertz*, Pennsylvania requires a private figure who brings a suit for defamation to bear the burden of proving negligence or malice by the defendant in publishing the statements at issue. As to falsity, Pennsylvania follows the common law's presumption that an individual's reputation is a good one. Statements defaming that person are therefore presumptively false, although a publisher who bears the burden of proving the truth of the statements has an absolute defense (defendant has the burden of proving the truth of a defamatory statement). . . . the trial court concluded that Pennsylvania's- statute giving the defendant the burden of proving the truth of the statements violated the Federal Constitution. The trial court therefore instructed the jury that the plaintiffs bore the burden of proving falsity.

. . . . the appellees here brought an appeal directly to the Pennsylvania Supreme Court. The trial court viewed *Gertz* as simply requiring the plaintiff to show fault in actions for defamation. It concluded that a showing of fault did not require a showing of falsity, held that to place the burden of showing truth on the defendant did not unconstitutionally inhibit free debate, and remanded the case for a new trial. We noted probable jurisdiction, and now reverse. . . .

One can discern in [our] decisions two forces that may reshape the common-law landscape to conform to the First Amendment. The first is whether the plaintiff is a public official or figure, or is instead a private figure. The second is whether the speech at issue is of public concern. When the speech is of public concern and the plaintiff is a public official or public figure, the Constitution clearly requires the plaintiff to surmount a much higher barrier before recovering damages from a media defendant than is raised by the common law. When the speech is of public concern but the plaintiff is a private figure, as in *Gertz*, the Constitution still supplants the standards of the common law, but the constitutional requirements are, in at least some of their range, less forbidding than when the plaintiff is a public figure and the speech is of public concern. When the speech is of exclusively private concern and the plaintiff is a private figure, as in Dun & Bradstreet, the constitutional requirements do not necessarily force any change in at least some of the features of the common-law landscape.

Our opinions to date have chiefly treated the necessary showings of fault rather than of falsity. Nonetheless, as one might expect given the language of the Court in *New York Times*, a public-figure plaintiff must show the falsity of the statements at issue in order to prevail in a suit for defamation. See *Garrison v. Louisiana* (1964) (reading *New York Times* for the proposition that "a public official [is] allowed the civil [defamation] remedy only if he establishes that the utterance was false").

. . . . There will always be instances when the factfinding process will be unable to resolve conclusively whether the speech is true or false; it is in those cases that the burden of proof is dispositive. Under a rule forcing the plaintiff to bear the burden of showing falsity, there will be some cases in which plaintiffs cannot meet their burden despite the fact that the speech is in fact false. The plaintiff's suit will fail despite the fact that, in some abstract sense, the suit is meritorious. Similarly, under an alternative rule placing the burden of showing truth on defendants, there would be some cases in which defendants could not bear their burden despite the fact that the speech is in fact true. Those suits would succeed despite the fact that, in some abstract sense, those suits are unmeritorious. Under either rule, then, the outcome of the suit will sometimes be at variance with the outcome that we would desire if all speech were either demonstrably true or demonstrably false.

This dilemma stems from the fact that the allocation of the burden of proof will determine liability for some speech that is true and some that is false, but all of such speech is unknowably true or false. Because the burden of proof is the deciding factor only when the evidence is ambiguous, we cannot know how much of the speech affected by the allocation of the burden of proof is true and how much is false. In a case presenting a configuration of speech and plaintiff like the one we face here, and where the scales are in such an uncertain balance, we believe that the Constitution requires us to tip them in favor of protecting true speech. To ensure that true speech on matters of public concern is not deterred, we hold that the common-law presumption that defamatory speech is false cannot stand when a plaintiff seeks damages against a media defendant for speech of public concern.

In the context of governmental restriction of speech, it has long been established that the government cannot limit speech protected by the First Amendment without bearing the burden of showing that its restriction is justified.

. . . . the need to encourage debate on public issues that concerned the Court in the governmental restriction cases is of concern in a similar manner in this case involving a private suit for damages: placement by state law of the burden of proving truth upon media defendants who publish speech of public concern deters such speech because of the fear that liability will unjustifiably result. . . .

We recognize that requiring the plaintiff to show falsity will insulate from liability some speech that is false, but unprovably so. Nonetheless, the Court's previous decisions on the restrictions that the First Amendment places upon the common law of defamation firmly support our conclusion here with respect to the allocation of the burden of proof.

To provide "'breathing space, New York Times (quoting NAACP v. Button), for true speech on matters of public concern, the Court has been willing to insulate even demonstrably false speech from liability, and has imposed additional requirements of fault upon the plaintiff in a suit for defamation. We therefore do not break new ground here in insulating speech that is not even demonstrably false.

We note that our decision adds only marginally to the burdens that the plaintiff must already bear as a result of our earlier decisions in the law of defamation. The plaintiff must show fault. A jury is obviously more likely to accept a plaintiff's contention that the defendant was at fault in publishing the statements at issue if convinced that the relevant statements were false. As a practical matter, then, evidence offered by plaintiffs on the publisher's fault in adequately investigating the truth of the published statements will generally encompass evidence of the falsity of the matters asserted. . . .

JUSTICE BRENNAN, with whom JUSTICE BLACKMUN joins, concurring. . . .

JUSTICE STEVENS, with whom THE CHIEF JUSTICE, JUSTICE WHITE, and JUSTICE REHNQUIST join, dissenting.

The issue the Court resolves today will make a difference in only one category of cases—those in which a private individual can prove that he was libeled by a defendant who was at least negligent. For unless such a plaintiff can overcome the burden imposed by Gertz v. Robert Welch, Inc. (1974), he cannot recover regardless of how the burden of proof on the issue of truth or falsity is allocated. By definition, therefore, the only litigants—and the only publishers—who will benefit from today's decision are those who act negligently or maliciously. . . .

While deliberate or inadvertent libels vilify private personages, they contribute little to the marketplace of ideas. In assaying the First Amendment side of the balance, it helps to remember that the perpetrator of the libel suffers from its failure to demonstrate the truth of its accusation only if the "private-figure" plaintiff first establishes that the publisher is at "fault," i. e., either that it published its libel with "actual malice" in the New York Times sense ("with knowledge that it was false or with reckless disregard of whether it was false or not," New York Times Co. v. Sullivan (1964)), or that it published with that degree of careless indifference characteristic of negligence. Far from being totally in the dark about "how much of the speech affected by the allocation of the burden of proof is true and how much is false," the antecedent fault determination makes irresistible the inference that a significant portion of this speech is beyond the constitutional pale. This observation is almost tautologically true with regard to libels published with "actual malice." For that standard to be met, the publisher must come close to willfully blinding itself to the falsity of its utterance. The observation is also valid, albeit to a lesser extent, with respect to defamations uttered with "fault." Thus, while the public's interest in an uninhibited press is at its nadir when the publisher is at fault or worse, society's "equally compelling" need for judicial redress of libelous utterances is at its zenith. *Time, Inc. v. Firestone* (1976).

To appreciate the thrust of the Court's holding, we must assume that a private-figure libel plaintiff can prove that a story about him was published with "actual malice"—that is, without the publisher caring in the slightest whether it was false or not. Indeed, in order to comprehend the full ramifications of today's decision, we should assume that the publisher knew that it would be impossible for a court to verify or discredit the story and that it was published for no other purpose than to destroy the reputation of the plaintiff. Even if the plaintiff has overwhelming proof of malice—in both the common-law sense and as the term was used in *New York Times Co. v. Sullivan*—the Court today seems to believe that the character assassin has a constitutional license to defame. . . .

Despite the obvious blueprint for character assassination provided by the decision today, the Court's analytical approach—by attaching little or no weight to the strong state interest in redressing injury to private reputation—provides a wholly unwarranted protection for malicious gossip. As I understand the Court's opinion, its counterintuitive result is derived from a straightforward syllogism. The major premise seems to be that "the First Amendment's protection of true speech on matters of public concern," is tantamount to a command that no rule of law can stand if it will exclude any true speech from the public domain. The minor premise is that although "we cannot know how much of the speech affected by the allocation of the burden of proof is true and how much is false," at least some unverifiable gossip is true. From these premises it necessarily follows that a rule burdening the dissemination of such speech would contravene the First Amendment. Accordingly, "a private-figure plaintiff must bear the burden of showing that the speech at issue is false before recovering damages for defamation from a media defendant."

The Court's result is plausible however, only because it grossly undervalues the strong state interest in redressing injuries to private reputations.

The error lies in its initial premise, with its mistaken belief that doubt regarding the veracity of a defamatory statement must invariably be resolved in favor of constitutional protection of the statement and against vindication of the reputation of the private individual. To support its premise, the Court relies exclusively on our precedents requiring the government to bear the burden of proving that a restriction of speech is justified. . . .

Even assuming that attacks on the reputation of a public figure should be presumed to be true, however, a different calculus is appropriate when a defamatory statement disparages the reputation of a private individual. In that case, the overriding concern for reliable protection of truthful statements must make room for "[t]he legitimate state interest underlying the law of libel"—"the compensation of individuals for the harm inflicted on them by defamatory falsehood." *Gertz v. Robert Welch, Inc.* A public official, of course, has no "less interest in protecting his reputation than an individual in private life." *Rosenbloom v. Metromedia* (1971) (opinion of BRENNAN, J.). But private persons are "more vulnerable to injury" and "more deserving of recovery"—more vulnerable because they lack "access to the channels of effective communication . . . to counteract false statements"; more deserving because they have "relinquished no part of [their] good name[s]" by "thrust[ing] themselves to the forefront of particular public controversies in order to influence the resolution of the issues involved." *Gertz v. Robert Welch, Inc.*

Recognition of the "strong and legitimate [state] interest in compensating private individuals for injury to reputation," exposes the untenability of the Court's methodology: the burden of proof in "private-figure" libel suits simply cannot be determined by reference to our precedents having the reputations of "public figures" in mind. . . .

In my view, as long as publishers are protected by the requirement that the plaintiff has the burden of proving fault there can be little, if any, basis for a concern that a significant amount of true speech will be deterred unless the private person victimized by a malicious libel can also carry the burden of proving falsity. The Court's decision trades on the good names of private individuals with little First Amendment coin to show for it. I respectfully dissent.

THE FLORIDA STAR V. B. J. F.

491 U.S. 524 (1989)

JUSTICE MARSHALL delivered the opinion of the Court.

Florida Stat. 794.03 (1987) makes it unlawful to "print, publish, or broadcast . . . in any instrument of mass communication the name of the victim of a sexual offense. Pursuant to this statute, appellant The Florida Star was found civilly liable for publishing the name of a rape victim which it had obtained from a publicly released police report. The issue presented here is whether this result comports with the First Amendment. We hold that it does not. . . .

On October 20, 1983, appellee B. J. F. reported to the Duval County, Florida, Sheriff's Department (the Department) that she had been robbed and sexually assaulted by an unknown assailant. The Department prepared a report on the incident which identified B. J. F. by her full name. The Department then placed the report in its pressroom. The Department does not restrict access either to the pressroom or to the reports made available therein.

A Florida Star reporter-trainee sent to the pressroom copied the police report verbatim, including B. J. F.'s full name, on a blank duplicate of the Department's forms. A Florida Star reporter then prepared a one-paragraph article about the crime, derived entirely from the trainee's copy of the police report. The article included B. J. F.'s full name. It appeared in the "Robberies" subsection of the "Police Report" section on October 29, 1983. . . .

On September 26, 1984, B. .J. F. filed suit in the Circuit Court of Duval County against the Department and The Florida Star, alleging that these parties negligently violated 794.03. Before trial, the Department settled with B. J. F. for $2,500. The Florida Star moved to dismiss, claiming, *inter alia*, that imposing civil sanctions on the newspaper pursuant to 794.03 violated the First Amendment. The trial judge rejected the motion. . . .

At the close of the newspaper's defense, the judge granted B. J. F.'s motion for a directed verdict on the issue of negligence, finding the newspaper per se negligent based upon its violation of 794.03. . . .

The jury awarded B. J. F. $76,000 in compensatory damages and $25,000 in punitive damages. . . .

We conclude that imposing damages on appellant for publishing B. J. F.'s name violates the First Amendment, although not for either of the reasons appellant urges.

. . . . one of the reasons we gave in *Cox Broadcasting* for invalidating the challenged damages award was the important role the press plays in subjecting trials to public scrutiny and thereby helping guarantee their fairness. That role is not directly compromised where, as here, the information in question comes from a police report prepared and disseminated at a time at which not only had no adversarial criminal proceedings begun, but no suspect had been identified.

Nor need we accept appellant's invitation to hold broadly that truthful publication may never be punished consistent with the First Amendment. . . . We continue to believe that the sensitivity and significance of the interests presented in clashes between First Amendment and privacy rights counsel relying on limited principles that sweep no more broadly than the appropriate context of the instant case. . . .

In our view, this case is appropriately analyzed with reference to such a limited

First Amendment principle. It is the one, in fact, which we articulated in *Daily Mail* in our synthesis of prior cases involving attempts to punish truthful publication: "[I]f a newspaper lawfully obtains truthful information about a matter of public significance then state officials may not constitutionally punish publication of the information, absent a need to further a state interest of the highest order." According the press the ample protection provided by that principle is supported by at least three separate considerations in addition to, of course, the overarching "public interest, seemed by the Constitution, in the dissemination of truth. . . ."

First, because the *Daily Mail* formulation only protects the publication of information which a newspaper has "lawfully obtain[ed]," the government retains ample means of safe-guarding significant interests upon which publication may impinge, including protecting a rape victim's anonymity. To the extent sensitive information rests in private hands, the government may under some circumstances forbid its nonconsensual acquisition, thereby bringing outside of the Dairy Mail principle the publication of any information so acquired. To the extent sensitive information is in the government's custody, it has even greater power to forestall or mitigate the injury caused by its release. The government may classify certain information, establish and enforce procedures ensuring its redacted release, and extend a damages remedy against the government or its officials where the government's mishandling of sensitive information leads to its dissemimation. Where information is entrusted to the government, a less drastic means than punishing truthful publication almost always exists for guarding against the dissemination of private facts. . . .

A second consideration undergirding the *Daily Mail* principle is the fact that punishing the press for its dissemination of information which is already publicly available is relatively unlikely to advance the interest in the service of which the State seeks to act. It is not, of course, always the case that information lawfully acquired by the press is known, or accessible, to others. But where the government has made certain information publicly available, it is highly anomalous to sanction persons other than the source of its release. . . .

A third and final consideration is the "timidity and self-censorship" which may result from allowing the media to be punished for publishing certain truthful information. *Cox Broadcasting* noted this concern with overdeterrence in the context of information made public through official court records, but the fear of excessive media self-suppression is applicable as well to other information released, without qualification, by the government. A contrary rule, depriving protection to those who rely on the government's implied representations of the lawfulness of dissemination, would force upon the media the onerous obligation of sifting through government press releases, reports, and pronouncements to prune out material arguably unlawful for publication. This situation could inhere even where the newspaper's sole object was to reproduce, with no substantial change, the government's rendition of the event in question.

Applied to the instant case, the *Daily Mail* principle clearly commands reversal. The first inquiry is whether the newspaper "lawfully obtain[ed] truthful information about a matter of public significance." It is undisputed that the news article describing the assault on. B. J. F. was accurate. In addition, appellant lawfully obtained B. J. F.'s name. . . .

It is, clear, furthermore, that the news article concerned "a matter of public significance," in the sense in which the *Daily Mail* synthesis of prior cases used that term. That is, the article generally, as opposed to the specific identity contained within it, involved a matter of paramount public import: the commission, and investigation, of a violent crime which had been reported to authorities. . . .

The second inquiry is whether imposing liability on appellant pursuant to 794.03 serves "a need to further a state interest of the highest order." *Daily Mail*. Appellee argues that a rule punishing publication furthers three closely related interests: the privacy of victims of sexual offenses; the physical safety of such victims, who may be targeted for retaliation if their names become known to their assailants; and the goal of encouraging victims of such crimes to report these offenses without fear of exposure.

We do not rule out the possibility that, in a proper case, imposing civil sanctions for publication of the name of a rape victim might be so overwhelmingly necessary to advance these interests as to satisfy the *Daily Mail* standard. For three independent reasons, however, imposing liability for publication under the circumstances of this case is too precipitous a means of advancing these interests to convince us that there is a "need" within the meaning of the *Daily Mail* formulation for Florida to take this extreme step. . . .

First is the manner in which appellant obtained the identifying information in question. As we have noted, where the government itself provides information to the media, it is most appropriate to assume that the government had, but failed to utilize, far more limited means of guarding against dissemination than the extreme step of punishing truthful speech. . . .

That appellant gained access to the information in question through a government news release makes it especially likely that, if liability were to be imposed, self-censorship would result. Reliance on a news release is a paradigmatically "routine newspaper reporting techniqu[e]." *Daily Mail*. The government's issuance of such a release, without qualification, can only convey to recipients that the government considered dissemination lawful, and indeed expected the recipients to disseminate the information further. . . .

A second problem with Florida's imposition of liability for publication is the broad sweep of the negligence *per se* standard applied under the civil cause of action implied from 794.03. Unlike claims based on the common-law tort of invasion of privacy, civil actions based on 794.03 require no case-by-case findings that the disclosure of a fact about a person's private life was one that a reasonable person would find highly offensive. On the contrary under the *per se* theory of negligence adopted by the courts below, liability follows automatically from publication. This is so regardless of whether the identity of the victim is already known throughout the community; whether the victim has voluntarily called public attention to the offense; or whether the identity of the victim has otherwise become a reasonable subject of public concern—because, perhaps, questions have arisen whether the victim fabricated an assault by a particular person. Nor is there a scienter requirement of any kind under 794.03, engendering the perverse result that truthful publications challenged pursuant to this cause of action are less protected by the First Amendment than even the least protected defamatory falsehoods: those involving purely private figures, where liability is evaluated under a standard, usually applied by a jury, of ordinary negligence. . . .

Third, and finally, the facial underinclusiveness of 794.03 raises serious doubts about whether Florida is, in fact, serving, with this statute, the significant interests which appellee invokes in support of affirmance. Section 794.03 prohibits the publication of identifying information only if this information appears in an "instrument of mass communication," a term the statute does not define. Section 794.03 does not prohibit the spread by other means of the identities of victims of sexual offenses. An individual who maliciously spreads word of the identity of a rape victim is thus not covered, despite the fact that the communication of such information to persons who live near, or work with, the victim may have consequences as devastating as the exposure of her name to large numbers of strangers. . . .

When a State attempts the extraordinary measure of punishing truthful publication in the name of privacy, it must demonstrate its commitment to advancing this interest by applying its prohibition evenhandedly, to the smalltime disseminator as well as the media giant. Where important First

Amendment interests are at stake, the mass scope of disclosure is not an acceptable surrogate for injury. A ban on disclosures effected by "instruments of mass communication" simply cannot be defended on the ground that partial prohibitions may effect partial relief. . . .

Our holding today is limited. We do not hold that truthful publication is automatically constitutionally protected, or that there is no zone of personal privacy within which the State may protect the individual from intrusion by the press, or even that a State may never punish publication of the name of a victim of a sexual offense. We hold only that where a newspaper publishes truthful information which it has lawfully obtained, punishment may lawfully be imposed if at all, only when narrowly tailored to a state interest of the highest order, and that no such interest is satisfactorily served by imposing liability under 794.03 to appellant under the facts of this case. . . .

JUSTICE SCALIA, concurring in part and concurring in the judgment.

I think it sufficient to decide this case to rely upon the third ground set forth in the Court's opinion: that a law cannot be regarded as protecting an interest "of the highest order," Smith v. Daily Mail Publishing Co., (1979), and thus as justifying a restriction upon truthful speech, when it leaves appreciable damage to that supposedly vital interest unprohibited. . . .

This law has every appearance of a prohibition that society is prepared to impose upon the press but not upon itself. Such a prohibition does not protect an interest "of the highest order. . . ."

JUSTICE WHITE, with whom THE CHIEF JUSTICE and JUSTICE O'CONNOR join, dissenting.

"Short of homicide, [rape] is the 'ultimate violation of self.'" Coker v. Georgia (1977). For B. J. F., however, the violation she suffered at a rapist's knifepoint marked only the beginning of her ordeal. A week later, while her assailant was still at large, an account of this assault—identifying by name B. J. F. as the victim—was published by The Florida Star. As a result, B. J. F. received harassing phone calls, required mental health counseling, was forced to move from her home, and was even threatened with being raped again. Yet today, the Court holds that a jury award of $75,000 to compensate B. J. F. for the harm she suffered due to the Star's negligence is at odds with the First Amendment. . . .

Cox Broadcasting stands for the proposition that the State cannot make the press its first line of defense in withholding private information from the public—it cannot ask the press to secrete private facts that the State makes no effort to safeguard in the first place. In this case, however, the State has undertaken "means which avoid [but obviously, not altogether prevent] public documentation or other exposure of private information." No doubt this is why the Court finally admits that "Cox Broadcasting . . . cannot fairly be read as controlling here."

. . . . at issue in Daily Mail was the disclosure of the name of the perpetrator of an infamous murder of a 15-year-old student. Surely the rights of those accused of crimes and those who are their victims must differ with respect to privacy concerns. That is, whatever rights alleged criminals have to maintain their anonymity pending an adjudication of guilt—and after Daily Mail, those rights would seem to be minimal—the rights of crime victims to stay shielded from public view must be infinitely more substantial. Daily Mail was careful to state that the "holding in this case is narrow . . . . there is no issue here of privacy." (emphasis added). But in this case, there is an issue of privacy—indeed, that is the principal issue—and therefore, this case falls outside of Daily Mail's "rule."

We are left, then, to wonder whether the three "independent reasons" the Court cites for reversing the judgment for B. J. F. support its result.

The first of these reasons relied on by the Court is the fact "appellant gained access to [B. J. F.'s name] through a government news release." "The government's issuance of such a release, without qualification, can only convey to recipients that the government considered dissemination lawful," the Court suggests. So described, this case begins to look like the situation in *Oklahoma Publishing*, where a judge invited reporters into his courtroom, but then tried to forbid them from reporting on the proceedings they observed. But this case is profoundly different. Here, the "release" of information provided by the government was not, as the Court says, "without qualification. As the State's own reporter conceded at trial, the crime incident report that inadvertently included B. J. F.'s name was posted in a room that contained signs making it clear that the names of rape victims were not matters of public record, and were not to be published. The State's reporter indicated that she understood that she "[was not] allowed to take down that information" (i. e., B. J. F.'s name) and that she "[was] not supposed to take the information from the police department." Thus, by her own admission the posting of incident report did not convey to the Star's reporter the idea that "the government considered dissemination lawful"; the Court's suggestion to the contrary is inapt. . . .

Instead, Florida has done precisely what we suggested, in *Cox Broadcasting*, that States wishing to protect the privacy rights of rape victims might do: "respond [to the challenge] by means which avoid public documentation or other exposure of private information. . . ."

By amending its public records statute to exempt rape victims names from disclosure and forbidding its officials from releasing such information, the State has taken virtually every step imaginable to prevent what happened here. This case presents a far cry, then, from *Cox Broadcasting*, or *Oklahoma Publishing*, where the State asked the news media not to publish information it had made generally available to the public: here, the State is not asking the media to do the State's job in the first instance. Unfortunately, as this case illustrates, mistakes happen: even when States take measures to "avoid" disclosure, sometimes rape victims' names are found out. As I see it, it is not too much to ask the press, in instances such as this, to respect simple standards of decency and refrain from publishing a victim's name, address, and/or phone number.

Second, the Court complains that appellant was judged here under too strict a liability standard. . . The short answer to this complaint is that whatever merit the Court's argument might have, it is wholly inapposite here, where the jury found that appellant acted with "reckless indifference towards the rights of others. . . ."

But even taking the Court's concerns in the abstract, they miss the mark. Permitting liability under a negligence *per se* theory does not mean that defendants will be held liable without a showing of negligence, but rather, that the standard of care has been set by the legislature, instead of the courts. The Court says that negligence *per se* permits a plaintiff to hold a defendant liable without a showing that the disclosure was "of a fact about a person's private life . . . that a reasonable person would find highly offensive." But the point here is that the legislature— reflecting popular sentiment—has determined that disclosure of the fact that a person was raped is categorically a revelation that reasonable people find offensive. . . .

Third, the Court faults the Florida criminal statute for being underinclusive: 794.03 covers disclosure of rape victim's names in "instruments of mass communication," but not other means of distribution, the Court observes.

 . . . . the Florida law evenhandedly covers all "instrument[s] of mass communication" no matter their form, media, content nature, or purpose. It excludes neighborhood gossips, because presumably the Florida Legislature has determined that neighborhood gossips do not pose the danger and intrusion to rape victims that ""instrument[s] of mass communication" do. Simply put: Florida wanted to prevent the widespread distribution of rape victims' names, and therefore enacted a statute tailored almost as precisely as possible to achieve that end. . . .

Florida does recognize a tort of publication of private facts. Thus, it is quite possible that the neighborhood gossip whom the Court so fears being left scot-free spread news of a rape victim's identity would be subjected to the same (or similar) liability regime under which appellant was taxed. The Court's myopic focus on 794.03 ignores the probability that Florida law is more comprehensive than the Court gives it credit for being. . .

.

At issue in this case is whether there is any information about people which—though true—may not be published in the press. By holding that only "a state interest of the highest older permits the State to penalize the publication of truthful information, and by holding that protecting a rape victim's right to privacy is not among those state interests of the highest order, the Court accepts appellant's invitation to obliterate one of the most noteworthy legal inventions of the 20th century: the tort of the publication of private facts.

I would find a place to draw the line, high enough to protect B. J. F.'s desire for privacy and peace-of-mind in the wake of a horrible personal tragedy. There is no public interest in publishing the names, addresses, and phone numbers of persons who are the victims of crime—and no public interest in immunizing the press from liability in the rare cases where a State's effort to protect a victim's privacy have failed.

11

PROTECTION FROM ASSAULTIVE AND UNWANTED STIMULI

More than a century ago Louis Brandeis and Samuel Warren extolled the right of privacy,[1] the "right to be let alone," as central to human freedom. For some fifty of those years the Supreme Court has struggled with the conflict between that right and the desires of persons to intrude on individual solitude in order to get across a message. The conflict, as the Court has dealt with it, has involved two particular forums in which privacy has been asserted to be superior to free communication: the home, where it has received its greatest protection, and that part of the public arena where it can be said that the individual is a "captive audience" deserving of at least some governmental protection from those whom he wishes to shut out.

The cases begin with <u>Martin v. City of Struthers</u> (1943), which arose out of a World War II attempt by an Ohio town to protect its citizens, and especially those who worked "swing" or "graveyard" shifts in defense plants, from being disturbed by persons going door-to-door and ringing doorbells. On their behalf, Struthers flatly banned door-to-door solicitations. Martin, a Jehovah's Witness, was convicted of violating the ordinance, but the Court reversed his conviction. The ordinance, said the Court, could not stand, at least where religious or political messages were concerned, for "doorbelling" was a traditional way for those with little money to get their messages across to others. And, said the Court, the city's purpose could be accomplished by other, more appropriate means.

For our purposes, the important thing about <u>Martin</u> is not its result, which appears correct on the facts of the case. Rather, it is the fact that both majority and minority expressly recognized the right of the householder to take measures, such as the posting of "No Peddlers" or "Do not disturb" signs at the entrance to his house, to fend off others. The city would then be free to enforce the householder's wishes. But the decision as to whether to welcome or to forbid such solicitation would, said the Court, be in the hands of the individual, "where it properly belongs."

The teachings of <u>Martin</u> must have been in the mind of Congress when it moved to prevent the mails from being used as a device to foist on unwilling receipients materials of an erotic or sexually explicit nature. The statute passed by Congress allowed postmasters, after being asked by an addressee to take such action, to order companies purveying such materials to remove that addressee from their mailing list. Failure to comply was a criminal offense.

The law was challenged, in <u>Rowan v. Post Office Department</u> (1970), by a seller of such materials who argued that the First Amendment protected the right to communicate with anyone by the best means available, and that the only proper recourse for the householder who objected to such material was to throw it away. The Court, however, "balanced" the interests of the purveyor against the householder's "right to be let alone" and upheld the statute. In doing so, it recognized that the statute inhibited, to some degree, the flow of information, and also that it was content-based. Despite this, the right of the householder to prevent the entering into his home of things to which he objected was held to prevail, over the dissent's argument that the flow of information was unnecessarily hindered in order to save the householder "the trip from his mailbox to the garbage can." Moreover, said the Court, no determination of "obscenity" other than that of the householder was required to implement the statute.

Does this interpretation leave the householder free to prevent anything (whether sexually explicit materials, political propaganda, or seed catalogues) from being delivered to his mailbox? One cannot be certain but, given the Court's language, the answer is almost surely "yes."[2] Together with <u>Martin</u>, <u>Rowan v. Post Office Department</u> stands for the proposition that the householder is master of what enters his home, and that the First Amendment is not violated by government action to enforce his or her wishes. It is, therefore, the first case excerpted in this chapter.

More complicated, and less capable of confident assessment, is the issue of communicative activity which does not directly enter into the household, but which may, because of noise or simple proximity, be viewed as to one degree or another assaultive of the integrity of the home. Twice since 1969 the Court has had the opportunity to deal with this issue. In both cases it declined.

The first case to present such an issue, Gregory v. City of Chicago (1969), arose from the activities of comedian and civil rights activist Dick Gregory. He and his supporters conducted a lengthy campaign in Chicago to promote the integration of that city's schools. Dissatisfied with the pace of desegregation, they assumed that Mayor Richard J. Daley (at the time the undisputed "boss" of all things political in and around Chicago) was at least partially responsible for delays. Accordingly, Gregory led a march from downtown Chicago, where he had unsuccessfully attempted to confront the mayor, to the "back of the yards" district on Chicago's South Side, where the mayor was born and still lived. The route led through an area full of hostile whites, and police eventually arrested Gregory for disturbing the peace. The Court avoided the issue of whether Gregory might have been convicted for demonstrating at the home of the mayor, reversing the conviction on the grounds that there was no evidence that Gregory and his supporters had caused any disturbance.

Justice Black concurred in the judgment, but objected to the Court's refusal to meet the issue of demonstrations at a home. His opinion aptly summarized the arguments for granting protection, even to the home of a public official:

> Were the authority of government so trifling as to permit anyone with a complaint to have the vast power to do anything he pleased, wherever he pleased, and whenever he pleased, our customs and our habits of conduct, social, political, ethical, and religious, would be wiped out . . . . churches would be compelled to welcome into their buildings invaders who came but to scoff and jeer; streets and highways and public buildings would cease to be available for the purposes for which they were constructed and dedicated whenever demonstrators and picketers wanted to use them for their own purposes. And perhaps worse than all other changes, homes, the sacred retreat to which families repair for their privacy and their daily way of living, would have to have their doors thrown open to all who desired to convert the occupants to new views, new morals, and a new way of life. Men and women who hold public office would be compelled, simply because they did hold public office, to lose the comforts and privacy of an unpicketed home. I believe that our Constitution . . . did not create a government with such monumental weaknesses. Speech and press are, of course to be free, so that public matters may be discussed with impunity. But picketing and demonstrations can be regulated like other conduct . . . I believe that the homes of men, sometimes the last citadel of the tired, the weary, and the

sick, can be protected by government from noisy, marching, tramping, threatening . . . demonstrators bent on filling the minds of men, women, and children with fears and the unknown.

In the more recent case of Carey v. Brown (1980), the Court avoided the issue of the constitutionality of a flat ban on picketing around city residences. This time the ordinance in question made an exception of picketing in labor disputes, thus violating equal protection standards.

We do not have, then, a decision on either a flat ban on residential picketing or on picketing around the homes of public officials, although, in Organization for a Better Austin v. O'Keefe (1971), the Court did address a somewhat related question. Austin involved actions taken by a suburban civic organization to pressure a person engaged in "blockbusting" to cease such tactics in their area. (Blockbusting is a device by which a real estate speculator seeks to take advantage of the fears of some whites that the value of their property will fall if a neighborhood is integrated. Typically, the "blockbuster" goes into an area, buys a house which is up for sale, and sells it to a Black. He then informs other neighborhood property owners that they had better sell out "before its too late." Under such circumstances, some property owners may be persuaded to sell for less than the market price, creating a handsome profit for the "blockbuster.")

In this case the members of the Organization for a Better Austin went, not to O'Keefe's home, but to those of his neighbors, distributing leaflets in which they accused him of being a "blockbuster" and pointed out the bases for their accusation. O'Keefe took exception to this assault on his reputation, and obtained an injunction against such action. The Supreme Court dissolved the injunction on the grounds that whatever interest O'Keefe might have had in not being subjected to pressure at his home, this interest did not extend to protecting him from the consequences of his neighbors being given truthful information.

One may applaud the consequence for O'Keefe, while expressing at least some doubt as to the soundness of the Court's decision. For surely a part of the interests that one has in the home involves the ability to live amicably with one's neighbors. On the other hand, the information was truthful, and the leafleting by itself caused no disturbance. Austin thus left open the possibility that activity directed against the home would be less favored.

That this reading of Austin is correct was established in Frisby v. Schultz

(1988), the second case excerpted in this chapter. In Frisby, all members of the Court agreed that government may give at least some protection to the householder who is a "captive audience," although the dissent of Brennan and Marshall would not have extended such protection simply against the householder's "knowledge that someone who disagreed with him was outside." In addition, all justices except Stevens considered even residential streets to be "public forums." This being the case, and since the statute at issue prohibited appellees (anti-abortion protesters who sought to influence a doctor living in a particular house to cease performing abortions) "from engaging in picketing on an issue of public concern," it must be judged by strict standards. The Court majority had no difficulty in finding that there were ample alternatives by which the picketers might get their message across. And, combining the interest in protecting the "well-being, tranquility, and privacy of the home" with the right of the unwilling recipient to reject communication, there was "simply no right to force speech into the home of an unwilling listener." Thus the statute at issue was narrowly focused on the evil involved.

Justice Brennan, dissenting, argued that the sole permissible result of a statute like that at issue was the prevention of the harassing or obnoxious intrusion of noises. This evil, he said, could have been dealt with by a statute dealing with the number of pickets, the noise level, and the character of the picketing. For him speech was of such great importance that even some intrusions on "psychological security" must be permitted. For the majority, the transcendent value was protection of the home and its occupants.

Frisby is an important case. But the limits of its recognition of the right to privacy in the home, particularly the majority's apparent assumption that demonstrators "walking a route in front of an entire block of houses" could not be banned, is still troubling. Suppose, for example, that we have a large group of angry people who repeatedly invade the residential streets of a neighborhood. Their very presence, given their anger, could be perceived as threatening. And their actions would, of course, impact the entire neighborhood regardless of the target of their grievance. Such "unfocused" picketing the Frisby opinion would seem to protect. But is there no interest in protecting a neighborhood from such disruption? It is in this context that Justice Steven's observation that ""one does not much advance the argument" by equating residential streets with the classic "public forum" has special force.

As might be expected, the right to be free from "unwanted stimuli" necessarily declines as one goes further and further away from the home. The activities of others, the noise that they make in the course of such activities, and even their attempts to communicate with us necessarily impinge on our capacity, and even more on our "right to be let alone" in the public forum. But, as the two "transition cases" which we will next consider illustrate, even here the Court has found a basis for some measure of protection for those who would reject unwanted communicative activity.

Saia v. New York (1948) and Kovacs v. Cooper (1949), involved the constitutionality of regulations directed against "sound trucks," devices which may intrude not only in the street, but also into the serenity of the home. In Saia the Supreme Court struck down a city ordinance which allowed sound trucks to operate only if their operator had received prior permission from the Chief of Police. Such an ordinance, said Justice Black for the Court, "established a previous restraint on the right of free speech" for there were no standards established for the exercise of the Chief's discretion, and the statute was "not narrowly drawn to regulate the hours or places of use of loud-speakers or the volume of sound (the decibels) to which they may be adjusted." Loudspeakers, said the Court, "are today indispensable instruments of effective public speech. . . .any abuses which . . . [they] . . . create can be controlled by narrowly drawn statutes."

Only two years later, in Kovacs, the Court distinguished Saia and upheld a Trenton, New Jersey, ordinance which imposed a flat ban on the use of "loud and raucus" soundtracks in any part of the city. Said the Court:

> While this Court . . . has invalidated an ordinance forbidding a distributor of pamphlets or handbills from summoning householders to their doors, this was on the ground that the home owner could protect himself from such an intrusion . . . . The Court never intimated that the visitor could insert a foot in the door and insist on a hearing. . . . We do not think that the Struthers case requires us to expand this interdiction of legislation to include ordinances against obtaining an audience for the broadcaster's ideas by way of sound trucks with loud and raucus noises on city streets. The unwilling listener is not like the passer-by who may be offered a pamphlet in the street but cannot be made to take it. In his home or on the street he is practically helpless to escape this interference with his privacy by loud speakers except through the protection of the municipality.

Justice Black, dissenting, argued that the flat ban on sound trucks was even more intrusive than the scheme outlawed in <u>Saia</u>, and that the two cases were in conflict with another. As Justice Jackson noted in his concurrence, Black was probably right, for all sound trucks would seem, by nature, to be "loud and raucus."

<u>Kovac's</u> reference to unwilling listeners "helpless to escape interference" laid the basis for the development, by the dissenters in a succeeding case, of the concept of the "captive audience" which, it was argued, should be protected even away from home. <u>Public Utilities Commission v. Pollak</u> (1952) involved the District of Columbia's practice of receiving and amplifying radio programs through the loudspeakers in its buses, thus making them audible to all those seated on the bus. Justice Burton's majority opinion upheld the practice. There was, said Burton, no proof that the programs interfered with free conversation between passengers. Nor was there any substantial claim that they were used for propaganda purposes. Rather, the claim was that the programs invaded the constitutional rights of privacy of those passengers who did not wish to listen. But, said Burton, the Constitution did not secure

> to each passenger on a public vehicle . . . a right of privacy substantially equal to the privacy to which he is entitled in his own home. However complete his right of privacy may be at home, it is substantially limited by the rights of others when its possessor travels on a public thoroughfare or rides in a public conveyance. Streetcars and buses . . . are for the common use of all their passengers. The . . . (government) . . . in its regulation of them is not only entitled, but is required to take into consideration the interests of all concerned.

The dissenting opinion of Justice Douglas, by contrast, emphasized the importance of privacy as contributing to a liberty which must mean more than "freedom from unlawful governmental restraint." And, while a person loses that privacy on the streets and in public places, even outside the home he may not be compelled to do certain things, like attend a religious service or accept one creed as against another. Thus the First Amendment honors the sanctity of thought and belief. And "the streetcar audience is a captive audience. It is there as a matter of necessity, not of choice." And unlike the person in the home who can turn off the radio, or one in a restaurant who can avoid its sounds by leaving, that audience "has no choice but to sit and listen, or perhaps to sit and try *not to listen*. . ."

The argument of Justice Douglas' bore fruit in the 1970's, a more privacy-

minded era, in the case of <u>Lehman v. City of Shaker Heights</u> (1974). Here
a municipality refused to sell advertising space on the inside of its city buses to a
political candidate. The city did so in part to maximize its revenues, on the belief
long-term commercial advertisements would give it a greater return. But it was also
motivated by the desire to avoid offending those riders who might have found such
ads offensive. Resurrecting the "captive audience" doctrine, the majority approved
both of these motivations. Justice Douglas concurred, emphasizing the right to
privacy, while Powell's dissent argued that the regulation was "content-based."

The majority opinion, its "content base" aside, has much to recommend it.
Yet, as Lawrence Tribe has noted, it may be criticized on the basis that the
distinction between "political" and "commercial" advertising is sometimes not
valid. It would appear, for example, that an advertisement for cigarettes is simply
"commercial," while one arguing for the banning of cigarettes is "political."
Similarly, an ad announcing the availability of abortions would seem to be
"commercial," one in opposition to abortion "political." Yet both the cigarette ad
and the ad for abortions say something on a matter of public policy, just as surely
as do the more overtly "political" ads.[3] <u>Lehman v. Shaker Heights</u> may, then,
represent the establishment of a desirable principle with respect to assaults on
"captive audiences" The implementation of that principle, at least as it articulated in
<u>Lehman</u>, may present considerable difficulty.[4]

The final case excerpted in this chapter involves, more than anything else, the
issue of "when is an audience a captive audience." In <u>Erznoznick v. City of
Jacksonville</u> (1975), the Florida municipality had an ordinance which forbade
those drive-in theatres with screens visible to the street from showing pictures in
which nudity occurred. The apparent purpose of the statute was to prevent offense
to passers-by who might object to seeing glimpses of sexually explicit nudity. The
ordinance was also justified as a traffic measure, on the theory that such nudity
could cause inattention to driving or other reactions inimicable to traffic safety.

The Court, *per* Powell, found the ordinance objectionable in several respects.
Any offense that was caused could be avoided simply by looking elsewhere. As to
traffic control, it could not be shown that nudity, any more than violence or any
other type of arresting on-screen activity, was particularly likely to cause problems.
The ordinance, which covered the showing of any kind of nudity (even a baby's
bottom), was fatally overbroad. And, of course, it was content based. A content

based restriction, said Powell, could be upheld only when it's object intruded on the home or when viewers could not easily avoid it.

Once again the Court drew a distinction which seems to have considerable merit, and the decision is no doubt correct on its face. But its implications for other situations are, as Justice White noted in dissent, potentially very disturbing. For what, under Erznoznick's "aversion of the eyes" principle, allows a city to prosecute a nude couple who engage in public sexual intercourse while "engaging in a valid political dialogue?" Professor Tribe would solve the problem, and allow the banning of this kind of nudity, on the ground that there are certain kinds of activities which we cannot get away from and that call for a response on our part.[5]

For Tribe, it is the fact that the activity at issue calls for such a response and thus allows others to see what our reaction is that constitutes an invasion of privacy and of our "right to be let alone." The explanation seems strained, and one may query whether all communicative activity does not "call for a response on our part" and potentially constitute an invasion of privacy. One tends to believe that the real reasons for objecting to such activity in public is simply that it is inappropriate and embarrassing, like a "pig in a parlor." But to base a prohibition on such considerations might make it "content" or "viewpoint" based. At any rate, the basis on which Erznoznick could be distinguished, so as to ban the "expressive nudity" of the example, remains unclear.

---

[1]Louis D. Brandeis and Samuel Warren, "The Right to Privacy," 4 Harvard Law Review 193 (1890).

[2]Consider, for example, the consequences of the Court's having held that, before the law could take effect against the materials, a determination of "obscenity" would have had to be made, by a postal official. Such a requirement , given the uncertainty (See Ch. 9) about the meaning of "obscenity." would have embroiled the matter in endless litigation. And, if the householder were required to make, or more likely to defend, such a determination, the result would be the same. Few householders would elect, in such circumstances, to save themselves the "trip to the garbage can."

[3]American Constitutional Law, 1st ed., 692.

[4]On the other hand, the difficulty may not be insurmountable. For, while the Lehman principle employs what I would consider to be a permissible "content" distinction, the First Amendment also has been construed to prohibit distinctions on the basis of "viewpoint." And permitting ads for cigarettes or abortion, while refusing to accept those opposing either of those two activities is assuredly "viewpoint based." Thus an equitable solution would be to refuse ads, political or not, which explicitly or implicitly take positions on matters of public controversy. This, of course, would present the question of whether one could successfully identify those implicating "public

continued on next page

controversy." But this problem, at least at first glance, would seem to be manageable. And such a solution would seem to be in accord with the purpose which Shaker Heights had sought to achieve, and of which the Supreme Court approved.

[5]*American Constitutional Law*, 2nd ed., 953-954.

ROWAN, DBA AMERICAN BOOK SERVICE, ET AL. V. UNITED STATES POST OFFICE DEPARTMENT ET AL.

397 U.S. 728 (1970)

MR. CHIEF JUSTICE BURGER delivered the opinion of the Court.

Appellants challenge the constitutionality of Title III of the Postal Revenue and Federal Salary Act of 1967, 81 Stat. 645, under which a person may require that a mailer remove his name from its mailing lists and stop all future mailings to the householder. The appellants are publishers, distributors, owners, and operators of mail order houses, mailing list brokers, and owners and operators of mail service organizations whose business activities are affected by the challenged statute.

A brief description of the statutory framework will facilitate our analysis of the questions raised in this appeal. Section 4009 is entitled "Prohibition of pandering advertisements in the mails." It provides a procedure whereby any householder may insulate himself from advertisements that offer for sale "matter which the addressee in his sole discretion believes to be erotically arousing or sexually provocative." 39 U. S. C. 4009 (a). Subsection (b) mandates the Postmaster General, upon receipt of a notice from the addressee specifying that he has received advertisements found by him to be within the statutory category, to issue on the addressee's request an order directing the sender and his agents or assigns to refrain from further mailings to the named addressee. Additionally, subsection (c) requires the Postmaster General to order the affected sender to delete the name of the designated addressee from all mailing lists owned or controlled by the sender and prohibits the sale, rental, exchange, or other transactions involving mailing lists bearing the name of the designated addressee.

If the Postmaster General has reason to believe that an order issued under this section has been violated, subsection (d) authorizes him to notify the sender by registered or certified mail of his belief and the reasons therefor, and grant him an opportunity to respond and have a hearing on whether a violation has occurred.

If the Postmaster General thereafter determines that the order has been or is being violated, he is authorized to request the Attorney General to seek an order from a United States District Court directing compliance with the prohibitory order. Subsection (e) grants to the district court jurisdiction to issue a compliance order upon application of the Attorney General.
. . .

The essence of appellants' argument is that the statute violates their constitutional right to communicate. One sentence in appellants' brief perhaps characterizes their entire position:
The freedom to communicate orally and by the written word and, indeed, in every manner whatsoever is imperative to a free and sane society.

Without doubt the public postal system is an indispensable adjunct of every civilized society and communication is imperative to a healthy social order. But the right of every person "to be let alone" must be placed in the scales with the right of others to communicate.

In today's complex society we are inescapably captive audiences for many purposes, but a sufficient measure of individual autonomy must survive to permit every householder to exercise control over unwanted mail. . .

In *Martin v. Struthers* (1943), MR. JUSTICE BLACK, for the Court, while supporting the "[f]reedom to distribute information to every citizen," acknowledged a limitation in terms of leaving "with the homeowner himself" the power to decide "whether distributors of literature may lawfully call at a home." Weighing the highly important right to communicate, but without trying to determine where it fits into constitutional imperatives, against the very basic right to be free from sights, sounds, and tangible matter we do not want, it seems to us that a mailer's right to communicate must stop at the mailbox of an unreceptive addressee.

The Court has traditionally respected the right of a householder to bar, by order or notice, solicitors, hawkers, and peddlers from his property. See *Martin v. Struthers*. In this case the mailer's right to communicate is circumscribed only by an affirmative act of the addressee giving notice that he wishes no further mailings from that mailer.

To hold less would tend to license a form of trespass and would make hardly more sense than to say that a radio or television viewer may not twist the dial to cut off an offensive or boring communication and thus bar its entering his home. Nothing in the Constitution compels us to listen to or view any unwanted communication, whatever its merit; we see no basis for according the printed word or pictures a different or more preferred status because they are sent by mail. The ancient concept that "a man's home is his castle" into which "not even the king may enter" has lost none of its vitality, and none of the recognized exceptions includes any right to communicate offensively with another. See *Camara v. Municipal Court* (1967).

Both the absoluteness of the citizen's right under 4009 and its finality are essential; what may not be provocative to one person may well be to another. In operative effect the power of the householder under the statute is unlimited; he may prohibit the mailing of a dry goods catalog because he objects to the contents—or indeed the text of the language touting the merchandise. Congress provided this sweeping power not only to protect privacy but to avoid possible constitutional questions that might arise from vesting the power to make any discretionary evaluation of the material in a governmental official.

In effect, Congress has erected a wall—or more accurately permits a citizen to erect a wall—that no advertiser may penetrate without his acquiescence. The continuing operative effect of a mailing ban once imposed presents no constitutional obstacles; the citizen cannot be put to the burden of determining on repeated occasions whether the offending mailer has altered its material so as to make it acceptable. Nor should the householder have to risk that offensive material come into the hands of his children before it can be stopped.

We therefore categorically reject the argument that a vendor has a right under the Constitution or otherwise to send unwanted material into the home of another. If this prohibition operates to impede the flow of even valid ideas, the answer is that no one has a right to press even "good" ideas on an unwilling recipient. That we are often "captives" outside the sanctuary of the home and subject to objectionable speech and other sound does I not mean we must be captives everywhere. See *Public Utilities Comm'n v. Pollak* (1952). The asserted right of a mailer, we repeat, stops at the outer boundary of every person's domain. . . .

There is no merit to the appellants' allegations that the statute is unconstitutionally vague. A statute is fatally vague only when it exposes a potential actor to some risk or detriment without giving him fair warning of the nature of the proscribed conduct. *United States v. Cardiff* (1952). Here the appellants know precisely what they must do on receipt of a prohibitory order. The complainants' names must be removed from the sender's mailing lists and he must refrain from future mailings to the named addressees. The sender is exposed to a contempt sanction only if he continues to mail to a particular addressee after administrative and judicial proceedings. Appellants run no substantial risk of miscalculation.

For the reasons stated, the judgment appealed from is affirmed. . . .

FRISBY ET AL. V. SCHULTZ ET AL.

487 U.S 474 (1988)

JUSTICE O'CONNOR delivered the opinion of the Court.

Brookfield, Wisconsin, has adopted an ordinance that completely bans picketing "before or about" any residence. This case presents a facial First Amendment challenge to that ordinance.

Brookfield, Wisconsin, is a residential suburb of Milwaukee. with a population of approximately 4,300. The appellees, Sandra C. Schultz and Robert C. Braun, are individuals strongly opposed to abortion and wish to express their views on the subject by picketing on a public street outside the Brookfield residence of a doctor who apparently performs abortions at two clinics in neighboring towns. Appellees and others engaged in precisely that activity, assembling outside the doctor's home on at least six occasions between April 20, 1985, and May 20, 1985, for periods ranging from one to one and a half hours. The size of the group varied from 11 to more than 40. The picketing was generally orderly and peaceful; the town never had occasion to invoke any of its various ordinances prohibiting obstruction of the streets, loud and unnecessary noises, or disorderly conduct. Nonetheless, the picketing generated substantial controversy and numerous complaints. The Town Board therefore . . . (passed) . . . the following flat ban:

"It is unlawful for any person to engage in picketing before or about the residence or dwelling of any individual in the Town of Brookfield."

The ordinance itself recites the primary purpose of this ban:

"the protection and preservation of the home through assurance 'that members of the community enjoy in their homes and dwellings a feeling of well-being,

tranquility, and privacy.' The Town Board believed that a ban was necessary because it determined that 'the practice of picketing before or about residences and dwellings causes emotional disturbance and distress to the occupants . . . [and] has as its object the harassing of such occupants.' The ordinance also evinces a concern for public safety, noting that picketing obstructs and interferes with the free use of public sidewalks and public ways of travel."

The antipicketing ordinance operates at the core of the First Amendment by prohibiting appellees from engaging in picketing on an issue of public concern. Because of the importance of "uninhibited, robust, and wide-open" debate on public issues, *New York Times Co. v. Sullivan* (1964), we have traditionally subjected restrictions on public issue picketing to careful scrutiny. . .

To ascertain what limits, if any, may be placed on protected speech, we have often focused on the "place" of that speech, considering the nature of the forum the speaker seeks to employ. . .

The relevant forum here may be easily identified: appellees wish to picket on the public streets of Brookfield. . . .

Our prior holdings make clear that a public street does not lose its status as a traditional public forum simply because it runs through a residential neighborhood. . . . No particularized inquiry into the precise nature of a specific street is necessary; all public streets are held in the public trust and are properly considered traditional public fora. Accordingly, the streets of Brookfield are traditional public fora. The residential character of those streets may well inform the application of the relevant test, but it does not lead to a different test; the antipicketing ordinance must be judged against the stringent standards we have established for restrictions on speech in traditional public fora. . . . Accordingly, we turn to consider whether the ordinance is "narrowly tailored to serve a significant government interest" and whether it "leave[s] open ample alternative channels of communication." *Perry.*

Because the last question is so easily answered, we address it first. Of course, before we are able to assess the available alternatives, we must consider more carefully the reach of the ordinance. The precise scope of the ban is not further described within the text of the ordinance, but in our view the ordinance is readily subject to a narrowing construction that avoids constitutional difficulties. Specifically, the use of the singular form of the words "residence" and "dwelling" suggests that the ordinance is intended to prohibit only picketing focused on, and taking place in front of, a particular residence.

So narrowed, the ordinance permits the more general dissemination of a message. . . the limited nature of the prohibition makes it virtually self-evident that ample alternatives remain. . . .

We readily agree that the ordinance preserves ample alternative channels of communication and thus move on to inquire whether the ordinance serves a significant government interest. We find that such an interest is identified within the text of the ordinance itself: the protection of residential privacy. . . .

"The State's interest in protecting the well-being, tranquility, and privacy of the home is certainly of the highest order in a free and civilized society."

One important aspect of residential privacy is protection of the unwilling listener. Although in many locations, we expect individuals simply to avoid speech they do not want hear. "That we are often 'captives' outside sanctuary of the home and subject to objectionable speech. . . does not mean we must be captives everywhere. " *Rowan v. Post Office Dept.* . . .

This principle is reflected even in prior decisions in which we have invalidated complete bans on expressive activity, including bans operating in residential areas. See, *e. g., Schneider v. State* (1939) (handbilling); *Martin v. Struthers* (1943) (door-to-door solicitation). In all such cases, we have been careful to acknowledge that unwilling listeners may be protected when within their own homes. In *Schneider,* for example, in striking down a complete ban on handbilling, we spoke of a right to distribute literature only "to one willing to receive it." Similarly, when we invalidated a ban on door-to-door solicitation in *Martin,* we did so on the basis that the "home owner could protect himself from such intrusion by an appropriate sign 'that he is unwilling to be disturbed.'" *Kovacs.* We have "never intimated that the visitor could insert a foot in the door and insist on a hearing." There simply is no right to force speech into the home of an unwilling listener.

It remains to be considered, however, whether the Brookfield ordinance is narrowly tailored to protect only unwilling recipients of the communications. A statute is narrowly tailored if it targets and eliminates no more than the exact source of the "evil" it seeks to remedy. *City Council of Los Angeles v. Taxpayers for Vincent* (1984). A complete ban can be narrowly tailored, but only if each activity within the proscription's scope is an appropriately targeted evil. . . .

The type of picketers banned by the Brookfield ordinance generally do not seek to disseminate a message to the general public, but to intrude upon the targeted resident, and to do so in an especially offensive way. Moreover, even if some such picketers have a broader communicative purpose, their activity nonetheless inherently ancl offensively intrudes on residential privacy. The devastating effect of targeted picketing on the quiet enjoyment of the home is beyond doubt.

In this case, for example, appellees subjected the doctor and his family to the presence of a relatively large group of protestors on their doorstep in an attempt to force the doctor to cease performing abortions. But the actual size of the group is irrelevant; even a solitary picket can invade residential privacy. The offensive

and disturbing nature of the form of the communication banned by the Brookfield ordinance thus can scarcely be questioned.
. . .

The First Amendment permits the government to prohibit offensive speech as intrusive when the "captive" audience cannot avoid the objectionable speech. The target of the focused picketing banned by the Brookfield ordinance is just such a "captive." The resident is figuratively, and perhaps literally, trapped within the home, and because of the unique and subtle impact of such picketing is left with no ready means of avoiding the unwanted speech. Thus, the "evil" of targeted residential picketing, "the very presence of an unwelcome visitor at the home," is "created by the medium of expression itself." See *Taxpayers for Vincent*. Accordingly, the Brookfield ordinance's complete ban of that particular medium of expression is narrowly tailored.

JUSTICE WHITE, concurring in the judgment. . . .

JUSTICE BRENNAN, with whom JUSTICE MARSHALL joins, dissenting.

The Court today sets out the appropriate legal tests and standards governing the question presented, and proceeds to apply most of them correctly. Regrettably, though, the Court errs in the final step of its analysis, and approves an ordinance banning significantly more speech than is necessary to achieve the government's substantial and legitimate goal. Accordingly, I must dissent. . . .

The mere fact that speech takes place in a residential neighborhood does not automatically implicate a residential privacy interest. It is the intrusion of speech into the home or the unduly coercive nature of a particular manner of speech around the home that is subject to more exacting regulation. . . . so long as the speech remains outside the home and does not unduly coerce the occupant, the government's heightened interest in protecting residential privacy is not implicated.

The foregoing distinction is crucial here because it directly affects the last prong of the time, place, and manner test:

whether the ordinance is narrowly tailored to achieve the governmental interest. I do not quarrel with the Court's reliance on *City Council of Los Angeles v. Taxpayers for Vincent* (1984), for the proposition that a blanket prohibition of a manner of speech in particular public fora may nonetheless be "narrowly tailored" if in each case the manner of speech forbidden necessarily produces the very "evil" the government seeks to eradicate. However, the application of this test requires that the government demonstrate that the offending aspects of the prohibited manner of speech cannot be separately, and less intrusively, controlled. Thus here, if the intrusive and unduly coercive elements of residential picketing can be eliminated without simultaneously eliminating residential picketing. . . .

Without question there are many aspects of residential picketing that, if unregulated, might easily become intrusive or unduly coercive. Indeed, some of these aspects are illustrated by this very case. As the District Court found, before the ordinance took effect up to 40 sign-carrying, slogan-shouting protestors regularly converged on Dr. Victoria's home and, in addition to protesting, warned young children not to go near the house because Dr. Victoria was a "baby killer." Further, the throng repeatedly trespassed onto the Victorias' property and at least once blocked the exits to their home. Surely it is within the government's power to enact regulations as necessary to prevent such intrusive and coercive abuses. Thus, for example, the government could constitutionally regulate the number of residential picketers, the hours during which a residential picket may take place, or the noise level of such a picket. In short, substantial regulation is permitted to neutralize the intrusive or unduly coercive aspects of picketing around the home. But to say that picketing may be substantially regulated is not to say that it may be prohibited in its entirety. Once size, time, volume, and the like have been controlled to ensure that the picket is no longer intrusive or coercive, only the speech itself remains, conveyed perhaps by a lone, silent individual, walking back and forth with a sign. Such speech, which no longer implicates the heightened governmental interest in residential privacy, is nevertheless banned by the Brookfield law. Therefore, the ordinance is not narrowly tailored.

. . . the ordinance applies to all picketers, not just those engaged in the protest giving rise to this challenge. Yet the Court cites no evidence to support its assertion that picketers generally, or even appellees specifically, desire to communicate only with the "targeted resident." (In fact, the District Court, on the basis of an uncontradicted affidavit, found that appellees sought to communicate with both Dr. Victoria and with the public) While picketers' signs might be seen from the resident's house, they are also visible to passersby. To be sure, the audience is limited to those within sight of the picket, but focusing speech does not strip it of constitutional protection. Even the site-specific aspect of the picket identifies to the public the object of the picketers' attention. *Boos v. Barry* (1988). Nor does the picketers' ultimate goal—to influence the resident's conduct—change the analysis; as the Court held in *Keefe*, such a goal does not defeat First Amendment protection.

A second flaw in the Court's reasoning is that it assumes that the intrusive elements of a residential picket are "inherent ". . . . Contrary to the Court's declaration in this regard, it seems far more likely that a picketer who truly desires only to harass those inside a particular residence will find that goal unachievable in the face of a narrowly tailored ordinance substantially limiting, for example, the size, time, and volume of the protest. If, on the other hand, the picketer intends to communicate generally, a carefully crafted ordinance will allow him or her to do so without intruding upon or unduly harassing the resident. Consequently, the discomfort to which the Court must refer is merely that of knowing there is a person outside who disagrees with someone inside. This may indeed be uncomfortable, but it does not implicate the town's interest in residential privacy and therefore does not warrant silencing speech. . . .

JUSTICE STEVENS, dissenting.

"GET WELL CHARLIE—OUR TEAM NEEDS YOU."

In Brookfield, Wisconsin, it is unlawful for a fifth grader to carry such a sign in front of a residence for the period of time necessary to convey its friendly message to its intended audience. . . .

The Court's analysis of the question whether Brookfield's ban on picketing is constitutional begins with an acknowledgment that the ordinance "operates at the core of the First Amendment," and that the streets of Brookfield are a "traditional public forum." It concludes, however, that the total ban on residential picketing is "narrowly tailored" to protect "only unwilling recipients of the communications." The plain language of the ordinance, however, applies to communications to willing and indifferent recipients as well as to the unwilling.

I do not believe we advance the inquiry by rejecting what JUSTICE BRENNAN calls the "rogue argument that residential streets are something less than public fora." See *Cornelius v. NAACP Legal Defense & Educational Fund, Inc.* (1985) (STEVENS, J., dissenting). The streets in a residential neighborhood that has no sidewalks are quite obviously a different type of forum than a stadium or a public park. Attaching the label "public forum" to the area in front of a single family dwelling does not help us decide whether the town's interest in the safe and efficient flow of traffic or its interest in protecting the privacy of its citizens justifies denying picketers the right to march up and down the streets at will.

Two characteristics of picketing—and of speech more generally—make this a difficult case. First, it is important to recognize that, "[l]ike so many other kinds of expression, picketing is a mixture of conduct and communication." *NLRB v. Retail Store Employees* (1980) (STEVENS, J., concurring in part and concurring in result). If we put the speech element to one side, I should think it perfectly clear that the town could prohibit pedestrians from loitering in front of a residence. On the other hand, it seems equally clear that a sign carrier has a right to march past a residence—and presumably pause long enough to give the occupants an opportunity to read his or her message—regardless of whether the reader agrees, disagrees, or is simply indifferent to the point of view being expressed. Second, it bears emphasis that: . . . . Picketing is a form of speech that, by virtue of its repetition of message and often hostile presentation, may be disruptive of an environment irrespective of the substantive message conveyed.

The picketing that gave rise to the ordinance enacted in this case was obviously intended to do more than convey a message of opposition to the character of the doctor's practice; it was intended to cause him and his family substantial psychological distress. As the record reveals, the picketers' message was repeatedly redelivered by a relatively large group—in essence, increasing the volume and intrusiveness of the same message with each repeated assertion, cf. *Kovacs v. Cooper* (1949). As is often the function of picketing, during the periods of protest the doctor's home was held under a virtual siege. I do not believe that picketing for the sole purpose of imposing psychological harm on a family in the shelter of their home is constitutionally protected. I do believe, however, that the picketers have a right to communicate their strong opposition to abortion to the doctor, but after they have had a fair

opportunity to communicate that message, I see little justification for allowing them to remain in front of his home and repeat it over and over again simply to harm the doctor and his family. Thus. I agree that the ordinance may be constitutionally applied to the kind of picketing that gave rise to its enactment.

On the other hand, the ordinance is unquestionably "overbroad" in that it prohibits some communication that is protected by the First Amendment. . . .

In this case the overbreadth is unquestionably "real." Whether or not it is "substantial" in relation to the "plainly legitimate sweep" of the ordinance is a more difficult question. My hunch is that the town will probably not enforce its ban against friendly, innocuous, or even brief unfriendly picketing, and that the Court may be right in concluding that its legitimate sweep makes its overbreadth insubstantial. But there are two countervailing considerations that are persuasive to me. The scope of the ordinance gives the town officials far too much discretion in making enforcement decisions; while we sit by and await further developments, potential picketers must act at their peril. Second, it is a simple matter for the town to amend its ordinance and to limit the ban to conduct that unreasonably interferes with the privacy of the home and does not serve a reasonable communicative purpose. Accordingly, I respectfully dissent.

ERZNOZNIK V. CITY OF JACKSONVILLE

422 U.S. 205 (1975)

MR. JUSTICE POWELL delivered the opinion of the Court.

This case presents a challenge to the facial validity of a Jacksonville, Fla., ordinance that prohibits showing films containing nudity by a drive-in movie theater when its screen is visible from a public street or place.

Appellant, Richard Erznoznik, is the manager of the University Drive-In Theatre in Jacksonville. On March 13,

1972, he was charged with violating 330.313 of the municipal code for exhibiting a motion picture, visible from public streets, in which "female buttocks and bare breasts were shown." The ordinance, adopted January 14, 1972, provides:

330.313 *Drive-In Theaters, Films Visible From Public Streets or Public Places*. It shall be unlawful and it is hereby declared a public nuisance for any ticket seller, ticket taker, usher, motion picture projection machine operator, manager, owner, or any other person connected with or employed by any drive-in theater in the City to exhibit, or aid or assist in exhibiting, any motion picture, slide, or other exhibit in which the human male or female bare buttocks, human female bare breasts, or human bare pubic areas are shown, if such motion picture, slide, or other exhibit is visible from any public street or public place. Violation of this section shall be punishable as a Class C offense.

Appellant, with the consent of the city prosecutor, successfully moved to stay his prosecution so that the validity of the ordinance could be tested in a separate declaratory action. In that action appellee, the city of Jacksonville, introduced evidence showing that the screen of appellant's theater is visible from two adjacent public streets and a nearby church parking lot. There was also testimony indicating that people had been observed watching films while sitting outside the theater in parked cars and in the grass.

The trial court upheld the ordinance as a legitimate exercise of the municipality's police power, and ruled that it did not infringe upon appellant's First Amendment

Appellee's primary argument is that it may protect its citizens against unwilling exposure to materials that may be offensive. Jacksonville's ordinance, however, does not protect citizens from all movies that might offend; rather it singles out films containing nudity, presumably because the lawmakers considered them especially offensive to passersby.

This Court has considered analogous issues—pitting the First Amendment rights of speakers against the privacy rights of those who may be unwilling viewers or auditors—in a variety of contexts.

Although each case ultimately must depend on its own specific facts, some general principles have emerged. A State or municipality may protect individual privacy by enacting reasonable time, place, and manner regulations applicable to all speech irrespective of content. See *Kovacs v. Cooper, Cox v. Louisiana*

(1965); *Adderley v. Florida* (1966).

But when the government, acting as censor, undertakes selectively to shield the public from some kinds of speech on the ground that they are more offensive than others, the First Amendment strictly limits its power. Such selective restrictions have been upheld only when the speaker intrudes on the privacy of the home, see *Rowan v. Post Office Dept.* (1970), or the degree of captivity makes it impractical for the unwilling viewer or auditor to avoid exposure.

. . . .discrimination cannot be justified as a means of preventing significant intrusions on privacy. The ordinance seeks only to keep these films from being seen from public streets and places where the offended viewer readily can avert his eyes. In short, the screen of a drive-in theater is not "so obtrusive as to make it impossible for an unwilling individual to avoid exposure to it." *Redrup v. New York* (1967). Thus, we conclude that the limited privacy interest of persons on the public streets cannot justify this censorship of otherwise protected speech on the basis of its content.

Appellee also attempts to support the ordinance as an exercise of the city's undoubted police power to protect children. Appellee maintains that even though it cannot prohibit the display of films containing nudity to adults, the present ordinance is a reasonable means of protecting minors from this type of visual influence.

In this case, assuming the ordinance is aimed at prohibiting youths from viewing the films, the restriction is broader than permissible. The ordinance is not directed against sexually explicit nudity, nor is it otherwise limited. Rather, it sweepingly forbids display of all films containing uncovered buttocks or breasts, irrespective of context or pervasiveness. Thus it would bar a film containing a picture of a baby's buttocks, the nude body of a war victim, or scenes from a culture in which nudity is indigenous. The ordinance also might prohibit newsreel scenes of the opening of an art exhibit as well as shots of bathers on a beach. Clearly all nudity cannot be deemed obscene even as to minors. Nor can such a broad restriction be justified by any other governmental interest pertaining to minors. Speech that is neither obscene as to youths nor subject to some other legitimate proscription cannot be suppressed solely to protect the young from ideas or images that a legislative body thinks unsuitable for them. In most circumstances, the values protected by the First Amendment are no less applicable when government seeks to control the flow of information to minors. *West Virginia Bd. of Ed. v. Barnette* (1943). Thus, if Jacksonville's ordinance is intended to regulate expression accessible to minors it is overbroad in its proscription. . . .

In concluding that this ordinance is invalid we do not deprecate the legitimate interests asserted by the city of Jacksonville. We hold only that the present ordinance does not satisfy the rigorous constitutional standards that apply when government attempts to regulate expression. Where First Amendment freedoms are at stake we have repeatedly emphasized that precision of drafting and clarity of purpose are essential. These prerequisites are absent here.

With whom MR. JUSTICE REHNQUIST joins, dissenting.

. . . . disregard of the admonition that "the nature of the forum and the conflicting interests involved have remained important in determining the degree of protection afforded by the [First] Amendment to the speech in question."

. . . .this case illustrates, for me, the inadequacy of the Court's rigidly simplistic approach. In the first place, the conclusion that only a limited interest of persons on the public streets is at stake here can be supported only if one completely ignores the unique visual medium to which the Jacksonville ordinance is directed. Whatever validity the notion that passersby may protect their sensibilities by averting their eyes may have when applied to words printed on an individual's jacket, see *Cohen v. California* (1971), or a flag hung from a second-floor apartment window, see *Spence v. Washington* (1974), it distorts

reality to apply that notion to the outsize screen of a drive-in movie theater. Such screens are invariably huge; indeed, photographs included in the record of this case show that the screen of petitioner's theater dominated the view from public places including nearby residences and adjacent highways. Moreover, when films are projected on such screens the combination of color and animation against a necessarily dark background is designed to, and results in holding the attention of all. . . .

So here, the screen of a drive-in movie theater is a unique type of eye-catching display that can be highly intrusive and distracting. Public authorities have a legitimate interest in regulating such displays under the police power; for example, even though traffic safety may not have been the only target of the ordinance in issue here, I think it not unreasonable for lawmakers to believe that public nudity on a giant screen, visible at night to hundreds of drivers of automobiles, may have a tendency to divert attention from their task and cause accidents.

No more defensible is the Court's conclusion that Jacksonville's ordinance is defective because it regulates only nudity. The significance of this fact is explained only in a footnote: "Scenes of nudity in a movie, like pictures of nude persons in a book, must be considered as a part of the whole work. . . . In this respect such nudity is distinguishable from the kind of public nudity traditionally subject to indecent-exposure laws."

Both the analogy and the distinction are flawed. Unlike persons reading books, passersby cannot consider fragments of drive-in movies as a part of the "whole work" for the simple reason that they *see* but do not *hear* the performance; nor do drivers and passengers on nearby highways see the whole of the visual display. The communicative value of such fleeting exposure falls somewhere in the range of slight to nonexistent. Moreover, those persons who legitimately desire to consider the "work as a whole" are not foreclosed from doing so. The record shows that the film from which appellant's prosecution arose was exhibited in several indoor theaters in the Jacksonville area. And the owner of a drive-in movie theater is not prevented from exhibiting nonobscene films involving nudity so long as he effectively shields the screen from public view. Thus, regardless of whether the ordinance involved here can be loosely described as regulating the content of a certain type of display it is not a restriction.

. . . . assuming *arguendo* that there could be a play performed in a theater by nude actors involving genuine communication of ideas, the same conduct in a public park or street could be prosecuted under an ordinance prohibiting indecent exposure. This is so because the police power has long been interpreted to authorize the regulation of nudity in areas to which all members of the public have access, regardless of any incidental effect upon communication. A nudist colony, for example, cannot lawfully set up shop in Central Park or Lafayette Park, places established for the public generally. *Paris Adult Theatre I v. Slaton,* (1973); *Roth v. United States* (1957). Whether such regulation is justified as necessary to protect public mores or simply to insure the undistracted enjoyment of open areas by the greatest number of people—or for traffic safety, its rationale applies *a fortiori* to giant displays which through technology are capable of revealing and emphasizing the most intimate details of humans. In sum, the Jacksonville ordinance involved in this case, although no model of draftsmanship, is narrowly drawn to regulate only certain unique public exhibitions of nudity; it would be absurd to suggest that it operates to suppress expression of *ideas. By* conveniently ignoring these facts and deciding the case on the basis of absolutes the Court adds nothing to First Amendment analysis and sacrificial legitimate state interests would affirm the judgment of the Florida Court of Appeals.

12

PROTECTION OF ECONOMIC AND PROPERTY RIGHTS

This chapter deals with the clash between First Amendment interests and
1) the desire of business persons to control the uses of commercial property, and
2) the perceived need for compulsory unionism in order to secure the economic
welfare of labor. The first of these is a part of the more general "right to property"
historically recognized in the United States. The second is a more recent
development, officially recognized by the national government only in the 1930's.[1]

The most drastic form of compulsory unionism is the "closed shop," in which
one must be a union member to be hired. Expressly legalized in the Wagner Act of
1935, the "closed shop" was prohibited with the passage, in 1947, of the Taft-
Hartley Act. Taft-Hartley, like the Railway Act of 1951, permitted the "union
shop," under which an employee was required to join a union after employment. It
was this arrangement that gave rise to the initial First Amendment challenges to
compulsory unionism, dealt with by the Court through statutory rather than
constitutional construction.

In Railway Employees Department v. Hanson (1956), the Court, *per*
Douglas, upheld a challenge to the "union shop" provision of the Railway Labor
Act, holding that the only condition of membership authorized by the act was the
payment of "dues, fees, and assessments" related to "the work of the union in the
realm of collective bargaining." In Machinists v. Street (1960), the Court construed
the Act to prohibit the use of moneys collected from dissidents for union activity
"not germane" to collective bargaining. In Ellis v. Railway Clerks (1984) the Court
construed the same law to allow the charging of dissidents for their part in financing

national union conventions and local union social activities, but not for general organizing efforts and non-contract related litigation. In all cases, the attendant infringement on First Amendment rights was held justified by the interest in labor peace and in preventing the problem of "free riders."

The decisions in the above cases have been adopted by the Court as reflecting constitutional requirements on the issue.[2] It is, therefore, appropriate to note that the approval of the "union shop" is arguably out of line with relevant First Amendment jurisprudence. It was proper for the Court to conclude that contributions by union dissidents are justifiable, lest "free riders" benefit from union activity without sharing the cost. But the Court has equated, in terms of impact on First Amendment rights, the "union" and the "agency" shop. ("Agency shop" agreements are those in which the dissident is required to pay fees, but not to join the union.) Such an equation seems unjustified, given the general rule that burdens must be "carefully tailored" and impinge no further than necessary on First Amendment rights. While these conditions are met by the agency shop, the union shop is a different matter. For, under the latter, the dissident must be a *member* of an organization to which he objects. To require such *membership* is to force the dissident to lend his name to objectionable activities. The number of members is, after all, a crucial component of union strength, one which can be used to further any union purpose.

Perhaps because of this, it has been the "agency shop" which has been involved in litigation about compulsory processes in *public employee* unionism. The seminal case is Abood v. Detroit Board of Education, decided in 1977, and excerpted in this chapter. In that case the Court majority, *per* Stewart, held agency shop provisions valid for such employees, but also determined that petitioners were entitled to relief on proof that some monies they were forced to pay were used for activities unrelated to collective bargaining. Justice Powell, for himself and Justice Blackmun, concurred only in the judgment. Majority and concurring opinions diverged chiefly in their perception of the difference between *public* and *private* sector unionism. As the opinions demonstrate, such differences have consequences, particularly with respect to the test which should be applied in determining whether union expenditures are "related to collective bargaining."

The Court has dealt with public employee unionism in two more recent cases. In Chicago Teachers Union v. Hudson (1986), a unanimous Court held a union-adopted procedure for dealing with dissidents and their contributions constitutionally inadequate. Said Justice Stevens:

> ... the constitutional requirements for the Union's collection of agency fees include an adequate explanation of the basis for the fee, a reasonable prompt opportunity to challenge the amount of the fee before an impartial decision-maker, and an escrow for the amounts reasonably in dispute while such challenges are pending.

In Lehnert v. Ferris Faculty Association, decided in 1991, the Court further defined the kinds of union activities "germane to collective bargaining," and thus proper subjects for dissident contributions. Approved were national union "program expenditures" directed for states other than that in which the objecting faculty members were located; information services relevant to the teaching profession and education generally; and participation in state and national meetings at which "bargaining strategies and representational policies" are determined. Held "not germane" and involving additional infringement of petitioner's First Amendment rights, were lobbying, electoral, and other union political activities outside the context of contract ratification and implementation; programs to secure funds for public education in general; and litigation not concerning petitioner's bargaining unit.

Perhaps most surprisingly, the Lehnert Court held that dissenters could be charged for expenses "incident to preparation for a strike which all concede would have been illegal under Michigan law. ..." Had the Faculty Association actually engaged in such a strike, said Justice Blackmun "the union clearly could not have charged the expenses incident to that strike to petitioners." But, in the absence of a state law prohibiting strike preparation, "these expenses are substantively indistinguishable from those appurtenant to collective-bargaining negotiations" in so far as they "aid in . . . negotiations and enure to the direct benefit of the dissenter's unit."[3]

Also arising out of unionization is the question of the rights of dissident employees to communicate views different than that of the union. In Madison Joint School District v. Wisconsin Employee Relations Commission (1976) the Court held that nonunion teachers could not be prevented from speaking on issues involved in pending labor negotiations at meetings opened to the public. But, in Minnesota State Board for Community Colleges v. Knight (1984), the Court upheld the provision of a collective bargaining agreement which forbade such dissidents from meeting with the relevant management unit to discuss such matters.

A closer question is presented by the issue of whether a collective bargaining agreement can lawfully prevent a rival union from using the same channels of communication to employees, as is authorized for use by the bargaining union. This was the issue in Perry Educator's Association v. Perry Local Educator's Association (1983), in which the specific "channel of communication" involved was the teachers' mailboxes. PEA, having won an election as exclusive bargaining representative, concluded an agreement with the school district that gave it access to the mailboxes, and to the interschool mail delivery system. The agreement stipulated that no other "school employee organizations" could use the mail system, and it was this provision which was challenged by PLEA.

The Supreme Court, in a five to four decision, reversed a Court of Appeals holding that opening of the mail system to one union made it a "public forum" and that, therefore, other entities must have access to its use. Justice White's majority opinion concluded that the mail system was a private rather than a public forum, and thus that the granting of exclusive access to the exclusive bargaining agent did not violate the Fourth Amendment. That opinion, and Justice Brennan's dissent, is excerpted herein.

In Railway Employees Department v. Hanson, Justice Douglas' majority opinion had asserted that "On the present record, there is no more an infringement or impairment of First Amendment rights than there would be in the case of a lawyer who by state law is required to be a member of an integrated bar." (An "integrated bar," common to most states, requires as a condition of admission to practice that all lawyers must belong to the state Bar Association.) Justice Douglas' words, though *dicta*, thus implied that "union fee" provisions would be applicable to entities other than labor unions. In Lathrop v. Donohue (1961), the Court upheld such a requirement against charges that it violated the First Amendment rights of dissenting lawyers. The state's interest in regulation of the legal profession, and the benefits of Bar Association membership justified, said the Court, compulsory membership and fee payment.

In Keller v. State Bar of California (1990), the Court had before it the question of whether Bar Associations could use mandatory dues to address public policy questions, and drew the lines as to permissible and forbidden uses in much the same way as it has done in the labor cases. The lines between association activities which lawyers could and could not be required to finance might, said the Chief Justice for a unanimous Court, not always be easy to discern. But:

> the extreme ends of the spectrum are clear: Compulsory dues may not be expended to endorse or advance a gun control or nuclear weapons freeze initiative; at the other end of the spectrum, petitioners have no valid constitutional objection to their compulsory dues being spent for activities connected with disciplining members of the bar or proposing ethical codes for the profession.

In Keller, the Court once again avoided the ultimate question of "free association" and compulsory membership. For petitioner also argued that the First Amendment prohibited compulsion to "associate with an organization that engages in political or ideological activities beyond those for which mandatory financial support is justified . . ." The fact that the state courts had not addressed the claim allowed the Supreme Court to "decline to do so in the first instance." But the issue, despite the Court's refusal to distinguish between "agency" and "union" shops, seems likely to return.

Particularly in view of its equation of the two types of "shops," the Court's record on the conflict between the organizational rights of labor and the First Amendment can be said to reflect a consistent solicitude for unionism. The same consistency has not been present in its holdings on the second "right of property" issue discussed in this chapter. Decisions on the right of the owners of business property to exclude others wishing to "communicate" from commercial premises changed radically between 1968 and 1976. First opting for an expansive view of the rights of the would be "communicators," the Court then retreated from, and finally abandoned that position.

The story of the conflict begins, however, with a much earlier case, the 1946 decision in Marsh v. Alabama. Marsh involved an attempt by a member of the Jehovah's Witnesses to distribute religious literature in a "company town." "Company towns" are an anachronism today, but were common in the late 19th and early 20th centuries. They were in all respects the functional equivalents of ordinary municipalities, but were wholly owned by the economic enterprise involved. In the case of Chickasaw, Alabama, the whole town, including its streets, residential areas, and the central business district, were owned by the Gulf Shipbuilding Corporation. In such circumstances, said Justice Black for the Marsh majority, the town exercised the same control as would the state, and thus it could not, any more than a conventional municipality, interfere with rights protected by the First Amendment.

The Marsh decision lay dormant for years, a little oddity in the law which depended on the convergence of a set of circumstances not likely to be repeated, "company towns" being a declining phenomena and those which continued to exist apparently having gotten the message. Then came the rise of the suburbs, and with them the shopping center and mall, the arrival of which once again blurred the distinction between "public" and "private" property.

The issue created by the rise of shopping centers was first faced by the Court in Amalgamated Food Employees v. Logan Valley Plaza (1968). In that case employees of a grocery chain were involved in a labor dispute with their employer, which operated one of two stores in Logan Valley Plaza. Wishing to take their case to customers of the grocery, the employees stationed pickets at the entrance to the store and in its "pick up" area. The Plaza's owners, together with the supermarket, objected on the grounds that the property was privately owned and could not be invaded without their permission.

By a six to three majority the Court found for the union, with Justice Marshall's majority opinion finding the situation here analogous to that in Marsh, the shopping center being the "functional equivalent" of the Chickasaw business district. In addition, noted Marshall, in what was to be for a time the crucial part of the holding, the message the employees wanted to convey to the public was intimately related to the function of the place in which they sought to picket. And, given the nature of the dispute, it could not be presented nearly so effectively in any place other than the environs of the market.

Justice Black, author of the Marsh opinion, dissented. He could see no similarity between the center at issue here and a "company town." In addition, he viewed as "contrary to common sense" the majority's position that, because the stores invited the public to come to shop, that invitation extended to those who came for other purposes.

Four years later the Court had before it Lloyd Corporation v. Tanner, a case which differed from Logan Valley in three respects. The property at issue was a self-enclosed shopping mall surrounded by a parking area bisected in places by public streets. As in most such malls, the owners had invited a number of noncommercial enterprises, including various social service organizations and the presidential candidates of the two major parties, to use mall facilities to deliver their messages. This opening of the mall to noncommercial activity was intended to create traffic in the mall and "build up good will." But the company had consistently refused to allow any distribution of literature or other kind of proselytizing in the mall. Finally, the respondents in Lloyd, unlike those in Logan Valley, were promulgating a message unrelated to the commercial purpose of the mall.

For the majority it was this latter fact that served to distinguish the previous case. Those who wished to spread their message of protest against the Vietnam war, said Justice Powell, could do so equally well in any public place. Indeed, they could have passed out leaflets to mall visitors as they drove in from the public streets. These things being so, Lloyd was distinguishable from Logan Valley, and the mall had not violated First Amendment rights.

Justice Powell's opinion is vulnerable on several counts. First, it is not wholly true that the protesters' message could have been conveyed equally well from the streets adjacent to the mall, for such activity would have exposed them to at least some danger from fast moving traffic. In addition, the "public invitation" issued by the mall owners in this case was much more open ended than that given by the stores in Logan Valley. Although the motives of the mall were commercial, many of those invited had presented noncommercial messages.

Given these considerations, Justice Marshall's dissent was probably correct in asserting that Logan Valley and Lloyd were irreconcilable. That, at any rate, was the conclusion reached by the Court in Hudgens v. National Labor Relations Board (1976), reproduced herein, in which a seven to two majority expressly overruled Logan Valley.

The facts in Hudgens made it a perfect vehicle for reconsideration of Logan Valley and Lloyd. The area involved was a shopping mall, as in Lloyd, and presumably operated in the way of most malls, inviting a variety of groups to use its common areas. But the entity that wished to convey its message was, as in Logan Valley, a labor union, specifically one representing the warehouse employees of Butler's, an Atlanta retail chain which leased space in the mall. When members of the union sought to picket at the Butler store they were asked to leave. Complying, they filed an unfair labor practice charge against Hudgens and with the

NLRB. The Labor Board found for the union and Hudgens appealed.

Justice Stewart's majority opinion first noted that the "constitutional guarantee of free speech is a guarantee only against government" and that, while statutory law might sometimes extend the guarantee against a private entity, "no such protection . . . is provided by the Constitution itself." The issue of whether the shopping mall was "public" or "private" was thus squarely presented and, said Stewart, " . . . we make clear now . . . that the rationale of Logan Valley did not survive the Court's decision in the Lloyd case." Rather, "the ultimate holding in Lloyd amounted to a total rejection of the holding in Logan Valley." Concluding that "under the present state of the law the constitutional guarantee of free expression has no part to play in a case such as this," the Court remanded the case for decision by the NLRB on the basis of statutory construction.

One is tempted to say that the Court's view of the First Amendment as having "no part to play" in cases like Logan Valley, Lloyd, and Hudgens, appears unwarranted. For, when the message sought to be conveyed, as in a labor dispute, directly relates to economic activity taking place in the "private arena" the location in question may be the only place in which those seeking to convey their message can do so effectively.[4] But the ultimate justification for the Hudgens result, and for the retreat from Logan Valley, is to be found in Justice Stewart's observation that the "constitutional guarantee of free speech is a guarantee only against government." A shopping center is not a "company town," and thus it remains essentially private property. That being so, the restrictions it places on communicative activity are not "state action," and thus are not covered by the Fourth Amendment.[5]

Somewhat the same argument might be made with respect to restrictions stemming from labor union agreements in the private sector, although such agreements, and such restrictions, are authorized by government. But the "public sector" union cases are a different matter. For here both the law and the agreement proceed from state action. In this situation the "agency," rather than the "union" shop, would seem the only system consistent with constitutional norms.

---

[1]There are, of course, many circumstances in which "economic rights" may conflict with the desire for freedom of communication. One case which raised the issue in a different context was Zacchini v. Scripps-Howard Publishing Co. (1977), in which the Court held that the First Amendment did

continued on next page

not give a television station the right to broadcast pictures of the entire "act" (being shot out of a cannon) on which petitioner depended for his livehihood.

For a decision upholding the right of Congress to grant exclusive use of the word "Olympic" and of the Olympic logo to the United States Olympic Committee, as against the free speech claim of an organization which wished to sponsor a "gay Olympics," see San Francisco Arts and Athletes v. United States Olympic Committee (1987)

[2]See the discussion of this matter in Justice Stewart's opinion for the Court in Abood v. Detroit Board of Education.

[3]The Court's logic on this point appears impeccable, but that does not wholly justify a practice which forces those who wish to have no part in an illegal activity to assist in paying for its preparation.

[4]Perhaps reflecting such considerations, the California Supreme Court has held its Constitution's "free communications" provisions applicable to shopping mall activity. The U.S. Supreme Court, in Pruneyard Shopping Center v. Robbins (1980), held that such a result was not foreclosed by Hudgens.

[5]In its most recent decision on communicative activity in shopping malls, Lechmere, Inc.v. National Labor Relations Board (1992), the Court held, on the basis of statutory construction, that a mall could prevent union organizers not themselves employed at the shopping center (though not those who were so employed) from seeking to present their message in the center and to its non-union employees. Neither the majority nor the dissenting opinion even mentioned the constitutional issue.

ABOOD ET AL. V. DETROIT BOARD OF EDUCATION ET AL.

431 U.S. 209 (1977)

MR. JUSTICE STEWART delivered the opinion of the Court.

The State of Michigan has enacted legislation authorizing a system for union representation of local governmental employees. A union and a local government employer are specifically permitted to agree to an "agency shop" arrangement, whereby every employee represented by a union—even though not a union member—must pay to the union, as a condition of employment, a service fee equal in amount to union dues. The issue before us is whether this arrangement violates the constitutional rights of government employees who object to public-sector unions as such or to various union activities financed by the compulsory service fees. . . .

Consideration of the question whether all agency-shop provision in a collective-bargaining agreement covering governmental employees is, as such, constitutionally valid must begin with two cases in this Court that on their face go far toward resolving the issue. The cases are *Railway Employees' Dept. v. Hanson*, and *Machinists v. Street*.

The designation of a union as exclusive representative carries with it great responsibilities. The tasks of negotiating and administering a collective-bargaining agreement and representing the interests of employees in settling disputes and processing grievances are continuing and difficult ones. They often entail expenditure of much time and money. The services of lawyers, expert negotiators, economists, and a research staff, as well as general administrative personnel, may be required. Moreover, in carrying out these duties, the union is obliged "fairly and equitably to represent all employees . . . union and nonunion," within the relevant unit. . . .

The same Important government interests recognized in the Hanson and Street cases presumptively support the impingement upon associational freedom created by the agency shop here at issue. Thus, insofar as the service charge is used to finance expenditures by the Union for the purposes of collective bargaining, contract administration, and grievance adjustment, those two decisions of this Court appear to require validation of the agency-shop agreement before us.

. . . . the appellants say that in the public sector collective bargaining itself is inherently "political," and that to require them to give financial support to it is to require the "ideological conformity" that the Court expressly found absent in the Hanson case.

The distinctive nature of public-sector bargaining has led to widespread discussion about the extent to which the law governing labor relations in the private sector provides an appropriate model. To take but one example, there has been considerable debate about the desirability of prohibiting public employee unions from striking, a step that the State of Michigan itself has taken. But although Michigan has not adopted the federal model of labor relations in every respect, it has determined that labor stability will be served by a system of exclusive representation and the permissive use of an agency shop in public employment. As already stated, there can be no principled basis for according that decision less weight in the constitutional balance than was given in Hanson to the congressional judgment reflected in the Railway Labor Act. The only remaining constitutional inquiry evoked by the appellants' argument therefore is whether a public employee has a weightier First Amendment interest than a private employee in not being compelled to contribute to the costs of exclusive union representation. We think he does not.

The very real differences between exclusive-agent collective bargaining in the public and private sectors are not such as to work any greater infringement upon the First Amendment interests of public employee who believes that a union representing him is urging a course that is unwise as a matter of public policy is not barred from expressing his viewpoint. Besides voting in accordance with his convictions every public employer is largely free to express his views, in public or private, orally or in writing. With some exceptions not pertinent here, public employees are free to participate in the full range of political activities open to other citizens. Indeed, just this Term we have held that the First and Fourteenth Amendments protect the right of a public school teacher to oppose at a public school board meeting, a position advanced by the teachers' union. *Madison School Dist. v. Wisconsin Employment Relations Comm'n*. In so ruling we recognized that the principle of exclusivity cannot constitutionally be used to muzzle a public employee who like any other citizen, might wish to express his view about governmental decisions concerning labor relations. . .

There can be no quarrel with the truism that because public employee unions attempt to influence governmental policymaking, their activities—and the views of members who disagree with them—may he properly termed political. But that characterization does not raise the ideas and belief of public employees onto a higher plane than the ideas and beliefs of private employees. It is no doubt true that a central purpose of the First Amendment "'was to protect the free discussion of governmental affairs.'". . .

But our cases have never suggested that expression about philosophical, social, artistic, economic, literary, or ethical matters—to take a nonexhaustive list of labels—is not entitled to full First Amendment protection. Union members in both the public and private sectors may find that a variety of union activities conflict with their beliefs. . .

The differences between public- and private-sector collective bargaining simply do not translate into differences in First Amendment rights. . . .

Because the Michigan Court of Appeals ruled that state law "sanctions the use of nonunion members' fees for purposes other than collective bargaining," and because the complaints allege that such expenditures were made, this case presents constitutional issues not decided in *Hanson* or *Street*. . . .

The appellants argue . . . . that they may constitutionally prevent the Union's spending a part of their required service fees to contribute to political candidates and to express political views unrelated to its duties as exclusive bargaining representative. We have concluded that this argument is a meritorious one.

One of the principles underlying the Court's decision in *Buckley v. Valeo*, was that contributing to an organization for the purpose of spreading a political message is protected by the First Amendment. Because "[m]aking a contribution . . . enables like-minded persons to pool their resources in furtherance of common political goals," the Court reasoned that limitations upon the freedom to contribute "implicate fundamental First Amendment interests."

The fact that the appellants are compelled to make, rather than prohibited from making, contributions for political purposes works no less an infringement of their constitutional rights. For at the heart of the First Amendment is the notion that an individual should be free to believe as he will, and that in a free society one's beliefs should be shaped by his mind and his conscience rather than coerced by the State. . . .

These principles prohibit a State from compelling any individual to affirm his belief in God, *Torcaso v. Watkins* . . . or to associate with a political party as a condition of retaining public employment. They are no less applicable to the case at bar, and they thus prohibit the appellees from requiring any of the appellants to contribute to the support of an ideological cause he may oppose as a condition of holding a job as a public school teacher.

We do not hold that a union cannot constitutionally spend funds for the expression of political views, on behalf of political candidates, or toward the advancement of other ideological causes not germane to its duties as collective-bargaining representative. Rather, the Constitution requires only that such expenditures be financed from charges, dues, or assessments paid by employees who do not object to advancing those ideas and who are not coerced into doing so against their will by the threat of loss of governmental employment.

There will, of course, be difficult problems in drawing lines between collective-bargaining activities, for which contributions may be compelled, and ideological activities unrelated to collective bargaining, for which such compulsion is prohibited. . . .

We have no occasion in this case, however, to try to define such a dividing line. . . .

All that we decide is that the general allegations in the complaints, if proved, establish a cause of action under the First and Fourteenth Amendments.

In determining what remedy will be appropriate if the appellants prove their allegations, the objective must be to devise a way of preventing compulsory subsidization of ideological activity by employees who object thereto without restricting the Union's ability to require every employee to contribute to the cost of collective-bargaining activities. This task is simplified by the guidance to be had from prior decisions. The Court in *Allen* described a "practical decree" that could properly be entered, providing for (1) the refund of a portion of the exacted funds in the proportion that union political expenditures bear to total union expenditures, and (2) the reduction of future exactions by the same proportion. Recognizing the difficulties posed by judicial administration of such a remedy, the Court also suggested that it would be highly desirable for unions to adopt a "voluntary plan by which dissenters would be afforded an internal union remedy." This last suggestion is particularly relevant to the case at bar, for the Union has adopted such a plan since the commencement of this litigation.

In holding that as a prerequisite to any relief each appellant must indicate to the Union the specific expenditures to which he objects, the Court of Appeals ignored the clear holding of *Allen*. As in *Allen*, the employees here indicated in their pleadings that they opposed ideological expenditures of any sort that are unrelated to collective bargaining. To require greater specificity would confront an individual employee with the dilemma of relinquishing either his right to withhold his support of ideological causes to which he objects or his freedom to maintain his own beliefs without public disclosure. It would also place on each employee the considerable burden of monitoring all of the numerous and shifting expenditures made by the Union that are unrelated to its duties as exclusive bargaining representative. . . .

MR. JUSTICE REHNQUIST, concurring . . . .

MR. JUSTICE STEVENS, concurring.

By joining the opinion of the Court, including its discussion of possible remedies I do not imply—nor do I understand the Court to imply—that the remedies described in Machinists v. Street and *Railway Clerks v. Allen* would necessarily be adequate in this case or in any other case. More specifically, the Court's opinion does not foreclose the argument that the Union should not be permitted to exact a service fee from nonmembers without first establishing a procedure which will avoid the risk that their funds will be used, even temporarily, to finance ideological activities unrelated to collective bargaining. . . .

MR. JUSTICE POWELL, with whom THE CHIEF JUSTICE and MR. JUSTICE BLACKMUN join, concurring in the judgment. . . .

The Court's extensive reliance on *Hanson* and *Street* requires it to rule that there is no constitutional distinction between what the government can require of its own employees and what it can permit private employers to do. To me the distinction is fundamental. Under the First Amendment the government may authorize private parties to enter into voluntary agreements whose terms it could not adopt as its own. . . .

The State in this case has not merely authorized agency shop agreements between willing parties; it has negotiated and adopted such an agreement itself. Acting through the *Detroit Board of Education*, the State has undertaken to compel employees to pay full fees equal in amount to dues to a Union as a condition of employment. Accordingly, the Board's collective-bargaining agreement, like any other enactment of state law is fully subject to the constraints that the Constitution imposes on coercive governmental regulation. . . .

The initial question is whether a requirement of a school board that all of its employees contribute to a teachers union as a condition of employment impinges upon the First Amendment interests of those who refuse to support the union whether because they disapprove of unionization of public employees or because they object to certain union activities or positions. The Court answers this question in the affirmative.

. . . . I agree with the Court as far as it goes, but I would make it more explicit that compelling a government employee to give financial support to a union in the public sector—regardless of the uses to which the union puts the contribution—impinges seriously upon interests in free speech and association protected by the First Amendment. . . .

The ultimate objective of a union in the public sector, like that of a political party, is to influence public decisionmaking in accordance with the views and perceived interests of its membership. Whether a teachers' union is concerned with salaries and fringe benefits, teacher qualifications and in-service training pupil-teacher ratios, length of the school day, student discipline, or the content of the high school curriculum, its objective is to bring school board policy and decisions into harmony with its own views. Similarly, to the extent that school board expenditures and policy are guided by decisions made by the municipal, State, and Federal Governments, the union's objective is to obtain favorable decisions—and to place persons in positions of power who will be receptive to the union's viewpoint. In these respects, the public-sector union is indistinguishable from the traditional political party in this country.

What distinguishes the public-sector union from the political party—and the distinction is a limited one—is that most of its members are employees who share similar economic interests and who may have a common professorial perspective on some issues of public policy. Public school teachers for example, have a common interest in fair teachers' salaries and reasonable pupil-teacher ratios. This suggests the possibility of a limited range of probable agreement among the class of individuals that a public-sector union is organized to represent. But I am unable to see why the likelihood of an area of consensus in the group should remove the protection of the First Amendment for the disagreements that inevitably will occur. Certainly, if individual teachers are ideologically opposed to public-sector unionism itself as are the appellants in this case, one would think that compelling them to affiliate with the union by contributing to it infringes their First Amendment rights to the same degree as compelling them to contribute to a political party. Under the First Amendment, the protection of speech does not turn on the likelihood or frequency of its occurrence.

Nor is there any basis here for distinguishing "collective bargaining activities" from "political activities" so far as the interests protected by the First Amendment are concerned. Collective bargaining in the public sector is "political" in any meaningful sense of the word. This is most obvious when public-sector bargaining extends—as it may in Michigan—to such matters of public policy as the educational philosophy that will inform the high school curriculum. But it is also true when public-sector bargaining focuses on such "bread and butter" issues as wages, hours vacations, and pensions. Decisions On such issues will have a direct impact on the level of public services, priorities within state and municipal budgets, creation of bonded indebtedness, and tax rates. The cost of public education is normally the largest element of a county or municipal budget. Decisions reached through collective bargaining in the schools will affect not only the teachers and the quality of education, but also the taxpayers and the beneficiaries of other important public services. Under our democratic system of government, decisions on these critical issues of public policy have been entrusted to elected officials who ultimately are responsible to the voters.

Disassociation with a public-sector union and the expression of disagreement with its positions and objectives therefore lie at "the core of those activities protected by the First Amendment." *Elrod v. Burns.*

As the Court points out, the interests advanced for the compulsory agency shop that the Detroit Board of Education has entered into are much the same as those advanced for federal legislation permitting voluntary agency-shop agreements in the private sector. The agency shop is said to be a necessary adjunct to the principle of exclusive union representation; it is said to reduce the risk that nonunion employees in become "free riders" by fairly distributing the costs of exclusive representation; and it is said to promote the cause of labor peace in the public sector. While these interests may well justify encouraging agency-shop arrangements in the private sector, there is far less reason to believe they justify the intrusion upon First Amendment rights that results from compelled support for a union as a condition of government employment. . . .

The Court points out that the minority employee is not barred by the exclusivity principle from expressing his viewpoint. In a limited sense, this may be true. The minority employee is excluded in theory only from engaging in a meaningful dialogue with his employer on the subjects of collective bargaining, a dialogue that is reserved to the union. It is possible that paramount governmental interests may be found—at least with respect to certain narrowly defined subjects of bargaining—that would support this restriction on First Amendment interests. But "the burden is On the government to show the existence of such an interest. . . ."

The same may be said of the asserted interests in eliminating the "free rider" effect and in preserving labor peace. It may be that the Board of Education is in a position to demonstrate that these interests are of paramount importance and that requiring public employees to pay certain union fees and dues as a condition of employment is necessary to serve those interests under an exclusive bargaining scheme. On the present record there is no assurance whatever that this is the case.

Before today it had been well established that when state law intrudes upon protected speech, the State itself must shoulder the burden of proving that its action is justified by overriding state interests. The Court, for the first time in a First Amendment case simply reverses this principle.

PERRY EDUCATION ASSOCIATION V. PERRY LOCAL EDUCATORS' ASSOCIATION ET AL.

460 U.S. 37 (1983)

JUSTICE WHITE delivered the opinion of the Court.

Perry Education Association is the duly elected exclusive bargaining representative for the teachers of the Metropolitan School District of Perry Township, Ind. A collective bargaining agreement with the Board of Education provided that Perry Education Association, but no other union, would have access to the interschool mail system and teacher mailboxes in the Perry Township schools. The issue in this case is whether the denial of similar access to the Perry Local Educators' Association, a rival teacher group, violates the First and Fourteenth Amendments.

The Metropolitan School District of Perry Township, Ind., operates a public school system of 13 separate schools. Each school building contains a set of mailboxes for the teachers. interschool delivery by school employees permits messages to be delivered rapidly to teachers in the District. The primary function of this internal mail system is to transmit official messages among the teachers and between the teachers and the school administration. In addition, teachers use the system to send personal messages, and individual school building principals have allowed delivery of messages from various private organizations. . . .

PEA and the School District negotiated a labor contract in which the School Board gave PEA "access to teachers' mailboxes in which to insert

material" and the right to use the interschool mail delivery system to the extent that the School District incurred no extra expense by such use. The labor agreement noted that these access rights were being accorded to PEA "acting as the representative of the teachers" and went on to stipulate that these access rights shall not be granted to any other "school employee organization"—a term of art defined by Indiana law to mean "any organization which has school employees as members and one of whose primary purposes is representing school employees in dealing with their school employer. . . ."

The exclusive-access policy applies only to use of the mailboxes and school mail system. PLEA is not prevented from using other school facilities to communicate with teachers. PLEA may post notices on school bulletin boards; may hold meetings on school property after school hours; and may, with approval of the building principals, make announcements on the public address system. Of course, PLEA also may communicate with teachers by word of mouth, telephone, or the United States mail. Moreover. under Indiana law, the preferential access the bargaining agent may continue only while its status as exclusive representative is insulated from challenge. While a representation contest is in progress, unions must be afforded equal access to such communication facilities.

PLEA and two of its members filed this action against PEA and individual members of the Perry Township School Board. Plaintiffs contended that PEA's preferential access to the internal mail system violates the First Amendment and the Equal Protection Clause of the Fourteenth Amendment. . . .

There is no question that constitutional interests are implicated by denying PLEA use of the interschool mail system. "It can hardly be argued that either students or teachers shed their constitutional rights to freedom of speech or expression at the schoolhouse gate." *Tinker v. Des Moines School District* (1969), *Healy v. James* (1972). The First Amendment's guarantee of free speech applies to teacher's mailboxes as surely as it does elsewhere within the school, *Tinker v. Des Moines School Dist.*, and on sidewalks outside, *Chicago v. Mosley* (1972). But this is not to say that the First Amendment requires equivalent access to all parts of a school building in which some form of communicative activity occurs. "[N]owhere [have we] suggested that students, teachers, or anyone else has an absolute constitutional right to use all parts of a school building or its immediate environs for . . . unlimited expressive purposes." *Grayned v. City of Rockford* (1972). The existence of a right of access to public property and the standard by which limitations upon such a right must be evaluated differ depending on the character of the property at issue.

In places which by long tradition or by government fiat have been devoted to assembly and debate, the rights of the State to limit expressive activity are sharply circumscribed. At one end of the spectrum are streets and parks which "have immemorially been held in trust for the use of the public and, time out of mind, have been used for purposes of assembly, communicating thoughts between citizens, and discussing public questions." *Hague v. CIO* (1939). In these quintessential public forums, the government may not prohibit all communicative activity. For the State to enforce a content-based exclusion it must show that its regulation is necessary to serve a compelling state interest and

that it is narrowly drawn to achieve that end. *Carey v. Brown* (1980). The State may also enforce regulations of the time, place, and manner of expression which are content-neutral, are narrowly tailored to serve a significant government interest, and leave open ample alternative channels of communication. . . .

A second category consists of public property which the State has opened for use by the public as a place for expressive activity. The Constitution forbids a State to enforce certain exclusions from a forum generally open to the public even if it as not required to create the forum in the first place . . . Although a State is not required to indefinitely retain the open character of the facility, as long as it does so it is bound by the same standards as apply in a traditional public forum. Reasonable time, place, and manner regulations are permissible, and a content-based prohibition must be narrowly drawn to effectuate a compelling state interest. Public property which is not by tradition or designation a forum for public communication is governed by different standards. We have recognized that the "First Amendment does not guarantee access to property simply because it is owned or controlled by the government." *United States Postal Service v. Council of Greenburgh Civic Assns.* In addition to time, place, and manner regulations, the State may reserve the forum for its intended purposes, communicative or otherwise, as long as the regulation on speech is reasonable and not an effort to suppress expression merely because public officials oppose the speaker's view. As we have stated on several occasions, "[t]he State, no less than a private owner of property, has power to preserve the property under its control for the use to which it is lawfully dedicated. . . ."

The school mail facilities at issue here fall within this third category. The use of the internal school mail by groups not affiliated with the schools is no doubt a relevant consideration. If by policy or by practice the Perry School District has opened its mail system for indiscriminate use by the general public, then PLEA could justifiably argue a public forum has been created. This, however, is not the case. As the case comes before us, there is no indication in the record that the school mailboxes and interschool delivery system are open for use by the general public. Permission to use the system to communicate with teachers must be secured from the individual building principal. There is no court finding or evidence in the record which demonstrates that this permission has been granted as a matter of course to all who seek to distribute material. We can only conclude that the schools do allow some outside organizations such as the YMCA, Cub Scouts, and other civic and church organizations to use the facilities. This type of selective access does not transform government property into a public forum. . . .

Moreover, even if we assume that by granting access to the Cub Scouts, YMCA's, and parochial schools, the School District has created a "limited" public forum, the constitutional right of access would in any event extend only to other entities of similar character. While the school mail facilities thus might be a forum generally open for use by the Girl Scouts, the local boys' club, and other organizations that engage in activities of interest and educational relevance to students, they would not as a consequence be open to an organization such as PLEA, which is concerned with the terms and conditions of teacher employment. . . .

In the Court of Appeals' view, however, the access policy adopted by the Perry schools favors a particular viewpoint, that of PEA, on labor relations, and consequently must be strictly scrutinized regardless of whether a public forum is involved. There is however, no indication that the School Board intended to discourage one viewpoint and advance another. We believe it is more accurate to characterize the access policy as based on the status of the respective unions rather than their views. Implicit in the concept of the nonpublic forum is the right to make distinctions in access on the basis of subject matter and speaker identity. These distinctions may be impermissible in a public forum but are inherent and inescapable in the process of limiting a nonpublic forum to activities

compatible with the intended purpose of the property. The touchstone for evaluating these distinctions is whether they are reasonable in light of the purpose which the forum at issue serves.

The differential access provided PEA and PLEA is reasonable because it is wholly consistent with the District's legitimate interest in " "preserv[ing] the property . . . for the use to is lawful dedicated." United States Postal Service. Use of school mail facilities enables PEA to perform effectively its obligations as exclusive representative of all Perry Township teachers. Conversely, PLEA does not have any official responsibility in connection with the School District and need not be entitled to the same rights of access to school mailboxes. We observe that providing exclusive access to recognized bargaining representatives is a permissible labor practice in the public sector. We have previously noted that the "designation of a union as exclusive representative carries with it great responsibilities. The tasks of negotiating and administering a collective-bargaining agreement and representing the interests of employees in settling disputes and processing grievances are continuing and difficult ones." *Abood v. Detroit Bd. of Ed.* (1977). Moreover, exclusion of the rival union may reasonably be considered a means of insuring labor peace within the schools. The policy "serves to prevent the District's schools from becoming a battlefield for inter-union squabbles."

Finally, the reasonableness of the limitations on PLEA's access to the school mail system is also supported by the substantial alternative channels that remain open for union-teacher communication to take place. These means range from bulletin boards to meeting facilities to the United States mail. During election periods, PLEA is assured of equal access to all modes of communication. There is no showing here that PLEA's ability to communicate with teachers is seriously impinged by the restricted access to the internal mail system. The variety and type of alternative modes of access present here compare favorably with those in other nonpublic forum cases where we have upheld restrictions on access. . . .

JUSTICE BRENNAN, with whom JUSTICE MARSHALL, JUSTICE POWELL, and JUSTICE STEVENS join, dissenting.

The Court today holds that an incumbent teachers' union may negotiate a collective-bargaining agreement with a school board that grants the incumbent access to teachers' mailboxes and to the interschool mail system and denies such access to a rival union. Because the exclusive-access provision in the collective-bargaining agreement amounts to viewpoint discrimination that infringes the respondents' First Amendment rights and fails to advance any substantial state interest, I dissent. . . .

City of Madison Joint School District v. Wisconsin Employment Relations Comm'n, considered the question of whether a State may constitutionally require a board of education to prohibit teachers other than union representatives from speaking at public meetings about matters relating to pending collective-bargaining negotiations. The board had been found guilty of a prohibited labor practice for permitting a teacher to speak who opposed one of the proposals advanced by the union in contract negotiations. The board was ordered to cease and desist from permitting employees, other than union representatives, to appear and to speak at board meetings on matters subject to collective bargaining. We held this order invalid. During the course of our opinion we stated: "Whatever its duties as an employer, when the board sits in public meetings to conduct public business and hear the views of citizens, it may not be required to discriminate between speakers on the basis of their employment, or the content of their speech. . . .

There is another line of cases, closely related to those implicating the prohibition against viewpoint discrimination, that have addressed the First Amendment principle of subject matter, or content neutrality. Generally, the concept of content-neutrality prohibits the government from choosing the subjects that are appropriate for public discussion. The content-neutrality cases frequently refer to the prohibition against viewpoint discrimination and both concepts have their roots in the First Amendment's bar against censorship. But unlike the viewpoint-discrimination concept, which is used to strike down government restrictions on speech by particular speakers, the content-neutrality principle is invoked when the government has imposed restrictions on speech related to an entire subject area. The content-neutrality principle can be seen as an outgrowth of the core First Amendment prohibition against viewpoint discrimination.

Once the government permits discussion of certain subject matter, it may not impose restrictions that discriminate among viewpoints on those subjects whether a nonpublic forum is involved or not. This prohibition is implicit in the *Mosley* line of cases, in *Tinker v. Des Moines School District*, and in those cases in which we have approved content-based restrictions on access to government property that is not a public forum. We have never held that government may allow discussion of a subject and then discriminate among viewpoints on that particular topic, even if the government for certain reasons may entirely exclude discussion of the subject from the forum. In this context, the greater power does not include the lesser because for First Amendment purposes exercise of the lesser power is more threatening to core values. Viewpoint discrimination is censorship in its purest form and government regulation that discriminates among view-points threatens the continued vitality of "free speech."

Against this background, it is clear that the Court's approach to this case is flawed. By focusing on whether the interschool mail system is a public forum, the Court disregards the independent First Amendment protection afforded by the prohibition against viewpoint discrimination. This case does not involve a claim of an absolute right of access to the forum to discuss any subject whatever. If it did, public forum analysis might be relevant. This case involves a claim of equal access to discuss a subject that the

Board has approved for discussion in the forum. In essence, the respondents are not asserting a right of access at all; they are asserting a right to be free from discrimination. The critical inquiry, therefore, is whether the Board's grant of exclusive access to the petitioner amounts to prohibited viewpoint discrimination.

. . . . whether the school mail system is a public forum or not the Board is prohibited from discriminating among viewpoints on particular subjects. Moreover, whatever the right of public authorities to impose content-based restrictions on access to government property that is a nonpublic forum, once access is granted to one speaker to discuss a certain subject access may not be denied to another speaker based on his viewpoint. Regardless of the nature of the forum, the critical inquiry is whether the Board has engaged in prohibited viewpoint discrimination. . . .

Addressing the question of viewpoint discrimination directly, free of the Court's irrelevant public forum analysis, it is clear that the exclusive-access policy discriminates on the basis of viewpoint. The Court of Appeals found that "[t]he access policy adopted by the Perry schools, in form a speaker restriction, favor a particular viewpoint on labor relations in the Perry schools . . . : the teachers inevitably will receive from [the petitioner] self-laudatory descriptions of its activities on their behalf and will be denied the critical perspective offered by [the respondents]." This assessment of the effect of the policy is eminently reasonable. Moreover, certain other factors strongly suggest that the policy discriminates among viewpoints.

On a practical level, the only reason for the petitioner to seek an exclusive-access policy is to deny its rivals access to an effective channel of communication. No other group is explicitly denied access to the mail system. In fact, as the Court points out, many other groups have been granted access to the system. Apparently, access is denied to the respondents because of the likelihood of their expressing points of view different from the petitioner's on a range of subjects. The very argument the petitioner advances in support of the

policy, the need to preserve labor peace, also indicates that the access policy is not viewpoint-neutral.

In short, the exclusive-access policy discriminates against the respondents based on their viewpoint. The Board has agreed to amplify the speech of the petitioner, while repressing the speech of the respondents based on the respondents' point of view. This sort of discrimination amounts to censorship and infringes the First Amendment rights of the respondents. In this light, the policy can survive only if the petitioner can justify it. . . .

The petitioner attempts to justify the exclusive-access provision based on its status as the exclusive bargaining representative for the teachers and on the State's interest in efficient communication between collective-bargaining representatives and the members of the unit. The petitioner's status and the State's interest in efficient communication are important considerations. They are not sufficient, however, to sustain the exclusive-access policy. . . .

While the Board may have a legitimate interest in granting the petitioner access to the system, it has no legitimate interest in making that access exclusive by denying access to the respondents. As the Court of Appeals stated: "Without an independent reason why equal access for other labor groups and individual teachers is undesirable, the special duties of the incumbent o not justify opening the system to the incumbent alone. . ." In this case, for the reasons discussed below, there is no independent reason for denying access to the respondents.

The petitioner also argues, and the Court agrees, that the exclusive-access policy is justified by the State's interest in preserving labor peace. As the Court of Appeals found, there is no evidence on this record that granting access to the respondents would result in labor instability. In addition, there is no reason to assume that the respondents' messages would be any more likely to cause labor discord when received by members of the majority union than the petitioner's messages would when received by the respondents. Moreover, it is noteworthy that both the petitioner and the respondents had access to the mail system for some time prior to the representation election. There is no indication that this policy resulted in disruption of the school environment.

Although the State's interest in preserving labor peace in the schools in order to prevent disruption is unquestionably substantial, merely articulating the interest is not enough to sustain the exclusive-access policy in this case. There must be some showing that the asserted interest is advanced by the policy. In the absence of such a showing, the exclusive-access policy must fall. . . .

Because the grant to the petitioner of exclusive access to the internal school mail system amounts to viewpoint discrimination that infringes the respondents' First Amendment rights and because the petitioner has failed to show that the policy furthers any substantial state interest, the policy must be invalidated as violative of the First Amendment. . . .

HUDGENS V. NLRB

424 U.S 507 (1976)

MR. JUSTICE STEWART delivered the opinion of the Court.

The petitioner, Scott Hudgens, is the owner of the North DeKalb Shopping Center, located in suburban Atlanta, Ga. The center consists of a single large building with an enclosed mall. Surrounding the building is a parking area which can accommodate 2,640 automobiles. The shopping center houses 60 retail stores leased to various businesses. One of the lessees is the Butler Shoe Co. Most of the stores, including Butler's, can be entered only from the interior mall.

In January 1971, warehouse employees of the Butler Shoe Co. went on strike to protest the company's failure to agree to demands made by their union in contract negotiations. The strikers decided to picket not only Butler's warehouse but its nine retail stores in the Atlanta area as well, including the store in the North DeKalb Shopping Center. On January 22, 1971, four of the striking warehouse employees entered the center's enclosed mall carrying placards which read: "Butler Shoe Warehouse on Strike, AFL—CIO, Local 315." The general manager of the shopping center informed the employees that they could not picket within the mall or on the parking lot and threatened them with arrest if they did not leave. The

employees departed but returned a short time later and began picketing in an area of the mall immediately adjacent to the entrances of the Butler store. After the picketing had continued for approximately 30 minutes, the shopping center manager again informed the pickets that if they did not leave they would be arrested for trespassing. The pickets departed. The union subsequently filed with the Board an unfair labor practice charge against Hudgens.

. . . . the history of this litigation has been a history of shifting positions on the part of the litigants, the Board, and the Court of Appeals. It has been a history, in short, of considerable confusion, engendered at least in part by decisions of this Court that intervened during the course of the litigation. In the present posture of the case the most basic question is whether the respective rights and liabilities of the parties are to be decided under the criteria of the National Labor Relations Act alone, under a First Amendment standard, or under some combination of the two. It is to that question, accordingly, that we now turn.

It is, of course, a commonplace that the constitutional guarantee of free speech is a guarantee only against abridgment by government, federal or state. See *Columbia Broadcasting System, Inc. v.*

Democratic National Comm. Thus, while statutory or common law may in some situations extend protection or provide redress against a private corporation or person who seeks to abridge the free expression of others, no such protection or redress is provided by the Constitution itself. . . .

It matters not that some Members of the Court may continue to believe that the *Logan Valley* case was rightly decided. Our institutional duty is to follow until changed the law as it now is, not as some Members of the Court might wish it to be. And in the performance of that duty we make clear now, if it was not clear before, that the rationale of *Logan Valley* did not survive the Court's decision in the *Lloyd* case. Not only did the *Lloyd* opinion incorporate lengthy excerpts from two of the dissenting opinions in *Logan Valley*; the ultimate holding in *Lloyd* amounted to a total rejection of the holding in *Logan Valley:*

"The basic issue in this case is whether respondents, in the exercise of asserted First Amendment rights, may distribute handbills on Lloyd's private property contrary to its wishes and contrary to a policy enforced against *all* handbilling. In addressing this issue, it must be remembered that the First and Fourteenth Amendments safeguard the rights of free speech and assembly by limitations on *state* action, not on action by the owner of private property used nondiscriminatory for private purposes only. . . .

Respondents contend . . . that the property of a large shopping center is open to the public, serves the same purposes as a 'business district' of a municipality and therefore has been dedicated to certain types of public use. The argument is that such a center has sidewalks, streets, and parking areas which are functionally similar to facilities customarily provided by municipalities. It is then asserted that all members of the public, whether invited as customers or not, have the same right of free speech as they would have on the similar public facilities in the streets of a city or town.

The argument reaches too far. The Constitution by no means requires such an attenuated doctrine of dedication of private property to public use. The closest decision in theory, *Marsh v. Alabama,* involved the assumption by a private enterprise of all of the attributes of a state-created municipality and the exercise by that enterprise of semiofficial municipal functions as a delegate of the State. In effect, the owner of the company town was performing the full spectrum of municipal powers and stood in the shoes of the State. In the instant case there is no comparable assumption or exercise of municipal functions or power.

We hold that there has been no such dedication of Lloyd's privately owned and operated shopping center to public use as to entitle respondents to exercise therein the asserted First Amendment rights. . . .

If a large self-contained shopping center *is* the functional equivalent of a municipality, as *Logan Valley* held, then the First and Fourteenth Amendments would not permit control of speech within such a center to depend upon the speech's content. For while a municipality may constitutionally impose reasonable time, place, and manner regulations on the use of its streets and sidewalks for First Amendment purposes, see *Cox v. New Hampshire,* and may even forbid altogether such use of some of its facilities, see *Adderley v. Florida*; what a municipality may *not* do under the First and Fourteenth Amendments is to discriminate in the regulation of expression on the basis of the content of that expression, *Erznoznik v. City of Jacksonville.* "[A]bove all else, the First Amendment means that government has no power to restrict expression because of its message, its ideas, its subject matter, or its content." *Police Dept. of Chicago v. Mosley.* It conversely follows, therefore, that if the respondents in the *Lloyd* case did not have a First Amendment right to enter that shopping center to distribute handbills concerning Vietnam, then the pickets in the present case did not have a First Amendment right to enter this shopping center for the purpose of advertising their strike against the Butler Shoe Co.

We conclude, in short, that under the present state of the law the constitutional guarantee of free expression has no part to play in a case such as this. . . .

For the reasons stated in this opinion, the judgment is vacated and the case is remanded to the Court of Appeals with directions to remand to the National Labor Relations Board, so that the case may be there considered under the statutory criteria of the National Labor Relations Act alone. MR. JUSTICE MARSHALL, with whom MR. JUSTICE BRENNAN joins dissenting.

The Court today holds that the First Amendment poses no bar to a shopping center owner's prohibiting speech within his shopping center. . . .

Turning to the constitutional issue resolved by the Court, I cannot escape the feeling that *Logan Valley* has been laid to rest without ever having been accorded a proper burial. . . .

In Logan Valley we recognized what the Court today refuses to recognize—that the owner of the modern shopping center complex, by dedicating his property to public use as a business district, to some extent displaces the "State" from control of historical First Amendment forums, and may acquire a virtual monopoly of places suitable for effective communication. The roadways, parking lots, and walkways of the modern shopping center may be as essential for effective speech as the streets and sidewalks in the municipal or company-owned town. I simply cannot reconcile the Court's denial of any role for the First Amendment in the shopping center with *Marsh's* recognition of a full role for the First Amendment on the streets and sidewalks of the company-owned town.

In the final analysis, the Court's rejection of any role for the First Amendment in the privately owned shopping center complex stems, I believe, from an overly formalistic view of the relationship between the institution of private ownership of property and the First Amendment's guarantee of freedom of speech. No one would seriously question the legitimacy of the values of privacy and individual autonomy traditionally associated with privately owned property.

But property that is privately owned is not always held for private use, and when a property owner opens his property to public use the force of those values diminishes. A degree of privacy is necessarily surrendered; thus, the privacy interest that petitioner retains when he leases space to 60 retail businesses and invites the public onto his land for the transaction of business with other members of the public is small indeed. *Paris Adult Theatre I v. Slaton* (1973). And while the owner of property open to public use may not automatically surrender any of his autonomy interest in managing the property as he sees fit, there is nothing new about the notion that that autonomy interest must be accommodated with the interests of the public. As this Court noted some time ago, albeit in another context:

"Property does become clothed with a public interest when used in a manner to make it of public consequence, and affect the community at large. When, therefore, one devotes his property to a use in which the public has an interest, he, in effect, grants to the public an interest in that use, and must submit to be controlled by the public for the common good, to the extent of the interest he has thus created." *Munn v. Illinois* (1877).

The interest of members of the public in communicating with one another on subjects relating to the businesses that occupy a modern shopping center is substantial. Not only employees with a labor dispute, but also consumers with complaints against business establishments, may look to the location of a retail store as the only reasonable avenue for effective communication with the public. As far as these groups are concerned, the shopping center owner has assumed the traditional role of the state in its control of historical First Amendment forums. *Lloyd* and *Logan Valley* recognized the vital role the First Amendment has to play in such cases, and I believe that this Court errs when it holds otherwise.

13

SEPARATISM, SECULARISM, AND ACCOMMODATION

A book on civil liberties in the Warren and Burger eras characterized Court decisions on the "religion clauses" as "Much Ado About Nothing," reflecting the author's view that few questions of real constitutional importance were involved.[1] But the Warren and Burger years saw changes in the doctrine of the religion clauses as profound as those in any area of constitutional law, changes that are by no means completed at this time. Those changes began, it may be argued, with the 1962 decision in Engel v. Vitale, and have continued through a spate of cases on both the establishment and free exercise clauses. Further, it is not just the constitutional law of the religion clauses that has changed. Rather, and partly in response to such changes in law, the entire "politics of religious conflict" has been altered, perhaps forever.[2]

Richard Morgan, writing more than two decades ago, could speak of three distinct attitudes toward the place of religion in America, attitudes that might be characterized as the Protestant, the Catholic, and the Jewish-secular. They are also attitudes that mirrored, to some extent, the divisions of colonial and constitutional times about the proper relation between church and state. For, contrary to the received wisdom, the historical tradition is not the simple, one-dimensional viewpoint encapsulated in the phrase "wall of separation." There were, by contrast, at least three traditions existent.

The oldest colonial tradition was one which today we would call "separatist," although with a slightly different twist than that to which we are accustomed. The spirit of this tradition is captured in the words of Roger Williams, who characterized church and state as "the garden and the wilderness," and believed that the two should be separate to spare the church (the garden) possible contamination by the state (the wilderness). Both at the time of its inception and today the separatist tradition has received its strongest support from religious dissidents and those whom the "mainline" churches decry as "fundamentalist," although its membership has included such presently "mainline" denominations as Baptists and Methodists.

A second tradition, represented by Jefferson's famous reference to the "wall of separation" which should exist between church and state, may be called the "Jewish-secularist," although historically, of course, it was not Jewish. This tradition in its pure form is the polar opposite of the "separatist," in that it evinces a distinct hostility toward religion and views the danger from union of church and state to be the contaminating effects of religion upon the state. It received its most explicit early support from Jefferson, who remains its principal spiritual antecedent. The tradition today receives strong support from the liberal-intellectual community, from atheists and agnostics, and from American Jewry. The last group, of course, bases its position not on hostility to religion but on appreciation of the historical fact that union, or close cooperation, of church and state has often meant persecution of Jews. That the secularist position is not a matter of principal or of religious doctrine for Jews is shown by the overwhelming Jewish acceptance of the united church-state of Israel.

A third tradition may be termed "accommodationist." It contrast to the others it regards neither state nor church as dangerous to the other. Rather, it views both as necessary and complimentary entities in the life of humanity. Its existence in the colonial and constitutional period is testified to by the existence of established churches (persisting in Massachusetts until 1826), by numerous statements by Madison and others of the founding fathers, and even on occasion by Jefferson, who in his "Notes on Virginia" recommended the establishment of a School of Divinity at the University of Virginia. In the past half-century it has probably been most identified with Roman Catholicism, a religion whose philosophic tradition never emphasized separation of the religious and the secular, and whose institutional requirements led it, in the United States as elsewhere, to argue for state support of quasi-church institutions such as schools.

Both the constitutional law and the politics of church-state relations have undergone a remarkable change in the past half-century. During the early part of the period the vast majority of cases coming before the Court involved the "free exercise" clause, particularly as employed by energetically proselytizing groups such as Jehovah's Witnesses. During this time the free exercise clauses seemed to work hand in hand with, and perhaps to be just a more specific expression of, the communications clauses. Here the Court seemed to see its role principally as keeping the church free from the nefarious influences or strictures of the state, and thus to be operating very much in the Roger Williams tradition.

Beginning, however, with Engel, the focus shifted to the establishment clause, and the "constitutional ball" has been carried chiefly by secularists seeking to keep the state, and especially the schools, free of the influence of religion. For a considerable period of time it appeared that the secularists were to win the day, as the Court struck down first one and then another practice said to violate the establishment clause.

Two principal factors appear to have caused the Court, in more recent times, to rethink its position on "establishment." First, the possible conflict between the establishment and free exercise clauses, always present and apparent to the thoughtful, has become more obvious as various state and national programs and policies have been seen to have implications for both. Thus the early issue of "Sunday closing laws," seen in secularist perspective purely as an example of an impermissible mixing of religious and state concerns, has been revealed, when applied to Orthodox Jewish merchants, to have overtones of freedom of religion. Similarly, and even more pointedly, there has been the issue of whether certain requirements of eligibility for welfare might operate to deny free exercise of religion, or, conversely, whether doing away with them might constitute favoritism amounting to establishment.

Perhaps more important is the fact that the political equation has, partly under the blow of Supreme Court decisions, changed radically. The Court's decisions in Engel and in School District of Abington Township v. Schempp (1963), effectively removing prayer from the public schools, have been coupled with increased secularization of those schools by professional administrators and educators. Leaders of "separatist" religions have sought to overturn decisions of this type, to assert the "free exercise" rights of religiously minded children in the public schools, and/or to set up their own schools. Thus the Catholic Church, which began its own school system as a protest against the "Protestantization" of the public schools, has now become an ally of the "religious right" in seeking a return of religious observances to the public schools and to public life generally. And Catholics have found an ally in Protestant groups faced with the problem of financing their own schools while continuing to pay taxes in support of a state school system from which they are increasingly alienated.

In general, the doctrines related to the "free exercise" clause tend to be less complex than those involved with the "establishment" clause. In part this may be simply because free exercise questions can be conceptualized in terms that are already familiar to us. As we have noted, many free exercise questions, particularly those involving rights of religious proselytization, can be dealt with using doctrinal approaches similar to those employed when dealing with questions of free expression. For example, although Cantwell v. Connecticut was the first case in which the free exercise clause was applied to the states, the substantive issue that it raised can also be seen one of "free communication." In addition, at least some of the more recent free exercise questions seem amenable to a kind of "equal protection" analysis. It is not that these last cases do not raise knotty problems. It is, rather, that governmental activity impinging on religious beliefs, or governmental prohibitions of religious activity, like those having to do with racial and other discriminations, can be more easily upheld if facially neutral and not aimed at religion in particular or at particular religious practices.

It is not surprising, therefore, that most of the doctrinal development that has taken place in recent years has been in the area of the establishment clause. Having developed such doctrines, the Court has had considerably difficulty in applying them. Thus there is room for, and the future will probably see, a good deal of experimentation with alternate doctrines, or with modifications of current ones, before the state of establishment law becomes settled.

In the Court's first full attempt to articulate doctrine relevant to the establishment clause, Justice Clark's majority opinion in Schempp, it was held that to avoid the strictures of the establishment clause a law or practice must be shown to have 1) a secular purpose; and 2) a primary effect that is similarly secular. The first test has been applied in a manner akin to the "rational basis" test used for determining the constitutionality of governmental actions involving economic regulation. Almost any law except the most blatant can be justified on the basis of some secular interest, and legislatures can be expected to carefully "make a record" reflecting a secular purpose. But the second has been applied only with considerably more difficulty, and in such a way as to raise the objection that whether a not an "effect" is primary or secondary depends simply on the reaction of the particular justices. Without impugning its considerable utility , the fact that the justices have split so deeply in applying the "effects" test lends credence to this criticism.

Perhaps in response to the perceived inadequacies of the Schempp tests, Chief Justice Burger, first in Walz v. Tax Commission (1970), and then in Lemon v. Kurtzmann (1971), suggested still another criterion of establishment. Assuming a secular purpose and primary effect, opined the Chief, the establishment clause could still be violated if the result of the governmental program or activity was an "excessive entanglement" with religion. The validity of the "excessive entanglement" doctrine rests on Burger's undoubtedly correct perception that a major purpose of the establishment (as well as of the free exercise) clause was to remove from American society the divisiveness that attends religious conflict. The test itself, however, has caused perhaps as much divisiveness as it has prevented. To begin with, it is obviously and almost necessarily vague. Although it is possible to argue, as would the pure secularist, that any entanglement between government and religion should be enough to invalidate a governmental activity, this would be almost certainly in conflict with the expectations of the Framers of the Constitution and would probably be politically impossible. Further, such a result would not fit with Burger's purpose, which was to widen, rather than to limit, the areas of permissible government-church cooperation. Thus the qualification "excessive," which only adds to the already considerable vagueness of the word "entanglement" itself.

The results of applications of the "Lemon tests" have thus been uneven. They have resulted in the invalidation of most programs aimed at assisting in the education of children attending religious schools. But they have failed to do so on anything approaching a principled basis, resulting in formalistic distinctions between approved and disapproved programs. And some applications of "excessive entanglement" seem at odds with full recognition that religiously motivated people, like others, retain their rights not only to free exercise of religion, but to freedom of expression, particularly political expression. Lawrence Tribe once advanced the argument (which he later modified) that, at least in some circumstances, legislation passed as a result of religious pressures could be held on that ground to be "excessively entangled" with religion, and therefore unconstitutional.[3] This position, if taken literally, would result in the constitutionally mandated removal of the influence of such people from the political process. Of course, as a formal matter they would remain free to attempt to get legislation passed. But their success would also be their failure, since the fact of that success, proceeding from an "impermissible motivation" having the effect of "excessive entanglement," would be sufficient reason for the courts to deny them the opportunity to enjoy the fruits of their victory.

The case of the "entanglement" test may serve to bring home an additional, and very fundamental, reason why the jurisprudence of the religious clauses is so complex. The two clauses may, and often will, appear to be partly in conflict; so much so that Tribe has also argued that interpretation of the two clauses will most often be successful only if they are considered together.[4]

But if they are potentially in conflict, it is of the greatest importance to determine which of the two clauses, in cases where they point in opposite directions, ought to have precedence. Here the intentions of the Framers, and the historical setting, of the religious clauses seems particularly helpful. The wording of the First Amendment places the establishment clause first. Despite this, it seems likely that the Framers, with the assistance of relatively recent history, saw that clause as secondary to, and indeed in aid of, the free exercise clause. Certainly that is the logical way of it. Except for a society that is professedly anti-religious (and we have the word of no less an authority than Justice Douglas that the United States is not such a society), there appears to be little of value in the prevention of an establishment of religion, except in so far as it is in aid of religious freedom. That non-establishment is such an aid would appear to be beyond contradiction, at least for a country such as the United States. But the fact that other nations, perhaps equally free, get along reasonably well under conditions of formal establishment, indicates that it is religious freedom that is indispensable.

To recognize this, however, is only to begin to understand the problem of the religion clauses. Complicating the equation is the fact that religious freedom must include a modicum of freedom from religion, and that allowance of a degree of "establishment" can, as is perhaps most obvious in the case of tax payments that go to support religiously oriented institutions, arguably interfere with the free exercise of "nonreligion."

We are left with a seemingly inevitable intermixture of the two clauses, and the discussion of doctrine in the case of one will ineluctably involve the discussion of doctrine in another. This perspective is reflected in the organizing principle of the chapters that follow. We begin with a series of cases, those involving the "rights and duties of citizens," in which government has attempted in various ways to minimize establishment only to be charged with having violated free exercise. The next chapter concerns governmental attempts to regulate, under the "police power," activities generally held regulable but arguably protected in specific cases by the demands of the free exercise. This is perhaps the only area in which free exercise can be considered alone, its interpretation relatively uncomplicated by the presence of establishment considerations.

The next chapter, on the relation of the religious clauses to the government's power to legislate for the general welfare, raises truly inseparable questions of both free exercise and establishment. In the concluding two chapters we confront the demands of establishment and free exercise in their most controversial forms, relating to the education of our children and to government involvement with religious observances. Other issues are important, but it is here, in questions of prayer and religious observances under public auspices, as well as the kinds of assistance to be given to those attending religiously oriented schools, that the demands of separatist, secularist, and accommodationist clash most sharply. It is here where the religious divisiveness that the First Amendment was intended to prevent is likely to occur in its most extreme form. It is here, therefore, that the doctrines formulated and applied by the Supreme Court must be most sensitive to conflicting demands. Given these factors, it is not surprising that doctrine and application in these areas is likely to be tentative, contradictory and, to admirers of logical consistency, less than satisfying.

---

[1]Richard Y. Funston, *Constitutional Counterrevolution? The Warren Court and the Burger Court: Judicial Policy Making in Modern America* (Cambridge, Mass., Schenkman Publishing Co, 1977), Ch. 6. Professor Funston quotes Robert McCloskey to the effect that, since the evil of church-state interrelationship is relatively small, it would have been better for the Court not to involve itself in the controversy. Such a policy would, in most cases, result in victory for the "accommodationist" position, which seems much stronger and better organized in the legislatures

continued on next page

and, arguably, in the minds of the people as a whole.

[2]This characterization, as well as the discussion which follows, of the various attitudes toward the place of religion in America, is based on Richard E. Morgan, *The Politics of Religious Conflict* (New York: Pegasus Books, 1968). See esp. Ch. 1.

[3]Lawrence Tribe, "The Supreme Court, 1972 Term - Foreword: Toward a Model of Roles in the Due Process of Life and Law," 87 *Harvard Law Review* 1, 21-25 (1973). Professor Tribe's specific reference was to anti-abortion legislation He later altered his view because it "appears to give too little weight to the value of allowing religious groups freely to express their convictions in the political process." Tribe, *American Constitutional Law* (2nd ed.), 1350.

[4]Tribe, *American Constitutional Law*, 1154-57.

14
THE RIGHTS AND DUTIES OF CITIZENS

Thus far we have proceeded as if the Constitution contains only two provisions related to religion, those parts of the First Amendment we have collectively denominated the "religion clauses." But there is contained in the original Constitution a prohibition bearing directly on the subject. At the end of Article VI the framers, in the course of requiring that all legislative, executive, and judicial officers of the United States take an oath (or affirmation) to support the Constitution, provided that "no religious Test shall ever be required as a Qualification of any Office or Public Trust under the United States." Several aspects of this provision are noteworthy. First, it's scope is extraordinarily wide, providing not only that such qualifications are forbidden for "public office," but also for any "public trust," and that the prohibition applies for "ever." Second, this sole "religion" provision of the original constitution seems rather clearly to be concerned with "free exercise of religion" rather than nonestablishment. This seems particularly significant given the fact that at the time the Constitution was adopted, a number of states had established churches. The bar to religious oaths may have been employed in recognition of such establishment, and in order to prevent it from encroaching on the "freedom of religion" which was to be the norm at the national level. The "no religious qualification" clause thus lends support to the argument that for the framers religious freedom was the primary concern.

The only Supreme Court decision to involve this clause, and the first that we use to illustrate the clash of constitutional prescriptions with the "rights and duties" of citizens, illustrates particularly well the tension between the existence of established religions in the states and the right to freely exercise religion. The state of Maryland, one of the antagonists in <u>Torcaso v. Watkins</u> (1961), never had a "religious establishment" in the sense of an official state church. But its constitutional requirement that all state officials take an oath of belief in God can, in historical context, be viewed as analogous to the much stricter establishment existing in other colonies. In deciding, for an all but unanimous court, that Maryland could not impose even the test of belief in God as a condition of public office, the Court thus evidenced an intention to remove one of the last remaining vestiges of "establishment" from states. Justice Black's majority opinion went much further than simply applying the relevant language of Article VI, and grounded the decision explicitly in free exercise values:

> We repeat and again reaffirm that "Neither a State nor the Federal government can constitutionally force a person "to profess a belief or disbelief in any religion." Neither can constitutionally pass laws or impose requirements which aid all religions as against non-believers, and neither can aid those religions based on a belief in the existence of God as against those religions founded on different beliefs.

<u>Torcaso</u> provides a good starting point for the discussion of our present topic, for it uniquely implicates all three of the constitutional provisions bearing on religion. In addition it raises, as seen in the final phrase quoted above, an issue of major importance which has given both Court and Congress no end of trouble, that of "defining religion." This issue, which we will meet in this chapter in the context of the matter of draft exemptions, also arose in relation to statutory provisions against fraud, as applied in the most difficult case of <u>United States v. Ballard</u> (1944). It has, in addition, been at least a "background" consideration in more recent cases.

Closer in tone to <u>Torcaso</u> is, however, <u>McDaniel v. Paty</u> (1978), which like <u>Torcaso</u> seemed to raise questions of "establishment" in its most classic sense. In <u>McDaniel</u>, it was not the reality but rather the fear of establishment that gave rise to the governmental regulation at issue. The Tennessee constitution contained a provision which prohibited "ministers of the gospel" from serving in state offices, a provision undoubtedly adopted in order to minimize religious influence.

It is worth noting, in this connection, that Tennessee is a "Bible Belt" state. It would thus be inaccurate to view the Tennessee provision as an expression of the hostility to religion characterized by the "secularist" position. Rather, the

Tennessee law faithfully reflected the "separatist" view of the "dissenting Protestants" who largely settled that state. In upholding the provision the Tennessee Supreme Court noted as much, opining that the state's interest in preventing the establishment of religion and in avoiding divisiveness and the channeling of political activity along religious lines were weighty enough to justify the disqualification of clergy from serving in governmental positions.

Nevertheless the Supreme Court, again unanimously, struck down the challenged provision. Here, said Chief Justice Burger for the plurality, the state had conditioned the exercise of one right, to be an office-holder, on the surrender of another. If the condition deprived the clergy *only* on the basis of belief, the statute would have to fall. But the law was directed not at beliefs but it acts and thus, following traditional lines of distinction, a sufficiently weighty state interest *could* serve to justify it. The acts involved, though, were central to religious activity, and only state interests of the "highest order" and not otherwise served could overbalance free exercise claims. And American experience provided "no persuasive support" for the view that the clergy, if allowed to serve in public positions, would be less protective than their "unordained counterparts" of anti-establishment interests, or less faithful to their oaths.

Burger's opinion seemed to recognize that the justification offered by Tennessee, pushed to its logical conclusion, could lead to all "religionists," or at least those whose motives for seeking public office might be shown to be religious, being banned from elective participation in public affairs. The opinion may therefore be read as a partial rejection of the secularist view that religious motivations in the promotion of public policy render that policy constitutionally suspect.

Justice Brennan's concurring opinion rejected as "sophistic" the plurality's distinction between acts and beliefs, and contended that the First Amendment "categorically prohibits" the hinging of political qualifications on the "act" of asserting a belief just as it does on the act of discussing that belief with others. Further, and more significantly for the development of law in the area, Brennan viewed the Tennessee law as manifesting "patent hostility, not neutrality," toward religion. While this position is, as we have seen, highly doubtful as a matter of historical fact, it does serve to introduce a discussion of "establishment" which has major implications for the validity of the Court's "entanglement" test. Excerpted herein along with Burger's opinion for the plurality, Brennan's opinion argued that the fact that the establishment clause has as a purpose the reducing of religious divisiveness cannot place religious "discussion, association, or political position" in a less advantageous position than such rights generally. While the Court's decisions on the establishment clause have been intended to reduce religious strife, "beyond enforcing these prohibitions . . . government may not go" for:

> The antidote which the Constitution provides against zealots who would inject sectarianism into the political process is to subject their ideas to refutation in the marketplace of ideas and their platforms to rejection at the polls. With these safeguards, it is unlikely that they will succeed in inducing government to act along religiously divisive lines, and, with judicial enforcement of the establishment Clause, any measure of success they achieve must be short-lived, at best.

This Janus-like statement seems to embrace the view that the fact of religious motivation, while it cannot be used as a device to prevent people so motivated from participating in politics, can properly be used by the Courts to invalidate measures proceeding from such motivations.[1] If this is what Justice Brennan meant, then the political freedom that he would grant to religious people is to be in form only. For it is difficult to see what remains of a freedom which can never hope to be effective. The problem, as we have seen, inheres not only in the view here expressed by Justice Brennan, but in the very nature of the Court's tests of establishment, particularly that of "entanglement." For if "entanglement" is to have independent meaning, it would appear to have the very consequences that Justice Brennan contemplates.[2]

McDaniel v. Paty has been little noted. Such is not the case, however, with the second group of cases dealt with in this chapter, in which the "free exercise of religion" clashes with the right of the state to demand support of its citizen in the form of military service. In political terms, of course, this is not surprising. McDaniel, like Torcaso, involved the kind of legal provision likely to be present only in a few jurisdictions, and unlikely in any event to effect the lives of many. By contrast, and particularly in a time when more and more people are questioning the validity of military service, the matter of "conscientious objection" is politically explosive. Given the traditional posture of Congress on the subject the Court has, with a single and now somewhat dated exception, been able to handle the issue by statutory, rather than constitutional, interpretation, and without attempting to determine whether a "right" to be an objector inheres in the free exercise of religion.

To the extent that the Court has expressed itself on the *constitutional* issue, there *does not* seem to be a constitutional right to be exempt from military service. It seems clear beyond dispute, and despite frequent challenges based on the theory that compulsory military service involves "involuntary servitude," that conscription considered alone is within the constitutional power of Congress. The early decision in Hamilton v. Board of Regents (1934), in which the Court held that the First Amendment did not prevent California from making compulsory military training a condition of attending a state college, argues strongly against a right of conscientious objection. To the same effect is Gillette v. United States (1971) in which the Court refused to recognize a right of conscientious objection to particular or "unjust" wars. Additionally *dicta* in a number of cases indicates that most justices would not have questioned Congress' right to end such exemption.[3]

But for political and policy reasons Congress, since the very beginning of conscription during the Civil War, has seen fit to give special consideration to the needs of the conscientious objector. In the past such consideration has taken the form of exemption from combatant status and/or the requirement of alternative service to the nation. In its present form, however, the exemption is an unqualified one adhering, according to the statutory language, to those who oppose all war because of "beliefs proceeding from religious conscience or from one's concept of duty to a Supreme Being." It is this qualification that has occasioned the Court's most recent pronouncements in this area. In the case of United States v. Seeger (1965), the Court was faced with the issue of whether one whose particular religion did not preach pacifism could avail himself of the exemption. The Court interpreted the statutory language to cover individuals whose personal interpretation of their relation to the Supreme Being was such that it led them to reject military activity.

At issue in Welsh v. United States was the somewhat more difficult question of whether one not formally affiliated with any religious group and not averring a belief in a Supreme Being nevertheless qualified for the exemption. Over the objection of Justice Harlan, concurring, and a powerful dissent by Justice White, the Court held that the statute covered all individuals whose objection to military service was based on ethical beliefs which, for the individual, occupied the same place in one's value system as did religion and belief in a Supreme Being for theists. Under the normal canons of statutory construction it would appear that the

Court construed the statute, as Harlan argued, in a manner not intended by Congress. But given the controversy over military service during the period of the Vietnam War, it may be that Congress breathed a figurative sigh of relief that the Court had relieved it of the necessity of determining whether the exemption should be so extended statutorily or whether it must be ended totally in light of the Court's expanded definition of "religion."

With more and more religious groups opposing American involvement in Central America, and with the ever present possibility that American troops might be sent to that troubled area, it is more than likely that Congress, the Court, or both, will be called upon to face again this particularly vexing issue. Thus we excerpt herein the principal opinions in Welsh.

The final case excerpted in this chapter involves that most pervasive of all duties toward government, the payment of taxes. Most of the discussion of taxes and the religion clauses have been concerned, as in Walz v. Tax Commission (to be discussed in Chapter 16) with the question of whether the extension of *tax exemptions* to religious entities violates the establishment clause. But several of the early decisions of the Court on religious proselytization did hold that, in the circumstances of those cases, a tax or "license fee" on the distribution of religious literature violated the free exercise clause.[4] The general issue of the obligation to pay taxes in the face of religiously based objections has been squarely faced only recently.

In Hernandez v. Commissioner of Internal Revenue, decided in 1989, a five to two majority, with Brennan and Kennedy not participating, upheld an IRS ruling that denied a tax exemption to adherents of the Church of Scientology for amounts they had contributed, under the Church's "doctrine of exchange" for "auditing" and "training" sessions conducted by the Church. Rejecting the argument that tax deductions must be allowed for *quid pro quo* payments in which the benefit received was purely spiritual, the Court held that the denial violated neither the free exercise nor the establishment clause. In Jimmy Swaggart Ministries v. Board of Equalization (1990), the Court unanimously upheld the application of a California sales and use tax on tangible property to religious items sold by the "televangilist" to citizens of California. Earlier cases which seemed to go the other way were distinguished on the grounds that they involved license taxes imposed as a *precondition* for permission to engage in religious evangelism. In Swaggart, by contrast, imposition of the tax imposed no significant burden on religious activity and was no different than that imposed by other general laws and regulations to which religious organizations must adhere. And, in United States v. Lee (1982), the final case to be excerpted in this chapter, a unanimous Court, with Burger writing the opinion and Stevens concurring in the judgment, concluded that an Amish citizen who objected on religious grounds to paying into and receiving benefits from the social security system could nevertheless be compelled to pay social security taxes for his Amish employees. Not all burdens on religion, said Burger, are unconstitutional, for government can justify limitations on religious liberty by showing them to be essential to accomplishing an overriding governmental interest. Such an interest was present in the necessity for a mandatory social security system. Prominently reflected in the Court's holding is concern as to the consequences that a contrary decision might have for the nation's tax structure generally. Given the loose definition of "religion" adopted in Seeger and Welsh, and the fact that it is not uncommon for citizens to oppose the spending of their tax money for purposes which they find offensive to their conscience, such a concern seems amply justified.[5]

---

[1]See the suggestion to this effect, made and later retracted by Lawrence Tribe, and discussed in Chapter 13.

[2]A common sense resolution of the problem would seem to be to make a distinction between the motives of legislators, or of those who try to influence them, (which may not be the basis for finding "entanglement,)" and the "purpose of the legislation", which may. In his dissenting opinion in Edwards v. Aguillard (1987), in which the Court invalidated a Louisiana statute requiring that "Creation Science" be given equal time with evolution in the state's schools, Justice Scalia, joined by Chief Justice Rehnquist, indicated his beliefthat it was inappropriate for the Court to invalidate legislation "on the basis of its motivation alone."

[3]See, e.g. Jacobson v. Massachusetts (1905), Welsh v. United States (1970)

[4]See, e.g. Murdock v. Pennsylvania (1943); Follett v. McCormick (1944)

[5]In his separate opinion in Lee, Justice Stevens argues that the fear of other claims for exemption is not a sufficient basis for denying that advanced by respondent, since "the Amish claim is readily distinguishable" from claims to general tax exemption in that , unlike here, the taxpayer in the typical case "is not in any position to supply the government with an equivalent substitute for the objectionable use of his money." For Stevens "the principal reason for adopting a strong presumption against such claims is not a matter of administrative convenience. It is the overriding interest in keeping the government . . . out of the business of evaluating the relative merits of differing religious claims".
   Whether one views the position of Burger or of Stevens as the correct one it appears certain,

continued on next page

given the current popularity of conscientiously based objections to taxes, that some device must be available to invalidate such claims, else the system of taxation could not survive. This would seem especially necessary given the wide interpretation which the Court has given, in the draft exemption cases, to the meaning of the term "religion."

McDANIEL V. PATY ET AL.

435 U.S. 619 (1978)

MR. CHIEF JUSTICE BURGER announced the judgment of the Court and delivered an opinion in which MR. JUSTICE POWELL, MR. JUSTICE REHNQUIST, and MR. JUSTICE STEVENS joined.

The question presented by this appeal is whether a Tennessee statute barring "Minister[s] of the Gospel, or priest[s] of any denomination whatever" from serving as delegates to the State's limited constitutional convention deprived appellant McDaniel, an ordained minister, of the right to the free exercise of religion guaranteed by the First Amendment and made applicable to the States by the Fourteenth Amendment. The First Amendment forbids all laws "prohibiting the free exercise" of religion. . . .

McDaniel, an ordained minister of a Baptist Church in Chattanooga, Tenn., filed as a candidate for delegate to the constitutional convention. An opposing candidate, appellee Selma Cash Paty, sued in the Chancery Court for a declaratory judgment that McDaniel as disqualified from serving as a delegate and for a judgment striking his name from the ballot. Chancellor Franks of the Chancery Court held that [the statute] violated the First and Fourteenth Amendments to the Federal Constitution and declared McDaniel eligible for the office of delegate. Accordingly, McDaniel's name remained on the ballot and in the ensuing election he was elected by a vote almost equal to that of three opposing candidates.

After the election, the Tennessee Supreme Court reversed the Chancery Court, holding that the disqualification of clergy imposed no burden upon "religious belief" and restricted "religious action . . .

[only] in the lawmaking process of government—where religious action is absolutely prohibited by the establishment clause. . . ." The State interests in preventing the establishment of religion and in avoiding the divisiveness and tendency to channel political activity along religious lines, resulting from clergy participation in political affairs, were deemed by that court sufficiently weighty to justify the disqualification notwithstanding the guarantee of the Free Exercise Clause.

. . . . the right to the free exercise of religion unquestionably encompasses the right to preach, proselyte, and perform other similar religious functions, or, in other words, to be a minister of the type McDaniel was found to be. *Murdoch v. Pennsylvania* (1943); *Cantwell v. Connecticut* (1940). Tennessee also acknowledges the right , of its adult citizens generally to seek and hold office as legislators or delegates to the state constitutional convention. Yet under the clergy-disqualification provision, McDaniel cannot exercise both rights simultaneously because the State has conditioned the exercise of one on the surrender of the other. . . .

If the Tennessee disqualification provision were viewed as depriving the clergy of a civil right solely because of their religious beliefs, our inquiry would be at an end. The Free Exercise Clause categorically prohibits government from regulating, prohibiting, or rewarding religious beliefs as such. *Cantwell v. Connecticut*. In *Torcaso v. Watkins* (1961), the Court reviewed the Maryland constitutional requirement that all holders of "any office of profit or trust in this

State" declare their belief in the existence of God. In striking down the Maryland requirement, the Court did not evaluate the interests assertedly justifying it but rather held that it violated freedom of religious belief.

In our view, however, *Torcaso* does not govern. By its terms, the Tennessee disqualification operates against McDaniel because of his status as a "minister" or "priest." The meaning of those words is, of course, a question of state law. And although the question has not been examined extensively in state-law sources, such authority as is available indicates that ministerial status is defined in terms of conduct and activity rather than in terms of belief. Because the Tennessee disqualification is directed primarily at status, acts and conduct it is unlike the requirement in *Torcaso*, which focused on belief. Hence, the Free Exercise Clause's absolute prohibition of infringements on the "freedom to believe" is inapposite here.

This does not mean, of course, that the disqualification escapes judicial scrutiny or that McDaniel's activity does not enjoy significant First Amendment protection. The Court recently declared in *Wisconsin v. Yoder* (1972): "The essence of all that has been said and written on the subject is that only those interests of the highest order and those not otherwise served can overbalance legitimate claims to the free exercise of religion."

Tennessee asserts that its interest in preventing the establishment of a state religion is consistent with the Establishment Clause and thus of the highest order. The constitutional history of the several States reveals that generally the interest in preventing establishment prompted the adoption of clergy disqualification ; Tennessee does not appear to be an exception to this pattern. There is no occasion to inquire whether promoting such an interest is a permissible legislative goal, however, for Tennessee has failed to demonstrate that its views of the dangers of clergy participation in the political process have not lost whatever validity the may once have enjoyed. The essence of the rationale underlying the Tennessee restriction on

ministers is that if elected to public office they will necessarily exercise their powers and influence to promote the interests of one sect or thwart the interests of another, thus pitting one against the others, contrary to the anti-establishment principle with its command of neutrality. *Waltz v. Tax Comm'n.* (1970). However widely that view may have been held in the 18th century by many, including enlightened statesmen of that day, the American experience provides no persuasive support for the fear that clergymen in public office will be less careful of anti-establishment interests or less faithful to their oaths of civil office than their unordained counterparts.

We hold that [the statute] violates McDaniel's First Amendment right to the free exercise of his religion made applicable to the States by the Fourteenth Amendment. Accordingly, the judgment of the Tennessee Supreme Court is reversed, and the case is remanded to that court for further proceedings not inconsistent with this opinion.

MR. JUSTICE BRENNAN, with whom MR. JUSTICE MARSHALL joins, concurring in the judgment. . . .

The plurality recognizes that *Torcaso* held "categorically prohibit[ed]," a provision disqualifying from political office on the basis of religious belief, but draws what I respectfully suggest is a sophistic distinction between that holding and Tennessee's disqualification provision. The purpose of the Tennessee provision is not to regulate activities associated with a ministry, such as dangerous snake handling or human sacrifice, which the State validly could prohibit, but to bar from political office persons regarded as deeply committed to religious participation because of that participation—participation itself not regarded as harmful by the State and which therefore must be conceded to be protected. As the plurality recognizes, appellant was disqualified because he "fill[ed] a 'leadership role in religion,' and . . . dedicated [himself] to the full time promotion of the religious objectives of a particular religious sect." According to the plurality, McDaniel could not be and was not in fact barred for *his* belief in religion, but was barred because of his commitment to persuade or lead others to accept that belief. I simply cannot fathom why the Free Exercise Clause "categorically prohibits" hinging qualification for office on the act of declaring a belief in religion, but not on the act of discussing that belief with others.

The State Supreme Court's justification of the prohibition echoed here by the State, as intended to prevent those most intensely involved in religion from injecting sectarian goals and policies into the law-making process, and thus to avoid fomenting religious strife or the fusing of church with state affairs, itself raises the question whether the exclusion violates the Establishment Clause. As construed, the exclusion manifests patent hostility toward, not neutrality respecting religion; forces or influences a minister or priest to abandon his ministry as the price of public office; and, in sum, has a primary effect which inhibits religion. . . .

Beyond these limited situations in which government may take cognizance of religion for purposes of accommodating our traditions of religious liberty, government may not use religion as a basis of classification for the imposition of duties, penalties, privileges or benefits. "State power is no more to be used so as to handicap religions than it is to favor them." *Everson v. Board of Education.*

Tennessee nevertheless invokes the Establishment Clause to excuse the imposition of a civil disability upon those deemed to be deeply involved in religion. In my view, that Clause not permit, much less excuse or condone, the deprivation of religious liberty here involved. . . .

That public debate of religious ideas, like any other, may arouse emotion, may incite, may foment religious divisiveness and strife does not rob it of constitutional protection. Cantwell v. Connecticut. The mere fact that a purpose of the Establishment Clause is to reduce or eliminate religious divisiveness or strife, does not place religious discussion, association, or political participation in a status less preferred the rights of discussion, association, and political participation generally. "Adherents of particular faiths and individual churches frequently take strong positions on public issues including . . . vigorous advocacy of legal or constitutional positions. Of course, churches as much as secular bodies and private citizens have that right." *Waltz v. Tax Comm'n.* (1970). . . .

Religionists no less than members of any other group enjoy the full measure of protection afforded speech, association, and political activity generally. The Establishment Clause, properly understood, is a shield against any attempt by government to inhibit religion as it has done here. *Abington School Dist. v. Schempp* (1963). It may not be used as a sword to justify repression of religion or its adherents from any aspect of public life.

Our decisions under the Establishment Clause prevent government from supporting or involving itself in religion or from becoming drawn into ecclesiastical disputes. These prohibitions naturally tend, as they were designed to, to avoid channeling political activity along religious lines and to reduce any tendency toward religious divisiveness in society. Beyond enforcing these prohibitions, however, government may not go. The antidote which the Constitution provides against zealots who would inject sectarianism into the political process is to subject their ideas to refutation in the marketplace of ideas and their platforms to rejection at the polls. With these safeguards, it is unlikely that they will succeed in inducing government to act along religiously divisive lines and, with judicial enforcement of the Establishment Clause, any measure of success they achieve must be short-lived, at best.

WELSH V. UNITED STATES

398 U.S. 333 (1970)

MR. JUSTICE BLACK announced the judgment of the Court and delivered an opinion in which M. JUSTICE DOUGLAS, MR. JUSTICE BRENNAN, and MR. JUSTICE MARSHALL join.

The petitioner, Elliott Ashton Welsh II, was convicted by a United States District Judge of refusing to submit to induction into the Armed Forces in violation of 50 U. S. C. App. 462(a), and was on June 1, 1966, sentenced to imprisonment for three years. One of petitioner's defenses to the prosecution was that 6(j) of the Universal Military Training and Service Act exempted him from combat and noncombat service because he was "by reason of religious training and belief . . . conscientiously opposed to participation in war in any form." After finding that there was no religious basis for petitioner's conscientious objector claim, the Court of Appeals, Judge Hamley dissenting, affirmed the conviction. We granted certiorari chiefly to review the contention that Welsh's conviction should be set aside on the basis of this Court's decision in *United States v. Seeger. . . .*

In *Seeger* the Court was confronted, first, with the problem that 6(j) defined "religious training and belief" in terms of a "belief in a relation to a Supreme Being . . . ," a definition that arguably gave a preference to those who believed in a conventional God as opposed to those who did not. Noting the "vast panoply of beliefs" prevalent in our country, the Court construed the congressional intent as being in "keeping with its long-established policy of not picking and choosing among religious beliefs," and accordingly interpreted "the meaning of religious training and belief so as to embrace *all* religions. . . ." But, having decided that all religious conscientious objectors were entitled to the exemption, we faced the more serious problem of determining which beliefs were "religious" within the meaning of the statute. This question was particularly difficult in the case of Seeger himself. Seeger stated that his was a "belief in and devotion to goodness and virtue for their own sakes, and a religious faith in a purely ethical creed. . . ."

In resolving the question whether Seeger and the other registrants in that case qualified for the exemption the Court stated that "[the] task is to decide whether the beliefs professed by a registrant are sincerely held and whether they are, *in his own scheme of things,* religious." The reference to the registrant's "own scheme of things" was intended to indicate that the central consideration in determining whether the registrant's beliefs are religious is whether these beliefs play the role of a religion and function as a religion in the registrant's life. . . .

What is necessary under *Seeger* for a registrant's conscientious objection to all war to be "religious" within the meaning of 6(j) is that this opposition to war stem from the registrant's moral, ethical, or religious beliefs about what is right and wrong and that these beliefs be held with the strength of traditional religious convictions. Most of the great religions of today and of the past have embodied the idea of a Supreme Being or a Supreme Reality—a God—who communicates to man in some way a consciousness of what is right and should be done, of what is wrong and therefore should be shunned. If an individual deeply and sincerely holds beliefs that are purely ethical or moral in source and content but that nevertheless impose upon him a duty of conscience to refrain from participating in any war at any time, those beliefs certainly occupy in the life of that individual "a place parallel to that filled by. . . God" in traditionally religious persons. Because his beliefs function as a religion in his life, such an individual is as much entitled to a "religious" conscientious objector exemption under 6(j) as is someone who derives his conscientious opposition to war from traditional religious convictions.

In the case before us the Government seeks to distinguish our holding in *Seeger* on basically two grounds, both of which were relied upon by the Court of Appeals in affirming Welsh's conviction. First, it is stressed that Welsh was far more insistent and explicit than Seeger in denying that his views were religious. For example, in filling out their conscientious objector applications, Seeger put quotation marks around the word "religious," but Welsh struck the word "religious" entirely and later characterized his beliefs as having been formed "by reading in the fields of history and sociology." The Court of Appeals found that Welsh had "denied that his objection to war was premised on religious belief" and concluded that "[t]he Appeal Board was entitled to take him at his word." 404 F. 2d, at 1082. We think this attempt to distinguish *Seeger* fails for the reason that it places undue emphasis on the registrant's interpretation of his own beliefs. The Court's statement in *Seeger* that a registrant's characterization of his own belief as "religious" should carry great weight, does not imply that his declaration that his views are nonreligious should be treated similarly. When a registrant states that his objections to war are "religious," that information is highly relevant to the question of the function his beliefs have in his life. But very few registrants are fully aware of the broad scope of the word "religious" as used in 6(j), and accordingly a registrant's statement that his beliefs are nonreligious is a highly unreliable guide for those charged with administering the exemption. Welsh himself presents a case in point. Although he originally characterized his beliefs as nonreligious, he later upon reflection wrote a long and thoughtful letter to his Appeal Board in which he declared that his beliefs were "certainly religious in the ethical sense of the word. . . ."

The Government also seeks to distinguish *Seeger* on the ground that Welsh's views, unlike Seeger's, were "essentially political, sociological, or philosophical views or a merely personal moral code." As previously noted, the Government made the same argument about Seeger, and not without reason, for Seeger's views had a substantial political dimension. In this case, Welsh's conscientious objection to war was undeniably based in part on his perception of world politics. . . .

We certainly do not think that 6(j)'s exclusion of those persons with "essentially political, sociological, or philosophical views or a merely personal moral code" should be read to exclude those who hold strong beliefs about our domestic and foreign affairs or even those whose conscientious objection to participation in all wars is founded to a substantial extent upon considerations of public policy . . . Once the Selective Service System has taken the first step and determined under the standards set out here and in *Seeger* that the registrant is a "religious" conscientious objector, it follows that his views cannot be "essentially political, sociological, or philosophical." Nor can they be a "merely personal moral code. . . ."

Welsh elaborated his beliefs in later communications with Selective Service officials. On the basis of these beliefs and the conclusion of the Court of Appeals that he held them "with the strength of more traditional religious convictions, "we think Welsh was clearly entitled to a conscientious objector exemption. Section 6(j) requires no more. That section exempts from military service all those whose consciences, spurred by deeply held moral, ethical, or religious beliefs, would give them no rest or peace if they allowed themselves to become a part of an instrument of war. . . .

MR. JUSTICE BLACKMUN took no part in the consideration or decision of this case.

MR. JUSTICE HARLAN, concurring in the result.

Candor requires me to say that I joined the Court's opinion in *United States v. Seeger*, 380 U. S. 163 (1965), only with the gravest misgivings as to whether it was a legitimate exercise in statutory construction, and today's decision convinces me that in doing so I made a mistake which I should now acknowledge. . . .

The natural reading of 6(j), which quite evidently draws a distinction between theistic and nontheistic religions, is the only one that is consistent with the legislative history. . . . it is a remarkable feat of judicial surgery to remove, as did *Seeger*, the theistic requirement of 6(j). The prevailing opinion today, however, in the name of interpreting the will of Congress, has performed a lobotomy and completely transformed the statute by reading out of it any distinction between religiously acquired beliefs and those deriving from "essentially political, sociological, or philosophical views or a merely personal moral code. . . ."

If an important congressional policy is to be perpetuated by recasting unconstitutional legislation, as the prevailing opinion has done here, the analytically sound approach is to accept responsibility for this decision. Its justification cannot be by resort to legislative intent, as that term is usually employed, but by a different kind of legislative intent, namely the presumed grant of power to the courts to decide whether it more nearly accords with Congress' wishes to eliminate its policy altogether or extend it in order to render what Congress plainly did intend, constitutional. . . .

The constitutional question that must be faced in this case is whether a statute that defers to the individual's conscience only when his views emanate from adherence to theistic religious beliefs is within the power of Congress. Congress, of course, could, entirely consistently with the requirements of the Constitution, eliminate *all* exemptions for conscientious objectors. Such a course would be wholly "neutral" and, in my view, would not offend the Free Exercise Clause. . . . However, having chosen to exempt, it cannot draw the line between theistic or nontheistic religious beliefs on the one hand and secular beliefs on the other. Any such distinctions are not, in my view, compatible with the Establishment Clause of the First Amendment. . . .

The "radius" of this legislation is the conscientiousness with which an individual opposes war in general, yet the statute, as I think it must be construed, excludes from its "scope" individuals motivated by teachings of nontheistic religions, and individuals guided by an inner ethical voice that bespeaks secular and not "religious" reflection. It not only accords a preference to the "religious" but also disadvantages adherents of religions that do not worship a Supreme Being. The constitutional infirmity cannot be cured, moreover, even by an impermissible construction that eliminates the theistic requirement and simply draws the line between religious and nonreligious. This in my view offends the Establishment Clause and is that kind of classification that this Court has condemned. . . .

If the exemption is to be given application, it must encompass the class of individuals it purports to exclude, those whose beliefs emanate from a purely moral, ethical, or philosophical source. The common denominator must be the intensity of moral conviction with which a belief is held. Common experience teaches that among "religious" individuals some are weak and others strong adherents to tenets and this is no less true of individuals whose lives are guided by personal ethical considerations. . . .

Where a statute is defective because of underinclusion there exist two remedial alternatives: a court may either declare it a nullity and order that its benefits not extend to the class that the legislature intended to benefit, or it may extend the coverage of the statute to include those who are aggrieved by exclusion. . . .

The appropriate disposition of this case, which is a prosecution for refusing to submit to induction and not an action for a declaratory judgment on the constitutionality of 6(j), is determined by the fact that at the time of Welsh's induction notice and prosecution the Selective Service was, as required by statute, exempting individuals whose beliefs were identical in all respects to those held by petitioner except that they derived from a religious source. Since this created a religious benefit not accorded to petitioner, it is clear to me that this conviction must be reversed under the Establishment Clause of the First Amendment unless Welsh is to go remediless. . . .

MR. JUSTICE WHITE, with whom THE CHIEF JUSTICE and MR. JUSTICE

STEWART join, dissenting. . . .

Our obligation in statutory construction cases is to enforce the will of Congress, not our own; and as MR. JUSTICE HARLAN has demonstrated, construing 6(j) to include Welsh exempts from the draft a class of persons to whom Congress has expressly denied an exemption.

For me that conclusion should end this case. Even if Welsh is quite right in asserting that exempting religious believers is an establishment of religion forbidden by the First Amendment, he nevertheless remains one of those persons whom Congress took pains not to relieve from military duty. Whether or not 6(j) is constitutional, Welsh had no First Amendment excuse for refusing to report for induction. If it is contrary to the express will of Congress to exempt Welsh, as I think it is, then there is no warrant for saving the religious exemption and the statute by redrafting it in this Court to include Welsh and all others like him. . . .

If I am wrong in thinking that Welsh cannot benefit from invalidation of 6(j) on Establishment Clause grounds, I would nevertheless affirm his conviction; for I cannot hold that Congress violated the Clause in exempting from the draft all those who oppose war by reason of religious training and belief. In exempting religious conscientious objectors, Congress was making one of two judgments, perhaps both. First, 6(j) may represent a purely practical judgment that religious objectors, however admirable, would be of no more use in combat than many others unqualified for military service. Exemption was not extended to them to further religious belief or practice but to limit military service to those who were prepared to undertake the fighting that the armed services have to do. On this basis, the exemption has neither the primary purpose nor the effect of furthering religion. As Mr. Justice Frankfurter, joined by MR. JUSTICE HARLAN, said in a separate opinion in the *Sunday Closing Law Cases*, an establishment contention "can prevail only if the absence of any substantial legislative, purpose other than a religious one is made to appear.

Second, Congress may have granted the exemption because otherwise religious objectors would be forced into conduct that their religions forbid and because in the view of Congress to deny the exemption would violate the Free Exercise Clause or at least raise grave problems in this respect. . . .

If there were no statutory exemption for religious objectors to war and failure to provide it was held by this Court to impair the free exercise of religion contrary to the First Amendment, an exemption reflecting this constitutional command would be no more an establishment of religion than the exemption required for Sabbatarians in *Sherbert v. Verner*. . . .

Surely a statutory exemption for religionists required by the Free Exercise Clause is not an invalid establishment because it fails to include nonreligious believers as well; nor would it be any less an establishment if camouflaged by granting additional exemptions for nonreligious, but "moral" objectors to war.

On the assumption, however, that the Free Exercise Clause of the First Amendment does not by its own force require exempting devout objectors from military service, it does not follow that 6(j) is a law respecting an establishment of religion within the meaning of the First Amendment. It is very likely that 6(j) is a recognition by Congress of free exercise values and its view of desirable or required policy in implementing the Free Exercise Clause. That judgment is entitled to respect. Congress has the power "To raise and support Armies" and "To make all Laws which shall be necessary and proper for carrying into Execution" that power. The power to raise armies must be exercised consistently with the First Amendment which, among other things, forbids laws prohibiting the free exercise of religion. It is surely essential therefore—surely "necessary and proper"— in enacting laws for the raising of armies to take account of the First Amendment and to avoid possible violations of the Free Exercise Clause. . . .

We have said that neither support nor

hostility, but neutrality, is the goal of the religion clauses of the First Amendment. "Neutrality," however, is not self-defining. If it is "favoritism" and not "neutrality" to exempt religious believers from the draft, is it "neutrality" and not "inhibition" of religion to compel religious believers to fight when they have special reasons for not doing so, reasons to which the Constitution gives particular recognition? It cannot be ignored that the First Amendment itself contains a religious classification. The Amendment protects belief and speech, but as a general proposition, the free speech provisions stop short of immunizing conduct from official regulation. The Free Exercise Clause, however, has a deeper cut: it protects conduct as well as religious belief and speech. "[I]t safeguards the free exercise of the chosen form of religion. Thus the Amendment embraces two concepts—freedom to believe and freedom to act. The first is absolute but, in the nature of things, the second cannot be." *Cantwell v. Connecticut*, (1940). Although socially harmful acts may as a rule be banned despite the Free Exercise Clause even where religiously motivated,

there is an area of conduct that cannot be forbidden to religious practitioners but that may be forbidden to others. . . .

We should thus not labor to find a violation of the Establishment Clause when free exercise values prompt Congress to relieve religious believers from the burdens of the law at least in those instances where the law is not merely prohibitory but commands the performance of military duties that are forbidden by a man's religion. . . .

The Establishment Clause as construed by this Court unquestionably has independent significance; its function is not wholly auxiliary to the Free Exercise Clause. It bans some involvements of the State with religion that otherwise might be consistent with the Free Exercise Clause. But when in the rationally based judgment of Congress free exercise of religion calls for shielding religious objectors from compulsory combat duty, I am reluctant to frustrate the legislative will by striking down the statutory exemption because it does not also reach those to whom the Free Exercise Clause offers no protection whatsoever. . . .

UNITED STATES V. LEE

455 U.S 252 (1982)

CHIEF JUSTICE BURGER delivered the opinion of the Court .

We noted probable jurisdiction to determine whether imposition of social security taxes is unconstitutional as applied to persons who object on religious grounds to receipt of public insurance benefits and to payment of taxes to support public insurance funds. The District Court concluded that the Free Exercise Clause prohibits forced payment of social security taxes when payment of taxes and receipt of benefits violate the taxpayer's religion. We reverse.

Appellee, a member of the Old Order Amish, is a farmer and carpenter. From 1970 to 1977, appellee employed several other Amish to work on his farm and in

his carpentry shop. He failed to file the quarterly social security tax returns required of employers, withhold social security tax from his employees, or pay the employer's share of social security taxes. . . .

The District Court held the statutes requiring appellee to pay social security and unemployment insurance taxes unconstitutional as applied. The court noted that the Amish believe it sinful not to provide for their own elderly and needy and therefore are religiously opposed to the national social security system. The court also accepted appellee's contention that the Amish religion not only prohibits the acceptance of social security benefits, but also bars all contributions by Amish to the social security system. The District Court observed that in light of their beliefs, Congress has accommodated self-employed Amish and self-employed members of other religious groups with similar beliefs by providing exemptions from social security taxes. The court's holding was based on both the exemption statute for the self-employed and the First Amendment. . . .

The exemption provided by 1402(g) is available only to self-employed individuals and does not apply to employers or employees. Consequently, appellee and his employees are not within the express provisions of 1402(g). Thus any exemption from payment of the employer's share of social security taxes must come from a constitutionally required exemption.

The preliminary inquiry in determining the existence of a constitutionally required exemption is whether the payment of social security taxes and the receipt of benefits interferes with the free exercise rights of the Amish. The Amish believe that there is a religiously based obligation to provide for their fellow members the kind of assistance contemplated by the social security system. Although the Government does not challenge the sincerity of this belief, the Government does contend that payment of social security taxes will not threaten the integrity of the Amish religious belief or observance. It is not within "the judicial function and judicial competence," however, to determine whether appellee or the Government has the proper interpretation of the Amish faith; "[c]ourts are not arbiters of scriptural interpretation." *Thomas v. Review Bd. of Indiana Employment Security Div.* (1981). We therefore accept appellee's contention that both payment and receipt of social security benefits is forbidden by the Amish faith. Because the payment of the taxes or receipt of benefits violates Amish religious beliefs, compulsory participation in the social security system interferes with their free exercise rights.

The conclusion that there is a conflict between the Amish faith and the obligations imposed by the social security system is only the beginning, however, and not the end of the inquiry. Not all burdens on religion are unconstitutional. The state may justify a limitation on religious liberty by showing that it is essential to accomplish an overriding governmental interest.

Because the social security system is nationwide, the governmental interest is apparent. The social security system in the United States serves the public interest by providing a comprehensive insurance system with a variety of benefits available to all participants, with costs shared by employers and employees. The social security system is by far the largest domestic governmental program in the United States today, distributing approximately $11 billion monthly to 36 million Americans. The design of the system requires support by mandatory contributions from covered employers and employees. This mandatory participation is indispensable to the fiscal vitality of the social security system. "[W]idespread individual voluntary coverage under social security . . . would undermine the soundness of the social security program." Moreover, a comprehensive national social security system providing for voluntary participation would be almost a contradiction in terms and difficult, if not impossible, to administer. Thus, the Government's interest in assuring mandatory and continuous participation in and contribution to the social security system is very high.

The remaining inquiry is whether accommodating the Amish belief will unduly interfere with fulfillment of the governmental interest. In *Braunfeld v. Brown* (1961), this Court noted that "to make accommodation between the religious action and an exercise of state authority is a particularly delicate task . . . because resolution in favor of the State results in the choice to the individual of either abandoning his religious principle or facing . . . prosecution."

The difficulty in attempting to accommodate religious beliefs in the area of taxation is that "we are a cosmopolitan nation made up of people of almost every conceivable religious preference." *Braunfeld.* The Court has long recognized that balance must be struck between the values of the comprehensive social security system, which rests on a complex of actuarial factors, and the consequences of allowing religiously based exemptions. To maintain an organized society that guarantees religious freedom to a great variety of faiths requires that some religious practices yield to the common good. Religious beliefs can be accommodated, but there is a point at which accommodation would "radically restrict the operating latitude of the legislature." *Braunfeld.*

Unlike the situation presented in *Wisconsin v. Yoder,* it would be difficult to accommodate the comprehensive social security system with myriad exceptions flowing from a wide variety of religious beliefs. The obligation to pay the social security tax initially is not fundamentally different from the obligation to pay income taxes; the difference—in theory at least—is that the social security tax revenues are segregated for use only in furtherance of the statutory program. There is no principled way, however, for purposes of this case, to distinguish between general taxes and those imposed under the Social Security Act. If, for example, a religious adherent believes war is a sin, and if a certain percentage of the federal budget can be identified as devoted to war-related activities, such individuals would have a similarly valid claim to be exempt from paying that percentage of the income tax. The tax system could not function if denominations were allowed to challenge the tax system because tax payments were spent in a manner that violates their religious belief. . . Because the broad public interest in maintaining a sound tax system is of such a high order, religious belief in conflict with the payment of taxes affords no basis for resisting the tax. . . .

Congress and the courts have been sensitive to the needs flowing from the Free Exercise Clause, but every person cannot be shielded from all the burdens incident to exercising every aspect of the right to practice religious beliefs. When followers of a particular sect enter into commercial activity as a matter of choice, the limits they accept on their own conduct as a matter of conscience and faith are not to be superimposed on the statutory schemes which are binding on others in that activity. Granting an exemption from social security taxes to an employer operates to impose the employer's religious faith on the employees. Congress drew a line in 1402(g), exempting the self-employed Amish but not all persons working for an Amish employer. The tax imposed on employers to support the social security system must be uniformly applicable to all, except as Congress provides explicitly otherwise. . . .

JUSTICE STEVENS, concurring in the judgment.

The clash between appellee's religious obligation and his civic obligation is irreconcilable. He must violate either an Amish belief or a federal statute. According to the Court, the religious duty must prevail unless the Government shows that enforcement of the civic duty "is essential to accomplish an overriding governmental interest." That formulation of the constitutional standard suggests that the Government always bears a heavy burden of justifying the application of neutral general laws to individual conscientious objectors. In my opinion, it is the objector who must shoulder the burden of demonstrating that there is a unique reason for allowing him a special exemption from a valid law of general applicability. . . .

The Court rejects the particular claim of this appellee, not because it presents any special problems, but rather because of the risk that a myriad of other claims would be too difficult to process. The Court overstates the magnitude of this risk because the Amish claim applies only to a small religious community with an established welfare system of its own. Nevertheless, I agree with the Court's conclusion that the difficulties associated with processing other claims to tax exemption on religious grounds justify a rejection of this claim. I believe, however, that this reasoning supports the adoption of a different constitutional standard than the Court purports to apply.

The Court's analysis supports a

holding that there is virtually no room for a "constitutionally required exemption" on religious grounds from a valid tax law that is entirely neutral in its general application. Because I agree with that holding, I concur in the judgment.

15

THE STATE'S POLICE POWER

Governments in the United States rarely, if ever, have attempted to inhibit religious practices solely for the sake of such inhibition. Thus controversy usually arises when a statute of general applicability under the "police power" or similar justification conflicts with an act required or permitted by the doctrine or practice of a particular religious body. The phrase "police power" generally connotes the power of government to enact legislation to protect public health, welfare, and morals; it is the basis on which the states exercise most of the powers reserved to them under our system. But it is worth recalling that the national government also exercises a "police power" in federal enclaves. It is in the context of one such enclave that the earliest "police power" controversies arose.

From its inception, the Church of Jesus Christ of Latter Day Saints (whose members are generally known as Mormons) taught the necessity of polygamous marriage, with a single husband having many wives, as a means of salvation. The practice was thought to be sanctioned by documents of special significance to the Mormon Church itself, as well as by the biblical injunction to "increase and multiply." Polygamy was a principal cause of the hostility encountered by Mormons in the more settled areas of the 19th century United States, and that hostility gave impetus to their move westward and to the establishment of the major Mormon settlement in what was to become Utah territory. There polygamy soon clashed with a federal statute which made plural marriage illegal. A result of that clash, Reynolds v. United States (1878) became the first case in which the Court dealt with the free exercise clause, and it did so at the expense of the religious freedom of Reynolds and other members of his church.

The Court began by making the familiar (and no doubt essential) distinction between the freedom of religious belief, which the religion clauses make absolute, and the freedom to act, which must be subject to governmental limitation, lest "free exercise" become a device for escaping the coverage of all laws. In this case, the Court held, there was a sufficient governmental interest (and a secular purpose), in preserving monogamous marriage and in preventing the exploitation of women to sustain the statute's prohibition of the *act of* as distinguished from the *belief in* polygamy.

In <u>Davis v. Beason</u> (1890), the Court held that appellant's Mormon beliefs respecting polygamy were not "according to the common tenets of mankind, religious tenets at all," and that even the teaching and counseling of polygamous activity could constitute criminal action. And in the same year, in <u>Late Corporation of the Church of Jesus Christ of Latter Day Saints v. United States</u>, the Court held valid the repeal of the Charter of the LDS Church on the grounds that it was "not a religion or charitable organization," since its tenet of polygamy was not "religious," but rather a "pretense, according to the enlightened sentiments of mankind."

It will have occurred to the student that the decisions in the above cases would today be of doubtful validity. In today's society it is at least arguable as to whether the protection of monogamy constitutes a state interest sufficient to interfere with religious belief, and statutes looking to prevent the "exploitation of women" are similarly somewhat suspect. Additionally, previously discussed cases on the "communications clauses" cast doubt on the degree to which government can make the mere teaching of *any* practice illegal. Finally, and most importantly, the Court's cavalier "definition" of what is and is not religion by reference to the "common tenets of mankind" would be unlikely to be accepted today.

The Court's increased sensitivity to the complex problems involved in defining "religion" is illustrated in <u>United States v. Ballard</u> (1944). In that case respondents were indicted and convicted for using and conspiring to use the mails to defraud, in that they had mailed literature making representations about religious matters and prophecies alleged to have been made to them by "St. Germain," and on that basis had sought contributions. The trial judge withdrew from the jury the issue of whether the allegations of the Ballards were true as a matter of fact, and submitted to it only the issue of the honest and good faith belief of the defendants in their religious representations. The Court of Appeals, however, held that the question of truth should have been submitted to the jury, and thus remanded the case for a new trial.

For the Supreme Court, Justice Douglas' majority opinion reinstated the conviction and held that for the triers of fact to attempt to determine the truth or falsity of religious belief would be to enter a "forbidden domain" in contravention of the free exercise clause. Chief Justice Stone's dissent argued that whether a physical act (related or unrelated to religion but said to have taken place) actually had occurred was a matter that courts (and juries) could properly determine. And the dissenting opinion of Justice Jackson, averring that it was impossible to "separate an issue as to what is believed from considerations as to what is believable" would have dismissed the indictment and had done "with this business of judicially examining other people's faiths." This despite Jackson's unequivocal assertion that the defendants did that for which they were convicted and that their teachings were "nothing but humbug, untainted by any trace of truth." Jackson's position, although appealing, is difficult to credit if government is to have any way of preventing fraudulent criminal activity committed in the name of religious belief.

Considerations of religious belief and sincerity were also involved in Cantwell v. Connecticut (1940), which presented the question of whether members of the Jehovah's Witnesses could be convicted of soliciting for funds without prior approval, and of preaching their religious doctrines in a manner which might be offensive to others. Cantwell was the first case in which the Supreme Court squarely held that the free exercise clause was applicable to the states and, in addition, was the first of a lengthy series in which the Court displayed sensitivity to the claims of those, like the Witnesses, whose religious beliefs required vigorous proselytization. On the issue of prior approval the Court, while conceding that the relevant statute was intended to prevent fraud nevertheless struck it down because the official charged with the approval function was empowered to determine whether the cause was in fact a religious one. "Such a censorship of religion," said the Court, "as the means of determining its right to survive is a denial of liberty. . ." One may, without in any way denying the validity of the decision on this point, query whether it was accurate to see at issue the right of the Jehovah's Witnesses "to survive."

Much more difficult for the Court was Prince v. Massachusetts (1944), the first case excerpted in this chapter. Prince presented in perhaps its purest form the clash between the police power and the right of religiously motivated individuals to act on their beliefs. The Court had no end of difficulty with the issue, but finally came down on the side of the state's right to protect children from injurious influences said to be present when the activity involved was the distribution of religious literature on the street. The dissenting opinion of Justice Murphy, stressing the importance of the religious activity involved to the children, as well as what he viewed as the lack of any real danger stemming from street proselytization in the company of their guardian, seems very persuasive.

Prince, as much as any other case arising from the religion clauses, illustrates the necessity of a "balancing approach." On one side was the state's powerful interest in protecting children from exploitation and from influences calculated to interfere with their healthy development. On the other was the right of the parent to provide for what she perceived to be the spiritual welfare of her charge, as well as the right of the child to engage in activity held by that child to be essential to spiritual health. And, although the issue was not mentioned in the Prince opinions, surely the spectre of what is a "reasonable religious belief" lurked in the background. What made Prince extraordinarily difficult, especially for a justice as sensitive to claims of individual rights as Wiley Rutledge, must have been the fact that the claims of Mrs. Prince, her children, and her ward were eminently reasonable. One wonders, if the activity for which protection had been sought had been the handling of "poisonous snakes" or the avoidance of blood transfusions, whether the Court would have had the same difficulty in arriving at its decision.

What was nascent in Prince became almost overt in Wisconsin v. Yoder, the second case excerpted herein. Like Prince, Yoder involved the right of parents to control the upbringing of their child. And unlike Cantwell, Yoder may very well have involved the very survival of a religious group. The Old Order Amish, of which Yoder and his children were members, substantially reject the modern world in favor of a rural existence more characteristic of 19th century America. For them, any way of life other than an agricultural one is a denial of tenets central to their faith. Like virtually all religious groups, the Amish seek to transmit their faith to their children by exposing them to traditional ways, while protecting them from outside and corruptive influences. The Old Order Amish favor such education as is necessary to compete as farmers in a modern economy. In the instant case the children involved had been educated through the eighth grade at a public school dominated by Amish educational theories, and stressing the basics of reading, writing, and arithmetical skills.

When Wisconsin, however, pursuant to its laws requiring school attendance through age 16, sought to force the Amish to send their children to the public high school, the stage was set for struggle. To the Amish, especially in the context of the "consolidated high school" which sends rural children to be educated in modern, urban, multi-purpose institutions, the survival of their very way of life was involved. Fortunately for them, the Wisconsin Supreme Court agreed, and struck down the state's attempt to enforce its laws. So also, ultimately, did the United States Supreme Court.

Like Prince, Yoder involved not only religious freedom but also the right of parents to control the upbringing of their children. In what was perhaps the most notable opinion of his tenure, Chief Justice Burger, with only Justice Douglas in partial dissent, came down squarely on the side of the Amish. Burger's opinion is replete with references to the centrality of the rural way of life to the religion of the Old Order Amish, the undoubted sincerity with which that belief and that way of life are practiced by the group in question, and the threat presented by public education beyond the elementary level to that way of life and therefore to the Amish religion. And the state's assertion that high school was necessary to self-reliance and self-sufficiency was inadequate to overcome this danger, particularly in the absence of a record suggesting that those educated in the Amish tradition tended to become public charges. This being so, said the Chief Justice, it was difficult to believe that a year or two of additional public education would further any of these goals sufficiently, while it might do incalculable harm to the concerns of the Amish.

Yoder is an extraordinarily interesting opinion on a subject of major importance, and would seem to be pregnant with possibilities for the development of this area of constitutional law. Its emphasis on Amish sincerity and on the laudable results of an Amish upbringing seems to recognize the necessity, even in the face of obvious danger, of the Court's making judgments about such matters as religious sincerity, and even about the end product of particular religious experience. This portion of the Chief Justice's opinion drew the wrath of Justice Douglas, who thought it wholly irrelevant to the decision. But surely the Court would have decided the case differently if it had been established that the Amish devotion to the simple life was merely pretense adopted for the purpose of keeping their children available for farm labor, or if it had been shown that the precepts taught by the Amish regularly resulted in their children becoming public charges. In such circumstance the decision would likely have gone the other way for the very reason stated by the majority. The interests of the state were real and considerable in the abstract, and would have become compelling given the proper factual situation. Thus, while it is understandable and salutary to avoid passing judgment on religious actions and their consequences, Yoder demonstrates the necessity of such judgments in the more difficult free exercise cases.

Such a situation, which might have involved just such a judgment, was presented in the recent case of Employment Division v. Smith, also excerpted in this chapter. In Smith the state of Oregon had denied unemployment benefits to appellee on the grounds of "misconduct." Smith's transgression had been to ingest peyote as a part of a religious ceremony of the Native American Church, an action for which he had lost his job. The majority of the Court, with Justice Scalia writing the opinion, held the denial of benefits lawful. The Court, said Scalia, had never held that a person's religious beliefs alone excuse from compliance with valid state law. Cantwell and other cases were distinguished on the grounds that they also involved freedom of communication, while Yoder implicated also the right to educate one's children. And the Sherbert test[1] that governmental action must be justified by a compelling state interest had been developed in a context that "lent itself to individualized governmental assessment of the reasons for the relevant conduct, and having nothing to do with across the board criminal prohibitions."

Scalia declined the opportunity to inquire into whether the ingestion of peyote was "central" to the individual's religion, on the grounds that the issue of centrality was not one appropriate for court decision. Blackmun's dissent, by contrast, emphasized that the court must consider the severe impact of the regulation of those for whom ingesting peyote is "an act of worship and communion."

The argument that the impact of a prohibition has a bearing on whether the prohibition may be applied to "religious" activity is appealing, and would almost certain be held determinative in cases involving less controversial activity and more "well established" religious bodies. Its presentation in the contexts of drug ingestion and a non-mainstream church indicates, as do other cases involving the beliefs and practices of the Native American Church, the extraordinary difficulty which the Court may have in applying conventional free exercise doctrine to "unconventional" religious activity.[2]

One final case deserves mention. The 1986 case of Goldman v. Weinberger involved not the national government's "police power," but rather its right to make regulations for the military forces.[3] Petitioner, a member of the Jewish faith who was also an Air Force medical officer, desired to wear the "yarmulke" indoors, in violation of an Air Force regulation. The Court divided five to four in upholding the regulation. For Chief Justice Rehnquist, who spoke for the majority, the necessity for deference to military judgments about military regulations, coupled with the fact that the Air Force had drawn a "reasonable and evenhanded" line between visible and nonvisible religious apparel, justified the denial of Goldman's free exercise claim.

Justice Brennan, for the four dissenters, argued that only conditions of "functional utility, health, safety, and professional appearance" were sufficient to justify such limitations on religious freedom." Whether such considerations would be sufficient to serve the perceived need for military uniformity seems doubtful. And, as Justice Stevens, concurring in the judgment, pointed out, adoption of the Brennan approach would necessarily involve considerations of "character and sincerity, as well as the probable reaction of the majority." Thus a more sensitive approach by the military to issues of religious sensibility might well embroil military authorities in making the kind of distinctions about religious activity that the Supreme Court itself undertakes only reluctantly.

---

[1]See the discussion of Sherbert v. Verner in Ch. 16.

[2]Precisely the same sort of difficulty can be seen in the case of Lyng v. Northwest Indian Cemetery Protective Association (1988), excerpted and discussed in Chapter 16. Indeed, it is exacerbated in that case. For the religious exercise at issue in Smith, the ingestion of a substance for religious purposes, is at least initially comparable to the Christian practice of the taking of wine as a commemorative ritual. But the claim made in Lyng, that certain publicly owned physical terrain must be recognized as of special significance to, and in part set aside for the use of, those of a particular religion, has no ready analogy in the Judaic-Christian tradition. In the same vein is Bowen v. Roy (1986), in which it was claimed that governmental assignment to and use of a social security number for an Indian child interfered with the spiritual development of that child. It is perhaps significant that in all three of these cases the claim based on religious freedom has been denied. While it might be argued that this result demonstrates the insensitivity of the Court to the religious values of Native Americans, it seems more likely that it is the adequacy of tests developed to solve quite different types of problems that is at issue.

continued on next page

[3]Of course, the national government does exercise a "police power" in federal enclaves, which include military bases. But, while the power which the military exerts in such locations is not unlike the "police power" it's power over its members is, as conceded by all the opinions in Goldman, considerably broader.

PRINCE V. MASSACHUSETTS

321 U.S. 158 (1944)

MR. JUSTICE RUTLEDGE delivered the opinion of the Court.

The case brings for review another episode in the conflict between Jehovah's Witnesses and state authority. This time Sarah Prince appeals from convictions for violating Massachusetts' child labor laws, by acts said to be a rightful exercise of her religious conviction. . . .

Sections 80 and 81 form parts of Massachusetts' comprehensive child labor law. They provide methods for enforcing the prohibitions of 69, which is as follows:

"No boy under twelve and no girl under eighteen shall sell, expose or offer for sale any newspapers, magazines, periodicals or any other articles of merchandise of any description, or exercise the trade of bootblack or scavenger, or any other trade, in any street or public place."

Sections 80 and 81, so far as pertinent, read:

"Whoever furnishes or sells to any minor any article of any description with the knowledge that the minor intends to sell such article in violation of any provision of sections sixty-nine to seventy-three, inclusive, or after having received written notice to this effect from any officer charged with the enforcement thereof, or knowingly procures or encourages any minor to violate any provisions of said sections, shall be punished by a fine of not less than ten nor more than two hundred dollars or by imprisonment for not more than two months, or both."

"Any parent, guardian or custodian having a minor under his control who compels or permits such minor to work in violation of any provision of sections sixty to seventy-four, inclusive, . . . shall for a first offense be punished by a fine of not less than two nor more than ten dollars or by imprisonment for not more than five days or both; . . ."

The story told by the evidence has become familiar. It hardly needs repeating, except to give setting to the variations introduced through the part played by a child of tender years. Mrs. Prince, living in Brockton, is the mother of two young sons. She also has legal custody of Betty Simmons, who lives with them. The children too are Jehovah's Witnesses and both Mrs. Prince and Betty testified they were ordained ministers. The former was accustomed to go each week on the streets of Brockton to distribute "Watchtower" and "Consolation," according to the usual plan. She had permitted the children to engage in this activity previously, and had been warned against doing so by the school attendance officer, Mr. Perkins. But, until December 18, 1941, she generally did not take them with her at night.

That evening, as Mrs. Prince was preparing to leave her home, the children asked to go. She at first refused. Childlike, they resorted to tears; and, motherlike, she yielded. Arriving downtown, Mrs. Prince permitted the children "to engage in the preaching work with her upon the sidewalks." That is, with specific reference to Betty, she and Mrs. Prince took positions about twenty feet apart near a street intersection. Betty held up in her hand, for passers-by to see, copies of "Watch Tower" and "Consolation." From her shoulder hung the usual canvas magazine bag, on which was printed: "Watchtower and Consolation 5 cents per copy." No one accepted a copy from Betty that evening and she received no money. Nor did her aunt. But on other occasions, Betty had received funds and given out copies.

Mrs. Prince and Betty remained until 8:45 p. m. A few minutes before this, Mr. Perkins approached Mrs. Prince. A discussion ensued. He inquired and she refused to give Betty's name. However, she stated the child attended the Shaw School. Mr. Perkins referred to his previous warnings and said he would allow five minutes for them to get off the street. Mrs. Prince admitted she supplied Betty with the magazines and said, "[N]either you nor anybody else can stop me . . . This child is exercising her God-given right and her constitutional right to preach the gospel, and no creature has a right to interfere with God's commands." However, Mrs. Prince and Betty departed. She remarked as she went, "I'm not going through this any more. We've been through it time and time again. I'm going home and put the little girl to bed." It may be added that testimony, by Betty, her aunt and others, was offered at the trials, and was excluded, to show that Betty believed it was her religious duty to perform this work and failure would bring condemnation "to everlasting destruction at Armageddon."

. . . . Appellant . . . . rests squarely on freedom of religion under the First Amendment, applied by the Fourteenth to the states. She buttresses this foundation, however, with a claim of parental right as secured by the due process clause of the latter Amendment. *Meyer v. Nebraska.* These guaranties, she thinks, guard alike herself and the child in what they have done. Thus, two claimed liberties are at stake. One is the parent's, to bring up the child in the way he should go, which for appellant means to teach him the tenets and the practices of their faith. The other freedom is the child's, to observe these; and among them is "to preach the gospel . . . by public distribution" of "Watchtower" and "Consolation," in conformity with the scripture: "A little child shall lead them."

To make accommodation between these freedoms and an exercise of state authority always is delicate. It hardly could be more so than in such a clash as this case presents. On one side is the obviously earnest claim for freedom of conscience and religious practice. With it is allied the parent's claim to authority in her own household and in the rearing of her children. The parent's conflict with the state over control of the child and his training is serious enough when only secular matters are concerned. It becomes the more 80 when an element of religious conviction enters. Against these sacred private interests, basic in a democracy, stand the interests of society to protect the welfare of children, and the state's assertion of authority to that end, made here in a manner conceded valid if only secular things were involved. The last is no mere corporate concern of official authority. It is the interest of youth itself, and of the whole community, that children be both safeguarded from abuses and given opportunities for growth into free and independent well-developed men and citizens. Between contrary pulls of such weight, the safest and most objective recourse is to the lines already marked out, not precisely but for guides, in narrowing the no man's land where this battle has gone on.

The rights of children to exercise their religion, and of parents to give them religious training and to encourage them in the practice of religious belief, as against preponderant sentiment and assertion of state power voicing it, have had recognition here, most recently in *West Virginia State Board of Education v. Barnette.* Previously in *Pierce v. Society of Sisters,* this Court had sustained the parent's authority to provide religious with secular schooling, and the child's right to receive it, as against the state's requirement of attendance at public schools. And in *Meyer v. Nebraska,* children's rights to receive teaching in languages other than the nation's common tongue were guarded against the state's encroachment. It is cardinal with us that the custody, care and nurture of the child reside first in the parents, whose primary function and freedom include preparation for obligations the state can neither supply nor hinder. *Pierce v. Society of Sisters.*

And it is in recognition of this that these decisions have respected the private realm of family life which the state cannot enter.

But the family itself is not beyond regulation in the public interest, as against a claim of religious liberty. And neither rights of religion nor rights of parenthood are beyond limitation. Acting to guard the general interest in youth's well being, the state as *parens patriae* may restrict the parent's control by requiring school attendance, regulating or prohibiting the child's labor and in many other ways. Its authority is not nullified merely because the parent grounds his claim to control the child's course of conduct on religion or conscience. Thus, he cannot claim freedom from compulsory vaccination for the child more than for himself on religious grounds. The right to practice religion freely does not include liberty to expose the community or the child to communicable disease or the latter to ill health or death. The catalogue need not be lengthened. It is sufficient to show what indeed appellant hardly disputes, that the state has a wide range of power for limiting parental freedom and authority in things affecting the child's welfare; and that this includes, to some extent, matters of conscience and religious conviction.

But it is said the state cannot do so here. This, first, because when state action impinges upon a claimed religious freedom, it must fall unless shown to be necessary for or conducive to the child's protection against some clear and present danger, and, it is added, there was no such showing here. The child's presence on the street, with her guardian, distributing or offering to distribute the magazines, it is urged, was in no way harmful to her, nor in any event more so than the presence of many other children at the same time and place, engaged in shopping and other activities not prohibited. Accordingly, in view of the preferred position the freedoms of the First Article occupy the statute in its present application must fall. . . .

The state's authority over children's activities is broader than over like actions of adults. This is peculiarly true of public activities and in matters of employment. A democratic society rests, for its continuance, upon the healthy, well-rounded growth of young people into full maturity as citizens, with all that implies. It may secure this against impeding restraints and dangers within a broad range of selection. Among evils most appropriate for such action are the crippling effects of child employment, more especially in public places, and the possible harms arising from other activities subject to all the diverse influences of the street. It is too late now to doubt that legislation appropriately designed to reach such evils is within the state's police power, whether against the parent's claim to control of the child or one that religious scruples dictate contrary action.

It is true children have rights, in common with older people, in the primary use of highways. But even in such use streets afford dangers for them not affecting adults. And in other uses, whether in work or in other things, this difference may be magnified. This is so not only when children are unaccompanied but certainly to some extent when they are with their parents. What may be wholly permissible for adults therefore may not be so for children, either with or without their parents' presence.

Street preaching, whether oral or by handing out literature, is not the primary use of the highway, even for adults. While for them it cannot be wholly prohibited, it can be regulated within reasonable limits in accommodation to the primary and other incidental uses. But, for obvious reasons, notwithstanding appellant's contrary view, the validity of such a prohibition applied to children not accompanied by an older person hardly would seem open to question. The case reduces itself therefore to the question whether the presence of the child's guardian puts a limit to the state's power. That fact may lessen the likelihood that some evils the legislation seeks to avert will occur. But it cannot forestall all of them. The zealous though lawful exercise of the right to engage in propagandizing the community, whether in religious, political or other matters. may and at times does create situations difficult enough for adults to cope with and wholly inappropriate for children, especially of tender years, to face. Other harmful possibilities could be stated, of emotional excitement and psychological or physical injury. Parents may be free to become martyrs themselves. But it does not follow they are free, in identical circumstances, to make martyrs of their children before they have reached the age of full and legal discretion when they can make that choice for themselves. Massachusetts has determined that an absolute prohibition, though one limited to streets and public places and to the incidental uses proscribed, is necessary to accomplish its legitimate objectives. Its power to attain them is broad enough to reach these peripheral instances in which the parent's supervision may reduce but cannot eliminate entirely the ill effects of the prohibited conduct. We think that with reference to the public proclaiming of religion, upon the streets and in other similar public places, the power of the state to control the conduct of children reaches beyond the scope of its authority over adults, as is true in the case of other freedoms, and the rightful boundary of its power has not been crossed in this case.

In so ruling we dispose also of appellant's argument founded upon denial of equal protection. It falls with that based on denial of religious freedom, since in this instance the one is but another phrasing of the other. Shortly, the contention is that the street, for Jehovah's Witnesses and their children, is their church, since their conviction makes it so; and to deny them access to it for religious purposes as was done here has the same effect as excluding altar boys, youthful choristers, and other children from the edifices in which they practice their religious beliefs and worship. The argument hardly needs more than statement, after what has been said, to refute it. However Jehovah's Witnesses may conceive them, the public highways have not become their religious property merely by their assertion. And there is no denial of equal protection in excluding their children from doing there what no other children may do.

MR. JUSTICE MURPHY, dissenting:

This attempt by the state of Massachusetts to prohibit a child from exercising her constitutional right to practice her religion on the public streets cannot, in my opinion, be sustained.

The record makes clear the basic fact that Betty Simmons, the nine-year old child in question, was engaged in a genuine religious, rather than commercial, activity. She was a member of Jehovah's Witnesses and had been taught the tenets of that sect by her guardian, the appellant. Such tenets included the duty of publicly distributing religious tracts on the street and from door to door. Pursuant to this religious duty and in the company of the appellant, Betty Simmons on the night of December 18, 1941, was standing on a public street corner and offering to distribute Jehovah's Witness literature to passersby. There was no expectation of pecuniary profit to herself or to appellant. It is undisputed, furthermore, that she did this of her own desire and with appellant's consent. She testified that she was motivated by her love of the Lord and that He commanded her to distribute this literature; this was, she declared, her way of worshipping God. She was occupied, in other words, in "an age-old form of missionary evangelism" with a purpose "as evangelical as the revival meeting. . . ."

As the opinion of the Court demonstrates, the power of the state lawfully to control the religious and other activities of children is greater than its power over similar activities of adults. But that fact is no more decisive of the issue posed by this case than is the obvious fact that the family itself is subject to reasonable regulation in the public interest. We are concerned solely with the reasonableness of this particular prohibition of religious activity by children.

In dealing with the validity of statutes which directly or indirectly infringe religious freedom and the right of parents to encourage their children in the practice of a religious belief, we are not aided by any strong presumption of the constitutionality of such legislation. *United States v. Carolene Products Co.* On the contrary, the human freedoms enumerated in the First Amendment and carried over into the Fourteenth Amendment are to be presumed to be invulnerable and any attempt to sweep away those freedoms is *prima facie* invalid. It follows that any restriction or prohibition must be justified by those who deny that the freedoms have been unlawfully invaded. The burden was therefore on the state of Massachusetts to prove the reasonableness and necessity of prohibiting children from engaging in religious activity of the type involved in this case.

The burden in this instance, however, is not met by vague references to the reasonableness underlying child labor legislation in general. The great interest of the state in shielding minors from the evil vicissitudes of early life does not warrant every limitation on their religious training and activities. The reasonableness that justifies the prohibition of the ordinary distribution of literature in the public streets by children is not necessarily the reasonableness that justifies such a drastic restriction when the distribution is part of their religious faith. *Murdock v. Pennsylvania*. If the right of a child to practice its religion in that manner is to be forbidden by constitutional means, there must be convincing proof that such a practice constitutes a grave and immediate danger to the state or to the health, morals or welfare of the child. . . .

The state, in my opinion, has completely failed to sustain its burden of proving the existence of any grave or immediate danger to any interest which it may lawfully protect. There is no proof that Betty Simmons' mode of worship constituted a serious menace to the public. It was carried on in an orderly, lawful manner at a public street corner. And "one who is rightfully on a street which the state has left open to the public carries with him there as elsewhere the constitutional right to express his views in an orderly fashion. This right extends to the communication of ideas by handbills and literature as well as by the spoken word." *Jamison v. Texas*. The sidewalk, no less than the cathedral or the evangelist's tent, is a proper place, under the Constitution, for the orderly worship of God. Such use of the streets is as necessary to the Jehovah's Witnesses, the Salvation Army and others who practice religion without benefit of conventional shelters as is the use of the streets for purposes of passage.

It is claimed, however, that such activity was likely to affect adversely the health, morals and welfare of the child. Reference is made in the majority opinion to "the crippling effects of child employment, more especially in public places, and the possible harms arising from other activities subject to all the diverse influences of the street." To the extent that they flow from participation in ordinary commercial activities, these harms are irrelevant to this case. And the bare possibility that such harms might emanate from distribution of religious literature is not, standing alone, sufficient justification for restricting freedom of conscience and religion. Nor can parents or guardians be subjected to criminal liability because of vague possibilities that their religious teachings might cause injury to the child. The evils must be grave, immediate, substantial. Yet there is not the slightest indication in this record, or in sources subject to judicial notice, that children engaged in distributing literature pursuant to their religious beliefs have been or are likely to be subject to any of the harmful "diverse influences of the street." Indeed, if probabilities are to be indulged in, the likelihood is that children engaged in serious religious endeavor are immune from such influences. Gambling, truancy, irregular eating and sleeping habits, and the more serious vices are not consistent with the high moral character ordinarily displayed by children fulfilling religious obligations. Moreover, Jehovah's Witness children invariably make their distributions in groups subject at all times to adult or parental control, as was done in this case. The dangers are thus exceedingly remote, to say the least. And the fact that the zealous exercise of the right to propagandize the community may result in violent or disorderly situations difficult for children to face is no excuse for prohibiting the exercise of that right. . . .

MR. JUSTICE JACKSON:
The novel feature of this decision is

this: the Court holds that a state may apply child labor laws to restrict or prohibit an activity of which, as recently as last term, it held: "This form of religious activity occupies the same high estate under the First Amendment as do worship in the churches and preaching from the pulpits. It has the same claim to protection as the more orthodox and conventional exercises of religion." ". . .the mere fact that the religious literature is 'sold' by itinerant preachers rather than 'donated' does not transform evangelism into a commercial enterprise. If it did, then the passing of the collection plate in church would make the church service a commercial project. The constitutional rights of those spreading their religious beliefs through the spoken and printed word are not to be gauged by standards governing retailers or wholesalers of books." *Murdock v. Pennsylvania.*

It is difficult for me to believe that going upon the streets to accost the public is the same thing for application of public law as withdrawing to a Private structure for religious worship. . . .

Our basic difference seems to be as to the method of establishing limitations which of necessity bound religious freedom.

My own view may be shortly put: I think the limits begin to operate whenever activities begin to affect or collide with liberties of others or of the public. Religious activities which concern only members of the faith are and ought to be free—as nearly absolutely free as anything can be. But beyond these, many religious denominations or sects engage in collateral and secular activities intended to obtain means from unbelievers to sustain the worshippers and their leaders. They raise money, not merely by passing the plate to those who voluntarily attend services or by contributions by their own people, but by solicitations and drives addressed to the public by holding public dinners and entertainments, by various kinds of sales and Bingo games and lotteries. All such money-raising activities on a public scale are, I think, Caesar's affairs and may be regulated by the state so long as it does not discriminate against one because he is doing them for a religious purpose, and the regulation is not arbitrary and capricious, in violation of other provisions of the Constitution. . . .

The Court in the *Murdock* case rejected this principle of separating immune religious activities from secular ones in declaring the disabilities which the Constitution imposed on local authorities. Instead, the Court now draws a line based on age that cuts across both true exercise of religion and auxiliary secular activities. I think this is not a correct principle for defining the activities immune from regulation on grounds of religion, and Mur*dock* overrules the grounds on which I think affirmance should rest. I have no alternative but to dissent from the grounds of affirmance of a judgment which I think was rightly decided, and upon right grounds, by the Supreme Judicial Court of Massachusetts.

MR. JUSTICE ROBERTS and MR. JUSTICE FRANKFURTER join in this opinion.

WISCONSIN V. YODER

406 U.S. 205 (1972)

MR. CHIEF JUSTICE BURGER delivered the opinion of the Court.

On petition of the State of Wisconsin, we granted the writ of certiorari in this case to review a decision of the Wisconsin Supreme Court holding that respondents' convictions of violating the State's compulsory school attendance law were invalid under the Free Exercise Clause of the First Amendment to the United States Constitution made applicable to the States by the Fourteenth Amendment. For the reasons hereafter stated we affirm the judgment of the

Supreme Court of Wisconsin.

Respondents Jonas Yoder and Wallace Miller are members of the Old Order Amish religion, and respondent Adin Yutzy is a member of the Conservative Amish Mennonite Church. They and their families are residents of Green County, Wisconsin. Wisconsin's compulsory school-attendance law required them to cause their children to attend public or private school until reaching age 16 but the respondents declined to send their children, ages 14 and 15, to public school after they completed the eighth grade. The children were not enrolled in any private school, or within any recognized exception to the compulsory-attendance law, and they are conceded to be subject to the Wisconsin statute.

Amish objection to formal education beyond the eighth grade is firmly grounded in these central religious concepts. They object to the high school, and higher education generally, because the values they teach are in marked variance with Amish values and the Amish way of life; they view secondary school education as an impermissible exposure of their children to a "worldly" influence in conflict with their beliefs. The high school tends to emphasize intellectual and scientific accomplishments, self-distinction, competitiveness, worldly success, and social life with other students. Amish society emphasizes informal learning-through-doing; a life of "goodness," rather than a life of intellect; wisdom, rather than technical knowledge; community welfare, rather than competition; and separation from, rather than integration with, contemporary worldly society.

Formal high school education beyond the eighth grade is contrary to Amish beliefs, not only because it places Amish children in an environment hostile to Amish beliefs with increasing emphasis on competition in class work and sports and with pressure to conform to the styles, manners, and ways of the peer group, but also because it takes them away from their community, physically and emotionally, during the crucial and formative adolescent period of life. During this period, the children must acquire Amish attitudes favoring manual work and self-reliance and the specific skills needed to perform the adult role of an Amish farmer or housewife. They must learn to enjoy physical labor. Once a child has learned basic reading, writing, and elementary mathematics, these traits, skills, and attitudes admittedly fall within the category of those best learned through example and "doing" rather than in a classroom. and, at this time in life, the Amish child must also grow in his faith and his relationship to the Amish community if he is to be prepared to accept the heavy obligations imposed by adult baptism. In short, high school attendance with teachers who are not of the Amish faith—and may even be hostile to it—interposes a serious barrier to the integration of the Amish child into the Amish religious community.

There is no doubt as to the power of a State, having a high responsibility for education of its citizens, to impose reasonable regulations for the control and duration of basic education. Providing public schools ranks at the very apex of the function of a State. Yet even this paramount responsibility was, in *Pierce,* made to yield to the right of parents to provide an equivalent education in a privately operated system. There the Court held that Oregon's statute compelling attendance in a public school from age eight to age 16 unreasonably interfered with the interest of parents in directing the rearing of their offspring, including their education in church-operated schools. As that case suggests, the values of parental direction of the religious upbringing and education of their children in their early and formative years have a high place in our society. See also *Ginsberg v. New York* (1968); *Meyer v. Nebraska* (1923). Thus, a State's interest in universal education, however highly we rank it, is not totally free from a balancing process when it impinges on fundamental rights and interests, such as those specifically protected by the Free Exercise Clause of the First Amendment, and the traditional interest of parents with respect to the religious upbringing of their children so long as they, in the words of *Pierce,* "prepare [them] for additional obligations."

It follows that in order for Wisconsin to compel school attendance beyond the eighth grade against a claim that such attendance interferes with the practice of a legitimate religious belief, it must appear either that the State does not deny the free exercise of religious belief by its requirement, or that there is a state interest of sufficient magnitude to override the interest claiming protection under the Free Exercise Clause.

. . . . the record in this case abundantly supports the claim that the traditional way of life of the Amish is not merely a matter of personal preference, but one of deep religious conviction, shared by an organized group, and intimately related to daily living. That the Old Order Amish daily life and religious practice stem from their faith is shown by the fact that it is in response to their literal interpretation of the Biblical injunction from the Epistle of Paul to the Romans, "be not conformed to this world. . . ." This command is fundamental to the Amish faith. Moreover, for the Old Order Amish, religion is not simply a matter of theocratic belief. As the expert witnesses explained, the Old Order Amish religion pervades and determines virtually their entire way of life, regulating it with the detail of the Talmudic diet through the strictly enforced rules of the church community.

The record shows that the respondents' religious beliefs and attitude toward life, family, and home have remained constant—perhaps some would say static—in a period of unparalleled progress in human knowledge generally and great changes in education. The respondents freely concede, and indeed assert as an article of faith, that their religious beliefs and what we would today call "life style" have not altered in fundamentals for centuries. Their way of life in a church-oriented community, separated from the outside world and "worldly" influences, their attachment to nature and the soil, is a way inherently simple and uncomplicated, albeit difficult to preserve against the pressure to conform. Their rejection of telephones, automobiles, radios, and television, their mode of dress, of speech, their habits of manual work do indeed set them apart from much of contemporary society; these customs are both symbolic and practical.

As the record so values of the modern secondary school are in sharp conflict with the fundamental mode of life mandated by the Amish religion; modern laws requiring compulsory secondary education have accordingly engendered great concern and conflict.

The conclusion is inescapable that secondary schooling, by exposing Amish children to worldly influences in terms of attitudes, goals, and values contrary to beliefs, and by substantially interfering with the religious development of the Amish child and his integration into the way of life of the Amish faith community at the crucial adolescent stage of development, contravenes the basic religious tenets and practice of the Amish faith, both as to the parent and the child.

The impact of the compulsory-attendance law on respondents' practice of the Amish religion is not only severe, but inescapable, for the Wisconsin law affirmatively compels them, under threat of criminal sanction, to perform acts undeniably at odds with fundamental tenets of their religious beliefs. See *Braunfeld v. Brown* (1961). Nor is the impact of the compulsory-attendance law confined to grave interference with important Amish religious tenets from a subjective point of view. It carries with it precisely the kind of objective danger to the free exercise of religion that the First Amendment was designed to prevent. As the record shows, compulsory school attendance to age 16 for Amish children carries with it a very real threat of undermining the Amish community and religious practice as they exist today; they must either abandon belief and be assimilated into society at large, or be forced to migrate to some other and more tolerant region.

In sum, the unchallenged testimony of acknowledged experts in education and religious history, almost 300 years of consistent practice, and strong evidence of a sustained faith pervading and regulating respondents' entire mode of life support the claim that enforcement of the State's requirement of compulsory formal education after the eighth grade would gravely endanger if not destroy the free exercise of respondents' religious beliefs.

We turn, then, to the State's broader contention that its interest in its system of compulsory education is, so compelling that even the established religious practices of the Amish must give way. Where fundamental claims of religious freedom are at stake, however, we cannot accept such a sweeping claim; despite its admitted validity in the generality of cases, we must searchingly examine the interests that the State seeks to promote by its requirement for compulsory education to age 16, and the impediment to those objectives that would flow from recognizing the claimed Amish exemption.

The State advances two primary arguments in support of its system of compulsory education. It notes, as Thomas Jefferson pointed out early in our history, that some degree of education is necessary to prepare citizens to participate effectively and intelligently in our open political system if we are to preserve freedom and independence. Further, education prepares individuals to be self-reliant and self-sufficient participants in society. We accept these propositions.

However, the evidence adduced by the Amish in this case is persuasively to the effect that an additional one or two years of formal high school for Amish children in place of their long-established program of informal vocational education would do little to serve those interests. Respondents' experts testified at trial, without challenge, that the value of all education must be assessed in terms of its capacity to prepare the child for life. It i8 one thing to say that compulsory education for a year or two beyond the eighth grade may be necessary when its goal is the preparation of the child for life in modern society as the majority live, but it is quite another if the goal of education be viewed as the preparation of the child for life in the separated agrarian community that is the keystone of the Amish faith. See *Meyer v. Nebraska.*

The State attacks respondents' position as one fostering "ignorance" from which the child must be protected by the State. No one can question the State's duty to protect children from ignorance but this argument does not square with the facts disclosed in the record. Whatever their idiosyncrasies as seen by the majority, this record strongly shows that the Amish community has been a highly successful social unit within our society, even if apart from the conventional "mainstream." Its members are productive and very law-abiding members of society; they reject public welfare in any of its usual modern forms. The Congress itself recognized their self-sufficiency by authorizing exemption of such groups as the Amish from the obligation to pay social security taxes.

It is neither fair nor correct to suggest that the Amish are opposed to education beyond the eighth grade level. What this record shows is that they are opposed to conventional formal education of the type provided by a certified high school because it comes at the child's crucial adolescent period of religious development.

The State, however, supports its interest in providing an additional one or two years of compulsory high school education to Amish children because of the possibility that some such children will choose to leave the Amish community, and that if this occur, they will be ill-equipped for life. The State argues that if Amish children leave their church they should not be in the position of making their way in the world without the education available in the one or two additional years the State requires.

There is nothing in this record to suggest that the Amish qualities of reliability, self-reliance, and dedication to work would fail to find ready markets in today's society. Absent some contrary evidence supporting the State's position, we are unwilling to assume that persons possessing such valuable vocational skills and habits are doomed to become burdens on society should they determine to leave the Amish faith, nor is there any basis in the record to warrant a finding that an additional one or two years of formal school education beyond the eighth grade would serve to eliminate any such problem that might exist.

Insofar as the State's claim rests on the view that a brief additional period of formal education is imperative to enable the Amish to participate effectively and intelligently in our democratic process, it must fall. The Amish alternative to formal secondary school education has enabled them to function effectively in their day-to-day life under self-imposed limitations on relations with the world, and to survive and prosper in contemporary society as a separate, sharply identifiable and highly self-sufficient community for more than 200 years in this country. In itself this is strong evidence that they are capable of fulfilling the social and political responsibilities of citizenship without compelled attendance beyond the eighth grade at the price of jeopardizing their free exercise of religious belief.

Finally, the State, on authority of *Prince v. Massachusetts*, argues that a decision exempting Amish children from the State's requirement fails to recognize the substantive right of the Amish child to a secondary education, and fails to five due regard to the power of the State as *parens patriae* to extend the benefit of secondary education to children regardless of the wishes of their parents.

. . . . it seems clear that if the State is empowered, *as parens patriae*, to "save" a child from himself or his Amish parents by requiring an additional two years of compulsory formal high school education, the State will in large measure influence, if not determine, the religious future of the child. Even more markedly than in *Prince*, therefore, this case involves the fundamental interest of parents, as contrasted with that of the State, to guide the religious future and education of their children. The history and culture of Western civilization reflect a strong tradition of parental concern for the nurture and upbringing of their children. This primary role of the parents in the upbringing of their children is now established beyond debate as an enduring American tradition. If not the first, perhaps the most significant statements of the Court in this area are found in *Pierce v. Society of Sisters*, in which the Court observed:

"Under the doctrine of *Meyer v. Nebraska* we think it entirely plain that the Act of 1922 unreasonably interferes with the liberty of parents and guardians to direct the upbringing and education of children under their control. As often heretofore pointed out, rights guaranteed by the Constitution may not be abridged by legislation which has no reasonable relation to some purpose within the competency of the State. The fundamental theory of liberty upon which all governments in this Union repose excludes any general power of the State to standardize its children by forcing them to accept instruction from public teachers only. The child is not the mere creature of the State; those who nurture him and direct his destiny have the right, coupled with the high duty, to recognize and prepare him for additional obligations."

The duty to prepare the child for "additional obligations," referred to by the Court, must be read to include the inculcation of moral standards, religious beliefs, and elements of good citizenship. *Pierce,* of course, recognized that where nothing more than the general interest of the parent in the nurture and education of his children is involved, it is beyond dispute that the State acts "reasonably" and constitutionally in requiring education to age 16 in some public or private school meeting the standards prescribed by the State.

However read, the Court's holding in *Pierce* stands as a charter of the rights of parents to direct the religious upbringing of their children. And, when the interests of parenthood are combined with a free exercise claim of the nature revealed by this record, more than merely a "reasonable relation to some purpose within the competency of the State" is required to sustain the validity of the State's requirement under the First Amendment. To be sure, the power of the parent, even when linked to a free exercise claim, may be subject to limitation under *Prince* if it appears that parental decisions will jeopardize the health or safety of the child, or have a potential for significant social burdens. But in this case, the Amish have introduced persuasive evidence undermining the in terms of the welfare of the child and society as a whole. The record strongly indicates that accommodating the religious objections of the Amish by forgoing one, or at most two, additional years of compulsory education will not impair the physical or mental health of the child, or result in an inability to be self-supporting or to discharge the duties and responsibilities of citizenship or in any other way materially detract from the welfare of society.

In the face of our consistent emphasis on the central values underlying the Religion Clauses in our constitutional scheme of government, we cannot accept a *parens patriae* claim of such all-encompassing scope and with such sweeping potential for broad and unforeseeable application as that urged by the State.

For the reasons stated we hold, with the Supreme Court of Wisconsin, that the First and Fourteenth Amendments prevent the State from compelling respondents to cause their children to attend formal high school to age 16.

MR. JUSTICE WHITE, with whom MR. JUSTICE BRENNAN and MR. JUSTICE STEWART join, concurring.

Decision in cases such as this and the administration of an exemption for Old Order Amish from the State's compulsory school-attendance laws will inevitably involve the kind of close and perhaps repeated scrutiny of religious practices, as is exemplified in today's opinion, which the Court has heretofore been anxious to avoid. But such entanglement does not create a forbidden establishment of religion where it is essential to implement free exercise values threatened by an otherwise neutral program instituted to foster some permissible, nonreligious state objective. I join the Court because the sincerity of the Amish religious policy here is uncontested, because the potentially adverse impact of the state requirement is great, and because the State's valid interest in education has already been largely satisfied by the eight years the children have already spent in school.

MR. JUSTICE DOUGLAS, dissenting in part.

I agree with the Court that the religious scruples of the Amish are opposed to the education of their children beyond the grade schools, yet I disagree with the Court's conclusion that the matter is within the dispensation of parents alone. The Court's analysis assumes that the only interests at stake in the case are those of the Amish parents on the one hand, and those of the State on the other. The difficulty with this approach is that, despite the Court's claim, the parents are seeking to vindicate not only their own free exercise claims, but also those of their high-school-age children.

It is the future of the student, not the future of the parents, that is imperiled by today's decision. If a parent keeps his child out of school beyond the grade school, then the child will be forever barred from entry into the new and amazing world of diversity that we have today. The child may decide that is the preferred course, or he may rebel. It is the student's judgment, not his parents', that is essential if we are to give full meaning to what we have said about the Bill of Rights and of the right of students to be masters of their own destiny. If he is harnessed to the Amish way of life by those in authority over him and if his education is truncated, his entire life may be stunted and deformed. The child, therefore, should be given an opportunity to be heard before the State gives the exemption which we honor today.

The views of the two children in question were not canvassed by the Wisconsin courts. The matter should be explicitly reserved so that new hearings can be held on remand of the case.

EMPLOYMENT DIVISION, DEPARTMENT OF HUMAN RESOURCES OF OREGON, ET AL. V. SMITH ET AL.

494 U.S. 872 (1990)

JUSTICE SCALIA delivered the opinion of the Court.

This case requires us to decide whether the Free Exercise Clause of the First Amendment permits the State of Oregon to include religiously inspired peyote use within the reach of its general criminal prohibition on use of that drug, and thus permits the State to deny unemployment benefits to persons dismissed from their jobs because of such religiously inspired use. . . .

Respondents Alfred Smith and Galen Black were fired from their jobs with a private drug rehabilitation organization because they ingested peyote for sacramental purposes at a ceremony of the Native American Church, of which both are members. When respondents applied to petitioner Employment Division for unemployment compensation, they were determined to be ineligible for benefits because they had been discharged for work-related "misconduct". The Oregon Court of Appeals reversed that determination, holding that the denial of benefits violated respondents' free exercise rights under the First Amendment.

On appeal to the Oregon Supreme Court, petitioner argued that the denial of benefits was permissible because respondents' consumption of peyote was a crime under Oregon law. The Oregon Supreme Court reasoned, however, that the criminality of respondents' peyote use was irrelevant to resolution of their constitutional claim—since the purpose of the "misconduct" provision under which respondents had been disqualified was not to enforce the State's criminal laws but to preserve the financial integrity of the compensation fund, and since that purpose was inadequate to justify the burden that disqualification imposed on respondents' religious practice. . . .

Respondents contend that their religious motivation for using peyote places them beyond the reach of a criminal law that is not specifically directed at their religious practice, and that is concededly

constitutional as applied to those who use the drug for other reasons. They assert, in other words, that "prohibiting the free exercise [of religion]" includes requiring any individual to observe a generally applicable law that requires (or forbids) the performance of an act that his religious belief forbids (or requires). As a textual matter, we do not think the words must be given that meaning. It is no more necessary to regard the collection of a general tax, for example, as "prohibiting the free exercise [of religion]" by those citizens who believe support of organized government to be sinful, than it is to regard the same tax as "abridging the freedom . . . of the press" of those publishing companies that must pay the tax as a condition of staying in business. It is a permissible reading of the text, in the one case as in the other, to say that if prohibiting the exercise of religion (or burdening the activity of printing) is not the object of the tax but merely the incidental effect of a generally applicable and otherwise valid provision, the First Amendment has not been offended. . . .

The only decisions in which we have held that the First Amendment bars application of a neutral, generally applicable law to religiously motivated action have involved not the Free Exercise Clause alone, but the Free Exercise Clause in conjunction with other constitutional protections, such as freedom of speech and of the press, see *Cantwell v. Connecticut* (invalidating a licensing system for religious and charitable solicitations under which the administrator had discretion to deny a license to any cause he deemed nonreligious); *Murdock v. Pennsylvania* (1943) (invalidating a flat tax on solicitation as applied to the dissemination of religious ideas); *Follett v. McCormick* (1944) (same), or the right of parents, acknowledged in *Pierce v. Society of Sisters* (1925), to direct the education of their children, see *Wisconsin v. Yoder* (1972) (invalidating compulsory school-attendance laws as applied to Amish parents who refused on religious grounds to send their children to school). . . .

The present case does not present such a hybrid situation, but a free exercise claim unconnected with any communicative activity or parental right. Respondents urge us to hold, quite simply, that when otherwise prohibitable conduct is accompanied by religious convictions, not only the convictions but the conduct itself must be free from governmental regulation. We have never held that, and decline to do so now. . . .

Respondents argue that even though exemption from generally applicable criminal laws need not automatically be extended to religiously motivated actors, at least the claim for a religious exemption must be evaluated under the balancing test set forth in *Sherbert v. Verner* (1963). Under the *Sherbert* test, governmental actions that substantially burden a religious practice must be justified by a compelling governmental interest. . . .

A system would be courting anarchy, but that danger increases in direct proportion to the society's diversity of religious beliefs, and its determination to coerce or suppress none of them. Precisely because "we are a cosmopolitan nation made up of people of almost every conceivable religious preference," *Braunfield v. Brown*, and precisely because we value and protect that religious divergence, we cannot afford the luxury of deeming presumptively invalid, as applied to the religious objector, every regulation of conduct that does not protect an interest of the highest order. The rule respondents favor would open the prospect of constitutionally required religious exemptions from civic obligations of almost every conceivable kind. . . .

Values that are protected against government interference through enshrinement in the Bill of Rights are not thereby banished from the political process. Just as a society that believes in the negative protection accorded to the press by the First Amendment is likely to enact laws that affirmatively faster the dissemination of the printed word, so also a society that believes in the negative protection accorded to religious belief can be expected to be solicitous of that value

in its legislation as well. It is therefore not surprising that a number of States have made an exception to their drug laws for sacramental peyote use. But to say that a nondiscriminatory religious-practice exemption is permitted, or even that it is desirable, is not to say that it is constitutionally required, and that the appropriate occasions for its creation can be discerned by the courts. It may fairly be said that leaving accommodation to the political process will place at a relative disadvantage those religious practices that are not widely engaged in; but that unavoidable consequence of democratic government must be preferred to a system in which each conscience is a law unto itself or in which judges weigh the social importance of all laws against the centrality of all religious beliefs.

Because respondents' ingestion of peyote was prohibited under Oregon law, and because that prohibition is constitutional, Oregon may, consistent with the Free Exercise Clause, deny respondents unemployment compensation when their dismissal results from use of the drug. . . .

JUSTICE O'CONNOR, with whom JUSTICE BRENNAN, JUSTICE MARSHALL, and JUSTICE BLACKMUN join as to Parts I and II, concurring in the judgment.

Although I agree with the result the Court reaches in this case, I cannot join its opinion. In my view, today's holding dramatically departs from well-settled First Amendment jurisprudence, appears unnecessary to resolve the question presented, and is incompatible with our Nation's fundamental commitment to individual religious liberty. . . .

Because the First Amendment does not distinguish between religious belief and religious conduct, conduct motivated by sincere religious belief, like the belief itself, must therefore be at least presumptively protected by the Free Exercise Clause.

The Court today, however, interprets the Clause to permit the government to prohibit, without justification, conduct mandated by an individual's religious beliefs, so long as that prohibition is generally applicable. . . .

The First Amendment, however, does not distinguish between laws that are generally applicable and laws that target particular religious practices. Indeed, few States would be so naive as to enact a law directly prohibiting or burdening a religious practice as such. Our free exercise cases have all concerned generally applicable laws that had the effect of significantly burdening a religious practice. If the First Amendment is to have any vitality, it ought not be construed to cover only the extreme and hypothetical situation in which a State directly targets a religious practice. . . .

The Court endeavors to escape from our decisions in *Cantwell* and *Yoder* by labeling them "hybrid" decisions, but there is no denying that both cases expressly relied on the Free Exercise Clause, and that we have consistently regarded those cases as part of the mainstream of our free exercise jurisprudence. Moreover, in each of the other cases cited by the Court to support its categorical rule, we rejected the particular constitutional claims before us only after carefully weighing the competing interests. . . . That we rejected the free exercise claims in those cases hardly calls into question the applicability of First Amendment doctrine in the first place Indeed, it is surely unusual to judge the vitality of a constitutional doctrine by looking to the win-loss record of the plaintiffs who happen to come before us.˅

. . . respondents invoke our traditional compelling interest test to argue that the Free Exercise Clause requires the State to grant them a limited exemption from its general criminal prohibition against the possession of peyote. The Court today, however, denies them even the opportunity to make that argument, concluding that "the sounder approach, and the approach in accord with the vast majority of our precedents, is to hold the [compelling interest] test inapplicable to" challenges to general criminal prohibitions.

In my view, however, the essence of a free exercise claim is relief from a burden imposed by government on religious practices or beliefs, whether the burden is imposed directly through laws that prohibit or compel specific religious practices, or indirectly through laws that, in effect, make abandonment of one's own religion or conformity to the religious beliefs of others the price of an equal place in the civil community. . . .

The Court's holding today not only misreads settled First Amendment precedent; it appears to be unnecessary to this case. I would reach the same result applying our established free exercise jurisprudence.

I would . . . hold that the State in this case has a compelling interest in regulating peyote use by its citizens and that accommodating respondents' religiously motivated conduct "will unduly interfere with fulfillment of the governmental interest." *Lee* (1982). Accordingly, I concur in the judgment of the Court.

JUSTICE BLACKMUN, with whom JUSTICE BRENNAN and JUSTICE MARSHALL join, dissenting.

This Court over the years painstakingly has developed a consistent and exacting standard to test the constitutionality of a state statute that burdens the free exercise of religion. Such a statute may stand only if the law in general, and the State s refusal to allow a religious exemption in particular, are justified by a compelling interest that cannot be served by less restrictive means.

. . . . I agree with JUSTICE O'CONNOR'S analysis of the applicable free exercise doctrine, and I join parts I and II of her opinion. As she points out, "the critical question in this case is whether exempting respondents from the State's general criminal prohibition 'will unduly interfere with fulfillment of the governmental interest," quoting *United States v. Lee* (1982). I do disagree, however, with her specific answer to that question.

In weighing respondents' clear interest in the free exercise of their religion against Oregon's asserted interest in enforcing its drug laws, it is important to articulate in precise terms the state interest involved. It is not the State's broad interest in fighting the critical "war on drugs" that must be weighed against respondents' claim, but the State's narrow interest in refusing to make an exception for the religious, ceremonial use of peyote. . . . "This Court has consistently asked the Government to demonstrate that unbending application of its regulation to the religious objector 'is essential to accomplish an overriding governmental interest. . . ."

The State's interest in enforcing its prohibition, in order to be sufficiently compelling to outweigh a free exercise claim, cannot be merely abstract or symbolic. The State cannot plausibly assert that unbending application of a criminal prohibition is essential to fulfill any compelling interest, if it does not, in fact, attempt to enforce that prohibition. In this case, the State actually has not evinced any concrete interest in enforcing its drug laws against religious users of peyote. Oregon has never sought to prosecute respondents, and does not claim that it has made significant enforcement efforts against other religious users of peyote. . . .

The State proclaims an interest in protecting the health and safety of its citizens from the dangers of unlawful drugs. It offers, however, no evidence that the religious use of peyote has ever harmed anyone. The factual findings of other courts cast doubt on the State's assumption that religious use of peyote is harmful. . . .

The fact that peyote is classified as a Schedule I controlled substance does not, by itself, show that any and all uses of peyote, in any circumstance, are inherently harmful and dangerous. The Federal Government, which created the classifications of unlawful drugs from which Oregon's drug laws are derived, apparently does not find peyote so dangerous as to preclude an exemption for religious use. . . .

The carefully circumscribed ritual context in which respondents used peyote is far removed from the irresponsible and unrestricted recreational use of unlawful drugs. The Native American Church's internal restrictions on, and supervision of, its members' use of peyote substantially obviate the State's health and safety concerns. . . .

Moreover, just as in *Yoder*, the values and interests of those seeking a religious exemption in this case are congruent; to a great degree, with those the State seeks to promote through its drug laws. See *Yoder* (since the Amish accept formal schooling up to 8th grade, and then provide "ideal" vocational education, State's interest in enforcing its law against the Amish is "less substantial than . . . for children generally") (WHITE, J., concurring opinion). Not only does the Church's doctrine forbid nonreligious use of peyote; it also generally advocates - self-reliance, familial responsibility, and abstinence from alcohol. . . .

The State also seeks to support its refusal to make an exception for religious use of peyote by invoking its interest in abolishing drug trafficking. The is, however, practically no illegal traffic in peyote. . . . Also, the availability of peyote for religious use, even if Oregon were to allow an exemption from its criminal laws, would still be strictly controlled by federal regulations. . . . Peyote simply is not a popular drug; its distribution for use in religious rituals has nothing to do with the vast and violent traffic in illegal narcotics that plagues this country. . . .

Finally, the State argues that granting an exception for religious peyote use would erode its interest in the uniform, fair, and certain enforcement of its drug laws. The State fears that, if it grants an exemption for religious peyote use, a flood of other claims to religious exemptions will follow. It would then be placed in a dilemma, it says, between allowing a patchwork of exemptions that would hinder its law enforcement efforts, and risking a violation of the Establishment Clause by arbitrarily limiting its religious exemptions. This argument, however, could be made in almost any free exercise case. . . .

The State's apprehension of a flood of other religious claims is purely speculative. Almost half the States, and the Federal Government, have maintained an exemption for religious peyote use for many years, and apparently have not found themselves overwhelmed by claims to other religious exemptions. Allowing an exemption for religious peyote use would not necessarily oblige the State to grant a similar exception to other religious groups. The unusual circumstances that make the religious use of peyote compatible with the State's interests in health and safety and in preventing drug trafficking would not apply to other religious claims.

. . . A showing that religious peyote use does not unduly interfere with the State's interests in "one that probably few other religious groups or sects could make. . ."

Finally, although I agree with JUSTICE O'CONNOR that courts should refrain from delving into questions of whether, as a matter of religious doctrine, a particular practice is "central" to the religion, I do not think this means that the courts must turn a blind eye to the severe impact of a State's restrictions on the adherents of a minority religion. see *Yoder* (since "education is inseparable from and a part of the basic tenets of their religion . . . [just as] baptism, the confessional, or a sabbath may be for others," enforcement of State's compulsory education law would "gravely endanger if not destroy the free exercise of respondents' religious beliefs").

Respondents believe, and their sincerity has *never* been at issue, that the peyote plant embodies their deity, and eating it is an act of worship and communion. Without peyote, they could not enact the essential ritual of their religion. See Brief for Association on American Indian Affairs, et al. "(To the members, peyote is consecrated with powers to heal body, mind and spirit. It is a teacher; it teaches the way to spiritual life through living in harmony and balance with the forces of the Creation. The rituals are an integral part of the life process. They embody a form of worship in which the sacrament Peyote is the means for communicating with the Great Spirit). . . ."

If Oregon can constitutionally prosecute them for this act of worship, they, like the Amish, may be "forced to migrate to some other and more tolerant region." *Yoder*. This potentially devastating impact must be viewed in light of the federal policy—reached in reaction to many years of religious persecution and intolerance—of protecting the religious freedom of Native Americans.

The American Indian Religious Freedom Act, in itself, may not create rights enforceable against government action restricting religious freedom, but this Court must scrupulously apply its free exercise analysis to the religious claims of Native Americans, however unorthodox they may be. Otherwise, both the First Amendment and the stated policy of Congress will offer to Native Americans merely an unfulfilled and hollow promise. . . .

For these reasons, I conclude that Oregon's interest in enforcing its drug laws against religious use of peyote is not sufficiently compelling to outweigh respondents' right to the free exercise of their religion. Since the State could not constitutionally enforce its criminal prohibition against respondents, the interests underlying the State's drug laws cannot justify its denial of unemployment benefits. Absent such justification, the State's regulatory interest in denying benefits for religiously motivated "misconduct," is indistinguishable from the state interests this Court has rejected in *Frazee*, *Hobbie*, *Thomas*, and *Sherbert*. The State of Oregon cannot, consistently with the Free Exercise Clause, deny respondents unemployment benefits.

16
THE GENERAL WELFARE

To some extent, and particularly as regards the states, the "police power" discussed in the last chapter can be considered equivalent to the power to legislate for the general welfare. The distinction between the two is nevertheless useful, and one which is based on valid analytical considerations. The cases discussed in our consideration of the religious clauses and the police power were concerned with situations in which an individual's religiously motivated desire to do something clashed with a statute prohibiting that activity. Thus the issue was, in each case, whether government could prevent the desired action without interfering impermissibly with the free exercise of religion. By contrast, in the cases with which we are presently concerned, government seeks to act affirmatively to achieve broad social goals. And the issue, although in certain factual circumstances involving free exercise, is broadly whether such governmental action involves the establishment of religion.

The case of <u>McGowan v. Maryland</u> (1961) is one of a series of cases which involved the constitutionality of the once very prevalent "Sunday closing" laws.[1] These statutes, though they differed in the degree of closure that was mandated and the kind of activity that was affected, had in common the legislative desire to recognize Sunday as a special day by restricting the types of commercial activity which could take place. Quite often, as in <u>McGowan</u> itself, the patterns of coverage and exception dictated by the laws were a crazy quilt with no discernible rationale. As such they were frequently attacked, as was the case in <u>McGowan</u>, as being impermissibly vague. But vagueness, though an important part of free communication doctrine, plays little role in the explication of the religious clauses and was not determinative here.

More important was McGowan's contention that his state's Sunday closing laws constituted an establishment of religion, a charge to which the law seemed particularly vulnerable. It had been enacted some years prior to the application of the "religion clauses" to the states and almost certainly with the intent, on the part of the enacting legislature, to aid religion. And there can be little doubt that Sunday closing laws give aid to religion. People who do not have to work on Sunday are more likely to attend religious services than those who have to sandwich church attendance into a crowded work schedule, and those foreclosed from shopping on Sunday are perhaps more likely to go to church. It appeared doubtful, therefore, that either prong of the "establishment test," which required that there be a valid secular legislative purpose and that the primary effect of the legislation not be to aid religion, could be met. (The third prong of establishment, that of "entanglement," was still years away.)

Nevertheless the Court, with Chief Justice Warren writing the opinion, upheld the validity of Sunday closing laws. On the issue of "secular legislative purpose" the Chief Justice concluded that, whatever the religious origins of such laws, they now had a purpose which was secular. That purpose was the state's legitimate interest in promoting for its citizens a common day of rest. Providing such a day would assure families of time to spend together in whatever pursuits they deemed desirable. Moreover all persons, singly or in groups, would thereby be more free from the ordinary distractions of the typical commercial day, and the civil community might, if it desired, have opportunity to celebrate the fact of its community.

Appellants further argued that the singling out of Sunday, in preference to any other day, demonstrated a preference for the day of worship of the dominant religious groups, and thus impermissibly aided religion. But, said Warren, Sunday was the day which most of the citizenry, by custom, observed as a day of rest, and the state was free to craft its laws in such a way that their enforcement would be aided, rather than hindered, by the customs of the majority. Thus, even if those religions which regarded Sunday as a special day were to some degree aided by the statutes, this was only a secondary and not the primary effect of the legislation.

The dissenting opinion of Justice Douglas saw the issue very differently. For

Douglas, the case raised both establishment and free exercise questions, with the second, it would seem, proceeding from the first. He saw the issue as whether a state could impose criminal sanctions on minorities who do not worship on Sunday, and so did not share the majority's religious scruples against Sunday activity. Seen in this light, Douglas appears to be right. His argument however, did not really meet that advanced by the majority, that the purpose and effect of the law were, at this time, secular.

Douglas argued further that there is an establishment of religion in the constitutional sense any time that the practice of any religious group has the sanction of law behind it. This position might be interpreted to call for the invalidation of any laws based on values held by religions. And there are those, of course, who would argue that this is the correct position. Its logical result though, could be the invalidation of statutes based on, for example, the values found in the Decalogue.[2]

A second case involving Sunday closing laws is Braunfeld v. Brown, decided the same day as McGowan, in which the practice was challenged on free exercise rather than establishment grounds. Braunfeld was an Orthodox Jew who, by the operation of a Pennsylvania statute, was forced to close his store on Sunday, while at the same time his religion mandated that the store be closed on Saturday, the Jewish day of worship. This, he argued, constituted an inhibition of his free exercise rights because the state's choice of Sunday as a day of rest forced him to choose between economic survival and closing on the day mandated by his religion.

The Court majority, with Warren again writing the opinion, upheld the statute. As to the plaintiff's "burden" argument, the Court observed that even if the statute did operate to place a burden on religious exercise, that itself was not dispositive. Some kinds of burdens on free exercise *are* absolutely prohibited, as would be compulsions to believe, or regulations absolutely forbidding certain kinds of religious activity. Here, however, it was Braunfeld who opted for the closing of his business on Saturday. Any choice made was made by him alone. In addition, the statute at issue regulated a secular activity; the opening and closing of a store. Thus the regulation was not one of a religious practice, in the way that Reynolds allowed the regulation of polygamy even though such activity was a positive duty which, for Mormons, arose out of their religious belief.

Finally, to recognize the argument of Braunfeld and force the state to grant him exemption from Sunday closing laws could, said Warren, lead to an establishment of religion, and even to involving the state in determining the validity of religious belief. For if others saw that those who worshipped on Saturday were gaining an economic advantage, they might also choose to close on Saturday, or on some other day so as to be open all weekend. Moreover, the business of involving the state in formulating its secular laws so as to avoid advantages or disadvantages based on the religion of its citizens, could involve it in a number of controversial matters, e.g. the effects of the practice of "tithing" on one's ability to pay taxes, or the obligation to support the public schools of one whose religion also obliged the supporting of a parochial school system.

The dissenters in Braunfeld saw the plaintiff, forced to choose between his religion and economic survival, as being faced with a "cruel choice." Their view is even more fully articulated in the majority opinion in Sherbert v. Verner (1963), a case in which the Court may have overruled Braunfeld *sub silentio*.

Sherbert involved a state statute which denied unemployment benefits to individuals who refused to work at jobs for which they were qualified and which were offered to them. The plaintiff, a member of the Sabbatarian Seventh Day Adventist Church, refused to take Saturday work and was denied compensation. Despite the fact that the case seems virtually "on all fours" with Braunfeld, a majority of the Court struck down the state law as an impermissible interference with the plaintiff's free exercise rights.

Justice Brennan's opinion began by quoting the majority opinion in Braunfeld, in which Chief Justice Warren had observed that if the purpose or effect of the law is to impede the observance of religion or discriminate invidiously between religions, the law is unconstitutional even though it places only an indirect burden on the individual. This, according to Brennan, was precisely what occurred in this case, for the statute as implemented put pressure on the Sabbatarian to forego her religious preference. That pressure, said Brennan, was the same as if a fine was imposed for Saturday worship. The case could be distinguished from Braunfeld in that allowing an exemption in the latter case might have given Braunfeld an economic advantage over his competitors, whereas in Sherbert the petitioner received only money, not an advantage in the employment market. Finally, in Braunfeld the allowance of an exemption for Sabbatarians was found to create an unbearable administrative burden on the state, whereas the exemption requested here could easily be implemented. This being so, there existed no state interest sufficient to overcome the free exercise interest safeguarded by allowing the exemption.

Justice Stewart, author of the Braunfeld dissent, concurred in Sherbert, but argued that Braunfeld was in fact put in a much less favorable position by state action than was Sherbert. All the latter could lose was 22 weeks of unemployment compensation. Braunfeld, by contrast, could have lost his business and his freedom, given the fact that the Pennsylvania statute was criminal in nature. Stewart also argued that the two cases were fundamentally incompatible, and that Braunfeld should be overruled.

Sherbert has been reaffirmed and extended in a number of cases and, rather than Braunfeld, is generally regarded as representing the preferable approach to the problem.[3] But the correctness of the Sherbert approach may be questioned. What, for example, if one accepts the viewpoint, largely accepted in the military draft cases, that religion should, for free exercise purposes, be broadly defined to include ethical, moral, and philosophical beliefs? On such an accounting, Sherbert might provide a precedent for exemptions from working on Monday, because that was thought to be the day that Socrates took the hemlock, or Wednesday, because that was the day of the death of Martin Luther King, or Friday, because that was the day Christ died. It is true that allowing for such exemptions would not, in the age of computers, create a major administrative burden. But, with religion defined in such a broad manner, opportunities for abuse would seem rampant. Further, as the final supposition above suggests, there would seem to be little basis for distinguishing between one whose religion or other beliefs prevented working on two rather than one day a week.

The case of Walz v. Tax Commission involved a challenge to what is perhaps the single most widespread policy which might be said to constitute establishment; the granting of tax exemptions to religious institutions. The petitioner argued both that such exemptions invaded his free exercise rights by forcing him to pay heavier taxes in lieu of those which otherwise would be paid by the affected institutions, and that the granting of such exemptions impermissibly aided such religions. The Court chose to deal with the issue principally in terms of establishment.

Chief Justice Burger's majority opinion averted to the long history of religious tax exemptions at all levels of American government and concluded that the legislative purpose of such exemptions was not sponsorship of religion. New York, said the Chief, had not singled out religious groups for special consideration, but treated them as part of a larger group of private, nonprofit organizations, the existence of which was considered beneficial in stabilizing the community.

Burger did not accept New York's invitation to justify the exemption on the basis of the social services provided by churches, which might otherwise have to be provided by the state. There are perhaps two reasons for this refusal. First, the acceptance of such a justification would be clearly relevant to the much more controversial issue of tax exemptions as a return for the costs of maintaining private schools systems, for if such were not maintained they would, of course, have to be replaced by the state. Second, all churches do not engage in social welfare activity to the same extent. To accept such a justification, therefore, would implicitly allow and perhaps require legislatures to distinguish between churches for tax purposes, on the basis of their degree of social welfare activity, a tactic that clearly could lead to much religious divisiveness. And the task of distinguishing between a social welfare service and a religious activity could prove most difficult, and almost necessarily would involve the state into on-going investigations into church activity.

It is the question of "entanglement" as applied to taxation that in fact gave Burger the most trouble. Entanglement must, he said, be avoided. But it is inevitably involved in the question of taxation. Taxing churches would necessarily mean governmental scrutiny of church affairs. The giving of exemptions unquestionably fosters religion and thus, in a sense, was itself entanglement. The dispositive question, therefore, was which policy would foster more, and which less entanglement. Exemption, Burger concluded, created only minimal, remote, and "one time" entanglement, and was thus to be preferred to taxation. The logical implication of such a position would seem to be that freedom from taxation may perhaps be an entitlement which religion must be given in order to avoid entanglement. That issue, however, was not before the Court.

The concurring opinion of Justice Brennan picked up and expanded on Burger's theme of religion as an element of social stability. Brennan began by observing that the framers intended to forbid three kinds of involvement with religion: that which serves the essentially religious activities of religious institutions; that which employs government to fulfill essentially religious ends; and that which uses essentially religious means to serve governmental ends when secular means would suffice. But for him, religious institutions serve the community in a variety of ways that the state cannot. Most importantly, religious institutions contribute to American pluralism simply by contributing to diversity. Just as racial and ethnic groups contribute a kind of diversity not otherwise available, so religious groupings contribute a kind of diversity which no one else can contribute. If, therefore, pluralism is one of the ends of our society, then government can recognize religions simply because they serve the interests of pluralism.

Additionally, Brennan argued that tax exemptions are not the same as subsidies, chiefly because subsidies are direct transfers and use funds obtained from taxpayers as a whole, while exemptions involve no such transfers and are essentially passive instruments. Taken literally, as Justice Douglas noted in his dissent, Brennan's distinction on this point is very close to being one without a difference. For churches are aided just as surely by exemptions as they are by subsidies, and, assuming a constant level of necessary governmental revenue, that which churches don't provide must be made up elsewhere.

The Brennan argument, however, has considerable strength if one is concerned not with reality, but with symbolism. As a symbolic matter, there is a great difference between the state directly giving money to a church, an act which might overwhelmingly convey the impression of state approval of, and support for that church, and the state's merely allowing the churches to keep that which they already have, which conveys no such message to most people. Despite this distinction, and Burger's argument about the lesser degree of "entanglement" involved in exemptions than in taxation, the Court has held that such exemptions are not mandated by the free exercise clause. The most recent decision on the subject is Jimmy Swaggart v. California Board of Equalization, discussed in Chapter 14. In Texas Monthly v. Bullock (1989) the Court took the perhaps more significant step of striking down a state statute which exempted religious periodicals, but only religious periodicals, from state taxation.

The Texas exemption, said Justice Brennan for the majority, was an impermissible establishment of religion on the basis of both the "purpose" and "effects" test. Walz was distinguished on the basis that, in that case, the tax exemption was a part of a host of such exemptions given to nonprofit, eleemosynary institutions, whereas here it applied only to religious entities. The dissent argued that the case represented a repudiation of the underlying principles of Walz. Justice Brennan, it will be recalled, had said in Walz that religious tax exemptions were justified by religion's promotion of a kind of pluralism *not obtainable from any other source*. It does seem that Brennan does not explain why the same interest is not sufficient to uphold the exemption at issue in Bullock.

The three recent cases which are excerpted in this chapter cover the broad area of disputes that have arisen in the context of free exercise, establishment, and the general welfare. The first such case, Corporation of the Presiding Bishop v. Amos (1987), is that rarity in religion clause jurisprudence: a decision by a unanimous Court (although there was no unanimity in the reasons for the decisions). It seems likely that, although the case was decided on the basis of the establishment clause, unspoken considerations of free exercise were also at work. The issue in Amos was whether a church could constitutionally be exempted from the operation of laws prohibiting religious discrimination in employment, in order that it might be free to give preference to its own members. More specifically, the case involved the validity of such a statutory exemption as applied to the secular, nonprofit activities of religious organizations, and in fact to a situation in which a religiously nonconforming individual had been discharged from the position of building engineer of a nonprofit gymnasium operated by the Mormon church.

Justice White's majority opinion rejected the district court's attempt to distinguish between "religious" and "non-religious" activities, largely on the grounds that requiring a religious group to predict how a court might rule on such an issue would involve a governmental interference with religion, the avoidance of which constituted a "secular legislative purpose." On the issue of "effect," White argued that the establishment clause does not foreclose the state from taking actions which have the effect of allowing the *religion*, as distinguished from the government, to better advance itself. Further, the law effectuated not entanglement, but a more complete separation of church and state.

In taking this position, White did not distinguish between the for profit and the nonprofit activities of churches. It was this distinction, however, which recommended itself to the concurring justices (particularly Brennan and Marshall), all of whom limited their concurrence to the validity of nonprofit activity. In addition, the concurrences questioned, with it would appear considerable validity, Justice White's distinction between a state's advancing religion and a state's passing laws which better enable a religion to advance itself. Students will wish to ponder whether invalidating the law as applied to "profitable" activities might not have the effect of necessitating governmental overseeing of religious activity and thus triggering the "Catch 22" feature of Lemon. Also worthy of note is Justice O'Connor's rejection of the Lemon test in favor of an emphasis on "governmental endorsement" of religion, a matter which increasingly seems to play a pivotal role in establishment cases.

The second case, Lyng v. Northwest Indian Cemetery Protective Association, was expressly a free exercise case, and presented in starkest form the difficulty involved in applying conventional juridical categories to "unconventional" religious activities. At issue in Lyng was the government's desire to allow timber cutting and road construction in a portion of a national forest traditionally used for religious purposes by Native Americans. That the government could not provide a "compelling interest" in its choice of a site for the activity desired was not, said Justice O'Connor for a majority of five, dispositive. For "incidental effects of governmental programs, which may make it more difficult to practice certain religions, but which have no tendency to coerce individuals into acting contrary to their religious beliefs" do not violate the free exercise clause. Justice O'Connor even found lurking in the claims of the Native Americans an establishment issue, in that recognition of the claims would constitute "*de facto* beneficial ownership," and thus a subsidy to the Indian religion. And she declined to adopt the test proposed by the dissent, under which the Courts would determine which public lands are "central" or "indispensable" to the religion in questions, for "the dissent offers us the prospect of this Court's holding that some sincerely held religious beliefs and practices are not 'central' to certain religions."

Recalling the difficulties involved in official definitions of religion, one may applaud Justice O'Connor's unwillingness to become involved in making such a determination. At the same time, students will want to assess the minority's argument that just such a determination is indispensable to a proper determination of this case.

In the final case excerpted here, Bowen v. Kendrick, the Court dealt with the degree to which the establishment clause permits government to accommodate, and even to employ, religious beliefs and feelings in the pursuit of a governmental end. There would seem to be little doubt that government has a "compelling interest" in

348

lessening the number of teenage pregnancies. Equally certain, it would seem, is the fact that religion might play a powerful role in the achievement of such a goal. Congress, then, seems to have been on solid ground when it determined that the participation of religiously based groups could be helpful in accomplishing the purposes of the Adolescent Family Life Act. The harder question was whether such participation could be utilized without violating the establishment clause. For Chief Justice Rehnquist and Justices White, O'Connor, Scalia, and Kennedy, the answer was a resounding yes. For Justices Blackmun, Brennan, Marshall, and Stevens, the answer was just as clearly no. Students will want to pay particular attention to the manner in which each of the two principal opinions uses precedent, especially in discussion the concept of "pervasive sectarianism" and its consequence for establishment jurisprudence. Beyond this, it is worth considering whether the majority opinion may not presage a new and perhaps quite different approach to the permissible range of "accommodation" under the establishment clause.[4]

---

[1] In addition to McGowan and Braunfeld v. Brown, also discussed herein, the other principal "Sunday Closing Cases" were Two Guys from Harrison-Allentown v. McGinley, and Gallagher v. Crown Kosher Market, both decided, as were McGowan and Braunfeld, in 1966. McGinley, like McGowan, involved principally "establishment" considerations, while Gallagher, like Braunfeld, was decided on the basis of "free exercise."

[2] It is, of course, not even remotely likely that laws against murder and theft could be thus invalidated. But the Decalogue also includes a prohibition of adultery, which might be much more vulnerable. The distinction that would be suggested is, of course, that the first two cause "harm" But, of course, adultery may, and probably does cause harm most of the time.

[3] Lawrence Tribe, for example, argues that Braunfeld (and Gallagher v. Crown Kosher Market) should, in the light of Scherbert, be overruled. Tribe, *The American Constitution*, 2nd ed., 1157.

[4] A recent argument for the view that traditional, Lemon-based, establishment jurisprudence has deprived the government of the necessary assistance of religion in the achievement of wholly secular goals, and implying, therefore, that results like that in Kendick are to be welcomed, is made in Richard Morgan, *Disabling America, the Rights Industry in Our Time* (New York: Basic Books, 1984), Ch. 2, esp. 41-42.

CORPORATION OF THE PRESIDING BISHOP OF THE CHURCH OF JESUS CHRIST OF LATTER-DAY SAINTS ET AL. V. AMOS ET AL.

483 U.S. 327 (1987)

JUSTICE WHITE delivered the opinion of the Court.

Section 702 of the Civil Rights Act of 1964, 78 Stat. 255, as amended, 42 U. S. C. 2000e-1, exempts religious organizations from Title VII's prohibition against discrimination in employment on the basis of religion. The question presented is whether applying the 702 exemption to the secular nonprofit activities of religious organizations violates the Establishment Clause of the First Amendment. The District Court held that it does, and these cases are here on direct appeal pursuant to 28 U. S. C. 1252. We reverse.

The Deseret Gymnasium (Gymnasium) in Salt Lake City, Utah, is a nonprofit facility, open to the public, run by the Corporation of the Presiding Bishop of The Church of Jesus Christ of Latter-day Saints (CPB), and the Corporation of the President of The Church of Jesus Christ of Latter-day Saints (COP). The CPB and the COP are religious entities associated with The Church of Jesus Christ of Latter-day Saints (Church), an unincorporated religious association sometimes called the Mormon or LDS Church.

Appellee Mayson worked at the Gymnasium for some 16 years as an assistant building engineer and then as building engineer. He was discharged in 1981 because he failed to qualify for a temple recommend, that is, a certificate that he is a member of the Church and eligible to attend its temples. . . .

Lemon requires first that the law at issue serve a "secular legislative purpose." This does not mean that the law's purpose must be unrelated to religion—that would amount to a requirement "that the government show a callous indifference to religious groups," *Zorach v. Clauson* (1952), and the Establishment Clause has never been so interpreted. Rather, *Lemon's* "purpose" requirement aims at preventing the relevant governmental decisionmaker—in this case, Congress—from abandoning neutrality and acting with the intent of promoting a particular point of view in religious matters.

Under the *Lemon* analysis, it is a permissible legislative purpose to alleviate significant governmental interference with the ability of religious organizations to define and carry out their religious missions. Appellees argue that there is no such purpose here because 702 provided adequate protection for religious employers prior to the 1972 amendment, when it exempted only the religious activities of such employers from the statutory ban on religious discrimination. We may assume for the sake of argument that the pre-1972 exemption was adequate in the sense that the Free Exercise Clause required no more. Nonetheless, it is a significant burden on a religious organization to require it, on pain of substantial liability, to predict which of its activities a secular court will consider religious. The line is hardly a bright one, and an organization might understandably be concerned that a judge would not understand its religious tenets and sense of mission. Fear of potential liability might affect the way an organization carried out what it understood to be its religious mission.

After a detailed examination of the legislative history of the 1972 amendment, the District Court concluded that Congress' purpose was to minimize governmental "interfer[ence] with the decision-making process in religions." We agree with the District Court that this purpose does not violate the Establishment Clause.

The second requirement under *Lemon* is that the law in question have "a principal or primary effect . . . that neither advances nor inhibits religion." Undoubtedly, religious organizations.are better able now to advance their purposes than they were prior to the 1972 amendment to 702. But religious groups have been better able to advance their purposes on account of many laws that have passed constitutional muster: for example, the property tax exemption at issue in *Walz v. Tax Comm'n, supra,* or the loans of schoolbooks to schoolchildren, including parochial school students, upheld in *Board of Education v. Allen* (1968). A law is not unconstitutional simply because it *allows* churches to advance religion, which is their very purpose. For a law to have forbidden "effects" under *Lemon,* it must be fair to say that the *government itself* has advanced religion through its own activities and influence. As the Court observed in *Walz,* for the men who wrote the Religion Clauses of the First Amendment the 'establishment' of a religion connoted sponsorship, financial support, and active involvement of the sovereign in religious activity.. . . .

We find no persuasive evidence in the record before us that the Church's ability to propagate its religious doctrine through the Gymnasium is any greater now than it was prior to the passage of the Civil Rights Act in 1964. In such circumstances, we do not see how any advancement of religion achieved by the Gymnasium can be fairly attributed to the Government, as opposed to the Church.

We find unpersuasive the District Court's reliance on the fact that 702 singles out religious entities for a benefit. Although the Court has given weight to this consideration in its past decisions, it has never indicated that statutes that give special consideration to religious groups are *per se* invalid. That would run contrary to the teaching of our cases that there is ample room for accommodation of religion under the Establishment Clause. Where, as here, government acts with the proper purpose of lifting a regulation that burdens the exercise of religion, we see no reason to require that the exemption come packaged with benefits to secular entities. . . .

It cannot be seriously contended that 702 impermissibly entangles church and state; the statute effectuates a more complete separation of the two and avoids the kind of intrusive inquiry into religious belief that the District Court engaged in in this case. The statute easily passes muster under the third part of the *Lemon* test. . . .

The judgment of the District Court is reversed, and the cases are remanded for further proceedings consistent with this opinion.

JUSTICE BRENNAN, with whom JUSTICE MARSHALL joins concurring in the judgment.

I write separately to emphasize that my concurrence in the judgment rests on the fact that these cases involve a challenge to the application of 702's categorical exemption to the activities of a *nonprofit* organization. I believe that the particular character of nonprofit activity makes inappropriate a case-by-case determination whether its nature is religious or secular. . . .

Ideally, religious organizations should be able to discriminate on the basis of religion *only* with respect to religious activities, so that a determination should be made in each case whether an activity is religious or secular. This is because the infringement on religious liberty that results from conditioning performance of *secular* activity upon religious belief cannot be defended as necessary for the community's self-definition. Furthermore, the authorization of discrimination in such circumstances is not an accommodation that simply enables a church to gain members by the normal means of prescribing the terms of membership for those who seek to participate in furthering the mission of the community. Rather, it puts at the disposal of religion the added advantages of economic leverage in the secular realm. As a result, the authorization of religious discrimination with respect to nonreligious activities goes beyond reasonable accommodation, and has the effect of furthering religion in violation of the Establishment Clause. See *Lemon v. Kurtzman* (1971).

What makes the application of a religious-secular distinction difficult is that the character of an activity is not self-evident. As a result, determining whether an activity is religious or secular requires a searching case-by-case analysis. This results in considerable ongoing government entanglement in religious affairs. Furthermore, this prospect of government intrusion raises concern that a religious organization may be chilled in its free exercise activity. While a church may regard the conduct of certain functions as integral to its mission, a court may disagree. A religious organization therefore would have an incentive to characterize as religious only those activities about which there likely would be no dispute, even if it genuinely believed that religious commitment was important in performing other tasks as well. As a result, the community's process of self-definition would be shaped in part by the prospects of litigation. A case-by-case analysis for all activities therefore would both produce excessive government entanglement with religion and create the danger of chilling religious activity.

The risk of chilling religious organizations is most likely to arise with respect to nonprofit activities. The fact that an operation is not organized as a profit-making commercial enterprise makes colorable a claim that it is not purely secular in orientation. In contrast to a for-profit corporation, a nonprofit organization must utilize its earnings to finance the continued provision of the goods or services it furnishes, and may not distribute any surplus to the owners. This makes plausible a church's contention that an entity is not operated simply in order to generate revenues for the church, but that the activities themselves are infused with a religious purpose. Furthermore, unlike for-profit corporations, nonprofits historically have been organized specifically to provide certain community services, not simply to engage in commerce. Churches often regard the provision of such services as a means of fulfilling religious duty and of providing an example of the way of life a church seeks to foster. . . .

While not every nonprofit activity may be operated for religious purposes, the likelihood that many are makes a categorical rule a suitable means to avoid chilling the exercise of religion.

Sensitivity to individual religious freedom dictates that religious discrimination be permitted only with respect to employment in religious activities. Concern for the autonomy of religious organizations demands that we avoid the entanglement and the chill on religious expression that a case-by-case determination would produce. We cannot escape the fact that these aims are in tension. Because of the nature of nonprofit activities, I believe that a categorical exemption for such enterprises appropriately balances these competing concerns. As a result, I concur in the Court's judgment. . . .

JUSTICE BLACKMUN, concurring in the judgment. . . .

JUSTICE O'CONNOR, concurring in the judgment. . . .

In *Wallace* v. *Jaffree*, I noted a tension in the Court's use of the *Lemon* test to evaluate an Establishment Clause challenge to government efforts to accommodate the free exercise of religion: On the one hand, a rigid application of the *Lemon*. test would invalidate legislation exempting religious observers from generally applicable government obligations. By definition, such legislation has a religious purpose and effect in promoting the free exercise of religion On the other hand, judicial deference to all legislation; that purports to facilitate the free exercise of religion would completely vitiate the Establishment Clause. Any statute pertaining to religion can be viewed as an 'accommodation of free exercise rights. *Wallace v. Jaffree*.

In my view, the opinion for the Court leans toward the second of the two unacceptable options described above. While acknowledging that "[u]ndoubtedly, religious organizations are better able now to advance their purposes than they were prior to the 1972 amendment to 702," the Court seems to suggest that the "effects" prong of the *Lemon* test is not at all implicated as long as the government action can be characterized as "allowing" religious organizations to advance religion, in contrast to government action directly advancing religion. This distinction seems to me to obscure far more than to enlighten. Almost any government benefit to religion could be recharacterized as simply "allowing" a religion to better advance itself, unless perhaps it involved actual proselytization by government agents. In nearly every case of a government benefit to religion, the religious mission would not be advanced if the religion did not take advantage of the benefit; even a direct financial subsidy to a religious organization would not advance religion if for some reason the organization failed to make any use of the funds. It is for this same reason that there is little significance to the Court's observation that it was the Church rather than the Government that penalized Mayson's refusal to adhere to Church doctrine. The Church had the power to put Mayson to a choice of qualifying for a temple recommend or losing his job because *the Government* had lifted from religious organizations the general regulatory burden imposed by 702.

The necessary first step in evaluating an Establishment Clause challenge to a government action lifting from religious organizations a generally applicable regulatory burden is to recognize that such government action *does* have the effect of advancing religion. The necessary second step is to separate those benefits to religion that constitutionally accommodate the free exercise of religion from those that provide unjustifiable awards of assistance to religious organizations. As I have suggested in earlier opinions, the inquiry framed by the *Lemon* test should be "whether government's purpose is to endorse religion and whether the statute actually conveys a message of endorsement."....

These cases involve a Government decision to lift from a nonprofit activity of a religious organization the burden of demonstrating that the particular nonprofit activity is religious as well as the burden of refraining from discriminating on the basis of religion. Because there is a probability that a nonprofit activity of a religious organization will itself be involved in the organization's religious mission, in my view the objective observer should perceive the Government action as an accommodation of the exercise of religion rather than as a Government endorsement of religion.

It is not clear, however, that activities conducted by religious organizations solely as profit-making enterprises will be as likely to be directly involved in the religious mission of the organization. While I express no opinion on the issue, I emphasize that under the holding of the Court, and under my view of the appropriate Establishment Clause analysis, the question of the constitutionality of the 702 exemption as applied to for-profit activities of religious organizations remains open.

LYNG, SECRETARY OF AGRICULTURE, ET AL. V. NORTHWEST INDIAN CEMETERY PROTECTIVE ASSN. ET AL.

485 U.S. 439 (1988)

JUSTICE O'CONNOR delivered the opinion of the Court.

This case requires us to consider whether the First Amendment's Free Exercise Clause prohibits the Government from permitting timber harvesting in, or constructing a road through, a portion of a National Forest that has traditionally been used for religious purposes by members of three American Indian tribes in northwestern California. We conclude that it does not. . . .

The Free Exercise Clause of the First Amendment provides that "Congress shall make no law . . . prohibiting the free exercise [of religion]." It is undisputed that the Indian respondents' beliefs are sincere and that the Government's proposed actions will have severe adverse effects on the practice of their religion. Those respondents contend that the burden on their religious practices is heavy enough to violate the Free Exercise Clause unless the Government can demonstrate a compelling need to complete the G-O road or to engage in timber harvesting in the Chimney Rock area. We disagree.

In *Bowen v. Roy* (1986), we considered a challenge to a federal statute that required the States to use Social Security numbers in administering certain welfare programs. Two applicants for benefits under these programs contended that their religious beliefs prevented them from acceding to the use of a Social Security number for their 2-year-old daughter because the use of a numerical identifier would "'rob the spirit' of [their] daughter and prevent her from attaining greater spiritual power." Similarly, in this case, it is said that disruption of the natural environment caused by the G-O road will diminish the sacredness of the area in question and create distractions that will interfere with "training and ongoing religious experience of individuals using [sites within] the area for personal medicine and growth . . . and as integrated parts of a system of religious belief and practice which correlates ascending degrees of personal power with a geographic hierarchy of power." ("Scarred hills and mountains, and disturbed rocks destroy the purity of the sacred areas, and [Indian] consultants repeatedly stressed the need of a training doctor to be undistracted by such disturbance"). The Court rejected this kind of challenge in *Roy:*

The Free Exercise Clause simply cannot be understood to require the Government to conduct its own internal affairs in ways that comport with the religious beliefs of particular citizens. Just as the Government may not insist that [the Roys] engage in any set form of religious observance, so [they] may not demand that the Government join in their chosen religious practices by refraining from using a number to identify their daughter. . . .

. . . The Free Exercise Clause affords an individual protection from certain forms of governmental compulsion; it does not afford an individual a right to dictate the conduct of the Government's internal procedures.

The building of a road or the harvesting of timber on publicly owned land cannot meaningfully be distinguished from the use of a Social Security number in *Roy*. In both cases, the challenged Government action would interfere significantly with private persons' ability to pursue spiritual fulfillment according to their own religious beliefs. In neither case, however, would the affected individuals be coerced by the Government's action into violating their religious beliefs; nor would either governmental action penalize religious activity by denying any person an equal share of the rights, benefits, and privileges enjoyed by other citizens.

We are asked to distinguish this case from *Roy* on the ground that the infringement on religious liberty here is "significantly greater," or on the ground that the Government practice in *Roy* was "purely mechanical" whereas this case involves "a case-by-case substantive determination as to how a particular unit of land will be managed." Similarly, we are told that this case can be distinguished from *Roy* because "the government action is not at some physically removed location where it places no restriction on what a practitioner may do.". . . In this case, however, it is said that the proposed road will "physically destro[y] the environmental conditions and the privacy without which the [religious] practices cannot be conducted."

These efforts to distinguish *Roy* are unavailing. This Court cannot determine the truth of the underlying beliefs that led to the religious objections here or in *Roy,* see *Hobbie v. Unemployment Appeals Comm'n of Fla.* (1987), and accordingly cannot weigh the adverse effects on the appellees in *Roy* and compare them with the adverse effects on the Indian respondents. Without the ability to make such comparisons, we cannot say that the one form of incidental interference with an individual's spiritual activities should be subjected to a different constitutional analysis than the other.

. . . . It is true that this Court has repeatedly held that indirect coercion or penalties on the free exercise of religion, not just outright prohibitions, are subject to scrutiny under the First Amendment. Thus, for example, ineligibility for unemployment benefits, based solely on a refusal to violate the Sabbath, has been analogized to a fine imposed on Sabbath worship. *Sherbert*. This does not and cannot imply that incidental effects of government programs, which may make it more difficult to practice certain religions but which have no tendency to coerce individuals into acting contrary to their religious beliefs, require government to bring forward a compelling justification for its otherwise lawful actions. The crucial word in the constitutional text is "prohibit": "For the Free Exercise Clause is written in terms of what the government cannot do to the individual, not in terms of what the individual can exact from the government." *Sherbert* (Douglas, J., concurring).

Whatever may be the exact line between unconstitutional prohibitions on the free exercise of religion and the legitimate conduct by government of its own affairs, the location of the line cannot depend on measuring the effects of a governmental action on a religious objector's spiritual development. . . .

Even if we assume that we should accept the Ninth Circuit's prediction, according to which the G-O road will "virtually destroy the . . . Indians' ability to practice their religion," (opinion below), the Constitution simply does not provide a principle that could justify upholding respondents' legal claims. However much we might wish that it were otherwise, government simply could not operate if it were required to satisfy every citizen's religious needs and desires. A broad range of government activities—from social welfare programs to foreign aid to conservation projects—will always be considered essential to the spiritual well-being of some citizens, often on the basis of sincerely held religious beliefs. Others will find the very same activities deeply offensive, and perhaps incompatible with their own search for spiritual fulfillment and with the tenets of their religion. The First Amendment must apply to all citizens alike, and it can give to none of them a veto over public programs that do not prohibit the free exercise of religion. The Constitution does not, and courts cannot, offer to reconcile the various competing demands on government, many of them rooted in

sincere religious belief, that inevitably arise in so diverse a society as ours. That task, to the extent that it is feasible, is for the legislatures and other institutions. The Federalist No. 10 (suggesting that the effects of religious factionalism are best restrained through competition among a multiplicity of religious sects).

Respondents attempt to stress the limits of the religious servitude that they are now seeking to impose on the Chimney Rock area of the Six Rivers National Forest. While defending an injunction against logging operations and the construction of a road, they apparently do not *at present* object to the area's being used by recreational visitors, other Indians, or forest rangers. Nothing in the principle for which they contend, however, would distinguish this case from another lawsuit in which they (or similarly situated religious objectors) might seek to exclude all human activity but their own from sacred areas of the public lands. The Indian respondents insist that *"[p]rivacy* during the power quests is required for the practitioners to maintain the purity needed for a successful journey." Similarly: "The practices conducted in the high country entail intense meditation and require the practitioner to achieve a profound awareness of the natural environment. Prayer seats are oriented so there is an unobstructed view, and the practitioner must be surrounded by *undisturbed* naturalness." No disrespect for these practices is implied when one notes that such beliefs could easily require *de facto* beneficial ownership of some rather spacious tracts of public property. Even without anticipating future cases, the diminution of the Government's property rights, and the concomitant subsidy of the Indian religion, would in this case be far from trivial: the District Court's order permanently forbade commercial timber harvesting, or the construction of a two-lane road, anywhere within an area covering a full 27 sections (*i.e.* more than 17,000 acres) of public land. . . .

The dissent proposes an approach to the First Amendment that is fundamentally inconsistent with the principles on which our decision rests. Notwithstanding the sympathy that we all must feel for the plight of the Indian respondents, it is plain that the approach taken by the dissent cannot withstand analysis. On the contrary, the path towards which it points us is incompatible with the text of the Constitution, with the precedents of this Court, and with a responsible sense of our own institutional role.

Perceiving a "stress point in the longstanding conflict between two disparate cultures," the dissent attacks us for declining to "balanc[e] these competing and potentially irreconcilable interests, choosing instead to turn this difficult task over to the Federal Legislature." Seeing the Court as the arbiter, the dissent proposes a legal test under which it would decide which public lands are "central" or "indispensable" to which religions, and by implication which are "dispensable" or "peripheral," and would then decide which government programs are "compelling" enough to justify "infringement of those practices." We would accordingly be required to weigh the value of every religious belief and practice that is said to be threatened by any government program. Unless a "showing of 'centrality,'" is nothing but an assertion of centrality, the dissent thus offers us the prospect of this Court's holding that some sincerely held religious beliefs and practices are not "central" to certain religions, despite protestations to the contrary from the religious objectors who brought the lawsuit. In other words, the dissent's approach would require us to rule that some religious adherents misunderstand their own religious beliefs. We think such an approach cannot be squared with the Constitution or with our precedents, and that it would cast the judiciary in a role that we were never intended to play.

JUSTICE KENNEDY took no part in the consideration or decision of this case.

JUSTICE BRENNAN, with whom JUSTICE MARSHALL and JUSTICE BLACKMUN join, dissenting.

"[T]he Free Exercise Clause," the Court explains today, "is written in terms of what the government cannot do to the individual, not in terms of what the individual can exact from the government." *Sherbert v. Verner* (1963) (Douglas, J., concurring). Pledging fidelity to this unremarkable constitutional principle, the Court nevertheless concludes that even where the Government uses federal land in a manner that threatens the very existence of a Native American religion, the Government is simply not "*doing*" anything to the practitioners of that faith. Instead, the Court believes that Native Americans who request that the Government refrain from destroying their religion effectively seek to exact from the Government *de facto* beneficial ownership of federal property. These two astonishing conclusions follow naturally from the Court's determination that federal land-use decisions that render the practice of a given religion impossible do not burden that religion in a manner recognizable under the Free Exercise Clause, because such decisions neither coerce conduct inconsistent with religious belief nor penalize religious activity. The constitutional guarantee we interpret today, however, draws no such fine distinctions between types of restraints on religious exercise, but rather is directed against any form of governmental action that frustrates or inhibits religious practice. Because the Court today refuses even to acknowledge the constitutional injury respondents will suffer, and because this refusal essentially leaves Native Americans with absolutely no constitutional protection against perhaps the gravest threat to their religious practices, I dissent.

The Court does not for a moment suggest that the interests served by the G-O road are in any way compelling, or that they outweigh the destructive effect construction of the road will have on respondents' religious practices. Instead, the Court embraces the Government's contention that its prerogative as landowner should always take precedence over a claim that a particular use of federal property infringes religious practices. Attempting to justify this rule, the Court argues that the First Amendment bars only outright prohibitions, indirect coercion, and penalties on the free exercise of religion. All other "incidental effects of government programs," it concludes, even those "which may make it more difficult to practice certain religions but which have no tendency to coerce individuals into acting contrary to their religious beliefs," simply do not give rise to constitutional concerns. Since our recognition nearly half a century ago that restraints on religious conduct implicate the concerns of the Free Exercise Clause, see *Prince v. Massachusetts* (1944), we have never suggested that the protections of the guarantee are limited to so narrow a range of governmental burdens.

. . . in *Wisconsin v. Yoder* (1972), we struck down a state compulsory school attendance law on free exercise grounds not so much because of the affirmative coercion the law exerted on individual religious practitioners, but because of "the *impact* that compulsory high school attendance could have on the continued survival of Amish communities." Like respondents here, the Amish view life as pervasively religious and their faith accordingly dictates their entire lifestyle. Detailed as their religious rules are, however, the parents in *Yoder* did not argue that their religion expressly proscribed public education beyond the eighth grade; rather, they objected to the law because "the *values* . . . of the modern secondary school are in sharp conflict with the fundamental *mode of life* mandated by the Amish religion." By exposing Amish children "to a 'worldly' influence in conflict with their beliefs," and by removing those children "from their community, physically and emotionally, during the crucial and formative adolescent period of life" when Amish beliefs are inculcated, the compulsory school law posed "a very real threat of undermining the Amish community and religious practice." Admittedly, this threat arose from the compulsory nature of the law at issue, but it was the "impact" on religious practice itself, not the source of that impact, that led us to invalidate the law.

I thus cannot accept the Court's premise that the form of the Government's restraint on religious practice, rather than its effect, controls our constitutional analysis. Respondents here have demonstrated that construction of the G-O

road will completely frustrate the practice of their religion, for as the lower courts found, the proposed logging and construction activities will virtually destroy respondents' religion, and will therefore necessarily force them into abandoning those practices altogether. Indeed, the Government's proposed activities will restrain religious practice to a far greater degree here than in any of the cases cited by the Court today. None of the religious adherents in *Hobbie, Thomas,* and *Sherbert,* for example, claimed or could have claimed that the denial of unemployment benefits rendered the practice of their religions impossible; at most, the challenged laws made those practices more expensive. Here, in stark contrast, respondents have claimed—and proved—that the desecration of the high country will prevent religious leaders from attaining the religious power or medicine indispensable to the success of virtually all their rituals and ceremonies. Similarly, in *Yoder* the compulsory school law threatened to "undermin[e] the Amish community and religious practice," and thus to force adherents to "abandon belief . . . or . . . to migrate to some other and more tolerant region." Here the threat posed by the desecration of sacred lands that are indisputably essential to respondents' religious practices is both more direct and more substantial than that raised by a compulsory school law that simply exposed Amish children to an alien value system. And of course respondents here do not even have the option, however unattractive it might be, of migrating to more hospitable locales; the site-specific nature of their belief system renders it nontransportable.

Ultimately, the Court's coercion test turns on a distinction between governmental actions that compel affirmative conduct inconsistent with religious belief, and those governmental actions that prevent conduct consistent with religious belief. In my view, such a distinction is without constitutional significance. The crucial word in the constitutional text, as the Court itself acknowledges, is "prohibit," a comprehensive term that in no way suggests that the intended protection is aimed only at governmental actions that coerce affirmative conduct. Nor does the Court's distinction comport with the principles animating the constitutional guarantee: religious freedom is threatened no less by governmental action that makes the practice of one's chosen faith impossible than by governmental programs that pressure one to engage in conduct inconsistent with religious beliefs. The Court attempts to explain the line it draws by arguing that the protections of the Free Exercise Clause "cannot depend on measuring the effects of a governmental action on a religious objector's spiritual development," for in a society as diverse as ours, the Government cannot help but offend the "religious needs and desires" of some citizens. While I agree that governmental action that simply offends religious sensibilities may not be challenged under the Clause, we have recognized that laws that affect spiritual development by impeding the integration of children into the religious community or by increasing the expense of adherence to religious principles—in short, laws that frustrate or inhibit religious *practice*— trigger the protections of the constitutional guarantee. Both common sense and our prior cases teach us, therefore, that governmental action that makes the practice of a given faith more difficult necessarily penalizes that practice and thereby tends to prevent adherence to religious belief. The harm to the practitioners is the same regardless of the manner in which the Government restrains their religious expression, and the Court's fear that an "effects" test will permit religious adherents to challenge governmental actions they merely find "offensive" in no way justifies its refusal to recognize the constitutional injury citizens suffer when governmental action not only offends but actually restrains their religious practices. Here, respondents have demonstrated that the Government's proposed activities will completely prevent them from practicing their religion, and such a showing, no less than those made out in *Hobbie, Thomas, Sherbert,* and *Yoder,* entitles them to the protections of the Free Exercise Clause. . .

Today the Court professes an inability

to differentiate *Roy* from the present case, suggesting that "[t]he building of a road or the harvesting of timber on publicly owned land cannot meaningfully be distinguished from the use of a Social Security number." I find this inability altogether remarkable. In *Roy,* w e repeatedly stressed the "internal" nature of the Government practice at issue: noting that *Roy* objected to "the widespread use of the social security number by the federal or state governments *in their computer systems,*" we likened the use of such recordkeeping numbers to decisions concerning the purchase of office equipment. When the Government processes information, of course, it acts in a purely internal manner, and any free exercise challenge to such internal recordkeeping in effect seeks to dictate how the Government conducts its own affairs. . . .

In the final analysis, the Court's refusal to recognize the constitutional dimension of respondents' injuries stems from its concern that acceptance of respondents' claim could potentially strip the Government of its ability to manage and use vast tracts of federal property. In addition, the nature of respondents' site-specific religious practices raises the specter of future suits in which Native Americans seek to exclude all human activity from such areas. These concededly legitimate concerns lie at the very heart of this case, which represents yet another stress point in the longstanding conflict between two disparate cultures—the dominant western culture, which views land in terms of ownership and use, and that of Native Americans, in which concepts of private property are not only alien, but contrary to a belief system that holds land sacred. Rather than address this conflict in any meaningful fashion, however, the Court disclaims all responsibility for balancing these competing and potentially irreconcilable interests, choosing instead to turn this difficult task over to the Federal Legislature. Such an abdication is more than merely indefensible as an institutional matter: by defining respondents' injury as "nonconstitutional," the Court has effectively bestowed on one party to this conflict the unilateral authority to resolve all future disputes in its favor, subject only to the Court's toothless exhortation to be "sensitive" to affected religions. In my view, however, Native Americans deserve—and the Constitution demands—more than this. . .

I believe it appropriate, therefore, to require some showing of "centrality" before the Government can be required either to come forward with a compelling justification for its proposed use of federal land or to forgo that use altogether. "Centrality," however, should not be equated with the survival or extinction of the religion itself. In *Yoder,* for example, we treated the objection to the compulsory school attendance of adolescents as "central" to the Amish faith even though such attendance did not prevent or otherwise render the practice of that religion impossible, and instead simply threatened to "undermine" that faith. Because of their perceptions of and relationship with the natural world, Native Americans consider all land sacred. Nevertheless, the Theodoratus Report reveals that respondents here deemed certain lands more powerful and more directly related to their religious practices than others. Thus, in my view, while Native Americans need not demonstrate, as respondents did here, that the Government's land-use decision will assuredly eradicate their faith, I do not think it is enough to allege simply that the land in question is held sacred. Rather, adherents challenging a proposed use of federal land should be required to show that the decision poses a substantial and realistic threat of frustrating their religious practices. Once such a showing is made, the burden should shift to the Government to come forward with a compelling state interest sufficient to justify the infringement of those practices.

The Court today suggests that such an approach would place courts in the untenable position of deciding which practices and beliefs are "central" to a given faith and which are not, and invites the prospect of judges advising some religious adherents that they "misunderstand their own religious beliefs." In fact, however, courts need not undertake any such inquiries: like all other religious adherents, Native Americans would be the arbiters of which practices are central to their faith, subject only to the normal requirement that their claims be genuine and sincere. The question for the courts, then, is not whether the Native American claimants understand their own religion, but rather, whether they have discharged their burden of demonstrating, as the Amish did with respect to the compulsory school law in *Yoder,* that the land-use decision poses a substantial and realistic threat of undermining or frustrating their religious practices. Ironically, the Court's apparent solicitude for the integrity of religious belief and its desire to forestall the possibility that courts might second-guess the claims of religious adherents leads to far greater inequities than those the Court postulates: today's ruling sacrifices a religion at least as old as the Nation itself, along with the spiritual well-being of its approximately 5,000 adherents, so that the Forest Service can build a 6-mile segment of road that two lower courts found had only the most marginal and speculative utility, both to the Government itself and to the private lumber interests that might conceivably use it.

BOWEN, SECRETARY OF HEALTH AND HUMAN SERVICES V.
KENDRICK ET AL.

487 U.S. 589 (1988)

CHIEF JUSTICE REHNQUIST delivered the opinion of the Court.

This case involves a challenge to a federal grant program that provides funding for services relating to adolescent sexuality and pregnancy. Considering the federal statute both "on its face" and "as applied," the District Court ruled that the statute violated the Establishment Clause of the First Amendment insofar as it provided for the involvement of religious organizations in the federally funded programs. We conclude, however, that the statute is not unconstitutional on its face, and that a determination of whether any of the grants made pursuant to the statute violate the Establishment Clause requires further proceedings in the District Court.

. . . the AFLA is essentially a scheme for providing grants to public or nonprofit private organizations or agencies "for services and research in the area of premarital adolescent sexual relations and pregnancy." S. Rep. No. 97-161 (1981) (hereinafter Senate Report). These grants are intended to serve several purposes, including the promotion of "self discipline and other prudent approaches to the problem of adolescent premarital sexual relations," 300z(b)(1), the promotion of adoption as an alternative for adolescent parents, 300z(b)(2), the establishment of new approaches to the delivery of care services for pregnant adolescents, 300z(b)(3), and the support of research and demonstration projects "concerning the societal causes and consequences of adolescent premarital sexual relations, contraceptive use, pregnancy, and child rearing," 300z(b)(4).

In pertinent part, grant recipients are to provide two types of services: "care services," for the provision of care to pregnant adolescents and adolescent parents, 300z1(a)(7), and "prevention services," for the prevention of adolescent sexual relations, 300z-1(a)(8). While the AFLA leaves it up to the Secretary of Health and Human Services (the Secretary) to define exactly what types of services a grantee must provide, the statute contains a listing of "necessary services" that may be funded. These services include pregnancy testing and maternity counseling, adoption counseling and referral services, prenatal and postnatal health care, nutritional information, counseling, child care, mental health services, and perhaps most importantly for present purposes, "educational services relating to family life and problems associated with adolescent premarital sexual relations," 300z-1(a)(4).

. . . .the AFLA expressly states that federally provided services in this area should promote the involvement of parents, and should "emphasize the provision of support by other family members, religious and charitable organizations, voluntary associations, and other groups." The AFLA implements this goal by providing in 300z-2 that demonstration projects funded by the government "shall use such methods as will strengthen the capacity of families to deal with the sexual behavior, pregnancy, or parenthood of adolescents and to make use of support systems such as other family members, friends, religious and charitable organizations, and voluntary associations." In addition, AFLA requires grant applicants, among other things, to describe how they will, "as appropriate in the provision of services[,] involve families of adolescents[, and] involve religious and charitable organizations, voluntary associations, and other groups in the private sector as well as services provided by publicly sponsored initiatives." This broad-based involvement of groups outside of the government was intended by Congress to "establish better coordination, integration, and linkages" among existing programs in the community, to aid in the development of "strong family values and close family ties," and to "help adolescents and their families deal with complex issues of adolescent premarital sexual relations and the consequences of such relations. . . ."

Since 1981, when the AFLA was adopted, the Secretary has received 1,088 grant applications and awarded 141 grants. Funding has gone to a wide variety of recipients, including state and local health agencies, private hospitals, community health associations, privately operated health care centers, and community and charitable organizations. It is undisputed that a number of grantees or subgrantees were organizations with institutional ties to religious denominations.

As we see it, it is clear from the face of the statute that the AFLA was motivated primarily, if not entirely, by a legitimate secular purpose—the elimination or reduction of social and economic problems caused by teenage sexuality, pregnancy, and parenthood. Appellees cannot, and do not, dispute that, on the whole, religious concerns were not the sole motivation behind the Act, nor can it be said that the AFLA lacks a legitimate secular purpose. . . .

Congress' decision to amend the statute in this way reflects the entirely appropriate aim of increasing broadbased community involvement "in helping adolescent boys and girls understand the implications of premarital sexual relations, pregnancy, and parenthood." In adopting the AFLA, Congress expressly intended to expand the services already authorized by Title VI, to insure the increased participation of parents in education and support services, to increase the flexibility of the programs, and to spark the development of new, innovative services. These are all legitimate secular goals that are furthered by the AFLA's additions to Title VI, including the challenged provisions that refer to religious organizations. There simply is no evidence that Congress' "actual purpose" in passing the AFLA was one of "endorsing religion."

. . . .there are two ways in which the statute, considered "on its face," might be said to have the impermissible primary effect of advancing religion. First, it can be argued that the AFLA advances religion by expressly recognizing that "religious organizations have a role to play" in addressing the problems associated with teenage sexuality. In this view, even if no religious institution receives aid or funding pursuant to the AFLA, the statute is invalid under the Establishment Clause because, among other things, it expressly enlists the involvement of religiously affiliated organizations in the federally subsidized programs, it endorses religious solutions to the problems addressed by the Act, or it creates symbolic ties between church and state. Secondly, it can be argued that the AFLA is invalid on its face because it allows religiously affiliated organizations to participate as grantees or subgrantees in AFLA programs. From this standpoint, the Act is invalid because it authorizes direct federal funding of religious organizations which, given the AFLA's educational function and the fact that the AFLA's "viewpoint" may coincide with the grantee's "viewpoint" on sexual matters, will result unavoidably in the impermissible "inculcation" of religious beliefs in the context of a federally funded program.

We consider the former objection first. As noted previously, the AFLA expressly mentions the role of religious organizations in four places. It states (1) that the problems of teenage sexuality are "best approached through a variety of integrated and essential services provided to adolescents and their families by [, among others, religious organizations," 300z(a)(8)(B), (2) that federally subsidized services "should emphasize the provision of support by[, among others,] religious and charitable organizations," (3) that AFLA programs "shall use such methods as will strengthen the capacity of families . . . to make use of support systems such as . . . religious . . . organizations," and (4) that grant applicants shall describe how they will involve religious organizations, among other groups, in the provision of services under the Act.

Putting aside for the moment the possible role of religious organizations as grantees, these provisions of the statute reflect at most Congress' considered judgment that religious organizations can help solve the; problems to which the AFLA is addressed. Nothing in our previous cases prevents Congress from making such a judgment or from recognizing the important part that religion or religious organizations may play in resolving certain secular problems. Particularly when, as Congress found, "prevention of adolescent sexual activity and adolescent pregnancy depends primarily upon developing strong family values and close family ties," it seems quite sensible for Congress to recognize that religious organizations can influence values and can have some influence on family life, including parents' relations with their adolescent children. To the extent that this congressional recognition has any effect of advancing religion, the effect is at most "incidental and remote." In addition, although the AFLA does require potential grantees to describe how they will involve religious organizations in the provision of services under the Act, it also requires grantees to describe the involvement of "charitable organizations, voluntary associations, and other groups in the private sector." In our view, this reflects the statute's successful maintenance of "a course of neutrality among religions, and between religion and nonreligion," *Grand Rapids School District v. Ball.* . . .

This brings us to the second ground for objecting to the AFLA: the fact that it allows religious institutions to participate as recipients of federal funds. The AFLA defines an "eligible grant recipient" as a "public or nonprofit private organization or agency" which demonstrates the capability of providing the requisite services. As this provision would indicate, a fairly wide spectrum of organizations is eligible to apply for and receive funding under the Act, and nothing on the face of the Act suggests it is anything but neutral with respect to the grantee's status as a sectarian or purely secular institution ("Religious affiliation is not a criterion for selection as a grantee . . ."). In this regard, then, the AFLA is similar to other statutes that this Court has upheld against Establishment Clause challenges in the past. . . .

We note in addition that this Court has never held that religious institutions are disabled by the First Amendment from participating in publicly sponsored social welfare programs.

Of course, even when the challenged statute appears to be neutral on its face, we have always been careful to ensure that direct government aid to religiously affiliated institutions does not have the primary effect of advancing religion.

. . . . a relevant factor in deciding whether a particular statute on its face can be said to have the improper effect of advancing religion is the determination of whether, and to what extent, the statute directs government aid to pervasively sectarian institutions. In *Grand Rapids School District*, for example, the Court began its "effects" inquiry with a consideration of the nature of the institutions in which the [challenged] programs "operate."

In this case, nothing on the face of the AFLA indicates that a significant proportion of the federal funds will be disbursed to pervasively "sectarian" institutions. Indeed, the contention that there is a substantial risk of such institutions receiving direct aid is undercut by the AFLA's facially neutral grant requirements, the wide spectrum of public and private organizations which are capable of meeting the AFLA's requirements, and the fact that, of the eligible religious institutions, many will not deserve the label of "pervasively sectarian. . . ."

Nor do we agree with the District Court that the AFLA necessarily has the effect of advancing religion because the religiously affiliated AFLA grantees will be providing educational and counseling services to adolescents. Of course, we have said that the Establishment Clause does "prohibit government-financed or government-sponsored indoctrination into the beliefs of a particular religious faith."

. . . But nothing in our prior cases warrants the presumption adopted by the District Court that religiously affiliated AFLA grantees are not capable of carrying out their functions under the AFLA in lawful, secular manner.

Only in the context of aid to "pervasively sectarian" institutions have we invalidated an aid program on the grounds that there was a "substantial" risk that aid to these religious institutions would, knowingly or unknowingly, result in religious indoctrination. . . .

We also disagree with the District Court's conclusion that the AFLA is invalid because it authorizes "teaching" by religious grant recipients on "matters [that] are fundamental elements of religious doctrine," such as the harm of premarital sex and the reasons for choosing adoption over abortion. On an issue as sensitive and important as teenage sexuality, it is not surprising that the Government's secular concerns would either coincide or conflict with those of religious institutions. But the possibility or even the likelihood that some of the religious institutions who receive AFLA funding will agree with the message that Congress intended to deliver to adolescents through the AFLA is insufficient to warrant a finding that the statute on its face has the primary effect of advancing religion. Nor does the alignment of the statute and the religious views of the grantees run afoul of our proscription against "fund[ing] a specifically religious activity in an otherwise substantially secular setting." The facially neutral projects authorized by the AFLA— including pregnancy testing, adoption counseling and referral services, prenatal and postnatal care, educational services, residential care, child care, consumer education, etc.—are not themselves "specifically religious activities," and they are not converted into such activities by the fact that they are carried out by organizations with religious affiliations.

As yet another reason for invalidating parts of the AFLA, the District Court found that the involvement of religious organizations in the Act has the impermissible effect of creating a "crucial symbolic link" between government and religion. If we were to adopt the District Court's reasoning, it could be argued that any time a government aid program provides funding to religious organizations in an area in which the organization also has an interest, an impermissible "symbolic link" could be created, no matter whether the aid was to be used solely for secular purposes. This would jeopardize Government aid to religiously affiliated hospitals, for example, on the ground that patients would perceive a "symbolic link" between the hospital—

part of whose "religious mission" might be to save lives—and whatever government entity is subsidizing the purely secular medical services provided to the patient. We decline to adopt the District Court's reasoning and conclude that, in this case, whatever "symbolic link" might in fact be created by the AFLA's disbursement of funds to religious institutions is not sufficient to justify striking down the statute on its face.

A final argument that has been advanced for striking down the AFLA on "effects" grounds is the fact that the statute lacks an express provision preventing the use of federal funds for religious purposes. Clearly, if there were such a provision in this statute, it would be easier to conclude that the statute on its face could not be said to have the primary effect of advancing religion, but we have never stated that a *statutory* restriction is constitutionally required. . . .

Unlike some other grant programs, in which aid might be given out in one-time grants without ongoing supervision by the Government, the programs established under the authority of the AFLA can be monitored to determine whether the funds are, in effect, being used by the grantees in such a way as to advance religion. Given this statutory scheme, we do not think that the absence of an express limitation on the use of federal funds for religious purposes means that the statute, on its face, has the primary effect of advancing religion.

This, of course, brings us to the third prong of the *Lemon* Establishment Clause "test"—the question whether the AFLA leads to "'an excessive government entanglement with religion.'" There is no doubt that the monitoring of AFLA grants is necessary if the Secretary is to ensure that public money is to be spent in the way that Congress intended and in a way that comports with the Establishment Clause. Accordingly, this case presents us with yet another "Catch-22" argument: the very supervision of the aid to assure, that it does not further religion renders the statute invalid. [But] there is no reason to assume that the religious organizations which may receive grants are "pervasively sectarian" in the same sense as the Court has held parochial schools to be. There is accordingly no reason to fear that the less intensive monitoring involved here will cause the Government to intrude unduly in the day-to-day operation of the religiously affiliated AFLA grantees. Unquestionably, the Secretary will review the programs set up and run by the AFLA grantees, and undoubtedly this will involve a review of, for example, the educational materials that a grantee proposes to use. The Secretary may also wish to have Government employees visit the clinics or offices where AFLA programs are being carried out to see whether they are in fact being administered in accordance with statutory and constitutional requirements. But in our view, this type of grant monitoring does not amount to "excessive entanglement," at least in the context of a statute authorizing grants to religiously affiliated organizations that are not necessarily "pervasively sectarian."

JUSTICE O'CONNOR, concurring. . . .

JUSTICE KENNEDY, with whom JUSTICE SCALIA joins, concurring. . . .

JUSTICE BLACKMUN, with whom JUSTICE BRENNAN, JUSTICE MARSHALL, and JUSTICE STEVENS join, dissenting. . . .

The majority first skews the Establishment Clause analysis by adopting a cramped view of what constitutes a pervasively sectarian institution. Perhaps because most of the Court's decisions in this area have come in the context of aid to parochial schools, which traditionally have been characterized as pervasively sectarian, the majority seems to equate the characterization with the institution. In support of that illusion, the majority relies heavily on three cases in which the Court has upheld direct government funding to liberal arts colleges with some religious affiliation, noting that such colleges were not "pervasively sectarian. . ."

In fact, the cases on which the majority relies have stressed that the institutions' "predominant higher education mission is to provide their students with a *secular* education." Tilton v. Richardson (1971) (emphasis added); *Roemer v. Maryland Public Works Board* (noting "high degree of institutional autonomy" and that "the encouragement of spiritual development is only one secondary objective of each college") (internal quotations omitted); *Hunt v. McNair* (finding no basis to conclude that the College's operations are oriented significantly towards sectarian rather than secular education"). In sharp contrast, the District Court here concluded that AFLA grantees and participants included "organizations with institutional ties to religious denominations *and corporate requirements that the organizations abide by and not contradict religious doctrines*. In addition, other recipients of AFLA funds, while not explicitly affiliated with a religious denomination, are religiously inspired *and dedicated to teaching the dogma that inspired them* (emphasis added)." On a continuum of "sectarianism" running from parochial schools at one end to the colleges funded by the statutes upheld in *Tilton, Hunt, and Roemer* at the other, the AFLA grantees described by the District Court clearly are much closer to the former than to the latter.

More importantly, the majority also errs in suggesting that the inapplicability of the label is generally dispositive. While a plurality of the Court has framed the inquiry as "whether an institution is so 'pervasively sectarian' that it may receive no direct state aid of any kind," *Roemer v. Maryland Public Works Board*, the Court never has treated the absence of such a finding as a license to disregard the potential for impermissible fostering of religion. The characterization of an institution as "pervasively sectarian" allows us to eschew further inquiry into the use that will be made of direct government aid. In that sense, it is a sufficient, but not a necessary, basis for a finding that a challenged program creates an unacceptable Establishment Clause risk.

The majority's holding that the AFLA is not unconstitutional on its face marks a sharp departure from our precedents. While aid programs providing nonmonetary, verifiably secular aid have been upheld notwithstanding the indirect effect they might have on the allocation of an institution's own funds for religious activities, see, *e.g., Board of Education v. Allen* (1968), (lending secular textbooks to parochial schools); *Everson v. Board of Education* (1947) (providing bus services to parochial schools), direct cash subsidies have always required much closer scrutiny into the expected and potential uses of the funds, and much greater guarantees that the funds would not be used inconsistently with the Establishment Clause. Parts of the AFLA prescribing various forms of outreach, education, and counseling services specifically authorize the expenditure of funds in ways previously held unconstitutional. For example, the Court has upheld the use of public funds to support a parochial school's purchase of secular textbooks already approved for use in public schools, see *Wolman v. Walter* (1977); *Meek v. Pittenger*, or its grading and administering of state-prepared tests, *Committee for Public Education & Religious Liberty v. Regan* (1980). When the books, teaching materials. or examinations were to government-sponsored religious indoctrination but, on the basis of little more than an indefensible assumption that AFLA recipients are not pervasively sectarian and consequently are presumed likely to comply with statutory and constitutional mandates, dismisses as insubstantial the risk that indoctrination will enter counseling. Similarly, the majority rejects the District Court's conclusion that the subject matter renders the risk of indoctrination unacceptable, and does so, it says, because "the likelihood that some of the religious institutions who receive AFLA funding will agree with the message that Congress intended to deliver to adolescents through the AFLA" does not amount to the advancement of religion. I do not think the statute can be so easily and conveniently saved.

The District Court concluded that asking religious organizations to teach and counsel youngsters on matters of deep religious significance, yet expect them to refrain from making reference to religion is both foolhardy and unconstitutional. . .

.
The majority rejects the District Court's assumptions as unwarranted outside the context of a pervasively sectarian institution. In doing so, the majority places inordinate weight on the nature of the institution receiving the funds, and ignores altogether the targets of the funded message and the nature of its content. . . .

The AFLA, unlike any statute this Court has upheld, pays for teachers and counselors, employed by and subject to the direction of religious authorities, to educate impressionable young minds on issues of religious moment. Time and again we have recognized the difficulties inherent in asking even the best-intentioned individuals in such positions to make "a total separation between secular teaching and religious doctrine.". . . Where the targeted audience is composed of children, of course, the Court's insistence on adequate safeguards has always been greatest. . . . In those cases in which funding of colleges with religious affiliations has been upheld, the Court has relied on the assumption that "college students are less impressionable and less susceptible to religious indoctrination. . . ."

By observing that the alignment of the statute and the religious views of the grantees do not render the AFLA a statute which funds "specifically religious activity," the majority makes light of the religious significance in the counseling provided by some grantees. Yet this is a dimension that Congress specifically sought to capture by enlisting the aid of religious organizations in battling the problems associated with teenage pregnancy. Whereas there may be secular values promoted by the AFLA, including the encouragement of adoption and premarital chastity and the discouragement of abortion, it can hardly be doubted that when promoted in theological terms by religious figures, those values take on a religious nature. . . .

It is true, of course, that the Court has recognized that the Constitution does not prohibit the government from supporting secular social-welfare services solely because they are provided by a religiously affiliated organization. But such recognition has been closely tied to the nature of the subsidized social service: "the State may send a cleric, indeed even a clerical order, to perform *a wholly secular task*" (emphasis added). Roemer v. *Maryland Public Works Board* (plurality opinion). There is a very real and important difference between running a soup kitchen or a hospital, and counseling pregnant teenagers on how to make the difficult decisions facing them. The risk of advancing religion at public expense, and of creating an appearance that the government is endorsing the medium and the message, is much greater when the religious organization is directly engaged in pedagogy, with the express intent of shaping belief and changing behavior, than where it is neutrally dispensing medication, food, or shelter.

There is also, of course, a fundamental difference between government's employing religion because of its unique appeal to a higher authority and the transcendental nature of its message, and government's enlisting the aid of religiously committed individuals or organizations without regard to their sectarian motivation. In the latter circumstance, religion plays little or no role; it merely explains why the individual or organization has chosen to get involved in the publicly funded program. In the former, religion is at the core of the subsidized activity, and it affects the manner in which the "service" is dispensed. For some religious organizations, the answer to a teenager's question "Why shouldn't I have an abortion?" or "Why shouldn't I use barrier contraceptives?" will undoubtedly be different from an answer based solely on secular considerations. Public funds may not be used to endorse the religious message.

Despite the glaring omission of a restriction on the use of funds for religious purposes, the Court attempts to resurrect the AFLA by noting a legislative intent not to promote religion, and observing that various reporting provisions of the statute "create a mechanism whereby the Secretary can police the grants." However effective this "mechanism" might prove to be in enforcing clear statutory directives, it is of no help where, as here, no restrictions are found on the face of the statute, and the Secretary has not promulgated any by regulation. . . .

Indeed, nothing in the AFLA precludes the funding of even "pervasively sectarian" organizations, whose work by definition cannot be segregated into religious and secular categories. . . .

To determine whether a statute fosters excessive entanglement, a court must look at three factors: (1) the character and purpose of the institutions benefited; (2) the nature of the aid; and (3) the nature of the relationship between the government and the religious organization. . .

It seems inherent in the pedagogical function that there will be disagreements about what is or is not "religious" and which will require an intolerable degree of government intrusion and censorship. . .

The AFLA, without a doubt, endorses religion. Because of its expressed solicitude for the participation of religious organizations in all AFLA programs in one form or another, the statute creates a symbolic and real partnership between the clergy and the fisc in addressing a problem with substantial religious overtones. Given the delicate subject matter and the impressionable audience, the risk that the AFLA will convey a message of Government endorsement of religion is overwhelming. The statutory language and the extensive record established in the District Court make clear that the problem lies in the statute and its systematically unconstitutional operation, and not merely in isolated instances of misapplication. I therefore would find the statute unconstitutional without remanding to the District Court. . . .

17

GOVERNMENTAL AID TO RELIGIOUS SCHOOLS

Religious schools exist because of a perceived need to educate children differently than in the public schools, in a manner more consonant with the religious beliefs of the subscribing parents and the sponsoring sects. They also provide, and are intended to provide, a way in which children are more firmly attached to the religious beliefs into which they were born. This being so, the impediments to state assistance to such schools would seem little short of overwhelming.

Yet the perceived need for such schools, and for such aid, has grown in the last quarter century. Catholics, finding themselves unable to carry the economic burden of a religiously-based alternative education, have seen the numbers of, and enrollment in their schools declining. But many Protestant denominations have reacted to decisions outlawing prayer and Bible in public schools, and to what they perceive as increasing secularist influences therein, by starting their own schools. Thus the number of people subjected to what Catholics used to call "double taxation" (i.e. the necessity of paying taxes for public schools while at the same time supporting religious schools), has grown, and pressures on the states for aid to religious schools has increased. At the same time these religious schools are increasingly seen by secularists and by champions of the public schools as inimical to their own goals. More than twenty years ago, Richard Morgan observed that the conflict over church-state relations is really a "struggle over funds." To the extent that this is still true, it is aid to schools which is at the cutting edge.[1]

In some part the Supreme Court is responsible for this state of affairs. It has been Supreme Court decisions which have led Protestants to join Catholics in seeking to establish their own schools and, once established, to search for ways to pay for them. At the same time, it has been Supreme Court decisions which, while striking down most of the stratagems used by the states to give such aid, have upheld others and thus held out the possibility that, if the right channels could be found, even more could be done to aid religious schools.

The story of the "school aid" issue began when the city of Patterson, New Jersey, already providing free public transportation for children attending public schools, decided to reimburse affected parents for the similar costs of transporting their children to parochial schools. Challenged by a taxpayer, the issue came to the Supreme Court in the seminal case of Everson v. Board of Education. Everson is important for a number of reasons. First, it was the earliest case in which the Court squarely held that the states were limited by the establishment clause. Second, the Court majority took the occasion to assert that the First Amendment was intended to establish what Jefferson called a "wall of separation" between church and state. Finally, the Court held that, despite the height and impregnability of that "wall," "New Jersey has not breached it here." That was so, said the Court, principally on the basis of the "child benefit" theory,[2] i.e. the aid directly benefited only children, and did so in the context of assuring their safety while going to and from school.

The Court did not again deal with the issue of aid to religious schools until the 1968 case of Board of Education v. Allen. In that case the state of New York required its local school districts to lend secular textbooks, free of charge, to all students in grades 7 through 12, including those in parochial schools. The texts were to be chosen by parochial school authorities who were limited in their choice to those which could be used in the public schools. Public school officials were to assure that the chosen books were appropriate, and no books were to be lent for the teaching of classes in religion.

Justice White, perhaps the most consistent "accommodationist" on the Warren and Burger Courts, spoke for the Court in Allen and upheld the textbook loan program. Applying the tests of Abington Township v. Schempp, White found that "the state does not lose its interest in the education of its children merely because they go to parochial schools." The "secular purpose" test was therefore satisfied, as it almost always is. In a similar vein, White found that the second of the Schempp tests was satisfied. Alhough the program assuredly aided religion, that aid was only secondary. The "primary effect," as in <u>Everson</u>, was to aid the children involved. That the choice of books was subject to ideological manipulation did not matter, said White, for there was no evidence that such manipulation had taken place, or that public officials would have allowed it to succeed.

The concurring opinion of Justice Harlan emphasized the necessity of neutrality in the government's attitude toward religion. And neutrality required that government neither engage in nor compel religious practices, effect no favoritism among sects or between religion and non-religion, and work no deterrence of religious beliefs. Thus, Harlan concluded, where the activity did not involve the state "so significantly and directly in the realm of the sectarian as to give rise to . . . divisive influences and inhibitions, it is not forbidden by the religious clauses."

Three years later, in <u>Lemon v. Kurtzman</u>, Justice Harlan's "involvement" idea now reformulated by Chief Justice Burger as "entanglement," became a part of the test by which all future establishment questions would be measured. <u>Lemon v. Kurtzman</u> has been of enormous significance in the jurisprudence of the religion clauses, and is the first case excerpted in this chapter.

At issue in <u>Lemon</u> were a variety of programs designed to aid religious schools, including salary supplements and loaned textbooks and instructional materials. The loaning of textbooks was upheld on the basis of <u>Allen</u>, but most of the other programs were struck down.

As always, the Court had little difficulty in finding a secular legislative purpose present in the statues. And it did not even attempt to determine whether the "primary effect" was to aid or to inhibit religion, as the second part of the <u>Lemon</u> test requires. Rather, it leapfrogged the "effects" test to hold that the programs presented the reality or the danger of "excessive entanglement." This was so, said the Court, because the very procedures designed to assure that the "primary effect" was not to aid religion were themselves indications of excessive entanglement. How, for example, could the state be assured that the teachers whose salaries were supplemented would not inject religious ideas into their presentations? The only way to do this was by long-term surveillance of activities in the religious schools. How could it be assured that instructional materials would not be chosen on the basis of religious orientation? The answer was the same.

Most importantly for the future of possible aid to sectarian schools, the Court observed that the possibility of entanglement was increased by the "divisive potential" of these programs. Partisans of church schools would seek to broaden the aid, and others would oppose such broadening. Thus there would be an increase in political debate and division which, when based on religious differences, was a major evil that the First Amendment was designed to prevent. And this potential was exacerbated by the necessity for continued annual appropriations and the likelihood of larger demands as costs and population grew.

It is assuredly true that the granting of some aid will foster requests for more, that people will line up on different sides of the issue, and that feelings will rise as the amounts in question increase. It seems likely, given his generally accommodationist position, that Chief Justice Burger's intent in formulating the "entanglement" test was to point the way toward, and lay a basis for the constitutionality of certain kinds of aid. To a very limited extent, his Lemon analysis was compatible with this goal. He did, after all, opine that one factor contributing to such "divisiveness" was the necessity of "annual appropriations" for expenditures, thus indicating that programs which could be established on a permanent basis were not so vulnerable. But in general, the "political divisiveness" factor, taken seriously, would seem to sound the death knell for any appropriation of money to aid religious schools.

Similarly, "entanglement" analysis, taken together with the "primary effect" test, creates a nearly insoluble situation for the proponents of aid to religious schools. For the very purpose of the regulations found indicative of "entanglement" in Lemon was to assure that the "primary effect" of the aid would be secular and not religious. If, however, such devices are taken to be evidences of entanglement, then what has been created is a "Catch 22," with the absence of such safeguards leading to a finding of an impermissible effect and their presence indicating entanglement.

What then, has been the use of the Lemon doctrine, as measured by its effect on later state efforts to assist religious schools? To this date, the Court has struck down the following programs: tuition rebates and reimbursements for the parents of children attending religious schools; tax exemptions for such parents; special counseling services for pupils in religious schools; the loan of educational equipment; counseling, testing, and remedial classes; financial aid for field trips and class paraphernalia; direct reimbursement for record keeping and testing services; and state-sponsored instructional services provided on the grounds of the religious school. It has upheld the following: the loan of secular textbooks, diagnostic and therapeutic testing services; reimbursement for expenses for testing and record keeping incurred due to state regulations; and an annual tax deduction of up to $700 per child for parents of children in elementary and secondary schools run by religious organizations.

This last decision, arrived at in the 1983 case of Mueller v. Allen, is the clearest single instance of the Court adopting an accommodationist position on the issue of aid to parochial schools, and is the second case excerpted in this chapter. In Mueller, a Minnesota statute allowed all taxpayers to deduct from their state income tax expenses incurred in providing tuition, texts, and transportation for any of their children attending primary schools. The deduction was limited to $500.00 in elementary, and $700.00 in secondary schools. It was available, where applicable, to all parents. Since tuition was the greatest single deductible expense, and was generally not required for attending public schools, the statute's impact was overwhelmingly skewed in favor of the parents of the 91,000 of the state's 820,000 school children who attended private schools, 91% of them in sectarian institutions.

By a vote of five to four, the Court upheld the statute. Justice Rehnquist's majority opinion first found a secular state interest in a well educated citizenry. Additionally, Rehnquist observed that "the state could (properly) conclude that it had a secular interest in the financial health of private schools which take some of the burdens from the state, and which act as an educational alternative and as competition for the public schools." As to secular effect, Rehnquist found that the fact that such aid was broadly available to all was an important index of secular effect, as was the fact that the money was channeled through the parents and became available to the religious schools only through individual choices not involving state approval. Both of these factors, in addition, tended to mitigate the possibility of the kind of government involvement that might lead to strife and strain in the political system. Finally, the only possible entanglement arose from the necessity of determining what books qualified for deductions, a problem deemed solvable in other cases. In a footnote, Rehnquist confined the relevance of the "political divisiveness" criterion to a situation where there was direct financial subsidy to schools or to teachers in such schools.

The dissenters, understandably, used the program's greatly disparate benefit to patrons of private as opposed to public schools to argue that the program in fact was intended to aid religion. Their argument seems nearly unassailable. Indeed, Rehnquist's only response to it was an assertion that an approach which grounded the "constitutionality of a facially neutral law on statistical analysis would not provide a principled basis for evaluation" and, somewhat surprisingly, that "private educational institutions and the parents who pay for them make special contributions to their local areas," contributions for which the tax deductions might be considered a rough return.

If Mueller indicated an emerging awareness by the Court of the contributions of religiously based primary and secondary schools, it was an awareness already testified to in the Court's several decisions on aid to religiously affiliated colleges and universities. On the same day it decided Lemon, the Court, in Tilton v. Richardson, gave general approval to governmental assistance to such entities. At issue was the constitutionality of the federal Higher Education Facilities Act, providing grants and long term, low interest loans to private institutions of higher education for the construction of academic facilities. The act provided that none of these facilities might be used as places for sectarian instruction or other religious purposes. Further, and to this end, the United States retained a 20 year interest in such facilities which entitled it to recover damages if the restrictions were violated. After twenty years the restriction, and the government interest, were no longer in effect. With the exception of the last provision, the Act was upheld.

The Act was passed in the aftermath of "Sputnik" and the perceived Soviet lead in space technology, a fact that made it easy for Chief Justice Burger, author of the plurality opinion, to find a secular state interest in the Act's stated purpose to "assure the security and welfare of the country through development of its citizen's intellectual capacity." As to its primary effect, the Court noted that the statute was "carefully drafted" to prevent use of facilities for religious purposes, and that there was no showing that any of the schools involved had violated that provision. More importantly, there was "no evidence" that religion so permeated the instruction involved as to make inseparable the school's religious and secular functions. Rather, the evidence was that courses were taught according to the academic requirements of the subject matter, the teachers' concepts of professional standards, and principles of academic freedom.

On the issue of excessive entanglement, Burger found significant differences between religious schools of higher learning and those on a lower level. College students were both less impressionable and susceptible and given much more freedom. Thus, there was less likelihood that religious indoctrination was a substantial purpose of the college. This, in turn, reduced the risk that government would inadvertently support religious activity, and mitigated the need for governmental surveillance and entanglement. Further, the aid was for the construction of buildings, which, like the bus rides approved in Everson, were viewed as ideologically neutral.

Finally, the potential for entanglement was reduced by the fact that the government aid at issue was a one-time, single-purpose construction grant, with no continuing financial relationship. Thus:

> . . . taken together, there is a narrow and limited relationship with government involving fewer and less significant contacts and thus less potential for realizing the substantive evils against which the religious clauses were intended to protect . . . . cumulatively these factors lesson the potential for divisive religious fragmentation, possibly because of the character of the recipient institutions, with a student constituency which is diverse and not local.

In a similar vein, the Court has upheld the issue of state bonds for the construction of academic buildings for non-religious and a state's allocation of general funds, for nonsectarian purposes, to religiously associated colleges and universities.[3]

That the Court has been exceptionally fragmented on the issue of aid to non-public schools can be seen not only in the large number of five to four votes in such cases, but also in its response to a single, multi-issued case, Wolman v. Walter. In Wolman, decided in 1977, the Court unanimously upheld the constitutionality of state-provided speech, hearing and psychological diagnostic testing on the property of religious schools; a six to three majority, composed of Burger, Stewart, White, Powell, Rehnquist, and Blackmun, with Brennan, Marshall, and Stevens dissenting, upheld the loan of secular textbooks and of payment for state mandated testing and scoring; a five to four majority, with Stewart joining in dissent, held constitutional therapeutic guidance and remedial services if held off (in mobile units placed in the street next to the religious school), but not if held on school property). A similar majority, with Blackmun joining the erstwhile dissenters, held unconstitutional the "loan" to pupils and their parents of educational materials like maps, tape recorders, etc., which could be stored in the religious school. And a like majority, with the addition of the Chief, held state financing of field trips unconstitutional.

One may agree that each of these programs merited separate inquiry, and that the "loaning" to parents and children of audio visual aids which, nevertheless, might be kept on school property, is a transparent fiction to do what otherwise might not be allowable. At the same time, it is little short of ridiculous to contend that services rendered by a professionally trained and state paid therapist unconnected with the school in question are constitutional when rendered "across the street" in a mobile trailer, but unconstitutional when made available on school grounds. Particularly is this true when the basis for the distinction is, as it was in Wolman, the alleged influence which the surroundings might have on the therapist's activity.

The possibility of such influence, and the steps necessary to combat it, resulted in the Court's decision in Aguilar v. Felton, the final case to be excerpted herein. Aguilar involved the use of public school teachers to provide remedial and enrichment classes to disadvantaged children. The program was federally funded under Title I of the Elementary and Secondary Education Act of 1965, and was not one of general assistance to students in nonpublic schools. Rather, it applied only to schools which were attempting to meet the needs of educationally deprived children from low-income families. The program reflected, therefore, Congress' judgment that federal grants directed to such schools could be useful in fighting the problem of inadequate education for, among others, members of minority groups.

For the majority, however, the "entanglement" of state and religion necessary to prevent religious indoctrination by teachers influenced by their environment triggered the "Catch 22" feature of the Lemon test, and made the program invalid. This despite the fact that, as emphasized in Justice O'Connor's dissent, the programs involved in the remedial program had operated for almost a decade with no showing of religious indoctrination, and only minimal intervention by public officials to assure that it did not occur.

Only two members of the Aguilar majority remain on the present Court, along with three justices who dissented. And the backgrounds of some of the newer appointees, most notably Justice Thomas, make likely their sympathy toward, and appreciation of the worth of religious schools. And the values in conflict in Aguilar go substantially beyond those traditionally at issue in "school aid" cases. Because of these factors, and because the assumption that the "pervasive atmosphere" of religious schools will dominate professional teachers seems particularly open to question, Aguilar seems a good candidate for reconsideration.

What, then, is the current status and probable future of aid to religiously oriented primary and secondary schools? The cases establish the following: First, a state may provide transportation and textbooks to children attending religious schools. Second, the provision of services directly impacting the health of the children, and of diagnostic services to determine the status of children's health, is constitutional; and services in remedy of psychological disorders are allowed if conducted off school property. Third, state money may be used to pay for state mandated activities when the nature of such activities makes it impossible to manipulate them in a way favorable to religion. And finally, state programs which benefit all educational consumers, which channel money to individuals or to parents, and which leave them genuinely free to make their own choice as to the ultimate receiver of the benefit, are likely to be constitutional.

In addition it may be, although there has been no decision directly on the point, that the interplay of Pierce v. Society of Sisters (1925) and Zorach v. Clauson (1952)[4] points to another area of permissible church-state cooperation. Pierce was originally decided partly on the basis of the right of teachers to pursue their craft. But, whatever its original meaning, it is now widely believed to establish the principal of parental choice in education. Zorach allowed for "released time" programs for public school students if held off school property. In combination, Pierce and Zorach lay the basis for an argument that a state may accommodate "free exercise" in the area of school choice by allowing children to receive instructions in some subjects (the social sciences and humanities, for example) at religious schools while exercising their right to attend the public schools for instruction in different areas (e.g. science and mathematics).[5]

It is not here contended that there is any state obligation to provide such programs, only that they might be permitted to do so. But the logistics of such arrangements would seem, in most cases, to be formidable. Perhaps for that reason the currently controversial "voucher systems," which could be structured to go directly to parents and thus to foster individual decisionmaking as to their eventual impact, seem more promising. Whether such systems would have to pass muster under the tri-partite Lemon test, or under a different one emphasizing, perhaps, the matter of "endorsement" of religious activity, is a matter yet to be decided. In this area, as in that of governmentally sponsored religious observances, the law appears to be in flux.

---

[1]Morgan, *The Politics of Religious Conflict*, 40.

[2]An even earlier application of the "child benefit" theory can be found in Cochran v. Louisiana, a 1930 case in which the Court upheld a similar type of state aid to parochial schools. Cochran was decided before the application of the "religious clauses" to the states and thus involved only the question of whether the Louisiana scheme violated the due process clause of the 14th Amendment.

[3]Hunt v. McNair, (1973), Roemer v. Board of Public Works (1976).

[4]See Ch. 18.

[5]This kind of program, generally known as "shared time" was not at issue in Grand Rapids v. Ball, the companion case ot Aguilar v. Felton. In Grand Rapids the Court held unconstitutional a "shared time" program in which public school teachers taught classes in the private schools, and the scheme thus shared the infirmity found to exist in Aguilar. It is true that the majority opinion in Grand Rapids expressed the view that one reason the system at issue was unconstitutional was that, by providing classes in "secular subjects" the public system freed private school funds for other purposes. But if this is to be the touchstone of unconstitutionality, then virtually all kinds of aid to religious schools is unconstitutional.

LEMON ET AL. V. KURTZMAN, SUPERINTENDENT OF PUBLIC INSTRUCTION OF PENNSYLVANIA, ET AL.

403 U.S. 602 (1971)

MR. CHIEF JUSTICE BURGER delivered the opinion of the Court.

These two appeals raise questions as to Pennsylvania and Rhode Island statutes providing state aid to church-related elementary and secondary schools. Both statutes are challenged as violative of the Establishment and Free Exercise Clauses of the First Amendment and the Due Process Clause of the Fourteenth Amendment.

Pennsylvania has adopted a statutory program that provides financial support to nonpublic elementary and secondary schools by way of reimbursement for the cost of teachers' salaries, textbooks, and instructional materials in specified secular subjects. Rhode Island has adopted a statute under which the State pays directly to teachers in nonpublic elementary schools a supplement of 15% of their annual salary. Under each statute state aid has been given to church-related educational institutions. We hold that both statutes are unconstitutional. . . .

In the absence of precisely stated constitutional prohibitions, we must draw lines with reference to the three main evils against which the Establishment Clause was intended to afford protection: "sponsorship, financial support, and active involvement of the sovereign in religious activity." *Walz v. Tax Commission,* (1970).

Every analysis in this area must begin with consideration of the cumulative criteria developed by the Court over many years. Three such tests may be gleaned from our cases. First, the statute must have a secular legislative purpose; second, its principal or primary effect must be one that neither advances nor inhibits religion, *Board of Education v. Allen* (1968); finally, the statute must not foster "an excessive government entanglement with religion." *Walz.*

Inquiry into the legislative purposes of the Pennsylvania and Rhode Island statutes affords no basis for a conclusion that the legislative purposes of the Pennsylvania and Rhode Island statutes affords no basis for a conclusion that the legislative intent was to advance religion. On the contrary, the statutes themselves clearly state that they are intended to enhance the quality of the secular education in all schools covered by the compulsory attendance laws. There is no reason to believe the legislatures meant anything else. A State always has a legitimate concern for maintaining minimum standards in all schools it allows to operate. As in *Allen,* we find nothing here that undermines the stated legislative intent; it must therefore be accorded appropriate deference.

In *Allen* the Court acknowledged that secular and religious teachings were not necessarily so intertwined that secular textbooks furnished to students by the State were in fact, instrumental in the teaching of religion. The legislatures of Rhode Island and Pennsylvania have concluded that secular and religious education are identifiable and separable. In the abstract we have no quarrel with this conclusion.

The two legislatures, however, have also recognized that church-related elementary and secondary schools have a significant religious mission and that a substantial portion of their activities is religiously oriented. They have therefore sought to create statutory restrictions designed to guarantee the separation between secular and religious educational functions and to ensure that State financial aid supports only the former. All these provisions are precautions taken in candid recognition that these programs approached, even if they did not intrude upon, the forbidden areas under the Religion Clauses. We need not decide whether these legislative precautions restrict the principal or primary effect of the programs to the point where they do not offend the Religion Clauses, for we conclude that the cumulative impact of the entire relationship arising under the statutes in each State involves excessive entanglement between government and religion. . . .

In order to determine whether the government entanglement with religion is excessive, we must examine the character and purposes of the institutions that are benefited, the nature of the aid that the State provides, and the resulting relationship between the government and the religious authority. MR. JUSTICE HARLAN, in a separate opinion in *Walz,* echoed the classic warning as to "programs, whose very nature is apt to entangle the state in details of administration. . . ." Here we find that both statutes foster an impermissible degree of entanglement.

(a) *Rhode Island program*

The District Court made extensive findings on the grave potential for excessive entanglement that inheres in the religious character and purpose of the Roman Catholic elementary schools of Rhode Island, to date the sole beneficiaries of the Rhode Island Salary Supplement Act.

The substantial religious character of these church-related schools gives rise to entangling church-state relationships of the kind the Religion Clauses sought to avoid. Although the District Court found that concern for religious values did not inevitably or necessarily intrude into the content of secular subjects, the considerable religious activities of these schools led the legislature to provide for careful governmental controls and surveillance by state authorities in order to ensure that state aid supports only secular education.

The dangers and corresponding entanglements are enhanced by the particular form of aid that the Rhode Island Act provides. Our decisions from *Everson* to *Allen* have permitted the States to provide church-related schools with secular, neutral, or nonideological services, facilities, or materials. Bus transportation, school lunches, public health services, and secular textbooks supplied in common to all students were not thought to offend the Establishment Clause. We note that the dissenters in *Allen* seemed chiefly concerned with the pragmatic difficulties involved in ensuring the truly secular content of the textbooks provided at state expense.

In *Allen* the Court refused to make assumptions, on a meager record, about the religious content of the textbooks that the State would be asked to provide. We cannot, however, refuse here to recognize that teachers have a substantially different ideological character from books. In terms of potential for involving some aspect of faith or morals in secular subjects, a textbook's content is ascertainable, but a teacher's handling of a subject is not. We cannot ignore the danger that a teacher under religious control and discipline poses to the separation of the religious from the purely secular aspects of pre-college education. The conflict of functions inheres in the situation.

In our view the record shows these dangers are present to a substantial degree. The Rhode Island Roman Catholic elementary schools are under the general supervision of the Bishop of Providence and his appointed representative, the Diocesan Superintendent of Schools. In most cases, each individual parish, however, assumes the ultimate financial responsibility for the school, with the parish priest authorizing the allocation of parish funds. With only two exceptions, school principals are nuns appointed either by the Superintendent or the Mother Provincial of the order whose members staff the school. By 1969 lay teachers constituted more than a third of all teachers in the parochial elementary schools, and their number is growing. They are first interviewed by the superintendent's office and then by the school principal. The contracts are signed by the parish priest, and he retains some discretion in negotiating salary levels. Religious authority necessarily pervades the school system. . . .

Several teachers testified, however, that they did not inject religion into their secular classes. And the District Court found that religious values did not necessarily affect the content of the secular instruction. But what has been recounted suggests the potential if not actual hazards of this form of state aid. The teacher is employed by a religious organization, subject to the direction and discipline of religious authorities, and works in a system dedicated to rearing children in a particular faith. These controls are not lessened by the fact that most of the lay teachers are of the Catholic faith. Inevitably some of a teacher's responsibilities hover on the border between secular and religious orientation.

We need not and do not assume that teachers in parochial schools will be guilty of bad faith or any conscious design to evade the limitations imposed by the statute and the First Amendment. We simply recognize that a dedicated religious person, teaching in a school affiliated with his or her faith and operated to inculcate its tenets, will inevitably experience Feat difficulty in remaining religiously neutral. Doctrines and faith are not inculcated or advanced by neutrals. With the best of intentions such a teacher would find it hard to make a total separation between secular teaching and religious doctrine. What would appear to some to be essential to good citizenship might well for others border on or constitute instruction in religion. Further difficulties are inherent in the combination of religious discipline and the possibility of disagreement between teacher and religious authorities over the meaning of the statutory restrictions.

A comprehensive, discriminating, and continuing state surveillance will inevitably be required to ensure that these restrictions are obeyed and the First Amendment otherwise respected. Unlike a book, a teacher cannot be inspected once so as to determine the extent and intent of his or her personal beliefs and subjective acceptance of the limitations imposed by the First Amendment. These prophylactic contacts will involve excessive and enduring entanglement between state and church. . . .

b) *Pennsylvania program*

The Pennsylvania statute also

provides state aid to church-related schools for teachers' salaries. The complaint describes an educational system that is very similar to the one existing in Rhode Island. According to the allegations, the church-related elementary and secondary schools are controlled by religious organizations, have the purpose of propagating and promoting a particular religious faith, and conduct their operations to fulfill that purpose. Since this complaint was dismissed for failure to state a claim for relief, we must accept these allegations as true for purposes of our review.

As we noted earlier, the very restrictions and surveillance necessary to ensure that teachers play a strictly nonideological role give rise to entanglements between church and state. The Pennsylvania statute, like that of Rhode Island, fosters this kind of relationship. Reimbursement is not only limited to courses offered in the public schools and materials approved by state officials, but the statute excludes "any subject matter expressing religious teaching, or the morals or forms of worship of any sect." In addition, schools seeking reimbursement must maintain accounting procedures that require the State to establish the cost of the secular as distinguished from the religious instruction.

The Pennsylvania statute, moreover, has the further defect of providing state financial aid directly to the church-related school. This factor distinguishes both *Everson* and *Allen,* for in both those cases the Court was careful to point out that state aid was provided to the student and his parents—not to the church-related school.

The history of government grants of a continuing cash subsidy indicates that such programs have almost always been accompanied by varying measures of control and surveillance. The government cash grants before us now provide no basis for predicting that comprehensive measures of surveillance and controls will not follow. In particular the government's post-audit power to inspect and evaluate a church-related school's financial records and to determine which expenditures are religious and which are secular creates an intimate and continuing relationship between church and state. . . .

A broader base of entanglement of yet a different character is presented by the divisive political potential of these state programs. In a community where such a large number of pupils are served by church-related schools, it can be assumed that state assistance will entail considerable political activity. Partisans of parochial schools, understandably concerned with rising costs and sincerely dedicated to both the religious and secular educational missions of their schools, will inevitably champion this cause and promote political action to achieve their goals. Those who oppose state aid, whether for constitutional, religious, or fiscal reasons, will inevitably respond and employ all of the usual political campaign techniques to prevail. Candidates will be forced to declare and voters to choose. It would be unrealistic to ignore the fact that many people confronted with issues of this kind will find their votes aligned with their faith.

Ordinarily political debate and division, however vigorous or even partisan, are normal and healthy manifestations of our democratic system of government, but political division along religious lines was one of the principal evils against which the First Amendment was intended to protect. The potential divisiveness of such conflict is a threat to the normal political process. . . .

Of course, as the Court noted in *Walz,* "[a]dherents of particular faiths and individual churches frequently take strong positions on public issues." *Walz v. Tax Commission.* We could not expect otherwise, for religious values pervade the fabric of our national life. But in *Walz* we dealt with a status under state tax laws for the benefit of all religious groups. Here we are confronted with successive and very likely permanent annual appropriations that benefit relatively few religious groups. Political fragmentation and divisiveness on religious lines are thus likely to be intensified.

The potential for political divisiveness related to religious belief and practice is aggravated in these two statutory programs by the need for continuing annual appropriations and the likelihood of larger and larger demands as costs and populations grow. The Rhode Island District Court found that the parochial school system's "monumental and deepening financial crisis" would "inescapably" require larger annual appropriations subsidizing greater percentages of the salaries of lay teachers. Although no facts have been developed in this respect in the Pennsylvania case, it appears that such pressures for expanding aid have already required the state legislature to include a portion of the state revenues from cigarette taxes in the program. . . .

MR. JUSTICE DOUGLAS, whom MR. JUSTICE BLACK joins, concurring. . . .

We have announced over and over again that the use of taxpayers' money to support parochial schools violates the First Amendment, applicable to the States by virtue of the Fourteenth.

We said in unequivocal words in *Everson v. Board of Education*, "No tax in any amount, large or small, can be levied to support any religious activities or institutions, whatever they may be called, or whatever form they may adopt to teach or practice religion." We reiterated the same idea in *Zorach v. Clauson,* and *McGowan v. Maryland,* and in *Torcaso v. Watkins.* We repeated the same idea in *McCollum v. Board of Education,* and added that a State's tax-supported public schools could not be used "for the dissemination of religious doctrines" nor could a State provide the church "pupils for their religious classes through use of the State's compulsory public school machinery."

Yet in spite of this long and consistent history there are those who have the courage to announce that a State may nonetheless finance the *secular* part of a sectarian school's educational program. That, however, makes a grave constitutional decision turn merely on cost accounting and bookkeeping entries. A history class, a literature class, or a science class in a parochial school is not a separate institute; it is part of the organic whole which the State subsidizes. The

funds are used in these cases to pay or help pay the salaries of teachers in parochial schools; and the presence of teachers is critical to the essential purpose of the parochial school, *viz.,* to advance the religious endeavors of the particular church. It matters not that the teacher receiving taxpayers' money only teaches religion a fraction of the time. Nor does it matter that he or she teaches no religion. The school is an organism living on one budget. What the taxpayers give for salaries of those who teach only the humanities or science without any trace of proselytizing enables the school to use all of its own funds for religious training. As Judge Coffin said, we would be blind to realities if we let "sophisticated bookkeeping" sanction "almost total subsidy of a religious institution by assigning the bulk of the institution's expenses to 'secular' activities." And sophisticated attempts to avoid the Constitution are just as invalid as simple-minded ones.

In my view the taxpayer's forced contribution to the parochial schools in the present cases violates the First Amendment.

MR. JUSTICE MARSHALL . . . concurs in MR. JUSTICE DOUGLAS' opinion covering No. 569.

MR. JUSTICE WHITE . . . dissenting.

. . . while the decision of the Court is legitimate, it is surely quite wrong in overturning the Pennsylvania and Rhode Island statutes on the ground that they amount to an establishment of religion forbidden by the First Amendment.

No one in these cases questions the constitutional right of parents to satisfy their state-imposed obligation to educate their children by sending them to private schools, sectarian or otherwise, as long as those schools meet minimum standards established for secular instruction. The States are not only permitted, but required by the Constitution, to free students attending private schools from any public school attendance obligation. *Pierce v. Society of Sisters,* (1925). The States may also furnish transportation for students, *Everson v. Board of Education* (1947), and books for teaching secular subjects to students attending parochial and other private as well as public schools, *Board of Education v. Allen* (1968); we have also upheld arrangements whereby students are released from public school classes so that they may attend religious instruction. *Zorach v. Clauson* (1952). Outside the field of education, we have upheld Sunday closing laws, *McGowan v. Maryland,* (1961), state and federal laws exempting church property and church activity from taxation, *Walz v. Tax Commission* (1970), and governmental grants to religious organizations for the purpose of financing improvements in the facilities of hospitals managed and controlled by religious orders. *Bradfield v. Roberts,* (1899).

Our prior cases have recognized the dual role of parochial schools in American society: they perform both religious and secular functions. See *Board of Education v. Allen,*. Our cases also recognize that legislation having a secular purpose and extending governmental assistance to sectarian schools in the performance of their secular functions does not constitute "law[s] respecting an establishment of religion" forbidden by the First Amendment merely because a secular program may incidentally benefit a church in fulfilling its religious mission. That religion may indirectly benefit from governmental aid to the secular activities of churches does not convert that aid into an impermissible establishment of religion.

This much the Court squarely holds in the *Tilton* case, where it also expressly rejects the notion that payments made directly to a religious institution are, without more, forbidden by the First Amendment. In *Tilton,* the Court decides that the Federal Government may finance the separate function of secular education carried on in a parochial setting. It reaches this result although sectarian institutions undeniably will obtain substantial benefit from federal aid; without federal funding to provide adequate facilities for secular education, the student bodies of those institutions might remain stationary or even decrease in size and the institutions might ultimately have to close their doors.

It is enough for me that the States and the Federal Government are financing a separable secular function of overriding importance in order to sustain the legislation here challenged. That religion and private interests other than education may substantially benefit does not convert these laws into impermissible establishments of religion.

It is unnecessary, therefore, to urge that the Free Exercise Clause of the First Amendment at least permits government in some respects to modify and mold its secular programs out of express concern for free-exercise values. . . .

Establishment Clause, however, coexists in the First Amendment with the Free Exercise Clause and the latter is surely relevant in cases such as these. Where a state program seeks to ensure the proper education of its young, in private as well as public schools, free exercise considerations at least counsel against refusing support for students attending parochial schools simply because in that setting they are also being instructed in the tenets of the faith they are constitutionally free to practice. . . .

The Court strikes down the Rhode Island statute on its face. No fault is found with the secular purpose of the program; there is no suggestion that the purpose of the program was aid to religion disguised in secular attire. Nor does the Court find that the primary effect of the program is to aid religion rather than to implement secular goals. The Court nevertheless finds that impermissible "entanglement" will result from administration of the program. The reasoning is a curious and mystifying blend, but a critical factor appears to be an unwillingness to accept the District Court's express findings that on the evidence before it none of the teachers here involved mixed religious and secular instruction. Rather, the District Court struck down the Rhode Island statute because it concluded that activities outside the secular classroom would probably have a religious content and that support for religious education therefore necessarily resulted from the financial aid to the secular programs, since that aid generally strengthened the parochial schools and increased the number of their students.

In view of the decision in *Tilton,* however, where these same factors were found insufficient to invalidate the federal plan, the Court is forced to other considerations. Accepting the District Court's observation in *DiCenso* that education is an integral part of the religious mission of the Catholic church—an observation that should neither surprise nor alarm anyone, especially judges who have already approved substantial aid to parochial schools in various forms—the majority then interposes findings and conclusions that the District Court expressly abjured, namely, that nuns, clerics, and dedicated Catholic laymen unavoidably pose a grave risk in that they might not be able to put aside their religion in the secular classroom. Although stopping short of considering them untrustworthy, the Court concludes that for them the difficulties of avoiding teaching religion along with secular subjects would pose intolerable risks and would in any event entail an unacceptable enforcement regime. Thus, the potential for impermissible fostering of religion in secular classrooms—an untested assumption of the Court— paradoxically renders unacceptable the State's efforts at insuring that secular teachers under religious discipline successfully avoid conflicts between the religious mission of the school and the secular purpose of the State's education program.

The difficulty with this is twofold. In the first place, it is contrary to the evidence and the District Court's findings in *DiCenso.* The Court points to nothing in this record indicating that any participating teacher had inserted religion into his secular teaching or had had any difficulty in avoiding doing so. The testimony of the teachers was quite the contrary. The District Court expressly found that "[t]his concern for religious values does not necessarily affect the content of secular subjects in diocesan schools. On the contrary, several teachers testified at trial that they did not inject religion into their secular classes, and one teacher deposed that he taught exactly as he had while employed in a public school. This testimony gains added credibility

from the fact that several of the teachers were non-Catholics. Moreover because of the restrictions of Rhode Island's textbook loan law . . . and the explicit requirement of the Salary Supplement Act, teaching materials used by applicants for aid must be approved for use in the public schools." *DiCenso v. Robinson,* (1970). Elsewhere, the District Court reiterated that the defect of the Rhode Island statute was "not that religious doctrine overtly intrudes into all instruction," but factors aside from secular courses plus the fact that good secular teaching was itself essential for implementing the religious mission of the parochial school.

Secondly, the Court accepts the model for the Catholic elementary and secondary schools that was rejected for the Catholic universities or colleges in the *Tilton* case. There it was urged that the Catholic condition of higher learning was an integral part of the religious mission of the church and that these institutions did everything they could to foster the faith. The Court's response was that on the record before it none of the involved institutions was shown to have complied with the model and that it would not purport to pass on cases not before it. Here, however, the Court strikes down this Rhode Island statute based primarily on its own model and its own suppositions and unsupported views of what is likely to happen in Rhode Island parochial school classrooms, although on this record there is no indication that entanglement difficulties will accompany the salary supplement program.

The Court thus creates an insoluble paradox for the State and the parochial schools. The State cannot finance secular instruction if it permits religion to be taught in the same classroom; but if it exacts a promise that religion not be so taught—a promise the school and its teachers are quite willing and on this record able to give and enforces it, it is then entangled in the "no entanglement" aspect of the Court's Establishment Clause jurisprudence.

Why the federal program in the *Tilton* case is not embroiled in the same difficulties is never adequately explained. Surely the notion that college students are more mature and resistant to indoctrination is a make-weight, for in *Tilton* there is careful note of the federal condition on funding and the enforcement mechanism available. If religious teaching in federally financed buildings was permitted, the powers of resistance of college students would in no way save the federal scheme. Nor can I imagine the basis for finding college clerics more reliable in keeping promises than their counterparts in elementary and secondary schools—particularly those in the Rhode Island case, since within five years the majority of teachers in Rhode Island parochial schools will be lay persons, many of them nonCatholic. . . .

Only teachers in those schools having per-pupil expenditures for secular subjects below the state average qualify under the system, an aspect of the state scheme which is said to provoke serious "entanglement." But this is also a slender reed on which to strike down this law, for as the District Court found, only once since the inception of the program has it been necessary to segregate expenditures in this manner.

The District Court also focused on the recurring nature of payments by the State of Rhode Island; salaries must be supplemented and money appropriated every year and hence the opportunity for controversy and friction over state aid to religious schools will constantly remain before the State. The Court in *DiCenso* adopts this theme, and makes much of the fact that under the federal scheme the grant to a religious institution is a one-time matter. But this argument is without real force. It is apparent that federal interest in any grant will be a continuing one since the conditions attached to the grant must be enforced. More important, the federal grant program is an ongoing one. The same grant will not be repeated, but new ones to the same or different schools will be made year after year. Thus the same potential for recurring political controversy accompanies the federal program. Rhode Island may have the problem of appropriating money each year to supplement the salaries of teachers, but the United States must each year seek financing for the new grants it desires to

make and must supervise the ones already on the record.

With respect to Pennsylvania, the Court, accepting as true the factual allegations of the complaint, as it must for purposes of a motion to dismiss, would reverse the dismissal of the complaint and invalidate the legislation. The critical allegations, as paraphrased by the Court, are that "the church-related elementary and secondary schools are controlled by religious organizations, have the purpose of propagating and promoting a particular religious faith, and conduct their operations to fulfill that purpose." From these allegations the Court concludes that forbidden entanglements would follow from enforcing compliance with the secular purpose for which the state money is being paid.

I disagree. There is no specific allegation in the complaint that sectarian teaching does or would invade secular classes supported by state funds. That the schools are operated to promote a particular religion is quite consistent with the view that secular teaching devoid of religious instruction can successfully be maintained, for good secular instruction is, as Judge Coffin wrote for the District Court in the Rhode Island case, essential to the success of the religious mission of the parochial school. I would no more here than in the Rhode Island case substitute presumption for proof that religion is or would be taught in state-financed secular courses or assume that enforcement measures would be so extensive as to border on a free exercise violation. We should not forget that the Pennsylvania statute does not compel church schools to accept state funds. I cannot hold that the First Amendment forbids an agreement between the school and the State that the state funds would be used only to teach secular subjects.

I do agree, however, that the complaint should not have been dismissed for failure to state a cause of action. Although it did not specifically allege that the schools involved mixed religious teaching with secular subjects, the complaint did allege that the schools were operated to fulfill religious purposes and one of the legal theories stated in the complaint was that the Pennsylvania Act "finances and participates in the blending of sectarian and secular instruction." At trial under this complaint, evidence showing such a blend in a course supported by state funds would appear to be admissible and, if credited, would establish financing of religious instruction by the State. Hence, I would reverse the judgment of the District Court and remand the case for trial, thereby holding the Pennsylvania legislation valid on its face but leaving open the question of its validity as applied to the particular facts of this case.

I find it very difficult to follow the distinction between the federal and state programs in terms of their First Amendment acceptability. My difficulty is not surprising, since there is frank acknowledgment that "we can only dimly perceive the boundaries of permissible government activity in this sensitive area of constitutional adjudication," *Tilton v. Richardson,*, and that "[j]udicial caveats against entanglement" are a "blurred, indistinct and variable barrier." I find it even more difficult, with these acknowledgments in mind, to understand how the Court can accept the considered judgment of Congress that its program is constitutional and yet reject the equally considered decisions of the Rhode Island and Pennsylvania legislatures that their programs represent a constitutionally acceptable accommodation between church and state.

MUELLER V. ALLEN

463 U.S. 388 (1983)

JUSTICE REHNQUIST delivered the opinion of the Court. Minnesota allows taxpayers, in computing their state income tax, to deduct certain expenses incurred in providing for the education of their children. (1982). The United States Court of Appeals for the Eighth Circuit held that the Establishment Clause of the First Amendment, as made applicable to the States by the Fourteenth Amendment, was not offended by this arrangement.

Minnesota, like every other state, provides its citizens with free elementary and secondary schooling. (1982). It seems to be agreed that about 820,000 students attended this school system in the most recent school year. During the same year, approximately 91,000 elementary and secondary students attended some 500 privately supported schools located in Minnesota, and about 95% of these students attended schools considering themselves to be sectarian.

Minnesota, by a law originally enacted in 1955 and revised in 1976 and again in 1978, permits state taxpayers to claim a I deduction from gross income for certain expenses incurred in I educating their children. The deduction is limited to actual I expenses incurred for the "tuition, textbooks and transportation" of dependents attending elementary or secondary schools. A deduction may not exceed $500 per dependent in grades K through 6 and $700 per dependent in grades 7 through 12.

Little time need be spent on the question of whether the Minnesota tax deduction has a secular purpose. Under our prior decisions, governmental assistance programs have consistently survived this inquiry even when they have run afoul of other aspects of the *Lemon* framework. This reflects, at least in part, our reluctance to attribute unconstitutional motives to the States, particularly when a plausible secular purpose for the State's program may be discerned from the face of the statute.

A State's decision to defray the cost of educational expenses incurred by parents— regardless of the type of schools their children attend—evidences a purpose that is both secular and understandable. An educated populace is essential to the political and economic health of any community, and a State's efforts to assist parents in meeting the rising cost of educational expenses plainly serves this secular purpose of ensuring that the State's citizenry is well educated. Similarly, Minnesota, like other States, could conclude that there is a strong public interest in assuring the continued financial health of private schools, both sectarian and nonsectarian. By educating a substantial number of students such schools relieve public schools of a correspondingly great burden—to the benefit of all taxpayers. In addition, private schools may serve as a benchmark for public schools, in a manner analogous to the "TVA yardstick" for private power companies. As JUSTICE POWELL has remarked:

"Parochial schools, quite apart from their sectarian purpose, have provided an educational alternative for millions of young Americans; they often afford wholesome competition with our public schools; and in some States they relieve substantially the tax burden incident to the operation of public schools. The State has, moreover, a legitimate interest in facilitating education of the highest quality for all children within its boundaries, whatever school their parents have chosen for them."

All these justifications are readily available to support 290.09, subd. 22, and each is sufficient to satisfy the secular purpose inquiry of *Lemon.*

We turn therefore to the more difficult but related question whether the Minnesota statute has "the primary effect of advancing the sectarian aims of the nonpublic schools. " In concluding that it does not, we find several features of the Minnesota tax deduction particularly significant. First, an essential feature of Minnesota's arrangement is the fact that 290.09, subd. 22, is only one among many deductions—such as those for medical expenses, 290.09, subd. 10, and charitable contributions, 290.21, subd. 3—available under the Minnesota tax laws. Our decisions consistently have recognized that traditionally "[l]egislatures have especially broad latitude in creating classifications and distinctions in tax statutes," *Regan v. Taxation With*

Representation of Wash. (1983), in part because the "familiarity with local conditions" enjoyed by legislators especially enables them to "achieve an equitable distribution of the tax burden." *Madden v. Kentucky,* (1940). Under our prior decisions, the Minnesota Legislature's judgment that a deduction for educational expenses fairly equalizes the tax burden of its citizens and encourages desirable expenditures for educational purposes is entitled to substantial deference.

Other characteristics of 290.09, subd. 22, argue equally strongly for the provision's constitutionality. Most importantly, the deduction is available for educational expenses incurred by *all* parents, including those whose children attend public schools and those whose children attend nonsectarian private schools or sectarian private schools.

We also agree with the Court of Appeals that, by channeling whatever assistance it may provide to parochial schools through individual parents, Minnesota has reduced the Establishment Clause objections to which its action is subject. It is true, of course, that financial assistance provided to parents ultimately has an economic effect comparable to that of aid given directly to the schools attended by their children. It is also true, however, that under Minnesota's arrangement public funds become available only as a result of numerous private choices of individual parents of school-age children. For these reasons, we recognized in *Nyquist* that the means by which state assistance flows to private schools is of some importance: we said that "the fact that aid is disbursed to parents rather than to . . . schools" is a material consideration in Establishment Clause analysis, albeit "only one among many factors to be considered." It is noteworthy that all but one of our recent cases invalidating state aid to parochial schools have involved the direct transmission of assistance from the State to the schools themselves. The exception, of course, was *Nyquist,* which, as discussed previously, is distinguishable from this case on other grounds. Where, as here, aid to parochial schools is available only as a result of decisions of individual parents no "imprimatur of state approval," *Widmar*, can be deemed to have been conferred on any particular religion, or on religion generally.

Petitioners argue that, notwithstanding the facial neutrality of 290.09, subd. 22, in application the statute primarily benefits religious institutions. Petitioners rely, as they did below, on a statistical analysis of the type of persons claiming the tax deduction. They contend that most parents of public school children incur no tuition expenses, see Minn. Stat. 120.06 (1982), and that other expenses deductible under 290.09, subd. 22, are negligible in value; moreover, they claim that 96% of the children in private schools in 1978-1979 attended religiously affiliated institutions. Because of all this, they reason, the bulk of deductions taken under 290.09, subd. 22, will be claimed by parents of children in sectarian schools. Respondents reply that petitioners have failed to consider the impact of deductions for items such as transportation, summer school tuition, tuition paid by parents whose children attended schools outside the school districts in which they resided, rental or purchase costs for a variety of equipment, and tuition for certain types of instruction not ordinarily provided in public schools.

We need not consider these contentions in detail. We would be loath to adopt a rule grounding the constitutionality of a facially neutral law on annual reports reciting the extent to which various classes of private citizens claimed benefits.

Finally, private educational institutions, and parents paying for their children to attend these schools, make special contributions to the areas in which they operate. "Parochial schools, quite apart from their sectarian purpose, have provided an educational alternative for millions of young Americans; they often afford wholesome competition with our public schools; and in some States they relieve substantially the tax burden incident to the operation of public schools." *Wolman,* (POWELL, J., concurring in part, concurring in judgment in part, and dissenting in part). If parents of children in private schools choose to take especial advantage of the relief provided by 290.09, subd. 22, it is no doubt due to the fact that they bear a particularly great financial burden in educating their children. More fundamentally, whatever unequal effect may be attributed to the statutory classification can fairly be regarded as a rough return for the benefits, discussed above, provided to the State and all taxpayers by parents sending their children to parochial schools. In the light of all this, we believe it wiser to decline to engage in the type of empirical inquiry into those persons benefited by state law which petitioners urge.

Thus, we hold that the Minnesota tax deduction for educational expenses satisfies the primary effect inquiry of our Establishment Clause cases.

Turning to the third part of the *Lemon* inquiry, we have no difficulty in concluding that the Minnesota statute does not "excessively entangle" the State in religion. The only plausible source of the "comprehensive, discriminating, and continuing state surveillance," 403 U. S., at 619, necessary to run afoul of this standard would lie in the fact that state officials must determine whether particular textbooks qualify for a deduction. In making this decision, state officials must disallow deductions taken for "instructional books and materials used in the teaching of religious tenets, doctrines or worship, the purpose of which is to inculcate such tenets, doctrines or worship." Minn. Stat. 290.09, subd. 22 (1982). Making decisions such as this does not differ substantially from making the types of decisions approved in earlier opinions of this Court. In *Board of Education v. Allen* (1968), for example, the Court upheld the loan of secular textbooks to parents or children attending nonpublic schools; though state officials were required to determine whether particular books were or were not secular, the system was held not to violate the Establishment Clause. See also *Wolman v. Walter* (1977); *Meek v Pittenger* (1975). The same result follows in this case.

For the foregoing reasons, the judgment of the Court of Appeals is

Affirmed.

JUSTICE MARSHALL, with whom JUSTICE BRENNAN, JUSTICE BLACKMUN, and JUSTICE STEVENS join, dissenting.

The Establishment Clause of the First Amendment prohibits a State from subsidizing religious education, whether it does so directly or indirectly. In my view, this principle of neutrality forbids not only the tax benefits struck down in *Committee for Public Education v. Nyquist* (1973), but any tax benefit, including the tax deduction at issue here, which subsidizes tuition payments to sectarian schools. I also believe that the Establishment Clause prohibits the tax deductions that Minnesota authorizes for the cost of books and other instructional materials used for sectarian purposes.

The majority first attempts to distinguish *Nyquist* on the ground that Minnesota makes all parents eligible to deduct up to $500 or $700 for each dependent, whereas the New York law allowed a deduction only for parents whose children attended nonpublic schools. Although Minnesota taxpayers who send their children to local public schools may not deduct tuition expenses because they incur none, they may deduct other expenses, such as the cost of gym clothes, pencils, and notebooks, which are shared by all parents of school-age children. This, in the majority's view, distinguishes the Minnesota scheme from the law at issue in *Nyquist.*

That the Minnesota statute makes some small benefit available to all parents cannot alter the fact that the most substantial benefit provided by the statute is available only to those parents who send their children to schools that charge tuition. It is simply undeniable that the single largest expense that may be deducted under the Minnesota statute is tuition. The statute is little more than a subsidy of tuition masquerading as a subsidy of general educational expenses. The other deductible expenses are *de minimis* in comparison to tuition expenses.

Contrary to the majority's suggestion, the bulk of the tax benefits afforded by the Minnesota scheme are enjoyed by parents of parochial school children not because parents of public school children fail to claim deductions to which they are entitled, but because the latter are simply *unable* to claim the largest tax deduction that Minnesota authorizes. Fewer than 100 of more than 900,000 school-age children in Minnesota attend public schools that charge a general tuition. Of the total number of taxpayers who are eligible for the tuition deduction, approximately 96% send their children to religious schools. Parents who send their children to free public schools are simply ineligible to obtain the full benefit of the deduction except in the unlikely event that they buy $700 worth of pencils, notebooks, and bus rides for their school-age children. Yet parents who pay at least $700 in tuition to nonpublic, sectarian schools can claim the full deduction even if they incur no other educational expenses.

That this deduction has a primary effect of promoting religion can easily be determined without any resort to the type of "statistical evidence" that the majority fears would lead to constitutional uncertainty. The only factual inquiry necessary is the same as that employed in *Nyquist* and *Sloan v. Lemon* (1973): whether the deduction permitted for tuition expenses primarily benefits those who send their children to religious schools. In *Nyquist* we unequivocally rejected any suggestion that, in determining the effect of a tax statute, this Court should look exclusively to what the statute on its face purports to do and ignore the actual operation of the challenged provision. In determining the effect of the New York statute, we emphasized that "virtually all" of the schools receiving direct grants for maintenance and repair were Roman Catholic schools, that reimbursements were given to parents "who send their children to nonpublic schools, the bulk of which is concededly sectarian in orientation," that "it is precisely the function of New York's law to provide assistance to private schools, the great majority of which are sectarian," and that "tax reductions authorized by this law flow primarily to the parents of children attending sectarian, nonpublic schools."

Similarly, in *Sloan v. Lemon*, we considered important to our "consider[ation of] the new law's effect . . . [that] more than 90% of the children attending nonpublic schools in the Commonwealth of Pennsylvania are enrolled in schools that are controlled by religious organizations or that have the purpose of propagating and promoting religious faith.

In this case, it is undisputed that well over 90% of the children attending tuition-charging schools in Minnesota are enrolled in sectarian schools. History and experience likewise instruct us that any generally available financial assistance for elementary and secondary school tuition expenses mainly will further religious education because the majority of the schools which charge tuition are sectarian. *Nyquist*; *Lemon v. Kurtzman* (Douglas, J., concurring). Because Minnesota, like every other State, is committed to providing free public education, tax assistance for tuition payments inevitably redounds to the benefit of nonpublic, sectarian schools and parents who send their children to those schools.

The majority also asserts that the Minnesota statute is distinguishable from the statute struck down in *Nyquist* in another respect: the tax benefit available under Minnesota law is a "genuine tax deduction," whereas the New York law provided a benefit which, while nominally a deduction, also had features of a "tax credit." Under the Minnesota law, the amount of the tax benefit varies directly with the amount of the expenditure. Under the New York law, the amount of deduction was not dependent upon the amount actually paid for tuition but was a predetermined amount which depended on the tax bracket of each taxpayer. The deduction was designed to yield roughly the same amount of tax "forgiveness" for each taxpayer.

AGUILAR ET AL. V. FELTON ET AL.

473 U.S. 402 (1985)

JUSTICE BRENNAN delivered the opinion of the Court.

The program at issue in this case, originally enacted as Title I of the Elementary and Secondary Education Act of 1965, authorizes the Secretary of Education to distribute financial assistance to local educational institutions to meet the needs of educationally deprived children from low-income families. The funds are to be appropriated in accordance with programs proposed by local educational agencies and approved by state educational agencies.

"To the extent consistent with the number of educationally deprived children in the school district of the local educational agency who are enrolled in private elementary and secondary schools, such agency shall make provisions for including special educational services and arrangements . . . in which such children can participate." The proposed programs must also meet the following statutory requirements: the children involved in the program must be educationally deprived, the children must reside in areas comprising a high concentration of low-income families, and the programs must supplement, not supplant, programs that would exist absent funding under Title I.

Since 1966, the City of New York has provided instructional services funded by Title I to parochial school students on the premises of parochial schools. Of those students eligible to receive funds in 1981-1982, 13.2% were enrolled in private schools. Of that group, 84% were enrolled in schools affiliated with the Roman Catholic Archdiocese of New York and the Diocese of Brooklyn and 8% were enrolled in Hebrew day schools. With respect to the religious atmosphere of these schools, the Court of Appeals concluded that "the picture that emerges is of a system in which religious considerations play a key role in the selection of students and teachers, and which has as its substantial purpose the inculcation of religious values."

The programs conducted at these schools include remedial reading, reading skills, remedial mathematics, English as a second language, and guidance services. These programs are carried out by regular employees of the public schools (teachers, guidance counselors, psychologists, psychiatrists, and social workers) who have volunteered to teach in the parochial schools. The amount of time that each professional spends in the parochial school is determined by the number of students in the particular program and the needs of these students.

The City's Bureau of Nonpublic School Reimbursement makes teacher assignments, and the instructors are supervised by field personnel, who attempt to pay at least one unannounced visit per month. The field supervisors in turn, report to program coordinators, who also pay occasional unannounced supervisory visits to monitor Title I classes in the parochial schools. The professionals involved in the program are directed to avoid involvement with religious activities that are conducted within the private schools and to bar religious materials in their classrooms. All material and equipment used in the programs funded under Title I are supplied by the Government and are used only in those programs. The professional personnel are solely responsible for the selection of the students. Additionally, the professionals are informed that contact with private school personnel should be kept to a minimum. Finally, the administrators of the parochial schools are required to clear the classrooms used by the public school personnel of all religious symbols. . . .

In *School District of Grand Rapids v. Ball*, the Court has today held unconstitutional under the Establishment Clause two remedial and enhancement programs operated by the Grand Rapids Public School District, in which classes were provided to private school children at public expense in classrooms located in and leased from the local private schools. The New York City programs challenged in this case are very similar to the programs we examined in *Ball*. In both cases, publicly funded instructors teach classes composed exclusively of private school students in private school buildings. In both cases, an overwhelming number of the participating private schools are religiously affiliated. In both cases, the publicly funded programs provide not only professional personnel, but also all materials and supplies necessary for the operation of the programs. Finally, the instructors in both cases are told that they are public school employees under the sole control of the public school system.

Appellants attempt to distinguish this case on the ground that the City of New York, unlike the Grand Rapids Public School District, has adopted a system for monitoring the religious content of publicly funded Title I classes in the religious schools. At best, the supervision in this case would assist in preventing the Title I program from being used, intentionally or unwittingly, to inculcate the religious beliefs of the surrounding parochial school. But appellants' argument fails in any event, because the supervisory system established by the City of New York inevitably results in the excessive entanglement of church and state, an Establishment Clause concern distinct from that addressed by the effects doctrine. Even where state aid to parochial institutions does not have the primary effect of advancing religion, the provision of such aid may nonetheless violate the Establishment Clause owing to the nature of the interaction of church and state in the administration of that aid.

The principle that the state should not become too closely entangled with the church in the administration of assistance is rooted in two concerns. When the state becomes enmeshed with a given denomination in matters of religious significance, the freedom of religious belief of those who are not adherents of that denomination suffers, even when the governmental purpose underlying the involvement is largely secular. In addition, the freedom of even the adherents of the denomination is limited by the governmental intrusion into sacred matters. . . .

In *Roemer v. Maryland Public Works*

Board (1976), the Court sustained state programs of aid to religiously affiliated institutions of higher learning. The State allowed the grants to be used for any nonsectarian purpose. The Court upheld the grants on the ground that the institutions were not "pervasively sectarian," and therefore a system of supervision was unnecessary to ensure that the grants were not being used to effect a religious end.. . . . Moreover, our holding in *Meek* invalidating instructional services much like those at issue in this case rested on the ground that the publicly funded teachers were "performing important educational services in schools in which education is an integral part of the dominant sectarian mission and in which an atmosphere dedicated to the advancement of religious belief is constantly maintained." *Meek*. The court below found that the schools involved in this case were "well within this characterization." Unlike the schools in *Roemer*, many of the schools here receive funds and report back to their affiliated church, require attendance at church religious exercises, begin the schoolday or class period with prayer, and grant preference in admission to members of the sponsoring denominations. In addition, the Catholic schools at issue here, which constitute the vast majority of the aided schools, are under the general supervision and control of the local parish.

The critical elements of the entanglement proscribed in *Lemon* and *Meek* are thus present in this case. First, as noted above, the aid is provided in a pervasively sectarian environment. Second, because assistance is provided in the form of teachers, ongoing inspection is required to ensure the absence of a religious message. In short, the scope and duration of New York City's Title I program would require a permanent and pervasive state presence in the sectarian schools receiving aid.

This pervasive monitoring by public authorities in the sectarian schools infringes precisely those Establishment Clause values at the root of the prohibition of excessive entanglement. Agents of the city must visit and inspect the religious school regularly, alert for the subtle or overt presence of religious matter in Title I classes. Lemon v. Kurtzman ("What would appear to some to be essential to good citizenship might well for others border on or constitute instruction in religion"). In addition, the religious school must obey these same agents when they make determinations as to what is and what is not a "religious symbol" and thus off limits in a Title I classroom. In short, the religious school, which has as a primary purpose the advancement and preservation of a particular religion must endure the ongoing presence of state personnel whose primary purpose is to monitor teachers and students in an attempt to guard against the infiltration of religious thought.

The administrative cooperation that is required to maintain the educational program at issue here entangles church and state in still another way that infringes interests at the heart of the Establishment Clause. Administrative personnel of the public and parochial school systems must work together in resolving matters related to schedules, classroom assignments, problems that arise in the implementation of the program, requests for additional services, and the dissemination of information regarding the program. Furthermore, the program necessitates "frequent contacts between the regular and the remedial teachers (or other professionals), in which each side reports on individual student needs, problems encountered, and results achieved."

We have long recognized that underlying the Establishment Clause is "the objective . . . to prevent, as far as possible, the intrusion of either [church or state] into the precincts of the other." *Lemon v. Kurtzman*. See also McCollum v. Board of Education. Although "[s]eparation in this context cannot mean absence of all contact," *Waltz v. Tax Comm'n*. (1970), the detailed monitoring and close administrative contact required to maintain New York City's Title I program can only produce "a kind of continuing day-to-day relationship which the policy of neutrality seeks to minimize." The numerous judgments that must be made by agents of the city concern matters that may be subtle and controversial, yet may be of deep religious significance to the controlling denominations. As government agents must make these judgments, the dangers of political divisiveness along religious lines increase. At the same time, "[t]he picture of state inspectors prowling the halls of parochial schools and auditing classroom instruction surely raises more than an imagined specter of governmental 'secularization of a creed.' *Lemon v. Kurtzman.*"

JUSTICE POWELL, concurring. . . .

(The) risk of entanglement is compounded by the additional risk of political divisiveness stemming from the aid to religion at issue here. I do not suggest that at this point in our history the Title I program or similar parochial aid plans could result in the establishment of a state religion. There likewise is small chance that these programs would result in significant religious or denominational control over our democratic processes. *Wolman v. Walter.* Nonetheless, there remains a considerable risk of continuing political strife over the propriety of direct aid to religious schools and the proper allocation of limited governmental resources. As this Court has repeatedly recognized, there is a likelihood whenever direct governmental aid is extended to some groups that there will be competition and strife among them and others to gain, maintain, or increase the financial support of government. In States such as New York that have large and varied sectarian populations, one can be assured that politics will enter into any state decision to aid parochial schools. Public schools, as well as private schools, are under increasing financial pressure to meet real and perceived needs. Thus, any proposal to extend direct governmental aid to parochial schools alone is likely to spark political disagreement from taxpayers who support the public schools, as well as from nonrecipient sectarian groups, who may fear that needed funds are being diverted from them. In short, aid to parochial schools of the sort at issue here potentially leads to "that kind and degree of government involvement in religious life that, as history teaches us, is apt to lead to strife and frequently strain a

political system to the breaking point. *Waltz v. Tax Comm'n.*" Although the Court's opinion does not discuss it at length, the potential for such divisiveness is a strong additional reason for holding that the Title I and Grand Rapids programs are invalid on entanglement grounds.

The Title I program at issue in this case also would be invalid under the "effects" prong of the test adopted in *Lemon v. Kurtzman.* As has been discussed thoroughly in *Ball*, with respect to the Grand Rapids programs, the type of aid provided in New York by the Title I program amounts to a state subsidy of the parochial schools by relieving those schools of the duty to provide the remedial and supplemental education their children require. This is not the type of "indirect and incidental effect beneficial to [the] religious institutions" that we suggested in *Nyquist* would survive Establishment Clause scrutiny. Rather, by directly assuming part of the parochial schools' education function, the effect of the Title I aid is "inevitably . . . to subsidize and advance the religious mission of [the] sectarian schools," even though the program provides that only secular subjects will be taught. As in *Meek v. Pittenger* (1975), the secular education these schools provide goes "hand in hand" with the religious mission that is the reason for the schools' existence. Because of the predominantly religious nature of the schools, the substantial aid provided by the Title I program "inescapably results in the direct and substantial advancement of religious activity." *Meek v. Pittenger.* . .

Our cases have upheld evenhanded secular assistance to both parochial and public school children in some areas. E.g., *Board of Education v. Allen*, (1968) (provision of secular textbooks); *Everson v. Board of Education* (1947) (reimbursements for bus fare to school). I do not read the Court's opinion as precluding these types of indirect aid to parochial schools. In the cases cited, the assistance programs made funds available equally to public and nonpublic schools without entanglement. The constitutional defect in the Title I program, as indicated above, is that it provides a direct financial subsidy to be administered in significant part by public school teachers within parochial schools—resulting in both the advancement of religion and forbidden entanglement. If, for example, Congress could fashion a program of evenhanded financial assistance to both public and private schools that could be administered, without governmental supervision in the private schools, so as to prevent the diversion of the aid from secular purposes, we would be presented with a different question. . . .

CHIEF JUSTICE BURGER, dissenting.

Under the guise of protecting Americans from the evils of an Established Church such as those of the 18th century and earlier times, today's decision will deny countless schoolchildren desperately needed remedial teaching services funded under Title I. The program at issue covers remedial reading, reading skills, remedial mathematics, English as a second language, and assistance for children needing special help in the learning process. The "remedial reading" portion of this program, for example, reaches children who suffer from dyslexia, a disease known to be difficult to diagnose and treat. Many of these children now will not receive the special training they need, simply because their parents desire that they attend religiously affiliated schools.

What is disconcerting about the result reached today is that, in the face of the human cost entailed by this decision the Court does not even attempt to identify any threat to religious liberty posed by the operation of Title I.

I cannot join in striking down a program that, in the words of the Court of Appeals, "has done so much good and little, if any, detectable harm." The notion that denying these services to students in religious schools is a neutral act to protect us from an Established Church has no support in logic, experience, or history. Rather than showing the neutrality the Court boasts of, it exhibits nothing less than hostility toward religion and the children who attend church-sponsored schools.

JUSTICE REHNQUIST, dissenting. . . .

In this case the Court takes advantage of the "Catch-22" paradox of its own creation, whereby aid must be supervised to ensure no entanglement but the supervision itself is held to cause an entanglement. The Court today strikes down nondiscriminatory nonsectarian aid to educationally deprived children from low-income families. The Establishment Clause does not prohibit such sorely needed assistance we have indeed traveled far afield from the concerns which prompted the adoption of the First Amendment when we rely on gossamer abstractions to invalidate a law which obviously meets an entirely secular need. I would reverse.

JUSTICE O'CONNOR, with whom JUSTICE REHNQUIST joins as to Parts II and III, dissenting.

Today the Court affirms the holding of the Court of Appeals that public school teachers can offer remedial instruction to disadvantaged students who attend religious schools "only if such instruction . . . [is] afforded at a neutral site off the premises of the religious school." This holding rests on the theory, enunciated in Part V of the Court's opinion in *Meek v. Pittenger* (1975), that public school teachers who set foot on parochial school premises are likely to bring religion into their classes, and that the supervision necessary to prevent religious teaching would unduly entangle church and state. Even if this theory were valid in the abstract, it cannot validly be applied to New York City's 19-year-old Title I program. The Court greatly exaggerates the degree of supervision necessary to prevent public school teachers from inculcating religion, and thereby demonstrates the flaws of a test that condemns benign cooperation between church and state. I would uphold Congress' efforts to afford remedial instruction to disadvantaged schoolchildren in both public and parochial schools. . . .

Indeed, in 19 years there has never been a single incident in which a Title I instructor "subtly or overtly" attempted to "indoctrinate the students in particular religious tenets at public expense. . . ."

Common sense suggests a plausible explanation for this unblemished record. New York City's public Title I instructors are professional educators who can and do follow instructions not to inculcate religion in their classes. They are unlikely to be influenced by the sectarian nature of the parochial schools where they teach, not only because they are carefully supervised by public officials, but also because the vast majority of them visit several different schools each week and are not of the same religion as their parochial students. In light of the ample record, an objective observer of the implementation of the Title I program in New York City would hardly view it as endorsing the tenets of the participating parochial schools. To the contrary, the actual and perceived effect of the program is precisely the effect intended by Congress: impoverished schoolchildren are being helped to overcome learning deficits, improving their test scores, and receiving a significant boost in their struggle to obtain both a thorough education and the opportunities that flow from it.

The only type of impermissible effect that arguably could carry over from the *Grand Rapids* decision to this litigation, then, is the effect of subsidizing "the religious functions of the parochial schools by taking over a substantial portion of their responsibility for teaching secular subjects. " That effect is tenuous, however, in light of the statutory directive that Title I funds may be used only to provide services that otherwise would not be available to the participating students. The Secretary of Education has vigorously enforced the requirement that Title I funds supplement rather than supplant the services of local education agencies.

Even if we were to assume that Title I remedial classes in New York City may have duplicated to some extent instruction parochial schools would have offered in the absence of Title I, the Court's delineation of this third type of effect proscribed by the Establishment Clause would be seriously flawed. Our Establishment Clause decisions have not barred remedial assistance to parochial school children, but rather remedial assistance *on the premises of the parochial school*. Under *Wolman v. Walter* (1977), the New York City classes prohibited by the Court today would have survived Establishment Clause scrutiny if they had been offered in a neutral setting off the property of the private school. Yet it is difficult to understand why a remedial reading class offered on parochial school premises is any more likely to supplant the secular course offerings of the parochial school than the same class offered in a portable classroom next door to the school. Unless *Wolman* was wrongly decided, the defect in the Title I program cannot lie in the risk that it will supplant secular course offerings.

Recognizing the weakness of any claim of an improper purpose or effect, the Court today relies entirely on the entanglement prong of *Lemon* to invalidate the New York City Title I program. The Court holds that the occasional presence of peripatetic public school teachers on parochial school grounds threatens undue entanglement of church and state because (1) the remedial instruction is afforded in a pervasively sectarian environment; (2) ongoing supervision is required to assure that the public school teachers do not attempt to inculcate religion; (3) the administrative personnel of the parochial and public school systems must work together in resolving administrative and scheduling problems; and (4) the instruction is likely to result in political divisiveness over the propriety of direct aid. . . .

It is not intuitively obvious that a dedicated public school teacher will tend to disobey instructions and commence proselytizing students at public expense merely because the classroom is within a parochial school. *Meek* is correct in asserting that a teacher of remedial reading "remains a teacher," but surely it is significant that the teacher involved is a professional, full-time public school employee who is unaccustomed to bringing religion into the classroom.

Given that not a single incident of religious indoctrination has been identified as occurring in the thousands of classes offered in Grand Rapids and New York City over the past two decades, it is time to acknowledge that the risk identified in

Meek was greatly exaggerated.

Just as the risk that public school teachers in parochial classrooms will inculcate religion has been exaggerated, so has the degree of supervision required to manage that risk. In this respect the New York City Title I program is instructive. What supervision has been necessary in New York City to enable public school teachers to help disadvantaged children for 19 years without once proselytizing? Public officials have prepared careful instructions warning public school teachers of their exclusively secular mission, and have required Title I teachers to study and observe them. Under the rules, Title I teachers are not accountable to parochial or private school officials; they have sole responsibility for selecting the students who participate in their class, must administer their own tests for determining eligibility, cannot engage in team teaching or cooperative activities with parochial school teachers, must make sure that all materials and equipment they use are not otherwise used by the parochial school, and must not participate in religious activities in the schools or introduce any religious matter into their teaching. To ensure compliance with the rules, a field supervisor and a program coordinator, who are full-time public school employees, make unannounced visits to each teacher's classroom at least once a month.

The Court's reliance on the potential for political divisiveness as evidence of undue entanglement is also unpersuasive. There is little record support for the proposition that New York .City's admirable Title I program has ignited any controversy other than this litigation. In *Mueller v. Allen* (1983), the Court cautioned that the "elusive inquiry" into political divisiveness should be confined to a narrow category of parochial aid cases. The concurring opinion in *Lynch v. Donnelly* (1984), went further, suggesting that Establishment Clause analysis should focus solely on the character of the government activity that might cause political divisiveness, and that "the entanglement prong of the *Lemon* test is properly limited to institutional entanglement."

I adhere to the doubts about the entanglement test that were expressed in *Lynch*. It is curious indeed to base our interpretation of the Constitution on speculation as to the likelihood of a phenomenon which the parties may create merely by prosecuting a lawsuit. My reservations about the entanglement test, however, have come to encompass its institutional aspects as well. As JUSTICE REHNQUIST has pointed out, many of the inconsistencies in our Establishment Clause decisions can be ascribed to our insistence that parochial aid programs with a valid purpose and effect may still be invalid by virtue of undue entanglement. . . .

Pervasive institutional involvement of church and state may remain relevant in deciding the effect of a statute which is alleged to violate the Establishment Clause, *Waltz v. Tax Comm'n* (1970), but state efforts to ensure that public resources are used only for nonsectarian ends should not in themselves serve to invalidate an otherwise valid statute. The State requires sectarian organizations to cooperate on a whole range of matters without thereby advancing religion or giving the impression that the government endorses religion. *Wallace v. Jaffree* (noting that state educational agencies impose myriad curriculum, attendance, certification, fire, and safety regulations on sectarian schools). If a statute lacks a purpose or effect of advancing or endorsing religion, I would not invalidate it merely because it requires some ongoing cooperation between church and state or some state supervision to ensure that state funds do not advance religion.

Today's ruling does not spell the end of the Title I program of remedial education for disadvantaged children. Children attending public schools may still obtain the benefits of the program. Impoverished children who attend parochial schools may also continue to benefit from Title I programs offered off the premises of their schools—possibly in portable classrooms just over the edge of school property. The only disadvantaged children who lose under the Court's holding are those in cities where it is not economically and logistically feasible to provide public facilities for remedial education adjacent to the parochial school. But this subset is significant, for it includes more than 20,000 New York City schoolchildren and uncounted others elsewhere in the country.

For these children, the Court's decision is tragic. The Court deprives them of a program that offers a meaningful chance at success in life, and it does so on the untenable theory that public school teachers (most of whom are of different faiths than their students) are likely to start teaching religion merely because they have walked across the threshold of a parochial school. I reject this theory and the analysis in Meek v. Pittenger on which it is based. I cannot close my eyes to the fact that, over almost two decades, New York City's public school teachers have helped thousands of impoverished parochial school children to overcome educational disadvantages without once attempting to inculcate religion. Their praiseworthy efforts have not eroded and do not threaten the religious liberty assured by the Establishment Clause.

(Justice White also dissented)

18
GOVERNMENTAL SPONSORSHIP OF RELIGIOUS ACTIVITIES

The American system, as Justice Douglas once remarked, is "honeycombed" with what might be considered governmental sponsorship of religion. By Congressional fiat, our coins proclaim "In God We Trust," and, according to the Pledge of Allegiance, we are "one nation, under God." The Congress, and many state legislatures, employ chaplains to open their sessions with prayer, and each branch of the military services has a "Chaplain's Corp" of commissioned officers whose major function is to provide religious services and spiritual assistance to those who seek their help.

Such practices, at least at the national level, have gone virtually unchallenged. But when local governments, commonly either municipalities or school districts, have acted in ways considered to foster religion, the Court has been asked to determine the constitutionality of such actions. Some of the practices challenged have involved governmental efforts to reflect the fact that, as Douglas also observed, "we are a religious people," by taking note of the religious character of certain national holidays. Others have involved religious observances in the public schools, particularly the saying of prayers. While the "school prayer" cases have had overtones of free exercise, the basis for the Court's resolution of both types of issues has been the establishment clause.

The Court's earliest decision on establishment, the 1947 case of Everson v. Board of Education, involved the issue of governmental aid to religious schools, and was discussed in Chapter 17. The Court's next consideration of the establishment question came in two cases involving "released time" from public school attendance for the purpose of religious instruction.

In the first of these cases, McCollum v. Board of Education (1948), the public schools of Champagne, Illinois, released students whose parents gave their permission for one half hour per week, to attend religious instruction given by representatives of the various faiths. The religious education classes were held in public school classrooms, with students whose parents did not wish them to participate going to "study hall."

For a majority of the Court, the Illinois program violated the establishment clause. Not only were the classes held on school property, but attendance was enforced by taking roll, with the religious instructors reporting attendance or absence to their public school counterparts. This, said Justice Black, was a utilization of the state's compulsory school system to assist religious organizations in promoting their faith. Not only were state buildings used for the inculcation of religious doctrine, but the system for enforcing attendance afforded incalculable aid in providing students for the religious program. Justice Reed's minority opinion, by contrast, saw the program as an example of government accommodation of its practices to the religious predilections of the people, likening it in this respect to the employment of chaplains by the military.

McCollum was soon followed by Zorach v. Clauson (1952), in which a narrowly divided court upheld a New York program in all respects similar, except that the religious instruction took place off, rather than on, school property. The New York program, said Justice Douglas' majority opinion, involved neither the use of public classrooms nor the expenditure of public funds. And the First Amendment, while "studiously defining" the specific ways in which state and church must not be united, did not mandate complete separation. Total separation would create hostility between the state and the church, and public schools would not be permitted to release children from their classrooms for individual attendance at religious services.

Without intimating that the decision in Zorach was wrong, it must be noted that there are serious problems with Douglas' opinion. While the New York program allowed no religious instruction on public property, public school teachers still recorded and transcribed reports of attendance at the religion classes. And Douglas was wrong in saying that striking down the program would necessarily prevent the state from accommodating the religious desires of children and their parents. It is one thing when such decisions are made individually, and when the result for the public school is the continuation of classes without interruption. It is another when a program is systematized and regularized, and when that program disrupts regular instruction.

Finally, and most fundamentally, Douglas' opinion does not deal with Black's McCollum argument that a regularized "released time" program is of powerful assistance to the churches in conveying their message. The various religions were, after all, free to conduct religious instruction after school hours (as many did and do), and there was a reason why the time chosen in each of the two programs was during hours of regular school instruction. That reason, it would seem, could only have derived from the undoubtedly correct perception that programs held after school hours would have been less attractive to both parent and child.

The distinctions which Douglas' offers seem, then, not very persuasive and Zorach, from a purely secularist perspective, was decided incorrectly. From another viewpoint, however, it was not Zorach but rather McCollum which represented an incorrect view of the meaning of the religion clauses. Walter Berns tells us that even Jefferson, generally credited as the most "secularist" of those whose views influenced the intent of the First Amendment, believed that the church could be useful to the state in providing certain essentials of character which, in a free society, could not be directly taught by the state.[1] Thus "released time" or similar programs not only might be considered as instances of an "accommodation" of religious beliefs, but as a way of accomplishing secular goals.

That, at any rate, was the belief of those who, for most of the history of the Amendment and of the public schools, fostered overtly religious exercises as a regular part of the public school curriculum. The saying of prayers and the reading of the Bible in the schools was a part of our history for nearly a century. The initial motivation for such practices may have been the preservation and advancement of Protestantism, the dominant religious belief. It was for that reason that early Catholic leaders founded their own school system. As the country became more pluralist, however, prayers and observances became more "religiously neutral" and more respecting of the views of all the major faiths. And their justification became one of molding character, rather than inculcating sectarian beliefs.

It was perhaps this motivation which, in the late 1950s, led to the New York

Board of Regent's designation of a prayer to be used in the state's schools. The prayer, composed by a committee representative of the three major faiths, stated in its entirety, "Almighty God, we acknowledge our dependence upon Thee, and we beg Thy blessings upon us, our parents, our teachers and our country." As utilized by the school district involved in Engel v. Vitale, the "Regents Prayer" was recited at the beginning of each school day by children wishing to participate. Those who objected were allowed to "stand aside" or to absent themselves from the room.

Neither its nondenominational character nor its voluntariness saved the "Regents Prayer" before the Supreme Court. For an all but unanimous majority Justice Black found that the saying of the prayer violated not the free exercise but the establishment clause. That clause, said Justice Black, "must at least mean that in this country it is no part of the business of government to compose official prayers for any group of the American people to recite as a part of a religious program carried on by government." Such an activity smacked too closely of the religious orthodoxy and persecution which motivated the establishment clause.

For Justice Douglas, concurring, the financing of religious activity, whether in the form at issue or in others common in the United States, was forbidden by the establishment clause, since "the person praying is a public official on the public payroll, performing a religious exercise in a governmental institution." Justice Stewart, the sole dissenter, complained that the decision refused to allow "a child who wanted to say a prayer, to say it."

The Engel decision evoked great protest. Religious leaders of many faiths condemned it, as did politicians more opposed (one would suspect) to the then controversial school integration decisions than to Engel itself. From the perspective of what was actually decided, however, it is as hard to understand the opposition as it is to credit the simplistic dissent of Justice Stewart. For, on almost any understanding of the meaning of the First Amendment, the New York practice was a violation. If it is unconstitutional for the state to establish an official church (and the Amendment, as Justice Black noted in Everson, must mean at least this), it is equally impermissible for the state to compose an official prayer. And even for those who believe that what the First Amendment prohibits is only preference for one religion over another, it is obvious that the prayer's terminology prefers the Judaic-Christian tradition over others.

It is likely, therefore, that opposition to Engel was based chiefly on a perception of what it presaged for other religious activities in the schools, particularly the widespread practice of beginning the school day with a recitation of the Lords Prayer or with a reading from the Bible. Within a year, both of these practices had been challenged and found constitutionally wanting in the combined cases of Abington Township v. Schempp and Murray v. Curlett (1963). In these cases, the school districts whose practices were challenged had attempted to make the programs as nondenominational as possible. The Bible used for the Murray program was, for example, the King James version, but Catholic students could use the Douay, and Jewish children could read from the Old Testament. Additionally, children who did not participate were excused from the classroom during the observance.

Despite these features, an argument can be made that Abington could, and perhaps should have been decided on the basis of the free exercise clause. Justice Frankfurter, in his McCollum concurrence, had argued that the presence of the "released time" program in the schools was at least subtly coercive, in that the minority of students who did not attend religious instruction were singled out as "different" from their peers, and thus would have some tendency to "go along" with their friends in order to avoid such a perception. If this was true in the case of a once a week program, it must have been even more true in the case of the daily practices at issue here. Perhaps one reason that the Court did not decide on this basis was the implication that such a decision might have had for Barnette and for continued recitation of the "Pledge of Allegiance."[2]

Justice Clark, for the Schempp majority, saw no evidence of coercion, and the case was decided on establishment grounds. The doctrines which it announced, along with one later addition, were to be the touchstones for determining the presence of establishment from that time forward. Thus the decision is excerpted herein.

Clark's opinion saw the test of establishment as being whether the questioned practice has 1) a secular legislative purpose, and 2) a primary effect which is neither the advancement nor the inhibition of religion. The legislatures in the instant cases had stated their purpose as providing for the moral and ethical training of the children concerned, and Clark did not argue that such was not a valid state purpose, nor that it might not be advanced by the practices here at issue. He conceded, furthermore, that the Bible could be studied in public schools as a matter of history or literature. Here, however, the effect of saying or reading these Judaic-Christian materials was inevitably to advance religion. Zorach was distinguished on the grounds that in that case the religious exercise was not part of the curriculum, was not held on school grounds, and involved no active participation by public school teachers.

The Court's decisions in Schempp and Murray are now almost thirty years old. In the intervening time few other cases have come to the Supreme Court on the issue of prayer or religious activity in the schools. The most noteworthy recent decision in the area was that in Wallace v. Jaffree (1985), in which the Court struck down an Alabama statute mandating a "moment of silence" at the beginning of the school day. In Wallace the Court, for the first time, found an alleged religious practice wanting in "secular purpose."

For the most part, however, the Court's energies have been devoted to the even more controversial issue of governmental aid to religious schools. Lower courts, though, have decided a number of cases presenting variation of the Schempp theme, expanding the meaning of Schempp to include even greater limitations on religious activity in the schools. [3]

Almost inevitably, such decisions provoked a clash with the "free exercise" rights of students, and, in the 1990 case of Board of Education v. Mergens, the Court was called upon to decide the difficult question of whether the state must, in order to avoid establishment, prohibit the formation and functioning on campus of religiously oriented organizations. At issue was the constitutionality of a Congressional statute mandating "equal access" to high school campuses by student religious organizations. The Court, per O'Connor, held that the presence of such groups, at least where the school permitted the formation of other organizations not related to the curriculum, did not violate establishment strictures. More than any other single case, Mergens illustrates the potential clash between establishment and free exercise concerns. For that reason, as well as its intrinsic importance, it is excerpted herein.

One who believes that in cases of collision free exercise should be preferred over nonestablishment can applaud the Mergens decision. And it would seem that the Court's distinction between situations where other non-curricular organizations are and are not allowed to exist would mitigate the likelihood that the presence of student religious organizations would be seen as school endorsement of religion.

But the decision may also, as the dissenters argued, serve as a basis for a future, and perhaps unfortunate, narrowing of the right of school officials to ban groups deemed inimical to the central functions of the schools. It is, we have previously noted, not unusual for religion cases to become precedents for those involving those of free speech and association.

If the Court has been relatively consistent in its application of the establishment clause to religious observances in the schools, the same cannot be said for its decisions with respect to other governmental activities said to be intertwined with religion. Its vacillation in such matters was sharply illustrated in the cases of <u>Lynch v. Donnelly</u> and <u>County of Allegheny v. American Civil Liberties Union</u>, both decided by five to four votes. At issue in both was the question of whether a city's use of admittedly religious symbols as part of a holiday observance constituted an "establishment of religion."

In <u>Lynch</u> the crèche, or Nativity scene, was owned by Pawtucket, R.I., and displayed by it on private property, along with scenes depicting Santa Claus, reindeer, a "talking wishing well" and a large Christmas tree. Chief Justice Burger's opinion upholding the practice began with an extensive canvassing of religion-related practices pursued by governments since adoption of the First Amendment. On the basis of this survey the Chief Justice reached the conclusion that history mandated accommodation, not merely tolerance, of religion, while forbidding hostility toward it. The Court, said Burger, had refused to apply the establishment clause so as to strike down all governmental conduct arguably conferring benefits on religion, but rather scrutinized them according to the three-prong <u>Lemon</u> test. Finding that inclusion of the crèche in the Pawtucket display supported the secular purpose of celebrating Christmas, and that there was little or no "entanglement" between church and state, the Chief devoted most of his attention to the issue of its "primary effect." Here, he concluded, there was less assistance to religion than in other instances where state recognition of religion had been held valid.

Justice Brennan's dissenting opinion began by asserting, partly on the basis of the religious nature of the crèche, and partly on the basis of statements made at trial by the Mayor of Pawtucket, that the city's purpose in exhibiting the crèche was to advance religion. Secondly, for Brennan the "primary effect" was to place the government's "imprimatur of approval" on the religious views which the crèche advanced. In support of this Brennan argued that "The effect on minority religious groups, as well as on those who may reject all religion, is to convey the message that their views are not similarly worthy of public recognition nor entitled to public support." Finally, for Brennan, inclusion of the crèche, posed "a significant threat of fostering 'excessive entanglement,'" principally because of the political wrangling that might result among groups wishing to have their views included in the display, and between advocates and opponents of such displays.

County of Allegheny v. American Civil Liberties Union (1989), excerpted in this chapter, also involved governmental display of a Nativity scene. But here the crèche, unlike that in Lynch, was the central, and for a time the only, figure in a Christmas display placed in the "choicest" location in the Allegheny County (Pa.) Courthouse. For Blackmun and the majority, this was enough to condemn it as an establishment of religion. The Jewish menorah, however, was placed next to a Christmas tree, which the Court deemed to be at present solely a secular sign of Christmas, and a sign proclaiming the virtues of liberty. Thus the menorah, in contrast to the crèche, had lost its religious character and its presence was seen only as part of a celebration of two *secular* holidays.

One must concede the validity of Blackmun's position as to the crèche. There is little doubt that the Courthouse display celebrated the Christian, and only the Christian, interpretation of Christmas. But it appears absurd to argue that a menorah in any context is *only* a secular symbol. Certainly Justice Kennedy is correct when he argues that it will not be so perceived by those casually acquainted with Judaism.

And it is *perception*, more than anything else, that ultimately determines the outcome in Allegheny County. Blackmun observed, with respect to the crèche: ". . . (Allegheny County) . . . has chosen to celebrate Christmas in a way that has the effect of endorsing a patently Christian message, "Glory to God for the birth of Jesus Christ." And, as to the menorah, he said, "Given all these considerations, it is not 'sufficiently likely' that residents of Pittsburgh will perceive the combined display of the tree, the sign, and the menorah as an "endorsement" or "disapproval" of their individual religious choices."

In County of Allegheny Blackmun adopted to his own purposes Justice O'Connor's concurring opinion in Lynch, which he characterized as providing "a sound analytical framework for evaluating governmental use of religious symbols." O'Connor, said Blackmun, rejected the idea that the Court tolerates any "endorsement of religion," for endorsement "sends a message to nonadherents that they are outsiders, not full members of the political community, and an accompanying message to adherents that they are insiders, favored members of the political community." That analysis, said Blackmun,"articulates a method for determining whether the government's use of an object with religious meaning has the effect of endorsing religion," which depends upon "what viewers may fairly understand to be the purpose of the display."

It may be that Blackmun's acceptance of the O'Connor position signals future employment of the "endorsement" in cases involving governmental use of religious symbols. Certainly that criterion is more sensitive to the issues involved in such cases than is the Lemon test considered alone. But even in the instant cases it is not free from difficulty, as O'Connor's concurrence in County of Allgheny demonstrates. While agreeing with Blackmun's conclusion, O'Connor asserts that what is demonstrated by the menorah display is not the celebration, as Blackmun would have it, of a secular holiday, but rather of "religious pluralism." It is difficult to see, with the very member of the Court who formulated the endorsement test disagreeing on its application in this case, how it can be ascertained what "viewers may fairly understand to be the purpose of" a symbol. Further, it does not follow that governmental recognition of a matter of special significance to some necessarily implies that others are "outsiders." St. Patrick's Day is of special significance to the Irish, and is celebrated as such by municipalities all over the country. Yet it would be difficult to contend that such celebration conveys, to those of us to whom "the wearing of the green" is inconsequential, that we are not "full members of the political community."[4] Finally, it is not certain whether the test of "endorsement" is to be applied independently, or as an explication of one of the three prongs of the Lemon test. Thus it is not clear what, if any role, it may play in future development of general principles relative to establishment.

[1] Berns, *The First Amendment and the Future of American Democracy* (N.Y., Basic Books, 1976); 12-15.

[2] We have, in this text, treated Barnette as a "freedom of communication" case. (See Chapter 7). But it is often discussed under the rubric of "free exercise of religion." From that perspective it would appear that the coercion said to operate implicitly on dissenting children in Barnette, and arguably present in the "school prayer" cases, should have resulted in the former as well as in the latter in the banning from schools of both the challenged practices. Indeed, as Carl Auerbach has

continued on next page

wisely remarked, peer pressure, among a group of schoolchildren, would likely have resulted in much greater "coercion" to perform the patriotic rather than the religious exercise. (Auerbach, "Teaching Constitutional Law: Some Uses of themes," 2 Constitutional Commentary, no. 1 (Winter, 1985), 25.

[3]See, e.g. Brandon v. Guilderland Bd. of Ed., 635 F. 2d 971 (1980), and Lubbock Civil Lib. Union v. Lubbock Indep. Sch. Dist., 669 F. 2d 1038 (1982).

[4]It is, of course, true that the "establishment clause," if it prohibits any "endorsements," proscribes only those relating to religion, and that St. Patrick's Day is not, except perhaps for relatively few, a "religious holiday." But the point is that, as a logical matter, governmental recognition that religion and religions play a role in the celebration of certain widely celebrated events, need not be seen as promoting the feeling that those who celebrate such events in other ways or do not celebrate them at all, are "outsiders." On the assumption that the Christmas tree is now a secular symbol, that would seem to recognize the views of that holiday of those to whom the birth of Christ has no significance. (Although, perhaps,, governmentally sponsored Christmas displays, in order to recognize all viewpoints, should be accompanied by a representation of Scrooge saying "Bah! Humbug!") In other words, it is difficult to see why the fact that governmentally sponsored displays recognize the historical fact that Christmas is for many Americans a "holy" day, if accompanied by recognition that for others it is not, is an "endorsement" of the religious position.

As to the utility of basing decisions on whether a particular symbol is likely to be perceived by the ordinary citizen as "religious" or "secular," it seems appropriate to note that there is no agreement on the Court itself as to the proper classification into which so common a symbol as the Christmas tree should be placed.

SCHOOL DISTRICT OF ABINGTON TOWNSHIP, PENNSYLVANIA, ET AL. V. SCHEMPP ET AL.

374 U.S. 203 (1963)

MR. JUSTICE CLARK delivered the opinion of the Court.

Once again we are called upon to consider the scope of the provision of the First Amendment to the United States Constitution which declares that "Congress shall make no law respecting an establishment of religion, or prohibiting the free exercise thereof . . . ." These companion cases present the issues in the context of state action requiring that schools begin each day with readings from the Bible. While raising the basic questions under slightly different factual situations, the cases permit of joint treatment. In light of the history of the First Amendment and of our cases interpreting and applying its requirements, we hold that the practices at issue and the laws requiring them are unconstitutional under the Establishment Clause, as applied to the States through the Fourteenth Amendment.

The Facts in Each Case: The Commonwealth of Pennsylvania by law, 24 Pa. Stat. 15-1516, as amended, Pub. Law 1928 Dec. 17, 1959, requires that "At least ten verses from the Holy Bible shall be read, without comment, at the opening of each public school on each school day. Any child shall be excused from such Bible reading, or attending such Bible reading, upon the written request of his parent or guardian. . . ."

The appellees Edward Lewis Schempp, his wife Sidney, and their children, Roger and Donna, are of the Unitarian faith and are members of the Unitarian Church in Germantown, Philadelphia, Pennsylvania, where they, as well as another son, Ellory, regularly attend religious services. The latter was originally a party but having graduated from the school system *pendente lite* was voluntarily dismissed from the action. The other children attend the Abington Senior High School, which is a public school operated by appellant district.

On each school day at the Abington Senior High School between 8:15 and 8:30 a.m., while the pupils are attending their home rooms or advisory sections, opening exercises are conducted pursuant to the statute. The exercises are broadcast into each room in the school building through an intercommunications system and are conducted under the supervision of a teacher by students attending the school's workshop studio for the exercises, which include readings by one of the students of 10 verses of the Holy Bible, broadcast to each room in the building. This is followed by the recitation of the Lord's Prayer, likewise over the intercommunications system, but also by the students in the various classrooms, who are asked to stand and join in repeating the prayer in unison. The exercises are closed with the flag salute and such pertinent announcements as are of interest to the students. Participation in the opening exercises, as directed by the statute, is voluntary. The student reading the verses from the Bible may select the passages and read from any version he chooses, although the only copies furnished by the school are the King James version, copies of which were circulated to each teacher by the school district. During the period in which the exercises have been conducted the King James, the Douay and the Revised Standard versions of the Bible have been used, as well as the Jewish Holy Scriptures. There are no prefatory statements, no questions asked or solicited, no comments or explanations made and no interpretations given at or during the exercises. The students and parents are advised that the student may absent himself from the classroom or, should he elect to remain, not participate in the exercises.

It appears from the record that in schools not having an intercommunications system the Bible reading and the recitation of the Lord's Prayer were conducted by the home-room teacher, who chose the text of the verses and read them herself or had students read them in rotation or by volunteers. This was followed by a standing recitation of the Lord's Prayer, together with the Pledge of Allegiance to the Flag by the class in unison and a closing announcement of routine school items of interest.

At the first trial Edward Schempp and the children testified as to specific religious doctrines purveyed by a literal reading of the Bible "which were contrary to the religious beliefs which they held and to their familial teaching." The children testified that all of the doctrines to which they referred were read to them at various times as part of the exercises. Edward Schempp testified at the second trial that he ad considered having Roger and Donna excused from attendance at the exercises but decided against it for several reasons, including his belief that the children's relationships with their teachers and classmates would be adversely affected.

. . .

In 1905 the Board of School Commisssioners of Baltimore City adopted a rule pursuant to Ar. 77, 202 of the Annotated Code of Maryland. The rule provided for the holding of opening exercises in the schools of the city, consisting primarily of the "reading, without comment, of a chpter in the Holy Bible and/or use of the Lord's Prayer." The petitioners, Mrs. Madalyn Murray and her son, William J. Murray III, are both professed atheists. Following unsuccessful attempts to have the respondent school board rescind the rule, this suit was filed for namdamus to compel its rescission and cancellation. It was alleged that William was a student in a public school of the city and Mrs. Murray, hismother, was a taxpayer therein; that it was the practice under the rule to have a reading on each school morning from the King James version of the Bible; that at petitioner's insistence the rule was amended to permit children to be excused from the exercise on request of the parent and that William had been excused pursuant thereto; that nevertheless the rule as amended was in violation of the petitioners' rights "to freedom of religion under the First and Fourteenth Amendments" and in violation of "the principle of sepatation between church and state, contained therein. . . ."

The wholesome "neutrality" of which this Court's cases speak stems from a recognition of the teachings of history that powerful sects or groups might bring about a fusion of governmental and religious functions or a concert or dependency of one upon the other to the end that official support of the State or Federal Government would be placed behind the tenets of one or of all orthodoxies. This the Establishment Clause progibits. And a further reason for neutrality is found in the Free Exercise Clause, which recognizes the balue of religious training, teaching and observance and, more particularly, the right of every person to freely choose his own course with reference thereto, free of any compulsion from the state. This the Free Exercise Clause guarantees. Thus, as we have seen, the two clauses may overlap. As we have indicated, the Establishment Clause has been directly considered by this Court eight times in the past score of years and, with only one Justice dissenting on the point, it has consistently held that the clause withdrew all legislative power respecting religious belief or the expression thereof. The test may be stated as follows: what are the purpose and the primary effect of the enactment? If either is the advancement or inhibition of relifion then the enactment exceeds the scope of legislative power as circumscribed by the Constitution. That is to say that to withstand the strictures of the Establishment Clause there must there must be a secular legislative purpose and a primary effect that neither advances nor inhibits religion. *Everson v. Board of Education, McGowan v. Maryland*. . . . Its purpose is to secure religious leberty in the individual by prohibiting any invasions thereof by civil authority. Hence it is necessary in a free exercise case for one to show the coercive effect of the enactment as it operates against him in the practice of his religion. The distiction between the two clauses is apparent–a violation of the Free Exercise Clause is predicated on coercion while the Establishment Clause violation need not be so attended.

Applying the Establishment Clause principles to the cases at bar we find that the States are requiring the selection and reading at the opening of the school day of verses from the Holy Bible and the recitation of the Lord's Prayer by the students inunison. These exercises are prescribed as part of the curricular activities of students who are required by law to attend school. They are held in the school buildings under the supervision and with the participation of teachers employed in those schools. None of these factors, other than compulsory school attendance, was present in the program upheld in *Zorach v. Clauson*. The trial court in No. 142 has found that such an opening exercise is a religious ceremony and was intended by the State to be so. We agree with the trial court's finding as to the religious ceremony and was intended by the State to be so. We agree with the trial court's finding as to the religious character of the exercises. Given that finding, the exercises and the law requiring them are in violation of the Establishment Clause.

There is no such specific finding as to the religious character of the exercises in No. 119, and the State contends (as does the State in No. 142) that the program is an effort to extend its benefits to all public school children without regard to their religious belief. Included within its secular purposes, it says, are the promotion of moral values, the contradiction to the materialistic trends of our times, the perpetuation of our institutions and the teaching of literature. The case came up on demurrer, of course, to a petition which alleged that the uniform practice under the rule had been to read from the King James version of the Bible and that the exercise was sectarian. The short answer, therefore, is that the religious character of the exercise was admitted by the State. But even if its purpose is not strictly religious, it is sought to be accomplished through readings, without comment, from the Bible. Surely the place of the Bible as an instrument of religion cannot be gainsaid, and the State's recognition of the pervading religious character of the ceremony is evident from the rule's specific permission of the alternative use of the Catholic Douay version as well as the recent ammendment permitting nonattendance at the exercises. None of these factors is consistent with the contention that the Bible is here used either as an instrument for nonreligious moral inspiration or as a reference for the teaching of secular subjects.

The conclussion follows that in both cases the laws require religious exercises andsuch exercises are being conducted in direct violation of the rights of the appellees and petitioners. Nor are these required exercises mitigated by the fact that individual students may absent themselves upon parental request, for that fact furnishes no defense to a claim of unconstitutionality under the Establishment Clause. See *Engel v. Vitale.* Further, it is no defense to urge that the religious practices here may be relatively minor encroachments on the First Amendment. The breach of neutrality that is today a trickling stream may all to soon become a raging torrent and, in the words of Madison, "it is proper to take alarm at the first experiment on our liberties." Memorial and Remonstrance Against Religious Assessments, quoted in *Everson.*

It is insisted that unless these religious exercises are permitted a "religion of secularism" is extablished in the schools. We agree of course that the State may not extablish a "religion of secularism" in the sense of affirmatively opposing or showing hostility to religion, thus "preferring those who believe in no religion over those who do believe." *Zorach v. Clauson.* We do not agree, however, that this decision in any sense has that effect. In addition, it might well be said that one's education is not complete without a study of comparative religion or the history of religion and its relationship to the advancement of civilization. It certainly may be said that the Bible is worthy of study for its literary and historic qualities. Nothing we have said here indicates that such study of the Bible or of religion, when resented

objectively as part of a secular program of education, may not be effected consistently with the First Amendment. But the exerciseshere do not fall into those categories. They are religious exercises, required by the States in violation of the command of the First Amendment that the Government maintain strict meutrality, neither aiding nor opposing religion.

Finally, we cannot accept that the concept of neutrality, which does not permit a State to require a religious exercise even with the consent of the majority of those affected, collides with the majority's right to free exercise of religion. While the Free Exercise Clause clearly prohibits the use of state action to deny the rights of free exercise to *anyone,* it has never meant that a majority could use the machinery of the State to practice its beliefs. . . .

The place of religion in our society is an exalted one, achieved through a long tradition of reliance on the home, the church and the inviolable citadel of the individual heart and mind. We have come to recognize through bitter experience that it is not within the power of government to invade that citadel, whether its purpose or effect be to aid or oppose, to advance or retard. In the relationship between man and religion, the State is firmly committed to a position of neutrality. Though the application of that rule requires interpretation of a delicate sort, the rule itself is clearly and concisely stated in the words of the First Amendment. Applying that rule to the facts of these cases, we affirm the judgment in No. 142. In No. 119, the judment is reversed and the cause remanded to the Maryland Court of Appeals for further proceedings consistent with this opinion.

MR. JUSTICE DOUGLAS, concurring. . . .

These regimes violate the Establishment Clause in two different ways. In each case the State is conducting a religious exercise; and, as the Court holds, that cannot be done without violating the "neutrality" required of the State by the balance of power between individual, church and state that has been struck by the First Amendment. But the

Establishment Clause is not limited to precluding the State itself from conducting religious exercises. It also forbids the State to employ its facilities or funds in a way that gives any church, or all churches, greater strength in our society than it would have by relying on its members alone. Thus, the present regimes must fall under that clause for the additional reason that public funds, though small in amount, are being used to promote a religious exercise. Through the mechanism of the State, all of the people are being required to finance a religious exercise that only some of the people want and that violates the sensibilities of others.

The most effective way to establish any institution is to finance it; and this truth is reflected in the appeals by church groups for public funds to finance their religious schools. Financing a church either in its strictly religious activities or in its other activities is equally unconstitutional, as I understand the Establishment Clause. Budgets for one activity may be technically separable from budgets for others. But the institution is an inseparable whole, a living organism, which is strengthened in proselytizing when it is strengthened in any department by contributions from other than its own members.

MR. JUSTICE BRENNAN, concurring. . .

MR. JUSTICE GOLBERG, with whom MR. JUSTICE HARLAN joins, concurring.

BOARD OF EDUCATION OF THE WESTSIDE COMMUNITY SCHOOLS (DIST. 66) ET AL. V. MERGENS

___U.S.___ (1990)

JUSTICE O'CONNOR delivered the opinion of the Court, except as to Part III.

This case requires us to decide whether the Equal Access Act prohibits Westside High School from denying a student religious group permission to meet on school premises during noninstructional time, and if so, whether the Act, so construed, violates the Establishment Clause of the First Amendment.

. . . . In January 1985, respondent Bridget Mergens met with Westside's principal, Dr. Findley, and requested permission to form a Christian club at the school. The proposed club would have the same privileges and meet on the same terms and conditions as other Westside student groups, except that the proposed club would not have a faculty sponsor. According to the students' testimony at trial, the club's purpose would have been, among other things, to permit the students to read and discuss the Bible, to have fellowship, and to pray together. Membership would have been voluntary and open to all students regardless of religious affiliation.

Findley denied the request, as did associate superintendent Tangdell. . . .In March 1985, Mergens appealed the denial of her request to the Board of Education, but the Board voted to uphold the denial.

Respondents, by and through their parents as next friends, then brought this suit . . . . The District Court entered judgment for petitioners. The, court held that the Act did not apply in this case because Westside did not have a "limited open forum" as defined by the Act—all of Westside's student clubs, the court concluded, were curriculum-related and tied to the educational function of the school. . .

The United States Court of Appeals for the Eighth Circuit reversed. The Court of Appeals held that the District Court erred in concluding that all the existing student clubs at Westside were curriculum-related. The Court of Appeals noted that the "broad interpretation" advanced by the Westside school officials "would make the [Equal Access Act] meaningless" and would allow any school to "arbitrarily deny access to school facilities to any unfavored student club on the basis of its speech content," which was "exactly the result that Congress sought to prohibit by enacting the [Act]." The Court of Appeals instead found that "[m]any of the student clubs at WHS, including the chess club, are noncurriculum-related." Accordingly, because it found that Westside maintained a limited open forum under the Act, the Court of Appeals concluded that the Act applied to "forbi[d] discrimination against [respondents'] proposed club on the basis of its religious content."

The Court of Appeals then rejected petitioners' contention that the Act violated the Establishment Clause. . . .

In *Widmar v. Vincent* (1981), we invalidated, on free speech grounds, a state university regulation that prohibited student use of school facilities "for purposes of religious worship or religious teaching." In doing so, we held that an "equal access" policy would not violate the Establishment Clause under our decision in *Lemon v. Kurtzman* (1971). In particular, we held that such a policy would have a secular purpose, would not have the primary effect of advancing religion, and would not result in excessive entanglement between government and religion. *Widmar*. We noted, however, that "[u]niversity students are, of course, young adults. They are less impressionable than younger students and should be able to appreciate that the University's policy is one of neutrality toward religion."

In 1984, Congress extended the reasoning of *Widmar* to public secondary schools. Under the Equal Access Act, a public secondary school with a "limited open forum" is prohibited from discriminating against students who wish to conduct a meeting within that forum on the basis of the "religious, political, philosophical, or other content of the speech at such meetings. . . ." The Act's obligation to grant equal access to student groups is therefore triggered if Westside maintains a "limited open forum"— i.e., if it permits one or more "noncurriculum related student groups" to meet on campus before or after classes.

Unfortunately, the Act does not define the crucial phrase "noncurriculum related student group." Our immediate task is therefore one of statutory interpretation. . .

The committee reports indicate that the Act was intended to address perceived widespread discrimination against religious speech in public schools, and, as the language of the Act indicates, its sponsors contemplated that the Act would do more than merely validate the status quo. The committee reports also show that the Act was enacted in part in response to two federal appellate court decisions holding that student religious groups could not, consistent with the Establishment Clause, meet on school premises during noninstructional time.

In light of this legislative purpose, we think that the term "noncurriculum related student group" is best interpreted broadly to mean any student group that does not directly relate to the body of courses offered by the school. In our view, a student group directly relates to a school's curriculum if the subject matter of the group is actually taught, or will soon be taught, in a regularly offered course; if the subject matter of the group concerns the body of courses as a whole; if participation in the group is required for a particular course; or if participation in the group results in academic credit. We think this limited definition of groups that directly relate to the curriculum is a commonsense interpretation of the Act that is consistent with Congress' intent to provide a low threshold for triggering the Act's requirements.

. . . . we think it clear that Westside's existing student groups include one or more "noncurriculum related student groups." Although Westside's physical education classes apparently include swimming, counsel stated at oral argument that scuba diving is not taught in any regularly offered course at the school. Based on Westside's own description of the group, Subsurfers does not directly relate to the curriculum as a whole in the same way that a student government or similar group might. Moreover, participation in Subsurfers is not required by any course at the school and does not result in extra academic credit. Thus, Subsurfers is a "noncurriculum related student group" for purposes of the Act. Similarly, although math teachers at Westside have encouraged their students to play chess, chess is not taught in any regularly offered course at the school, and participation in the chess club is not required for any class and does not result in extra credit for any class. The chess club is therefore another "noncurriculum related student group" at Westside. Moreover, Westside's principal acknowledged at trial that the Peer Advocates program—a service group that works with special education classes—does not directly relate to any courses offered by the school and is not required by any courses offered by the school (participation in Peer Advocates is not required for any course and does not result in extra credit in any course). Peer Advocates would therefore also fit within our description of a "noncurriculum related student group." The record therefore supports a finding that Westside has maintained a limited open forum under the Act. . . .

The remaining statutory question is whether petitioners' denial of respondents' request to form a religious group constitutes a denial of "equal access" to the school's limited open forum. Although the school apparently permits respondents to meet informally after school, respondents seek equal access in the form of official recognition by the school. Official recognition allows student clubs to be part of the student activities program and carries with it access to the school newspaper, bulletin boards, the public address system, and the annual Club Fair. Given that the Act explicitly prohibits denial of "equal access . . . to . . . any students who wish to conduct a meeting within [the school's] limited open forum" on the basis of the religious content of the speech at such meetings, we hold that Westside's denial of respondents' request to form a Christian club denies them "equal access" under the Act.

Because we rest our conclusion on statutory grounds, we need not decide—and therefore express no opinion on—whether the First Amendment requires the same result.

Petitioners contend that even if Westside has created a limited open forum within the meaning of the Act, its denial of official recognition to the proposed Christian club must nevertheless stand because the Act violates the Establishment Clause of the First Amendment, as applied to the States through the Fourteenth Amendment. Specifically, petitioners maintain that because the school's recognized student activities are an integral part of its educational mission, official recognition of respondents' proposed club would effectively incorporate religious activities into the school's official program, endorse participation in the religious club, and provide the club with an official platform to proselytize other students.

We disagree. In *Widmar*, we applied the three-part Lemon test to hold that an "equal access" policy, at the university level, does not violate the Establishment Clause. . . .

We think the logic of *Widmar* applies with equal force to the Equal Access Act. As all initial matter, the Act's prohibition of discrimination on the basis of "political, philosophical, or other" speech as well as religious speech is a sufficient basis for meeting the secular purpose prong of the Lemon test. . . . Even if some legislators were motivated by a conviction that religious speech in particular was valuable and worthy of protection, that alone would not invalidate the Act, because what is relevant is the legislative purpose of the statute, not the possibly religious motives of the legislators who enacted the law. Because the Act on its face grants equal access to both secular and religious speech, we think it clear that the Act's purpose was not to "endorse or disapprove of religion. . . ."

Petitioners' principal contention is that the Act has the primary effect of advancing religion. Specifically, petitioners urge that, because the student religious meetings are held under school aegis, and because the state's compulsory attendance laws bring the students together (and thereby provide a ready-made audience for student evangelists), an objective observer in the position of a secondary school student will perceive official school support for such religious meeting. . . .

We disagree. First, although we have invalidated the use of public funds to pay for teaching state-required subjects at parochial schools, in part because of the risk of creating a crucial symbolic link between government and religion, thereby enlisting—at least in the eyes of impressionable youngsters—the powers of government to the support of the religious denomination operating the school, *Grand Rapids School Dist. v. Ball* (1985), there is a crucial difference between government speech endorsing religion, which the Establishment Clause forbids, and private speech endorsing religion, which the Free Speech and Free Exercise Clauses protect. We think that secondary school students are mature enough and are likely to understand that a school does not endorse or support student speech that it merely permits on a nondiscriminatory basis. . . .

Second, we note that the Act expressly limits participation by school officials at meetings of student religious groups, and that any such meetings must be held during "noninstructional time." The Act therefore avoids the problems of "the students' emulation of teachers as role models" and "mandatory attendance requirements." *Edwards v. Aguillard*; see also *Illinois ex rel. McCollum v. Board of Education* (1948) (release time program invalid where students were "released in part from their legal duty [to attend school] upon the condition that they attend the religious classes"). To be sure, the possibility of student peer pressure remains, but there is little if any risk of official state endorsement or coercion where no formal classroom activities are involved and no school officials actively participate. Moreover, petitioners' fear of a mistaken inference of endorsement is largely self-imposed, because the school itself has control over any impressions it gives its students. . . .

Third, the broad spectrum of officially recognized student clubs at Westside, and the fact that Westside students are free to initiate and organize additional student clubs counteract any possible message of official endorsement of or preference for religion or a particular religious belief. . .

Petitioners' final argument is that by complying with the Act's requirement, the school risks excessive entanglement between government and religion. The proposed club, petitioners urge, would be required to have a faculty sponsor who would be charged with actively directing the activities of the group, guiding its leaders, and ensuring balance in the presentation of controversial ideas. Petitioners claim that this influence over the club's religious program would entangle the government in day-to-day surveillance of religion of the type forbidden by the Establishment Clause.

Under the Act, however, faculty monitors may not participate in any religious meetings, and nonschool persons may not direct, control, or regularly attend activities of student groups. Moreover, the Act prohibits school "sponsorship" of any religious meetings, which means that school officials may not promote, lead, or participate in any such meeting. Although the Act permits "[t]he assignment of a teacher, administrator, or other school employee to the meeting for custodial purposes," such custodial oversight of the student-initiated religious group, merely to ensure order and good behavior, does not impermissibly entangle government in the day-to-day surveillance or administration of religious activities. See *Tony and Susan Alamo Foundation v. Secretary of Labor* (1985). Indeed, as the Court noted in *Widmar*, a denial of equal access to religious speech might well create greater entanglement problems in the form of invasive monitoring to prevent religious speech at meetings at which such speech might occur. *Widmar*.

Accordingly, we hold that the Equal Access Act does not on its face contravene the Establishment Clause. Because we hold that petitioners have violated the Act, we do not decide respondents' claims under the Free Speech and Free Exercise Clauses. . . .

JUSTICE KENNEDY, with whom JUSTICE SCALIA joins, concurring in part and concurring in the judgment. . . .

I agree with the plurality that a school complying with the statute does not violate the Establishment Clause. The accommodation of religion mandated by the Act is a neutral one, and in the context of this case it suffices to inquire whether the Act violates either one of two principles. The first is that the government cannot "give direct benefits to religion in such a degree that it in fact 'establishes a [state] religion or religious faith, or tends to do so. . . .'" Any incidental benefits that accompany official recognition of a religious club under the criteria set forth do not lead to the establishment of religion under this standard. *Widmar*. The second principle controlling the case now before us, in my view, is that the government cannot coerce any student to participate in a religious activity. *County of Allegheny*. The Act is consistent with this standard as well. Nothing on the face of the Act or in the facts of the case as here presented demonstrate that enforcement of the statute will result in the coercion of any student to participate in a religious activity. The Act does not authorize school authorities to require, or even to encourage, students to become members of a religious club or to attend a club's meetings; the meetings take place while school is not in session, and the Act does not compel any school employee to participate in, or to attend, a club's meetings or activities.

The plurality uses a different test, one which asks whether school officials, by complying with the Act, have endorsed religion. It is true that when government gives impermissible assistance to a religion it can be said to have "endorsed religion; but endorsement cannot be the test. The word endorsement has insufficient content to be dispositive. And for reasons I have explained elsewhere, its literal application may result in neutrality in name but hostility in fact when the question is the government's proper relation to those who express some religious preference.

I should think it inevitable that a public high school "endorses" a religious club, in a common-sense use of the term, if the club happens to be one of many activities that the school permits students to choose in order to further the development of their intellect and character in an extracurricular setting. But no constitutional violation occurs if the school's action is based upon a recognition

of the fact that membership in a religious club is one of many permissible ways for a student to further his or her own personal enrichment. The inquiry with respect to coercion must be whether the government imposes pressure upon a student to participate in a religious activity. This inquiry, of course, must be undertaken with sensitivity to the special circumstances that exist in a secondary school where the line between voluntary and coerced participation may be difficult to draw. No such coercion, however, has been shown to exist as a necessary result of this statute, either on its face or as respondents seek to invoke it on the facts of this case.

For these reasons, I join Parts I and II of the Court's opinion, and concur in the judgment.

JUSTICE MARSHALL, with whom JUSTICE BRENNAN joins, concurring in the judgment.

I agree with the majority that "noncurriculum" must be construed broadly to "prohibit schools from discriminating on the basis of the content of a student group's speech." As the majority demonstrates, such a construction "is consistent with Congress' intent to provide a low threshold for triggering the Act's requirements." In addition, to the extent that Congress intended the Act to track this Court's free speech jurisprudence, as the dissent argues, the majority's construction is faithful to our commitment to nondiscriminatory access to open fora in public schools. *Widmar v. Vincent*. When a school allows student-initiated clubs not directly tied to the school's curriculum to use school facilities, it has "created a forum generally open to student groups" and is therefore constitutionally prohibited from enforcing a "content-based exclusion" of other student speech. In this respect, the Act as construed by the majority simply codifies in statute what is already constitutionally mandated: schools may not discriminate among student-initiated groups that seek access to school facilities for expressive purposes not directly related to the school's curriculum. . . .

The Act's low threshold for triggering

equal access, however, raises serious Establishment Clause concerns where secondary schools with fora that differ substantially from the forum in *Widmar* are required to grant access to student religious groups. Indeed, as applied in the present case, the Act mandates a religious group's access to a forum that is dedicated to promoting fundamental values and citizenship as defined by the school. The Establishment Clause does not forbid the operation of the Act in such circumstances, but it does require schools to change their relationship to their fora so as to disassociate themselves effectively from religious clubs' speech. Thus, although I agree with the plurality that the Act as applied to Westside *could* withstand Establishment Clause scrutiny, I write separately to emphasize the steps Westside must take to avoid appearing to endorse the Christian Club's goals.

This case involves the intersection of two First Amendment guarantees—the Free Speech Clause and the Establishment Clause. We have long regarded free and open debate over matters of controversy as necessary to the functioning of our constitutional system. . . .

But the Constitution also demands that the State not take action that has the primary effect of advancing religion. *Lemon v. Kurtzman.* The introduction of religious speech into the public schools reveals the tension between these two constitutional commitments, because the failure of a school to stand apart from religious speech can convey a message that the school endorses rather than merely tolerates that speech. . . .

The plurality suggests that our conclusion in *Widmar* controls this case. But the plurality fails to recognize that the wide-open and independent character of the student forum in *Widmar* differs substantially from the forum at Westside.

Westside currently does not recognize any student club that advocates a controversial viewpoint. . . .

Given the nature and function of student clubs at Westside, the school makes no effort to disassociate itself from the activities and goals of its student clubs.

The entry of religious clubs into such a realm poses a real danger that those clubs will be viewed as part of the school's effort to inculcate fundamental values. The school's message with respect to its existing clubs is not one of toleration but one of endorsement. As the majority concedes, the program is part of the "district's commitment to teaching academic, physical, civic, and personal skills and values." But although a school may permissibly encourage its students to become well-rounded as student-athletes, student-musicians, and student-tutors, the Constitution forbids schools to encourage students to become well-rounded as student-worshippers. Neutrality toward religion, as required by the Constitution, is not advanced by requiring a school that endorses the goals of some noncontroversial secular organizations to endorse the goals of religious organizations as well. . . .

Thus, the underlying difference between this case and *Widmar* is not that college and high school students have varying capacities to perceive the subtle differences between toleration and endorsement, but rather that the University of Missouri and Westside actually choose to define their respective missions in different ways. That high schools tend to emphasize student autonomy less than universities may suggest that high school administrators tend to perceive a difference in the maturity of secondary and university students. But the school's behavior, not the purported immaturity of high school students, is dispositive. If Westside stood apart from its club program and expressed the view, endorsed by Congress through its passage of the Act, that high school students are capable of engaging in wide-ranging discussion of sensitive and controversial speech, the inclusion of religious groups in Westside's forum would confirm the school's commitment to nondiscrimination. Here, though, the Act requires the school to permit religious speech in a forum explicitly designed to advance the school's interest in shaping the character of its students.

The comprehensiveness of the access afforded by the Act further highlights the Establishment Clause dangers posed by the Act's application to fora such as

Westside's. The Court holds that "[o]fficial recognition allows student clubs to be part of the student activities program and carries with it access to the school newspaper, bulletin boards, the public address system, and the annual Club Fair." Students would be alerted to the meetings of the religion club over the public address system; they would see religion club material posted on the official school bulletin board and club notices in the school newspaper; they would be recruited to join the religion club at the school-sponsored Club Fair. If a school has a variety of ideological clubs, as in *Widmar*, I agree with the plurality that a student is likely to understand that "a school does not endorse or support student speech that it merely permits on a nondiscriminatory basis." When a school has a religion club but no other political or ideological organizations, however, that relatively fine distinction may be lost.

Moreover, in the absence of a truly robust forum that includes the participation of more than one advocacy-oriented group, the presence of a religious club could provide a fertile ground for peer pressure, especially if the club commanded support from a substantial portion of the student body. . . .

Given these substantial risks posed by the inclusion of the proposed Christian Club within Westside's present forum, Westside must redefine its relationship to its club program. The plurality recognizes that such redefinition is necessary to avoid the risk of endorsement and construes the Act accordingly. The plurality holds that the Act "limits participation by school officials at meetings of student religious groups," and requires religious club meetings to be held during noninstructional time, ate. It also holds that schools may not sponsor any religious meetings. Finally, and perhaps most importantly, the plurality states that schools bear the responsibility for taking whatever further steps are necessary to make clear that their recognition of a religious club does not reflect their endorsement of the views of the club's participants.

Westside thus must do more than merely prohibit faculty members from actively participating in the Christian Club's meetings. It must fully disassociate itself from the Club's religious speech and avoid appearing to sponsor or endorse the Club's goals. It could for example, entirely discontinue encouraging student participation in clubs and clarify that the clubs are not instrumentally related to the school's overall mission. Or, if the school sought to continue its general endorsement of those student clubs that did not engage in controversial speech, it could do so if it also affirmatively disclaimed any endorsement of the Christian Club. . . .

JUSTICE STEVENS, dissenting.

The dictionary is a necessary, and sometimes sufficient, aid to the judge confronted with the task of construing an opaque act of Congress. In a case like this, however, I believe we must probe more deeply to avoid a patently bizarre result. Can Congress really have intended to issue an order to every public high school in the nation stating, in substance, that if you sponsor a chess club, a scuba diving club, or a French club—without having formal classes in those subjects—you must also open your doors to every religious, political, or social organization, no matter how controversial or distasteful its views may be? I think not. A fair review of the legislative history of the Equal Access Act discloses that Congress intended to recognize a much narrower forum than the Court has legislated into existence today. . . .

My construction of the Act makes it unnecessary to reach the Establishment Clause question that the Court decides. It is nevertheless appropriate to point out that the question is much more difficult than the Court assumes. The Court focuses upon whether the Act might run afoul of the Establishment Clause because of the danger that some students will mistakenly believe that the student-initiated religious clubs are sponsored by the school. I believe that the majority's construction of the statute obliges it to answer a further question: whether the Act violates the Establishment Clause by authorizing religious organizations to meet on high school grounds even when the high school's teachers and administrators deem it unwise to admit controversial or partisan organizations of any kind.

Under the Court's interpretation of the Act, Congress has imposed a difficult choice on public high schools receiving federal financial assistance. If such a school continues to allow students to participate in such familiar and innocuous activities as a school chess or scuba diving club, it must also allow religious groups to make use of school facilities. Indeed, it is hard to see how a cheerleading squad or a pep club, among the most common student groups in American high schools could avoid being "noncurriculum related" under the majority's test. The Act, as construed by the majority, comes perilously close to an outright command to allow organized prayer, and perhaps the kind of religious ceremonies involved in *Widmar*, on school premises. . . .

There is an additional reason, also grounded in constitutional structure, why the Court's rendering of the Act is unsatisfying: so construed, the Act alters considerably the balance between state and federal authority over education, a balance long respected by both Congress and this Court.

The Court's construction of this Act, however, leads to a sweeping intrusion by the federal government into the operation of our public schools, and does so despite the absence of any indication that Congress intended to divest local school districts of their power to shape the educational environment. If a high school administration continues to believe that it is sound policy to exclude controversial groups, such as political clubs, the Ku Klux Klan, and perhaps gay rights advocacy groups, from its facilities, it now must also close its doors to traditional extracurricular activities that are noncontroversial but not directly related to any course being offered at the school. . . .

COUNTY OF ALLEGHENY ET AL. V. AMERICAN CIVIL LIBERTIES UNION, GREATER PITTSBURGH CHAPTER, ET AL.

492 U.S. 573 (1989)

JUSTICE BLACKMUN announced the judgment of the Court and delivered the opinion of the Court with respect to Parts III-A, IV, and V, an opinion with respect to Parts I and II, in which JUSTICE STEVENS and JUSTICE O'CONNOR join, an opinion with respect to Part III-B, in which JUSTICE STEVENS joins, an opinion with respect to Part VII, in which JUSTICE O'CONNOR joins, and an opinion with respect to Part VI.

This litigation concerns the constitutionality of two recurring holiday displays located on public property in downtown Pittsburgh. The first is a crèche placed on the Grand Staircase of the Allegheny County Courthouse. The second is a Chanukah menorah placed just outside the City-County Building, next to a Christmas tree and a sign saluting liberty. The Court of Appeals for the Third Circuit ruled that each display violates the Establishment Clause of the First Amendment because each has the impermissible effect of endorsing religion. We agree that the crèche display has that unconstitutional effect but reverse the Court of Appeals' judgment regarding the menorah display.

. . . .The crèche in the county courthouse, like other crèches, is a visual representation of the scene in the manger in Bethlehem shortly after the birth of Jesus, as described in the Gospels of Luke and Matthew. The crèche includes figures of the infant Jesus, Mary, Joseph, farm animals, shepherds, and wise men, all placed in or before a wooden representation of a manger, which has at its crest an angel bearing a banner that proclaims "Gloria in Excelsis Deo!"

During the 1986-198 holiday season, the crèche was on display on the Grand Staircase from November 26 to January 9.

It had a wooden fence on three sides and bore a plaque stating: "This Display Donated by the Holy Name Society." Sometime during the week of December 2, the county placed red and white poinsettia plants around the fence. The county also placed a small evergreen tree, decorated with a red bow, behind each of the two end-posts of the fence. These trees stood alongside the manger backdrop and were slightly shorter than it was. The angel thus was at the apex of the crèche display. Altogether, the crèche, the fence, the poinsettias, and the trees occupied a substantial amount of space on the Grand Staircase. No figures of Santa Claus or other decorations appeared on the Grand Staircase.

The City-County Building is separate and a block removed from the county courthouse and, as the name implies, is jointly owned by the city of Pittsburgh and Allegheny County. The city's portion of the building houses the city's principal offices, including the mayor's. The city is responsible for the building's Grant Street entrance which has three rounded arches supported by columns.

For a number of years, the city has had a large Christmas tree under the middle arch outside the Grant Street entrance. Following this practice, city employees on November 17, 1986, erected a 45-foot tree under the middle arch and decorated it with lights and ornaments. A few days later, the city placed at the foot of the tree a sign bearing the mayor's name and entitled "Salute to Liberty." Beneath the title, the sign stated: "During this holiday season, the city of Pittsburgh salutes liberty. Let these festive lights remind us that we are the keepers of the flame of liberty and our legacy of freedom. JEV 41."

At least since 1982, the city has expanded its Grant Street holiday display to include a symbolic representation of Chanukah, an 8-day Jewish holiday that begins on the 25th day of the Jewish lunar month of Kislev. . . .

Lighting the menorah is the primary tradition associated with Chanukah. . . .

Chanukah, like Christmas, is a cultural event as well as a religious holiday. Indeed, the Chanukah story always has had a political or national, as well as a religious, dimension: "it tells of national heroism in addition to divine intervention." Also, Chanukah, like Christmas, is a winter holiday; according to some historians, it was associated in ancient times with the winter solstice. Just as some Americans celebrate Christmas without regard to its religious significance, some nonreligious American Jews celebrate Chanukah as an expression of ethnic identity, and "as a cultural or national event, rather than as a specifically religious event. . . ."

On December 22 of the 1986 holiday season, the city placed at the Grant Street entrance to the City-County Building an 18-foot Chanukah menorah of an abstract tree-and-branch design The menorah was placed next to the city's 45-foot Christmas tree. . . .

In recent years, we have paid particularly close attention to whether the challenged governmental practice either has the purpose or effect of "endorsing" religion, a concern that has long had a place in our Establishment Clause jurisprudence. See *Engel v. Vitale*. Thus, in *Wallace v. Jaffree*, the Court held unconstitutional Alabama's moment-of-silence statute because it was "enacted . . . for the sole purpose of expressing the State's endorsement of prayer activities." The Court similarly invalidated Louisiana's "Creationism Act" because it "endorses religion" in its purpose. *Edwards v. Aguillard* (1987). And the educational program in *School Dist. of Grand Rapids v. Ball* (1985), was held to violate the Establishment Clause because of its "endorsement" effect. See also *Texas Monthly, Inc. v. Bullock* (1989) (plurality opinion) (tax exemption limited to religious periodicals "effectively endorses religious belief").

Of course, the word "endorsement" is not self-defining. (But) . . . Whether the key word is "endorsement," "favoritism," or "promotion," the essential principle remains the same. The Establishment Clause, at the very least, prohibits government from appearing to take a position on questions of religious belief or from "making adherence to a religion relevant in any way to a person's standing in the political community." Lynch v. Donnelly (O'CONNOR, J., concurring).

We have had occasion in the past to apply Establishment Clause principles to the government's display of objects with religious significance. In Stone v. Graham (1980), we held that the display of a copy of the Ten Commandments on the walls of public classrooms violates the Establishment Clause. Closer to the facts of this litigation is Lynch. v. Donnelly, supra, in which we considered whether the city of Pawtucket, R. I., had violated the Establishment Clause by including a crèche in its annual Christmas display, located in a private park within the downtown shopping district. By a 5-to-4 decision in that difficult case, the Court upheld inclusion of the crèche in the Pawtucket display, holding, *inter alia*, that the inclusion of the crèche did not have the impermissible effect of advancing or promoting religion.

The rationale of the majority opinion in Lynch is none too clear: the opinion contains two strands, neither of which provides guidance for decision in subsequent cases. First, the opinion states that the inclusion of the crèche in the display was "no more an advancement or endorsement of religion" than other "endorsements" this Court has approved in the past—but the opinion offers no discernible measure for distinguishing between permissible and impermissible endorsements. Second, the opinion observes that any benefit the government's display of the crèche gave to religion was no more than "indirect, remote, and incidental," without saying how or why.

Although JUSTICE O'CONNOR joined the majority opinion in Lynch, she wrote a concurrence that differs in significant respects from the majority opinion. The main difference is that the concurrence provides a sound analytical framework for evaluating governmental use of religious symbols.

First and foremost, the concurrence squarely rejects any notion that this Court will tolerate some government endorsement of religion. Rather, the concurrence recognizes any endorsement of religion as "invalid," because it "sends a message to nonadherents that they are outsiders, not full members of the political community, and an accompanying message to adherents that they are insiders, favored members of the political community."

Second, the concurrence articulates a method for determining whether the government's use of an object with religious meaning has the effect of endorsing religion. The effect of the display depends upon the message that the government's practice communicates: the question is "what viewers may fairly understand to be the purpose of the display." That inquiry, of necessity, turns upon the context in which the contested object appears: "[A] typical museum setting, though not neutralizing the religious content of a religious painting, negates any message of endorsement of that content."

The concurrence thus emphasizes that the constitutionality of the crèche in that case depended upon its "particular physical setting," and further observes: "Every government practice must be judged in its unique circumstances to determine whether it [endorses] religion."

The concurrence applied this mode of analysis to the Pawtucket crèche, seen in the context of that city's holiday celebration as a whole. In addition to the crèche, the city's display contained: a Santa Claus house with a live Santa distributing candy; reindeer pulling Santa's sleigh; a live 40 foot Christmas tree strung with lights; statues of carolers in old-fashioned dress; candy-striped poles; a "talking" wishing well; a large banner proclaiming "SEASONS GREETINGS"; a miniature "village" with several houses and a church; and various "cut-out" figures, including those of a clown, a dancing elephant, a robot, and a teddy bear. The concurrence concluded that both because the crèche is "a traditional symbol" of Christmas, a holiday with strong secular elements, and because the crèche was "displayed along with purely secular symbols," the crèche's setting "changes what viewers may fairly understand to be the purpose of the display" and "negates any message of endorsement" of "the Christian beliefs represented by the crèche."

The four Lynch dissenters agreed with the concurrence that the controlling question was "whether Pawtucket ha[d] run afoul of the Establishment Clause by endorsing religion through its display of the crèche." The dissenters also agreed with the general proposition that the context in which the government uses a religious symbol is relevant for determining the answer to that question. They simply reached a different answer: the dissenters concluded that the other elements of the Pawtucket display did not negate the endorsement of Christian faith caused by the presence of the crèche. They viewed the inclusion of the crèche in the city's overall display as placing "the government's imprimatur of approval on the particular religious beliefs exemplified by the crèche." Thus, they stated: "The effect on minority religious groups, as well as on those who may reject all religion, is to convey the message that their views are not similarly worthy of public recognition nor entitled to public support."

Thus, despite divergence at the bottom line, the five Justices in concurrence and dissent in Lynch agreed upon the relevant constitutional principles: the government's use of religious symbolism is unconstitutional if it has the effect of endorsing religious beliefs, and the effect of the government's use of religious symbolism depends upon its context.

. . . . Accordingly, our present task is to determine whether the display of the crèche and the menorah, in their respective "particular physical settings," has the effect of endorsing or disapproving religious beliefs.

We turn first to the county's crèche display. There is no doubt, of course, that the crèche itself is capable of communicating a religious message. See *Lynch*. Indeed, the crèche in this lawsuit uses words, as well as the picture of the nativity scene, to make its religious meaning unmistakably clear. "Glory to God in the Highest!" says the angel in the crèche—Glory to God because of the birth of Jesus. This praise to God in Christian terms is indisputably religious—indeed sectarian—just as it is when said in the Gospel or in a church service.

Under the Court's holding in *Lynch*, the effect of a crèche display turns on its setting. Here, unlike in *Lynch*, nothing in the context of the display detracts from the crèche's religious message. The *Lynch*. display comprised a series of figures and objects, each group of which had its own focal point. Santa's house and his reindeer were objects of attention separate from the crèche, and had their specific visual story to tell. Similarly, whatever a "talking" wishing well may be, it obviously was a center of attention separate from the crèche. Here, in contrast, the crèche stands alone: it is the single element of the display on the Grand Staircase.

The floral decoration surrounding the crèche cannot be viewed as somehow equivalent to the secular symbols in the overall Lynch display. The floral frame, like all good frames, serves only to draw one's attention to the message inside the frame. The floral decoration surrounding the crèche contributes to, rather than detracts from, the endorsement of religion conveyed by the crèche. It is as if the county had allowed the Holy Name Society to display a cross on the Grand Staircase at Easter, and the county had surrounded the cross with Easter lilies. The county could not say that surrounding the cross with traditional flowers of the season would negate the endorsement of Christianity conveyed by the cross on the Grand Staircase. Its contention that the traditional Christmas greens negate the endorsement effect of the crèche fares no better.

Nor does the fact that the crèche was the setting for the county's annual Christmas-carol program diminish its religious meaning. First, the carol program in 1986 lasted only from December 3 to December 23 and occupied at most one hour a day. The effect of the crèche on those who viewed it when the choirs were not singing—the vast majority of the time—cannot be negated by the presence of the choir program. Second, because some of the carols performed at the site of the crèche were religious in nature, those carols were more likely to augment the religious quality of the scene than to secularize it.

Furthermore, the crèche sits on the Grand Staircase, the "main" and "most beautiful part" of the building that is the seat of county government. No viewer could reasonably think that it occupies this location without the support and approval of the government. Thus, by permitting the "display of the crèche in this particular physical setting, the county sends an unmistakable message that it supports and promotes the Christian praise to God that is the crèche's religious message."

. . . . JUSTICE KENNEDY'S reasons for permitting the crèche on the Grand Staircase and his condemnation of the Court's reasons for deciding otherwise are so far reaching in their implications that they require a response in some depth.

. . . . Although JUSTICE KENNEDY'S misreading of *Marsh* is predicated on a failure to recognize the bedrock Establishment Clause principle that, regardless of history, government may not demonstrate a preference for a particular faith, even he is forced to acknowledge that some instances of such favoritism are constitutionally intolerable. He concedes also that the term "endorsement" long has been another way of defining a forbidden "preference" for a particular sect, but he would repudiate the Court's endorsement inquiry as a "jurisprudence of minutiae," because it examines the particular contexts in which the government employs religious symbols.

. . . . The Justice would substitute the term "proselytization" for "endorsement," post, but his "proselytization" test suffers from the same "defect," if one must call it that, of requiring close factual analysis. . .

Indeed, perhaps the only real distinction between JUSTICE KENNEDY'S "proselytization" test and the Court's "endorsement" inquiry is a burden of "unmistakable" clarity that JUSTICE KENNEDY apparently would require of government favoritism for specific sects in order to hold the favoritism in violation of the Establishment Clause. The question whether a particular practice "would place the government's weight behind an obvious effort to proselytize for a particular religion," is much the same as whether the practice demonstrates the government's support, promotion, or "endorsement" of the particular creed of a particular sect—except to the extent that it requires an "obvious" allegiance between the government and the sect.

Our cases, however, impose no such burden on demonstrating that the government has favored a particular sect or creed. On the contrary, we have expressly required "strict scrutiny" of practices suggesting "a denominational preference," *Larson v. Valente*, in keeping with " 'the unwavering vigilance that the Constitution requires'" against any violation of the Establishment Clause. Bowen v. Kendrick (1988) (O'CONNOR, J., concurring). Thus, when all is said and done, JUSTICE KENNEDY'S effort to abandon the "endorsement" inquiry in favor of his "proselytization" test seems nothing more than an attempt to lower considerably the level of scrutiny in Establishment Clause cases. We choose, however, to adhere to the vigilance the Court has managed to maintain thus far, and to the endorsement inquiry that reflects our vigilance.

The display of the Chanukah menorah in front of the City-County Building may well present a closer constitutional question. The menorah, one must recognize, is a religious symbol: it serves to commemorate the miracle of the oil as described in the Talmud. But the menorah's message is not exclusively religious. The menorah is the primary visual symbol for a holiday that, like Christmas, has both religious and secular dimensions.

Moreover, the menorah here stands next to a Christmas tree and a sign saluting liberty. While no challenge has been made here to the display of the tree and the sign, their presence is obviously relevant in determining the effect of the menorah's display. The necessary result of placing a menorah next to a Christmas tree is to create an "overall holiday setting" that represents both Christmas and Chanukah—two holidays, not one. See Lynch (O'CONNOR, J., concurring).

The mere fact that Pittsburgh displays symbols of both Christmas and Chanukah does not end the constitutional inquiry. If the city celebrates both Christmas and Chanukah as religious holidays, then it violates the Establishment Clause. The simultaneous endorsement of Judaism and Christianity is no less constitutionally infirm than the endorsement of Christianity alone.

Conversely, if the city celebrates both Christmas and Chanukah as secular holidays, then its conduct is beyond the reach of the Establishment Clause. . . .

Accordingly, the relevant question for Establishment Clause purposes is whether the combined display of the tree, the sign, and the menorah has the effect of endorsing both Christian and Jewish faiths, or rather simply recognizes that both Christmas and Chanukah are part of the same winter-holiday season, which has attained a secular status in our society. Of the two interpretations of this particular display, the latter seems far more plausible and is also in line with *Lynch*.

The Christmas tree, unlike the menorah, is not itself a religious symbol. Although Christmas trees once carried religious connotations, today they typify the secular celebration of Christmas. . . . Indeed, a 40-foot Christmas tree was one of the objects that validated the crèche in *Lynch*. The widely accepted view of the Christmas tree as the preeminent secular symbol of the Christmas holiday season serves to emphasize the secular component of the message communicated by other elements of an accompanying holiday display, including the Chanukah menorah.

The tree, moreover, is clearly the predominant element in the city's display. The 45-foot tree occupies the central position beneath the middle archway in front of the Grant Street entrance to the City-County Building; the 18-foot menorah is positioned to one side. Given this configuration, it is much more sensible to interpret the meaning of the menorah in light of the tree, rather than vice versa. In the shadow of the tree, the menorah is readily understood as simply a recognition that Christmas is not the only traditional way of observing the winter-holiday season. In these circumstances, then, the combination of the tree and the menorah communicates, not a simultaneous endorsement of both the Christian and Jewish faiths, but instead, a secular celebration of Christmas coupled with an acknowledgment of Chanukah as a contemporaneous alternative tradition.

Although the city has used a symbol with religious meaning as its representation of Chanukah, this is not a case in which the city has reasonable alternatives that are less religious in nature. It is difficult to imagine a predominantly secular symbol of Chanukah that the city could place next to its Christmas tree. An 18-foot dreidel would look out of place and might be interpreted by some as mocking the celebration of Chanukah. The absence of a more secular alternative symbol is itself part of the context in which the city's actions must be judged in determining the likely effect of its use of the menorah. Where the government's secular message can be conveyed by two symbols, only one of which carries religious meaning, an observer reasonably might infer from the fact that the government has chosen to use the religious symbol that the government means to promote religious faith. But where, as here no such choice has been made, this inference of endorsement is not present.

The mayor's sign further diminishes the possibility that the tree and the menorah will be interpreted as a dual endorsement of Christianity and Judaism. The sign states that during the holiday season the city salutes liberty. Moreover, the sign draws upon the theme of light, common to both Chanukah and Christmas as winter festivals, and links that theme with this Nation's legacy of freedom, which allows an American to celebrate the holiday season in whatever way he wishes, religiously or otherwise. While no sign can disclaim an overwhelming message of endorsement, see Stone v. Graham, an "explanatory plaque" may confirm that in particular contexts the government's association with a religious symbol does not represent the government's sponsorship of religious beliefs. Here, the mayors sign serves to confirm what the context already reveals: that the display of the menorah is not an endorsement of religious faith but simply a recognition of cultural diversity. . . .

JUSTICE O'CONNOR, with whom JUSTICE BRENNAN and JUSTICE STEVENS join as to Part II, concurring in part and concurring, in the judgment.

In my concurrence in Lynch, I suggested a clarification of our Establishment Clause doctrine to reinforce the concept that the Establishment Clause "prohibits government from making adherence to a religion relevant in any way to a person's standing in the political community."

The government violates this prohibition if it endorses or disapproves of religion. "Endorsement sends a message to nonadherents that they are outsiders, not full members of the political community, and an accompanying message to adherents that they are insiders, favored members of the political community. Ibid."
Disapproval of religion conveys the opposite message. Thus, in my view, the central issue in Lynch was whether the city of Pawtucket had endorsed Christianity by displaying a crèche as part of a larger exhibit of traditional secular symbols of the Christmas holiday season.

In Lynch., I concluded that the city's display of a crèche in its larger holiday exhibit in a private park in the commercial district had neither the purpose nor the effect of conveying a message of government endorsement of Christianity or disapproval of other religions. The purpose of including the crèche in the larger display was to celebrate the public holiday through its traditional symbols, not to promote the religious content of the crèche. Nor, in my view, did Pawtucket's display of the crèche along with secular symbols of the Christmas holiday objectively convey a message of endorsement of Christianity.

For the reasons stated in Part IV of the Court's opinion in these cases, I agree that the crèche displayed on the Grand Staircase of the Allegheny County Courthouse, the seat of county government, conveys a message to nonadherents of Christianity that they are not full members of the political community, and a corresponding message to Christians that they are favored members of the political community. In

contrast to the crèche in Lynch, which was displayed in a private park in the city's commercial district as part of a broader display of traditional secular symbols of the holiday season, this crèche stands alone in the county courthouse. The display of religious symbols in public areas of core government buildings runs a special risk of "mak[ing] religion relevant, in reality or public perception, to status in the political community.". . . .

An Establishment Clause standard that prohibits only "coercive" practices or overt efforts at government proselytization, , but fails to take account of the numerous more subtle ways that government can show favoritism to particular beliefs or convey a message of disapproval to others, would not, in my view, adequately protect the religious liberty or respect the religious diversity of the members of our pluralistic political community. Thus, this Court has never relied on coercion alone as the touchstone of Establishment Clause analysis.

. . . . Moreover, as even JUSTICE KENNEDY recognizes, any Establishment Clause test limited to "direct coercion" clearly would fail to account for forms of "[s]ymbolic recognition or accommodation of religious faith" that may violate the Establishment Clause.

I continue to believe that the endorsement test asks the right question about governmental practices challenged on Establishment Clause grounds, including challenged practices involving the display of religious symbols. . . .
JUSTICE KENNEDY submits that the endorsement test is inconsistent with our precedents and traditions because, in his words, if it were "applied without artificial exceptions for historical practice," it would invalidate many traditional practices recognizing the role of religion in our society. This criticism shortchanges both the endorsement test itself and my explanation of the reason why certain longstanding government acknowledgments of religion do not, under that test, convey a message of endorsement. Practices such as legislative prayers or opening Court sessions with "God save the United States and this honorable Court" serve the secular

purposes of "solemnizing public occasions" and "expressing confidence in the future," Lynch (concurring opinion). These examples of ceremonial deism do not survive Establishment Clause scrutiny simply by virtue of their historical longevity alone. Historical acceptance of a practice does not in itself validate that practice under the Establishment Clause if the practice violates the values protected by that Clause, just as historical acceptance of racial or gender based discrimination does not immunize such practices from scrutiny under the 14th Amendment. As we recognized in Waltz v. Tax Comm'n of New York City (1970), "[N]o one acquires a vested or protected right in violation of the Constitution by long use, even when that span of time covers our entire national existence and indeed predates it."

Under the endorsement test, the "history and ubiquity" of a practice is relevant not because it creates an "artificial exception" from that test. On the contrary, the "history and ubiquity" of a practice is relevant because it provides part of the context in which a reasonable observer evaluates whether a challenged governmental practice conveys a message of endorsement of religion. It is the combination of the longstanding existence of practices such as opening legislative sessions with legislative prayers or opening Court sessions with "God save the United States and this honorable Court," as well as their nonsectarian nature, that leads me to the conclusion that those particular practices, despite their religious roots, do not convey a message of endorsement of particular religious beliefs. See Lynch (concurring opinion). Similarly, the celebration of Thanksgiving as a public holiday, despite its religious origins, is now generally understood as a celebration of patriotic values rather than particular religious beliefs. The question under endorsement analysis, in short is whether a reasonable observer would view such longstanding practices as a disapproval of his or her particular religious choices, in light of the fact that they serve a secular purpose rather than a sectarian one and have largely lost their religious significance over time.

Although the endorsement test requires careful and often difficult line drawing and is highly context specific, no alternative test has been suggested that captures the essential mandate of the Establishment Clause as well as the endorsement test does, and it warrants continued application and refinement.

Contrary to JUSTICE KENNEDY'S assertions, neither the endorsement test nor its application in this case reflects "an unjustified hostility toward religion." Instead, the endorsement standard recognizes that the religious liberty so precious to the citizens who make up our diverse country is protected, not impeded, when government avoids endorsing religion or favoring particular beliefs over others. Clearly, the government can acknowledge the role of religion in our society in numerous ways that do not amount to an endorsement. See Lynch, (concurring opinion). Moreover, the government can accommodate religion by lifting government imposed burdens on religion.

Indeed, the Free Exercise Clause may mandate that it do so in particular cases. In cases involving the lifting of government burdens on the free exercise of religion, a reasonable observer would take into account the values underlying the Free Exercise Clause in assessing whether the challenged practice conveyed a message of endorsement.

For reasons which differ somewhat from those set forth in Part VI of JUSTICE BLACKMUN'S opinion, I also conclude that the city of Pittsburgh's combined holiday display of a Chanukah menorah, a Christmas tree, and a sign saluting liberty does not have the effect of conveying an endorsement of religion. . . . Although JUSTICE BLACKMUN'S opinion acknowledges that a Christmas tree alone conveys no endorsement of Christian beliefs, it formulates the question posed by Pittsburgh's combined display of the tree and the menorah as whether the display "has the effect of endorsing both Christian and Jewish faiths, or rather simply recognizes that both Christmas and Chanukah are part of the same winter-holiday season, which has attained a secular status in our society."

That formulation of the question disregards the fact that the Christmas tree is a predominantly secular symbol and, more significantly, obscures the religious nature of the menorah and the holiday of Chanukah.

In my view, the relevant question for Establishment Clause purposes is whether the city of Pittsburgh's display of the menorah, the religious symbol of a religious holiday, next to a Christmas tree and a sign saluting liberty sends a message of government endorsement of Judaism or whether it sends a message of pluralism and freedom to choose one's own beliefs.

One need not characterize Chanukah as a "secular" holiday or strain to argue that the menorah has a "secular" dimension, in order to conclude that the city of Pittsburgh's combined display does not convey a message of endorsement of Judaism or of religion in general.

In setting up its holiday display, which included the lighted tree and the menorah, the city of Pittsburgh stressed the theme of liberty and pluralism by accompanying the exhibit with a sign bearing the following message: "During this holiday season, the city of Pittsburgh salutes liberty. Let these festive lights remind us that we are the keepers of the flame of liberty and our legacy of freedom."
This sign indicates that the city intended to convey its own distinctive message of pluralism and freedom. By accompanying its display of a Christmas tree—a secular symbol of the Christmas holiday season—with a salute to liberty, and by adding a religious symbol from a Jewish holiday also celebrated at roughly the same time of year, I conclude that the city did not endorse Judaism or religion in general, but rather conveyed a message of pluralism and freedom of belief during the holiday season.

The message of pluralism conveyed by the city's combined holiday display is not a message that endorses religion over nonreligion. Just as government may not favor particular religious beliefs over others, "government may not favor religious belief over disbelief. " Here, by displaying a secular symbol of the Christmas holiday season rather than a religious one, the city acknowledged a public holiday celebrated by both religious and nonreligious citizens alike, and it did so without endorsing Christian beliefs. A reasonable observer would, in my view, appreciate that the combined display is an effort to acknowledge the cultural diversity of our country and to convey tolerance of different choices in matters of religious belief or nonbelief by recognizing that the winter holiday season is celebrated in diverse ways by our citizens.

My conclusion does not depend on whether or not the city had "a more secular alternative symbol" of Chanukah, just as the Court's decision in Lynch clearly did not turn on whether the city of Pawtucket could have conveyed its tribute to the Christmas holiday season by using a "less religious" alternative to the crèche symbol in its display of traditional holiday symbols.

In my view, JUSTICE BLACKMUN'S new rule, that an inference of endorsement arises every time government uses a symbol with religious meaning if a "more secular alternative" is available is too blunt an instrument for Establishment Clause analysis, which depends on sensitivity to the context and circumstances presented by each case. Indeed, the opinion appears to recognize the importance of this contextual sensitivity by creating an exception to its new rule in the very case announcing it: the opinion acknowledges that "a purely secular symbol" of Chanukah is available, namely, a dreidel or four-sided top, but rejects the use of such a symbol because it "might be interpreted by some as mocking the celebration of Chanukah." This recognition that the more religious alternative may, depending on the circumstances, convey a message that is least likely to implicate Establishment Clause concerns is an excellent example of the need to focus on the specific practice in question in its particular physical setting and context in determining whether government has conveyed or attempted to convey a message that religion or a particular religious belief is favored or preferred. . . .

JUSTICE BRENNAN, with whom

JUSTICE MARSHALL and JUSTICE STEVENS join, concurring in part and dissenting in part. . . .

I continue to believe that the display of an object that "retains a specifically Christian [or other] religious meaning," is incompatible with the separation of church and state demanded by our Constitution. I therefore agree with the Court that Allegheny County's display of a crèche at the county courthouse signals an endorsement of the Christian faith in violation of the Establishment Clause, and join Parts III-A, IV, and V of the Court's opinion. I cannot agree, however, that the city's display of a 45 foot Christmas tree and an 18-foot Chanukah menorah at the entrance to the building housing the mayor's office shows no favoritism towards Christianity, Judaism, or both. Indeed, I should have thought that the answer as to the first display supplied the answer to the second.

. . . . the decision as to the menorah rests on three premises: the Christmas tree is a secular symbol; Chanukah is a holiday with secular dimensions, symbolized by the menorah; and the government may promote pluralism by sponsoring or condoning displays having strong religious associations on its property. None of these is sound.

While acknowledging the religious origins of the Christmas tree, JUSTICES BLACKMUN and O'CONNOR dismiss their significance. In my view, this attempt to take the "Christmas" out of the Christmas tree is unconvincing. That the tree may, without controversy, be deemed a secular symbol if found alone does not mean that it will be so seen when combined with other symbols or objects. Indeed, JUSTICE BLACKMUN admits that "the tree is capable of taking on a religious significance if it is decorated with religious symbols."

The notion that the Christmas tree is necessarily secular is, indeed, so shaky that, despite superficial acceptance of the idea, JUSTICE O'CONNOR does not really take it seriously. While conceding that the "menorah standing alone at city hall may well send" a message of endorsement of the Jewish faith she nevertheless concludes: "By

accompanying its display of a Christmas tree—a secular symbol of the Christmas holiday season—with a salute to liberty, and by adding a religious symbol from a Jewish holiday also celebrated at roughly the same time of year, I conclude that the city did not endorse Judaism or religion in general, but rather conveyed a message of pluralism and freedom of belief during the holiday season."

But the "pluralism" to which JUSTICE O'CONNOR refers is religious pluralism, and the "freedom of belief" she emphasizes is freedom of religious belief The display of the tree and the menorah will symbolize such pluralism and freedom only if more than one religion is represented; if only Judaism is represented, the scene is about Judaism, not about pluralism. Thus, the pluralistic message JUSTICE O'CONNOR stresses depends on the tree's possessing some religious significance.

JUSTICE BLACKMUN believes that it is the tree that changes the message of the menorah, rather than the menorah that alters our view of the tree. After the abrupt dismissal of the suggestion that the flora surrounding the crèche might have diluted the religious character of the display at the county courthouse, his quick conclusion that the Christmas tree had a secularizing effect on the menorah is surprising. The distinguishing characteristic, it appears, is the size of the tree. The tree, we are told, is much taller—2 1/2 times taller, in fact—than the menorah, and is located directly under one of the building's archways, whereas the menorah "is positioned to one side . . . [i]n the shadow of the tree."

As a factual matter, it seems to me that the sight of an 18 foot menorah would be far more eye catching than that of a rather conventionally sized Christmas tree. It also seems to me likely that the symbol with the more singular message will predominate over one lacking such a clear meaning. . . .

The second premise on which today s decision rests is the notion that Chanukah is a partly secular holiday, for which the menorah can serve as a secular symbol. It is no surprise and no anomaly that Chanukah has historical and societal roots that range beyond the purely religious. I would venture that most, if not all, major religious holidays have beginnings and enjoy histories studded with figures, events, and practices that are not strictly religious. It does not seem to me that the mere fact that Chanukah shares this kind of background makes it a secular holiday in any meaningful sense. The menorah is indisputably a religious symbol, used ritually in a celebration that has deep religious significance. That, in my view, is all that need be said. Whatever secular practices the holiday of Chanukah has taken on in its contemporary observance are beside the point. . . .

JUSTICE BLACKMUN, in his acceptance of the city's message of "diversity," and, even more so, JUSTICE O'CONNOR, in her approval of the "message of pluralism and freedom to choose one's own beliefs," , appear to believe that, where seasonal displays are concerned, more is better. Whereas a display might be constitutionally problematic if it showcased the holiday of just one religion, those problems vaporize as soon as more than one religion is included. I know of no principle under the Establishment Clause, however, that permits us to conclude that governmental promotion of religion is acceptable so long as one religion is not favored. We have, on the contrary, interpreted that Clause to require neutrality, not just among religions, but between religion and nonreligion. . . .

The uncritical acceptance of a message of religious pluralism also ignores the extent to which even that message may offend. . . To lump the ritual objects and holidays of religions together without regard to their attitudes toward such inclusiveness, or to decide which r religions should be excluded because of the possibility of offense, is not a benign or beneficent celebration of pluralism: it is instead an interference in religious matters precluded by the Establishment Clause.

The government-sponsored display of the menorah alongside a Christmas tree also works a distortion of the Jewish religious calendar.

December is not the holiday season for Judaism. Thus, the city's erection alongside the Christmas tree of the symbol of a relatively minor Jewish religious holiday, far from conveying "the city's secular recognition of different traditions for celebrating the winter-holiday season," (BLACKMUN, J.), or "a message of pluralism and freedom of belief", (O'CONNOR, J.), has the effect of promoting a Christianized version of Judaism. The holiday calendar they appear willing to accept revolves exclusively around a Christian holiday. And those religions that have no holiday at all during the period between Thanksgiving and New Year's Day will not benefit, even in a second-class manner, from the city's once-a-year tribute to "liberty" and "freedom of belief." This is not "pluralism" as I understand it.

JUSTICE STEVENS, with whom JUSTICE BRENNAN and JUSTICE MARSHALL join, concurring in part and dissenting in part. . . .

In my opinion the Establishment Clause should be construed to create a strong presumption against the display of religious symbols on public property. There is always a risk that such symbols will offend nonmembers of the faith being advertised as well as adherents who consider the particular advertisement disrespectful. Some devout Christians believe that the crèche should be placed only in reverential settings, such as a church or perhaps a private home; they do not countenance its use as an aid to commercialization of Christ's birthday. In this very suit, members of the Jewish faith firmly opposed the use to which the menorah was put by the particular sect that sponsored the display at Pittsburgh's City-County Building. Even though "[p]assersby who disagree with the message conveyed by these displays are free to ignore them, or even to turn their backs," displays of this kind inevitably have a greater tendency to emphasize sincere and deeply felt differences among individuals than to achieve an ecumenical goal. The Establishment Clause does not allow public bodies to foment such disagreement.

Application of a strong presumption against the public use of religious symbols scarcely will "require a relentless extirpation of all contact between government and religion," for it will prohibit a display only when its message, evaluated in the context in which it is presented, is nonsecular. For example, a carving of Moses holding the Ten Commandments, if that is the only adornment on a courtroom wall, conveys an equivocal message, perhaps of respect for Judaism, for religion in general, or for law. The addition of carvings depicting Confucius and Mohammed may honor religion, or particular religions, to an extent that the First Amendment does not tolerate. . . .

Placement of secular figures such as Caesar Augustus, William Blackstone, Napoleon Bonaparte, and John Marshall alongside these three religious leaders, however, signals respect not for great proselytizers but for great lawgivers. It would be absurd to exclude such a fitting message from a courtroom, as it would to exclude religious paintings by Italian Renaissance masters from a public museum.

I cannot agree with the Court's conclusion that the display at Pittsburgh's City-County Building was constitutional. Standing alone in front of a governmental headquarters, a lighted, 45-foot evergreen tree might convey holiday greetings linked too tenuously to Christianity to have constitutional moment. Juxtaposition of this tree with an 18-foot menorah does not make the latter secular, as JUSTICE BLACKMUN contends. Rather, the presence of the Chanukah menorah, unquestionably a religious symbol, gives religious significance to the Christmas tree. The overall display thus manifests governmental approval of the Jewish and Christian religions. . . .

Although it conceivably might be interpreted as sending "a message of pluralism and freedom to choose one's own beliefs" (O'CONNOR, J., concurring in part and concurring in judgment), the message is not sufficiently clear to overcome the strong presumption that the display, respecting two religions to the exclusion of all others, is the very kind of double establishment that the First Amendment was designed to outlaw.

JUSTICE KENNEDY, with whom THE CHIEF JUSTICE, JUSTICE WHITE, and JUSTICE SCALIA join, concurring in the judgment in part and dissenting in part. . .

Rather than requiring government to avoid any action that acknowledges or aids religion, the Establishment Clause permits government some latitude in recognizing and accommodating the central role religion plays in our society. *Lynch v. Donnelly*; *Waltz v. Tax Comm'n of New York City*. Any approach less sensitive to our heritage would border on latent hostility toward religion, as it would require government in all its multifaceted roles to acknowledge only the secular, to the exclusion and so to the detriment of the religious. A categorical approach would install federal courts as jealous guardians of an absolute "wall of separation," sending a clear message of disapproval. In this century, as the modern administrative state expands to touch the lives of its citizens in such diverse ways and redirects their financial choices through programs of its own, it is difficult to maintain the fiction that requiring government to avoid all assistance to religion can in fairness be viewed as serving the goal of neutrality.

The ability of the organized community to recognize and accommodate religion in a society with a pervasive public sector requires diligent observance of the border between accommodation and establishment. Our cases disclose two limiting principles: government may not coerce anyone to support or participate in any religion or its exercise; and it may not, in the guise of avoiding hostility or callous indifference, give direct benefits to religion in such a degree that it in fact "establishes a [state] religion or religious faith, or tends to do so." *Lynch v. Donnelly*. These two principles, while distinct, are not unrelated, for it would be difficult indeed to establish a religion without some measure of more or less subtle coercion, be it in the for-m of taxation to supply the substantial benefits that would sustain a state-established faith, direct compulsion to observance, or governmental exhortation to religiosity that amounts in fact to proselytizing.

AS JUSTICE BLACKMUN

observes, some of our recent cases reject the view that coercion is the sole touchstone of an Establishment Clause violation. See *Engel v. Vitale*, (rejecting, without citation of authority, proposition that coercion is required to demonstrate an Establishment Clause violation). That may be true if by "coercion" is meant direct coercion in the classic sense of an establishment of religion that the Framers knew. But coercion need not be a direct tax in aid of religion or a test oath. Symbolic recognition or accommodation of religious faith may violate the Clause in an extreme case. I doubt not, for example, that the Clause forbids a city to permit the permanent erection of a large Latin cross on the roof of city hall. This is not because government speech about religion is per se suspect, as the majority would have it, but because such an obtrusive year-round religious display would place the government's weight behind an obvious effort to proselytize on behalf of a particular religion.

Speech may coerce in some circumstances but this does not justify a ban on all government recognition of religion. As Chief Justice Burger wrote for the Court in *Waltz:*

"The general principle deducible from the First Amendment and all that has been said by the Court is this: that we will not tolerate either governmentally established religion or governmental interference with religion. Short of those expressly proscribed governmental acts there is room for play in the joints productive of a benevolent neutrality which will permit religious exercise to exist without sponsorship and without interference."

This is most evident where the government's act of recognition or accommodation is passive and symbolic, for in that instance any intangible benefit to religion is unlikely to present a realistic risk of establishment. Absent coercion, the risk of infringement of religious liberty by passive or symbolic accommodation is minimal. Our cases reflect this reality by requiring a showing that the symbolic recognition or accommodation advances religion to such a degree that it actually "establishes a religion or religious faith, or tends to do

so." *Lynch.*

In determining whether there exists an establishment, or a tendency toward one, we refer to the other types of churchstate contacts that have existed unchallenged throughout our history, or that have been found permissible in our case law. In *Lynch*, for example, we upheld the city of Pawtucket's holiday display of a crèche, despite the fact that "the display advance[d] religion in a sense." We held that the crèche conferred no greater benefit on religion than did governmental support for religious education, legislative chaplains, "recognition of the origins of the [Christmas] Holiday itself as 'Christ's Mass," or many other forms of symbolic or tangible governmental assistance to religious faiths that are ensconced in the safety of national tradition. And in *Marsh v. Chambers*, we found that Nebraska's practice of employing a legislative chaplain did not violate the Establishment Clause, because "legislative prayer presents no more potential for establishment than the provision of school transportation, beneficial grants for higher education, or tax exemptions for religious organizations (citations omitted)." Noncoercive government action within the realm of flexible accommodation or passive acknowledgment of existing symbols does not violate the Establishment Clause unless it benefits religion in a way more direct and more substantial than practices that are accepted in our national heritage.

These principles are not difficult to apply to the facts of the cases before us. In permitting the displays on government property of the menorah and the crèche, the city and county sought to do no more than "celebrate the season," and to acknowledge, along with many of their citizens, the historical background and the religious, as well as secular, nature of the Chanukah and Christmas holidays. This interest falls well within the tradition of government accommodation and acknowledgment of religion that has marked our history from the beginning. It cannot be disputed that government, if it chooses, may participate in sharing with its citizens the joy of the holiday season, by declaring public holidays, installing or permitting festive displays, sponsoring celebrations and parades, and providing holiday vacations for its employees. All levels of our government do precisely that. As we said in Lynch, "Government has long recognized—indeed it has subsidized—holidays with religious significance."

If government is to participate in its citizens' celebration of a holiday that contains both a secular and a religious component, enforced recognition of only the secular aspect would signify the callous indifference toward religious faith that our cases and traditions do not require; for by commemorating the holiday only as it is celebrated by nonadherents, the government would be refusing to acknowledge the plain fact, and the historical reality, that many of its citizens celebrate its religious aspects as well. Judicial invalidation of government's attempts to recognize the religious underpinnings of the holiday would signal not neutrality but a pervasive intent to insulate government from all things religious. The Religion Clauses do not require government to acknowledge these holidays or their religious component; but our strong tradition of government accommodation and acknowledgment permits government to do so. . . .

There is no realistic risk that the crèche and the menorah represent an effort to proselytize or are otherwise the first step down the road to an establishment of religion. Lynch is dispositive of this claim with respect to the crèche, and I find no reason for reaching a different result with respect to the menorah. Both are the traditional symbols of religious holidays that over time have acquired a secular component. Without ambiguity Lynch instructs that "the focus of our inquiry must be on the [religious symbol] in the context of the [holiday] season," 465 U. S., at 679. In that context, religious displays that serve "to celebrate the Holiday and to depict the origins of that Holiday" give rise to no Establishment Clause concern. If Congress and the state legislatures do not run afoul of the Establishment Clause when they begin each day with a state-sponsored prayer for divine guidance offered by a chaplain whose salary is paid at government expense, I cannot comprehend how a menorah or a crèche, displayed in the limited context of the holiday season, can be invalid.

Respondents say that the religious displays involved here are distinguishable from the crèche in Lynch because they are located on government property and are not surrounded by the candy canes, reindeer, and other holiday paraphernalia that were a part of the display in Lynch. Nothing in Chief Justice Burger's opinion for the Court in Lynch provides support for these purported distinctions. After describing the facts, the Lynch opinion makes no mention of either of these factors. It concentrates instead on the significance of the crèche as part of the entire holiday season.

Indeed, it is clear that the Court did not view the secular aspects of the display as somehow subduing the religious message conveyed by the crèche, for the majority expressly rejected the dissenters' suggestion that it sought "'to explain away the clear religious import of the crèche'" or had "equated the crèche with a Santa's house or reindeer." Crucial to the Court's conclusion was not the number, prominence, or type of secular items contained in the holiday display but the simple fact that, when displayed by government during the Christmas season, a crèche presents no realistic danger of moving government down the forbidden road toward an establishment of religion. Whether the crèche be surrounded by poinsettias, talking wishing wells, or carolers, the conclusion remains the same, for the relevant context is not the items in the display itself but the season as a whole. . . .

Even if Lynch did not control, I would not commit this Court to the test applied by the majority today. The notion that cases arising under the Establishment Clause should be decided by an inquiry into whether a "'reasonable observer'" may "'fairly understand'" government action to "'sen[d] a message to nonadherents that they are outsiders, not full members of the political community,'" is a recent, and in my view most unwelcome, addition to our tangled Establishment Clause jurisprudence. Although a scattering of our cases have used "endorsement" as another word for "preference" or "imprimatur," the endorsement test applied by the majority had its genesis in JUSTICE O'CONNOR'S concurring opinion in *Lynch.*

For the reasons expressed below, I submit that the endorsement test is flawed in its fundamentals and unworkable in practice. The uncritical adoption of this standard is every bit as troubling as the bizarre result it produces in the cases before us. . . .

I take it as settled law that, whatever standard the Court applies to Establishment Clause claims, it must at least suggest results consistent with our precedents and the historical practices that, by tradition, have informed our First Amendment jurisprudence. It is true that, for reasons quite unrelated to the First Amendment, displays commemorating religious holidays were not commonplace in 1791. . . .

But the relevance of history is not confined to the inquiry into whether the challenged practice itself is a part of our accepted traditions dating back to the Founding.

Our decision in *Marsh. v. Chambers* illustrates this proposition. The dissent in that case sought to characterize the decision as "carving out an exception to the Establishment Clause rather than reshaping Establishment Clause doctrine to accommodate legislative prayer," but the majority rejected the suggestion that "historical patterns ca[n] justify contemporary violations of constitutional guarantees." *Marsh* stands for the proposition, not that specific practices common in 1791 are an exception to the otherwise broad sweep of the Establishment Clause, but rather that the meaning of the Clause is to be determined by reference to historical practices and understandings. Whatever test we choose to apply must permit not only legitimate practices two centuries old but also any other practices with no greater potential for an establishment of religion. The First Amendment is a rule, not a digest or compendium. A test for implementing the protections of the Establishment Clause

that, if applied with consistency, would invalidate longstanding traditions cannot be a proper reading of the Clause.

If the endorsement test, applied without artificial exceptions for historical practice, reached results consistent with history, my objections to it would have less force. But, as I understand that test, the touchstone of an Establishment Clause violation is whether nonadherents would be made to feel like "outsiders" by government recognition or accommodation of religion. Few of our traditional practices recognizing the part religion plays in our society can withstand scrutiny under a faithful application of this formula.

Some examples suffice to make plain my concerns. Since the Founding of our Republic, American Presidents have issued Thanksgiving Proclamations establishing a national day of celebration and prayer. . . . "It requires little imagination to conclude that these proclamations would cause nonadherents to feel excluded, yet they have been a part of our national heritage from the beginning."

The Executive has not been the only Branch of our Government to recognize the central role of religion in our society. The fact that this Court opens its sessions with the request that "God save the United States and this honorable Court" has been noted elsewhere. See *Lynch.* The Legislature has gone much further, not only employing legislative chaplains, but also setting aside a special prayer room in the Capitol for use by Members of the House and Senate. . . .

Some endorsement is inherent in these reasonable accommodations, yet the Establishment Clause does not forbid them.

The United States Code itself contains religious references that would be suspect under the endorsement test. Congress has directed the President to set aside and proclaim a suitable day each year . . . as a National Day of Prayer, on which the people of the United States may turn to God in prayer and meditation at churches, in groups, and as individuals.

This statute does not require anyone to pray, of course, but it is a straightforward endorsement of the concept

of "turn[ing] to God in prayer. " Also by
statute, the Pledge of Allegiance to the
Flag describes the United States as "one
Nation under God." To be sure, no one is
obligated to recite this phrase, see *West
Virginia State Board of Education v.
Barnette*, but it borders on sophistry to
suggest that the "'reasonable'" atheist
would not feel less than a "'full member]
of the political community'" every time
his fellow Americans recited, as part of
their expression of patriotism and love for
country, a phrase he believed to be false.
Likewise, our national motto, "In God we
trust," which is prominently engraved in
the wall above the Speaker's dais in the
Chamber of the House of Representatives
and is reproduced on every coin minted and
every dollar printed by the Federal
Government, must have the same effect.

If the intent of the Establishment
Clause is to protect individuals from mere
feelings of exclusion, then legislative
prayer cannot escape invalidation. It has
been argued that "[these] government
acknowledgments of religion serve, in the
only ways reasonably possible in our
culture, the legitimate secular purposes of
solemnizing public occasions, expressing
confidence in the future, and encouraging
the recognition of what is worthy of
appreciation in society." Lynch
(O'CONNOR, J., concurring). I fail to see
why prayer is the only way to convey
these messages; appeals to patriotism,
moments of silence, and any number of
other approaches would be as effective,
were the only purposes at issue the ones
described by the Lynch concurrence. Nor is
it clear to me why "encouraging the
recognition of what is worthy of
appreciation in society" can be
characterized as a purely secular purpose, if
it can be achieved only through religious
prayer. No doubt prayer is "worthy of
appreciation," but that is most assuredly
not because it is secular. Even accepting
the secular-solemnization explanation at
face value, moreover, it seems incredible
to suggest that the average observer of
legislative prayer who either believes in
no religion or whose faith rejects the
concept of God would not I receive the
clear message that his faith is out of step
with the political norm. Either the

endorsement test must invalidate scores of
traditional practices recognizing the place
religion holds in our culture e, or it must
be twisted and stretched to avoid
inconsistency with practices we know to
have been permitted in the past, while
condemning similar practices with no
greater endorsement effect simply by
reason of their lack of historical
antecedent. Neither result is acceptable.

In addition to disregarding precedent
and historical fact, the majority's approach
to government use of religious symbolism
threatens to trivialize constitutional
adjudication. By mischaracterizing the
Court's opinion in Lynch as an
endorsement-in-context test, JUSTICE
BLACKMUN embraces a jurisprudence of
minutiae. A reviewing court must consider
whether the city has included Santas,
talking wishing wells, reindeer, or other
secular symbols as "a center of attention
separate from the crèche." After
determining whether these centers of
attention are sufficiently "separate" that
each "had their specific visual story to
tell," the court must then measure their
proximity to the crèche. A community
that wishes to construct a constitutional
display must also take care to avoid floral
frames or other devices that might insulate
the crèche from the sanitizing effect of the
secular portions of the display. . . .

Another important factor will be the
prominence of the setting in which the
display is placed. In this case, the Grand
Staircase of the county courthouse proved
too resplendent. Indeed, the Court finds
that this location itself conveyed an
"unmistakable message that [the county]
supports and promotes the Christian praise
to God that is the crèche's religious
message." . . . Deciding cases on the
basis of such an unguided examination of
marginalia is irreconcilable with the
imperative of applying neutral principles
in constitutional adjudication. . . .

The approach adopted by the majority
contradicts important values embodied in
the Clause. Obsessive, implacable
resistance to all but the most carefully
scripted and secularized forms of
accommodation requires this Court to act
as a censor, issuing national decrees as to
what is orthodox and what is not. What is

orthodox, in this context, means what is secular; the only Christmas the State can acknowledge is one in which references to religion have been held to a minimum. The Court thus lends its assistance to an Orwellian rewriting of history as many understand it.

. . . The Court also assumes the difficult and inappropriate task of saying what every religious symbol means. Before studying this case, I had not known the full history of the menorah, and I suspect the same was true of my colleagues. More important, this history was, and is, likely unknown to the vast majority of people of all faiths who saw the symbol displayed in Pittsburgh. Even if the majority is quite right about the history of the menorah, it hardly follows that this same history informed the observers' view of the symbol and the reason for its presence. This Court is ill equipped to sit as a national theology board, and I question both the wisdom and the constitutionality of its doing so.

EPILOGUE
THE FIRST AMENDMENT IN THE BALANCE

To "balance," as the word implies, is to "weigh" two entities, and thus to determine which is "heavier," of more "importance," or should take precedence. That "balancing" is a necessary, indeed an indispensable technique in constitutional interpretation is crystal clear when the things to be balanced are the "religion clauses" of the constitution. First and foremost, this is so because the two clauses do, as we have noted, frequently clash with each other. In such circumstances an "absolutist" approach to either is not only undesirable, but impossible, for to adopt such an approach is to prefer one at the expense of the other. Thus, for example, in Widmar v. Vincent, the predecessor case to the Equal Access Act and thus to Board of Education v. Mergens, to have held that colleges could deny student religious groups the right to meet on campus on the same footing as other groups would have been to hold that "free exercise" rights must take a back seat to fears of "establishment." And, of course, the Court, in deciding Widmar as it did, "preferred" the free exercise right to that of "establishment. To the same effect, it would seem, were the Court's decisions in such cases as Presiding Bishop v. Amos, and Scherbert v. Verner. Whether or not they were articulated in the decisions of these cases, surely the interest of church and citizen in being free to pursue their religiously mandated courses were of major consideration.

But the same necessity for "weighing" is seen in those cases where there is no arguable conflict between the two religious clauses. As we have already observed, this can be most clearly seen in Prince v. Massachusetts, in which the Court necessarily had to weigh petitioners enormously important interest in following their conscience against the states unquestioned, and unquestionable, interest in protecting children. There was simply no way to decide the case except to assess the weight of each of these interests and to determine, in the specific context created by the facts, which ought to take precedence. Nor, it would seem, was there any way to avoid the same process in such diverse cases as Lyng v. Northwest Indian Cemetery Protective Association, involving a clash between the government's right to develop its property in a certain way with the religious needs of Native Americans, and Bowen v. Kendrick, in which the danger of establishment clashed with governmental need to address a vexing social problem in the most effective ways possible. And how, to use the language of the Lemon test, is one to determine if the "effect" of a law aids religion "primarily" or only "secondarily" except with reference to the interests which the law is intended to secure?

In the same way decisions on the "communications clauses" have depended on one or another type of balancing. If the necessity for "balancing" is, in these cases, a bit less clear, it is because the clauses do not contain any internal contradiction. But, as has been demonstrated, they may, interpreted in particular ways, clash with such other constitutionally protected interests as that of a "fair trial," or privacy. How, except on a "balancing" basis, can the Court choose between clashing constitutional rights?

In addition, many of the doctrines developed to aid in the decision of communications cases require "balancing." How, for example, is one to decide that there is a "clear and present danger" of a "serious evil" that government may prevent (the formulation of "clear and present danger espoused by Justice Brandeis in Whitney) except by reference to some kind of weighing. Nor, it would seem, can the "weighing" be accomplished by taking into consideration *only* the "seriousness" of the evil. If that were the case, the governmental interest in, for example, keeping the streets clean, could never outweigh the right of an individual to make dirty those streets in the process of "communication."[1] Nor could the Court look, as it has, to the availability of adequate alternative outlets for speech in determining whether particular kinds of communication could be prohibited, without some concept of the importance of the non-speech interest.

And the "preferred position" doctrine which has played such an important role in the jurisprudence of the communications clauses is unintelligible except in the context of a "balancing process." For if there is no need to weigh, there is no need to assign preference. Similarly, the requirement that the interest sought by the government be "compelling" implies that it must be weighed. And how are we to determine its "weight" except in reference to that against which it is arrayed.

The need for, and the presence of the balancing process in the decision of communications cases can be perhaps best be seen in the context of those cases involving what we have called "desirable" governmental goals. Surely the reason for allowing less constitutional protection for "private speech" which is also libelous than for the same type of speech on public matters is bound up with the determination that "private speech," although constitutionally protected, is of less moment than is speech on public issues. It is the weighty interest in the latter that accounts for the limits put on the reach of libel law in New York Times Co. v. Sullivan and later cases, just as he reason for the holding that Robert Welch's libel of Elmer Getz did not merit the same kind of protection is related to its "private" character.

In a similar vein, it does not seem possible that the Court's decisions on the contributions by dissidents in the "compulsory unionism" cases could have been reached without balancing the need for such contributions against the First Amendment interests of dissenters. Indeed, the Court, in construing the Railway Act to allow for such contributions, said as much, as it also did in determining that forced contributions could be justified only when "related to collective bargaining.

But even in cases balancing required governmental activity against the interest in communication, the necessity of balancing can be seen. Rightly or wrongly, the Court in the Dennis case "balanced" what it perceived to be a national security need against communications interest. Similarly, in its decision in Tinker v. Community School District, it had to weigh the asserted interest in "order" in the schools against free communications interests. And in Buckley v. Valeo, the Court explicitly balanced the degree to which contributions and expenditures contributed to free communication, as well as the extent to which each might threaten the integrity of elections, in concluding that limitations on the former were acceptable, while those on the latter were not.

But, while "balancing" must be accepted as both a fact and a necessity of constitutional life, several caveats need to be entered. First, "definitional balancing," because it allows for judgment relatively free of the influence of current controversy, is much to be preferred to *ad hoc* balancing. Second, so long as judicial review is an instrument of government in our nation, it is the Court, and not other agencies, that must strike the final balance. And the Court should not, in reaching its decision, assume that the legislature (or other governmental entity) is correct. To do so is, indeed, to pretend that the First Amendment does not exist. Always, at least in those situations in which constitutionally protected rights are not in conflict, there must be a "thumb on the scale" in favor of rights of communication.

Finally, although one is always free to disagree with the balance that the Court has reached, the importance of the fact that it has done so, and was available to do so, cannot be overestimated. One may conclude, as I would, that the Court during the McCarthy period vastly overestimated the danger from Communism, and thus approved statutes and regulations that were unnecessary and not in the public interest. Or one may contend, as I also would, that the Court has, especially in cases related to fair trial and privacy interests, so overbalanced the interests of the media and the public, that it can justly be accused of giving little or no weight to competing values. Or, one may assert, as I again would, that the balance reached by the Court in many of the "establishment" cases is to some extent devoid of intelligible principle. But no one, whether adherent or opponent of these positions, who carefully reads and assesses the decisions of the Court, can in the last analysis be anything but grateful that it has so carefully and conscientiously performed the "balancing act" assigned to it in the American system of government.

---

[1]In the early case of Lovell v. City of Griffin (1938) the Court did hold that the fear of littering did not suffice to validate a licensing system directed, in part, at the distribution of handbills. But Lovell involved only the apprehension of an evil, not its reality. And there may be circumstances in which the nonspeech interest would seem to clearly outweigh the interest in communicating in a particular way. If, for example, the chosen mode of "expression" was the placing of obnoxious material on public byways, or the covering of city owned property with graffiti, and if this activity was repeated incessantly, at some point the citizens' interest in a clean and present atmosphere, and the government's interest in saving some of its money for purposes other than cleanup would be entitled to consideration.

BIBLIOGRAPHICAL NOTE

There is no dearth of scholarly commentary on the First Amendment. Much of that which is most valuable appears in periodicals published by the nation's law schools. It thus may be available only to undergraduates who attend universities where such schools are located. But most undergraduate libraries will have a few such journals, and virtually all will contain *The Supreme Court Review*, published by the School of Law of the University of Chicago, and *Constitutional Commentary*, published by the University of Minnesota Law School. Both these publications, as their titles imply, are concerned exclusively with constitutional matters. Both are of high quality and frequently contain articles dealing with First Amendment problems.

Of the many books which are available on First Amendment issues, I have found the following particularly useful. On the communications clauses two early volumes by political scientists, Walter Berns' *Freedom, Virtue, and the First Amendment* (Chicago: Henry Regnery Co., 1965), and Martin Shapiro, *Freedom of Speech: Judicial Review and the Supreme Court* (Englewood Cliffs, N.J.: Prentice-Hall Pub. Co., 1966)), shaped my thinking and still provide a good basis for evaluating the various "tests" employed by the Court in its "free speech" decisions. Because of their contrasting viewpoints, they are particularly valuable when read in tandem. More recent works which are both challenging and useful include Thomas Emerson's *The System of Freedom of Expression*, (New York, Random House Vintage Books, 1971), the first attempt by any scholar to evaluate the entire range of "communications clause" jurisprudence; and Franklyn Haiman, *Speech and Law in a Free Society* (Chicago: University of Chicago Press, 1981), a similarly wide-ranging effort which sought to build and to improve on Emerson's work, and which argues for an even broader protection of communicative activity. Frederick Schauer's *Free Speech: A Philosophical Inquiry* (Cambridge: England: Cambridge University Press, 1982) provides, as its title implies, a rigorous philosophical basis for evaluating "free communications" claims, a basis which I have tried to reflect in this text. And two recent works by Donald Alexander Downs, *Nazis in Skokie: Freedom, Community, and the First Amendment* (South Bend, Indiana: University of Notre Dame Press, 1985), and *The New Politics of Pornography* (Chicago: University of Chicago Press, 1989) utilize recent and current controversies to highlight both the content and the possible shortcomings of the "modern doctrine of free speech."

On the "religion" clauses the scholarly commentary reflects, as does the Supreme Court's own approach to the problem, an emphasis on constitutional history. That history seemed largely settled until the appearance, in 1982, of Robert Cord's *Separation of Church and State: Historical Fact and Current Fiction* (New York: Lambeth Press, 1982), which challenged the conventional view of the "wall of separation" as largely accepted by both Court and commentators. Leonard Levy, perhaps the most renowned historian of constitutional rights and liberties, has challenged Cord's conclusions and presented the evidence for a more conventional position in his *The Establishment Clause: Religion and the First Amendment* (New York: Macmillan Publishing Co., 1986). Also useful on the historical question are Walter Berns, *The First Amendment and the Future of American Democracy* (New York: Basic Books, 1976), and Thomas Curry: *The First Freedoms*, (New York: Oxford University Press, 1986), which examines the history of religious freedom and establishment in colonial times. An indispensable starting-place for an understanding of the jurisprudence of the religion clauses is Donald Gianella, "Religious Liberty, Nonestablishment, and Doctrinal Development." Part I of Professor Giannella's work, entitled "The Religious Liberty Guarantee," appeared in 80 *Harvard Law Review* 1381 (1967). Part II, "The Nonestablishment Principle," is in 81 *Harvard Law Review* 513 (1968). Both, but especially the second, are more than worth the trip to the law library. And, on the interrelationship between politics and the religious clauses I have found especially useful Richard Morgan's *The Politics of Religious Conflict* (New York: Pegasus Books, 1968) and Ch. 2 of his more recent work, *Disabling America: The*

Rights Industry in Our Time (New York: Basic Books, 1984)Another book useful for bringing the jurisprudence of the religion clauses into contemporary perspective is James A. Hunter and Os Guinness, eds., *Articles of Faith, Articles of Peace* (Washington, D.C.: The Brookings Institution, 1990).

Finally, no student of the First Amendment should be unaware of Lawrence Tribe's *The American Constitution* (Mineola, N.Y.: The Foundation Press, 2nd ed., 1988.) Professor Tribe's discussion of "Rights of Communication and Expression" and of "Rights of Religious Autonomy" is found in Chapters 12 and 14, respectively, of his treatise. Copiously annotated, Professor Tribe's discussion is exhaustive in its coverage, rigorous in its analysis, and challenging in its conclusions.

TABLE OF CASES

ABOOD v. DETROIT BOARD OF EDUCATION, 431 U.S. 209 (1977), 268, 275
Abrams v. United States , 250 U.S. 616 (1919), 9, 16, 28-29
Adderly v. Florida, 385 U.S. 39 (1966), 78-80
Adler v. Board of Education, 342 U.S. 485 (1952), 27
AGUILAR v. FELTON, 473 U.S. 402 (1985), 374-376
Albertson v. Subversive Activities Control Board, 382 U.S. 70, (1965), 34
Amalgamated Food Employees v. Logan Valley Plaza, 391 U.S. 308 (1968), 272-274
American Booksellers Association v. Hudnut, 771 F. 2d323 (1985), 189
American Party of Texas v. White, 415 U.S. 767 (1974), 133
Aptheker v. Secretary of State, 378 U.S. 500 (1964), 27
Associated Press v. Walker, Curtis Publishing Co. v. Butts, 388 U.S. 130 (1967), 224, 231
Baggett v. Bullitt, 377 U.S. 360 (1964), 34
Barnes v. Glen Theatre, 110 S.Ct. 2456 (1991), 22, 205
Barenblatt v. United States, 360 U.S.109 (1959), 28
BEAUHARNAIS v. ILLINOIS, 343 U.S. 250 (1952), 182-183, 188
BETHEL SCHOOL DISTRICT v. FRASER, 478 U.S. 675 (1986), 83
Board of Education v. Allen, 392 U.S. 236 (1968), 368-369
BOARD OF EDUCATION OF WESTSIDE COMM. SCHOOLS v. MERGENS 110 S.Ct. 2536
    (1990), 402, 435
BOOS v. BARRY, 485 U.S. 312 (1987), 33
BOWEN v. KENDRICK, 487 U.S. 589 (1988), 347-348, 436
Bowen v. Roy, 476 U.S. 693 (1986), 321
Brandenburg v. Ohio, 395 U.S. 444 (1969), 21, 23, 31
Brandon v. Guilderland Bd. of Ed., 635 F. 2d 971 (1980), 406
Branti v. Finkel, 445 U.S. 507 (1980), 127-128
Braunfeld v. Brown, 366 U.S. 599 (1961), 341-343, 348
Bridges v. California, Times-Mirror Co. v. California, 314 U.S. 252 (1941), 97-98
Broadrick v. Oklahoma, 413 U.S. 601 (1973), 24
Brown v. Louisiana, 383 U.S. 131 (1966), 78
BUCKLEY v. VALEO, 424 U.S. 1 (1976), 18, 23, 131-133, 437
Butler v. Michigan, 352 U.S. 380 (1957), 201
California v. LaRue, 409 U.S. 109 (1972), 205
Cameron v. Johnson, 390 U.S. 611 (1968), 78-79, 163-166
Cantwell v. Connecticut, 310 U.S. 296 (1940), 292,317-318, 320
Carey v. Brown, 447 U.S. 455 (1980), 250
Central Hudson Gas & Electric Corp. v. Public Service Commission, 447 U.S. 557 (1980), 23
Chaplinsky v. New Hampshire, 315 U.S. 568 (1942), 14, 22, 54, 158, 201-202, 223
Chicago Police Department v. Mosely 408 U.S. 92 (1972), 81
Chicago Teachers Union v. Hudson, 475 U.S. 291 (1986), 268
CITY OF LAKEWOOD v. CLEVELAND PLAIN DEALER, 468 U.S. 750 (1988), 53
CITY OF RENTON v. PLAYTIME THEATRES, 475 U.S. 41 (1986), 205
Civil Service Comm. v. Nat'l Ass'n of Letter Carriers, 413 U.S. 548 (1973), 124
CLARK v. COMMITTEE FOR CREATIVE NON-VIOLENCE, 468 U.S. 288 (1984), 59
Cochran v. Louisiana, 281 U.S. 370 (1930), 376
Cohen v. California, 403 U.S. 15 (1971), 10, 22
Cohen v. Cowles Media Co., 111 S.Ct. 2513 (1991), 105
Cole v. Richardson, 405 U.s. 676 (1972), 28
Collin v. Smith, 578 F. 2d 1197, 447 F. Supp. 676 (1978), 60, 188
Communist Party v. Subversive Activities Control Board, 367 U.S. 1 (1961), 27
CORNELIUS v. N. A. A. C. P. LEGAL DEFENSE FUND, 473 U.S. 788 (1985), 84
CORP. OF THE PRESIDING BISHOP v. AMOS, 483 U.S. 327 (1987), 346, 435
COUNTY OF ALLEGHENY v. AMERICAN CIVIL LIBERTIES UNION, 492 U.S. 573
    (1989), 404

Cox v. New Hampshire, 312 U.S. 569 (1941), 53
Cox v. Louisiana I, 379 U.S. 536 (1965), 76, 78
Cox v. Louisiana II, 379 U.S. 559 (1965), 76, 78
Craig v. Harney, 331 U.S. 367 (1947), 98
Davis v. Beason, 133 U.S. 333 (1890), 316
Davis v. Massachusetts, 167 U.S.43 (1897), 53
DENNIS v. UNITED STATES, 341 U.s. 494 (1951), 16, 23, 29-31
Doe v. University of Michigan, 721 F. Supp. 852 (1989), 189
Edwards v. Aguillard, 482 U.S. 578 (1987), 303
EDWARDS v. SOUTH CAROLINA, 372 U.S. 229 (1963), 75-78
Elfbrandt v. Russell, 384 U.S. 11 (1966), 34
Ellis v. Railway Clerks , 466 U.S. 435 (1984), 267
Elrod v. Burns, 427 U.S. 347 (1976), 125-128
EMPLOYMENT DIVISION v. SMITH, 494 U.S. 872 (1990), 320-321
Engel v. Vitale, 370 U.S. 421 (1962), 289, 291, 400
ERZNOZNIK v. CITY OF JACKSONVILLE, 422 U.S. 205 (1975), 254-255
Eu v. San Francisco County Democratic Comm., 489 U.S. 214 (1989), 128-130
Everson v. Board. of Education, 330 U.S. 1 (1947), 368-369, 373, 397, 400
Fed. Election Comm. v. Nat'l Conservative Pol. Action Comm., 470 U.S. 480 (1985), 132
Feiner v. New York, 340 U.S. 315 (1951), 55-56, 75
First National Bank v. Belotti, 435 U.S. 765, (1978), 24
Follett v. McCormick, 321 U.S. 573 (1944), 303
FRISBY v. SCHULTZ, 487 U.S. 474 (1988), 250-251
Gallagher v. Crown Kosher Market, 366 U.S. 617 (1961), 348
Gannet Co. v. DiPasquale, 443 U.S. 368 (1979), 100
GENTILE v. STATE BAR OF NEVADA, 111 S.Ct. 2720 (1991), 104
Gertz v. Robert Welch, Inc., 408 U.S. 323 (1974), 226-227, 231
Gillette v. United States, 401 U.S. 437 (1971), 301
Ginsberg v. New York, 390 U.S. 629 (1968), 201
Ginzburg v. United States, 383 U.S. 463 (1966), 207
Gitlow v. New York, 268 U.S. 652 (1925), 9, 28-29
GLOBE NEWSPAPERS v. SUPERIOR COURT, 457 U.S. 596 (1982), 102
Goldman v. Weinberger, 475 U.S. 503 (1986), 321-322
Gooding v. Wilson, 405 U.S. 518, (1972), 55
Grand Rapids School District v. Ball, 473 U.S. 373 (1985), 376
Grayned v. City of Rockford, 408 U.S. 104 (1972), 81-82
Greer v. Spock, 424 U.S. 828 (1976), 79-80
Gregory v. City of Chicago (1969), 394 U.S. 111 (1969), 249
Hague v. Committee for Industrial Organization, 307 U.S. 496 (1939), 53, 59-60, 75, 83
Hamilton v. Regents of Univ. of California, 293 U.S. 245 (1934), 301
Harte-Hanke Pub. Co. v. McNaughton, 491 U.S. 657 (1989), 231
Hazelwood School District v. Kuhlmeier, 484 U.S. 260 (1988), 83
HEFFRON v. INT'L SOCIETY. FOR KRISHNA CONSCIOUSNESS, 452 U.S. 640 1981), 59
Hernandez v. Comm. of Internal Revenue, 490 U.S. 680 (1989), 302
Houchins v. KQED, 483 U.S. 1 (1978), 84
Hess v. Indiana, 414 U.S. 105 (1973), 58
HUDGENS V. NATIONAL LABOR RELATIONS BD., 424 U.S. 507 (1976), 273-274
Hunt v. McNair, 413 U.S. 734 (1973), 376
Hustler Magazine v. Falwell, 485 U.S. 40 (1988), 230
In the Matter of the Welfare of R.A.V. v. City of St. Paul, 464 NW 2d 507 (1991), 187, 189
International Ass'n of Machinists v. Street, 367 U.S. 740 (1960), 162
Irvin v. Dowd, 366 U.S. 717 (1961), 98
Jacobellis v. Ohio,378 U.S. 184 (1964), 201
Jacobson v. Massachusetts, 197 U.S. 11 (1905), 303
Jenkins v. Georgia, 418 U.S. 153 (1974), 204

Jenness v. Fortson, 403 U.S. 431 (1971), 133
Jimmy Swaggart Ministries v. California Bd. of Equalization, 493 U.S. 378 (1990), 302, 345
Keller v. State Bar of California,110 S.Ct. 2228 (1990), 270
Keyeshian v. Board of Regents, 385 U.S. 589 (1967), 27
Kovacs v. Cooper, 336 U.S. 77 (1949), 253
Landmark Communications Co. v. Virginia, 435 U.S. 829 (1978), 105
Late Corporation of the Church Of Jesus Christ of Latter Day Saints v. United States, 136 U.S. 1
    (1890), 316
Lathrop v. Donohue, 367 U.S. 820 (1961), 270
Lechmere, Inc. v. National Labor Relations Board, 112 S.Ct. 841 (1992), 275
Lehman v. City of Shaker Heights, 418 U.S. 298 (1974), 254-255
Lehnert v. Ferris Faculty Association, 111 S.Ct. 1950(1991), 269
LEMON v. KURTZMAN, 403 U.S. 602 (1971), 293, 347-348, 369-370, 372, 374, 376, 403,
    405, 436
LINMARK ASSOCIATES V. WILLINGBORO, 431 U.S. 85 (1977), 186
Lloyd Corporation v. Tanner, 407 U.S. 551 (1972), 272-274
Lovell v. City of Griffin, 303 U.S. 444 (1938), 438
Lubbock Civil Lib. Union v. Lubbock Indep. Sch. Dist., 669 F. 2d 1038 (1982), 406
Lynch v. Donnelly, 465 U.S. 668 (1984), 403-404
LYNG v. NORTHWEST INDIAN CEMETERY PROTECTIVE ASSOCIATION, 485 U.S. 439
    (1988), 321, 347, 436
Madison Joint. Sch. District v. Wisconsin Employee Rel. Comm., 429 U.S. 167 (1976), 269
Marsh v. Alabama, 326 U.S. 501 (1946), 271-272
Masson v. New Yorker Magazine, 111 S.Ct. 2419 (1990), 229-230
Martin v. City of Struthers, 319 U.S. 141 (1943), 24, 247-248
McCollum v. Board of Education, 333 U.S. 203 (1948), 398
McDANIEL v. PATY, 435 U.S. 619 (1978), 298, 300
McGowan v. Maryland, 366 U.S. 420 (1961), 339, 341, 348
Memoirs v. Massachusetts, 383 U.S. 413, (1966). 202, 207
MILLER v. CALIFORNIA, 413 U.S. 15 (1973), 203-207
Minersville School District v. Gobitis, 310 U.S. 586 (1940), 159-160, 166
Minnesota State Board for Community Colleges v. Knight, 465 U.S. 271 (1984), 269
Mishkin v. New York, 383 U.S. 502 (1966), 207
MUELLER v. ALLEN, 463 U.S. 388 (1983), 371-372
MUNRO v. SOCIALIST PARTY,479 U.S. 189 (1986), 130
Murdock v. Pennsylvania, 319 U.S. 105 (1943), 303
Near v. Minnesota, 283 U.S. 697 (1931), 23
NEBRASKA PRESS ASS'N v. STUART, 427 U.S. 539 (1976), 99-101, 105
New York v. Ferber, 458 U.S. 747 (1982), 201
NEW YORK STATE CLUB ASSOCIATION v. CITY OF NEW YORK, 487 U.S 1 (1988), 188
New York State Liquor Authority v. Bellanco, 452 U.S. 714 (1981), 205
NEW YORK TIMES CO. v. SULLIVAN, 376 U.S. 264, (1964), 8-9, 19-20, 224, 228, 231-
    232, 437
New York Times Co. v. United States, 403 U.S. 713 (1971), 23, 32
Noto v. United States, 367 U.S. 290 (1961), 26-27
Oklahoma Publishing Co. v. District Court, 430 U.S. 308 (1977), 105
Organization for a Better Austin v. O'Keefe, 402 U.S. 415 (1971), 250
Osborne v. Ohio, 110 S.Ct. 1691 (1990), 201
Papachristou v. City of Jacksonville, 405 U.S. 156 (1972), 24
PARIS ADULT THEATRE v. SLATON, 413 U.S. 49 (1973), 203, 207
Pell v. Procunier, 417 U.S. 817 (1974), 84
Pennekamp v. Florida, 328 U.S. 331 (1946), 97
PERRY ED. ASSOCIATION v. PERRY LOCAL EDUCATORS ASSOCIATION, 460 U.S. 37
    (1983), 84, 270
PHILADELPHIA NEWSPAPERS INC., v. HEPPS, 475 U.S. 767 (1986), 228, 230

Pierce v. Society of Sisters, 268 U.S. 510 (1925), 375
Pittsburgh Press Co. v. Pittsburgh Comm. on Human Relations, 413 U.S. 376 (1973), 183, 185-186
Pope v. Illinois, 481 U.S. 497, (1987), 204
Press-Enterprise Co. v. Superior Court, 464 U.S. 501 (1984), 103
Press-Enterprise Co. v. Superior Court, 477 U.S. 648 (1986), 103
PRINCE v. MASSACHUSETTS, 321 U.S. 158 (1944), 23, 317-319, 435
Pruneyard Shopping Center v. Robbins, 447 U.S. 74 (1980), 275
Public Utilities Comm. v. Pollak, 343 U.S. 451 (1952), 253
Railway Employees Dept. v. Hanson, 351 U.S. 225 (1956), 267, 270
Redrup v. New York, 386 U.S. 767 (1967), 202
Reynolds v. United States, 98 U.S. 145 (1878), 315
Richmond Newspapers v. Virginia, 448 U.S. 555 (1980), 101-102
Roberts v. United States Jaycees, 468 U.S. 609 (1984). 188
Roemer v. Board of Public Works, 426 U.S. 736 (1976), 376
Rosenfeld v. New Jersey, 408 U.S. 901 (1972), 55
Roth v. United States, 354 U.S. 476 (1957), 201
ROWAN v. POST OFFICE DEPT., 397 U.S. 728 (1970), 248
Runyon v. McCrary, 427 U.S. 160 (1976), 186
RUTAN v. REPUBLICAN PARTY OF ILLINOIS, 110 S.Ct. 2729 (1990), 128
SABLE COMMUNICATIONS CO. v. FED. COMMUNICATIONS COMMISSION, 492 U.S. 115 (1989), 206
San Francisco Arts and Athletes v. U.S. Olympic Committee, 483 U.S. 522 (1987), 275
Scales v. United States, 367 U.S. 203 (1961), 26-27
Schacht v. United States, 398 U.S. 58 (1970), 163
Schad v. Borough of Mt. Ephraim, 452 U.S. 61 (1981), 205
Schenck v. United States, 249 U.S. 47 (1919), 15-16, 28
SCH. DIST OF ABINGTON TWP v. SCHEMPP, MURRAY v. CURLETT, 374 U.S. 203 (1963), 401-402
Saia v. New York, 334 U.S. 558 (1948), 252-253
Sheppard v. Maxwell, 384 U.S. 333 (1966), 99, 103
Scherbert v. Verner, 374 U.S. 398, (1963), 321, 348, 435
Smith v. Allwright, 321 U.S. 649 (1944), 129, 133
Smith v. Goguen, 415 U.S. 566 (1974), 163
SPENCE v. WASHINGTON, 418 U.S. 405 (1974), 163
Staub v. City of Baxley, 355 U.S. 313 (1958), 53
Street v. New York, 394 U.S. 576 (1969), 162
Tashjian v. Republican Party of Connecticut, 479 U.S. 208 (1986), 128-130
Terminiello v. Chicago, 337 U.S. 1 (1949), 56-58, 75
Terry v. Adams, 345 U.S. 461 (1953), 133
TEXAS v. JOHNSON, 491 U.S.397 (1989), 163-166
Texas Monthly v. Bullock, 489 U.S. 1 (1989), 345-346
THE FLORIDA STAR v. B.J.F..491 U.S. 524 (1989), 105, 231
Thornhill v. Alabama, 310 U.S. 88 (1940), 23
Time, Inc. v. Hill, 385 U.S. 374 (1967), 225-227
Time, Inc. v. Firestone, 424 U.S. 448 (1976), 226
Tilton v. Richardson, 403 U.S. 672 (1971), 372
Tinker v. Des Moines Comm. School District, 393 U.S. 503 (1969), 82-83, 437
Torcaso v. Watkins, 367 U.S. 488 (1961), 298, 300
Turner v. Safley, 482 U.S. 78 (1987), 84
Two Guys from Harrison-Allentown v. McGinley, 366 U.S. 582 (1961), 348
United Public Workers v. Mitchell, 330 U.S. 75 (1947), 124
United States v. Ballard, 322 U.S. 78 (1944), 298, 316
United States v. Brown, 381 U.S. 437 (1965), 34, 78
United States v. Carolene Products Co., 304 U.S. 144 (1938), 21, 23

United States v. Classic, 313 U.S. 299 (1941), 133
United States v. Eichman, 110 S.Ct. 287 (1990), 164, 166
UNITED STATES v. LEE, 455 U.S. 252 (1982), 303
UNITED STATES v. O'BRIEN, 391 U.S. 367 (1968), 12, 32, 34, 205
United States v. Robel, 389 U.S. 258 (1967), 27
United States v. Seeger, 380 U.S. 163 (1965), 301, 303
Univ. of Wisconsin-Madison *Post* v. Bd. of Regents, 774 F. Supp. 1173 (1991), 189
Valentine v. Christensen, 316 U.S. 52 (1942), 22
Virginia State Board of Pharmacy v. Virginia Citizens Consumer Council, 425 U.S.748 (1976), 22, 185
Wallace v. Jaffree, 472 U.S. 38 (1985), 402
Walz v. Tax Commission, 397 U.S. 664 (1970), 293, 302, 343, 345-346
Watkins v. United States, 354 U.S. 178 (1957), 28
Ways v. City of Lincoln, 705 F. Supp 1420 (1988), 189
WELSH v.UNITED STATES, 398 U.S. 333 (1970), 301-303
Westmoreland v. Columbia Broadcasting System, 752 F. 2d 16 (1984), 231
WEST VIRGINIA BOARD OF EDUCATION v. BARNETTE, 319 U.S. 624 (1943), 159-161, 164-166, 181, 401, 405
Whitney v. California, 274 U.S. 357 (1927), 16, 28-29, 31
Widmar v. Vincent, 454 U.S. 263 (1981), 82, 435
WISCONSIN v. YODER, 406 U.S. 205 (1972), 318-320
Wolman v. Walter, 433 U.S. 229 (1977), 373-374
Wood v. Georgia, 370 U.S. 375 (1962), 98
Wooley v. Maynard, 430 U.S. 705 (1977), 160-161, 166
Yates v.United States, 354 U.S. 298 (1957), 30
Young v. American Mini-Theatres, 427 U.S. 50 (1976), 204
Zacchini v. Scripps-Howard Pub. Co., 433 U.S. 562 (1977), 275
Zorach v. Clauson, 343 U.S. 306 (1952), 375, 398, 399, 402